The Refugee in International Law

THE
REFUGEE
IN
INTERNATIONAL
LAW

SECOND EDITION

GUY S. GOODWIN-GILL

OXFORD
UNIVERSITY PRESS

OXFORD

UNIVERSITY PRESS

Great Clarendon Street, Oxford OX2, 6DP

Oxford University Press is a department of the University of Oxford.
It furthers the University's objective of excellence in research, scholarship,
and education by publishing worldwide in

Oxford New York

Auckland Bangkok Buenos Aires Cape Town Chennai
Dar es Salaam Delhi Hong Kong Istanbul Karachi Kolkata
Kuala Lumpur Madrid Melbourne Mexico City Mumbai Nairobi
São Paulo Shanghai Taipei Tokyo Toronto

Oxford is a registered trade mark of Oxford University Press
in the UK and in certain other countries

Published in the United States
by Oxford University Press Inc., New York

British Library Cataloguing in Publication Data

Data available

Library of Congress Cataloging in Publication Data

Data available

ISBN 0-19-826019-9

N 0-19-826020-2 (Pbk)

9 10 8

Printed in Great Britain by Biddles Ltd., King's Lynn, Norfolk

PREFACE

The refugee in international law occupies a legal space characterized, on the one hand, by the principle of State sovereignty and the related principles of territorial supremacy and self-preservation; and, on the other hand, by competing humanitarian principles deriving from general international law (including the purposes and principles of the United Nations) and from treaty. Refugee law nevertheless remains an incomplete legal regime of protection, imperfectly covering what ought to be a situation of exception. It goes some way to alleviate the plight of those affected by breaches of human rights standards or by the collapse of an existing social order in the wake of revolution, civil strife, or aggression; but it is incomplete so far as refugees and asylum seekers may still be denied even temporary refuge or temporary protection, safe return to their homes, or compensation.[1]

The international legal status of the refugee necessarily imports certain legal consequences, the most important of which is the obligation of States to respect the principle of *non-refoulement* through time. In practice, the (legal) obligation to respect this principle, independent and compelling as it is, may be difficult to isolate from the (political) options which govern the availability of solutions. The latter necessarily depends upon political factors, including the conditions which gave rise to the refugee's flight, while for any solution to be ultimately satisfactory, the wishes of the individual, for example, in the light of connections which he or she may have with one or another State, cannot be disregarded entirely.

The existence of the class of refugees not only entails legal consequences for States, but also the entitlement and the responsibility to exercise protection on behalf of refugees. The Office of the United Nations High Commissioner for Refugees (UNHCR) is the agency presently entrusted with this function, as the representative of the international community, but States also may have a protecting role, even though their material interests are not engaged, and notwithstanding their common reluctance to take up the cause.

The study of refugee law invites a look not only at States' obligations with regard to admission and treatment after entry, but also at the potential responsibility in international law of the State whose conduct or omissions cause an outflow. It is easy enough to prescribe a principle of responsibility for 'creating' refugees, but considerably harder to offer a more precise formulation of the

---

[1] To what extent one should seek to fill every gap is a moot point, and indeed may compromise another objective, namely, the right of everyone 'to belong—or alternatively to move in an orderly fashion to seek work, decent living conditions and freedom from strife': Sadruddin Aga Khan, *Study on Human Rights and Mass Exoduses*: UN doc. E/CN.4/1503, para. 9.

underlying rights and duties. Writing nearly sixty years ago, Jennings posited liability on the repercussions which a refugee exodus has on the material interests of third States. In his view, conduct resulting in 'the flooding of other States with refugee populations' was illegal, '. . . *a fortiori* where the refugees are compelled to enter the country of refuge in a destitute condition'.[2]

With developments since 1939, the bases for the liability of source countries now lie not so much in the doctrine of abuse of rights, as Jennings then suggested, as in the breach of original obligations regarding human rights and fundamental freedoms. Legal theory nevertheless remains imperfect, given the absence of clearly correlative rights in favour of a subject of international law competent to exercise protection, and the uncertain legal consequences which follow where breach of obligations leads to a refugee exodus.[3] States are under a duty to co-operate with one another in accordance with the UN Charter, but the method of application of this principle in a given refugee case requires care. The promotion of 'orderly departure programmes', as an example of co-operation, supposes a degree of recognition of the right to leave one's country *and* to enter another which is not generally and currently justified by State practice.[4] Principles of reparation for loss suffered by receiving States also remain undeveloped.[5]

Established rules of international law nevertheless permit the conclusion that States are bound by a general principle not to create refugee outflows and to co-operate with other States in the resolution of such problems as they emerge. First, by analogy with the rule enunciated in the *Corfu Channel* case, responsibility may be attributed whenever a State, within whose territory substantial transboundary harm is generated, has knowledge or means of knowledge of the harm

---

[2] Jennings, R.Y., 'Some International Law Aspects of the Refugee Question', 20 *BYIL* 98, 111 (1939); see also at 112–13: 'Domestic rights must be subject to the principle *sic utere tuo ut alienum non laedas*. And for a State to employ these rights with the avowed purpose of saddling other States with unwanted sections of its population is as clear an abuse of right as can be imagined.'

[3] On developments in the international law of State responsibility having relevance to the flight or displacement of people, see *Report* of the International Law Commission, 41st Sess., 2 May–21 July 1989, UNGAOR: UN doc. A/44/10, para. 302 (text of draft articles provisionally adopted), specifically art. 5(2)(e)(ii),(iii), defining 'injured State'; art. 7 (restitution in kind), and para. 280; also *Report* of the International Law Commission, 42nd Sess., 1 May–20 July 1990: UN doc. A/45/11, para. 324, art. 8 (reparation by equivalent, or pecuniary compensation); art. 10 (satisfaction and guarantees of non-repetition); and comment at para. 393.

[4] The Director of the Intergovernmental Committee established by the 1938 Evian Conference was charged with undertaking 'negotiations to improve the present conditions of exodus (of refugees from Germany and Austria) and to replace them by orderly emigration'. Orderly departure was also proposed (and adopted, though with some slow starts), as an alternative to the departure of refugees from Vietnam by boat. See further below on Indo-chinese refugees and the Comprehensive Plan of Action.

[5] See above, note 3. Cf. Brownlie, I., *Principles of Public International Law*, (4th edn. 1990), 520: 'Expulsion [of non-nationals] which causes specific loss to the national state receiving groups without adequate notice would ground a claim for indemnity as for incomplete privilege.' Such a claim would in principle be stronger where the expulsion is itself unlawful, as in the case of nationals.

and the opportunity to act.[6] Secondly, even if at a somewhat high level of generality, States now owe to the international community the duty to accord to their nationals a certain standard of treatment in the matter of human rights. Thirdly, a State owes to other States at large (and to particular States after entry), the duty to re-admit its nationals. Fourthly, every State is bound by the principle of international co-operation.

A *rule* to the effect that 'States shall not create refugees' is too general and incomplete. An ambulatory principle nevertheless operates, obliging States to exercise care in their domestic affairs in the light of other States' legal interests,[7] and to co-operate in the solution of refugee problems. Such co-operation might include, as appropriate, assisting in the removal or mitigation of the causes of flight, contributing to the voluntary return of nationals abroad, and facilitating, in agreement with other States, the processes of orderly departure and family reunion.

Given the uncertain (and perhaps unpromising) legal situation that follows flight, increasing attention now focuses on the ways and means to *prevent* refugee outflows.[8] The enjoyment of human rights and fundamental freedoms is conditioned, in part at least, upon the opportunity of individuals and groups to participate in and benefit from the nation and body politic, and from the sensible premise that the authority to govern derives from the will of the people as expressed in periodic and genuine elections. The responsibility of States, in turn, springs from the fact of control over territory and inhabitants. *A priori*, individuals and groups ought to be free to enjoy human rights in the territory with which they are connected by the internationally relevant social fact of attachment; and it is probably self-evident that this is most likely to be attained, not by imposition from outside, but where local democratic and representative government, civil society and the rule of law flourish locally.

---

[6] Cf. Stockholm Declaration: 'States have . . . the responsibility to ensure that activities within their jurisdiction or control do not cause damage to the environment of other States or of areas beyond the limits of national jurisdiction': *Report* of the UN Conference on the Human Environment: UN doc. A/CONF.48/14/Rev. 1 and Corr. 1, Principle 21, 5. To compare the flow of refugees with the flow of, for example, noxious fumes may appear invidious; the basic issue, however, is the responsibility which derives from the fact of control over territory, a point clearly made by the International Court of Justice in its Advisory Opinion in the *Namibia Case*, ICJ *Rep.*, 1971, 16, at 54 (para. 118).

[7] Cf. International Law Commission, 'International Liability for Injurious Consequences arising out of acts not prohibited by international law': UN doc. A/36/10, 334ff (1981).

[8] A number of attempts have been made to devise more 'equitable' systems for dealing with the effects of refugee movements, for example, by the allocation of refugees to States in light of their relative well-being, space and capacity; see, for example, Grahl-Madsen, A., *Territorial Asylum*, (1980), 102–14; Hathaway, J., 'A Reconsideration of the Underlying Premise of Refugee Law', 31 *Harv. Int.L.J.* 129 (1990). See also Denmark's 1986 proposal for 'regional United Nations processing centres', intended to manage a global resettlement scheme on the basis of annual quotas to be offered by Member States: 'International Procedures for the Protection of Refugees': UN doc. A/C.3/41/L.51, 12 Nov. 1986. None of these proposals has struck a responsive chord with other States or non-State actors. For discussion of related developments to avert new flows of refugees, see below, Ch. 7, s. 3.5.

Essential as it is to the preservation of life and liberty, the right to seek asylum from persecution and the threat of torture or other relevant harm is no substitute for the fullest protection of human rights at home. Population pressure is not just a matter of numbers, but also of rural–urban migration, military and social conflict, under-development, deficient or faltering democratization, and peoples' perception that they are not or no longer able to influence their own life–plans. Equally clearly, however, the responses of the more developed world seem frequently limited to measures at their own front or back door; hence, the concentration on adding locks and bolts, on building higher walls and stronger fences, on palliatives and not remedies.

This all adds up to a less than healthy background against which to portray the panorama of rules and principles that do comprise the international legal regime of refugee protection. The sceptic may consider the ambition entirely quixotic, finding the field of population displacement dominated by narrow national ideologies and the play of market forces. The preface to the first edition of this book, written in 1982 by a much younger person, looked forward to a time when human rights and basic freedoms might be attainable, 'on behalf of every man, woman, and child who has not yet chosen flight from their homeland'. Fourteen or so years later, this implicit optimism, premised on a profound belief in the human capacity to resolve problems, is certainly harder to sustain. No international lawyer, however, can help but be impressed by the extent to which human rights and individual welfare have risen higher on the political and legal agenda, and by the expanding commitment, particularly among non-governmental organizations and in regional supervisory mechanisms, to ensure that rules are followed and standards maintained. One can only be concerned, therefore, by the piecemeal but persistent undermining of rules taken as fundamental just a decade and a half ago, all the while without apparent serious intent to face up to the social reality for which those rules exist.

The community of nations is responsible in a general sense for finding solutions and in providing international protection to refugees. This special mandate was entrusted to UNHCR in relatively unambiguous terms in 1951, which makes it all the more troubling when, even if for the best of all possible reasons, this agency is now to be found spending most of its time and resources on 'additional activities', such as general relief programmes and the fanciful ways of 'prevention'. As an actor on the international plane whose practice necessarily contributes as much to the formation as to the dismantling of legal structures, UNHCR's recent activities are bound to have an influence on the development of rules and standards; at the time of writing, however, a protection audit of recent activities seems overdue, while it is by no means clear that the end result will have been positive for refugees in the sense of international law.

This is not to argue that internally displaced persons should not be protected and assisted wherever possible; or that 'causes' cannot be dealt with. Rather, it is to raise the question of mandates, accountability, and the appropriateness of assumptions of responsibility and service on behalf of donor clients with agendas, worthy enough in themselves perhaps, which yet do not include *protection* among their primary objectives.

Besides attempting to capture these and other developments since 1982, the present edition differs in a number of important respects. The overall structure remains the same, although with the addition of a new Chapter 7 on 'Protection, Solutions, Prevention and Co-operation', and a number of consequential changes. The elapse of time since the previous edition has necessitated a complete revision of substance and assessment. First, this edition attempts to reflect the phenomenal growth in refugee literature and jurisprudence as coherently as possible, although understandably the final selection of sources and citations may not satisfy every reader. Secondly, municipal law in all its varieties has manifested an infinite capacity for revision and amendment. In 1982, it was possible to describe national laws and procedures with a degree of certainty and some prospect of accuracy over a reasonable period to come. That is no longer the case; the descriptions of national procedures have therefore been abandoned, and former Chapter VIII on 'Protection in Municipal Law' (now Chapter 9) has been entirely re-written in order to focus thematically on the sorts of procedural and substantive issues, such as due process, admissibility, credibility, and emergent social groups, that daily confront those involved in the determination of refugee status at the national level.

The Annexes have also been considerably expanded, and relevant documents are now grouped in six categories, with a separate Table of Contents appearing at pages 375–8. Perhaps the most important addition here is the selection of UNHCR Executive Committee Conclusions on International Protection. The full text of Conclusions cited simply by reference to their number (for example, Executive Committee Conclusion No. 24 (1981) on family reunification) can be found in Annexe 3, while references to source are provided for all others.

The aim of this second edition remains the same as that of the first: to describe the foundations and the framework of international refugee law by concentrating on three core issues; the definition of refugees, 'asylum' for refugees, and the protection of refugees. I still hope, too, that it will serve not only as an authoritative statement of the current law, but also as a pointer to the future, as a basis for further enquiry, the development of appropriate principles and solutions, and a world in which the *necessity* for flight, as a rational choice between alternative fates, may indeed be reduced.

Ferney-Voltaire
April 1996

Guy S. Goodwin-Gill

ACKNOWLEDGEMENTS

For having more than doubled the size of the original work, the author owes at least an apology, if not also some explanation for the time that has elapsed since the first edition appeared in 1983. In many respects, both size and time are due to the extraordinary growth in refugee studies, literature and case law during the period, itself a reflection of the continuing crises of coerced displacement, the search for solutions, and the reluctance or inability of States to perfect the regime of refugee protection by the addition, either of a right to asylum, or of meaningful alternatives to flight in search of safety.

Many individuals have contributed, directly and indirectly, to this second edition, some by their persistent (and insistent) encouragement, others by their enthusiasm and readiness to share thinking and experience, to discuss developments and to plan for the future. Among the first, in particular, is Professor Ian Brownlie, Chichele Professor of International Law in the University of Oxford, who has provided support for my practical and academic work over the years, for which I am continually appreciative. I am also indebted to Professor James Crawford, Whewell Professor of International Law in the University of Cambridge, for his readiness at all times to share his views and experience.

Although I left the Office of the United Nations High Commissioner for Refugees in 1987, I have nevertheless been able to count on old and new colleagues in that organization, not least by way of my editorship of the *International Journal of Refugee Law*, the contributors to which figure frequently in the text that follows. Anders Johnsson, on whose initiative the *IJRL* first saw the light of day, has generously given his help over the years, in his time in UNHCR's Division of International Protection, as a member of the *IJRL* Editorial Board, and latterly in his capacity as Deputy Secretary General of the Inter-Parliamentary Union. I am grateful also to other members of the Board with whom I have been able to work closely over the last years, particularly Patricia Hyndman, Arthur Helton, and Walter Kälin, as well as all past and present members who have helped to establish the journal as the major focus for legal writing, research and promotion, and to spread the word among those with experience and critical perceptions seeking a channel for dissemination.

Although no financial grant or research assistance has been received or employed in the preparation of this work, the drafting of this second edition has drawn upon a fair range of professional papers and opinions prepared for governments, international and non-governmental organizations, counsel and administrative agencies. Chapter 4, in particular, relies extensively on a review of the status of the principle of *non-refoulement* in international law drafted for the

UNHCR Division of International Protection and at the request of Leonardo Franco, former Director of the Division, and Pierre Bertrand, former Chief of the General Legal Advice Section. The sections dealing with international co-operation owe much to original work done with Professor Louis Sohn, Thomas Burgenthal, the American Society of International Law and the John D. and Catherine T. MacArthur Foundation, in a pilot project on the governing rules of international law. Some of the ideas in that work were in turn developed in a paper prepared jointly for UNHCR and the International Organization for Migration, as a contribution to the debate on migration and refugee issues within the CSCE (thanks to Anders Wenström and Jan Henneman, both then with IOM and UNHCR respectively). Those ideas later acquired a practical orientation in a contribution to strategic planning and management for UNHCR's Regional Bureau for Europe, at the request of John Horekens, Director of the Bureau, and in collaboration with human resources management expert Piers Campbell.

An early focus on a number of substantive and procedural matters was actively encouraged by John Scratch, QC, and Martin Low, QC, Head and former Head respectively of the Human Rights Law Section of the Department of Justice of Canada, for which I continue to be especially grateful. In like manner, I am happy to record my deep appreciation for the opportunity to participate in the establishment of Canada's Immigration and Refugee Board (IRB), and in particular for the ready support and confidence provided by Gordon Fairweather, the IRB's first Chair, and Peter Harder, its first Executive Director. Despite my recent absence from Canada, this positive association has continued thanks to the current Chairperson, Nurjehan Mawani, and the Deputy Chair and former Law Reform Commissioner, John Frecker.

In another but related context, I would like to express my thanks to Alan Dingle and John Lawford of QuickLaw (QL Systems Ltd), with whom I worked in the first stages of establishing a publicly available electronic record of refugee decisions in Canada. They have since greatly facilitated my access to a wide range of legal databases, the results of which will soon be apparent to the reader.

My work with the IRB included not only a fruitful series of training sessions with new members and staff, but also a close association with the then fledgling Documentation Centre, since renamed the Documentation, Information and Research Branch (DIRB). Graham Howell, then and now Director General of the Centre/DIRB, and Sharon Rusu, Director of Research, together with their colleagues, provided many occasions on which to develop some of the thinking that appears in the following pages. Other challenges came about through my participation in training sessions with the new Asylum Corps of the United States Immigration and Naturalization Service, where Gregg Beyer was an able initiator; and with Australian decision-makers, courtesy of Libby Lloyd and the Department of Immigration, Local Government and Ethnic Affairs.

Documentation, country of origin information, and standards of analysis and dissemination play an increasingly important role in the determination of refugee status and the development of refugee and related policies. In this field, a substantial contribution has been made and continues to be made by UNHCR's Centre for Documentation on Refugees (CDR). Its Chief for many years, Hans Thoolen, provided friendly and co-operative assistance both to my own work and to that of the *IJRL*. His successor, Sharon Rusu (the same), continued and enhanced that relationship, and I am especially grateful to her and her team not only for information shared, but also for the frequent, excellent opportunities to participate in constructing the future. It was particularly rewarding to be involved with CDR's CD-ROM team, the producers of *RefWorld/Refmonde*, including Udo Janz, Julian Durand, Jerome Sabety, Ian Myles, Elisa Mason, Susin Park, Andrei Dmitrichev, Martha Percival, Ann Encontre, Zak Kawi and Christophe Beau. Other members of CDR also readily put their skills at my disposal, including Anne Fati (for many an information request), Gogo Hukportie, Geneviève Bador, Houssam Mu'allem, Victoria Bonomo, Suzanne Mesli, Nathalie Bernard-Bonpain, Catherine Meylan, Chandrasekaran Nagarajan and Diane Trevellyan.

The opportunity to get to grips with this revision is due in large measure to the Department of Law of Carleton University, Ottawa, and to Brettel Dawson and Ron Saunders, Chair and former Chair respectively, for the kind support and approval of an extended period of leave of absence. A different sort of opportunity was provided by the Stichting Bijzondere Leerstoel Asielrecht, a unique and innovative foundation set up in the Netherlands by five non-governmental organizations (Vereniging VluchtelingenWerk Nederland, Vereniging Nederlands Juristencomité voor de Mensenrechten, Vereniging Amnesty International Afdeling Nederland, and Stichting voor Vluchteling-Studenten UAF), for the express purpose of endowing a Chair of Asylum Law. It was my good fortune to be elected as the first incumbent of this post, which continues to provide me with a very rewarding teaching experience. I am particularly grateful to Foundation members Hanneke Steenbergen, Ted Badoux, Frits Florin and Paul Schaink for their assistance and positive support, and to my colleagues in the Vakgroep Bestuursrecht, Universiteit van Amsterdam, for the friendly and stimulating work environment.

As always, it has been a pleasure to work with the staff of Oxford University Press in the preparation of this edition, and my thanks go to Richard Hart and Kristin Clayton for their patience and perseverance.

Finally, as so many of us who write will know, there is no way this second edition would ever have been finished, had it not been for the love and support of my family. For my wife Sharon, providing endless encouragement professionally but above all personally, and for our boys, Adam and Nathaniel, who even came to miss the late-night tapping at the keyboard, this at last will close not just a chapter!

I have attempted to state the law as it stood on 31 December 1995. Notwithstanding the many who have contributed to my thinking over the years, I alone am responsible for the views expressed herein, as also for such errors and omissions as remain.

*   *   *

The first reprinting of this work has permitted the correction of a number of typographical errors, and for the information in Annexe 6 to be updated to 1 June 1997.

CONTENTS

PART 3: PROTECTION

TABLE OF TREATIES AND OTHER
INTERNATIONAL INSTRUMENTS

[The full text or relevant extracts of instruments marked with an asterisk can be found in the Annexes]

TABLE OF CASES

[Judicial and administrative decisions cited only from secondary sources, such as articles and case commentaries, are generally not included in the following list]

SELECTED ABBREVIATIONS

AJIL	American Journal of International Law
ASEAN	Association of South East Asian States
Asyl	*Schweizerische Zeitschrift für Asylrecht und-praxis/Revue suisse pour la pratique et le droit d'asile*
AsylVfG	*Asylverfahrensgesetz* (Asylum Procedure Law of the Federal Republic of Germany)
AuslG	*Ausländergesetz* (Aliens Law of the Federal Republic of Germany)
BDIL	*British Digest of International Law*, vols. 2b–7, London, 1965, 1967 (C. Parry, ed.)
BGBl	*Bundesgesetzblatt* (published laws of the Federal Republic of Germany and/or Austria)
BVerfGE	*Entscheidungen des Bundesverfassungsgerichts* (decisions of the Federal Constitutional Court of the Federal Republic of Germany)
BVerwGE	*Entscheidungen des Bundesverwaltungsgerichts* (decisions of the Federal Administrative Court of the Federal Republic of Germany)
BYIL	*British Yearbook of International Law*
CDR	Centre for Documentation on Refugees (UNHCR)
CE	Council of Europe
CFR	Code of Federal Regulations (USA)
CIREFCA	International Conference on Refugees in Central America
CPA	Comprehensive Plan of Action for Indo-chinese Refugees
CRDD	Convention Refugee Determination Division (IRB, Canada)
CRR	Commission des recours des réfugiés (France)
CSCE	Conference on Security and Co-operation in Europe (later the OSCE—Organization for Security and Co-operation in Europe)
CTD	Convention Travel Document (issued under article 28 of the 1951 Convention relating to the Status of Refugees)
D.Ct.	District Court (USA)
DHA	Department of Humanitarian Affairs (United Nations)

DIRB	Documentation, Information and Research Branch (see IRBDC)
DISERO	Disembarkation Resettlement Offers
Doc. réf.	*Documentation réfugiés*
DORS Committee	Determination of Refugee Status Committee (Australia)
ECHR	European Convention on Human Rights
ECtHR	European Court of Human Rights
ECOSOC	Economic and Social Council of the United Nations
ETS	European Treaty Series
EU	European Union
FAO	Food and Agriculture Organization
FC-TD	Federal Court—Trial Division (Canada)
FCA	Federal Court of Appeal (Canada)
FCJ	Judgments of the Federal Court of Canada (Court of Appeal and Trial Division), as cited online by QuickLaw
Hackworth, *Digest*	G.H. Hackworth, *Digest of International Law*, 8 vols., Washington, 1940–4
HC	House of Commons
HC Deb.	Parliamentary Debates, House of Commons, 5th series
HCR	High Commissioner for Refugees
HL Deb.	Parliamentary Debates, House of Lords, 5th series
HRQ	*Human Rights Quarterly*
ICEM	Inter-governmental Committee for European Migration
ICJ	International Court of Justice
ICLQ	*International and Comparative Law Quarterly*
IDPs	Internally displaced persons
IFA	Internal flight alternative
IGCR	Inter-governmental Committee on Refugees
IJRL	*International Journal of Refugee Law*
ILC	International Law Commission
ILO	International Labour Organization
ImmAR	Immigration Appeals Reports
IMCO	Intergovernmental Maritime Consultative Organization (renamed in 1982 as the International Maritime Organization—IMO)
IMO	See IMCO
IMT	International Military Tribunal
INA	Immigration and Nationality Act 1952 (USA)
INS	Immigration and Naturalization Service (USA)
IRB	Immigration and Refugee Board (Canada)
IRBDC	Immigration and Refugee Board Documentation

	Centre (later DIRB)
IRO	International Refugee Organization
JRS	*Journal of Refugee Studies*
LN	League of Nations
LNTS	League of Nations Treaty Series
MEI	Minister of Employment and Immigration (Canada)
Moore, *Arbitrations*	John Bassett Moore, *History and Digest of the International Arbitrations to which the United States has been a Party*, Washington, 1898.
Moore, *Digest*	John Bassett Moore, *Digest of International Law*, 8 vols., Washington, 1906.
NGO	Non-governmental organization
OAS	Organization of American States
OAU	Organization of African Unity
OFPRA	*Office français de protection des réfugiés et apatrides*
OJ	Official Journal
ORCI	Office for Research and Collection of Information (United Nations)
OSCE	See CSCE
PCIJ	Permanent Court of International Justice
QL	QuickLaw (QL Systems Ltd.) online database service (Canada)
RASRO	Rescue at Sea Resettlement Offers
RDDE	*Revue du droit des étrangers*
RSAC	Refugee Status Advisory Committee (Canada)
RSQ	*Refugee Survey Quarterly*
SC res.	Security Council resolution
SCJ	Judgments of the Supreme Court of Canada, as cited online by QuickLaw
UN	United Nations
UNBRO	United Nations Border Relief Operation
UNCCP	United Nations Conciliation Commission for Palestine
UNDP	United Nations Development Programme
UNDRO	Office of the United Nations Disaster Relief Co-ordinator
UNGA res.	United Nations General Assembly resolution
UNHCR	Office of the United Nations High Commissioner for Refugees
UNHCR, *Collection*	UNHCR, *Collection of International Instruments concerning Refugees*, 2nd edn., Geneva, 1979
UNHCR, *Conclusions*	UNHCR, *Conclusions on International Protection adopted by the Executive Committee of the Programme of the High Commissioner*, Geneva, 1979–

UNHCR, *Handbook*	UNHCR, *Handbook on Procedures and Criteria for Determining Refugee Status*, Geneva, 1979
UNICEF	United Nations Children's Fund
UNKRA	United Nations Korean Reconstruction Agency
UNPROFOR	United Nations Protection Force in Former Yugoslavia
UNRRA	United Nations Relief and Rehabilitation Administration
UNRWA	United Nations Relief and Works Agency for Palestine Refugees in the Near East
UNTS	United Nations Treaty Series
USCR	United States Committee for Refugees
VG	*Verwaltungsgericht* (Administrative Court, Federal Republic of Germany)
WFP	World Food Programme
Whiteman, *Digest*	Marjorie M. Whiteman, *Digest of International Law*, 15 vols., Washington, 1963–73
WHO	World Health Organization
ZaöRV	*Zeitschrift für ausländisches öffentliches Recht und Völkerrecht*

PART ONE

REFUGEES

Chapter 1

DEFINITION AND DESCRIPTION

1. Refugees

The term 'refugee' is a term of art, that is, a term with a content verifiable according to principles of general international law. In ordinary usage, it has a broader, looser meaning, signifying someone in flight, who seeks to escape conditions or personal circumstances found to be intolerable. The destination is not relevant; the flight is to freedom, to safety. Likewise, the reasons for flight may be many; flight from oppression, from a threat to life or liberty, flight from prosecution; flight from deprivation, from grinding poverty; flight from war or civil strife; flight from natural disasters, earthquake, flood, drought, famine. Implicit in the ordinary meaning of the word 'refugee' lies an assumption that the person concerned is worthy of being, and ought to be, assisted, and, if necessary, protected from the causes and consequences of flight. The 'fugitive' from justice, the person fleeing criminal prosecution for breach of the law in its ordinary and non-political aspect, is therefore often excepted from this category of refugees.[1]

For the purposes of international law, States have further limited the concept of the refugee. For example, 'economic refugees'—the term is generally disfavoured—are not included. The solution to their problem, perhaps, lies more within the province of international aid and development, rather than in the institution of asylum, considered as protection of whatever duration on the territory of another State.

Defining refugees may appear an unworthy exercise in legalism and semantics, obstructing a prompt response to the needs of people in distress. States have nevertheless insisted on fairly restrictive criteria for identifying those who benefit from refugee status and asylum or local protection. For the victims of natural calamities,[2] the very fact of need may be the sufficient indicator, but for the

---

[1] The *New Shorter Oxford English Dictionary* (1993) defines a refugee as 'a person driven from his or her home to seek refuge, esp. in a foreign country, from war, religious persecution, political troubles, natural disaster, etc.' and 'refuge' as 'shelter from danger or trouble; protection, aid . . .'

[2] The Office of the Disaster Relief Co-ordinator (UNDRO) was established further to UNGA res. 2816(XXVI), 14 Dec. 1971, in recognition of the necessity 'to ensure prompt, effective and efficient response to a Government's need for assistance, at the time of a natural disaster or other disaster situation'. For critical assessments of its performance, see for example the report of the Joint Inspection Unit: JIU/REP/80/11; UN doc. A/36/73 and Add. 1. In 1981, the General Assembly resolved to strengthen the capacity of the UN system to respond to natural disasters and other disaster situations (UNGA res. 36/225, 17 Dec. 1981), but only in 1992 was it decided to appoint a co-ordinator and to establish the UN Department of Humanitarian Affairs (incorporating UNDRO), with the requisite levels of responsibility. See generally Macalister-Smith, P., *International Humanitarian Assistance* (1985); and for recent developments, below Ch. 6, s. 1.3.

victims of conditions or disasters with a human origin, additional factors are required. The purpose of any definition or description of the class of refugees is thus to facilitate, and to justify, aid and protection; moreover, in practice, satisfying the relevant criteria ought to indicate entitlement to the pertinent rights or benefits. In determining the content in international law of the class of refugees, therefore, the traditional sources—treaties and the practice of States—must be examined, with account taken also of the practice and procedures of the various bodies established by the international community to deal with the problems of refugees.

2. Refugees defined in international instruments 1922–46

In treaties and arrangements concluded under the auspices of the League of Nations, a group or category approach was adopted. That someone was (a) outside their country of origin and (b) without the protection of the government of that State, were sufficient and necessary conditions. A Russian refugee, for example, was defined in 1926 to include 'any person of Russian origin who does not enjoy or who no longer enjoys the protection of the Government of the Union of Socialist Soviet Republics and who has not acquired another nationality'.[3] In this instance, presence outside the country of origin was not explicitly required, but was implicit in the objectives of the arrangements, namely, the issue of identity certificates for the purpose of travel and resettlement.[4]

A similar approach was employed in 1936 arrangements for those fleeing Germany,[5] which were later developed by article 1 of the 1938 Convention, to cover:

(a) Persons possessing or having possessed German nationality and not possessing any other nationality who are proved not to enjoy, in law or fact, the protection of the German government.
(b) Stateless persons not covered by previous conventions or agreements who have left German territory after being established therein and who are proved not to enjoy, in law or in fact, the protection of the German government.[6]

---

[3] Arrangement relating to the issue of identity certificates to Russian and Armenian refugees, 12 May 1926: 84 *LNTS* No. 2004. The definition of 'Armenian refugee' was to like effect: ibid. 'Assyrian, Assyro-Chaldean, and assimilated refugee' was defined in the Arrangement concerning the Extension to other Categories of Refugees of certain Measures taken in favour of Russian and Armenian Refugees of 30 June 1928: 89 *LNTS* No. 2006. Cf. art. 1, 1933 Convention relating to the International Status of refugees, and reservations thereto: 159 *LNTS* No. 3663. See also Marrus, M., *The Unwanted—European Refugees in the Twentieth Century*, (1985), 74–81, 119–21; Hathaway, J., 'The Evolution of Refugee Status in International Law,' 33 *ICLQ* 348 (1984).

[4] Certificates ceased to be valid if the bearers returned to their country of origin; see form and wording of the certificate attached to the arrangement of 5 July 1922: 13 *LNTS* No. 355; res. 9 of the arrangement of 30 June 1928: 89 *LNTS* No. 2005; certificate attached to the Convention concerning the Status of Refugees coming from Germany of 10 Feb. 1938: 192 *LNTS* No. 4461.

[5] Art. 1, Provisional Arrangement concerning the Status of Refugees coming from Germany, 4 July 1936: 171 *LNTS* No. 3952.

[6] 1938 Convention concerning the Status of Refugees coming from Germany: 191 *LNTS* No.

Article 1(2) excluded from the definition persons who left Germany for reasons of purely personal convenience.

At a meeting in Evian in the same year, participating States resolved to establish an Inter-governmental Committee on Refugees with, as its primary objective, 'facilitating involuntary emigration from Germany (including Austria)'.[7] Included within the scope of the Committee's activities were those who had yet to emigrate on account of their political opinions, religious beliefs, or racial origin, as well as those who had already left for these reasons and had not established themselves elsewhere.[8] A major review at the Bermuda Conference in April 1943 expanded the mandate to include 'all persons, wherever they may be, who, as a result of events in Europe, have had to leave, or may have to leave, their country of residence because of the danger to their lives or liberties on account of their race, religion or political beliefs'.[9]

Commenting on definitions, Simpson observed already in 1938 that they each had certain inherent deficiencies. He stressed the importance of keeping in view the 'essential quality' of the refugee as one 'who has sought refuge in a territory other than that in which he was formerly resident as a result of political events which rendered his continued residence in his former territory impossible or intolerable'.[10] This description is in turn something of an abstraction from what

4461. The Convention was expanded the following year to include Austrian refugees after the *Anschluss*; see the Additional Protocol, 14 Sept. 1939: 198 *LNTS* No. 4634.

[7] (1938) 19 (8–9) LNOJ 676–7. For a full account of the IGCR, see Sjöberg, T., *The Powers and the Persecuted: The Refugee Problem and the Intergovernmental Committee on Refugees (IGCR), 1938–47*, (1991). On 'orderly departure' from Vietnam, see further below, Ch. 5, s. 3. Speaking in 1979 to the Geneva Conference on Refugees and Displaced Persons in Southeast Asia, United States Vice-President Mondale characterized the 1938 Evian Conference as a failure: 'The civilized world', he said, 'hid in a cloak of legalism': UN Press Release SG/REF/3, 21 Jul. 1979. See also Marrus, *The Unwanted*, 166–70.

[8] Para. 8, res. adopted by the Intergovernmental Meeting at Evian, 14 Jul. 1938: LNOJ, 19, nos. 8–9: Aug.–Sept. 1938, 676–7. See also art. 1, Agreement relating to the issue of Travel Documents to Refugees who are the Concern of the Intergovernmental Committee on Refugees, 15 Oct. 1946: 11 *UNTS* 73; Marrus, *The Unwanted*, 170–7.

[9] Sjöberg, *The Powers and the Persecuted*, 16 and Ch. 4. The functions of the organization were also rewritten: IGCR was 'to undertake negotiations with neutral or Allied States or with organizations, and to take such steps as may be necessary to preserve, maintain and transport' refugees within its mandate. The United Nations Relief and Rehabilitation Administration (UNRRA), established in Nov. 1943 with forty-four governments signing the constituent agreement, was principally concerned with assistance to civilian nationals of the allied nations and to displaced persons in liberated countries, and with the repatriation and return of prisoners of war. It was not authorized to resettle the displaced or to deal with or find solutions for refugees, considered as those who, 'for any reason, definitely cannot return to their homes, or have no homes to return to, or no longer enjoy the protection of their Governments . . .' See para. 22, proposal concerning refugees submitted by the United Kingdom: UN doc. A/C.3/5, annexed to GAOR, Third Committee, 1st Sess., 1st Part, 1946, Summary Records: UN doc. A/C.3/SR.1–11. UNRRA nevertheless increasingly faced these issues as east Europeans fled or refused to return to communism; see Salomon, K., *Refugees in the Cold War: Toward a New International Refugee Regime in the Early Postwar Era*, (1991), 46–54 and *passim*; Woodbridge, G., *The History of the United Nations Relief and Rehabilitation Administration*, 3 vols., (1950); Marrus, *The Unwanted*, 317–24.

[10] Simpson, J.H., *Refugees—A Preliminary Report of a Survey* (1938), 1.

was known then about the 'political events' producing refugees. While the notion of the impossibility or intolerability of continued residence illustrates the problem of the refugee in broad strokes, after the Second World War more precise criteria emerged. This is evident first in the Constitution of the International Refugee Organization (IRO), then in the Statute of the Office of the United Nations High Commissioner for Refugees (UNHCR), and finally in the provisions of the 1951 Convention relating to the Status of Refugees. In a little less than five years, the preferred approach to refugee definition moved from a basis in flexible or open groups and categories, to an apparently more closed and legalistic one.

The Constitution of the IRO continued the practice of earlier instruments, and specified certain categories to be assisted. 'Refugees' thus included victims of the Nazi, Fascist, or Quisling regimes which had opposed the United Nations, certain persons of Jewish origin, or foreigners or stateless persons who had been victims of Nazi persecution, as well as persons considered as refugees before the outbreak of the Second World War for reasons of race, religion, nationality, or political opinion. The IRO was also competent to assist 'displaced persons', including those deported or expelled from their own countries, some of whom had been sent to undertake forced labour.[11] In addition, the IRO Constitution included as refugees those unable or unwilling to avail themselves of the protection of the government of their country of nationality or former residence. It expressly recognized that individuals might have 'valid objections' to returning to their country of origin, including 'persecution or fear based on reasonable grounds of persecution because of race, religion, nationality or political opinions,' and objections 'of a political nature judged by the [IRO] to be valid'.[12]

In 1949, the UN began to look forward to a post-IRO period. Several States were opposed to the adoption of a broad approach, considering it essential to identify refugees who were in need of international protection. The United States favoured a narrow definition of those who would fall within the competence of a new, temporary agency, a de-emphasis of resettlement, and concentration on 'legal protection' pending integration in countries of refuge, as opposed to assistance or similar activities; the main purpose was to prevent refugees becoming a liability to the international community. Other refugee categories, such as those created by population transfers, were mostly entitled to rights afforded by their countries of residence, and thus in no need of interna-

---

[11] On the re-emergence of the term 'displaced persons' see further below, s. 3.2.

[12] For full text, see below, Annexe 1, No. 1. Generally, see Holborn, L. W., *The International Refugee Organization: A Specialized Agency of the United Nations. Its History and Work 1946–52*, (1956); Salomon, K., *Refugees in the Cold War: Toward a New International Refugee Regime in the Early Postwar Era*, (1991). For a brief account of the politicized debates in the UN on refugee definition in the 1940s, see Goodwin–Gill, G. S., 'Different Types of Forced Migration Movements as an International and National Problem', in Rystad, G., ed., *The Uprooted: Forced Migration as an International Problem in the Post-War Era*, (1990), 15, 22–9.

tional protection.[13] Apart from those countries actually having to deal with large populations of 'national refugees',[14] a consensus emerged that such refugees were not 'an international problem', and did not require international protection.

3.   Refugees for the purposes of the United Nations

The Office of the United Nations High Commissioner for Refugees (UNHCR) succeeded the IRO as the principal UN agency concerned with refugees; the scope and extent of its competence are considered more fully below, taking account of the impact of developments within the UN, such as article 14(1) of the Universal Declaration of Human Rights,[15] the relation of 'asylum'[16] to persecution, and the 1967 Declaration on Territorial Asylum. The bases for an international legal concept of the refugee are thus to be found in treaties, State and United Nations practice, and in the Statute of the UNHCR.[17]

3.1 STATUTE OF THE UNITED NATIONS HIGH COMMISSIONER FOR REFUGEES (UNHCR)

UNHCR was established by the General Assembly to provide 'international protection' and to seek 'permanent solutions for the problem of refugees'. According to its Statute, the work of the Office shall be of an entirely non-political character—it is to be 'humanitarian' and 'social' and to relate, as a rule, to groups and categories of refugees.[18]

The Statute first brings within UNHCR's competence refugees covered by various earlier treaties and arrangements. It next includes refugees resulting from events occurring before 1 January 1951, who are outside their country of

---

[13] GAOR, 5th Sess., Third Committee, Summary Records, 324th Meeting, 22 Nov. 1950, paras. 44–9; see also 326th Meeting, 24 Nov. 1950, para. 31f (United States). At the 329th Meeting, 29 Nov. 1950, the US representative, Eleanor Roosevelt, criticized the UK proposal to include refugees requiring assistance, but not protection. She noted that refugees in Germany, India, Pakistan and Turkey had serious problems of integration, but they enjoyed the rights of nationals. Any specific relief programmes should be formulated within the overall economic framework of the countries concerned, and were beyond the competence of the High Commissioner. Ibid., paras. 34–6.

[14] Cf. the views of India: ibid., 332nd Meeting, 1 Dec. 1950, paras. 26–7.

[15] 'Everyone has the right to seek and to enjoy in other countries asylum from persecution'.

[16] See below, Ch. 5.

[17] An understanding of the historical context of UNHCR's creation is also important; see Salomon, K., *Refugees in the Cold War: Toward a New International Refugee Regime in the Early Postwar Era*, (1991); Sjöberg, T., *The Powers and the Persecuted: The Refugee Problem and the Intergovernmental Committee on Refugees (IGCR), 1938–47*, (1991) (both reviewed by the present writer in 6 *IJRL* 311 (1994); Rystad, G., ed., *The Uprooted: Forced Migration as an International Problem in the Post-War Era*, (1990).

[18] UNGA res. 428(V), annexe, paras. 1, 2; for full text, see below, Annexe 1, No. 3. For brief background, see Goodwin-Gill, G.S., 'Different Types of Forced Migration Movements as an International and National Problem,' in Rystad, G., ed., *The Uprooted: Forced Migration as an International Problem in the Post-War Era*, (1990), 15.

origin[19] and unable or unwilling to avail themselves of its protection 'owing to a well-founded fear of being persecuted' or 'for reasons other than personal convenience'.[20] Finally, the Statute extends to:

Any other person who is outside the country of his nationality, or if he has no nationality, the country of his former habitual residence, because he has or had a well-founded fear of persecution by reason of his race, religion, nationality or political opinion and is unable or, because of such fear, is unwilling to avail himself of the protection of the government of the country of his nationality, or, if he has no nationality, to return to the country of his former habitual residence.

This description is of universal application, containing neither temporal nor geographical limitations. The substantive or ideological criteria are nevertheless a significant restriction on the scope of refugees 'strictly so-called', who must establish a well-founded fear of persecution on one or more of the stated grounds.

The definition remains a critical point of departure in determining who is entitled to the protection and assistance of the United Nations, for it is the lack of protection by their own government which distinguishes refugees from ordinary aliens. In attempting to make good this deficiency, the appropriate international agency will aim generally to protect the refugee's basic human rights, including the right to life, liberty, and security of the person.[21] Simultaneously, 'protection activities' may focus on specific issues peculiar to the refugee: for example, ensuring that no refugee is returned to a country in which he or she will be in danger; ensuring that asylum seekers have access to an informed procedure and that every refugee is recognized as such, that asylum is granted, that expulsion is prevented, that travel and identity documents are issued. Any intervention with governments must therefore have a sound jurisdictional base, especially when made in a political context that is hostile to asylum, or in which laws, regulations and practice may be oriented to summary dismissal.

3.2 DEVELOPMENT OF THE STATUTORY DEFINITION AND EXTENSION OF THE MANDATE

The UNHCR Statute nevertheless contains an apparent contradiction. On the one hand, it affirms that the work of the Office shall relate, as a rule, to groups and categories of refugees. On the other hand, it proposes a definition of the refugee which is essentially individualistic, seeming to require a case by case examination of subjective and objective elements. The frequency of large-scale refugee crises over the last 45 years, together with a variety of political and

---

[19] The phrase 'country of origin' is used for convenience here and throughout the text; it signifies, as appropriate, the refugee's country of nationality or, if he or she has no nationality, his or her country of former habitual residence.

[20] This latter provision would cover the situation of a person who, by reason of persecution already suffered, remains unwilling to return even though the circumstances which gave rise to his or her refugee status have ceased to exist. Cf. art. 1C(5), (6), 1951 Convention; and below, Ch. 3, s. 2.

[21] See further below, Ch. 6.

humanitarian considerations, has necessitated flexibility in the administration of UNHCR's mandate. In consequence, there has been a significant broadening of what may be termed the concept of 'refugees of concern to the international community'.

A major role in these developments has been played by the United Nations General Assembly and the Economic and Social Council, whose policy directions the High Commissioner is required to follow.[22] More recently, a similar influence has been exercised by the Executive Committee of the High Commissioner's Programme. Established in 1957,[23] the Executive Committee's terms of reference include advising the High Commissioner, on request, in the exercise of the statutory functions; and advising on the appropriateness of providing international assistance through UNHCR in order to solve such specific refugee problems as may arise.[24]

It was also in 1957 that the General Assembly first authorized the High Commissioner to assist refugees who did not come fully within the statutory definition, but whose situation was 'such as to be of concern to the international community'.[25] The case involved large numbers of mainland Chinese in Hong Kong whose status as 'refugees' was complicated by the existence of two Chinas, each of which might have been called upon to exercise protection. Given the need for assistance, express authorization to the High Commissioner 'to use his good offices to encourage arrangements for contributions' was an effective, pragmatic solution.[26] Assistance to other specific groups was authorized in the years that followed.[27] Concurrently, the General Assembly developed the notion of the

[22] UNHCR Statute, para. 3.
[23] UNGA res. 1166(XII), 26 Nov. 1957. The General Assembly decided on 23 Dec. 1994 to enlarge membership of the Executive Committee from forty-seven to fifty States: UNGA res. 49/171. See below, Annexe 6.
[24] On the conclusions of the Executive Committee and their role in setting protection standards, see further below, Ch. 6.
[25] UNGA res. 1167(XII), 26 Nov. 1957. Cf. UNGA res. 1129(XI), 21 Nov. 1956, approving UNHCR action already taken to assist Hungarian refugees. In UNGA res. 1784(XVII), 7 Dec. 1962, the General Assembly again acknowledged that the situation of Chinese refugees was of concern to the international community, recognized the continuing need for emergency and long-term assistance, and requested UNHCR to use its good offices in the provision thereof.
[26] See Hambro, E., *The Problem of Chinese Refugees in Hong Kong*, (1955), for background.
[27] For example, to Algerians fleeing to Tunisia and Morocco to escape the effects of the struggle for liberation: UNGA resolutions 1286(XIII), 5 Dec. 1958, 1389(XVI), 20 Nov. 1959, 1500(XV), 5 Dec. 1960, 1672(XVI), 18 Dec. 1961; and to Angolan refugees in the Congo: UNGA res. 1671(XVI), 10 Dec. 1961. Using recently declassified archival material in London, Paris and Washington, as well as interviews with officials (including August Lindt, the High Commissioner of the day), Ruthström-Ruiz has shown that earlier explanations attributing UNHCR's involvement with Algerian refugees to a 'good offices' basis are 'incomplete, and partly incorrect': *Beyond Europe: The Globalization of Refugee Aid*, (1993), 103f; reviewed by the present writer in 7 *IJRL* 168 (1995). Following an on-site investigation in Tunisia, the High Commissioner initially decided that the Algerians were indeed within his mandate as refugees with a well-founded fear of persecution, only to change tack later. UNHCR's inconsistent interpretation and application of its Statute satisfied client governments, including those who, while critical of French policy in Algeria, either did not want France accused of persecution or were themselves uncertain whether Algerians who fled were 'refugees'.

High Commissioner's 'good offices' as an umbrella idea under which to bring refugees who did not come within the competence, or 'immediate competence',[28] of the United Nations. The type of assistance which might be given was initially limited, often to the transmission of financial contributions, but that restriction was soon dropped.[29]

In 1959, in anticipation of World Refugee Year, the General Assembly called for special attention to be given 'to the problems of refugees coming within the competence' of UNHCR, while simultaneously authorizing the High Commissioner to use his good offices in the transmission of contributions for the assistance of refugees 'who do not come within the competence of the United Nations'.[30] On the same day, the General Assembly had no hesitation in recommending that the High Commissioner continue his efforts on behalf of refugees from Algeria in Morocco and Tunisia, pending their return to their homes.[31] As more than the mere transmission of contributions was involved, these refugees, who had fled a particularly violent national liberation struggle,[32] were clearly considered to fall within the competence of the United Nations. Indeed, there is little to distinguish the resolution in question from that adopted three years earlier on refugees from Hungary.[33] After the reference to 'good offices refugees' in the General Assembly's 1963 resolution on the report of UNHCR,[34] the term does not recur again until its final appearance in 1973.[35] The 1965 resolution referred generically to the protection of refugees and to solutions for the 'various groups of refugees within (UNHCR) competence'.[36] Thereafter the language changed, became more composite and began to reflect the notion of refugees 'of concern' to UNHCR.[37]

---

[28] The term is employed but not defined in UNGA res. 1499(XV), 5 Dec. 1960.

[29] Compare UNGA resolutions 1167(XII), 26 Nov. 1957 and 1784(XVII) 7 Dec. 1962.

[30] UNGA res. 1388(XIV), 20 Nov. 1959.

[31] UNGA res. 1389(XIV), 20 Nov. 1959. See also UNGA resolutions 1286(XIII), 5 Dec. 1958, 1500(XV), 5 Dec. 1960 and 1672(XVI), 18 Dec. 1961.

[32] The details are well summarized in Ruthström-Ruiz, C., *Beyond Europe: The Globalization of Refugee Aid*, (1993), 81–93.

[33] See UNGA resolutions 1129(XI), 21 Nov. 1956; 1499(XV), 5 Dec. 1960; res. 1673(XVI), 18 Dec. 1961; 1783(XVII), 7 Dec. 1962.

[34] UNGA res. 1959(XVIII), 12 Dec. 1963, requesting the High Commissioner to continue to afford international protection to refugees and to pursue efforts on behalf of refugees within his mandate and of those for whom he extends his good offices, by giving particular attention to new refugee groups, in conformity with relevant General Assembly resolutions and Executive Committee directives (para. 1).

[35] UNGA res. 3143(XXVIII), 14 Dec. 1973, requesting the High Commissioner to continue his assistance and protection activities in favour of refugees within his mandate as well as for those to whom he extends his good offices or is called up to assist in accordance with relevant resolutions of the General Assembly.

[36] UNGA res. 2039(XX), 7 Dec. 1965.

[37] UNGA resolutions 2197(XXI), 16 Dec. 1966; 2294(XXII), 11 Dec. 1967 (continuing UNHCR and requesting protection, assistance and efforts towards solutions for refugees who are UNHCR's concern); 2399(XXIII), 6 Dec. 1968 (to similar effect, calling also for 'special attention to new groups of refugees, particularly in Africa', in conformity with relevant General Assembly resolutions and Executive Committee directives); 2594(XXIV), 16 Dec. 1969 (noting results obtained in regard to

General Assembly resolutions are rarely consistent in their language, and their rationale, too, is often hidden. The nature of the activities in which UNHCR was involved, however, suggests that the class of refugees assisted were either clearly not within the Statute or else had not been specifically determined to be within the Statute, perhaps for political or logistical reasons.[38] At the same time, the situations in question shared certain factors in common: the people in need (a) had crossed an international frontier, (b) as a result of conflicts, or radical political, social, or economic changes in their countries of origin. The very size of refugee problems in Africa in the 1960s made individual assessment of refugee status impractical, as did the absence of appropriate machinery. Moreover, the pragmatic, rather than doctrinal, approach to the new problems was almost certainly influenced by factors such as the desire to avoid the imputation carried by every determination that a well-founded fear of persecution exists;[39] and the feeling, not always made manifest, that while 'political conditions' had compelled the flight of the entire group in question, it might not be possible to establish a well-founded fear on an individual case-by-case basis. The 'group approach', by concentrating on the fact that those concerned are effectively without the protection of their own government, thus avoids the restrictions of the legal definition.[40]

From the mid-1970s, the General Assembly has spoken of and unanimously commended the High Commissioner's activities on behalf of 'refugees and displaced persons of concern' to the Office. The reference to 'displaced persons' dates at least from 1972, when the Economic and Social Council acted both to promote the voluntary repatriation of refugees to the Sudan, including measures of rehabilitation and assistance, and also to extend the benefit of such measures to 'persons displaced within the country'.[41] The ECOSOC lead was followed by the General Assembly[42] in the first of references to displaced persons which were soon to acquire a regularity and substance of their own. In 1974 and 1975 the General Assembly reiterated its recognition of refugees of concern to UNHCR, and acknowledged an additional category of 'special humanitarian tasks' undertaken by the High Commissioner.[43] ECOSOC took another consolidating step forward in 1976 when it recognized the importance of UNHCR's activities in

the international protection of refugees within the mandate, and requesting continued protection and assistance for refugees who are UNHCR's concern); 2650(XXV), 30 Nov. 1970; 2789(XXVI), 6 Dec. 1971; 2956(XXVII), 12 Dec. 1972.

[38] Cf. Ruthström-Ruiz, *Beyond Europe*, 96–123.

[39] This was certainly a factor with respect to France and refugees from Algeria: Ruthström-Ruiz, *Beyond Europe*, 96–109.

[40] Schnyder, F., 'Les aspects juridiques actuels du problème des réfugiés', Hague *Recueil* (1965–I) 339–450, at 426–43; Sadruddin Aga Khan, 'Legal Problems relating to refugees and displaced persons', Hague *Recueil* (1976–I) 287–352, at 306, 339–43.

[41] ECOSOC resolutions 1655(LII), 1 Jun. 1972; 1705(LII), 27 Jul. 1972; 1741(LIV), 4 May 1973; 1799(LV), 30 Jul. 1973; 1877(LVII), 16 Jul. 1974.

[42] UNGA res. 2958(XXVII), 12 Dec. 1972.

[43] UNGA resolutions 3271(XXIX), 10 Dec. 1974; 3454(XXX), 9 Dec. 1975. UNHCR had meanwhile served as focal point for assistance operations in India/Bangladesh, and in Cyprus.

'the context of man-made disasters, in addition to its original functions'. The High Commissioner was commended for his efforts 'on behalf of refugees and displaced persons, victims of man-made disasters', and requested to continue his activities 'for alleviating the suffering of all those of concern to his Office'.[44] In November 1976 the General Assembly formally endorsed the ECOSOC resolution and recognized the need to strengthen further the international protection of refugees.[45]

In 1975, in a short resolution, the General Assembly approved continued humanitarian assistance to 'Indo-chinese displaced persons'.[46] Originally intended as after the fact legislative approval for UNHCR activities *inside* Laos and Vietnam,[47] it has come to be seen as contributing an international dimension to the notion of displaced persons by its apparent recognition of the fact of *external* displacement. If the term was intended to cover groups, besides refugees, who had crossed international frontiers, then at the time it may have been something of a misnomer. 'Displaced persons' had a special meaning in the Constitution of the IRO, but had otherwise been commonly employed to describe those displaced within their own country, for example, by the effects of civil strife or natural disasters.[48]

Whatever its current dimensions, the 'displaced persons' category was initially introduced to deal with two problematic but related areas of activity. First, it was addressed to the situation of countries divided in fact, if not in law; this included countries split by civil war, such as the Sudan,[49] or Vietnam and, to a lesser extent, Laos prior to 1975. In the case of Vietnam, the legal situation was complicated by the respective constitutions and laws of the divided parts, each of which purported to acknowledge the existence of only one legitimate, truly representative entity. Again in the case of Vietnam, necessity required that UNHCR, as occasion demanded, deal with three different parties—the north Vietnamese, the south Vietnamese and the Provisional Revolutionary Government. The 'displaced persons' category, with its foundations in humanitarian necessity, was the natural successor to the 'good offices' approach; in its

---

[44] ECOSOC res. 2011(LXI), 2 Aug. 1976.   [45] UNGA res. 31/35, 30 Nov. 1976.

[46] UNGA res. 3455(XXX), 9 Dec. 1975. Chooi Fong, 'Some Legal Aspects of the Search for Admission into other States of Persons leaving the Indo-Chinese Peninsular in Small Boats', 52 *BYIL* 53, 80–5 (1982)—discusses the meaning of 'displaced persons,' with particular reference to UNGA res. 3454(XXX) and the mandate of UNHCR.

[47] UNHCR had become involved in the region, at the request of the governments concerned, and was promoting assistance programmes for those displaced by the effects of war. See the High Commissioner's statement to the 25th Session of the Executive Committee (1974): UN doc. A/AC. 96/511, annexe; *Report* of the High Commissioner to the General Assembly (1975): E/5688, Add. 1, paras. 34–43. Such assistance was undertaken 'within the framework of [UNHCR's] "good offices" function', and 'on a purely humanitarian basis'.

[48] See n. 57 below and accompanying text. In debate on the successor to the IRO in 1950, several countries, including India, Pakistan and Greece, argued for the inclusion of 'internal refugees', but it was the insistence on the absence of *legal* protection that prevailed; for a summary account, see Goodwin-Gill, 'Different Types of Forced Migration,' 27.

[49] See above, n. 41.

time, 'good offices' had accommodated the need for *prima facie* eligibility, while 'displaced persons' came in to describe UNHCR action on the ground— providing humanitarian assistance to those displaced within divided countries, by the effects of civil war or insurgency. In this practical context, protection was of secondary or incidental concern; there is indeed no necessary or inextricable link between protection and assistance, even if these notions have come to run together with the refugee and displaced persons categories in the General Assembly resolutions which succeeded and consolidated these developments.

The refugee crises in the period 1975–1995 illustrate both the development in the refugee definition and the problems that arise in applying it consistently to large numbers of asylum seekers. Over one and a half million people left Cambodia, Laos, and Vietnam, beginning in April 1975.[50] Already involved in the region, with the turn of events in the spring of 1975, UNHCR was called upon to assist many who had left their countries of origin, in particular by securing asylum,[51] providing care and maintenance, and promoting resettlement; the Provisional Revolutionary Government in South Vietnam also requested UNHCR to promote voluntary repatriation.

Official documentation of the period reveals a reluctance to apply the term 'refugee' to those assisted by UNHCR. Instead, the papers refer, for example, to 'displaced persons from Indo-China outside their country of origin',[52] and to 'persons leaving the Indo-China peninsula in small boats'.[53] UNHCR's operations were never challenged on the basis that the persons concerned might not fall within the mandate of the Office, however, and assistance and protection continued to be extended on the basis of that somewhat ambiguous resolution adopted by the General Assembly in December 1975.[54] The Executive Committee, however, began to employ more specific language in its annual

---

[50] A summary of the background is provided in *Report* of the Secretary-General on the Meeting on Refugees and Displaced Persons in South East Asia, Geneva, 20–1 July 1979, and Subsequent Developments: UN doc. A/34/627. See also Osborne, M., 'The Indochinese Refugees: Causes and Effects', *International Affairs*, 1980, 37–53; Grant, B., *The Boat People* (1980); Garcia Marquez, G., 'The Vietnam Wars', *Rolling Stone*, May 1980; Thayer, C., 'Dilemmas of Development in Vietnam', 75 *Current History*, no. 442, (1978); id., 'Vietnam—Beleaguered Outpost of Socialism', 79 *Current History*, no. 461, (1980); Foreign Language Press, Hanoi, *The Hoa in Vietnam*, Dossiers I and II, (1978); id., *Those who Leave*, (1979); id., *With Firm Steps: Southern Vietnam since Liberation 1975–1977*, (1978); 'Human Rights, War and Mass Exodus', *Transnational Perspectives*, (1982), 34–8.

[51] Already difficulties had been encountered in obtaining even temporary admission for those arriving by small boat or rescued at sea: UN doc. A/AC.96/516/Add. 1, para. 92.

[52] UN docs. A/AC.96/516/Add. 1; A/AC.96/INF.147. The High Commissioner's report to the General Assembly (1976) refers to 'special operations within the framework of the High Commissioner's good offices function' and to 'displaced persons who face problems analogous to those of refugees': E/5853, paras. 170ff.

[53] UN doc. A/AC.96/534, para. 57 (1976). 'Displaced persons' and 'boat people' terminology prevailed through 1977 and 1978 (see E/5987, paras. 6, 185, 207, 212, 214; A/AC.96/553/Add. 1), with the composite 'refugees and displaced persons' also appearing.

[54] UNGA res. 3455(XXX), 9 Dec. 1975, on humanitarian assistance to the Indo-Chinese displaced persons.

conclusions. In 1976, it spoke of 'asylum seekers' who had left their country in small boats,[55] and in 1977 referred expressly to the problems of refugees from Indo-China.[56]

In that year, the High Commissioner for Refugees also requested the Executive Committee to clarify the distinction between refugees and displaced persons. No formal advice was tendered, although there was considerable support for the view that refugees had crossed an international frontier, whereas displaced persons had not.[57] Notwithstanding the focus on *internally displaced persons* in the 1990s, which has been accompanied by the search for a jurisdictional base, a competent protecting and assisting agency, and an applicable body of rules and standards,[58] by 1977 UNHCR responsibilities for refugees and displaced persons had clearly established their place in the language of the General Assembly.[59] They have remained ever since, with the incremental recognition of others requiring protection, including returnees, women and children, asylum seekers and those displaced.[60]

[55] UN doc. A/AC.96/534, para. 87(f).

[56] UN doc. A/AC.96/549, para. 36(b). In 1980, the General Assembly referred to 'boat and land cases in South East Asia' as 'refugees': UNGA res. 35/41, 25 Nov. 1980, para. 8. The causes of population displacements naturally change over time; a 1985 internal UNHCR survey of motivations for departure from Vietnam looked at ethnic and religious discrimination, amongst others, but found that severe economic conditions were mentioned by practically all as a factor in the decision to leave. A review of refugee claims carried out by several officials working independently found that some 8% of cases had a clear claim to refugee status; 31% could qualify on basis of a 'very liberal interpretation'; and that 61% 'clearly' did not qualify: UNHCR, 'Assessment of Current Arrivals in South East Asian Countries of Persons leaving the SRVN by Boat', Sept. 1985.

[57] See the High Commissioner's statement to the Executive Committee in 1977: UN doc. A/AC.96/549, annexe, and for summary of the views of States: ibid., paras. 21, 26. For more detailed statements, see UN docs. A/AC.96/SR.284, paras. 13, 25 *bis*, 46; SR.287, paras. 26, 35; SR.288, paras. 30, 57; SR.291, para. 6. See also the High Commissioner's statement to the 31st Session of the Executive Committee (1980): UN doc. A/AC.96/588, annexe 5. At that session, the representative for Turkey expressed the view that 'the time had come to ensure that UNHCR did not, by virtue of precedents, become a body which cared for anyone compelled for whatever reason to leave his country or even to move to a different area inside his country': UN doc. A/AC.96/SR.319, paras. 12–15.

[58] See further below, Ch. 7, s. 2.

[59] In 1973, the General Assembly requested the High Commissioner 'to continue his assistance *and protection* activities in favour of refugees within his mandate as well as for those to whom he extends his good offices or is called upon to assist in accordance with relevant resolutions of the General Assembly': UNGA res. 3143(XXVIII), 14 Dec. 1973. UNGA res. 32/68, 8 Dec. 1977, continued UNHCR's mandate and noted 'the outstanding work ... performed ... in providing international *protection* to refugees and displaced persons'. UNGA res. 35/41, 25 Nov. 1980, refers to UNHCR's responsibilities 'for *protecting* and assisting refugees and displaced persons throughout the world'. Cf. paras. 28–32, CIREFCA Plan of Action; below, Annexe 5, No. 2.

[60] UNGA resolutions 33/26, 29 Nov. 1978; 34/60, 29 Nov. 1979; 35/41, 25 Nov. 1980; 35/135, 11 Dec. 1980 (refugee and displaced women); 35/187, 15 Dec. 1980 (refugee and displaced children); 36/125, 14 Dec. 1981 (including also the protection of asylum seekers in large-scale influx); 37/195, 18 Dec. 1982 (refugees, returnees and displaced persons of concern to the Office); 37/196, 18 Dec. 1982; 38/121, 16 Dec. 1983; 39/105, 14 Dec. 1984; 39/140, 14 Dec. 1984; 40/118, 13 Dec. 1985; 41/124, 4 Dec. 1986; 42/108, 7 Dec. 1987 (protection and material assistance to refugees and displaced persons); 43/117, 8 Dec. 1988 (also noting the close connection between the problems of refugees and stateless persons); 44/137, 15 Dec. 1989; 45/140, 14 Dec. 1990; 46/106,

The field of UNHCR competence, and thus the field of its responsibilities, has broadened considerably since the Office was established. Briefly, the movement has been from the Statute through good offices and assistance, to protection and solutions. The class of beneficiaries has moved from those defined in the Statute, through those outside competence assisted on a good offices basis, those defined in relevant resolutions of the General Assembly and directives of the Executive Committee, arriving finally at the generic class of refugees, displaced and other persons of concern to UNHCR.[61]

Apart from purely humanitarian considerations, this tendency shows awareness of the difficulty of determining in the case of a massive exodus that each and everyone has a well-founded fear of persecution in the sense of the UNHCR Statute. It also suggests that something more general, such as lack of protection, should serve as the criterion for identifying persons 'of concern' to the High Commissioner. This is not immediately obvious from the resolutions themselves, but appears to be confirmed by UNHCR and international agency practice, for example, in Rwanda and Zaire, Northern Iraq, Somalia and former Yugoslavia.

The lack of protection may occur as a matter of law, for example, in the case of stateless persons; or as a matter of fact, where individuals or groups are unable or unwilling to avail themselves of the protection of the government of their country. This may be due to a well-founded fear of persecution for reasons of race, religion, nationality or political opinion; or to some man-made disaster, such as conflict or violence resulting from a variety of sources. For example, in establishing a Group of Governmental Experts on International Co-operation to Avert New Flows of Refugees in 1981, the General Assembly reaffirmed its strong condemnation of 'policies and practices of oppressive and racist regimes, as well as aggression, colonialism, *apartheid*, alien domination, foreign intervention and occupation', which it identified among the root causes of refugee movements.[63] In its 1986 Report,[64] this Group avoided definitional problems, concentrating instead on 'coerced movements', where the element of compulsion 'was to be

---

16 Dec. 1991; 47/105, 16 Dec. 1992; 48/116, 20 Dec. 1993 (refugees and other persons to whom UNHCR is called upon to provide assistance and protection, including 'persons displaced within their own country in specific situations calling for the Office's particular expertise'); 49/169, 23 Dec. 1994 (noting that the situation of 'refugees and other persons to whom the Office of the High Commissioner is called upon to provide assistance and protection' has continued to be seriously jeopardized).

[61] The incremental, 'after the event', and sometimes accidental growth in UNHCR's area of institutional responsibility might have been more efficiently organized had the General Assembly maintained the approach to 'competence' proposed in the 1949 draft statute: '... for the time being, refugees and displaced persons defined in [the IRO Constitution] and, thereafter, such persons as the General Assembly may from time to time determine, including any persons brought under the jurisdiction of the High Commissioner's Office under the terms of international conventions or agreements approved by the General Assembly': UNGA res. 319(IV), 3 Dec. 1949, Annex, para. 3.

[62] That is, a general sense that something must be done, even if those in need of protection or assistance do not fall squarely within the letter of legal regimes of competence or obligation.

[63] UNGA res. 36/148, 16 Dec. 1981.

[64] UN doc. A/41/324 (May 1986); see below, Annexe 4, No. 2.

understood in a wide sense covering a variety of natural, political and socio-economic factors which directly or indirectly force people to flee . . . in fear for life, liberty and security'. Wars and armed conflicts were cited as a major cause of refugee flows, for flight was often the only way to escape danger to life or extensive restrictions of human rights.[65]

Lack of protection by the government of the country of origin is already an element in the statutory definition of the refugee. Given the impracticability of individual determinations in the case of large scale movements of asylum seekers, that element acquires great significance. 'Protection' here implies both 'internal protection', in the sense of effective guarantees in matters such as life, liberty, and security of the person; and 'external protection', in the sense of diplomatic protection, including documentation of nationals abroad and recognition of the right of nationals to return. The 'right to return', in particular, is accepted as a normal incident of nationality. In the case of those leaving Vietnam, however, that right was initially subject to significant qualification. Although in 1975 the Provisional Revolutionary Government of South Vietnam requested UNHCR to promote voluntary repatriation, it stressed at the time that authorization to return fell within its sovereign rights and that each case would need to be examined separately.[66] Many of those who left Chile following the 1973 coup were also 'listed' as prohibited from returning, although they retained their citizenship.[67] These factors alone may justify protection and assistance by UNHCR, particularly where, in individual cases, further evidence is available of measures seriously affecting certain racial, social or political groups.

Although no objection was raised to UNHCR's activities on behalf of persons leaving Indo-China, challenges to the Office's competence have arisen with respect to other groups. In discussion of the High Commissioner's report in the Third Committee in 1979, for example, the representative of Afghanistan referred to UNHCR's 'assistance to fugitive insurgents in Pakistan'.[68] Recalling article 1F of the 1951 Convention, he observed that assistance to those committing acts of aggression against Afghanistan contravened the UNHCR Statute, the 1951 Convention, and the UN Charter. At the Executive Committee in 1984 the observer for Afghanistan claimed that Afghans in Iran and Pakistan, if not insurgents, were nomads and migrant workers; this was roundly rejected by

---

[65] The Group separated man-made causes and factors, sub-divided into political causes and socio-economic factors, from natural causes. Within the man-made category were wars, colonialism, the treatment of minorities (for example, under *apartheid*), discrimination and internal conflict, violation of human rights and fundamental freedoms, and expulsions. Socio-economic factors relevant to these causes were those that threatened the physical integrity and survival of individuals and groups, underdevelopment, particularly the legacy of colonialism, the absence of adequate economic infrastructures, and the perilous state of the world economy.

[66] See statement by the observer for the Democratic Republic of Vietnam at the 26th Session of the Executive Committee (1975): UN doc. A/AC.96/521, para. 105.

[67] See further below, Ch. 3, s. 1.

[68] UN doc. A/C.3/34/SR.46, para. 58f.

representatives of the receiving and other countries.[69] More recent exchanges and interventions have focused on the status of Bulgarians of Turkish origin and Romanians of Hungarian origin.[70]

Despite the protests of individual governments, the international community at large has not hitherto demurred when UNHCR has exercised its protection and assistance functions in cases of large-scale movements of asylum seekers. This, together with other developments, permits the conclusion that the class of persons within the mandate of, or of concern to, UNHCR includes: (1) those who, having left their country, can, on a case-by-case basis, be determined to have a well-founded fear of persecution on certain specified grounds; and (2) those often large groups or categories or persons who, likewise having crossed an international frontier, can be determined or presumed to be without, or unable to avail themselves of, the protection of the government of their State of origin. This is the broad meaning of the term 'refugee' for the purposes of the United Nations, and this is the class for which UNHCR will in principle seek the immediate protection of temporary refuge, treatment in accordance with minimum standards, and appropriate long-term solutions. The preceding *functional* description of the scope of UNHCR's responsibilities towards refugees and the displaced begs a number of key questions relating to the international obligations of States, which are dealt with more fully below. For the present, it is sufficient to note that both the activities of UNHCR and the responses of States with regard to refugees in the broad sense may be limited to the provision of

[69] See UN docs. A/AC.96/SR.371, paras. 92–7, 107; SR.372, para. 60; SR.373, paras. 34, 78; similar exchanges occurred in 1987; UN doc. A/AC.96/SR.416, paras. 38–41, 82. Also in 1984, Morocco objected to use of the word 'refugee' in describing UNHCR assistance to Sahrawis in the Tindouf: UN doc. A/AC.96/SR.376, paras. 2–7, claiming that not enough was being done by Algeria to encourage their voluntary repatriation; see further ibid., paras. 8–15; SR.377, paras. 55–61, 67–69; SR.378, paras. 77–81. The dispute continued in later years; see UN docs. A/AC.96/SR.394, 59–71; SR.399, paras. 46–8 (1985); SR.403, paras. 65–6; SR. 407, paras. 81–3, 91–4 (1986); SR.414, para. 29; SR.415, para. 73; SR.420, paras. 7–9, 53 (1987). In 1986, Iraq claimed that the 'Iraqi refugees' referred to by Iran were in fact Iranians who had been living in Iraq and who had been expelled for having committed acts of terrorism and threatening security: SR.409, paras. 34, 94–103. The following year, Iran claimed that most so-called Iranian refugees were 'members of rival political groups, supported from outside . . . , attempting to infiltrate Iranian territory in order to commit subversive acts': UN doc. A/AC.96/SR.418, para. 105. Israel objected when Palestinians began to appear in the annual Executive Committee General Conclusion on International Protection (usually expressing concern about the lack of adequate international protection); see *Report* of the 39th Session of the Executive Committee: UN doc. A/AC/96/721, 13 Oct. 1988, paras. 22, 36. The last express reference to Palestinians was recorded in the 1992 General Conclusion; see *Report* of the 43rd Session of the Executive Committee: UN doc. A/AC.96/804, 15 Oct. 1992, para. 21; in contrast to its previous practice, Israel raised no objection on this occasion. For relevant texts, see 2 *IJRL* 144, 156–7 (1990); 3 *IJRL* 141, 143 (1991); 4 *IJRL* 103, 104 (1992); 5 *IJRL* 129, 145 (1993).

[70] For Turkey/Bulgaria, see UN docs. A/AC.96/SR.438, para. 81; SR.440, paras. 93–7; SR.441, paras. 60–4, 65, 66 (1989). For Hungary/Romania, see SR.440, paras. 49–51, 112 (1989); SR.457, paras. 49–57 (1990). 'Inclusion' claims are also made from time to time; regarding 'Russians living in other republics', see SR.466, paras. 47–8 (1991); similarly, for Ukrainians, see SR.484, para. 20 (1993), touching also on the plight of Crimean Tatars, Germans, Greeks, Bulgarians deported from the Ukraine during the Second World War.

temporary refuge and material assistance, and the pursuit of voluntary repatriation. The refugee with a well-founded fear of persecution alone, perhaps, enjoys the full spectrum of protection and the expectation of a lasting solution in a country of asylum or resettlement,[71] although that presumption too may be questioned today in the light of more recent State practice.[72]

4. Refugees in the sense of the 1951 Convention and the 1967 Protocol relating to the Status of Refugees

The States which acceded to or ratified the 1951 Convention agreed that the term 'refugee' should apply, first to any person considered a refugee under earlier international arrangements; and, secondly, to any person who, broadly speaking, qualifies as a refugee under the UNHCR Statute.[73] In discussions leading up to agreement on the definition in the *Ad hoc* committee on refugees and stateless persons, the United States remained concerned that 'too vague a definition' would entail unknowable (and excessive) responsibilities, and provoke disagreements between governments with respect to its interpretation and application.[74] However, the definition should not be narrow or the field of application of the Convention excessively restricted. It proposed four categories of refugees outside their country 'because of persecution or fear of persecution',[75] which were intended also to include those who had fled since the beginning of the Second World War or 'who might be obliged to flee from their countries for similar reasons in the future'.[76] The United Kingdom proposed an alternative, general definition,[77] and a working group was set up within the *Ad hoc* committee to resolve differences. Its provisional draft identified a number of categories, such as the victims of the Nazi or Falangist regimes and by reference to previous international agreements, but also adopted the criterion of well-founded fear and lack of protection.[78] The drafters thus used the IRO Constitution as a model for the formulation of certain categories of existing refugees,[79] while the

---

[71] Reservations about the implications of an expanded refugee definition were expressed at the 32nd Session of the Executive Committee in 1981: UN doc. A/AC.96/601, para. 48, and at the 35th Session in 1984: UN doc. A/AC.96/651, para. 81. See further below, s. 7.

[72] See below, Ch. 5.   [73] Art. 1A(2) of the Convention.   [74] Below, n. 76, para. 40.

[75] See United States of America, *Memorandum on the Definition Article of the Preliminary Draft Convention Relating to the Status of Refugees (and Stateless Persons)*: UN doc. E/AC.32/L.4 (18 Jan. 1950). The four categories were (1) refugees from the period of the first world war; (2) inter-war refugees; (3) 'neo-refugees'; and (4) displaced persons and unaccompanied minors.

[76] UN doc. E/AC.32/SR.3, para. 45 (Mr Henkin).

[77] The UK definition would have included 'a person who, having left the country of his ordinary residence on account of persecution or well-founded fear of persecution, either does not wish to return to that country for good and sufficient reason or is not allowed by the authorities of that country to return there and who is not a national of any other country'. See UN docs. E/AC.32/L.2 (17 Jan. 1950) and E/AC.32/L.2/Rev.1 (19 Jan. 1950).

[78] See UN doc. E/AC.32/L.6, 23 Jan. 1950 (provisional draft of parts of the definition article). Various exclusions and limitations, including geographical, temporal and nationality factors, were also mentioned.

[79] For the IRO Constitution, see below, Annexe 1, No. 1.

general criterion of persecution or fear of persecution, neither narrow nor exces-sively restricted, according to the United States delegate, was considered broad enough for post-Second World War and future refugees.

Originally, the definition, like the first part of that in the Statute, limited appli-cation of the Convention to the refugee who acquired such status 'as a result of events occurring before 1 January 1951'. An optional geographical limitation also permitted States, on ratification, to limit their obligations to refugees result-ing from 'events occurring in Europe' prior to the critical date.[80] Finally, the substantive or ideological basis for the essential 'well-founded fear of persecu-tion' differs slightly from that in the UNHCR Statute, by including the criterion 'membership of a particular social group' in addition to race, religion, national-ity, or political opinion. The differences between the two definitions are due to amendments accepted by the Conference of Plenipotentiaries which adopted the final draft of the Convention.[81] The reference to 'membership of a particular social group' is analyzed more fully below;[82] it makes little practical difference in the respective areas of competence of UNHCR and States parties to the Convention.

From the outset, it was recognized that, given its various limitations, the Convention definition would not cover every refugee. The Conference of Plenipotentiaries therefore recommended in the Final Act that States should apply the Convention beyond its strictly contractual scope, to other refugees within their territory.[83] Many States relied upon this recommendation in the case of refugee crises precipitated by events after 1 January 1951, until the 1967 Protocol expressly removed that limitation. It may still be invoked to support extension of the Convention to groups or individuals who do not fully satisfy the definitional requirements.[84]

Convention refugees are thus identifiable by their possession of four elemental characteristics: (1) they are outside their country of origin; (2) they are unable or

---

[80] Art. 1B. The Convention is frequently criticized for its 'European bias', but another view was apparent in 1951. Mr Rochefort, the French representative, remarked that although more than 80 invitations had been sent out, the Conference gave the appearance of nothing more than a 'slightly enlarged' meeting of the Council of Europe. He observed that only a small fraction of the 41 gov-ernments that had voted for art. 1 in the General Assembly had been willing to come to Geneva to sign the Convention and nearly all were European. In his view, those who argued for deletion of the geographical limitation, 'had done so without any feeling of definite responsibility'. The system of generalized protection had failed; because the non-European countries were absent and because of the attitudes of the immigration countries (they claimed to have no protection problems), there was no practical possibility of 'giving refugees in general, and European refugees in particular, a truly international status': UN doc. A/CONF.2/SR.3, p. 12.

[81] Cf. Grahl-Madsen, A., *The Status of Refugees in International Law*, vol. 1, (1966), 217.

[82] See further below, Ch. 2, s. 4.2.4.   [83] Recommendation E of the Final Act.

[84] Although qualification as a Convention definition is often the sufficient condition for the grant of asylum, States also generally claim the right to grant asylum to others, for example, for 'human-itarian reasons'. Thus, art. 2 of the Declaration on Territorial Asylum adopted by the Committee of Ministers of the Council of Europe on 18 Nov. 1977, reaffirms the right to grant asylum in respect of Convention refugees 'as well as to any other person [considered] worthy of receiving asylum for humanitarian reasons'. See Annexe 4, No. 6, below.

unwilling to avail themselves of the protection of that country, or to return there; (3) such inability or unwillingness is attributable to a well-founded fear of being persecuted; and (4) the persecution feared is based on reasons of race, religion, nationality, membership of a particular social group, or political opinion.

5. Regional approaches

The 1951 Convention and the 1967 Protocol remain the principal international instruments benefiting refugees, and their definition has been expressly adopted in a variety of regional arrangements aimed at further improving the situation of recognized refugees. It forms the basis for article I of the 1969 OAU Convention on Refugee Problems in Africa, although it has there been realistically extended to cover those compelled to leave their country of origin on account of external aggression, occupation, foreign domination, or events seriously disturbing public order.[85]

Latin America has long been familiar with the practice of diplomatic asylum[86] and with the concept of *asilado*. The Montevideo Treaty of 1889 acknowledged that 'political refugees shall be accorded an inviolable asylum',[87] while other agreements have dealt expressly with asylum granted in diplomatic premises or other protected areas.[88] The beneficiaries are usually described as being sought 'for political reasons' or 'for political offences', although the 1954 Caracas Convention on Territorial Asylum expressly refers to persons coming from a State 'in which they are persecuted for their beliefs, opinions, or political affiliations, or for acts which may be considered as political offences'.[89]

The refugee crisis in Central America during the 1980s led in due course to one of the most encompassing approaches to the refugee question. The *1984*

---

[85] Generally, see Arboleda, E., 'Refugee Definition in Africa and Latin America: The Lessons of Pragmatism,' 3 *IJRL* 185 (1991); Rwelamira, M., '1989—An Anniversary Year: The 1969 OAU Convention on the Specific Aspects of Refugee Problems in Africa,' 1 *IJRL* 557 (1989); also, OAU/UNHCR, 'The Addis Ababa Symposium 1994,' 7 *IJRL Special Issue—Summer 1995*, (1995).

[86] See further below Ch. 5, s. 1.

[87] See art. 16, 1889 Montevideo Treaty on International Penal Law: *OAS Official Records* OEA/Ser.X/1. Treaty Series 34; revised by the 1940 Montevideo Treaty on International Penal Law: ibid., art. 20 of which excludes extradition for 'political crimes'.

[88] See, for example, 1954 Caracas Convention on Diplomatic Asylum; text below, Annexe 2, No. 4.

[89] Art. 2. Arboleda notes that despite the appearance of a broader definition, 'virtually all Latin American scholars equate the Caracas Convention with earlier treaties'; see Arboleda, E., 'The Cartagena Declaration of 1984 and its Similarities to the 1969 OAU Convention—A Comparative Perspective,' 7 *IJRL Special Issue—Summer 1995*, 87, n. 6 (1995). See also arts. 4, 5, 6, 1981 Inter-American Convention on Extradition; below, Annexe 2, No. 15. Extradition is commonly the background to these regional agreements, non-extradition of political offenders being one part of the wider topic of asylum. Developments in the legal concept of the refugee have likewise had a corresponding influence on extradition arrangements. On the one hand, there has been a tendency to expand protection beyond the limitations which afflict the notion of political offence; on the other hand, international action to suppress the hijacking of aircraft, to counteract terrorism, and to protect diplomats, has imposed new limitations upon the class of those entitled to international protection. See further below, Ch. 2, s. 4.2.

Cartagena Declaration proposed a significant broadening, analogous to that of the OAU Convention.[90] But this *Declaration* emerged not from within a regional organization, but out of an *ad hoc* group of experts and representatives from governments in Central America, meeting together in a colloquium in Colombia.[91] It is not a formally binding treaty, but represents endorsement by the States concerned of appropriate and applicable standards of protection and assistance.[92] Moreover, it recommends that the definition of a refugee to be used in the region include, in addition to the elements of the 1951 Convention and the Protocol, persons who have fled their country, because their lives, safety or freedom have been threatened by generalized violence, foreign aggression, internal conflicts, massive violation of human rights or other circumstances seriously disturbing public order.

This expanded definition, which clearly matches the developments within the UN, has also been proposed as the criterion generally applicable in situations of mass influx, although care is required in calculating the precise legal implications.[93]

6. Refugees in municipal law: some examples

The municipal law practice of non-extradition of political offenders is one antecedent to current principles protecting refugees from return to a State in which they may face persecution. It remains doubtful whether the narrow principle of non-extradition reflects a rule of international law, despite its wide acceptance in municipal law, but apart from the extradition context, many States have nevertheless recognized that the refugee is someone worthy of protection and assistance. In some countries, the principle of asylum for refugees is expressly acknowledged in the constitution.[94] In others, ratification of the 1951 Convention and the 1967 Protocol has direct effect in local law, while in still other cases, ratifying States may follow up their acceptance of international

[90] For text see Annexe 2, No. 7. Also, para. 6, CPA; below, Annexe 5, No. 1.

[91] The Colloquium was co-sponsored by the University of Cartagena, the Regional Center for Third World Studies and the Office of the United Nations High Commissioner for Refugees, and held under the auspices of the Colombian government; see *La Protección Internacional de los Refugiados en América Central, México y Panamá: Problemas Jurídicos y Humanitarios*, National University of Colombia, (1984), 42. See also Gros Espiell, H, Picado, s. and Valladares Lanza, L., 'Principles and Criteria for the Protection of and Assistance to Central American Refugees and Displaced Persons in Latin America', 2 *IJRL* 83 (1990); Cuellar, R., García–Sayán, D., Montaño, J., Dieguez, M., and Valladares Lanza, L., 'Refugee and Related Developments in Latin America: Challenges Ahead', 3 *IJRL* 484 (1991).

[92] The OAS General Assembly has consistently endorsed the Cartagena Declaration; see, for example, 1991 Legal Resolution of Situation of Refugees, Repatriated and Displaced Persons in the American Hemisphere, AG/RES.1103 (XXI–0/91) (7 Jun. 1991).

[93] See also Executive Committee Conclusion No. 22 (1981) on the protection of asylum seekers in situations of large-scale influx; text below, Annexe 3. See also Ch. 5, s. 5.

[94] See, for example, the provisions listed in preparation for the 1977 Conference on Territorial Asylum: *A Select Bibliography on Territorial Asylum* (1977): UN doc. ST/GENEVA/LIB/SER.B/Ref.9, 68–74.

obligations with the enactment of specific refugee legislation or the adoption of appropriate administrative procedures.

The Federal Republic of Germany, for example, has both constitutional and enacted law provisions benefiting refugees, both of which were amended in 1992/93. The 1949 Constitution prescribes that the politically persecuted enjoy the right of asylum,[95] and the 1992 Asylum Procedure Law provides that those recognized shall enjoy the status provided for by the 1951 Convention, as a minimum standard.[96] The recent amendments, however, establish a geographical limitation by prescribing that the right to asylum may not be invoked by one who enters from a European Union State or from a third country where application of the 1951 Convention and of the 1950 European Convention on Human Rights is guaranteed.[97]

The Preamble to the 1958 Constitution of France acknowledges the principle of asylum, while a 1952 law establishing the *Office français de protection des réfugiés et apatrides* (OFPRA) declares that refugees within the competence of the Office shall include those within the mandate of UNHCR, as well as those within article 1 of the 1951 Convention.[98]

The United States Refugee Act 1980 abandoned the earlier ideologically and geographically based definition of refugees[99] in favour of that offered by the Convention and Protocol.[100] At the same time, it goes beyond international instruments by offering 'resettlement' opportunities to those who might qualify as Convention refugees, save for the fact that they have not yet left their country of origin.[101] Canada also adopted the Convention definition in the 1976

[95] See art. 16a (formerly art. 16(2)): *'Politisch Verfolgte geniessen Asylrecht'*; interpretations of the constitutional provision are often at variance with those of art. 1A(2) of the 1951 Convention; see, among others, Frowein, J. Abr. & Kühner, R., 'Drohende Folterung als Asylgrund und Grenze für Auslieferung und Ausweisung', 35/36 *ZaöRV* 538, arguing that while the human right to be protected against torture does not always provide a basis for political asylum, it may be an aspect of persecution, and the threat of torture limits the rights of expulsion and extradition. On legal changes, see Federal Ministry of the Interior, 'Recent Developments in the German Law on Asylum and Aliens,' 6 *IJRL* 265 (1994); Ablard, T. and Novak, A., ' L'évolution du droit d'asile en Allemagne jusqu'à la réforme de 1993', 7 *IJRL* 260 (1995); Blay, S. and Zimmermann, A., 'Recent Changes in German Refugee Law: A Critical Assessment', 88 *AJIL* 361 (1994).

[96] *'Asylberchtigte genießen im Bundesgebiet die Rechtstellung nach dem Abkommen über die Rechtstellung der Flüchtlinge vom 28. June 1951 . . .'* Art. 2(1), *Asylverfahrensgesetz (AsylVfG)* vom 26. Juni 1992: *BGBl.* I s. 1126; amended 30 Jun. 1993: *BGBl.* I s. 1062 and subsequently. For detailed analysis and commentary, see Marx, R., *Kommentar zum Asylverfahrensgesetz*, (3., erw. Aufl., 1995).

[97] The latter countries are to be determined by law and approved by the *Bundesrat*, which is also empowered to list States which will be presumed not to engage in political persecution or inhuman or degrading treatment or punishment. A claimant from such a State has the additional evidentiary burden of overcoming that presumption: art. 16a(2),(3).

[98] *Loi no. 52–893*, 25 Jul. 1952, art. 2; see also *loi no. 70–107*, 25 Nov. 1970, authorizing accession to the 1967 protocol.

[99] Refugees were limited to those fleeing from the Middle East or from Communist or Communist-dominated countries.

[100] See s. 101(a)(42), Immigration and Nationality Act, as amended: 8 USC §1101; also 8 CFR §223a.1.

[101] Ibid. This expanded category is dependent upon 'appropriate consultations' taking place between the President and Congress: ibid., and s. 207(e). See also Refugee Policy Group, 'U.S.

Immigration Act,[102] where it serves both as a criterion for selection under admission programmes and as the basis for formal recognition of refugee status and the grant of residence to those already in Canada.[103] In addition, Canadian law makes provision for the designation of other classes whose admission to Canada would be in keeping with humanitarian tradition.[104]

In other countries, the admission of refugees and special groups is often decided by the government in the exercise of broad discretionary powers. Although the Convention and Protocol are not formally incorporated in United Kingdom law, the rules adopted for implementation of the 1971 Immigration Act have traditionally referred to the Convention definition in the context of applications for entry, for extensions of stay, and against deportation. The Asylum and Immigration Appeals Act 1993 does not define refugees as such, but a claim for asylum is described as 'a claim made by a person ... that it would be contrary to the United Kingdom's obligations under the Convention for him to be removed from, or required to leave, the United Kingdom'. Section 2 in turn provides that, 'Nothing in the immigration rules ... shall lay down any practice which would be contrary to the Convention.'[105]

In its 1979 law on asylum,[106] Switzerland elaborated on the Convention definition. Article 3 declares,

Refugee Admissions: Processing in Europe', (Mar. 1985); Immigration and Naturalization Service, Department of Justice, *Worldwide Guidelines for Overseas Refugee Processing*, (Aug. 1983), 59–62, identifying, among others, certain general characteristics qualfiying applicants for refugee status.

[102] S. 2(1). The Act contains a statement of the objectives of Canadian immigration policy in s. 3, which includes the need 'to fulfil Canada's international legal obligations with respect to refugees and to uphold its humanitarian tradition with respect to the displaced and the persecuted'.

[103] See now *Immigration Act*, ss. 57–69.3

[104] See now ss. 6(3), 114(1)(d). The following 'designated classes' have been identified at various times since 1978: *Indo-Chinese* (SOR/78–931), *Latin Americans* (SOR/78–932), *Self-exiled Persons* (SOR/78–933), and *Political Prisoners and Oppressed Persons* (SOR/82–977). The classes are generally described by reference to their country of origin, as persons who are outside Canada and not still present in their country of origin, are unable or unwilling to return to their country, have not become permanently resettled, and are seeking resettlement in Canada. The *Political Prisoners and Oppressed Persons Designated Class* provided resettlement opportunities to certain categories of persons who had not yet left their country of origin and who therefore would not qualify as refugees under international legal criteria. The class applied to applicants who were citizens of, and still within, a listed country (El Salvador, Uruguay, or Guatemala), who either met the Convention refugee definition, apart from the requirement of presence outside the country in which persecution is feared; or 'as a direct result of acts that in Canada would be considered a legitimate expression of free thought or a legitimate exercise of civil rights pertaining to dissent or to trade union activity, have been (i) detained or imprisoned for a period exceeding 72 hours with or without charge, or (ii) subjected to some other recurring form of penal control': SOR/82–977, s. 2(a). An exceptional designated class, the *Refugee Claimants Designated Class* (SOR/89–744), was introduced temporarily to deal with the backlog of refugee claimants in Canada whose applications were outstanding on 1 Jan. 1989, the date of the entry into force of a revised procedure. On proposals for change, see Employment and Immigration Canada, *Canada's Resettlement Programs: New Directions*, Ottawa, (Jan. 1993), and further below, Ch. 7, s. 3.3.

[105] *Statement of Changes in Immigration Rules*: HC 725; (see now Immigration Rules, HC 395, in force 1 Oct. 1994); Asylum Appeals Procedure Rules: SI 1661 (in force 26 July 1993).

[106] See Kälin, W., 'The Legal Condition of Refugees in Switzerland,' 24 *Swiss Reports presented at the XIVth International Congress of Comparative Law*, 57–73 (1994); Achermann, A. and Hausammann,

1. Sont des réfugiés les étrangers qui, dans leur pays d'origine ou le pays de leur dernière résidence, sont exposés à de sérieux préjudices ou craignent à juste titre de l'être en raison de leur race, de leur religion, de leur nationalité, de leur appartenance à un groupe social déterminé ou de leurs opinions politiques.

2. Sont considérés notamment comme sérieux préjudices la mise en danger de la vie, de l'intégrité corporelle ou de la liberté, de même que les mesures qui entraînent une pression psychique insupportable.

3. Sont également reconnus comme réfugiés, à moins que des circonstances particulières ne s'y opposent, les conjoints des réfugiés et leurs enfants mineurs.[107]

Many other similar instances can be cited. Botswana's Refugees (Recognition and Control) Act, for example, defines the refugee in Convention terms, as do the laws of Japan[108] and Spain.[109] Section 3 of Lesotho's 1983 Refugee Act adopts both 1951 Convention and 1969 OAU criteria with respect to individuals, and likewise as to classes so declared by the Minister. The 1983 Zimbabwe Refugee Act, section 3, is very similar, containing particularly detailed provision for class determinations. Despite its Central American location, the 1991 Belize Refugees Act incorporates the 1951 Convention definition and not the Cartagena Declaration extensions, as might have been expected, but the broader terms of the 1969 OAU Convention (section 4). Article 15 of Norway's Immigration Act extends protection to refugees having a fear of persecution, as well to foreign nationals who, 'for reasons similar to those given in the definition of a refugee are in considerable danger of losing their lives or of being made to suffer inhuman treatment'. Bolivian law provides also for both Convention and extended definitions.[110] The 1990 law on refugees of the Czech Republic adopts the 1951 Convention approach in section 2, while section 3 provides that refugee status may also be granted for reasons of protection of human rights or for humanitarian reasons to an individual who does not satisfy the Convention conditions.[111] The Danish Aliens Act likewise provides addi-

C., *Handbuch des Asylrechts,* (1991), 71ff; Bersier, R., *Droit d'asile et statut de refugié,* (1991), 43ff; Kälin, W., *Grundriss des Asylverfahrens,* (1990), 23ff. Despite the different wording, the content of the Swiss law is generally seen as identical with the 1951 Convention.

[107] *Loi sur l'asile du 5 octobre 1979: FF 1979 II 977.* Peruvian law uses almost identical terminology; see, for example, art. 11, *Decreto Pres. No.1 Situation Juridica De Los Refugiados*: 'Para los efectos dispuestos en el articulo 7, se considera particularmente como serios perjuicios el hallarse en peligro la vida, la integridad fisica o la libertad personal, al igual que las medidas que acarrean una presión psíquica intolerable'.

[108] Immigration Control and Refugee Recognition Act, art. 2(3)–2.

[109] Ley 5/1984 sobre el derecho de asilo, art. 3 (Causas que justifican la concesión de asilo y su denegación).

[110] See Decreto Presidencial No. 19640 (in force 4 July 1983), art. 1 and the extended definition in art. 2: 'Se considerará también refugiados por razones humanitarios a todas aquellas personas que se hayan visto forzadas a huir de su país a causa de conflictos armados internos; agresión, ocupación o dominación extranjeras, violación masiva de los derechos humanos; o en razón de acontecimientos fr naturaleza política que alteren gravemente el orden público en el país de origen o procedencia'.

[111] Act No. 498 of 16 Nov. 1990; amended by Act No. 317/1993 Sb., 8 Dec. 1993. See also Nagy, B., 'Asylum Seekers and Refugees: Hungarian Dilemmas,' 34 *Acta Juridica Hungarica,*

tionally for the issue of a residence permit to non-nationals who, 'for reasons similar to those listed in the Convention or for other weighty reasons', ought not to be required to return to the country of origin.[112]

This far from comprehensive selection illustrates the extent to which certain States have translated their concern for the international problem of refugees into action on the municipal level. Many immigration and non-immigration countries have incorporated the Convention definition, with occasional slight modifications, into their laws and policies. That definition may be used both as a basis for overseas selection and for the purposes of determining claims to asylum and/or refugee status raised by persons physically present or arriving in their territory. A further notable feature is the tendency of States to take account of the plight of others, who are either not recognized or not strictly refugees in the sense of the Convention, but who have valid humanitarian reasons for being offered resettlement opportunities or protection.[113] The tension between obligation and discretion nevertheless contributes a measure of uncertainty to the debate,[114] which is amplified by recent tendencies on the part of States effectively to qualify the refugee definition by reference to other, exclusionary criteria, such as a continuing need for protection or the absence of another State with actual or assumed protection responsibilities.[115]

7. 'Refugees' and international obligations

Voting patterns in the General Assembly on UNHCR and related topics confirm that the majority of States clearly want the United Nations to assume responsibilities for a broad category of persons obliged to flee their countries for a variety of reasons. Indeed, the scope of those who might count on

(1992), No. 1–2, 27—s. 65 of the Hungarian Constitution refers to persecution for 'linguistic' reasons, in addition to racial, religious, national and political grounds; Nagy, B., 'Before or After the Wave? The Adequacy of the New Hungarian Refugee Law', 3 *IJRL* 529 (1991).

[112] Denmark: Aliens Act, art. 7. These and many other examples are available on-line in REF-LEG, one of many databases, collectively known as REFWORLD, developed and maintained by UNHCR's Centre for Documentation on Refugees. A substantial part of these databases was opened for access on the INTERNET during 1995, and included in UNHCR's CD-ROM, *RefWorld/RefMonde*, published in Jan. 1996.

[113] See Weis, P., 'The Legal Aspects of the Problems of *de facto* Refugees', in International University Exchange Fund, *Problems of Refugees and Exiles in Europe*, (1974). The notion of 'valid reasons' is expanded at 3–5 and would include (1) a person's reasonable belief that he or she would be prejudiced in the exercise of human rights, would suffer discrimination, or be compelled to act against conscience; and (2) war or warlike conditions, foreign or colonial occupation, or serious disturbance of public order in part or all of the person's country of origin. See also UNHCR, 'Note on Consultations on the Arrivals of Asylum-seekers and Refugees in Europe': UN doc. A/AC.96/INF.174 (July 1985), Annexe V.

[114] See 'Report on the situation of asylum-seekers whose asylum applications have been rejected', Rapporteur: Mr Flückiger: Parliamentary Assembly of the Council of Europe, CE Doc. 7044, 21 Mar. 1994—refers to the practice of allowing rejected asylum seekers who nonetheless need protection to remain exceptionally on humanitarian grounds, concludes that this is not generally satisfactory, and that there is a 'legal vacuum'.

[115] See further below, Ch. 4, s. 5; Ch. 9, s. 2.1.1.

international protection is expanding even to include the internally displaced, at least in certain circumstances. In each case, however, there is a clear gap between what may be called *functional* responsibilities and expectations, on the one hand, and the legal obligations of States, on the other hand.

That UNHCR's competence and responsibility have evolved is beyond question,[116] and neither the Executive Committee nor the General Assembly has resiled from this position. However, as States endorsed a wider role for UNHCR, so they began also to express their reservations about a general widening of the refugee definition.[117] At the UNHCR Executive Committee in 1985, for example, several States expressed concern about abuse of asylum procedures, but still agreed that those fleeing armed conflict or internal disturbances deserved protection.[118] The Netherlands suggested that protection in such cases was based not so much on international obligations, as on national asylum policies. The universally accepted definition of a refugee should not be applied, lest this diminish the readiness of governments to grant asylum.[119]

[116] In 1980, the UNHCR Executive Committee noted continuing large-scale movements from man-made disasters; it stressed the necessity for co-ordination among UN bodies concerned with such emergencies and those involving refugees and displaced persons in refugee-like situations, and 'emphasized . . . the leading responsibility of (UNHCR) in emergency situations which involve refugees in the sense of its Statute or of General Assembly resolution 1388(XIV) and its subsequent resolutions': *Report* of the 31st Session: UN doc. A/AC.96/588, paras. 29.A(c), 29.B(c)(e)(f)). The other resolutions cited by the Executive Committee tracked the High Commissioner's good offices work; see above, s. 3.2. Executive Conclusion No. 22 on the protection of asylum seekers in situations of large-scale influx expressly recognizes that such flows will include both Convention/Protocol refugees as well as others who flee for reasons such as those mentioned in art. I(2) of the 1969 OAU Convention.

[117] Already in 1982 some States were emphasizing that UNHCR's mandate was 'sufficiently flexible and adaptable to changing requirements', that no change there or in the refugee definition was called for; see *Report* of the 33rd Session: UN doc. A/AC.96/614 (1982), para. 43(f); also UN doc. A/AC.96/SR.344, para. 11 (USA); SR.352, paras. 60–2 (UK). Cf. Hailbronner, K., 'Rechtsfragen —der Aufnahme von "Gewaltflüchtlingen" in Westeuropa—am Beispiel Jugoslawien', (1993) *Schweizerische Zeitschrift für internationales und europäisches Recht*, 517–38—discusses the meaning respectively of *Gewaltflüchtlingen* = refugee from violence and *de facto* refugee, recognizing that protection needs do not always coincide with legal categories (523–4); also Gattiker, M. and Illes, R., 'Kosovo: Trends in der deutschen und schweizerischen Asylrechtsprechung', *Asyl* (1993/2), 32–40.

[118] See Summary Records, 36th Session (1985): UN doc. A/AC.96/SR.391, paras. 50–1 (Switzerland); also para. 42 (Australia), confirming UNHCR's protecting role for the broader class, but considering it 'undesirable to define those groups of persons as "refugees" and to grant them the full range of protection available to victims of individual persecution'; also SR.464, para. 14 (1991), where Australia suggested priority for those in the broader class should be 'relief and humanitarian assistance and repatriation when that is possible in reasonably safe conditions'. Compare the contrasting positions of Tunisia and France in 1984: A/AC.96/SR.374, paras. 57–60.

[119] Ibid., para. 72. Not many States appear fully to have recognized the distinction between the *functional* responsibilities of UNHCR, which they themselves have determinedly enlarged, and the precise scope of their own *legal* obligations, which are to be assessed in the light of treaty and customary international law. Cf. ibid., paras. 77–8 (Federal Republic of Germany: even if UNHCR's competence were extended, no legal obligations could be implied on the basis of the 1951 Convention with regard to the acceptance of asylum seekers); and para. 82 (Italy, suggesting an additional type of legal status to deal with new categories). The confusion of UNHCR's mandate with States' obligations seems to continue; see *Report* of the Sub-Committee of the Whole: UN doc. A/AC.96/717, paras. 25–6 (1988).

For the last decade or so, the developed States in particular have continued to complain about abuse and the numbers of asylum applications.[120] The Federal Republic of Germany, for example, said that States' adherence to existing texts offered an 'unprecedented degree of security to genuine refugees', while the numbers of arrivals left it with little leeway for additional obligations.[121] The Netherlands stressed the importance of distinguishing refugees and asylum seekers from persons leaving for socio-economic or personal reasons,[122] and insisted the following year that its restrictive measures were a good faith effort to balance control and respect for the principle of asylum. Switzerland argued that the 'dilution' of the refugee concept would not solve the dilemma facing States.[123] Refugees defined in the Convention 'should be able to count on protection in a host country against persecution'. The acceptance of other foreigners for humanitarian reasons would be based, not on any Convention obligation, but on considerations of humanitarian law or international solidarity; that is, 'on a free decision by the State concerned'.[124] Canada has also warned against the

[120] At the 37th Session of the Executive Committee (1986), see UN doc. A/AC.96/SR.401, para. 70 (UK); SR.403, para. 19 (Belgium) and para. 22 (Norway). Some of the reaction in 1986 may have been due to references in the High Commissioner's opening statement, in which he suggested, not without reason, that the concept of individual persecution had been overtaken by forced mass migration; and that, while still useful, the 1951 Convention no longer fully matched realities; see *Report* of the 37th Session, Annex, 2–3: UN doc. A/AC.96/688 and /Corr.1. At the 38th Session (1987), see UN doc. A/AC.96/SR.414, para. 39 (Sweden); para. 49 (Switzerland); SR.417, para. 83 (UK); paras. 84–5 (Sweden). At the 39th Session (1988), see UN doc. A/AC.96/SR.426, para. 81 (Norway); para. 88 (Belgium); SR.430, para. 41 (Switzerland); para. 51 (UK).

[121] UN doc. A/AC.96/SR.406 (1986), para. 22; also SR.402, para. 32. Cf. Hailbronner, K., 'Perspectives of a Harmonization of the Law of Asylum after the Maastricht Summit,' 29 *CMLR* 917, 930 (1992), considering shelter for humanitarian refugees as a humanitarian obligation of west European States on the basis of *political* guidelines, and 'decidedly not a legal title which could be taken to court by any individual'.

[122] UN doc. A/AC.96/SR.406 (1986), paras. 36 *et seq.* The Netherlands did not address the question of those falling between the two extremes, but did argue that asylum in Europe should be considered on an individual basis. Cf. its views on 'national asylum policies': above, text to note 119. With a masterful combination of understatement and question-begging, Switzerland urged a clear distinction between Convention refugees and 'persons attempting to escape from an insecure or distressing situation created by political, social, ecological or economic circumstances': UN doc. A/AC.96/SR.406, para. 87.

[123] Or, as France appropriately described it in 1987, the 'confusion' prevalent in developed countries: UN doc. A/AC.96/SR.426, para. 72. See also Arboleda, E. and Hoy, I., 'The Convention Refugee Definition in the West: Disharmony of Interpretation and Application', 5 *IJRL* 66 (1993).

[124] UN doc. A/AC.96/SR.430, para. 42 (1988); also SR.455, para. 50 (1990), noting increasing difficulty in distinguishing between Convention refugees, displaced persons and others forced to flee by conflicts or disasters. Similarly Sweden: SR.464, para. 31 (1991). See the views of the Federal Republic of Germany at the 38th Session (1987), on UNHCR's reference to the 'right of asylum' in that year's *Note on International Protection* (UN doc. A/AC.96/694). In its opinion, what counted was not any such right, but the 'prerogative of sovereign States to regulate the entry of aliens': UN doc. A/AC.96/SR.418, para. 71. Since 1990, art. 14a, para. 4 of the Swiss Aliens Act has made special provision for those fleeing violence. Further to para. 5, the Federal Council may, after consultations with UNHCR and after taking into account the practice of other States, determine categories of persons who will be temporarily admitted if they meet certain criteria. They must apply for asylum, but will otherwise be admitted without further investigation. Kälin has noted the reluctance of the Swiss

notion, 'that more persons could be assisted by simply broadening the definition'.[125]

Following on a working group report that identified some seven categories of persons falling, in various degrees, within UNHCR's area of operations,[126] a discussion paper on 'persons of concern' to the Office was submitted to an intersessional meeting of the Executive Committee in April 1992.[127] It noted the disjuncture between the 'obligation' of the international community to provide protection, and the discretionary responses of States. The debate revealed general recognition of the need to deal with the protection issues, but no great willingness to move speedily in the direction of a separate regime, for example in Europe, that would combine criteria, burden sharing, identification of safe countries or areas, and evaluation of safe return possibilities.[128] The practical value of 'guidelines' suggested by one participant,[129] was taken up in a comprehensive review of protection submitted by UNHCR to the Executive Committee in 1994.[130] Noting that, while there was broad consensus on the need to provide protection, States had little inclination to adopt a new convention, it proposed 'the adoption of guiding principles embodied in a global or regional declaration';[131] this idea in turn received support from many States in the Executive Committee in 1994 and 1995.[132]

authorities to take decisions on those fleeing violence, preferring to leave cases pending in the hope that the situation will improve; see Kälin, W., 'Safe Return for Refugees of Violence: A Blueprint for Action,' in Gowlland, V. and Sampson, K., *Problems and Prospects of Refugee Law*, (1992), 125; Gattiker, M. & Illes, R., 'Kosovo: Trends in der deutschen und schweizerischen Asylrechtsprechung', *Asyl*, 1993/2, 32.

[125] UN doc. A/AC.96/463, para. 61 (1991).

[126] Convention/Protocol refugee, OAU/Cartagena refugees, refugees from man-made disasters, persons in flight from natural disasters, rejected cases, internally displaced persons, stateless persons: *Report* of the Working Group on Solutions and Protection: UN doc. EC/SCP/64 (12 Aug. 1991), paras. 8–53. The *Report* was 'accepted with appreciation', rather than adopted by the Sub-Committee of the Whole on International Protection, which recommended further discussions: *Report* of the Sub-Committee: UN doc. A/AC.96/781 (9 Oct. 1991), paras. 2–18.

[127] 'Protection of Persons of Concern to UNHCR who fall outside the 1951 Convention: A Discussion Note': EC/SCP/1992/CRP.5; the African Group and the Latin America Group also submitted a paper on the scope, respectively, of the OAU Convention and the Cartagena Declaration: EC/SCP/1992/CRP.6.

[128] *Report* of the 13–14 April Meeting: UN doc. EC/SCP/71 (7 Jul. 1992), paras. 31–44.

[129] Ibid., para. 39.

[130] UNHCR, *Note* on International Protection: UN doc. A/AC.96/830 (7 Sept. 1994), paras. 19–43, 54–7; published also in 6 *IJRL* 679 (1994).

[131] Ibid., para. 57.

[132] *Report* of the Sub-Committee of the Whole on International Protection: UN doc. A/AC.96/837 (4 Oct. 1994), para. 19, Executive Committee General Conclusion on International Protection, *Report* of the 45th Session: UN doc. A/AC.96/839 (11 Oct. 1994), para. 19 (k)–(q); UN doc. A/AC.96/SR.490, para. 8 (Canada); SR.491, para. 35 (Norway); SR.492, para. 16 (Switzerland); see also UNGA res. 49/169, 23 Dec. 1994, paras. 6, 7.

8. Summary conclusions on the refugee definition for the purposes of general international law

Refugees within the mandate of UNHCR, and therefore eligible for protection and assistance by the international community, include not only those who can, on a case-by-case basis, be determined to have a well-founded fear of persecution on certain grounds (so-called 'statutory refugees'); but also other often large groups of persons who can be determined or presumed to be without, or unable to avail themselves of, the protection of the government of their State of origin (now often referred to as 'displaced persons' or 'persons of concern').[133] In each case, it is essential that the persons in question should have crossed an international frontier and that, in the case of the latter group, the reasons for flight should be traceable to conflicts, or radical political, social, or economic changes in their own country. With fundamental human rights at issue, the key remains violence, or the risk or threat of violence, but only in certain cases; those who move because of pure economic motivation, pure personal convenience or criminal intent are excluded.

UNHCR may also assist persons displaced *within* their own countries and contribute to the rehabilitation and reintegration of returning refugees and 'externally' displaced persons.[134] Recent practice indicates that in some circumstances UNHCR may exercise a protection function with respect to the internally displaced, but its legal standing in that context is less certain.[135] Assistance and protection activities on behalf of the internally displaced, once exceptional, are now increasingly common, and although they are highly significant in determining the role and responsibility of UNHCR and in allocating resources, they are of limited relevance to the precise question of the international legal status of refugees.[136]

On the basis of State and international organization practice, the above core of meaning represents the content of the term 'refugee' in general international law. Grey areas nevertheless remain. The class of persons 'without, or unable to avail themselves of, the protection of the government of their State of origin'

---

[133] Cf. Goodwin-Gill, G.S., 'Chi é un rifugiato', *Politica internazionale*, No. 5. sett-ott. 1991, 41–62.

[134] The facilitation and promotion of voluntary repatriation are prescribed functions of UNHCR (paras. 1 and 8(c) of the Statute), which may extend to a period after initial return, when technically the persons in question will have ceased to be refugees; see further below Ch. 7, s. 3.1.

[135] See below, Ch. 7, s. 2.

[136] The question of institutional responsibilities for humanitarian emergencies is not unrelated to the refugee issue, however. On proposed reforms, see Refugee Policy Group. 'Humanitarian Action in the Post Cold War Era.' Background Paper and Conference Summary. Bellagio, Italy, May 1992, proposing six major overlapping categories of persons of 'humanitarian concern'; also, Beyer, G. A., 'Improving International Response to Humanitarian Situations,' Refugee Policy Group. (Dec. 1989), 14–17, who favours developing a consensus on 'additional categories' of persons of potential humanitarian concern, relative to the needs of each for international protection. These would include Convention refugees, victims of civil strife, conscientious objectors, self-exiles, victims of natural disasters (including both internally and externally displaced), and migrants (including legal and illegal migrants).

begs many questions. Moreover, the varying content of the term 'refugee' may likewise import varying legal consequences, so that the obligations of States in matters such as *non-refoulement*, non-rejection at the frontier, temporary refuge or asylum, and treatment after entry will depend upon the precise status of the particular class. In many situations, UNHCR's institutional responsibilities will be complemented by the obligations of States under the 1951 Convention/1967 Protocol, or supplemented by regional arrangements. This is by no means a complete legal regime, however. The disjuncture between the obligations of States and the institutional responsibilities of UNHCR is broadest and most clearly apparent in regard to refugees, other than those having a well-founded fear of persecution or falling within regional arrangements. The disjuncture is compounded by disputes as to the criteria determining the limits of the class, and as to the applicability of certain basic principles of human rights, including rights to refuge and protection. UNHCR has been accorded a functional role and responsibility by the international community, but it remains dependent upon the resources and the political will of States to work out the practical problems of protection, assistance and solutions. UN General Assembly resolutions may impose obligations on UNHCR, its subsidiary organ, but they do not thereby directly impose obligations on States.[137]

As shown below, however, the principle of *non-refoulement*, (in its generic form of 'refuge') is the foundation stone of international protection and applies across a broad class, even if the resulting regime of law and practice is far from adequate either for States or individuals. Certain factual elements may be necessary before the principle is triggered—for example, mass movement to or across an international frontier and some evidence of relevant and valid reasons for flight, such as human rights violations in the country of origin—but it would not be permissible for a State to seek to avoid its obligations, either by declining to make a formal determination of refugee status or by ignoring and acting in disregard of the development of the refugee concept in State and international organization practice.

Recent examples show that, while States are conscious of the potential threat to their own security that a massive influx can pose, none claims an absolute right to return a refugee, as such, to persecution. A State may try to assert for itself greater freedom of action, however, by avoiding any use of refugee terminology. Asylum seekers are thus classified as 'displaced persons', 'illegal immigrants', 'economic migrants', 'quasi-refugees', 'aliens', 'departees', 'boat-people', or 'stowaways'.

Similarly, the developed world has expended considerable energy in trying to find ways to prevent claims for protection being made at their borders, or to allow for them to be summarily passed on or back to others. 'Interdiction', 'visa

---

[137] See also by the present writer, 'The Language of Protection,' 1 *IJRL* 6 (1989); and 'Refugees: The Functions and Limits of the Existing Protection System,' in Nash, A., *Human Rights and the Protection of Refugees under International Law*, (1988), 149–82.

requirements', 'carrier sanctions', 'safe third country' concepts, 'security zones', 'international zones', and the like are among the armoury of measures recently employed. The intention may be either to forestall arrivals, or to allow those arriving to be dealt with at discretion, but the clear implication is that, for States at large, refugees are protected by international law and, as a matter of law, entitled to a better and higher standard of treatment.

Chapter 2

DETERMINATION OF REFUGEE STATUS: ANALYSIS AND APPLICATION

The legal consequences[1] which flow from the formal definition of refugee status are necessarily predicated upon determination by some or other authority that the individual or group in question satisfies the relevant legal criteria. In principle, a person becomes a refugee at the moment when he or she satisfies the definition, so that determination of status is declaratory, rather than constitutive;[2] problems arise, however, where States decline to determine refugee status, or where different determinations are reached by States and by UNHCR.[3]

1. Respective competence of UNHCR and of States parties to the Convention and Protocol

The UNHCR Statute and the 1951 Convention contain very similar definitions of the term 'refugee'. It is for UNHCR to determine status under the Statute and any relevant General Assembly resolutions, and for States parties to the Convention and the Protocol to determine status under those instruments.[4]

---

[1] To the drafters of the 1951 Convention, at least initially, the absence of a clear legal status necessarily had repercussions on the refugee's right to recognition as a person before the law, as required by art. 6 of the Universal Declaration of Human Rights, while such status was also essential in order to enable the refugee 'to lead a normal and self-respecting life'. See UN doc. E/AC.32/2, 3 Jan. 1950, *Ad Hoc* Committee on Statelessness and Related Problems. Memorandum by the Secretary-General; Annex; Preliminary Draft Convention, para. 13. These references were dropped from the final version of the Preamble; today, although 'refugee status' is understood more as the formal confirmation of entitlement to international protection or asylum in the sense of solution, than as a particular civil quality, its absence or denial may well entail the marginalization of substantial numbers of individuals otherwise in need of refuge.

[2] See UNHCR, *Handbook*, para. 28; Grahl-Madsen, A., *The Status of Refugees in International Law*, vol. 1, (1966), 340; Tribunal civil, Verviers, 15 nov. 1989, *X c/ Etat belge:* 55 *Revue du droit des étrangers* (RDDE), sept.–oct. 1989, 242.

[3] See generally, Grahl-Madsen, *Status of Refugees*, vol. 1, (1966); Weis, P., 'The Concept of the Refugee in International Law', *Journal du droit international,* (1960) 1; Schnyder, F., 'Les aspects juridiques actuels du problème des réfugiés', Hague *Recueil* (1965–I) 339; Sadruddin Aga Khan, 'Legal Problems relating to Refugees and Displaced Persons Hague', *Recueil* (1976–I) 287; Aleinikoff, T. A. and Martin, D. A., *Immigration: Process and Policy,* (2nd ed., 1991), 789–853; Carlier, J.-Y., *Droit des réfugiés,* (1989); European Council on Refugees and Exiles, *Asylum in Europe,* 2 vols., (1994); Hathaway, J., *The Law of Refugee Status,* (1991); Kälin, W., *Grundriss des Asylverfahrens,* (1990); Marx, R., *Asylrecht,* (5. Aufl., 1991); Tiberghien, F., *La protection des réfugiés en France,* (2e ed., 1988); UNHCR, *Handbook on Procedures and Criteria for Determining Refugee Status,* (1979).

[4] The situation of refugees acknowledged under earlier arrangements and formally included in both Statute and Convention is not examined further; cf. Statute, para. 6(a)(1) and 1951 Convention, art. 1A(1): below, Annexe 1, Nos. 3 and 4; Grahl-Madsen, *Status of Refugees*, vol. 1, 108–41; Tiberghien, *La protection des réfugiés,* 401–41.

Given the differences in definition, an individual may be recognized as both a mandate,[5] and a Convention[6] refugee; or as a mandate refugee but not as a Convention refugee.[7] The latter can arise, for example, where the individual is in a non-contracting State or a State which adheres to the temporal or geographical limitations permitted under the Convention.[8] Divergence between mandate and Convention status can also result from differences of opinion between States and UNHCR, although a number of factors ought in principle to reduce that possibility. UNHCR, for example, has the statutory function of supervising the application of international conventions for the protection of refugees,[9] and States parties to the Convention and Protocol formally undertake to facilitate this duty.[10] Moreover, many States accept direct or indirect participation by UNHCR in procedures for the determination of refugee status, so that the potential for harmonization of decisions is increased. The problem of divergent positions is more likely, however, where States decline to determine refugee status for any reason; or where refugees whose claims are well-founded under a regional regime move elsewhere.[11]

2. Determination of refugee status by UNHCR

The basic elements of the refugee definition are common to States and to UNHCR and are examined more fully in Section 3. UNHCR itself will be concerned to determine status (1) as a condition precedent to providing international protection (for example, intervention with a government to prevent expulsion); or (2) as a prerequisite to providing assistance to a government which requests it in respect of certain groups within its territory. Except in individual cases, formal determination of refugee status may not be necessary. Intervention to secure temporary refuge or temporary protection,[12] for example, can be based on prima facie elements in the particular case—the fact of flight across an international frontier, evidence of valid reasons for flight from the country of origin, and the material needs of the group in question. Where assistance is expressly requested by a receiving country, that invitation alone would justify UNHCR's involvement in the absence of hard evidence that those to be helped were not

---

[5] The term 'mandate refugee' will signify a refugee within the competence of UNHCR according to its Statute, or according to specific General Assembly resolutions.

[6] The term 'Convention refugee' will signify a refugee within the meaning of the 1951 Convention and/or 1967 Protocol.

[7] Recognition as a Convention, but not as a mandate refugee would import no consequences of significance.

[8] These optional limitations are not discussed further; see Grahl-Madsen, *Status of Refugees*, vol. 1, 164–72. States parties maintaining the limitations are listed below in Annexe 6.

[9] Para. 8(a).

[10] Art. 35 of the Convention; art. II of the Protocol.   [11] Cf. Ch. 6, s. 6.1.

[12] The terms 'temporary refuge' and 'temporary protection' are used interchangeably; see further below, Ch. 5, s. 5.

refugees or displaced persons, or of any coherent, persuasive opposition by the country of origin or other members of the international community.[13]

Formal determination of mandate status, however, is often necessary in individual cases. Only comparatively few States have instituted procedures for assessing refugee claims, so that intervention by UNHCR on the basis of a positive determination of refugee status may be required to protect the individual. Occasionally, access to national refugee resettlement programmes may be conditional upon certification by the UNHCR office in the country of first admission that the individuals in question fall within the mandate of the High Commissioner.[14]

3. Determination of refugee status by States

The 1951 Convention defines refugees and provides for certain standards of treatment to be accorded to refugees. It says nothing about procedures for determining refugee status, and leaves to States the choice of means as to implementation at the national level.[15] Given the nature of the definition, the assessment of claims to refugee status thus involves a complex of subjective and objective factors, while the context of such assessment—interpretation of an international instrument with fundamentally humanitarian objectives—implies certain ground rules.[16]

Clearly, the onus is on the applicant to establish his or her case, but practical considerations and the trauma which can face a person in flight, impose a cor-

[13] Cf. various state objections, cited above, Ch. 1, ns. 68–70.

[14] UNHCR's determination operates as a filter in such cases, although the final decisions on both status and acceptance are increasingly taken by governments themselves. See, for example, Australia, Ministerial Statement on Refugee Policy *Parliamentary Debates*, 16 Mar. 1982, 989–94 (House of Representatives). See also *Loi no. 52–893*, 25 juill. 1951, as modified by *Loi no. 93–1027*, 24 août 1993, according to which the *Office français de protection des réfugiés et apatrides* (OFPRA), 'reconnaît le qualité de réfugié à toute personne sur laquelle le Haut Commissariat des Nations unies pour les réfugiés exerce son mandat aux terms des articles 6 et 7 de son statut . . . ou qui répond aux définitions de l'article 1er de la Convention de Genève du 28 juillet 1951 . . .' See also CRR, 16 mai 1988, 38.367, *Kazilbash, Doc. réf.* no. 79, 4/13 juill. 1989, Suppl., JC, 1—Afghan asylum seeker received UNHCR protection in India, but claim in France rejected. CRR held that OFPRA was required not only to determine whether claimant was within the Convention, but also whether within mandate of UNHCR.

[15] See further below, Ch. 6, s. 2.2, and Ch. 9.

[16] Cf. art. 31(1), Vienna Convention on the Law of Treaties. The UNHCR *Handbook on Procedures and Criteria for Determining Refugee Status* was prepared at the request of States members of the Executive Committee of the High Commissioner's Programme, for the guidance of governments: UNHCR Executive Committee, *Report of the 28th Session*: UN doc. A/AC.96/549 (1977), para. 53.6(g). First published in 1979, it has been reprinted several times in many languages, generally with a new foreword by the current Director of International Protection and updated lists of States parties. The content, however, is unchanged, being based on material and analysis available at the date of preparation, including UNHCR experience, State practice in regard to the determination of refugee status, exchanges of views between the Office and the competent authorities of Contracting States, and relevant literature. The *Handbook* has been widely circulated and approved by governments, is frequently referred to in refugee status proceedings throughout the world, and has been cited with approval by a variety of courts in many jurisdictions; see further below, Ch. 9.

responding duty upon whomever must ascertain and evaluate the relevant facts and the credibility of the applicant.[17] Given 'protection' of refugees as one of the Convention's objectives, a liberal interpretation of the criteria is called for. A decision on the well-foundedness or not of a fear of persecution is essentially an essay in hypothesis, an attempt to prophesy what might happen to the applicant in the future, if returned to his or her country of origin. Particular care needs to be exercised, therefore, in applying the correct standard of proof.

In civil and criminal cases, two 'standards of proof' are commonly advanced: 'proof on a balance of probability' for the former, and 'proof beyond a reasonable doubt' for the latter. In practice, there can be no absolute standard in either case, and it will vary with the subject-matter. In the United Kingdom, for example, in *habeas corpus* proceedings, the applicant must cast some doubt on the validity of his or her detention. But in matters of fact, it is enough that the applicant presents such evidence as raises the possibility of a favourable inference. It then falls to the respondent, the detaining authority, to rebut that inference.[18] It might be argued that, in a refugee status case, the 'likelihood of persecution' must be established on a balance of probabilities. In civil cases, the typical issue is whether a close, legally relevant relation exists between past causes and past effects.[19] The applicant for refugee status, however, is adducing a future speculative risk as the basis for a claim to protection. Analogous issues were considered as long ago as 1971 in the United Kingdom by the House of Lords in an extradition case, *Fernandez* v. *Government of Singapore*.[20] Here, Lord Diplock noted that the phrase 'balance of probability' was 'inappropriate when applied not to ascertaining what has happened, but to prophesying what, if it happens at all, can only happen in the future'.[21] He went on to note that the relevant provision of the Fugitive Offenders Act:

. . . calls upon the court to prophesy what will happen to the fugitive in the future if he is returned . . . The degree of confidence that the events specified will occur which the court should have to justify refusal to return the fugitive . . . should, as a matter of common sense and common humanity, depend upon the gravity of the consequences contemplated on the one hand of permitting and on the other hand of refusing, the return of the fugitive if the court's expectation should be wrong. The general policy of the Act, viz. that persons against whom a prima facie case is established that they have committed a crime . . . should be returned to stand their trial . . . , is departed from if the return

---

[17] UNHCR, *Handbook*, paras. 195–205.

[18] *R.* v. *Governor of Brixton Prison, ex parte Ahsan* [1969] 2 QB 222 per Goddard LCJ at 233.

[19] For example, did war service cause or contribute to cancer of the gullet leading to death? Cf. *Miller* v. *Minister of Pensions* [1947] 2 All ER 372.

[20] [1971] 1 WLR 987. The Court considered and applied section 4(1)(c) of the Fugitive Offenders Act 1967 which provides: 'A person shall not be returned under this Act . . . if it appears . . . that he might, if returned, be prejudiced at his trial or punished, detained or restricted in his personal liberty by reason of his race, religion, nationality or political opinion.'

[21] [1971] 1 WLR 987, at 993–4. Cf. the quantification of future losses, both pecuniary and non-pecuniary, which courts undertake in personal injury claims; see for example, *Davies* v. *Taylor* [1972] All ER 836, *Jefford* v. *Gee* [1970] 2 QB 130.

of a person who will not be detained or restricted for any of the reasons specified in paragraph (c) is refused. But it is departed from only in one case. On the other hand, detention or restriction in his personal liberty, the consequence which the relevant words are intended to avert, is grave indeed to the individual fugitive concerned.

One significant difference between the principle of non-extradition and that of protection of refugees lies in the risk to society if return is refused when, in fact, persecution would not have occurred. On the one hand, a suspected or actual criminal is allowed to remain, while on the other hand, someone who is innocent and against whom no allegations are made is allowed to remain. The attitude to the asylum seeker should be at least as benevolent as that accorded to the fugitive from justice. Lord Diplock took account of the relative gravity of the consequences of the court's expectations proving wrong either one way or the other, and concluded that the appellant need not show that it was more likely than not that he or she would be detained or restricted if returned. A lesser degree of likelihood sufficed such as 'a reasonable chance', 'substantial grounds for thinking', or 'a serious possibility'.[22] Considered in isolation, these terms lack precision. In practice, however, they are appropriate, beyond the context of municipal law, for the unique task of assessing a claim to refugee status. While the facts on which the claimant relies may be established on a balance of probability, the decision-maker must then make a reasoned guess as to the future, taking account also of the element of relativity between the degree of persecution feared (whether death, torture, imprisonment, discrimination, or prejudice, for example), and the degree of likelihood of its eventuating.

In 1984, UNHCR submitted an *amicus curiae* brief to the US Supreme Court, arguing against the balance of probability, or clear probability, test as the criterion for the grant of asylum. The Court concluded that the well-founded fear standard, which is incorporated into the Refugee Act 1980 as the criterion for the grant of asylum, does not apply to applications for relief from deportation under section 243(h) of the Immigration and Nationality Act; in such cases, relief is conditional on the applicant showing 'a clear probability' of persecution. However, the Court also emphasized that eligibility for asylum under section 208 of the Act remained an entirely separate issue.[23]

Following this ruling, courts and administrative authorities were divided. Officials insisted that well-founded fear requires applicants to show that it is more likely than not that they will be singled out for persecution, a view also followed by the Immigration and Naturalization Service and the Board of

[22] Cf. art. 2, Draft Convention on Territorial Asylum, proposing a 'definite possibility of persecution' as the criterion for the grant of asylum; also art. 3, UN Convention against Torture; art. 3, European Convention on Human Rights. For texts, see below, Annexe 1, Nos. 6 & 7; Annexe 2, No. 8. See also Jackman, B., 'Well-founded fear of persecution and other standards of decision-making: A North American perspective', in Bhabha, J. and Coll, G., *Asylum Law and Practice in Europe and North America*, (1992), 44.

[23] *INS* v. *Stevic* 467 US 407 (1984); Weinman, S.C., '*INS* v. *Stevic*: A Critical Assessment', 7 *HRQ* 391 (1985).

Immigration Appeals. In *Acosta*, for example, the applicant appealed against denial both of his application for asylum and for withholding of deportation to El Salvador.[24] His claim was based on active participation in a co-operative organization of taxi-drivers, threatened by anti-government forces seeking to disrupt transportation; a number of taxis were burnt and drivers killed, and the applicant testified to having received a beating and various threats. The Board of Immigration Appeals (BIA) found the applicant's testimony, which was corroborated by other objective evidence in the record, to be worthy of belief; however, it considered this insufficient to meet the statutory standards of eligibility for asylum and withholding of deportation.

The Board referred to the *Stevic* case, but remarked that, 'as a practical matter the showing contemplated by the phrase "a well-founded fear" of persecution converges with the showing described by the phrase "a clear probability" of persecution'. The asylum seeker's fear must be *well-founded* in the sense that, 'an individual's fear of persecution must have its basis in external, or objective, facts that show there is a realistic likelihood he will be persecuted on his return'.

... the evidence must demonstrate that (1) the alien possesses a belief or characteristic a persecutor seeks to overcome in others by means of punishment of some sort; (2) the persecutor is already aware, or could easily become aware, that the alien possesses this belief or characteristic; (3) the persecutor has the capability of punishing the alien; and (4) the persecutor has the inclination to punish the alien.

Subjective fears alone were not enough; they must 'have a sound basis in personal experience or in other external facts or events'. The various competing standards of proof (likelihood of persecution, clear probability of persecution, persecution as more likely than not), did not reflect meaningful distinctions in practice.

Although the Board's reasoning is well thought out and retains a persuasive and pervasive logic, yet it finally demands too much of the asylum seeker and pays too little attention to the essentially future-oriented and hypothetical assessment attaching to the determination that a well-founded fear of persecution exists.[25]

In due course, the US Supreme Court was called on to rule precisely on the difference, if any, between a 'well-founded fear', and a 'clear probability' of

---

[24] *Re Acosta-Solorzano*, Int. Dec. no. 2986, 1 Mar. 1985.

[25] Cf. *Bolanos-Hernandez* v. *Immigration and Naturalization Service*, 749 F.2d 1316 (9th Cir., 1984). The Court of Appeals held that while evidence of a general level of violence was not alone enough, the uncontroverted evidence of a threat to the applicant's own life was sufficient to establish a likelihood of persecution. The documentary evidence submitted also illustrated the likely fate of those who refused to co-operate with the non-governmental forces, and that the guerrillas had both the ability and the will to carry out their threats; to require further corroborative evidence would impose an impossible burden. See also *Hernandez-Ortiz* v. *INS* 777 F.2d 509 (9th Circ., 1985); *Kiala*, 16,580, Commission des recours, 7 Jan. 1983—documentary evidence of the general situation in the country of origin and without specific reference to the claimant is insufficient: cited in Tiberghien, *La protection des réfugiés*, 377.

persecution. UNHCR's *amicus curiae* brief in *INS* v. *Cardoza-Fonseca* examined the negotiating history of article 1 of the Convention, and demonstrated that the status of refugee had been intended for a person who has been persecuted or who has 'good reason' to fear persecution, and that the subjective fear should be based on an objective situation, which in turn made that fear plausible and reasonable in the circumstances. It concluded,

No statistical definition is . . . appropriate to determine the reasonableness of an applicant's fear, given the inherently speculative nature of the exercise. The requisite degree of probability must take into account the intensity of the fear, the nature of the projected harm (death, imprisonment, torture, detention, serious discrimination, etc.), the general history of persecution in the home country, the applicant's personal experience and that of his or her family, and all other surrounding circumstances.[26]

The Supreme Court confirmed its earlier judgment in *Stevic*, but rejected the Government's argument that the clear probability standard also controlled applications for asylum. The 'ordinary and obvious meaning' of the words used in the Refugee Act, its legislative history and the provisions of the Convention and Protocol, showed that Congress intended to establish a broad class of refugees eligible for the discretionary grant of asylum, and a narrower class with the statutory right not to be deported. Giving the judgment of the Supreme Court, Justice Stevens emphasized the role of discretion. There is no entitlement to asylum, although its benefits once granted are broader than simple relief under section 243(h); the latter is 'country-specific', and merely prohibits deportation to the country or countries in which life or freedom would be threatened. Moreover, while it constrains discretion in the matter of *non-refoulement*, 'the Protocol does not require the granting of asylum to anyone'. The Court found very different meanings in the statutory language. The 'would be threatened' criterion of section 243(h) (and article 33 of the Convention) contains no subjective element; objective evidence showing persecution as more likely than not is therefore required. By contrast, the reference to fear in section 208(a), 'obviously makes the eligibility standard turn to some extent on the subjective mental state' of the applicant. The 'well-founded' qualifier does not entail a clear probability standard: 'One can certainly have a well-founded fear of an event happening when there is a less than 50% chance of the occurrence taking place'.

The Court did not elaborate the standard of proof more precisely, being of the view that a term like 'well-founded fear' is ambiguous to a point, and can only be given concrete meaning through a process of case-by-case adjudication; abstract speculation on the differences between the two standards has its limits,

---

[26] See UNHCR, *Handbook*, para. 42: 'In general, the applicant's fear should be considered well-founded if he can establish, *to a reasonable degree*, that his continued stay in his country of origin has become intolerable to him for the reasons stated in the definition, or would for the same reasons be intolerable if he returned there.' (Emphasis supplied). See also, Gibney, M., 'A "Well-founded Fear" of persecution', 10 *HRQ* 109 (1988).

and it remains for the responsible authorities to develop a standard whose 'final contours are shaped by application to the facts of specific cases'.

The debate regarding the standard of proof reveals some of the inherent weaknesses of a system of protection founded upon essays in prediction. It is no easy task to determine refugee status; decision-makers must assess credibility and will look to the demeanour of the applicant. Information on countries of origin will often be lacking or deficient, so that it is tempting to demand impossible degrees of corroboration. The applicant's testimony may seem unduly self-serving, though it could scarcely be otherwise, absent anyone else to speak on his or her behalf.[27] The onus of establishing a well-founded fear of persecution is on the applicant, and some objective evidence is called for; but documentary corroboration is frequently unavailable or too general to be conclusive in the individual case.

Credibility remains problematic, but the nature of the exercise in prediction and the objective of protection call for account to be taken of consequences, and of degrees of likelihood far short of any balance of probability.[28] This indeed seems now to have been recognized in most jurisdictions involved in individual refugee determination. In *Adjei* v. *Minister of Employment and Immigration*, for example, the Canadian Federal Court of Appeal approved 'good grounds for fearing persecution' as a description of what the evidence must show to support a claim to be a Convention refugee, posing the question, 'Is there a reasonable chance that persecution would take place were the applicant returned to his country?'[29] The Australian High Court has applied the notion of a 'real chance', understood to mean a less than fifty per cent possibility,[30] while the United Kingdom House of Lords has confirmed the approach initiated in *Fernandez:* The 'well-founded'

---

[27] In their own way, both *Acosta* and *Bolanos-Hernandez* underline the importance of personal testimony and documentary evidence.

[28] Cf. Inter-American Court of Human Rights, *Velasquez Rodriguez,* (Forced Disappearance and Death of Individual in Honduras, 29 Jul. 1988): 28 *ILM* 291 (1989)—with respect to the standard of proof, international jurisprudence recognizes the power of the courts to weigh the evidence freely. The standard adopted should take into account the seriousness of the finding; not only direct, but also circumstantial evidence, indicia and presumptions may be considered, and are especially important where the type of repression is characterized by attempts to suppress all information and the State controls the means to verify acts occurring within territory. The object of the proceedings is not to punish, 'but to protect the victims and to provide for the reparation of damages'.

[29] [1989] 2 FC 680, 683. Speaking for the Court, MacGuigan J. said, 'It was common ground that the objective test is not so stringent as to require a probability of persecution. In other words, *although an applicant has to establish his case on a balance of probabilities, he does not nevertheless have to prove that persecution would be more likely than not* . . . We would adopt that phrasing, which appears to us to be equivalent to that employed by Pratte J. A. in *Seifu* v. *Immigration Appeal Board* (A-277-822, dated 12 Jan. 1983): '[I]n order to support a finding that an applicant is a Convention refugee, the evidence must not necessarily show that he "has suffered or would suffer persecution"; what the evidence must show is that the applicant has good grounds for fearing persecution for one of the reasons specified in the Act.' (Emphasis supplied). See also *Salibian* v. *MEI*, [1990] 3 FC 250.

[30] *Chan* v. *Minister for Immigration and Ethnic Affairs*, (1989) CLR 379—real, that is, substantial chance includes less than 50% likelihood.

requirement, 'means no more than that there has to be demonstrated a reason-able degree of likelihood of . . . persecution . . .'[31]

4. Preliminary analysis of the definition

4.1 GENERAL MATTERS

A claimant to refugee status must be 'outside' his or her country of origin, and the fact of having fled, of having crossed an international frontier, is an intrinsic part of the quality of refugee, understood in its ordinary sense. Certain States may provide for those who would be considered as refugees once they took flight,[32] and a growing body of practice has aimed to bring some measure of protection and assistance to the internally displaced, but this in no way alters the basic international rule.[33]

The Convention requires neither that the putative refugee shall have fled by reason of fear of persecution, nor that persecution should have actually occurred. The fear may derive from conditions arising during an ordinary absence abroad (for example, as student, diplomat or holiday-maker), while the element of well-foundedness looks more to the future, than to the past. Subjective and objective factors are thus combined. Fear, reflecting the focus of the refugee definition in part at least on factors personal to the individual, and the degree to which it is felt, are incapable of precise quantification.[34] Fear may be exaggerated or under-stated, but still be reasonable.[35] It is by no means clear, however, whether from the definition, jurisprudence or commentary, how much of a role the subjective element is expected to play in a determination process that is practically oriented to the assessment of *risk*. If the applicant's statements in regard to his or her fear are consistent and credible, then little more can be required in the way of formal proof.[36] What seems to be intended, however, is not so much evidence of

---

[31] *R.* v. *Secretary of State for the Home Department, ex parte Sivakumaran et al,* [1988] 1 All ER 193. In a 1990 decision, the Administrative Appeals Court of Hesse in the Federal Republic of Germany ruled that the test of persecution was a 'reasonable likelihood': *Hessischer Verwaltungsgerichtshof,* 13 UE 1568/84, 2 May 1990. In a 1989 judgment, the *Tribunal Supremo* of Spain ruled that asylum seekers coming from countries in turmoil need only establish a prima facie case in order to qualify for asylum or be granted refugee status: *Tribunal Supremo, Recurso de apelación 2403/88: La Ley,* vol. X, No. 2276 (1989); *Aranzadi,* Tomo LVI, v. III, (1989). The standard of proof for art. 3 claims before the European Court of Human Rights is considerably higher, however; see further below, Ch. 8, s. 2.2.1.

[32] See US Refugee Act 1980 s. 201. UK immigration rules on asylum have been held not to apply to a refugee in a third country (*Secretary of State* v. *Two citizens of Chile* [1977] Imm AR 36) or to a would-be refugee in his or her country of origin (*Secretary of State* v. *X. (a Chilean citizen)* [1978] Imm AR 73).

[33] On the question of *non-refoulement* and the rejection of refugees at the frontier, see further below, Ch. 4, s. 2.1.

[34] The relevance or value of such an exercise is questionable in cases involving minority or mental disturbance. On children, see further below, Ch. 9, s. 3.1.

[35] UNHCR, *Handbook,* paras. 37–41.

[36] Hathaway, *Law of Refugee Status,* 65–97, argues that 'Well-founded fear has nothing to do with the state of mind of the applicant for refugee status . . .', save so far as the claimant's testimony may be evidence of conditions in the country of origin, and that, 'The concept of well-founded fear is

subjective fear, as evidence of the subjective aspects of an individual's life, including beliefs and commitments. These help not only to locate the claimant in a social and political context, but also go to the double issue of personal credibility and credible, reasonable fear.[37] For the heart of the question is whether that 'subjective' fear is well-founded; whether there are sufficient facts to permit the finding that the applicant faces a serious possibility of persecution.[38]

Problems of assessment cannot be pursued very far in the abstract. All the circumstances of the case have to be considered, including the relation between the nature of the persecution feared and the degree of likelihood of its happening. At each stage, hard evidence is likely to be absent, so that finally the asylum seeker's own statements, their force, coherence, and credibility must be relied on, in the light of what is known generally, from a variety of sources, regarding conditions in the country of origin.[39]

4.1.1 Statelessness

Article 1A(2) of the Convention makes separate provision for refugees with a nationality and for those who are stateless. For the former, the relevant criterion is that they should be unable or unwilling to avail themselves of the protection of their State of nationality, while the latter should be unable or unwilling to return to their State of former residence.[40] In cases of dual or multiple

rather inherently objective, and was intended to restrict the scope of protection to persons who can demonstrate a present or prospective risk of persecution irrespective of the extent or nature of mistreatment, if any, that they have suffered in the past.'

[37] On the assessment of claims, see further below, Ch. 9, s. 2.2.

[38] The *Ad Hoc* Committee referred to a refugee as a person who 'has either actually been a victim of persecution or can show good reasons why he fears persecution': UN doc. E/1618, 39. Evidence of past persecution alone has been considered sufficient in some circumstances; for example, in *Matter of Chen*, Int. Dec. No. 3104 (1989), the Board of Immigration Appeals declared that past persecution established eligibility for asylum, stating further that past persecution established a rebuttable presumption of reason to fear future persecution. See also the 1990 Final Regulations on Asylum: 8 CFR, §208.13(b)(1)(i), to like effect.

[39] On the sources and uses of documentary information, see further below, Ch. 9, s. 2.2.2. The UNHCR *Handbook* suggests that 'Determination of refugee status will . . . primarily require an evaluation of the applicant's statements rather than a judgement on the situation prevailing in the country of origin' (paras. 37, 42). This apparent attempt to 'depoliticize' the process in no way reflects the practical reality of refugee determination, however, which is precisely an essay in the assessment and evaluation of the situation prevailing in the country of origin.

[40] See report of the *Ad Hoc* Committee: UN doc. E/1618, 39: 'The Committee agreed that for the purposes [of this provision], and therefore the draft Convention as a whole, "unable" refers primarily to stateless refugees but includes also refugees possessing a nationality who are refused passports or other protection by their own government. "Unwilling" refers to refugees who refuse to accept the protection of the government of their nationality.' A number of decisions, particularly in Canada, have recognized that 'inability' also describes the situation of claimants who cannot obtain protection, for example, because the government or authorities of their country are non-existent, ineffective, or in active or passive collusion with the persecutors. *Zalzali* v. *Minister of Employment and Immigration* [1991] FCJ No. 341, involved a claimant from Lebanon who had been threatened by different militia at a time when the Lebanese government exercised effective control over no part of the country. Décary J. A. in the Federal Court of Appeal observed that, 'the natural meaning of the words "is unable" assumes an objective inability on the part of the claimant, and the fact that "is unable" is, in contrast to "is unwilling", not qualified by "by reason of that fear",

nationality, refugee status will only arise where the individual in question is unable or unwilling, on the basis of well-founded fear, to secure the protection of any of the States of nationality. In this context, whether the link of nationality is effective in the sense of general international law will be a relevant consideration.[41]

Statelessness and refugee status are by no means identical phenomena.[42] On occasion, those fleeing may be deprived of their nationality, but it is quite common also for the formal link to remain. Following the Russian revolution in 1917, large numbers of citizens were stripped of their status and for years Soviet Jews leaving the country permanently were required to renounce their citizenship. Refugee status in such cases might appear determinable in the light of the situation prevailing in the country of origin as the 'country of former habitual residence'.[43] However, in addition to internal repressive measures applied to those seeking to leave that country,[44] the denationalization itself provided compelling testimony of denial of protection. Whether it severs the effective link for all purposes of international law, including the responsibility of States, is less clear, but the expulsion of an unwanted minority could not justifiably be predicated upon the municipal act of deprivation of citizenship.[45]

seems to me to confirm that the inability in question is governed by objective criteria which can be verified independently of the fear experienced . . .' Statelessness represents one type of inability, and anarchy or the disintegration of State and civil authority, another. See further below, s. 5.2.

[41] Cf. Goodwin-Gill, G.S., *International Law and the Movement of Persons between States*, (1978), 46–9.

[42] A stateless person has been defined as 'a person who is not considered as a national by any State under the operation of its law' in art. 1, 1954 Convention relating to the Status of Stateless Persons: 360 *UNTS* 117. By 16 votes to 1 with 4 abstentions the Conference preceding the Convention adopted a recommendation that each contracting State 'when it recognises as valid the reasons for which a person has renounced the protection of the State of which he is a national' should consider sympathetically extending the Convention to such persons. See also the 1961 Convention on the Reduction of Statelessness: UN doc. A/CONF.9/15, Final Act, where the Conference recommended that 'persons who are stateless *de facto* should as far as possible be treated as stateless *de jure* to enable them to acquire an effective nationality'. Cf. Weis, who for long criticized the terminology of *de facto* and *de jure* statelessness, for example, in 72 *AJIL* 680–1 (1978), reviewing Mutharika, *The Regulation of Statelessness under International and National Law: Texts and Documents* (1977); see also Weis's articles in 30 *BYIL* 480 (1953); 10 *ICLQ* 255 (1961); 11 *ICLQ* 1073 (1962).

[43] There is no historical, textual or commonsensical basis for one commentator's view that because a stateless person is not 'returnable' to his or her country of former habitual residence, so he or she is not in danger of being *refouled* and is therefore not a refugee: Hathaway, *Law of Refugee Status*, 59–63. None of the citations or references to the *travaux préparatoires* provides any support for the 'returnability' gloss. Although this notion was adopted by some members of Canada's Convention Refugee Determination Division, principally as a ground for denying protection to Palestinians expelled from the Gulf States, it has since been categorically rejected by the Federal Court; see, for example, *Desai v. Canada (Minister of Citizenship and Immigration)* [1994] FCJ No. 2032.

[44] For details of practice in an earlier period, see *Religious Minorities in the Soviet Union*, (Minority Rights Group, report no. 1, rev. ed. 1977), 18–20.

[45] See Fisher Williams, J., 'Denationalization', 8 *BYIL* 45 (1927).

4.2 REASONS FOR PERSECUTION

The Convention identifies five relevant grounds of persecution, all of which, in varying degrees, have been correspondingly developed in the field of non-discrimination.[46]

4.2.1 *Race*

With regard to *race* for example, account should be taken of article 1 of the 1965 Convention on the Elimination of All Forms of Racial Discrimination which defines that practice to include distinctions based on 'race, colour, descent, or national or ethnic origin'. Given legal developments over the last thirty years, the broad meaning can be considered valid also for the purposes of the 1951 Convention. Persecution on account of race is all too frequently the background to refugee movements in all parts of the world.[47] The international community has expressed particular abhorrence at discrimination on racial grounds, as evidenced by repeated resolutions of the General Assembly, but whether such practices amount to persecution of themselves is more controversial.[48]

---

[46] See generally, UNHCR, *Handbook*, paras. 66–86; Grahl–Madsen, *Status of Refugees*, vol. 1, (1966), 217–53; Hathaway, *Law of Refugee Status*, 135–88. The substantive linkage to non-discrimination was recognized by the Canadian Supreme Court in *Attorney-General* v. *Ward* [1993] 2 SCR 689. On the specific issue, see also Vierdag, E. W., *The Concept of Discrimination in International Law*, (1973); McKean, W. A., 'The Meaning of Discrimination in International and Municipal Law', 44 *BYIL* 177 (1970); Goodwin-Gill, *Movement of Persons*, 75–87.

[47] For example, Ugandan citizens of Asian origin were persecuted and expelled in 1972: see Goodwin-Gill, *Movement of Persons*, 212-16. The same year, large numbers of Burundi citizens of the Hutu tribe were massacred, while many others fled into neighbouring countries: *Selective Genocide in Burundi*, Minority Rights Group, report no. 20, 1974; cf. US Committee for Refugees, 'Transition in Burundi: The Context for a Homecoming,' Sept., 1993. The combination of genocidal massacres in Rwanda in 1994 and successful military resistance caused the internal and external displacement of many thousands of both Hutu and Tutsi citizens: Prunier, G., 'La crise rwandaise: Structures et déroulment', 13 *RSQ*, Nos. 2 and 3, 13 (1994); Degni-Ségui, R., 'Rapports sur la situation des droits de l'homme au Rwanda du 28 juin 1994 et du 12 août 1994', ibid., 116. After 1975 thousands of Vietnamese citizens of Chinese ethnic origin felt compelled, along with many others, to seek protection in the countries of South East Asia: see above, Ch. 1, n. 50, and sources cited. In apartheid South Africa, institutionalized discrimination and its politics of repression likewise contributed to large-scale exodus: 'Human Rights, War and Mass Exodus', *Transnational Perspectives* (1982), 11, 14. See also Tiberghien, *La protection des réfugiés*, 87f, 329–35.

[48] See further below, s. 5.2. In the view of the European Commission on Human Rights, discrimination on racial grounds could, in certain circumstances, constitute degrading treatment within the meaning of art. 3 of the European Convention on Human Rights: Decision on Admissibility, *Patel* (application 4403/70) *et al* v. *United Kingdom* Oct. 1970, p. 30. Cf. *Ali* v. *Secretary of State* [1978] Imm AR 126 (discrimination likely to be faced by Kenyan citizen of Asian origin did not amount to persecution).

4.2.2 Religion

Religion has long been the basis upon which governments and peoples have sin-gled out others for persecution. In 1685, thousands of Huguenots fled from France to England and Prussia after revocation of the Edict of Nantes opened the way to massacre and oppression. The late nineteenth century witnessed pogroms of Jews in Russia and of Armenian Christians in Ottoman Turkey. The present century has likewise seen large-scale persecution of Jews under the hege-mony of Nazi and Axis powers up to 1945, while more recent targets have included Jehovah's Witnesses in Africa,[49] Moslems in Burma,[50] Baha'is in Iran,[51] Ahmadis in various Islamic countries,[52] believers of all persuasions in totalitarian and self-proclaimed atheist States.

Article 18 of the 1966 Covenant on Civil and Political Rights, elaborating article 18 of the Universal Declaration of Human Rights, prescribes that every-one shall have the right to freedom of thought, conscience, and religion, which shall include the freedom to have or adopt a religion or belief of choice and the freedom to manifest such religion or belief.[53] Moreover, no one is to be subject to coercion which would impair the freedom to have or adopt a religion or belief of choice. In 1962, the General Assembly requested the Commission on Human Rights to draw up a draft declaration and draft convention on the elimination of all forms of intolerance based on religion or belief,[54] and in 1967 it took note of the Preamble and article 1 of a proposed convention,[55] in which the Third Committee had suggested that the expression 'religion or belief' should include

---

[49] *Jehovah's Witnesses in Central Africa* (Minority Rights Group, report no. 29, 1976).

[50] Piper, T., 'Myanmar: Exodus and Return of Muslims from Rakhine State', 13 *RSQ*, No. 1, 11 (1994).

[51] Parliamentary Human Rights Group, 'The Abuse of Human Rights in Iran', (1986); Baha'i International Community, *The Baha'is in Iran: A Report on the Persecution of a Religious Minority*, (2nd ed., 1982); Final Report on the Situation of Human Rights in Iran: UN docs. E/CN.4/1993/41 (28 Jan. 1993), paras. 218–30; E/CN.4/1994/50 (2 Feb. 1994), paras. 144–70.

[52] Commission de l'immigration et du statut de réfugié, 'Ahmadis du Pakistan: mise à jour décem-bre 1991 à octobre 1993', (1994); Yahya Hassan Bajwa, 'Zur Situation der Ahmadi-Muslime in Pakistan', *Asyl*, 1994/3, 65.

[53] See to similar effect art. 9, European Convention on Human Rights, which also expressly re-cognizes the freedom to change religion or belief. Note, however, that a distinction may be drawn between the freedom to practice religious belief and the right to proselytise; see *Kokkinakis* v. *Greece* (3/1992/348/421), Judgment of the European Court of Human Rights, 25 May 1993: The Court considered the conviction of a Jehovah's Witness for 'proselytism'. Art. 9(2) of the European Convention permits limitations, not on freedom of conscience or belief as such, but on the freedom to manifest one's religion or belief. The Court was of the view that where several religions coexist within one population, restrictions on this freedom may be necessary in order to reconcile the inter-ests of the various groups and ensure that everyone's beliefs are respected (para. 33). A distinction should be drawn between 'bearing Christian witness and improper proselytism' (para. 48); although the impugned measure was in pursuit of a legitimate aim (protection of the rights and freedoms of others: para. 44), in the circumstances the conviction did not appear to have been justified by a pressing social need, and was not proportionate (para. 49).

[54] UNGA res. 1781(XVII), 7 Dec. 1962.   [55] UNGA res. 2295(XXII), 11 Dec. 1967.

'theistic, non-theistic and atheistic beliefs'.[56] The content of the right to freedom of thought, conscience, and religion continues to be a subject in many human rights enquiries,[57] and the Declaration on the Elimination of All Forms of Intolerance and of Discrimination Based on Religion or Belief, adopted in 1981, indicates the interests to be protected, the infringement of which may signal persecution.[58]

4.2.3 *Nationality*

The reference to persecution for reasons of *nationality* is somewhat odd, given the absurdity of a State persecuting its own nationals on account of their membership of the body politic. Those who possess the nationality of another State will, in normal circumstances, be entitled to its protection and so fall outside the refugee definition. Conceivably, the nationals of State B resident in State A could find themselves persecuted on account of their nationality, driven out to a neighbouring country and yet still denied the protection of State B, particularly that aspect which includes the right of nationals to enter their own State.[59] However, nationality in article 1A(2) of the 1951 Convention is usually interpreted broadly, to include origins and the membership of particular ethnic, religious, cultural, and linguistic communities.[60] It is not necessary that those persecuted should constitute a minority in their own country, for oligarchies

[56] Article reproduced in *Elimination of All Forms of Religious Intolerance, Note by the Secretary-General*: UN doc. A/8330, 8. This article, which includes definitions of discrimination on religious grounds and of religious intolerance, was adopted by 91 votes in favour, 2 against, with 6 abstentions.
[57] See, for example, Implementation of the Declaration on the Elimination of all Forms of Intolerance and of Discrimination based on Religion or Belief. *Reports* of the Special Rapporteur of the Commission on Human Rights on religions and intolerance: UN doc. E/CN.4/1993/62 (6 Jan. 1993); Add.1 (29 Jan. 1993); *Report* on the Situation of Human Rights in the Sudan: UN doc. E/CN/.4/1994/48 (1 Feb. 1994), para. 79—apostasy; see also UN doc. E/CN.4/1992/52.
[58] Declaration adopted without vote by UNGA res. 36/55 of 25 Nov. 1981; see further below, s. 5.1; also Tiberghien, *La protection des réfugiés*, 185ff: *Nahmany*, Commission des recours, 30 juill. 1982: given the values upon which the State of Israel is founded and the fact that Jews who convert to Christianity face serious discrimination, the applicants have good ground to fear persecution by reason of their religion.
[59] Such denial of protection could easily arise through the haphazard workings of citizenship and immigration laws; cf. the situation of citizens of the UK and colonies resident in East Africa, discussed in Goodwin-Gill, *Movement of Persons*, 101–3, 164–7. See also *Huang*, 12, 935 and 13, 451, 26 janv. 1982, cited by Tiberghien, *La protection des réfugiés*, 318.
[60] Cf. *London Borough of Ealing v. Race Relations Board* [1972] AC 342, in which the court *excluded* nationality from the generic term 'national origin'. Note art. 27 of the 1966 Covenant on Civil and Political Rights: 'In those States in which ethnic, religious or linguistic minorities exist, persons belonging to such minorities shall not be denied the right, in community with the other members of their group, to enjoy their own culture, to profess and practise their own religion, or to use their own language.' See also Grahl-Madsen, *Status of Refugees*, vol. 1, (1966), 218–19; Capotorti, *Study on the Rights of Persons belonging to Ethnic, Religious and Linguistic Minorities* (1978): UN doc. E/CN/4/Sub. 2/384/Rev. 1, 5–15, 95–6; Rights of Persons belonging to National and Ethnic, Religious and Linguistic Minorities: UN doc. E/CN.4/1994/72 (13 Dec. 1993). Cf. Martinez Cobo, *Study of the Problem of Discrimination against indigenous Populations* (1979): UN doc. E/CN.4/Sub. 2/L. 707; Elles, *International Provisions protecting the Human Rights of Non-Citizens* (1980): UN doc. E/CN.4/Sub. 2/392/Rev. 1, 25f.

traditionally tend to resort to oppression.[61] Nationality, interpreted broadly, illustrates the points of distinction which can serve as the basis for the policy and practice of persecution.[62] There may be some overlap between the various grounds and, likewise, factors derived from two or more of the criteria may contribute cumulatively to a well-founded fear of persecution.

4.2.4 Membership of a particular social group

Further potential overlap lies in the criterion, *membership of a particular social group*.[63] The 1951 Convention is not alone in recognizing 'social' factors as a potential irrelevant distinction giving rise to arbitrary or repressive treatment. Article 2 of the 1948 Universal Declaration of Human Rights includes 'national or social origin, property, birth or other status' as prohibited grounds of distinction,[64] a form of words repeated in article 2 of the 1966 Covenants on Economic, Social, and Cultural Rights and Civil and Political Rights; it also appears in article 26 of the latter Covenant, which calls for equality before and equal protection of the law.

The *travaux préparatoires* provide little explanation for why 'social group' was included. The Swedish delegate to the 1951 Conference simply stated that social group cases existed, and that the Convention should mention them explicitly.[65] The lack of substantive debate on the issue suggests that contemporary examples of such persecution may have been in the minds of the drafters, such as resulted from the 'restructuring' of society then being undertaken in the socialist States and the special attention reserved for landowners, capitalist class members, independent business people, the middle class and their families.

The initial intention may thus have been to protect known categories from

---

[61] *Selective Genocide in Burundi*, above, n. 47; see also the analysis in *The two Irelands—the double Minority*, (Minority Rights Group, report no. 2, rev. ed., 1979).

[62] Grahl-Madsen notes that persecution for reasons of nationality is also understood to include persecution of lack of nationality, that is, by reason of statelessness: *Status of Refugees*, vol. 1, 219. See further on the particular situation of Palestinians, below, Ch. 6, s. 3.

[63] Tajfel, in *The Social Psychology of Minorities*, (Minority Rights Group, report no. 38, 1978), cites at p. 3 Simpson and Yinger, *Racial and Cultural Minorities*, (1965), 17, for the following set of definitional criteria appropriate for the identification of social minorities: '(1) Minorities are subordinate segments of complex state societies; (2) minorities have special physical or cultural traits which are held in low esteem by the dominant segments of the society; (3) minorities are self-conscious units bound together by the special traits which their members share and by the special disabilities which these bring; (4) membership in a minority is transmitted by a rule of descent which is capable of affiliating succeeding generations even in the absence of readily apparent special cultural or physical traits; (5) minority peoples, by choice or necessity, tend to marry within the group'. See further below, Ch. 9, s. 3.2.

[64] During debate on the Universal Declaration, the USSR stressed the importance of abolishing 'differences based on social conditions as well as the privileges enjoyed by certain groups in the economic and legal fields.'

[65] UN docs. A/CONF.2/SR.3, p.14—Mr Petren (Sweden): 'experience had shown that certain refugees had been persecuted because they belonged to particular social groups. The draft Convention made no provision for such cases, and one designed to cover them should accordingly be included'; also SR.19, p.14; SR.23, p.8—Swedish amendment adopted by 14–0–8; A/CONF.2/9—text of amendments.

known forms of harm; less clear is whether the notion of 'social group' was expected or intended to apply generally to then unrecognized groups facing new forms of persecution. The answer to that question will never be found, but there is no reason in principle why this ground, like every other, should not be progressively developed. The experience of 1951 is also illustrative, for its implicit reference to the perception or attitude of the persecuting authority. It is still not unusual for governments publicly to write off sections of their population—the petty bourgeoisie, for example, or the class traitors; and even more frequent will be those occasions on which the identification of groups to be neutralised takes place covertly. In eastern Europe in the late 1940s and the 1950s, groups and classes and their descendants were *perceived* to be a threat to the new order, whatever their individual qualities or beliefs. In Vietnam in the late 1970s, the bourgeoisie were similarly seen as an obstacle to economic and social restructuring (in circumstances in which class and ethnicity happened to combine). The *characteristics* of the group and its individual members were what counted. As paragraph 78 of the UNHCR *Handbook* puts it,

Membership of a particular social group may be at the root of persecution because there is no confidence in the group's loyalty to the government or because the political outlook, antecedents or economic activity of its members, or the very existence of the social group as such, is held to be an obstacle to the Government's policies.

Especially important is the conjunction of 'internal' characteristics and 'external' perceptions. *Linking*, rather than unifying, characteristics, more accurately represent social reality, while circumstances external to the group may have isolated it from the rest of society, or may lead to its separate treatment.

A superficial linguistic analysis suggests people in a certain relation or having a certain degree of similarity, or a coming together of those of like class or kindred interests. A fully comprehensive definition is impracticable, if not impossible, but the essential element in any description would be the factor of shared interests, values, or background—a combination of matters of choice with other matters over which members of the group have no control. In determining whether a particular group of people constitutes a 'social group' within the meaning of the Convention, attention should therefore be given to the presence of linking and uniting factors such as ethnic, cultural, and linguistic origin; education; family background; economic activity; shared values, outlook, and aspirations.[66] Also highly relevant are the attitude to the putative social group of other groups in the same society and, in particular, the treatment accorded to it by State authorities. The importance, and therefore the identity, of a social group may well be in direct proportion to the notice taken of it by others—the view which others have of us—particularly at the official level. The notion of social group thus possesses an element of open-endedness potentially capable of

[66] The US Board of Immigration Appeals adopted very similar language in *Acosta*, Int. Dec. No. 2986 (1 Mar. 1985); see further below.

expansion in favour of a variety of different classes susceptible to persecution.[67] How far decision-makers are prepared to go is another matter, but in arguing for expansion appropriate reference could be made to the linking factors of the group in question and to the elements of distinction which make it the object of persecution.[68]

Jurisprudence on the interpretation of the term 'social group', once sparse, is growing rapidly and is reviewed below in Chapter 9.[69]

4.2.5 *Political opinion*

Finally, the Convention adduces fear of persecution for reasons of *political opin-ion*. Article 19 of the Universal Declaration of Human Rights provides that: 'Everyone has the right to freedom of opinion and expression; the right includes freedom to hold opinions without interference and to seek, receive and impart information and ideas through any media and regardless of frontiers'. The basic

[67] In *Acosta*, Int. Dec. No. 2986 (1 Mar. 1985) the US Board of Immigration Appeals, applying the *ejusdem generis* rule, limited its understanding of the term 'social group' to reflect a common, immutable characteristic, that is, one which it is either beyond the power of an individual to change, or which is so fundamental to individual identity or conscience that changing it should not be required. This might include sex, class, kinship or even shared past experience, but membership of a taxi-drivers' co-operative, or a particular manner of wage-earning, did not fall within such a class of characteristics. Many commentators, if not decision-makers, have favoured a broad approach; cf. Grahl-Madsen, *Status of Refugees*, vol. 1, (1966), 219—'the notion . . . is of broader application than the combined notions of racial, ethnic and religious groups . . .'; Helton, A. C., 'Persecution on Account of Membership in a Social Group as a Basis for Refugee Status', 15 *Col. Hum. Rts. L.R.* 39 (1983). Hathaway, on the other hand, inclines against social group 'as an all-encompassing residual category,' arguing that the original intent was to protect refugees 'from *known* forms of harm': *Law of Refugee Status*, 159 (emphasis supplied). See also Fullerton, M., 'Persecution due to membership in a particular social group: Jurisprudence in the Federal Republic of Germany', 4 *Georgetown Imm. L.J.* 381 (1990); Fullerton, M., 'A Comparative Look at Refugee Status based on Persecution due to Membership in a Particular Group', 26 *Cornell Int'l L.J.* 505 (1993); Iogna-Prat, M., 'The Notion of "Membership of a Particular Social Group" from the Point of View of European Jurisprudence', in Bhabha, J. and Coll, G., eds., *Asylum Law and Practice in Europe and North America*, (1992), 87; Blum, C. P., 'Refugee Status based on Membership in a Particular Social Group: A North American Perspective', in Bhabha, J. and Coll, G., eds., *Asylum Law and Practice in Europe and North America*, (1992), 98.

[68] Again there may be a relation of degree between the nature of the particular group and the type of persecution alleged.

[69] See below, Ch. 9, s. 3.2. For earlier cases, cf. Grahl-Madsen, *Status of Refugees*, vol. 1, 219–20. For more recent examples, see *Lai* v. *Minister of Employment and Immigration* [1989] FCJ No. 826—cap-italist background in China resulted in persecution due to family's social position; *De Valle* v. *INS* 901 F.2d 787 (9th Cir., 1990)—family members of deserters manifest diverse and different life-styles and varying interests and therefore do not constitute a social group; *Ramirez–Rivas* v. *INS* 899 F.2d 864 (9th Cir., 1990)—name association with family subject to persecution sufficient to support social group claim; *Z* v. *Secretary of State*, TH/19404/86—'westernized Iranians' failed to satisfy the 'cohe-siveness' test; *M.M.G.* v. *Secretary of State* TH/9515/85—although women in Iran are discriminated against and may be persecuted, 'westernized women' do not constitute a social group, so far as they are not identified with some common practice or belief and opposition to Islamic rules remains indi-vidually based; *Cheung* v. *Minister for Employment and Immigration* [1993] 2 FC 314—women in China who have more than one child and are faced with forced sterilization are a social group; *Attorney-General of Canada* v. *Ward* [1993] 2 SCR 689—members of terrorist movement are not a particular social group, for membership was not characterized by an innate characteristic or an unchangeable historical fact, and its objectives also were not fundamental to human dignity; *Chan* v. *Minister of Employment and Immigration* [1993] 3 FC 675—social group cannot be defined by fact of persecution.

principle is restated in article 19 of the Covenant on Civil and Political Rights, but the right to freedom of expression is qualified there by reference to 'special duties and responsibilities'. Certain types of opinion may therefore be judged unacceptable.[70]

In the 1951 Convention, 'political opinion' should be understood in the broad sense, to incorporate, within substantive limitations now developing generally in the field of human rights, any opinion on any matter in which the machinery of State, government, and policy may be engaged.[71] The typical 'political refugee' is one pursued by the government of a State or other entity on account of his or her opinions, which are an actual or perceived threat to that government or its institutions, or to the political agenda and aspirations of the entity in question. Political opinions may or may not be expressed, and they may be rightly or wrongly attributed to the applicant for refugee status.[72] If they have been expressed, and if the applicant or others similarly placed have suffered or been threatened with repressive measures, then a well-founded fear may be made out. Problems arise, however, in assessing the value of the 'political act', particularly if the act itself stands more or less alone, unaccompanied by evident or overt expressions of opinion.[73]

4.3 INITIAL PROBLEMS OF INTERPRETATION AND APPLICATION

The substantial growth and elaboration of refugee determination procedures in the developed world, and the equally substantial body of jurisprudence that has accompanied it at various levels of appeal, have exposed the words of the 1951 Convention to close scrutiny, often apparently at one or more removes from its protection objectives. Besides the standard of proof question examined above, national determination bodies have also considered, among others, the questions of attribution and causation—whether a claimant, for example, in fact fears persecution for reasons of or on account of his or her political opinion, and what

---

[70] Cf. art. 4, Convention on the Elimination of All Forms of Racial Discrimination; art. 10, European Convention on Human Rights; *Handyside* v. *U.K.*, European Court of Human Rights, 7 Dec. 1976, Ser. A No. 24; *Sunday Times* v. *U.K.*, European Court of Human Rights, 26 Apr. 1979, Ser. A No. 30; *Arrowsmith* v. *U.K.* (7050/75) European Commission on Human Rights, 12 Oct. 1978, 19 *Decisions and Reports* 5.

[71] This wording was adopted and endorsed by the Supreme Court of Canada in *Canada (Attorney-General)* v. *Ward* [1993] 2 SCR 689.

[72] In *Ward*, the Supreme Court of Canada held that circumstances should be examined from the perspective of the persecutor, since this perspective is determinative in inciting the persecution: [1993] 2 SCR 689, 747.

[73] It is not always appropriate to view the (objective) political act as equivalent to the (subjective) notion of political opinion, for the asylum seeker's actual motivation can make such an approximation pure fiction. The same applies in the case of the individual who is likely to be persecuted for political opinions *wrongly* attributed to him or her. The humanitarian aspects of such cases may be better accommodated in a liberal asylum practice, than in a forced interpretation of refugee status criteria. Cf. *INS* v. *Elias-Zacarias*, 112 S.Ct. 812 (1992), in which a majority of the US Supreme Court held that resisting forced recruitment by guerillas did not, on the facts, necessarily imply a political opinion. Musalo, K., 'Irreconcilable Differences? Divorcing Refugee Protections from Human Rights Norms', 15 *Mich. J. Int. Law* 1179 (1994).

was the motive of the persecutor; whether prosecution and punishment under a law of general application can amount to persecution, in the absence of evidence of discriminatory application; whether a single act of an otherwise non-political claimant should be characterized as (sufficiently) political to qualify the resulting treatment or punishment as persecution within the Convention; whether conscientious objection to military service can form a sufficient basis for a refugee claim, and if so, in what circumstances; whether 'political offenders' are refugees; and whether the notion of particular social group is flexible enough to encompass women generally or any particular sub-group of women, or to protect men and women liable to involuntary sterilization under national family planning policies, or homosexuals.

4.3.1 Fear, intent and motive, and the rationale for persecution

Applications for refugee status are sometimes denied on the ground that the claimant has failed to prove either that the law was enacted with intent to persecute, or that the authorities in his or her country of origin themselves *intended* to persecute the individual for one or other Convention reason. Proof of legislative or organizational intent is notoriously hard to establish and while evidence of such motivation may be sufficient to establish a claim to refugee status, it cannot be considered a *necessary* condition.

Nowhere in the drafting history[74] of the 1951 Convention is it suggested that the motive or intent of the persecutor was ever to be considered as a *controlling* factor in either the definition or the determination of refugee status. The debate in the *Ad hoc* committee regarding the 'precedent' of the IRO Constitution's approach to classification and description, considered in context, reveals itself as a debate, not about fear, intention or motive, but one between those who, like the United Kingdom, France and Belgium, favoured a definition in general terms; and those who, like the United States, preferred a detailed statement of the various categories of refugees who should receive international protection.

As revised, the definition that emerged on 30 January 1950 was substantially that which was adopted in July 1951, at the Conference of Plenipotentiaries.[75] As the Israeli delegate observed at the time, 'All the *objective* factors which would make it possible to characterize a person as a refugee were now known . . . (and) . . . contained in paragraph 1'.[76] The only *subjective* elements of relevance, for this delegate, went to the 'horrifying memories' of past persecution which might justify non-return to the country of origin. The (subjective) state of the *persecutor's*

---

[74] The 'drafting history' includes, in particular, debates in the United Nations Economic and Social Council (ECOSOC) in 1950, the two sessions of the *Ad hoc* Committee on Statelessness and Related Problems (in Jan.–Feb. and Aug. 1950; the Committee was renamed the *Ad hoc* Committee on Refugees and Stateless Persons), and the Conference of Plenipotentiaries which settled the final text of the Convention in July 1951.

[75] See UN doc. E/AC.32/L.6/Rev.1 (30 Jan. 1950).

[76] See UN doc. E/AC.32/SR.18, para. 10 (31 Jan. 1950)—Mr Robinson (emphasis supplied).

mind was never mentioned. As the *Ad hoc* committee stated to ECOSOC in its comments on the draft,

The expression 'well-founded fear of being the victim of persecution for reasons of race, religion, nationality or political opinion' means that a person has either been actually a victim of persecution or can show good reason why he fears persecution.[77]

Persecution for Convention reasons has sometimes been read to mean 'the infliction of suffering *because of or on account of* the victim's race, beliefs or nationality, etc.'[78] Such a seemingly innocuous change in the wording, however, distorts the natural meaning of the language and can create additional evidentiary burdens for the claimant. In particular, perhaps unwittingly, it may import a *controlling* intent on the part of the persecutor, as an element in the definition.

Of course, intent is relevant; indeed, evidence of persecutory intent may be conclusive as to the existence of well-founded fear, but its absence is not necessarily conclusive the other way. A persecutor may intend to harm an individual because of/for reasons of/on account of that person's race or religion.[79] Similarly, a persecutor may intend to harm an individual because of an opinion expressed, or a decision or action taken, irrespective or regardless of that individual's actual motivation or conviction. If that opinion, decision, or action falls within the category of protected interests (freedom of religion, expression, opinion, conscience, and so forth), and *if* the harm visited or feared is in fact of a degree to amount to persecution, then a sufficient link may be inferred on which to base a well-founded fear of persecution within the meaning of the Convention. There are slight but important differences between the terms *on account of* and *for reasons of.* 'On account of', which is *not* the language of the Convention, implies an element of conscious, individualized direction which is often conspicuously absent in the practices of mass persecution.

The Convention definition offers a series of objective elements by which to describe the refugee. The *travaux préparatoires* suggest that the only relevant intent

---

[77] See UN doc. E/1618 (17 Feb. 1950), Annex.

[78] For reasons that are not clear, s. 101 of the 1980 United States Refugee Act employs 'on account of' in preference to 'for reasons of' in its statement of the refugee definition. This harkens back to one of the first US contributions to the definitions debate in 1950; see United States of America, *Memorandum on the Definition Article of the Preliminary Draft Convention Relating to the Status of Refugees (and Stateless Persons)*: UN doc. E/AC.32/L.4 (18 Jan. 1950).

[79] This is the sense of *Acosta*, above note 24 and accompanying text, in which the BIA emphasized the relevance of 'a belief or characteristic a persecutor seeks to overcome', and of the persecutor having 'the inclination to punish' the claimant. Referring to persecution for reasons of political opinion in the *Ward* case, the Supreme Court of Canada noted that the 'examination of the circumstances should be approached from the perspective of the persecutor, since that is the perspective that is determinative in inciting the persecution': [1993] 2 SCR 689, 740f. See also, Kälin, W., Comment on Bundesverfassungsgericht (BRD) v. 10.7.1989—2 BvR 502/86 u.a. (EuGRZ 1989, S.444–455): *Asyl*, 1990/4, 13; *INS* v. *Elias-Zacarias*, 112 S.Ct. 812 (1992); 908 F.2d 1452 (9th Cir. 1990); Case Abstract No. *IJRL/0114*: 4 *IJRL* 263 (1992); Anker, D., Blum, C. P. and Johnson, K. R., '*INS* v. *Zacarias*: Is There Anyone Out There?' ibid., 266; von Sternberg, Mark R., 'Emerging Bases of "Persecution" in American Refugee Law: Political Opinion and the Dilemma of Neutrality', 13 *Suffolk Transnat'l L.J.* 1 (1989).

or motive would be that, not of the persecutor, but of the refugee or refugee claimant: one motivated by personal convenience, rather than fear, might be denied protection;[80] while one with horrifying memories of past persecution might yet continue to receive protection, notwithstanding a change of circumstances in the country of origin.[81] Otherwise, the governing criterion remains that of a serious possibility of persecution, not proof of intent to harm on the part of the persecutor.

4.3.2 Persecution and laws of general application

Applications for refugee status are often denied on the ground that the claimant fears not persecution, but prosecution under a law of general application. Experience shows, however, that the law can as well be the instrument of persecution as any other arbitrary measure. The question then is, if some laws can be the instruments of persecution, which are they?[82]

Nowhere perhaps has this question been more controversial in recent years, than with respect to the alleged impact of China's 'one child policy'. Claimants in different jurisdictions argued that their being liable to forcible sterilization for breach of this policy amounted to persecution within the meaning of the Convention, and decisions in the matter have also been open to political considerations. In *Matter of Chang*, for example, the US Board of Immigration Appeals held that the policy is not persecutory and does not, by itself, create a well-founded fear of persecution, 'even to the extent that involuntary sterilization may occur'. To qualify for asylum, the claimant must show that he or she is at risk because the policy is being selectively applied on Convention grounds, or being used to punish for those reasons.

Every government has the right to enact, implement and enforce its own legislation, inherent in its sovereignty and in the principle of the reserved domain of domestic jurisdiction. Notwithstanding the presumption of legitimacy in the legislative field, the discriminatory application of law or the use of law to promote discrimination may tend to persecution.[83] In this sense, a human rights

---

[80] See the US draft: UN doc. E/AC.32/L.4, para. B. Cf. the views of the UK: UN docs. E/AC.32/SR.6, para. 5; E/AC.32/L.2/Rev.1.

[81] See UN doc. E/AC.32/SR.18, paras. 10–16 (Mr Robinson); art. 1C(5),(6), 1951 Convention relating to the Status of Refugees; and further below, Ch. 3, s. 2.

[82] In *Zolfagharkhani* v. *Minister for Employment and Immigration* [1993] FCJ No. 584, the Canadian Federal Court of Appeal offered the following propositions with respect to persecution and an ordinary law of general application: (1) the Convention refugee definition makes the intent or any principal effect of an ordinary law of general application, rather than the motivation of the claimant, relevant to the existence of persecution; (2) the neutrality of such law vis-à-vis the five Convention grounds must be judged objectively; (3) an ordinary law of general application, even in non-democratic societies, should be presumed valid and neutral, and it is for the claimant to show that the law is persecutory, either inherently or for some other reason; and (4) the claimant must show not that a particular regime is generally oppressive, but that the law in question is persecutory in relation to a Convention ground: ibid., paras. 20–3.

[83] Cf. CRR, 26 juill. 1990, *Gambini*, 93.031, *Doc. réf.* no. 145, 28 avr./7 mai 1991, Suppl., JC, 4—lack of legislative provision for transsexuals in Argentina a situation of a general character and

perspective can inform the approach to persecution, for example, by indicating which rights are absolute, which may be 'subject to such restrictions as are prescribed by law and reasonably necessary in a democratic society', whether restrictions are reasonably necessary, and whether any prohibition or penalty is proportional to the (social) objective that the legislation aims to achieve.

4.3.2.1 'Republikflucht'

The issue of *Republikflucht* illustrates the case. Totalitarian States severely restrict travel abroad by their nationals. Passports are difficult to obtain, while illegal border-crossing and absence abroad beyond the validity of an exit permit can attract heavy penalties.[84] The question is, whether fear of prosecution and punishment under such laws can be equated with a well-founded fear of persecution on grounds of political opinion, especially where the claim to refugee status is based on nothing more than the anticipation of such prosecution and punishment. It may be argued that the individual in question, if returned, would be subject merely to prosecution for breach of a law of general application; he or she would not be 'singled out' for treatment amounting to persecution. Alternatively, more weight might be accorded to the object and purpose of such laws,[85] and a context in which the fact of leaving or staying abroad is seen as a *political act*. It may reflect an actual and sufficient political opinion on the part of the individual, or dissident political opinion may be attributed to the individual by the authorities of the State of origin;[86] in practice, however, many States are wary of recognizing refugee status in such cases, for fear of attracting asylum seekers motivated by purely economic considerations.

not discriminatory; CRR, 23 mai 1988, *Gungor*, 74.537—flight because of homosexuality did not fall within the Convention, for in Tiberghien's view (ibid.), 'un vide législatif n'est pas assimilable à une persécution, sauf si ce vide législatif est délibérément maintenu par un Etat pour persécuter une fraction de la population qu'il prive ainsi de protection.' Cf. *Tobosco-Alfonso*, Int. Dec. (1990), 3222 in which BIA found that a Cuban homosexual was persecuted as a result of government's desire that all homosexuals be forced to leave their homeland.

[84] The issue is less relevant today, with the progressive spread of democratization. For examples of laws, see the first edition of this work. Amnesty International has often taken up the cases of those punished under this rubric; see *1979 Report*, 123, 133; *1980 Report*, 255, 269f., 277f., 291, 303; *1982 Report*, 270f., 286f., and later *Reports*.

[85] In one case in the Federal Republic of Germany in 1971, the Court observed, '[Die Bestrafung wegen Republikflucht] dient dem Zweck, die politische Herrschaft des Kommunismus zu sichern. Sie ist nicht vergleicher mit Strafen, durch die auch in Rechsstaaten dem unerlaubten Grenzubertritt gewehrt wird.' [Punishment for the crime of flight from the Republic] serves the goal of securing the political sovereign authority of communism. It is not comparable with the penalties with which, even in "constitutional States", unauthorized border crossing is punished.' *BVerwGE*, Bd.39, S.27, 28–9. The nature of such penalties was to be distinguished by reference to their purpose, which should not be to hinder or prevent journeys abroad.

[86] In Austria an earlier directive of the Minister of the Interior expressly provided for recognition of refugee status where penal sanctions applied to overstayers, where the asylum seeker overstayed, and where he or she expressed unwillingness to return to the country of origin for political reasons considered in the widest sense: Directive of the Minister of the Interior: 22.501/4–II/0/75, part ii.

4.3.2.2 Conscientious objectors

Issues of 'causation,' attribution and the motives for treatment amounting to persecution are also raised by asylum seekers who base their claim upon the fear of prosecution and punishment for conscientious objection to military service, or upon fear of sanctions imposed by non-governmental armed opposition elements. Objectors may be motivated by reasons of conscience or convictions of a religious, ethical, moral, humanitarian, or philosophical nature;[87] they may be opposed to their own government, or to its policy on this occasion; they may object to all wars or to particular wars; they may be opposed to the methods of warfare, or they may simply not want to kill or be killed.[88] Against their claim to be refugees, it may be argued that they are punished not on account of their beliefs, but because of their failure to obey a law of universal application; that the 'right' to refuse to do military service is not a recognized human right; and that punishment does not necessarily amount to persecution.

In 1976, the United Kingdom's Immigration Appeal Tribunal found that, on the basis of the law and practice then applying in Greece,[89] punishment of conscientious objectors amounted to persecution. However, the Tribunal doubted that this was persecution for reasons of religion or political opinion. The 'immediate cause of the persecution,' it said, 'is a refusal to obey the law of the land, and the fact that such refusal may be due to religious beliefs or political opinion is . . . only the secondary cause'. It also considered that the relevant law was not discriminatory, because 'other religious beliefs with similar views . . . and indeed persons with no religious beliefs at all . . . , would all be treated in the same way'.[90] Some commentators and national decision-makers also look for a

---

[87] See Human Rights Committee General Comment No. 22 (48) on art. 18(1)—freedom of thought, conscience and religion. The Committee believes that a right of conscientious objection, 'can be derived from article 18, inasmuch as the obligation to use lethal force may seriously conflict with the freedom of conscience and the right to manifest one's religion or belief. When this right is recognized by law or practice, there shall be no differentiation among conscientious objectors on the basis of the nature of their particular beliefs': UN doc. CCPR/C//21/Rev.1/Add.4, 27 Sept. 1993, para. 11.

[88] UNHCR, *Handbook*, paras. 167–74; Grahl-Madsen, *Status of Refugees*, vol. 1, 231–8; Hathaway, *Law of Refugee Status*, 174–85; Köfner & Nicolaus, *Grundlagen des Asylrechts*, 511–81; Marx, *Asylrecht*, 1600–14.

[89] Art. 13 of the Constitution of the Republic of Greece, which deals with freedom of conscience, provides in para. 4 that 'No person shall, by reason of his religious convictions, be exempt from discharging his obligations to the State, or refuse to comply with the laws'. Art. 4(6) obliges every Greek able to bear arms to assist in the defence of the nation. Practice has often resulted in conscientious objectors being sentenced to repeated terms of four and one-half years imprisonment throughout the period of military age. See generally Amnesty International, *5000 years in prison: Conscientious objectors in Greece*, Mar. 1993; also, Amnesty International, *Report 1994*, 140–2.

[90] *Dounetas* v. *Secretary of State*, approved and applied in *Atibo* v. *Immigration Officer, London (Heathrow) Airport* [1978] Imm AR 93. The Tribunal in *Dounetas* also suggested that 'If the Jehovah's Witnesses in Greece were being persecuted for reasons of religion, we would expect that their teachings and meetings would be proscribed. This is evidently not the case . . .' Cf. *Kokkinakis* v. *Greece* (3/1992/348/421), judgment of the European Court of Human Rights, 25 May 1993 (above n. 53).

close connection between the refusal to serve and a Convention-based motiva-tion.[91]

No international human rights instrument yet recognizes the right of consci-entious objection to military service, even though the right to freedom of con-science itself is almost universally endorsed.[92] The exercise of that latter right, however, may be subject to certain legal limitations, such as those necessary to protect the rights or freedoms of others, and a conflict of competing interests is perhaps inevitable.[93] The international community nevertheless appears to be moving towards acceptance of a right of conscientious objection, particularly as

[91] The UNHCR *Handbook*, paras. 167–74, is far from clear on this point, and has generated some narrow interpretations. A 'dislike' of military service will not suffice, unless accompanied by dispro-portionate punishment on Convention grounds (paras. 168–9). 'Genuine' convictions or 'valid rea-sons of conscience' may be enough, however, if the military action in question is condemned by the international community; or if religious convictions are not taken into account by the authorities (paras. 171–2). Hathaway interprets the *Handbook* as requiring refusal to serve to be 'grounded in civil or political status': *Law of Refugee Status*, 179. Reviewing recent jurisprudence of the French *Commission des recours*, Tiberghien also concludes that if desertion or conscientious objection is not linked to a Convention reason, refugee status will not be upheld: Tiberghien, F., 'La crise yougoslave devant la Commission des recours', *Doc. réf.*, no. 223, 17/30 août 1993, Suppl., CJ, 1–10. What is required is either 'un motif politique ou de conscience qui soit personnel au requérant': cf. CRR, Sections reunies, 29 janv. 1993, 217.894, *Sporea*, ibid., 7—member of Romanian minority in Voivodina, opposed to ethnic and cultural hegemony and unwilling to serve for political reasons. Appeal against refusal of refugee status upheld. An unwillingness to fight Croats ('fellow compatri-ots') is not enough, despite the fact that the UN has condemned the conflict: CRR, Sections reunies, 29 janv. 1993, 229.937, *Djukic*, ibid., 6. But the possibility of sanctions on family members in another State may support refugee status on the basis of a 'conscientious' objection to service; see CRR, Sections reunies, 29 janv. 1993, 229.956, *Dabetic*, ibid., 6: Claimant's family members resided in dif-ferent States (Croatia and Montenegro); he left Croatia to avoid conscription, and if returned to Yugoslavia, was likely to be conscripted into the *federal* army with resulting sanctions on relations in Zagreb. See also CRR, Sections reunies, 12 fév. 1993, 216.617, *Dzebric*, ibid., 9: refusal to serve in the militia of a *de facto* authority upheld, on the ground that the legal authority can offer no protec-tion against reprisals.

[92] See art. 18, 1948 Universal Declaration of Human Rights; art. 18, 1966 Covenant on Civil and Political Rights, art. 12, 1969 American Convention on Human Rights, and art. 9, 1950 European Convention on Human Rights. The following expanded analysis draws in part on the *ami-cus curiae* brief submitted by UNHCR in 1989 to the US Court of Appeals for the Ninth Circuit in *Cañas-Segovia* v. *United States Immigration and Naturalization Service*, in the drafting of which the author participated together with Susan Timberlake and Ralph Steinhardt; for the brief in full, see 2 *IJRL* 341 (1990); see also Musalo, K., 'Swords into Ploughshares: Why the United States should provide refuge to young men who refuse to bear arms for reasons of conscience', 26 *San Diego L.Rev.* 849 (1989).

[93] Note also art. 4, European Convention, prohibiting slavery, servitude, forced or compulsory labour. Art. 4(3)(b) provides that the term 'forced or compulsory labour' shall not include 'any ser-vice of a military character or, in case of conscientious objectors in countries where they are recog-nized, service exacted instead of compulsory military service'. Art. 4(3) also excludes work required to be done during detention, or service exacted in emergencies, or as part of normal civic obliga-tions. Fawcett has observed that this 'implies that such conscientious objection is an exercise of free-dom of conscience under Art. 9, but that a State may restrict it by allowing no exemption from military service, if it is necessary for the public safety . . .' Fawcett, J., *The Application of the European Convention on Human Rights*, (2nd. ed., 1987), 64.

a result of the standard-setting activities of United Nations and regional bodies.[94]

It is increasingly accepted in a variety of different contexts that it may be unconscionable to require the individual to change, or to exercise their freedom of choice differently. The question is, how to distinguish between those opponents of State authority who do, and those who do not, require international protection. For sincerely held reasons of conscience may motivate the individual who refuses to pay such proportion of income tax as is destined for military expenditures; or the shopkeeper who wishes to trade on Sundays; or the parents who, on grounds of religious conviction, refuse to send their children to public schools.

To a degree, the conflict between these individuals and the State is attributable to the 'choice' of the individual, who elects to place matters of principle or belief over obligations in law. The unrecognized conscientious objector is constrained, in a direct physical sense, to act either in a way contrary to conscience or to face punishment. The objector must choose either to participate in the violence opposed, or to suffer the sanction. The reluctant taxpayer, on the other hand, has only to tolerate the use of funds for military purposes,[95] while the would-be Sunday trader is restrained from transacting business at will.[96] Again,

[94] For background, see *Conscientious Objection to Military Service*: UN doc. E/CN.4/Sub.2/1983/30/Rev.1 (the Eide/Mubanga-Chipoya report); *Report of the Secretary-General, The Role of Youth in the Promotion and Protection of Human Rights, including the Question of Conscientious Objection to Military Service*: UN doc. E/CN.4/1989/30 (20 Dec. 1988); *Report of the United Nations Commission on Human Rights*: UN doc. E/CN.4/1989/L.10/Add.15 (9 Mar. 1989). At its 1995 session, the Commission on Human Rights renamed the agenda item, which appears every two years, as 'The question of conscientious objection to military service', dropping the more general reference to the role of youth, etc. Resolution 1995/83 clarified that the religious, ethical, or similar motives that may be the basis for conscientious objection also included humanitarian motives, and that the principle was equally applicable to those already serving in the armed forces. The Commission endorsed Human Rights Committee General Comment No. 22 (48) (above n. 87), and requested the Secretary-General to submit an updated version of the information annexes to the Eide/Mubonga-Chipoya report to its 1997 session. With respect to Europe, see Committee of Ministers Recommendation No. R(87)8 (9 Apr. 1987); Council of Europe, Conscientious Objection to Military Service, Explanatory Report: CE Doc. 88.C55 (1988); Parliamentary Assembly of the Council of Europe. CE Doc. 7102, 10 Jun. 1994. Report on deserters and draft resisters from the republics of the former Yugoslavia. Rapporteur: Mr Franck—recommends that 'refusal to take part in a fratricidal war condemned by the international community because of serious violations of humanitarian law in the former Yugoslavia should be considered as grounds for granting asylum.' The Report recalls Rec. 816 (1977) on the right of conscientious objection, calls on Croatia to establish a conscientious objector status, and on Serbia and Montenegro to recognize the right in practice and to amnesty deserters and draft resisters.

[95] In *Prior v. Canada*, [1988] FCJ No. 107, the court considered the claim of the taxpayer who, on grounds of conscience, objected to contributing to the government's military expenditures. In striking out the claim as disclosing no reasonable cause of action, the court found no 'offence to conscience', no being 'forced to act in a way contrary to . . . beliefs.' The Canadian Constitution does not guarantee that the State will not act inimically to a citizen's standards of proper conduct, but merely that a citizen will not be required to do something contrary to those standards, subject to the reasonable limitations recognized by s. 1 of the *Canadian Charter of Rights and Freedoms*.

[96] See *The Queen v. Big M Drug Mart*, [1985] 1 SCR 295; *Edwards Books and Art Limited v. The Queen et al*, [1986] 2 SCR 713. In *Jones v. The Queen*, [1986] 2 SCR 284, the issue of compulsory school

the conscientious objector is distinguishable because the State requires his or her *active* complicity in military service, not just tolerance or restraint or restrictions on certain conduct.

A 1988 Council of Europe report emphasized the centrality of 'compelling reasons of conscience' in this context, in preference to a listing of 'acceptable' reasons for objection.[97] Leaving aside any cumulative factors supporting refugee status (such as personal, social, religious or political background), the conscientious objector is also distinguishable from the 'mere' draft evader or deserter by the sincerely-held opinion. This locates the conflict of individual and State within the realm of competing (but legitimate) rights or interests, and separates out others whose motivations may be purely self-regarding and devoid of any recognized human rights interest, such as conscience or religion.

Military service and objection thereto, seen from the point of view of the State, are also issues which go to the heart of the body politic. Refusal to bear arms, however motivated, reflects an essentially political opinion regarding the permissible limits of State authority; it is a political act.[98] The 'law of universal application' can thus be seen as singling out or discriminating against those holding certain political views. While the State has a justifiable interest in the maintenance of its own defence,[99] the measures taken to that end should at least be

---

attendance was examined, in a context closer to the experience of the conscientious objector. The legislation in question was held to be a reasonable limitation on a parent's religious convictions regarding the education of children. The authorities did not purport to exercise absolute control, and there was no absolute obligation to attend public schools. Instruction could be given elsewhere, including at home, provided it was certified as efficient; the appellant objected, again on religious grounds, to seeking such certification, but the Court found this to be demonstrably justifiable under Canadian law.

[97] 'Compelling' here being used in the sense of 'impossible to resist': Council of Europe, *Explanatory Report*, paras. 15–17. In a 1985 report on *Conscientious Objection to Conscripted Military Service*, the Australian Senate Standing Committee on Constitutional and Legal Affairs referred to the individual's right not to be compelled by law to act contrary to a conscientiously held position in such a way that this would 'fundamentally impair his sense of integrity as a human being.' The Committee also rejected a 'list approach' to the bases for conscientious objection (paras. 2.2, 2.4, 2.29). In describing what was meant by conscientious belief, the Committee placed particular weight on the following analysis: '. . . the only possible definition of a conscientious belief is a belief based on a seriously held moral conviction. That is, of course, very broad and it is perhaps best understood if we see what it leaves out. What it leaves out most clearly are beliefs based on selfish desires of one sort or another, personal interest, belief based on emotions like fear or ambition . . . beliefs which are whimsical or based on impulse.' Testimony of Prof. Peter Singer, Professor of Philosophy, Monash University: quoted ibid., para. 2.13.

[98] This approach was cited with approval by the Canadian Federal Court of Appeal in *Zolfagharkhani* v. *Minister for Employment and Immigration* [1993] FCJ No. 584, para. 36.

[99] The converse is that no State has the right to wage a war of aggression, or to employ unlimited choice of weapons. In *Zolfagharkhani* v. *Minister for Employment and Immigration* [1993] FCJ No. 584, the court found that, 'The probable use of chemical weapons . . . is clearly judged by the international community to be contrary to basic rules of human conduct, and consequently the ordinary Iranian conscription law of general application, as applied to a conflict in which Iran intended to use chemical weapons, amounts to persecution for political opinion': para. 34.

'reasonably necessary in a democratic society';[100] specifically, there ought to exist a reasonable relationship of proportionality between the end and the means.[101] The element of proportionality is especially important in this context of competing interests, where the right in question has not yet been generally accepted by States as falling within the corpus of fundamental human rights.[102]

Alternative service can help to reconcile the situation in a way that promotes community interests in defence and equality of treatment, and the individual's interest in his or her own conscience. Whether alternative service meets international standards is a question of fact in each case, having regard to conditions, nature and duration.[103] In the absence of alternative service, or where insufficient weight is given to a sincerely held belief going to conscience, the likelihood of prosecution and punishment must be examined in order to determine whether they amount to persecution. This may be the case where the treatment is disproportionate, excessive or arbitrary, and whether it derives from official or unofficial sources.

Once having recognized the protected interest of freedom of conscience, it is but a short step to the critical issue, namely, the circumstances under which the punishment or treatment, legal or extra-legal, feared by the claimant amounts to persecution.

---

[100] Cf. *Akar* v. *Attorney-General of Sierra Leone* [1970] AC 853, in which the Privy Council declined to accept that a law dealing with citizenship was *by that fact alone* 'reasonably necessary in a democratic society' so as to avoid constitutional limitations, including provisions on discrimination. The European Court of Human Rights interprets this phrase to mean 'justified by a pressing social need and, in particular, proportionate to the legitimate aim pursued'. See *Moustaquim* v. *Belgium* (31/1989/191/291), 18 Feb. 1991, para. 43; *Beldjoudi* v. *France* (55/1990/246/317), 26 Mar. 1992; *Berrehab case* (3/1987/126/177), 21 Jun. 1988, paras. 25, 29.

[101] In the UK, throughout the Second World War, conscientious objectors were permitted the alternative of civilian service. Exemption from that was also permitted if reasons of religion or conscience demanded, while the criterion for exemption was the honesty or sincerity, rather than the 'validity' of the views held. See Gattiker, M. and Illes, R., 'Kosovo: Trends in der deutschen und schweizerischen Asylrechtsprechung', *Asyl* (1993/2), 32–40, referring to the 28 Oct. 1992 Swiss Federal Council decision (renewed 21 Apr. 1993), to the effect that deserters and objectors from former Yugoslavia (with the exception of Slovenia and Macedonia) should be accepted if their objections are credible.

[102] In a case in the Federal Republic of Germany in 1976 (*Verwaltungsgericht, Ansbach Nr.* AN3220–II(IV)/73, cited with approval by the same court in 1977: *VG Ansbach Nr.* AN8341–IV/76, the court expressly conceded the widest discretion to other States in the regulation of military service, which it considered to fall within the reserved domain of domestic jurisdiction (*innerstaatliche Rechtsordnung*). The court declined to apply the standard of exemption recognized by art. 4 of the 1949 Constitution of the Federal Republic; its reasoning would not appear wholly consistent with that adopted in cases of *Republikflucht*, but seems well established. See also *BVerwGE*, Bd. 62. 5. 123 (1981).

[103] See on alternative service, Sub-Commission on the Prevention of Discrimination and the Protection of Minorities, *Conscientious Objection to Military Service*: UN doc. E/CN.4/Sub.2/1983/30/Rev.1, paras. 104–15, 150–3; but see also *Appl. 24630* v. *Belgium*, in which the European Commission on Human Rights declared inadmissible an application by a Jehovah's Witness imprisoned for refusal to do either military or alternative service; and *JPK* v. *Netherlands*, Communication no. 401/1990, Decision on admissibility, 7 Nov. 1991, Human Rights Committee—requirement to do military service does not violate arts. 6, 7, 1966 Covenant on Civil and Political Rights.

States are free to recognize conscientious objection in itself as a sufficient ground upon which to base recognition of refugee status. In this sense, they are free to attribute such value to the fundamental right to freedom of conscience that any measures having as their object to compel the individual to act contrary to sincerely held belief, or any punishment, such as deprivation of liberty, imposed to that end, amounts to persecution within the meaning of the 1951 Convention, regardless of its duration.

Alternatively, and short of such position of principle, international human rights law attaches special importance to the individual's freedom of conscience. The standards of reasonableness and proportionality must be applied to the particular circumstances of each individual case. Whether prosecution and punishment amount to persecution in the sense of the Convention will depend on the object and purpose of the law, the precise motivation of the individual who breaches such law, the 'interest' which such individual asserts and the nature and extent of the punishment. This in turn invites attention to (1) the genuineness of the applicant's beliefs, as a manifestation of freedom of conscience; (2) the nature of the individual's objection, so far as it may be relevant to the nature of the military conflict at issue (if any) or the way in which war is being waged; (3) the legality of the military action (if any) for which conscription is employed; (4) the scope and manner of implementation of military service laws; (5) the selective conscription of particular groups within society, and the bases of such distinctions; (6) the extent to which the right of conscientious objection is recognized, if at all; (7) the type of alternative service available, if any, its length and conditions by comparison with military service, and the treatment of conscientious objectors performing such service; (8) the manner of prosecution and the proportionality and likelihood of punishment of conscientious objectors in the absence of alternative service; (9) the treatment of conscientious objectors subject to such punishment, including the extra-legal activities of paramilitary groups or sections of the populace; and (10) the extent to which penalties for conscientious objection may be employed selectively, against specific racial, religious, social, or political groups.

4.3.2.3 Political and non-political offenders

Similar considerations apply to the related question of non-extradition of political offenders. The IRO Constitution excluded 'ordinary criminals who are extraditable by treaty' as well as 'war criminals, quislings, and traitors' and a variety of other 'undeserving' groups; the UNHCR Statute and the 1951 Convention contain equivalent provisions.[104] The exception in favour of political offenders developed in the nineteenth century in the context of bilateral extradition arrangements, and is not the consequence of any rule of general international law. No duty obliges States to surrender fugitive criminals and

---

[104] Para. 7(d) and art. 1F, respectively. See further below, Ch. 3, s. 4.2.

extradition itself has traditionally been seen as a gloss upon the rule which permits the grant of territorial asylum.[105] In practice, characterization of an offence as 'political' is left to the authorities of the State from which extradition is requested, and the function of characterization itself is evidently one in which political considerations will be involved, including the self-interest of the requested State as reflected by its military and other alliances.[106] Not surprisingly, divergent attitudes are revealed in municipal law. For example, the political offence exception did not figure in the extradition arrangements existing between eastern European socialist States,[107] although their constitutions commonly recognized the institution of asylum.[108] In contrast, certain Western European States developed an elaborate comprehensive approach to purely political offences, complex political offences, and related political offences, all of which might justify non-extradition.[109] Nevertheless, the weight to be accorded to the motives of the offender varies from jurisdiction to jurisdiction,[110] as does the practice on substantive limitations to the political offence exception. Some States have long excluded assassination of the head of State, while others have explicitly excluded acts of barbarism or offences the suppression of which is required under international obligations.[111] Moreover, appreciation of the political character of offences is clearly likely to vary according to the particular perspective of the requested State.[112]

[105] O'Connell, D. P., *International Law*, (2nd ed., 1970), 720; *Asylum* case, ICJ *Rep.*, 1950, 266, at 274; Lauterpacht, H., 'The Law of Nations and the Punishment of War Crimes', 21 *BYIL* (1944). Bassiouni, M. C., *Crimes against Humanity in International Criminal Law*, (1992).

[106] Goodwin-Gill, *Movement of Persons*, 143ff, 226–8; Corey, J. M., 'INS v Doherty: The Politics of Extradition, Deportation and Asylum', 16 *Maryland J.Int'l. L & Trade* 83 (1992).

[107] See Shearer, I. A., *Extradition in International Law* (1971) 65–6; Epps, V., 'The Validity of the Political Offence Exception in Extradition Treaties in Anglo-American Jurisprudence,' 20 *Harv. ILJ* (1979) 61, 86; Gold, 'Non-extradition for political offences: the Communist perspective,' 11 *Harv. ILJ* (1970) 191.

[108] See the provisions listed in *A Selected Bibliography on Territorial Asylum* (1977): UN doc. ST/GENEVA/LIB.SER.B/Ref.9, 68–74.

[109] See, in particular, the Swiss cases: *Pavan*, Ann. Dig., 1927–8, 347 (in which the theory of predominance is advanced); *Ficorilli*, 18 ILR 345 (1951); *Kavic*, 19 ILR 371 (1952); also, Whiteman, M., *Digest of International Law*, vol. 6, 799ff.

[110] In *Giovanni Gatti*, Ann. Dig. 1947 case no. 70; Kiss, *Répertoire de la pratique française en matière de droit international public*, (1966), vol. 2, 213–14, the Court of Appeal of Grenoble took the view that motive alone does not give a common crime the character of a political offence; such offence springs from the nature of the rights of the State which are injured. Cf. *Public Prosecutor* v. *Zind* 40 ILR 214.

[111] Kiss, *Répertoire de la pratique française*, vol. 2, 210, 212, 216–17; cf. art. 3, 1957 European Convention on Extradition.

[112] See *VerwRspr*, Bd. 20, S. 332 (OVG Münster, 1968). A Belgian was sentenced to 12 years imprisonment for having served in the *Wehrmacht* during the Second World War. Released on parole, he was subsequently sentenced to serve the remainder of his sentence. He fled to the Federal Republic of Germany where the court upheld his appeal against expulsion and noted that he would in any event be immune from extradition by reason of the political character of his offence. Cf. *In re Pohle*, 46 *BVerfGE*, 214, noted 73 *AJIL* 305–6 (1979), where the Federal Constitutional Court, in an appeal by a convicted member of the Baader-Meinhof group subsequently extradited from Greece, maintained the traditional rule that extradition treaties confer no rights on individuals, save if expressly mentioned. It construed the treaty with Greece as neither conferring rights on political offenders nor as barring a request for surrender of an offender who might be covered by an

Much of the early debates and the jurisprudence concentrated on acts committed during the course of an insurrection.[113] Successive decisions of courts in the United Kingdom have limited the exception to offences committed in the context of parties in opposition and conflict.[114] To a significant extent, this approach is confirmed in the jurisprudence of the United States and other countries. The offence should have been committed in the course of some political dispute or conflict, and have been related to the promotion of political ends. Intention or motive is not conclusive, however, and there is a presumption against classifying as political those offences which may be loosely described as common law crimes, such as murder and robbery. Inherent limitations on the category of political offences, by reference to their nature and circumstances, are increasingly accepted.

In the Federal Republic of Germany, for example, the extradition law expressly excludes murder and attempted murder, unless they occur in open combat.[115] Judicial decisions confirm that to qualify as political offences, the actions in question must be directed against the organization of the State ('unmittelbar gegen . . .').[116] The Federal Administrative Court has also ruled against the grant of asylum to those who commit offences in a fight against

---

exception clause. It further held that membership in a 'criminal organization', even if politically motivated, did not constitute a political offence from the perspective of the German legal system. See also the 'collaboration cases' cited in Goodwin-Gill, *Movement of Persons*, 143, n. 2.

[113] See, for example, debates in the UK, summarized in 6 *British Digest of International Law*, 661ff.

[114] In the leading cases, *Re Castioni* [1891] 1 QB 149 and *Re Meunier* [1894] 2 QB 415, the court emphasized that, to qualify for non-extradition, the offences in question must be 'incidental to and . . . part of political disturbances', involving two or more parties. In *R v. Governor of Brixton Prison, ex parte Schtraks* [1964] AC 556, it was suggested that the word 'political', 'indicate[s] . . . that the requesting State is after [the fugitive] for reasons other than the enforcement of the criminal law in its ordinary, . . . common or international aspect'. In each case, the fundamental requirement was that of political disturbance and opposition. See also *Cheng* v. *Governor of Pentonville Prison* [1973] 2 All ER 204, at 209; Lord Diplock said that an offence could not be considered political 'unless the only purpose sought to be achieved by the offender . . . were to change the government of the *state in which it was committed* . . .' (emphasis supplied).

[115] Art. 3(3), *Deutsches Auslieferungsgesetz 1929:* '. . . im offenen Kampf'.

[116] See the following two extradition cases: OLG Frankfurt, 8.6.1973; *NJW* 1973, 1568; cited in Marx, *Asylrecht*, (5. Aufl. 1991), Bd. 2, 352: neither attacks on banks nor explosives offences are political offences as such, and do not become political because committed by radical anarchists with the aim of altering society and having the intention to combat with force all manifestations of State authority. See similarly, BGH, 17.8.1978; ibid., 355, a case involving the Croatian Revolutionary Brotherhood, whose goals and methods included bomb attacks on innocent civilians: '. . . sind als politisches Taten aber nur strafbare Angriffe anzusehen, die sich *unmittelbar* gegen den Bestand oder die Sicherheit des Staates richten, soweit sie nicht im offenen Kampf begangen worden sind.' ('Unless they occur during open combat, criminally punishable acts are only to be considered as political offences if they are *directly* targeted on the organization and security of the State.' Author's translation). The court also ruled that for extradition purposes, more than mere membership in such a terrorist organization is required before an individual can be returned on the ground of involvement in an offence against life.

democracy in other countries, and, in the absence of any evidence of persecution, face prosecution for such offences.[117]

The French Extradition Law of 1927 provides that there shall be no extradition, 'Lorsque le crime ou délit a un caractère politique ou lorsqu'il résulte des circonstances que l'extradition est demandée dans un but politique . . .'[118] Acts committed during civil war or insurrection may benefit, unless they amount to 'odious barbarism'.[119] Decisions on claims to asylum and refugee status have been founded on a similar principle. In a 1958 decision, for example, the *Office français de protection des réfugiés et apatrides* (OFPRA) applied the rule that,

Par crime de droit commun . . . il y a lieu d'entendre toute infraction qui n'est pas commise à l'occasion de la lutte de l'intéressé contre les autorités responsables des persécutions dont l'intéressé est ou a été victime, sans d'ailleurs qu'il y ait lieu de donner au mot 'crime' le sens précis que lui prête le droit interne français.[120]

Homicides and, in particular, the deaths of civilians or even State officials chosen at random, have been consistently found to fall outside the protection of the political offence.[121] Commenting on exclusion jurisprudence in 1988, Tiberghien concluded:

. . . dans toutes les affaires jugées jusqu'ici par la Commission des recours et par le Conseil d'Etat, les assassinats et les attentats visaient soit des civils innocents, soit des représentants de l'ordre public choisis au hasard et non pas pour leur qualité de responsables de persécutions infligées aux auteurs des assassinats.[122]

The case of *Urizar-Murgoitio*, decided by the *Conseil d'Etat* on 14 December 1987, is illustrative. The appellant, from the Basque country in Spain, was accused of the death by shooting of a naval officer and a bar-owner, a suspected informer, and of a bomb attack against the police, which left two children victims, one dead, and the other disabled and blind. The *Conseil d'Etat* noted:

---

[117] BVerwG 17.5.1983; BVerwGE 76, 184; Marx, *Asylrecht*, Bd. 2, 1116; the Federal Administrative Court confirmed the interpretations of art. 3 of the extradition law described above. In *Quinn* v. *Wren* [1985] IR 322 the court refused to accord immunity from extradition to those whose objectives included the destruction of the very constitution under which they now claimed protection. In a later decision of the Supreme Court, the Chief Justice ruled that personal, mental reservations regarding the overthrow of the Irish Constitution were insufficient to allow the appellant thereby to rely on the principle of non-extradition for political offences: *Russell* v. *Fanning* [1988] IR 333, 340.

[118] Art. 5(2), loi du 10 mars 1927; Kiss, *Répertoire de la pratique française en matière de droit international public*, vol. 2, 204.

[119] Such as killing a wounded policeman, 'un crime de droit commun . . . un acte de barbarie odieux contraire aux lois de l'honneur et de la guerre, depuis longtemps indiscutées par les nations civilisées': *Morelli*, Cour d'Aix, arrêt du 15 nov. 1928: *Clunet 1930*, 108–9.

[120] *Gardai*, 2.800, 7 fév. 1958; cited in Tiberghien, *La protection des réfugiés*, 104, 468. So far, no decision has 'upheld' an offence committed against the authors of persecution.

[121] Cf. *McMullen* v. *INS* 788 F.2d 591, 597 (9th Cir., 1986): 'There is a meaningful distinction between terrorist acts directed at the military or official agencies of the State, and random acts of violence against ordinary citizens that are intended only "to promote social chaos".'

[122] Tiberghien, F., *Doc. réf.*, No. 43, 9/18 juill. 1988, Supp., pp. 3–4.

... la circonstance que ces crimes, qui ne sont pas politiques par leur nature, auraient été commis dans le cadre d'une lutte pour l'indépendance du pays basque et au sein d'une organisation armée, ne suffit pas, compte tenu de leur gravité, à les faire regarder comme ayant un caractère politique.[123]

Neither intention, nor the presence or absence of political motives will determine the characterization of the offence.[124] In *McMullen* v. *INS*, the US Court of Appeals for the Ninth Circuit expressly rejected 'the argument that places the determination ... on the alien's state of mind. The law focuses on the circumstances surrounding the acts'.[125] Quoting the first edition of this work,[126] among other sources, the court further observed,

Of course, for a criminal act to be 'political', the individual must have been motivated by political reasons ... However, 'motivation is not itself determinative of the political character of any given act.' ... The critical issue is 'whether there is a close and direct causal link between the crime committed and its alleged political purpose and object.'

Notwithstanding certain contradictory elements, United States jurisprudence generally supports the view that indiscriminate violence is not a protected political act. In *Eain* v. *Wilkes*, a member of the PLO who planted a bomb in a market-place, which killed two young boys and wounded many other people, was extradited precisely on this ground.[127] *Quinn* v. *Robertson* casts some doubt on the validity of the general proposition,[128] but has itself been apparently confined to the extradition context by the decision of the same circuit in *McMullen* v. *INS*, cited above.

McMullen concerned a former member of the Provisional IRA, who had successfully resisted extradition from the United States, and who now sought

---

[123] *Rec. Dalloz Sirey*, 1988, Inf. rap., p. 20; extract of decision in *Documentation réfugiés*, (*Doc. réf.*), No. 43, 9/18 juill. 1988, Supp., p. 6. To similar effect, *Lujambio Galdeano*, Conseil d'Etat (CE), 25 sept. 1984, 62.847: *Rec. Lebon*, p. 308; Tiberghien, *La protection des réfugiés*, 254f. This case involved 'assassinat par groupes armées'; such crimes were not inherently political and did not become so, merely by reason of their commission in the context of an independence struggle. See also *Croissant*, CE, 7 juill. 1978, 10.079: *Rec. Lebon*, p. 292; *(Gabor) Winter*, CE, 15 fév. 1980, 17.224: *Rec. Lebon*, p. 87. In the *Commission des recours* decision in *Assad (Kayed)*, 16 Nov. 1987, the claimant's conviction for murder and attempted murder of members of the Palestine Liberation Organization in France was held sufficient to justify the denial of refugee status; extract of decision in *Doc. réf.* no. 43, 9/18 juill. 1988, Supp., p. 5. The application of art. 1F(b) to those who commit serious non-political crimes *in* France has been controversial for some years: Tiberghien, 102–3, 468; also the case of presumed ETA leader, Santiago Arrposide Sarasola (Santi Potros): *Doc. réf.* no. 126: 20/29 oct. 1990; and below, Ch. 3, s. 4.2.

[124] Cf. *Giovanni Gatti*, in which the Cour de Grenoble in 1947 observed, 'Le caractère politique d'un acte ne dépend pas de l'existence ou de la non-existence de motifs politiques, qui sont le secret de la pensée de l'auteur, mais uniquement de l'acte considéré en lui-même ...': Ch. des mises en accusation, arrêt de 13 janv. 1947; Kiss, *Répertoire de la pratique française en matière de droit international public*, vol. 2, 213.

[125] *McMullen* v. *INS*, 788 F.2d 591, 597.   [126] At 60–1; see now Ch. 3, s. 4.2.

[127] 641 F.2d 504 (7th Cir., 1981). Cf. UNGA res. 26/171, 16 Dec. 1981. Question of human rights relating to the case of Mr Ziad Abu Eain. Annexes. Notes Verbales: 21 *ILM* 442 (1982).

[128] 783 F.2d 776 (9th Cir., 1986).

asylum and withholding of deportation to the Republic of Ireland.[129] The Ninth Circuit addressed precisely the issue, whether the petitioner was ineligible for asylum by reason of there being serious reasons to consider that he had committed a serious non-political crime.[130] Emphasizing the asylum context, the Court favoured the use of a balancing approach to the alleged serious non-political crime, in which the proportionality of the act to its objective and the degree of atrocity would be taken into account. It noted that terrorist activities were involved, including indiscriminate bombing campaigns, murder, torture, and maiming of innocent civilians who disagree with the objectives and methods of the Provisional IRA. In the view of the Court, 'such acts are beyond the pale of protectable "political offence".' There was no sufficient link between the acts and the political objective; they were so barbarous, atrocious and disproportionate as to amount to serious non-political crimes. At several places, the court stresses the civilian targets of PIRA terrorist activities, in a manner that recalls the special protection accorded to civilians under the laws of war, and presents an analogy with the mandatory exclusion from the Convention of those who have committed war crimes.[131]

At one time, Irish courts tended to disregard the nature of the offences that were the subject of extradition requests by the British authorities.[132] They now accept, however, as do courts in many other countries, that not every charge connected with terrorism is to be considered a political offence. In *McGlinchey* v. *Wren*, for example, the murder of an elderly postmistress by the PIRA was ruled not to fall within the political offence exception.[133] This was followed in *Shannon* v. *Fanning*, which involved the murder of a former Speaker of the Northern Ireland House of Commons, and of his son, a former MP. In the view of the court,

... the circumstances of the murders ... were so brutal, cowardly and callous that it would be a distortion of language if they were to be accorded the status of political offences or offences connected with political offences.[134]

---

[129] The facts are set out in full in 658 F.2d 1312 (1981).

[130] Under s. 243(h)(2)(c) of the Immigration and Nationality Act, withholding of deportation (the statutory protection against *refoulement*) may be denied to those who have persecuted others; those who fall within the terms of art. 33(2) of the 1951 Convention; those who come within art. 1F(b); and those who are a danger to the security of the US.

[131] In a 1989 extradition case, the Court ruled that an act properly punishable even in the context of declared war, or in the heat of open military conflict, cannot fall within the political offence exception: *Mahmoud Abed Atta*, 706 F. Supp. 1032 (D.Ct., EDNY, 1989). The case involved an attack in Israel on a bus, in which the driver was killed and a passenger wounded. The court opted for a qualitative standard, that takes account of 'our own notions of civilised strife'. It also ruled that, even if one or more of the passengers might have been a non-civilian, this did not make the bus a military vehicle at the time of the attack, so exposing it to indiscriminate attack. Cf. *Gonzalez* v. *Minister of Employment and Immigration* [1994] FCJ No. 765.

[132] See, for example, *O'Neill* v. *Attorney-General*, *The Times*, 30 Jul. 1974 (deaths of passers-by in bombing attack on police station).

[133] [1982] IR 154.   [134] [1984] IR 569, 581.

In the European context, the development, or consolidation, of a limitative approach to the political offence has reflected regional developments, such as the 1977 European Convention on the Suppression of Terrorism, as well as recognition of the new dimension of terrorist violence introduced by military and para-military organizations. From an international legal perspective, this progression is by no means new; already in 1948, States had agreed that genocide should not be considered a political offence for extradition purposes, and subsequent years have seen broad agreement on the depoliticization of other offences, such as hijacking, hostage-taking, and offences against diplomats.[135]

In general, it may be concluded that an offence will not be considered political if (1) it is *remote*, in the sense that there is no sufficient 'close and direct causal link between the crime committed and its alleged political purpose'; and (2) if it is *disproportionate* in relation to the political aims.

In one British case, Lord Diplock explained that the political offence exception had the dual purpose of avoiding the United Kingdom's involvement in the internal political conflicts of foreign States; and preventing, on humanitarian grounds, the surrender of an offender to a jurisdiction in which trial and punishment might be unfairly prejudiced by political considerations.[136] As regards the latter, international legal principles relating to the protection of refugees are immediately involved. Not only must the offence in respect of which extradition is requested be examined, but also the broader context, with due consideration given to humanitarian issues and the fundamental rights of the individual.[137] The good faith and motives of the requesting State may require investigation, and although some courts are wary of this highly political arena,[138] others have been prepared to apply 'persecution criteria' more generously. State practice suggests, at the least, that these factors should be taken into account at some level, either judicial or executive.[139]

[135] The European Convention on the Suppression of Terrorism, for example, provides that the following offences shall not be considered as political offences: offences against internationally protected persons; kidnapping, hostage-taking; the use of explosives or automatic firearms, if such use endangers persons; and attempts to commit any of the above. Other offences may also be excluded if they involve collective danger to the life, physical integrity, or liberty of persons; if those affected are foreign to the motives of those responsible; and if cruel or vicious means are employed.

[136] *Cheng* v. *Governor of Pentonville Prison* [1973] 2 All ER 204, at 209. Cf. United Kingdom Fugitive Offenders Act 1967, s. 4.

[137] See Austria, Extradition Law 1979, s. 14; 1979 *BGBl* 2551ff; Austria-Poland Extradition Treaty 1980, arts. 4, 5; *BGBl* 1104ff; Austria-Hungary Extradition Treaty 1976, art. 3; *BGBl* 1262ff. Cf. Blum, C. P., 'License to Kill: Asylum Law and the Principle of Legitimate Governmental Authority to "Investigate its Enemies" ', 28 *Willamette L.R.* 719 (1992), discussing the argument that a government which defends itself against sedition and revolution does not engage in persecution and criticizing two BIA decisions in that sense, *Maldonado-Cruz*, Int. Dec. No. 3041 (1988) and *Izatula*, Int. Dec. No. 3127 (1990).

[138] See, for example, *Re Arton* [1896] 1 QB 108, 110, 115; *R.* v. *Governor of Brixton Prison, ex parte Kotronis* [1971] AC 250; *Zacharia* v. *Cyprus* [1962] 2 All ER 438; *R.* v. *Governor of Brixton Prison, ex parte Keane* [1971] 2 WLR 1243; similarly in the US, see *Re Lincoln* 228 F. 70 (1915); *Re Gonzalez* 217 F. Supp. 717 (1963).

[139] Moore, *Digest*, iv., s. 604; 6 *BDIL* 665-8 (US–UK discussions 1870–6); cf. art. 3, 1957 European Convention on Extradition.

The international community does not exist for the purpose of preserving established governments, and the political offence exception may be considered valuable for its dynamic quality.[140] International law, however, provides no guidance on the substance of the concept, other than its outermost limits; States retain the broadest discretion, almost a 'unilateral right of qualification'.[141] Nevertheless, exclusive attention to the concept should not lead to total disregard of the broader humanitarian issues which underlie it. It is arguable (though few might care to do so), that the mere commission of a political offence is not sufficient to qualify a person for refugee status, which arises only where the anticipated punishment shades into persecution. Alternatively, it may be that certain offences are inherently political, that their commission reflects the failure of a State to protect a greater and more valued interest, so that any punishment would be equivalent to persecution.

5. Persecution

'Persecution' is not defined in the 1951 Convention or in any other international instrument.[142] Articles 31 and 33 of the Convention refer to those whose life or freedom 'was' or 'would be' threatened,[143] and the 1984 UN Convention against Torture defines that term as covering,

any act by which severe pain or suffering, whether physical or mental, is intentionally inflicted on a person . . . It does not include pain or suffering arising only from, inherent in or incidental to lawful sanctions.[144]

---

[140] Many earlier treaties, however, were intended precisely to ensure the survival of rulers. See, for example, art. 3, 1765 Treaty between the Nabob Shujah-ul-Dowla, the Nabob Nudjum-ul-Dowla, and the English Company, executed at Illiabad: 'His Highness solemnly engages never to entertain or receive Cossim Ally Khan, the late Soubahday of Bengal, etc., Sombre, the assassin of the English, nor any of the European deserters, within his dominions, nor to give the least countenance, support, or protection to them. He likewise solemnly engages to deliver up to the English whatever Europeans may in future desert from them into his country': Aitchison, C. U., *A Collection of Treaties, Engagements and Sanads Relating to India and Neighbouring Countries*, 4th ed., Calcutta, 1909, vol. I., 89-91. Also, 1816 Treaty of Perpetual Defensive Alliance between the Honorable English East India Company and His Highness Maharajah Pursojee Bhooslah, his heirs and successors, which, after providing in art. 1 that 'The friends and enemies of either shall be the friends and enemies of both . . .', continues in art. 14: 'The British Government agrees not to give aid or countenance to any discontented subjects or dependants of the Maharajah, or any members of His Highness' family or relations or servants of His Highness, who, in like manner, engages to refuse protection to any persons who may be in a state of rebellion against the British Government or its allies, or to any fugitives from their respective territories': ibid., vol. I, 419-24.
[141] See further below, Ch. 4, s. 6.
[142] UNHCR, *Handbook*, paras. 51-65; Grahl-Madsen, *Status of Refugees*, vol. 1, 188-216; Hathaway, *Law of Refugee Status*, 99-134.
[143] Cf. UNHCR, *Handbook*, para. 51: '. . . it may be inferred that a threat to life or freedom on account of race, religion, nationality, political opinion or membership of a particular social group is always persecution. Other serious violations of human rights—for the same reasons—would also constitute persecution.'
[144] Art. 1; for full text, see below, Annexe 1, No. 7. The Convention requires a linkage between the act and a public official or other person acting in an official capacity.

Although discrimination may be a factor, torture, unlike Convention refugee status, need not necessarily be linked to specific indices such as race, religion, nationality, social group or political opinion.[145] Other acts amounting to persecution on the particular facts of the case may include those covered by the prohibition of cruel, inhuman or degrading treatment or punishment,[146] or punishment or repeated punishment for breach of the law, which is out of proportion to the offence.

In other respects, however, a wide margin of appreciation is left to States in interpreting this fundamental term, and practice reveals no coherent or consistent jurisprudence.[147] Specific decisions by national authorities are some evidence of the content of the concept, as understood by States, but comprehensive analysis requires the general notion of persecution to be related to developments within the broad field of human rights.

Fear of persecution and lack of protection are themselves interrelated elements, as article 1A(1) of the 1951 Convention makes clear. The persecuted clearly do not enjoy the protection of their country of origin, while evidence of the lack of protection on either the internal or external level may create a presumption as to the likelihood of persecution and to the well-foundedness of any fear.[148] The core meaning of persecution readily includes the threat of

---

[145] Given that the Committee against Torture now has the competence to review State actions, including refusal of admission, deportation or removal which may involve return to face the risk of torture, a new formal category of refugee is thus in the making. Cf. Frowein, J. Abr. and Kühner, R., 'Drohende Folterung als Asylgrund und Grenze für Auslieferung und Ausweisung', 35/36 *ZaöRV* 538, arguing with reference to the Federal Republic of Germany that the human right to be protected against torture does not always provide a basis for political asylum, although it may well be an aspect of persecution. The threat of torture, however, does limit the right of expulsion and extradition. See further below, Ch. 4, s. 3.2.6.

[146] See, for example, art. 16, 1984 Convention against Torture; art. 7, 1966 Covenant on Civil and Political Rights; art. 3, 1950 European Convention on Human Rights; art. 5, 1969 American Convention on Human Rights.

[147] In *Acosta*, Int. Dec. No. 2986, 1 Mar. 1985, the Board of Immigration Appeals described persecution as meaning, 'the infliction of suffering or harm in order to punish an individual for possessing a particular belief or characteristic the persecutor seeks to overcome'. Experience is not quite so mechanical. See also Tiberghien, F., 'Le champ d'application de l'article 1er, A, 2 de la Convention de Genève': *Doc. réf.* no. 49, Suppl., CJ, 1–24—an extensive review of decisions of the *Commission des recours*, mostly showing what is not persecution. For example, CRR, 26 nov. 1987, 56.191, *Avakian*, ibid., 6—injured by revolutionary guards for failure to respect islamic dress standards: not persecution; CRR, 23 nov. 1987, 58.649, *Skiba*, ibid., 15—left Poland for economic reasons and to join relative in France: not within Convention; CRR, 29 sept. 1987, 66,701, *Shan*, ibid., 17. PRC legislation on family planning is of a general character and it is not claimed that it was applied in a discriminatory manner linked to the grounds set forth in the Convention; CRR, 10 nov. 1987, 67.843, *Yu*, ibid., 17—similarly; CRR, 3 dec. 1987, 30.620, *Simon*, ibid., 11—Romanian adventist refused passport: not sufficient to amount to persecution; CRR, 30 avr. 1987, 49.936, *Tawileh*, ibid.—similarly.

[148] This passage was not clearly understood by Urie, J. A. in *Canada (Attorney General)* v. *Ward* [1990] 2 FC 667 (Federal Court of Appeal). He said that it was important to avoid confusing 'the determination of persecution and ineffective protection', that 'the two concepts must be addressed and satisfied independently,' and that the absence of protection did not serve as a presumption of persecution (at 680–1). On appeal, the Supreme Court of Canada, quoting the passage in the text, stated that having established that the claimant has a fear, the decision-maker is 'entitled to presume

deprivation of life or physical freedom.[149] In its broader sense, however, it remains very much a question of degree and proportion; less overt measures may suffice, such as the imposition of serious economic disadvantage, denial of access to employment, to the professions, or to education, or other restrictions on the freedoms traditionally guaranteed in a democratic society, such as speech, assembly, worship, or freedom of movement.[150] Whether such restrictions amount to persecution within the 1951 Convention will again turn on an assessment of a complex of factors, including (1) the nature of the freedom threatened, (2) the nature and severity of the restriction, and (3) the likelihood of the restriction eventuating in the individual case.

5.1 PROTECTED INTERESTS

The references to 'race, religion, nationality, membership of a particular social group, or political opinion' illustrate briefly the characteristics of individuals and groups which are considered worthy of special protection.[151] These same factors have figured in the development of the fundamental principle of non-discrimination in general international law,[152] and have contributed to the formulation of other fundamental human rights. In a judgment in 1970, the International Court of Justice referred to the outlawing of genocide, slavery, and racial discrimination as falling within the emergent notion of obligations *erga omnes*.[153] The resulting rights, so far as they are embodied in international conventions, figure generally among those from which no derogation is permitted, even in exceptional circumstances.[154] These basic rights include: the right to life, to the

that persecution will be *likely* and the fear *well-founded* if there is an absence of state protection. The presumption goes to the heart of the inquiry, which is whether there is a likelihood of persecution . . . . The presumption is not a great leap . . . Of course, the persecution must be real—the presumption cannot be built on fictional events—but the *well-foundedness* of the fears can be established through the use of such a presumption': *Ward,* [1993] SCR 689, 708 (emphasis in original). See also *Zalzali* v. *Minister for Employment and Immigration* [1991] FCJ No. 341.

    149 See Grahl-Madsen, *Status of Refugees,* vol. 1, 193, quoting Zink's 'restrictive' interpretation.
    150 Ibid., citing the liberal interpretations of Weis, P., in 'The concept of the refugee in international law,' 87 *Clunet* 928 (1960): 'other measures in disregard of human dignity'; and Vernant, J., *The Refugee in the Post-War World,* (1953), 8: 'severe measures and sanctions of an arbitrary nature, incompatible with the principles set forth in the Universal Declaration of Human Rights'.
    151 In an otherwise extensive analysis of the scope and purpose of the refugee definition, Hathaway rationalizes the limited protection available under the Convention to persons affected by 'forms of fundamental disfranchisement', in which marginalization is defined by reference to norms of non-discrimination: *Law of Refugee Status,* 136. If the danger that a claimant faces cannot be linked to his or her 'socio-political situation and resultant marginalization', the refugee claim must fail: ibid., 137. It seems doubtful whether anything is gained by formally interposing a notion of membership and/or 'civil or political status' between claimant and claim. Not only does the idea run up against common usage (someone who holds political opinions is not generally thought of on that account as someone having a particular 'civil or political status'), but through the natural tendency of ideas to reify, runs the further risk of placing yet another conceptual hurdle in the path of one who seeks protection.
    152 Cf. Goodwin-Gill, *Movement of Persons,* 66–87.
    153 *Barcelona Traction* case, ICJ *Rep.* (1970) 3, at 32.
    154 Cf. art 15(2), European Convention on Human Rights; art. 4, Covenant on Civil and Political Rights; art. 27, American Convention of Human Rights. But see also Meron, T., 'On a Hierarchy

extent that the individual is protected against 'arbitrary' deprivation;[155] the right to be protected against torture, or cruel or inhuman treatment or punishment;[156] the right not to be subjected to slavery or servitude;[157] the right not to be subjected to retroactive criminal penalties;[158] the right to recognition as a person before the law;[159] and the right to freedom of thought, conscience, and religion.[160] Although not included within the same fundamental class, the following rights are also relevant in view of the frequent close connection between persecution and personal freedom: the right to liberty and security of the person, including freedom from arbitrary arrest and detention;[161] and the right to freedom from arbitrary interference in private, home and family life.[162]

Recognition of these rights is essential to the maintenance of the integrity and inherent human dignity of the individual. Persecution within the Convention thus comprehends measures, taken on the basis of one or more of the stated grounds, which threaten deprivation of life or liberty; torture or cruel, inhuman, or degrading treatment; subjection to slavery or servitude; non-recognition as a person (particularly where the consequences of such non-recognition impinge directly on an individual's life, liberty, livelihood, security, or integrity); and oppression, discrimination, or harassment of a person in his or her private, home, or family life.[163]

5.2 THE WAYS AND MEANS OF PERSECUTION

There being no limits to the perverse side of human imagination, little purpose is served by attempting to list all known measures of persecution. Assessments must be made from case to case by taking account, on the one hand, of the notion of individual integrity and human dignity and, on the other hand, of the manner and degree to which they stand to be injured. A straightforward threat to life or liberty is widely accepted, and the repeated condemnation of a wide range of activities involving violation of international humanitarian law, genocide, crimes against humanity and related offences should also be taken into account, given the recognition of responsibility at both State and individual level.

The International Tribunal for Rwanda, for example, has competence to prosecute persons responsible for serious violations of international humanitarian

of International Human Rights', 80 *AJIL* 1 (1987), with discussion of International Law Institute proposals for non-extradition 'where there is a well-founded fear of the violation of the fundamental human rights of an accused in the territory of the requesting State' (17–18); Weil, P., 'Towards Relative Normativity in International Law?' 77 *AJIL* 413 (1985).

[155] Art. 6, Covenant on Civil and Political Rights.   [156] Ibid., art. 7.
[157] Ibid., art. 8.   [158] Ibid., art. 15.
[159] Ibid., art. 16. See above, n. 1.   [160] Ibid., art. 18.
[161] Ibid., art. 9.   [162] Ibid., art. 17.
[163] Cf. Martin, DA, 87 *AJIL* 348 (1993), review of Hathaway, *Law of Refugee Status*, criticizing too tight a linkage with the Covenants, drafted without reference to asylum, noting discrepancies in the lists of non-derogable rights, and concluding that 'the concept of "persecution" simply does not implicate the full range of rights listed in the Covenants'. (350).

law;[164] genocide, including conspiracy, incitement, attempts and complicity with intent to destroy, in whole or in part, a national, ethnical, racial or religious group;[165] crimes against humanity, when committed as part of a widespread or systematic attack against any civilian population on national, political, ethnic, racial or religious grounds;[166] and violations of article 3 common to the Geneva Conventions and of Additional Protocol II.[167]

Certain measures, such as the forcible expulsion of an ethnic minority or of an individual, will clearly show the severance of the normal relationship between citizen and State, but the relation of cause and effect may be less clear in other cases. For example, expulsion may be encouraged indirectly, either by threats[168] or by the implementation of apparently unconnected policies. Thus, in Vietnam after 1978, State policies aimed at the restructuring of society and the abolition of the bourgeoisie[169] began to be implemented, giving rise among those affected to serious concern for their future life and security. Those in any way associated with the previous government of South Vietnam were already liable not only to 're-education',[170] but thereafter also to surveillance, to denial of access to employment and the ration system, or to relocation in a 'new economic zone'.[171] The situation of ethnic Chinese was exacerbated by the deterioration in relations and subsequent armed conflict with the People's Republic of China.[172] The net result was a massive exodus of asylum seekers by boat and land to countries in the region.

5.2.1 Agents of persecution and non-State entities

Cause and effect are yet more indirect where the government of the country of origin cannot be immediately implicated. Refugees, for example, have fled mob

---

[164] SC res. 955, 8 Nov. 1994, Annex, Statute of the International Tribunal for Rwanda, art. 1. See art. 6 on the principle of individual criminal responsibility, and below, Ch. 3, s. 4.1.3.

[165] Ibid., art. 2. The following acts are covered: killing; causing serious bodily or mental harm; deliberately inflicting on the group conditions of life calculated to bring about its physical destruction in whole or in part; imposing measures intended to prevent births; forcibly transferring children to another group. LeBlanc, LJ, 'The Intent to Destroy Groups in the Genocide Convention: The Proposed U.S. Understanding', 78 *AJIL* 369 (1984).

[166] Statute of the International Tribunal for Rwanda, art. 3. The following are included: murder, extermination, enslavement, deportation, imprisonment, torture, rape, persecutions on political, racial and religious grounds, and other inhumane acts.

[167] Ibid., art. 4. Such violations include but are not limited to violence to the life, health and physical or mental well-being of persons, in particular, murder and cruel treatment such as torture, mutilation or any form of corporal punishment; collective punishments; taking of hostages; acts of terrorism; outrages upon personal dignity, in particular humiliating and degrading treatment, rape, enforced prostitution and any form of indecent assault; pillage; the passing of sentences and the carrying out of executions without previous judgment pronounced by a regularly constituted court, affording all the judicial guarantees which are recognized as indispensable by civilized peoples; and threats to commit any of the above.

[168] As was done by President Amin in the case of the Ugandan expulsions in 1972.

[169] Foreign Language Press, Hanoi, *The Hoa in Vietnam,* (1978), 12.

[170] Cf. Amnesty International, *1980 Report,* 241–6; *1982 Report,* 249–52.

[171] Grahl-Madsen includes 'removal to a remote or designated place within the home country' in a list of measures which may amount to persecution: *Status of Refugees,* vol. 1, 201.

[172] Osborne, M., 'Indo-China's refugees: causes and effects', *International Affairs,* (1980) 37, 38–44.

violence[173] or the activities of so-called 'death squads'.[174] Governments may be unable to suppress such activities, they may be unwilling or reluctant to do so, or they may even be colluding with those responsible. In such cases, where protection is in fact unavailable, persecution within the Convention can result, for it does not follow that the concept is limited to the actions of governments or their agents.[175]

The term, 'agent of persecution', is somewhat misleading. An 'agent' usually acts for and on behalf of another, the 'principal'. In the law of contract, for example, an agent is empowered to represent and to conclude agreements that bind the principal. In some cases, the agent who acts beyond the bounds of specific authority may also bind the principal, and even on occasion one who, having no authority, holds him- or herself out as representing a principal may also bind the latter, unless the principal takes steps to avoid responsibility. In agency cases, therefore, the essential link is the actual or implied conferral of authority to act upon another.

Neither the 1951 Convention nor the *travaux préparatoires* say much about the source of the persecution feared by the refugee,[176] and no necessary linkage

---

[173] Cf. *The Biharis in Bangladesh* (Minority Rights Group, report no. 11, 1977).

[174] 'Death squads' have been particularly active in Latin American countries; see, for example, Amnesty International, *Guatemala: A government program of political murder*, (1981). Jonas, S., *The Battle for Guatemala: Rebels Death Squads and U.S. Power*, (1991). See also the UN Commission on Human Rights Working Groups and Special Rapporteurs, including for example, *Report* on extrajudicial, summary or arbitrary executions: UN doc. E/CN.4/1994/7 (7 Dec. 1993); *Report* on developments in the human rights situation in El Salvador: UN doc. E/CN.4/1994/11 (3 Feb. 1994); *Report* of the Working Group on Enforced or Involuntary Disappearances: *Report* of the Special Rapporteur on Torture: UN doc. E/CN.4/1994/26 (22 Dec. 1993); E/CN.4/1994/31 (6 Jan. 1994); *Report* of the Working Group on Enforced or Involuntary Disappearances: UN doc. E/CN.4/1993/25 (7 Jan. 1993); *Report* on the visit to Sri Lanka by three members of the Working Group on Enforced or Involuntary Disappearances: UN doc. E/CN.4/1993/25/Add.1 (30 Dec. 1992); *Report* on extrajudicial, summary or arbitrary executions: UN doc. E/CN.4/1993/46 (23 Dec. 1992).

[175] Persecution for reasons of race or religion will often spring from hostile sections of the populace, while that for reasons of political opinion will more commonly derive from direct, official action. See Cons. d'Etat, *Dankha*, 42,074, 27 mai 1983; Commission des recours, *Duman*, 9,744, 3 avr. 1979, cited in Tiberghien, *La protection des réfugiés*, 247, 394, respectively. See also CRR, 18 sept. 1991, *Mlle. **, 164.078, *Doc. réf.* no. 187, 20/29 juin 1992, Suppl., CJ, 1—pressure to submit to excision in Mali; if the requirement to submit came from public authority or if it was encouraged or even tolerated by public authority, it would constitute persecution within the meaning of the Convention provided that the claimant(s) had been personally at risk, contrary to their wishes.

[176] One exception is acknowledged in art. 1C(5),(6); UNHCR, *Handbook*, para. 136, according to which refugee status may continue, notwithstanding a change of circumstances, in the case of 'compelling reasons arising out of previous persecution'; see further below, Ch. 3, s. 2. The Convention also does not specify *where* the threat or persecution must take place. Tiberghien, F., 'Le lieu d'exercise des persecutions': *Doc. réf.* no. 67, 6/15 mars 1989, 1–5—notes acceptance of the idea that a threat or other act committed in France can be equated with persecution in the country of origin, for example, (1) where the authorities of the country of origin undertake their activities abroad through groups which they control or manipulate; (2) where the persecutor is the country of residence, and the country of origin does not protect. Cf. Conseil d'Etat, 4 dec. 1987, 61.376, *Urtiaga Martinez*, ibid., 3—Basque threatened in France by group tolerated or encouraged by Spanish authorities, and name found on list in possession of suspected counter-terrorist group member; refugee status upheld.

between persecution and government authority is formally required. On the other hand, the Convention does recognize the relation between protection and fear of persecution. A Convention refugee, by definition, must be *unable* or *unwilling* to avail him- or herself of the protection of the State or government. In the view of the *Ad hoc* committee in 1950, '. . . "unable" refers primarily to stateless refugees but includes also refugees possessing a nationality who are refused passports or *other* protection by their own government . . .'[177]

Grahl-Madsen ties persecution 'to acts or circumstances for which the government (or, in appropriate cases, the ruling party) is responsible, that is, . . . acts committed by the government (or the party) or organs at its disposal, or behaviour tolerated by the government in such a way as to leave the victims virtually unprotected by the agencies of the State'.[178] The decisive factor, in his view, is the 'place' of the acts or atrocities in the general situation prevailing in the country of origin, for example, whether they are sporadic and rapidly terminated, or 'continue over a protracted period without the government being able to check them effectively', thereby amounting to a flaw in the organization of the State.[179]

The jurisprudence of the French *Commission des recours,* drawing on the references to protection in article 1A(2) and 1C(1), implies that persecution not deriving from public authorities or officials cannot form the basis of a Convention refugee claim. The 'public authorities' have been interpreted to include the government, the administration and the military, but not political parties, participants in civil conflict, criminals and extremists.[180] Two exceptions have been recognized, however. First, mistreatment repeated and systematically organized by the population against a minority, on the ground that such systematic ill-treatment is necessarily dependent on passive compliance (*la passivité complaisante*) by the authorities.[181] This approach was confirmed and extended by the Conseil d'Etat in the case of *Dankha* in 1983, on reviewing a *Commission des recours* finding that the facts alleged by the claimant could not be imputed to the official authorities. The *commissaire du gouvernement,* M. Genevois, noted that the 1951 Convention did not limit the concept of refugee to those persecuted at the hands of official authorities; it simply required a well-founded fear of persecution in the country of origin. Besides 'official' persecution, he proposed, and the *Section contentieux* agreed, that account be taken, 'des persécutions exercées par des particuliers dès lors qu'elles sont encouragées ou tolérées par l'autorité publique, si bien que la personne intéressée n'est pas en mesure de se réclamer de la pro-

---

177   Report of the *Ad hoc* Committee: UN doc. E/1618, para. 39.
178   Grahl-Madsen, *Status of Refugees,* vol. 1, 189; also Hathaway, *Law of Refugee Status,* 125–33.
179   Grahl-Madsen, *Status of Refugees,* vol. 1, 192.
180   Tiberghien, *La protection des réfugiés,* 93–6, 247, 394.
181   *Duman,* 9, 744, 3 avr. 1979: Tiberghien, *La protection des réfugiés,* 394. Cf. the views of Hailbronner, M. A., former president of the *Commission,* cited ibid., 94: 'La Commission en a concluque les persécutions doivent être le fait de l'Etat, étant bien entendu que l'inaction de l'Etat, sa complicité de fait avec ces émeutiers, peut faire regarder les persécutions comme émanant de lui.'

tection de l'Etat dont elle a la nationalité'.[182] Later jurisprudence, however, confirms how difficult it is for claimants to establish the requirements of passive compliance, encouragement or willing toleration.[183]

5.2.1.1 Agents of persecution and State responsibility

The purpose is not to attribute responsibility, in the sense of State responsibility,[184] for the persecution. If it were, then qualifying as a refugee would be conditional on the rules of attribution, and protection would be denied in cases where, for any reason, the actions of the persecutors were not such as to involve the responsibility of the State.[185] As with the putative question of persecutory intent, so the issue of State responsibility for persecution, relevant though it may be in other circumstances, is not part of the refugee definition. Analogous aspects may arise, however, in considering the availability and/or sufficiency of local protection. Here, the law of State responsibility provides some parallel illustrations; for example, if the acts of private groups or individuals are attributable to the State, then the lack of adequate local protection can be inferred. Likewise, where the State is either unable or unwilling to satisfy the standard of due diligence in the provision of protection, the circumstances may equally found an international claim, as provide a basis for fear of persecution within the meaning of the Convention. The correlation is coincidental, however, not normative. The central issue remains that of *risk of harm amounting to persecution*; the principles and practice of State responsibility can contribute to that assessment, for example, by confirming the level of protection and judicial or other guarantees that may be due under universal and regional human rights instruments.

Moreover, while the inability in fact of a State to exercise control in certain circumstances may entail an absence of responsibility vis-à-vis the rights of other States,[186] there is no basis in the 1951 Convention, or in general international

---

[182] Tiberghien, *La protection des réfugiés*, 95, 247.

[183] Tiberghien cites only two cases, one where the involvement of the police was clear, and one where the authorities had taken no steps to disarm a group: ibid., 96. Instances of criminal aggression, the dangers due to civil war, the destruction of property by private individuals, and religious riots that were not tolerated, have all been held insufficient to support a claim to refugee status. Cf. CRR, 18 sept. 1991, *Mlle.* *, 164.078, *Doc. réf.* no. 187, 20/29 juin 1992, Suppl., CJ, 1, above note 175. The case law of the Federal Republic of Germany provides some additional twists. For example, if the State is unwilling to provide protection, that unwillingness must be shown to be politically motivated, that is, itself transformed into political persecution. On the other hand, the motivation of the persecuting individuals or groups is irrelevant, for the State is equally responsible for the protection of its inhabitants against criminal, as against politically motivated violence. Only where the State is willing, but for whatever reason, unable to provide protection, is the (political) motivation of the actual persecutor to be taken into account. See Köfner, G. and Nicolaus, P., *Grundlagen des Asylrechts in der Bundesrepublik Deutschland,* (1986), 436–40.

[184] By 'State responsibility' is understood the body of principles which determines when and how one State may be liable to another for breach of an international obligation deriving either from treaty or from customary law.

[185] See Brownlie, I., *System of the Law of Nations: State Responsibility, Part I,* (1983), 159–79.

[186] Note, however, that a successful insurrectional movement is liable for its activities *before* its assumption of power; see Borchard, E. M., *The Diplomatic Protection of Citizens Abroad,* 241; *Bolívar Railway Co. Case (Great Britain v. Venezuela)*, Ralston's *Report*, 388, 394, per Umpire Plumley.

law, for requiring the existence of effective, operating institutions of government as a pre-condition to a successful claim to refugee status.[187] In the same way, the existence or non-existence of governmental authority is irrelevant to the issue of individual responsibility for genocide, war crimes, or other serious violations of international humanitarian law including, as article 3 of the Statute of the International Tribunal for Rwanda notes, 'persecutions on political, racial and religious grounds'.[188]

5.2.2 *Internal flight alternative*

There is also no reason in principle why the fear of persecution should relate to the whole of the asylum seeker's country of origin;[189] for various reasons, it may be unreasonable to expect the asylum seeker to move internally, rather than to cross an international frontier.[190] Different jurisdictions have thus held that the relevant criterion is the availability in fact of protection in another region, *and* the chance of maintaining some sort of social and economic existence.[191] Canadian courts consider that an internal flight alternative (IFA) is part of the general question of whether the claimant is a refugee; consequently the burden of proof remains with the claimant, 'to show, on a balance of probabilities, that

[187] See further below.

[188] SC res. 955 (1994), Annex. To make 'persecution' contingent upon the existence of governmental institutions is likely also to have the absurd consequence that those responsible for persecuting others during periods of anarchy or State disintegration could themselves later claim not to be *excluded* from refugee status; the reason being that the persecution for which they were responsible was not persecution within the meaning of the Convention . . .

[189] In *Acosta*, Int. Dec. No. 2986 (1 Mar. 1985), the US Board of Immigration Appeals saw the requirement of international protection as inherent in the refugee concept, because the claimant's country of origin was no longer safe. The criterion of inability or unwillingness to return to a particular 'country' implied further that the claimant 'must do more than show a well-founded fear of persecution in a particular place . . . within a country; he must show that the threat of persecution exists for him country-wide.'

[190] Cf. OAU Convention, art. I(2); see also Köfner, G. and Nicolaus, P., *Grundlagen des Asylrechts in der Bundesrepublik Deutschland,* 360–84; Marx, R., *Kommentar zum Asylverfahrensgesetz,* 3. Aufl. 1995, 56. Cf. UNHCR, *Handbook,* para. 91; *R. v. Immigration Appeal Tribunal, ex p. Jonah* [1985] ImmAR 7 (QBD, Nolan J)—finding that protection available elsewhere in country of origin reversed on ground that to obtain same would have required claimant to live in a remote village away from wife and to give up trade union activities, which was unreasonable; also *R. v. Secretary of State for the Home Department, ex p. Yurekli* [1990] Imm AR 334 (QBD, Otton J)—a Kurd persecuted in his own village moved to Istanbul, leaving wife and children behind. Although safe from persecution, he was not able to find secure employment, apparently because of ethnic origin. The Secretary of State's argument that such harassment did not amount to persecution upheld as not manifestly unreasonable.

[191] See decision of the Bundesverfassungsgericht = Federal Constitutional Court, 10 Jul. 1989, *BVerfGE* 2 BvR 502/86, 2 BvR 1000/86, 2 BvR 961/86, noting that an internal flight alternative presupposes that the territory in question offers the asylum seeker reasonable protection against persecution: Case Abstract No. *IJRL/0084*: 3 *IJRL* 343 (1991); also *Rasaratnam v. Canada (Minister of Employment and Immigration)* [1992] 1 FC 706, 710, in which the Canadian Federal Court of Appeal held that for an internal flight alternative to exist, the decision-maker should be satisfied, 'on a balance of probabilities that there was no serious possibility of the applicant being persecuted in Colombo, and that, in all the circumstances, including circumstances particular to him, conditions in Colombo were such that it would not be unreasonable for the Appellant to seek refuge there': Case Abstract No. *IJRL/0099*: 3 *IJRL* 95 (1992).

there is a serious possibility of persecution throughout the country, including the area which is alleged to afford an IFA'.[192] If there is an area in their own country in which asylum claimants would be safe from persecution, they will be expected to go there, 'unless they can show that it is objectively unreasonable for them to do so.'[193] The claimant need not undergo great physical danger or hardship, cross battle lines or hide out in isolated areas, but he or she may be expected to put up with certain difficulties, for example, in finding suitable employment.[194]

5.2.3 *Flight from civil war*

The fact of having fled from civil war is not incompatible with a well-founded fear of persecution in the sense of the 1951 Convention.[195] Too often, the existence of civil conflict is perceived by decision-makers as giving rise to situations of general insecurity that somehow exclude the possibility of persecution.[196] A closer look at the background to the conflict, however, and the ways in which it is fought, will often establish a link to the Convention.[197] As the Canadian Federal Court of Appeal stated in one case, 'a situation of civil war . . . is not an obstacle to a claim provided that the fear is not that felt indiscriminately by all citizens as a consequence . . . , but that felt by the applicant himself, by a group with which he is associated, or, even by all citizens on account of a risk of persecution based on one of the reasons stated . . . '[198] It nevertheless remains for the applicant to show that he or she is unable to obtain the protection of the State, and to establish the requisite Convention link.[199]

---

[192] *Rasaratnam*, above note 191, explained further in *Thirunavukkarasu* v. *Canada (Minister of Employment and Immigration)* [1993] FCJ No. 1172 (FCA), paras. 2–6. The claimant must nevertheless be given notice of intent to raise the possibility of internal flight, in order to be able to meet the claim.

[193] *Thirunavukkarasu*, para. 12.

[194] Ibid., paras. 14–15. In the particular circumstances of the appellant, a Sri Lankan Tamil, the court in *Thirunavukkarasu* found that Colombo did *not* constitute an internal flight alternative, and he was declared to be a Convention refugee.

[195] See generally, UNHCR, *Handbook*, paras. 164–6; also Bodart, S., 'Les réfugiés apolitiques: guerre civile et persécution de groupe au regard de la Convention de Genève', 7 *IJRL* 39 (1995); Hathaway, *Law of Refugee Status*, 185–8; von Sternberg, MR, 'Political Asylum and the Law of Internal Armed Conflict: Refugee Status, Human Rights and Humanitarian Law Concerns,' 5 *IJRL* 153 (1993); Kälin, W., 'Refugees and Civil Wars: Only a Matter of Interpretation?' 3 *IJRL* 435 (1991).

[196] See CRR, 21 fev. 1984, *Waked*, 21.951, *Doc. réf.*, no. 7, 15/24 juill. 1987, Suppl., CJ., 2—'les faits ainsi allégués sont des conséquences de la guerre civile qui déchire le Liban depuis de longue années et ne constituent pas des persécutions émanant directement des autorités publiques ou exercées par des particuliers avec l'encouragement ou la tolérance volontaire de ces autorités . . .' CRR, 15 sept. 1986, *Chahine*, 33.958, *Doc. réf.*, no. 7, 15/24 juill. 1987, Suppl., CJ., 4—'la requérante décrit une situation générale d'insécurité et ne fait état d'aucun mauvais traitement dont elle aurait été victime personnellement . . .'

[197] See also below, Ch. 9, s. 2.2.2.

[198] *Salibian* v. *Minister for Employment and Immigration* [1990] 3 FC 250, 258; also, Conseil d'Etat, 26 mai 1993, No. 43.082 (3è ch.), *Muric c/ Etat belge*, 74 *Revue du droit des étrangers*, jan–avr 1993, 336.

[199] See *Isa* v. *Canada (Secretary of State)* [1995] FCJ No. 254 (FC-TD); *Rizkallah* v. *Minister of Employment and Immigration* [1992] FCJ No. 412 (FCA); *Zalzali* v. *Canada (Minister of Employment and Immigration)* [1991] 3FC 605 (FCA); *Canada (Attorney General)* v. *Ward* [1993] 2 SCR 689.

In other situations, it may be argued that the Convention does not and cannot apply to a conflict between two competing groups, or when there is no effective government responsible for the implementation of international obligations relating to human rights. A number of German and French decisions and commentators, for example, have drawn distinctions between the civil war in Liberia and that in Somalia, finding for refugee status in the former (where rival factions have divided power between themselves and now compete for supremacy);[200] and denying it in the latter (where competing clans, sub-clans and factions compete amongst themselves, but none emerges as an authority in fact, controlling territory and possessing a minimum of organization).[201] This reasoning, which draws on the 'old' legal history of civil war and recognition of belligerency, has no obvious relevance to the 1951 Convention.

5.2.4 *The individual and the group*

Wherever large numbers of people are affected by repressive laws or practices of general or widespread application, the question arises whether each member of the group can, by reason of such membership alone, be considered to have a well-founded fear of persecution; or does persecution necessarily imply a further act of specific discrimination, a singling out of the individual?[202] Where large groups are seriously affected by a government's political, economic, and social policies or by the outbreak of uncontrolled communal violence, it would appear wrong in principle to limit the concept of persecution to measures immediately identifiable as direct and individual.[203] General measures, aimed as often at 'restructuring' society as at maintaining the *status quo*,[204] will frequently be

---

[200] See for example, CRR, 4 sept. 1991, *Freemans;* CRR, 30 sept. 1991, *Togbah,* discussed in Tiberghien, F., 'Les situations de guerre civile et la reconnaissance de la qualité de réfugié', *Doc. réf.,* no. 181, 21/30 avr. 1992, Suppl., CJ, 4.

[201] CRR, Sections reunies, 26 nov. 1993, *Ahmed Abdullah,* 229.619, *Doc. réf.,* no. 237, 1er/14 mars 1994, Suppl., CJ, 1. See also Hailbronner, K., 'Rechtsfragen der Aufnahme von "Gewaltflüchtlingen" in Westeuropa—am Beispiel Jugoslawien', (1993) *Schweizerische Zeitschrift für internationales und europäisches Recht* 517, 527–9, citing decisions of the Federal Constitutional Court, and arguing that protection against violations of human rights in open civil war does not come within the scheme of protection of the 1951 Convention, unless a government responsible for the implementation of international obligations can still be identified.

[202] See Crawford, J. and Hyndman, P., 'Three Heresies in the Application of the Refugee Convention', 1 *IJRL* 152 (1989).

[203] Grahl-Madsen, *Status of Refugees,* vol. 1, 213. In *R.* v. *Secretary of State for the Home Department, ex p. Jeyakumaran,* No. CO/290/84, QBD, 28 June 1985, Taylor J. referred to the singling out requirement as a 'startling proposition. It can be little comfort to a Tamil family to know that they are being persecuted simply as Tamils rather than as individuals. How can this dismal distinction bear upon whether the applicant has a well-founded fear of persecution?' The court held that 'the evidence clearly shows the reason for oppression to have been simply membership of the Tamil minority'.

[204] Economic reasons or motivation alone will not entitle a person to refugee status; but a government's 'economic measures' may well be the cloak for action calculated to destroy the economic livelihood of specific groups; in such cases, a fear of persecution can be well founded. Cf. Palley, *Constitutional Law and Minorities* (Minority Rights Group, report no. 36, 1978) on the subject of laws and administrative action designed to remedy economic imbalances, at 10: 'If the emphasis is on remedying disadvantage and lack of opportunity (such as special educational programmes, special

directed at groups identifiable by reference to the Convention reasons for persecution, and carried through with the object, express or implied, of excluding them from or forcing them into the mainstream of the new society. Where individual or collective measures of enforcement are employed, such as coercion by denial of employment or education, restrictions on language and culture, denial of access to food supplies, expropriation of property without compensation, and forcible or involuntary relocation, then fear of persecution in the above sense may exist; mere membership of the affected group can be sufficient. Likewise, where punishment under a law of general application may result, any necessary condition of singling out would be met by the decision to prosecute in a given case. The 1990 US Asylum Regulations explicitly dispense with the 'singling out' or 'targeting' requirement, if the applicant can show 'a pattern or practice . . . of persecution of persons *similarly situated* to the applicant,' and his or her 'own inclusion in or identification with such group of persons such that . . . fear of persecution upon return is reasonable.'[205] Whether a well-founded fear of persecution exists will depend upon an examination of the class of persons in fact affected, of the interests in respect of which they stand to be punished, of the likelihood of punishment, and the nature and extent of the penalties.

6. Persecution and lack of protection

Persecution under the Convention is thus a complex of reasons, interests, and measures. The measures affect or are directed against groups or individuals for reasons of race, religion, nationality, membership of a particular social group, or political opinion. These reasons in turn show that the groups or individuals are identified by reference to a classification which ought to be irrelevant to the enjoyment of fundamental, protected interests. Persecution results where the measures in question harm those interests and the integrity and inherent dignity of the human being to a degree considered unacceptable under prevailing international standards or under higher standards prevailing in the State faced with determining a claim to asylum or refugee status.[206] An element of relativity is perhaps inherent and

technical assistance programmes, special loan programmes in setting up co-operatives) or is protective (protection of native land against sale to capitalist entrepreneurs) it can be more readily tolerated by non-recipients. If it becomes an instrument of economic attack on other communities by denial of the right to engage in their traditional occupations, then it is proper to describe the technique as one of domination'.

[205] 8 CFR §208.13(b)(2)(i); §208.16(3)(i)(ii). Note the approach adopted in INS, Department of Justice, *Worldwide Guidelines for Overseas Refugee Processing*, Aug. 1983. See also *Gonzalez* v. *Minister of Employment and Immigration* [1991] FCJ No. 408 (FCA): 'Where the applicant makes a refugee claim on the basis of being a member of a particular social group, evidence regarding the experience of other members of that group is material to the applicant's claim.'

[206] For details of 'ethnic cleansing' and other events in former Yugoslavia, see the reports by Tadeusz Mazowiecki, Special Rapporteur of the UN Commission on Human Rights: UN docs. E/CN.4/1992/S–1/9 (28 Aug. 1992); E/CN.4/1992–/S–1/10 (27 Oct. 1992). The following historical examples provide illustrations of measures which may amount to persecution: the treatment accorded to those returned to the USSR after the Second World War: Bethell, N., *The Last Secret*

inescapable in determining the value to be attributed to the protected interest (for example, life and freedom of conscience), and the nature or severity of the measure threatened (for example, death and some lesser interference).

Although persecution itself is undefined by any international instrument, an approach in terms of *reasons, interests,* and *measures* receives support by analogy from the human rights field. The International Convention on the Suppression and Punishment of the Crime of Apartheid,[207] for example, identifies the 'crime of apartheid' very much in these terms. The *reasons* are self-evident—race and racial domination; the *interests* threatened and in need of protection include the right to life; liberty of the person; freedom; dignity; participation in political, social, economic and cultural rights; the right to work; the right to form trade unions; the right to education; the right to a nationality; freedom of movement and residence; freedom of opinion and expression; freedom of peaceful assembly and association; and non-discrimination. The measures that were used to defend apartheid and achieve its objectives included inhuman acts; systematic oppression; denial of rights; murder; infliction of serious bodily or mental harm; torture; cruel, inhuman or degrading treatment or punishment; arbitrary arrest; illegal imprisonment; deliberate imposition of substandard living conditions; legislative measures denying participatory rights; denial of development; segregation on racial lines; prohibition of mixed marriages; expropriation of landed property; forced labour; and denial of rights to political opponents.

The criteria for refugee status posited by article 1 of the 1951 Convention have the individual asylum seeker very much in mind. In the case of large numbers of asylum seekers, establishing a well-founded fear of persecution on a case-by-case basis can be impossible and impracticable. A prima facie or group determination, based on evidence of lack of protection, may therefore be the answer.[208] This solution is implied by the second leg of the refugee definition adopted in the 1969 OAU Convention and by the Cartagena Declaration, which extends to 'every person who, owing to external aggression, occupation,

(1974); Tolstoy, N., *Victims of Yalta* (rev. ed. 1979); relocation of national minorities in the USSR: *The Crimean Tatars, Volga Germans and Meskhetians* (Minority Rights Group, Report No. 6, rev. ed. 1980); mob and institutionalized attacks on members of the Baha'i faith in Iran: *The Baha'is in Iran* (Baha'i International Community, June 1981 and update); measures taken against ethnic minorities: *Selective Genocide in Burundi* (Minority Rights Group, Report No. 20, 1974); *What future for the Amerindians of South America?* (Minority Rights Group, Report No. 15, rev. ed. 1977); institutional and individual measures of repression against religious groups: *Religious Minorities in the Soviet Union*, (Minority Rights Group, Report No. 1, rev. ed. 1977); *Jehovah's Witnesses in Central Africa* (Minority Rights Group, Report No. 29. 1976); economic measures affecting Asians in East and Central Africa: *The Asian Minorities of East and Central Africa* (Minority Rights Group, Report No. 4, 1971); *Problems of a Displaced Minority: The new position of East Africa's Asians*, (Minority Rights Group, Report No. 16, rev. ed. 1978); the complex of measures aimed or calculated to deny self-determination: *The Kurds* (Minority Rights Group, Report No. 23, rev. ed. 1981); *The Namibians of South West Africa* (Minority Rights Group, Report No. 19, rev. ed. 1978); *The Palestinians* (Minority Rights Group, Report No. 24, rev. ed. 1979).

[207] Adopted by the UN General Assembly on 30 Nov. 1973: res. 3068(XXVIII). The Convention entered into force on 18 July 1976; by 30 Nov. 1995, 98 States were parties to the Convention.
[208] Cf. Sadruddin Aga Khan, Hague *Recueil* (1965–I) at 341.

foreign domination, or events seriously disturbing public order in either part or the whole of his country of origin or nationality', is compelled to seek refuge in another country.[209] Certainly, a group determination may be called for in the initial stages of any movement where protection and material assistance are the first priorities. It may also be appropriate in other contexts, for example, either where the need for protection is expected to be short-term and prospects for return in security are good; or, on the contrary, where the situation in the country of origin is so bad that practical realities dictate a prompt move in the direction of local asylum or resettlement. Establishing that civil war has broken out, that law and order have broken down, or that aggression is under way is relatively simple. The notion of lack of protection, however, is potentially wider and invites attention to the general issue of a State's duty to protect and promote human rights. Clearly, not every failure by the State to promote and protect, for example, the various rights recognized by the 1966 Covenants, will justify flight across an international frontier and a claim to refugee status. Not all the rights are fundamental, some are subject to progressive implementation only, while others may in turn be the subject of permissible derogations.[210]

The list of fundamental protected interests proposed above can be expanded in the future, as hitherto unrecognized groups and individuals press their claims, and as the value of certain economic and social rights is increasingly accepted. As noted above,[211] however, States are not currently willing to accept any formal extension of the 1951 Convention refugee definition, even as their practice commonly reflects recognition of the protection needs and entitlements of a broader class. Nevertheless, one legal implication of developments in favour of refugees and of human rights generally is that there are limits to the legitimate or permissible extent of State power. If individuals, social groups, and classes are at the absolute disposal of the State, then repression, re-education, relocation or even expulsion aimed at the restructuring of society can be considered comprehensible, even acceptable. But where there are limits to State power, and individuals and groups have rights against the State or interests entitled to recognition and protection, then such measures may amount to persecution. The traditional response to those who flee in fear of persecution has been to grant protection; increasingly, the international community now focuses its attention on the possibility of dealing with causes at source.

[209] For full texts, see Annexe 2, Nos. 1 and 7.

[210] Both the protection due to certain rights and the circumstances of permitted derogation are of course subject to development in international law. See, for example, the 1994 OAS Inter-American Convention on the Forced Disappearance of Persons: 22 *ILM* 1529 (1994); the preamble characterizes the act as a crime against humanity; art. II links the concept to 'agents of the State or . . . persons or groups of persons acting with the authorization, support, or acquiescence of the State', and art. X provides that exceptional circumstances do not justify forced disappearance, and that effective judicial procedures must be retained. Also, Inter-American Court of Human Rights, Advisory Opinion on Habeas Corpus in Emergency Situations, 30 Jan. 1987, AO OC-8/87: 27 *ILM* 512 (1988), noting that 'essential judicial remedies' should remain in force: paras. 27–30.

[211] See above, Ch. 1, s. 7.

Chapter 3

LOSS AND DENIAL OF REFUGEE
STATUS AND ITS BENEFITS

Most recent international instruments not only define refugees, but also provide
for the circumstances in which refugee status shall terminate or in which the
benefits of status shall be denied or withdrawn.[1] The IRO Constitution, for
example, described the circumstances in which refugees and the displaced would
'cease to be the concern' of the organization, and excluded various others,
including 'war criminals, quislings and traitors', and 'ordinary criminals . . .
extraditable by treaty'.[2] Article 14 of the Universal Declaration of Human
Rights prohibits invocation of the right of asylum 'in the case of prosecutions
genuinely arising from non-political crimes or from acts contrary to the purposes
and principles of the United Nations'. These categories have been expanded in
other instruments and in State practice so that, broadly, there are four sets of
circumstances in which refugee status may be lost or denied: (1) by reason of
voluntary acts of the individual; (2) by reason of change of circumstances; (3) by
reason of protection accorded by other States or international agencies; and (4)
in the case of criminals or other undeserving cases.

1. Voluntary acts of the individual

Both the UNHCR Statute and the 1951 Convention provide for loss of refugee
status where the individual, by his or her own actions, indicates that a well-
founded fear of persecution no longer exists or that international protection is
no longer required.[3] The circumstances include voluntary reavailment of the
protection of the country of origin, voluntary reacquisition of nationality, acquisition of a new nationality and the protection which derives therefrom, and voluntary re-establishment in the country of origin.

For the purposes of *reavailment of protection*, the refugee must not only act vol-

---

[1] See generally, Grahl-Madsen, A., *The Status of Refugees in International Law*, vol. 1, (1966),
262–304, 367–412; UNHCR, *Handbook on Procedures and Criteria for Determining Refugee Status*, (1979),
paras. 111–63; Weis, P., 'The Concept of the Refugee in International Law', *Journal du dr. inter.*,
(1960) 1, at 25–30; Tiberghien, F., *La protection des réfugiés en France* (2e. éd., 1988), 101–34, 441–76;
Hathaway, J., *The Law of Refugee Status*, (1991), 189–229.

[2] IRO Constitution, Section D; Part II.

[3] Statute, para. 6(a)–(d); Convention, art. 1 C (1)–(4). The French *Commission des recours* has held
that withdrawal in cases of fraud is also permitted: CRR, 2 mai 1988, *Dogan*, 59.037, *Doc. réf.* no.
79, 4/13 juill. 1989, Suppl., JC, 2.

untarily, but must also intend to and actually obtain protection.[4] Protection comprises all such actions by the refugee as indicate the establishment of normal relations with the authorities of the country of origin, such as registration at consulates or application for and renewal of passports or certificates of nationality. Sometimes, however, a refugee may be unwillingly obliged to seek a measure of protection from those authorities, as where a passport or travel document is essential to obtain the issue of a residence permit in the country of asylum.[5] Being involuntary, the protection obtained should not bring refugee status to an end.

In other cases of application for and obtaining a national passport or the renewal of a passport, it may be presumed, in the absence of evidence to the contrary, that reavailment of protection is intended. The presumption may be strengthened where the refugee in fact makes use of the passport for travel, or for return to the country of origin, or in order to obtain some advantage in the country of asylum that is dependent on nationality. Possession of a national passport and a visit to the country of origin would seem conclusive as to cessation of refugee status. Grahl-Madsen, however, suggests that 'physical presence in the territory of the home country does not *per se* constitute reavailment of protection . . . it is the conscious subjection under the government of that country . . . the normalization of the relationship between State and individual which matters'.[6] Indeed, on leaving the country of origin for the second time, the individual in question may well be able to show that he or she, still or once again, has a well-founded fear of persecution within the Convention.[7]

All the circumstances of the contact between the individual and the authorities of the country of origin must be taken into account. It is therefore relevant

[4] UNHCR, *Handbook*, paras. 118–25.
[5] Earlier decisions were abstracted in *Jurisprudence de la Commission de Recours des Réfugiés* (1961); a more accessible source today is Tiberghien, F., *La protection des réfugiés en France*, (2e. éd., 1988). See, for example, *Chimeno*, 1.208, 1.209, 25 oct. 1956—nationality certificate obtained at request of French authorities but not used to obtain any advantage not reavailment; *Grunberg*, 185, 19 janv. 1954—passport for journey to third country obtained from consular authorities at invitation of *Préfecture de Police* not reavailment: Tiberghien, *La protection des réfugiés*, 442–8; also at 396–8. See *Jagir Singh*, TH. 60274/92, 16 Jun. 1994, where the UK adjudicator held that renewal of passport during the asylum process for purpose of travel to a third State amounted to reavailment of protection; and similarly in Belgium: C.P.R., 2 ch., 11 déc. 1991, R226; V.B.C., 2 ch., 1er juin 1992, W526; cf. Conseil d'Etat, 13 janv. 1989, *Thevarayan*, 78.055, *Doc. réf.* no. 79, 4/13 juill. 1989, Suppl., JC, 6—fact of requesting issue or renewal of passport from diplomatic or consular authorities generally sufficient to raise presumption that the individual has re-availed himself or herself of the protection of their country of origin, but such presumption can be rebutted. It is error of law not to enquire into the reasons why.
[6] *Status of Refugees*, vol. 1, 384 f. See also *Dominquez del Rey*, 593, 29 jan. 1955—brief, clandestine return journeys to the country of origin not reavailment of protection; *Vallejo Leon*, 15.683, 26 Aug. 1982—return to country of origin following death of mother and to assist father, himself in ill health, also not reavailment: Tiberghien, *La protection des réfugiés*, 447; UNHCR, *Handbook*, para. 125.
[7] Note that art. 1C(4) of the Convention, which provides for cessation of refugee status on 'voluntary re-establishment' in the country of origin, clearly implies something more than mere presence.

to consider the age of the refugee,[8] the object to be attained by the contact,[9] whether the contact was successful,[10] whether it was repeated,[11] and what advantages were actually obtained.[12] In cases involving passports, it will be relevant if the refugee's country of residence is a party to the 1951 Convention and/or the 1967 Protocol, and so bound under article 28 to issue travel documents to refugees lawfully staying in its territory.[13] If not a party, that State may yet issue aliens passports or certificates of identity which enable the refugee to avoid recourse to his or her national authorities. In addition, it will be necessary to determine whether the national passport which the refugee obtains in fact reflects the full measure of national protection, for example, by enabling him or her to return freely to the country of issue.

These various issues were illustrated in the late 1970s when many Chilean refugees were found to be obtaining and renewing national passports, apparently without difficulty. In 1976 the Chilean Government had decided that passports might be issued or renewed for citizens abroad, even if they had refugee status and asylum in their country of residence. However, under a 1973 legislative decree,[14] persons who had left Chile to seek asylum, who had left illegally or been expelled or forced to leave, were prohibited from returning without express

[8] See *Ibanez bel Ramon*, 4.145, 18 oct. 1960; *Lopez Perez*, 2.049 et 2.423, 7 fév. 1958—only from age 18 should the individual be considered as understanding the nature of their acts: Tiberghien, *La protection des réfugiés*, 463, 471. The fact that the contact has been made on behalf of the refugee by a third party is not generally sufficient to rebut a finding of reavailment of protection; see *Morales*, 135, 19 jan. 1954: ibid., 443, 448.

[9] See *Borensztajn*, 3.355, 3 déc. 1959—passport renewed in order to obtain foreign visas for urgent journeys for professional purposes not reavailment: Tiberghien, *La protection des réfugiés*, 472; *Mendez Perez*, 1.486, 26 mars 1957—passport obtained and renewed by seaman for whom such document essential to pursue his profession not reavailment, particularly as document not valid for return to home country: ibid., 444.

[10] See *Bata Lojos*, 1.727, 24 oct. 1957—unsuccessful approach to consular authorities with view to repatriation not considered reavailment; *Kjosev*, 534, 29 jan. 1955—repatriation requested and passport permitting return obtained amounted to reavailment in absence any proof that refugee acted in moment of severe depression; *Michalska*, 6.681, 16 déc. 1969—single reference to consular authorities by mistake, in order to obtain renewal of residence permit in France not reavailment: Tiberghien, *La protection des réfugiés*, 443, 445.

[11] See *Llesta Escanilla*, 288, 21 juin 1954—nationality certificate obtained, apparently to facilitate reunion with minor daughter, but twice renewed and considered reavailment of protection; *Rebay Lazlo*, 55, 16 oct. 1953—unsuccessful application for passport but stated intention to apply again indicative of absence of fear, thus justifying refusal of recognition of refugee status; *Caballero Martin*, 133, 19 jan. 1954—obtaining and renewing passport amounted to reavailment of protection: Tiberghien, *La protection des réfugiés*, 209, 471.

[12] See *Roldan*, 271, 21 juin 1954—nationality certificate obtained to complete sale of property in country of origin, but not renewed or used to obtain any other advantage, not considered reavailment. Cf. *Rodriguez Martin*, 291, 21 juin 1954—nationality certificate obtained and used to renew residence permit amounted to reavailment; *Callado Sierra*, 562, 29 jan. 1955—similarly; *Codina Bea*, 941, 12 avr. 1956—initial reference to consular authorities with agreement of *Office français de protection des réfugiés et apatrides* followed by second reference with object of benefitting from advantages granted to those of applicant's nationality considered reavailment of protection: Tiberghien, *La protection des réfugiés*, 442, 444, 446.

[13] See further below, Ch. 8, s. 1.2.1.

[14] Art. 3 of Decree Law no. 81 of 11 Oct. 1973; *Diario Oficial*, no. 28694, 6 Nov. 1973.

authorization by the Minister of the Interior. Moreover, those returning without such permission were liable to prosecution.[15] Holding a Chilean passport could thus still be compatible with refugee status, although the holder might reasonably be required to explain why alternative documentation had not been obtained.[16]

Voluntary action is also explicitly required in respect of *re-acquisition of nationality*.[17] Such an act is more immediately verifiable than the notion of reavailment of protection, yet perhaps constitutes the supreme manifestation of the latter. There is less scope for explanation of extenuating circumstances: the intention of the individual and the effectiveness of the act will suffice in most cases.[18]

In the case of *acquisition of a new nationality*,[19] however, the individual must also enjoy protection by virtue of that status. The new nationality must be effective, in that at least the fundamental incidents of nationality should be recognized, including the right of return and residence in the State.[20] In a number of decisions in the 1950s, the French *Commission des recours* considered the refugee status of Jews who had travelled to and resided in Israel. The general view was that acquisition of Israeli nationality under the provisions of the Law of Return brought the individuals within the scope of article 1C(3), particularly where Israeli passports were later used.[21] In one case, the Commission held that the 'très graves difficultés d'existence' which had motivated the individual to leave

---

[15] Cf. Amnesty International *1978 Report*, 111; *1980 Report*, 118; *1981 Report*, 122–3.

[16] See *Petrow*, 637, 1er avr. 1955, where the *Commission des recours* took the view that use of a 'passport of convenience' issued by a third State had no effect on the holder's true nationality such as to remove the basis for her claim to refugee status; see also *Berline*, 577, 25 fév. 1955; *Ekmekdjian*, 313, 3 mars 1954: Tiberghien, *La protection des réfugiés*, 313, 474. In a series of cases in 1980, the Australian DORS Committee considered the weight to be accorded to Taiwanese passports held by Indo-Chinese seeking refugee status in Australia. The Committee noted that the Taiwanese authorities issued two types of passport, only one of which (the so-called 'MFA' passport) enabled the holder to return to and reside in Taiwan. Other passports, issued freely to 'overseas Chinese', amounted to no more than a travel facility and could not be equated with the full protection normally accorded to passport holders by the state of issue. Cf. *Hong*, 11.517, 21 avr. 1981—claimant, born in Vietnam of Chinese parents issued with passport by authorities in Taiwan where he had lived one year with his parents after leaving Vietnam. It was not alleged that the passport had been obtained by fraud or that it was a mere passport of convenience. Moreover, the document carried the mention, 'Overseas Chinese who has resided in the mother country', indicating that he was recognized as a Chinese national, having the right to reside in Taiwan and otherwise entitled to its protection: Tiberghien, at 473. See generally, Goodwin-Gill, *Movement of Persons*, 24–50; and on the nationality question, Tang Lay Lee, 'Stateless Persons and the Comprehensive Plan of Action–Part 1: Chinese Nationality and the Republic of China (Taiwan)', 7 *IJRL* 201 (1995).

[17] Statute, para. 6(b); Convention, art. 1C(2); UNHCR, *Handbook*, 126–8.

[18] Cf. *Gorbatcheff*, 772, 8 mars. 1955—nationality acquired on marriage lost following remarriage with refugee after divorce from first husband: Tiberghien, *La protection des réfugiés*, 450.

[19] Statute, para. 6(c); Convention, art. 1C (3); UNHCR, *Handbook*, 129–32.

[20] Cf. Goodwin-Gill, *Movement of Persons*, 45–9.

[21] See *Breitholz*, 208, 30 avr. 1954; *Schapira*, 237, 31 mai 1954—no steps taken to avoid the acquisition of nationality; 473 *Mincu*, 432, 21 juill. 1954—similarly, and no evidence that the individual applied for or was refused a Convention Travel Document: Tiberghien, *La protection des réfugiés*, 432, 449–51, 474.

Israel were not attributable to the political or administrative authorities and could not be equated with persecution or lack of protection.[22]

Finally, refugee status may be lost by *voluntary re-establishment in the country of origin*.[23] Something more than a visit or mere presence is required; the individual must have settlement on a permanent basis in view, with no evident intention of leaving.[24] Should the individual leave again and claim refugee status, the case will need to be considered in the light of events subsequent to re-establishment.

2. Change of circumstances

The 'change of circumstances' anticipated is clearly intended to comprehend fundamental changes in the country which remove the basis of any fear of persecution.[25] The replacement of a tyrannical by a democratic regime is an obvious example,[26] but the process of change may be more subtle and reflected over a number of years by legal reforms and gradual improvements in human rights. Amnesties are important and, provided they are effective, may also indicate that the grounds for refugee status have disappeared.[27]

A UNHCR discussion note on change of circumstances, presented to the Sub-Committee on International Protection in January 1992, noted that the cessation clauses were exhaustive, and that a strict approach to their application was called for.[28] This was endorsed by the Executive Committee later that year, when it stressed that,[29]

States must carefully assess the fundamental character of the changes in the country of nationality or origin, including the general human rights situation, as well as the partic-

[22] See *Arbusoff*, 11.898, 12 fév. 1981: Tiberghien, *La protection des réfugiés*, 239, 473.

[23] Statute, para. 6(d); Convention, art. 1C(4); UNHCR, *Handbook*, 133–4. Cf. IRO Constitution, part I D, below, Annexe 1, No. 1.

[24] See *Maqueda*, 59, 1er oct. 1953—two years' clandestine but voluntary residence amounted to voluntary re-establishment; cf. *Dominquez del Rey*, 593, 29 jan. 1955—short, clandestine visits to help family leave for France not reavailment: Tiberghien, *La protection des réfugiés*, 451, 447.

[25] Statute, para. 6(e), (f); Convention, art. 1C(5), (6). The difference in the wording of the two paragraphs reflects that between refugees with and refugees without a nationality.

[26] Cf. IRO Constitution, Annexe 1, No. 1, below, part 1 C 2.

[27] For example, after President Masie Nguema of Equatorial Guinea was overthrown in 1979, the new government enacted a general amnesty for all who had fled abroad for political reasons during the previous eleven years: Ministerial decree 45/1979, 10 Oct. 1979. The law was required to be transmitted to interested governments, the United Nations Secretary-General, the OAU Secretary-General, and UNHCR. See Amnesty International, *1979 Report*, 46–7; *1980 Report*, 43–4; for UNHCR's involvement in repatriation to Equatorial Guinea, see UN doc. A/AC.96/575, para. 381 (Aug. 1980).

[28] 'Discussion Note on the Application of the "ceased circumstances" Cessation Clause in the 1951 Convention': UN doc. EC/SCP/1992/CRP.1 (20 Dec. 1991). Some UNHCR official appears to blame for the linguistic aberration, 'ceased circumstances', inelegant in itself, and also somewhat misleading in its reference to the Convention provisions, which predicate the end or 'cessation' of refugee status on a sufficient change *in the factual base for a well-founded fear of persecution.*

[29] Executive Committee Conclusion No. 69 (1992) on Cessation of Status; for full text see below, Annexe 3. The draft conclusion was revised in two earlier inter-sessional meetings; see 'Report of the 13–14 April Meeting': UN doc. EC/SCP/71 (7 Jul. 1992), paras. 6–11; 'Report of the 25 June Meeting': UN doc. EC/SCP/76 (13 Oct. 1992), paras. 20–2.

ular cause of fear of persecution, in order to make sure in an objective and verifiable way that the situation which justified the granting of refugee status has ceased to exist . . . (A)n essential element in such assessment by States is the fundamental, stable and durable character of the changes . . .

UNHCR had argued that special weight should be attached to 'the level of democratic development in the country, its adherence to international human rights (including refugee) instruments and access allowed for independent national or international organizations freely to verify and supervise the respect for human rights'. Other, more specific factors might include declarations of amnesty, the repeal of repressive legislation, the annulment of judgments against political opponents and the general re-establishment of legal protection and guarantees. UNHCR emphasized 'that a minimum period of 12 to 18 months (always depending on the circumstances) should normally elapse before a judgment . . . can be considered reliable'. Conclusion No. 69, however, emphasizes that application of the cessation clauses is a matter 'exclusively' for States, although the High Commissioner should be appropriately involved.[30] States also considered that no particular time frame could be laid down as a condition of durable change,[31] but they accepted that every refugee affected by a cessation decision should be able 'to have such application in their cases reconsidered on grounds relevant to their individual case'.[32]

UNHCR noted that voluntary repatriation, as a matter of fact, often does away with the need for formal decisions by the Office on cessation, which had anyway been relatively rare.[33] At the same time, however, the Executive Committee acknowledged that a declaration by UNHCR that its statutory competence with regard to certain refugees had ceased to apply might be useful to States in applying the clauses.[34]

In practice, States rarely have recourse to cessation, particularly if recognition of refugee status has exhausted itself in the grant of permanent or indefinite residence, but provision for termination is often included in municipal legislation. Canadian law, for example, provides that a person ceases to be a refugee when

[30] UNHCR's offer to share its country of origin information with States was generally welcomed: 'Report of the 23 January Meeting': UN doc. EC/SCP/70 (7 Jul. 1992), para. 20; Executive Committee Conclusion No. 69, para. (b).

[31] 'Report of the 23 January Meeting': UN doc. EC/SCP/70, para. 20; see also generally paras. 11, 12, 14, 15.

[32] Executive Committee Conclusion No. 69, para. (d). A parallel paper introduced by the Swiss government in the Sub-Committee also emphasized the right to request reconsideration; see 'Report of the 23 January Meeting': UN doc. EC/SCP/70, para. 8.

[33] 'Discussion Note': UN doc. EC/SCP/1992/CRP.1, para. 19. UNHCR cited the following examples of formal determinations of cessation: Zimbabweans (1981), Argentinians (1984), Uruguayans (1985), Czechs (1991), Hungarians (1991) and Poles (1991). For UNHCR's involvement in repatriation of refugees from Angola and Zaire, see UN docs. A/AC.96/564, paras. 4–5, 255–6, 262, 275–80 (1979); A/AC.96/577, paras. 6–8, 20–2, 304, 315, 321–5 (1980); and in repatriation of Zimbabweans following independence: ibid., paras. 368–75.

[34] Executive Committee Conclusion No. 69, Preamble, third paragraph; see also 'Discussion Note': UN doc. EC/SCP/1992/CRP.1, para. 3.

'the reasons for the person's fear of persecution . . . cease to exist'.[35] The choice of words, varying slightly from those of the Convention, locates the issue firmly in a *procedural* context; and notwithstanding the rubric 'cessation', in Canada change of circumstances is considered as relevant to the existence of a well-founded fear of persecution on initial determination,[36] as to any later decision to bring refugee status to an end.

Canadian courts have several times reviewed the criteria by which to evaluate later events, much of it turning on whether the changes must be 'of substantial political significance', 'truly effective', and 'durable'.[37] The question frequently asked is whether there is a *prescriptive* sense to these factors, so that cessation is contingent on their existence; or whether they are merely *illustrative*.[38] In practice, the problem is essentially procedural, and goes to the burden and standard of proof: who must prove what, and when? Cessation or change of circumstances acquires meaning only in context, that is, first, where the claimant seeks to show today that he or she has a well-founded fear of persecution; or secondly, where the appropriate authority seeks to show that a previously recognized refugee should no longer be considered as such.

[35] Canada, *Immigration Act*, s. 2(2)(e). See also France, Ministère de l'Intérieur, Circulaire: NOR: INTD9000176C (non publiée), Objet: Réfugiés polonais, hongrois et tchécoslovaques. Cessation du statut de réfugié: *Doc. réf.* no. 135, 18/27 janv. 1991, annexe I—emphasizes that change of circumstances in no way prejudices the entitlement of citizens of the countries concerned to claim refugee status; also, that authority for withdrawal of refugee status rests with OFPRA, but that change of circumstances does not itself permit withdrawal or refusal of resident permits. This does not exclude the possibility of expelling otherwise deportable 'former refugees'; OFPRA, 'Note de Service: Procédure de retrait de la qualité de réfugié aux ressortissants de Pologne, Hongrie et Tchécoslovaquie', *Doc. réf.* no. 134, 8/17 janv. 1991, annexe II; Tiberghien, *La protection des réfugiés*, 114–34, 451–9.

[36] See *Mileva* v. *Canada* 15 Imm L.R. (2d) 204, 208 (1991): 'The question . . . is not whether the claimant had reason to fear persecution in the past, but rather whether he now, at the time his claim is being decided, has good grounds to fear persecution in the future . . .'

[37] The Canadian courts have concentrated in particular on the three-part test laid out in Hathaway, *Law of Refugee Status*, 199–203. On the general applicability of change of circumstances, see also CRR, 13 juill. 1989, *Derda*, 90.196, *Doc. réf.* no. 79, 4/13 juill. 1989, Suppl., JC, 2—fear of persecution by reason of activities with Solidarity at time when not officially recognized; even if true, no longer any fear of persecution given change of circumstances; CRR, 16 juin 1989, *Ahmad*, 86.625, *Doc. réf.* no. 79, 4/13 juill. 1989, Suppl., JC; 2; 1 juin 1989, *Ahmed*, 91.934, ibid., 3—political changes in Pakistan not such as to benefit the Ahmadi community.

[38] The change of circumstances cessation clause was first proposed by the French representative in the Third Committee: UN doc. A/C.3/L.123 (27 Nov. 1950), and was incorporated, apparently without debate, in a revised draft drawn up by an informal working group: UN doc. A/C.3/L.131/Rev.1, 1 Dec. 1950, and duly adopted in UNGA res. 429(V), 14 Dec. 1950, Annex, recommending the draft definition to the Conference of Plenipotentiaries to be held in July 1951. Apart from isolated references to the restoration of democracy, the *travaux préparatoires* do not deal with how or when change of circumstances should result in cessation of refugee status. France, for example, simply thought that a country which had 'returned to democratic ways' should 'take over the burden' of its nationals: UN doc. A/CONF.2/SR.28, pp. 12, 13. It had earlier explained this proposal by 'its desire to allow only persons who were still refugees to keep that status', while accepting that, 'in no case could the victims of racial persecution be compelled to resume their former nationality or resettle in countries where they had suffered so bitterly': ECOSOC, 406th Mtg., UN doc. E/OR(XI), p. 276, para. 58. Cf. Israel's view: UN doc. A/CONF.2/SR.23, pp. 20–1.

In the first instance, the burden of proof is on the claimant, and the standard of proof remains that of showing that the changes in question nevertheless leave open the existence of a serious risk or possibility of persecution. In the second instance, the burden is on the authority concerned, and the standard of proof for bringing refugee status to an end is the balance of probabilities—is the nature of the changes such that it is more likely than not that the pre-existing basis for fear of persecution has been removed? In either case, change alone may be insufficient; it is relevant only in relation to the claim, as part of the evidence of the existence or non-existence of risk. The central issue remains that of risk, the assessment of which is a matter of fact; no other *legal* condition is required, such as any degree of permanence, or the holding of elections.[39] Whether the change is significant, effective, durable or substantial is merely another way of describing its evidential weight.

The UNHCR Statute and the 1951 Convention deal somewhat differently with those who, having fled, may still be considered as having valid reasons for continuing to enjoy the status of refugee, any change in their country of origin notwithstanding. The Convention expressly acknowledges the weight to be accorded to 'compelling reasons arising out of previous persecution',[40] yet perversely limits the right to invoke such reasons to refugees recognized under earlier agreements. The Statute refers to 'grounds other than those of personal convenience' as justifying a refusal to have recourse to the protection of the country of origin, but without limiting their availability.[41] The object of this exception to the effects of a change of circumstances is clearly the continuation of protection for those who have suffered most seriously in their country of origin. One early commentator suggested that the provision is 'mainly intended to cover the case of victims of racial persecution where, unlike political persecution, the population as well as the government often took an active part'.[42] The severe and continuing nature of the injuries often suffered by the persecuted is also a reason for the exception to be widely applied, as was recognized by the Executive Committee[43] and is the case today in several jurisdictions.[44]

[39] In *Yusuf* v. *Canada (Minister of Employment and Immigration)* [1995] FCJ No. 35, the Federal Court of Appeal of Canada noted that 'the issue of so-called "changed circumstances" seems to be in danger of being elevated, wrongly in our view, into a question of law when it is, at bottom, simply one of fact'. The fundamental issue is the possibility or risk of persecution: 'there is no separate legal "test" by which any alleged change in circumstances must be measured. The use of words such as "meaningful", "effective" or "durable" is only helpful if one keeps clearly in mind that the only question, and therefore the only test, is . . . does the claimant now have a well founded fear of persecution?' To similar effect, see Conseil d'Etat, 19 déc. 1986, *Zapirain Elisalde*, 72.149: *Doc. réf.* no.1, 12/25 mai 1987, Suppl., Chronique de jurisp.

[40] Cf. IRO Constitution, Annexe 1, No.1, below, Part 1 C (a) (iii).

[41] The precise relationship between the various parts of para. 6 is far from clear.

[42] Pompe, C. A., 'The Convention of 28 July 1951 and the international protection of refugees', HCR/INF/42 (May 1958) 10, n. 3; originally published in Dutch in *Rechtsgeleerd Magazyn Themis*, (1956), 425–91.

[43] Executive Committee Conclusion No. 69, para. (e); the principle of 'acquired rights' was also recognized: ibid. See further 'Discussion Note': UN doc. EC/SCP/1992/CRP.1, paras. 5, 10–15.

[44] See UNHCR, *Handbook*, para. 136; also *Ibarguren Aguirre*, 10.884, 28 févr. 1984—the words,

3. Protection or assistance by other States or United Nations agencies

3.1 THE COUNTRY OF FIRST ASYLUM PRINCIPLE[45]

States have so far not accepted an obligation to grant asylum to refugees, and, otherwise than on a regional basis, have likewise failed to agree upon principles which would establish the appropriate State to consider applications in any given case. Article 31 of the 1951 Convention relating to the Status of Refugees requires refugees present or entering illegally not to be penalized, but is limited to those 'coming directly from a territory where their life or freedom was threatened'.[46] In discussions on this issue at the 1951 Conference of Plenipotentiaries, the then High Commissioner for Refugees, Mr van Heuven Goedhart, expressed his concern about the occasions when transit was necessary. Recalling that he himself had fled the Netherlands in 1944 to escape persecution, he told how, still at risk, he had been helped by the resistance to move on from Belgium to France, then Spain and finally to safety in Gibraltar. It would be unfortunate, said the High Commissioner, if refugees in similar circumstances were penalized for not proceeding 'directly' to a country of refuge.[47] At the time, however, a number of States were concerned that refugees 'who had settled temporarily in a receiving country' or 'found asylum', should not be accorded a 'right of immigration' that might be exercised for reasons of mere personal convenience.[48] The final wording of article 31 is in fact something of a compromise, limiting the benefits of non-penalization to refugees 'coming directly', but without further restricting its application to the country of origin.

With the background of this somewhat ambiguous reference, a practice developed in certain States of excluding from consideration the cases of those who have found or are deemed to have found asylum or protection elsewhere, or who are considered to have spent too long in transit.[49] Asylum and resettlement pol-

---

'compelling reasons arising out of previous persecution' apply to both statutory and non-statutory refugees, and also extend to violent persecution against the refugee or members of his or her family: Tiberghien, *La protection des réfugiés*, 252, and cases cited at 457–9. Canada's *Immigration Act* adopts the exception without limitation as to the class of refugees; see s. 2(3).

[45] On identification of the State responsible to determine an asylum claim, with reference also to the Dublin and Schengen Conventions, see below, Ch. 9, s. 2.1.1.

[46] For text, see below, Annexe 1, No. 4.   [47] UN doc. A/CONF.2/SR.14, pp. 4–5.

[48] France first favoured a limitation to refugees coming directly from their *country of origin*, objecting to the first draft which would have allowed the refugee, 'to move freely from one country to another without having to comply with frontier formalities': UN doc. A/CONF.2/SR.13, p. 13. This position was moderated in acceptance of the present wording, which is capable also of covering unsafe transit countries. What remains unclear is whether the refugee is entitled to invoke art. 31 when continued flight has been dictated more by the refusal of other countries to consider the claim or to grant asylum, for example, because of time limits, or exclusionary provisions such as those on safe third country, or safe country of origin.

[49] In the Federal Republic of Germany, asylum may not be claimed where the applicant comes from a safe third State, or has already found protection against persecution: *AsylVfG* 1993, art. 26a. Besides the Member States of the European Union, the following States had been listed as safe at 31 Jan. 1995: Czech Republic, Norway, Poland, Switzerland. Residence for three months or more raises a presumption that protection has been found, which can be rebutted by credible

icy tends to concentrate on refugees 'still in need of protection'. Consequently, a refugee formally recognized by one State, or who holds an identity certificate or travel document issued under the 1951 Convention,[50] generally has no claim to transfer residence to another State, otherwise than in accordance with normal immigration policies. Much the same approach has also been applied to refugees and asylum seekers who, though not formally recognized, have found protection in another State.[51] In resettlement countries, too, eligibility for special entry programmes may be conditional upon the refugee not otherwise having found a durable solution. Under United States law, a refugee has long been liable to refusal of admission if already established in another State.[52] A temporary refuge may not prejudice the claim to resettlement, but this will depend on all the circumstances, including whether the individual has established any business, or held an official position inconsistent with status, and the duration of stay.[53] This

evidence of a risk of expulsion to a State in which the claimant fears persecution: ibid., art. 27. In other countries, an applicant for refugee status may be barred from submitting or pursuing a claim if it is not made within a determined period after departure from the country of origin, or after the occurrence of events there which give rise to the fear of persecution, or after entry to the potential asylum country. See Amnesty International, 'Japan: Inadequate Protection for Refugees and Asylum Seekers', (1993); also published in 5 *IJRL* 205 (1993); Yamagami, Susumu, 'Determination of Refugee Status in Japan', 7 *IJRL* 60 (1995). For earlier accounts of the problem, see Melander, G., *Refugees in Orbit*, (1978); also, Grahl-Madsen, A., *Territorial Asylum*, (1980), 95–101; Raoul Wallenberg Institute, *Responsibility for Examining an Asylum Request*, Report of a Seminar in Lund, 24–6 April 1985, Report No. 1 (1986); Uibopuu, H. -J., 'Ss. 7(2) Asylgesetz und der "anderweitige Schutz" des Asylbewerbers', 34 *Österr. Z. Recht und Völkerrecht* 30 (1984); Kooijmans, P. H., 'Ambiguities in Refugee Law: Some Remarks on the Concept of the Country of First Asylum', in Nowak, M., Steurer, D., and Tretter, H., eds., *Fortschritt im Bewusstsein der Grund- und Menschenrechte. Progress in the Spirit of Human Rights. Festschrift für Felix Ermacora*, (1988), 401–14.

[50] 1951 Convention, arts. 27, 28; see further below, Ch. 8, s. 1.2.1.

[51] Effective 'protection' in this context would appear to entail the right of residence and re-entry, the right to work, guarantees of personal security and some form of guarantee against return to a country of persecution; see Uibopuu, above n. 49, proposing as conditions for an international standard that protection must be explicit, stay in the third State must have been of a particular duration, accompanied by residence permit and/or work permit and/or other possibility to integrate; and above all, protection against expulsion, extradition or *refoulement* to a State where life or freedom would be endangered. See also Tiberghien, *La protection des réfugiés*, 110–12, 466f. During the 1980s, German courts developed particularly strong, qualitative principles of protection on behalf of individual asylum seekers, thereby rendering 'protection elsewhere' ineffective as a basis for summary exclusion from the asylum procedure; see Marx, R., *Asylrecht*, (5. Aufl., 1991), vol. 1, 163–200. The 1993 constitutional changes, however, significantly strengthened limitations on access; see Ablard, T. and Novak, A., 'L'évolution du droit d'asile en Allemagne jusqu'à la réforme de 1993', 7 *IJRL* 260, 276–87 (1995).

[52] *Rosenberg v. Yee Chien Woo* 402 US 49 (1971): 65 *AJIL* 828 (1971): US Supreme Court held that presence in the United States must be a consequence of the flight in search of refuge, 'reasonably proximate to the flight and not following a flight remote in point of time or intervening residence in a third country reasonably constituting a termination of the original flight in search of refuge'. For early UK practice, see 469 HC Deb. col. 811 (1949).

[53] In 1979, the Australian DORS Committee disregarded the fact that various Indo-Chinese applicants had spent some time in camps in Malaysia and Thailand before travelling on by boat to Australia, on the ground that the 'transit' States could not be considered as potential countries of asylum. The *Conseil d'Etat* has held on several occasions that the mere fact of having resided in an intermediate country is not alone sufficient to justify refusal of refugee status; see *Conté*, 20.527, 16 janv. 1981; *Chin Wei*, 21.154, 27 mars 1981: Tiberghien, *La protection des réfugiés*, 238, 239, 466–7.

limitation now appears in the United States 1980 Refugee Act and regulations made thereunder,[54] and has also been used as a criterion for qualification in Canada's designated classes.[55]

Article 31 contains an obligation of essentially negative scope, prescribing what States shall *not* do with respect to certain refugees. Today, the problem is no longer non-penalization, but that of identifying which State is 'responsible' for determining a claim to asylum and ensuring protection for those found eligible. The 1951 Convention as a whole is silent with respect to such positive obligations, save so far as article 31 has come to be seen by some States parties as implicitly endorsing a concept of 'first country of asylum' and various legal consequences.

Problems arise, however, where the candidate for refugee status has not been formally recognized, has no asylum or protection elsewhere, but is nevertheless unilaterally considered by the State in which application is made to be some other State's responsibility. Individuals can end up in limbo, unable to return to the alleged country of asylum or to pursue an application and regularize status in the country in which they now find themselves. The absence of any convention or customary rule on responsibility in such cases, the variety of procedural limitations governing applications for refugee status and asylum, as well as the tendency of States to interpret their own and other States' duties in the light of sovereign self-interest, all contribute to a negative situation potentially capable of leading to breach of the fundamental principle of *non-refoulement*.

At the abortive 1977 United Nations Conference on Territorial Asylum, States reached a measure of agreement on the principle that,

---

[54] S. 201 introducing new s. 207(c) into the Immigration and Nationality Act 1952. The combined effect of statute and regulations is to disqualify refugees 'firmly resettled' in third countries from overseas admission. The individual will be considered 'firmly resettled' if, before seeking admission, he or she entered another State with, or received while there, an offer of permanent residence, citizenship or other type of permanent resettlement. The person concerned will not be considered firmly resettled, however, if he or she can show, either that entry into the other State was a necessary consequence of flight, that he or she remained there only so long as was necessary to arrange onward travel, and that no significant ties were established; or that the conditions of residence there were so 'substantially and consciously restricted by the authority of the country of refuge', that he or she was not in fact resettled. Relevant factors for consideration by the decision-maker include the living conditions of residents, type of housing and employment available, property and other rights and privileges, such as travel documents, rights of entry and return, education, public relief: 8 CFR §208.15. A similar disqualification applies to asylum, and the regulations require mandatory denial if 'the applicant has been firmly resettled within the meaning of §208.15': INA §207(c), §208(a); 8 CFR §208.14(c)(2). One denied asylum under 8 CFR §208.14(c)(2) may still be entitled to the benefit of withholding of deportation under INA §243(h); see Anker, D. E., 'First Asylum Issues under United States Law', in Bhabha, J. and Coll, G., eds., *Asylum Law and Practice in Europe and North America*, (1992), 150. Similarly, a refugee recognized in Canada, but denied landing under *Immigration Act*, s. 46.04(1)(d), is nevertheless entitled to non-removal under s. 53: 'no person who is finally determined . . . to be a Convention refugee . . . shall be removed from Canada to a country where the person's life or freedom would be threatened . . .'

[55] The Indo-Chinese and Self-Exiled Designated Classes regulations (SOR/78–931 and 933) referred to persons who 'have not become permanently resettled'.

Asylum should not be refused ... solely on the ground that it could be sought from another State. However, where it appears that a person before requesting asylum from a Contracting State already has a connection or close links with another State, the Contracting State may, if it appears fair and reasonable, require him first to request asylum from that State.[56]

The UNHCR Executive Committee adopted much the same approach in its 1979 Conclusion No. 15 on refugees without an asylum country, stressing the need for agreement on criteria to allow positive identification of the responsible State, taking account of the duration and nature of any stay in another country, as well as of the asylum seeker's intentions.

3.2 REFUGEES RECEIVING UNITED NATIONS PROTECTION AND ASSISTANCE

Palestinians are the only group in effect excluded by the words of the Statute and the Convention. The competence of the High Commissioner in the political issues surrounding the Palestinian question was once thought incompatible with the proclaimed non-political character of UNHCR's work,[57] but other factors were also at play. Egypt and members of the Arab group were wary, for example, lest the refugee definition then being debated in the United Nations lose sight of groups which were the particular concern of the General Assembly, and whose right to repatriate had been recognized in various resolutions. They therefore successfully argued that both the High Commissioner's mandate and the draft convention should exclude refugees falling within the competence of other United Nations agencies.[58] Solutions to the Palestinian problem by way of repatriation or indemnification were under consideration at the time,[59] and Palestinians were the responsibility of, and received assistance from, the United Nations Relief and Works Agency (UNRWA), established as a subsidiary organ by the General Assembly in 1949.[60]

UNHCR's competence under paragraph 6 of its Statute was therefore limited by paragraph 7(1), which provides that such competence shall not extend to a person, 'who continues to receive from other organs or agencies of the United Nations protection or assistance'. This exclusion also had a functional aspect and served to delimit the respective areas of responsibility of UNHCR, the

---

[56] See below, Annexe 4, No. 1.   [57] UN doc. E/AC.7/SR.172.

[58] Ibid., 328th Meeting, 27 Nov. 1950, paras. 37 (Egypt), 45–7 (Lebanon), 54–5 (Saudi Arabia). See also GAOR, 5th Sess., Plenary, Summary Records, 325th Meeting, 14 Dec. 1950, paras. 187–92 (Iraq). As early as 1946, in the Third Committee, the Egyptian, Iraqi and Lebanese representatives wanted a clear distinction to be made between 'the political and humanitarian aspects of the Jewish question': UN doc. A/C.3/SR.7, pp. 18–20, (4 Feb. 1946). Support for this approach was by no means limited to Arab States; the US, for example, endorsed the exclusion of certain groups, such as Palestinians, for whom the UN had made special arrangements. See for example, *Ad hoc* Committee on Statelessness and Related Problems: UN doc. E/AC.32/SR.3, paras. 35–48 (26 Jan. 1950).

[59] See, for example, UNGA resolutions 194(III), 11 Dec. 1948, and 393(V), 2 Dec. 1950; Radley, K. R., 'The Palestinian Refugees: The Right to Return in International Law', 72 *AJIL* 586 (1978).

[60] UNGA res. 302(IV), 8 Dec. 1949; see further below, Ch. 6, s. 1.2.

UNRWA, and the United Nations Conciliation Commission for Palestine (UNCCP).

At the 1951 Conference of Plenipotentiaries it was likewise decided to exclude Palestinians from the application of the 1951 Convention relating to the Status of Refugees.[61] Although political reasons were again involved, the pertinent issue this time was not that of inter-agency competence, but of rights and status. Hence the rider to article 1D:

When such protection or assistance has ceased for any reason, without the position of such persons being definitively settled in accordance with the relevant resolutions adopted by the General Assembly of the United Nations, these persons shall *ipso facto* be entitled to the benefits of this Convention.

In practice, assistance has been provided to Palestinian refugees by UNRWA, within the area of its operations and subject to the conditions of entitlement and registration.[62] No international agency has been charged with providing protection to Palestinian refugees, although elements of that function were entrusted to UNCCP.[63]

Article 1D is not free from ambiguity, however. On the one hand, it premises exclusion upon the continuing receipt of protection *or* assistance; on the other hand, it premises entitlement to the benefits of the Convention on the cessation *ipso facto* of protection *or* assistance, without the situation of such persons having been resolved, for example, through legal provision for and recognition of a separate nationality.

UNHCR has taken the view that a refugee from Palestine outside the UNRWA area 'may be considered for determination of refugee status under the criteria (well-founded fear of persecution) of the 1951 Convention'.[64] This interpretation does not appear to be correct on a literal reading of article 1D.

Palestinian refugees who leave UNRWA's area of operations, being without protection and no longer in receipt of assistance, would seem to fall by that fact alone within the Convention, whether or not they qualify independently as refugees with a well-founded fear of persecution. In practice, however, many States have resisted providing automatic Convention protection, contrary to what appears to be the clear intent of its terms.[65] For such States, the key issue

---

[61] Art. 1D: 'persons who are at present receiving from organs of the United Nations other than the United Nations High Commissioner for Refugees protection or assistance'.

[62] See below, Ch. 6, s. 1.2.

[63] But see Takkenberg, L., 'The Protection of Palestine Refugees in the Territories Occupied by Israel', 3 *IJRL* 414 (1991).

[64] UNHCR, *Handbook*, para. 143. This paragraph continues: 'It should normally be sufficient to establish that the circumstances which originally made him qualify for protection or assistance from UNRWA still persist and that he has neither ceased to be a refugee under one of the cessation clauses nor is excluded from the application of the Convention under one of the exclusion clauses'.

[65] See Marx, R., *Asylrecht*, (5. Aufl., 1991), Bd. 3, 1048–66; *BVerwG*, B.v.8.10.1974—'Er genießt im Libanon Schutz und Beistand der UNRWA' (at 1048–9); *BVerwG*, B.v.7.7.1987—art. 1A(2) of the 1951 Convention identifies the indices of political persecution for the purposes of art. 16 of the *Grundgesetz*. It does not follow, however, that other factual matters, which may be sufficient for

is not so much the status of Palestinians as refugees, but whether they are able to return to their (former) State of residence, or are, as stateless persons, claiming to be refugees as against that country. Article 1D of the 1951 Convention is thus not so much an 'exclusion' clause, as a contingent inclusion clause, merely postponing the incorporation of Palestinian refugees.[66]

The legal situation of Palestinians with respect to the 1951 Convention became somewhat more complex with the signing on 13 September 1993 of the *Declaration of Principles on Interim Self-Government Arrangements* in the West Bank and Gaza.[67] Notwithstanding the changed political situation, UNRWA retains competence with respect to those who left Palestine as a result of the 1948 conflict, and it continues to operate in Jordan, Syria, Lebanon, and the Gaza Strip.[68] Depending on future political developments, article 1D will likely continue to raise problems of interpretation and application.[69]

3.3 OTHER REFUGEES NOT CONSIDERED TO REQUIRE INTERNATIONAL PROTECTION

Finally, the Statute and the Convention exclude from any entitlement to protection those who, in their country of residence, are considered by the competent authorities 'as having the rights and obligations which are attached to the possession of the nationality of that country'.[70] The reference is clearly intended to take account of an effective nationality, such as that enjoyed by the so-called *Volksdeutsche*, or ethnic Germans, under article 116 of the Constitution of the

Convention refugee status, automatically satisfy the political persecution criterion: 'Nur aus den genannten Gründen verfolgungsbedrohte Personenkreis kommt nämlich in der BRD für die förmlich Anerkennung als Asylberechtigter in Betracht'. See also Tiberghien, *La protection des réfugiés*, 102, 466 (*Kassem*, 10, 451, 22 janv. 1980—no denial of protection by the *Lebanese* (sic) authorities. Compare Grahl-Madsen, *Status of Refugees*, vol. 1, 140–2, who is of the opinion that the words '*ipso facto*' in art. 1D imply that 'no new screening is required for the persons concerned to become entitled to the benefits of the Convention', and that on the cessation of UNRWA assistance and/or protection, those concerned 'will become a kind of "statutory refugees" . . .' Statutory refugees are those within the scope of article 1A(1) of the Convention, having qualified or been treated as refugees under earlier treaties and arrangements. Grahl-Madsen also suggests that the cessation of protection or assistance may result from departure from UNRWA's area of operations: ibid., 263–5.

[66] See, for example, the views of the French representative at the 1951 Conference: UN doc. A/CONF.2/SR.19, pp. 11–12; and of the Egyptian and Iraqi representatives: ibid., 16–17. Egypt proposed an amendment to the initial draft of article 1D, with the expressed object of ensuring that 'Arab refugees from Palestine who were still refugees when the organs or agencies of the United Nations at present providing them with protection or assistance ceased to function, would automatically come within the scope of the Convention'. See ibid., SR.29, pp. 5–9. The question is whether, without those organs or agencies ceasing to function as such, the requisite protection or assistance should be deemed to have terminated, either because of voluntary removal from the jurisdiction of UNRWA, or because of expulsion or denial of return to a country of residence, such as Lebanon.

[67] For text see 32 *ILM* 1520 (1993); 'The Civilian Judicial System in the West Bank and Gaza: Present and Future', International Commission of Jurists/Centre for the Independence of Judges and Lawyers, June 1994, 108.

[68] By UNGA res. 2252(ES–V), 4 Jul. 1967, the mandate for assistance was extended to other persons in the area in serious need as a result of the June 1967 war; operations were extended to Egypt on behalf of those displaced from the Gaza Strip.

[69] See further below, Ch. 6, s. 3.   [70] Statute, para. 7(b); Convention, art. 1E.

Federal Republic of Germany.[71] The IRO Constitution excluded Germans by name,[72] as did earlier drafts of the 1951 Convention,[73] but the general scope of the later provision is capable of extending to many other groups. The British Nationality Act 1948, for example, declared the citizens of independent Commonwealth countries to be British subjects or Commonwealth citizens, the expressions having the same meaning.[74] The assimilation of Commonwealth citizens to United Kingdom nationals strictly so-called was most fully realized in the years up to 1962, when all British subjects (Commonwealth citizens) had the unrestricted right of entry into the United Kingdom, whatever their country of origin. They were free to settle, they enjoyed the right to work and the right to vote, and they were not subject to removal; they also enjoyed the right after 12 months of residence to register as citizens of the United Kingdom. However, the most important of these indices of nationality have now been specifically removed, namely, the right to enter freely and the right not to be expelled. The distinction between non-patrial Commonwealth citizens and patrial citizens of the United Kingdom and Colonies is stated clearly in the Immigration Act 1971 which limits the 'right of abode' to the latter.[75] Simply describing non-patrial Commonwealth citizens as 'British subjects' did not constitute them nationals of the United Kingdom for the purposes of international law generally or article 1E of the 1951 Convention in particular. The term was a matter of internal law, from which the United Kingdom derived none of the rights (such as that of protection) or obligations (such as the duty of admission) that are the normal attributes of nationality in international law.[76] In 1981, a new 'British citizenship' was introduced, which became the sole criterion for the right of entry and residence in the United Kingdom.[77]

Article 1E of the Convention and the corresponding statutory provision do not require that the individuals in question should enjoy the full range of rights incidental to citizenship. Given the fundamental objective of protection, how-

[71] See further, Goodwin-Gill, *Movement of Persons*, 16–20. The agency responsible for refugees in the Federal Republic of Germany is correspondingly known as the *Bundesamt für ausländische Flüchtlinge* = Federal Office for *Foreign* Refugees. It is not competent for German 'refugees', whether they fled from the German Democratic Republic before reunification, or from German minority communities elsewhere in eastern Europe.

[72] Annexe I, part II, s. 4; see below, Annexe 1, No. 1. See also de Zayas, A., *Die Anglo-Amerikaner und die Vertreibung der Deutschen*, (1977); published in English as *Nemesis at Potsdam: the Anglo-Americans and the Expulsion of the Germans*, (1977).

[73] See, for example, Second Report of the Social Committee to ECOSOC: UN doc. E/1814, para. 4 (10 Aug. 1950).

[74] S. 1(2).

[75] S. 1(1), (2). Non-patrials are also liable to deportation; ibid. s. 3(5). Exemptions from deportation provided by s. 7 are limited to those ordinarily resident in the UK on 1 Jan. 1973.

[76] See Goodwin-Gill, *Movement of Persons*, 174–5.

[77] The British Nationality Act 1981 abandoned use of the term 'British subject' as a common description of all Commonwealth citizens, with certain savings. In 1979, changes in the UK immigration rules provided for the first time for the recognition of refugees from Commonwealth countries, who even if granted asylum had not previously been accepted under the Convention, because of their status as 'British subjects'; see 967 HC Deb. cols. 1379–80 (1979).

ever, the right of entry to the State and freedom from removal are to be considered essential.

4. Undeserving cases

A different drafting approach is used in the Statute and the Convention to describe those not deserving the benefits of refugee status,[78] but without great differences of substance.

4.1 CRIMES AGAINST PEACE, WAR CRIMES, AND CRIMES AGAINST HUMANITY

4.1.1 *The drafting history of article 1F(a)*

The Constitution of the International Refugee Organization, adopted by the UN General Assembly in 1946, explicitly excluded 'war criminals, quislings and traitors', those who had assisted the enemy in persecuting civilian populations, ordinary criminals extraditable by treaty, and those who had participated in any organization having the purpose of overthrowing by force the government of a UN Member State, or who had participated in any terrorist organization.[79] The exclusion of war criminals from the benefits of the 1951 Convention was first considered by the *Ad hoc* Committee on Statelessness and Related Problems at its initial session in January–February 1950, when article 14(2) of the Universal Declaration of Human Rights was cited.[80]

France submitted an alternative draft convention which would have denied recognition as a refugee to any person to whom article 14(2) applied.[81] 'War criminals', noted the French representative, 'would naturally be excluded'.[82] The representative for the United States, on the other hand, thought that as there were no longer any unpunished war criminals, there was no need to exclude them; common law criminals subject to extradition, however, should be excepted.[83] Not surprisingly, the United States position was challenged as premature by the Israeli delegate, who suggested that those guilty of persecuting others should also be expressly mentioned.[84] The draft duly prepared by an *Ad hoc* Committee Working Group proposed to frame exclusion by reference to the commission of crimes 'specified in Article VI of the London Charter of the International Military Tribunal or any other act contrary to the purposes and

---

[78] Statute, para. 7(d); Convention, art. 1F; UNHCR, *Handbook*, paras. 147–63, 175–80.

[79] IRO Constitution, Annex I, Pt. II.

[80] See *Memorandum by the Secretary-General*: UN doc. E/AC.32/2, 2 Jan. 1950, pp. 15–18, 22–3. 'Exclusion' was not mentioned as such. Art. 14(2), which provides that the right to seek and to enjoy asylum 'may not be invoked in the case of prosecutions genuinely arising from non-political crimes or from acts contrary to the purposes and principles of the United Nations', was cited in the context of admission of refugees.

[81] UN doc. E/AC.32/L.3, 17 Jan. 1950, 3.

[82] UN doc. E/AC.32/SR.4, 26 Jan. 1950, para. 25.

[83] UN doc. E/AC.32/SR.5, 26 Jan. 1950, para. 16.

[84] Ibid., para. 45. The French representative concurred: para. 73.

principles of the United Nations'.[85] Again, the United States had reservations regarding mandatory exclusion, preferring that each receiving State retain discretion in the matter.[86] This also produced a reaction,[87] leading France to counter with an amendment confirming an *obligation* not to apply the Convention to war criminals.[88]

In August 1950, the Economic and Social Council and the Third Committee each revised the exclusion provisions of the refugee definition, which now included references both to the IMT Charter and the Universal Declaration:[89]

The provisions of this Convention shall not apply to any person with respect to whom there are serious reasons for considering that (a) he has committed a crime specified in article VI of the London Charter of the International Military Tribunal; or (b) he falls under the provisions of article 14, paragraph 2, of the Universal Declaration of Human Rights.

In December 1950, this was duly recommended by the General Assembly to the Conference of Plenipotentiaries scheduled to meet in July 1951.[90]

At the 1951 Conference, the representative of the Federal Republic of Germany suggested referring to the 1949 Geneva Conventions as an alternative to the IMT Charter. 'By associating the Geneva Conventions with the work of the Conference, the humanitarian aims which should govern the Convention would be stressed.'[91] He emphasized nonetheless that all war criminals should be excluded from the Convention, and objected essentially to the *source* of the applicable rules.[92]

[85] UN doc. E/AC.32/L.6, 23 Jan. 1950.

[86] UN doc. E/AC.32/SR.17, 6 Feb. 1950, para. 37.

[87] See UN doc. E/AC.32/SR.17, para. 38 (Israel); ibid., SR.18 (France).

[88] The proposed French amendment provided that, 'The High Contracting Parties shall not apply the present convention in the case of a person they consider a war criminal . . .' Ibid., para. 5. It was adopted by the Committee: UN doc. E/AC.32/L.20/Rev.1.

[89] See UN docs. E/1814; A/1682. The Third Committee took note also of the Second Session of the *Ad hoc* Committee (UN docs. E/1850 and E/1850/Annex).

[90] UNGA res. 429(V), 14 Dec. 1950. The text of the draft convention was submitted to the Conference of Plenipotentiaries by the Secretary-General: UN doc. A/CONF.2/1, 12 Mar. 1951. It comprised the Preamble, adopted by ECOSOC in res. 319(XI)B II, 11 Aug. 1950; art. 1, the definition, adopted by the General Assembly; and the text of the remaining articles and annex, prepared by the *Ad hoc* Committee: *Report* of the Second Session, 14–25 Aug. 1950: UN doc. E/1850 and Annex.

[91] Conference of Plenipotentiaries on the Status of Refugees and Stateless Persons: UN doc. A/CONF.2/SR.19, p. 26; the German proposal is in UN doc. A/CONF.2/76.

[92] See A/CONF.2/SR.24, p. 7. As the representative for Germany pointed out, even art. 6 mentioned crimes committed 'before or during *the war*' (emphasis supplied). The representative of the Consultative Council of Jewish Organizations argued strongly against deletion of the reference to the London Charter, on the ground that its principles had since been twice confirmed by the UN General Assembly, and formulated by the International Law Commission (see UNGA resolutions 95(I), 11 Dec. 1946, and 177(II), 21 Nov. 1947); neither the Geneva Conventions nor the UN Genocide Convention had the same 'solid foundation': UN doc. A/CONF.2/SR.21, pp. 7–11, a view later reiterated by the Israeli delegate: A/CONF.2/SR.24, pp. 14–15. The Federal Republic of Germany replied that the objective would be as well met by a provision excluding anyone who had committed non-political crimes or acts contrary to the purposes and principles of the United Nations: A/CONF.2/SR.24, pp. 6–8.

The issue was referred to a working group,[93] which recommended the phrasing now found in article 1F(a).[94] It was adopted by twenty votes to one against, with two abstentions, the Israeli representative explaining that his negative vote was due to the omission of all reference to the London Charter, and to its possible political and moral implications.[95]

4.1.2 *The scope of article 1F(a)*

Even though the final text of article 1F(a) omitted all mention of the IMT Charter, the participating States clearly saw it as an appropriate and relevant source of international law.[96] Excluded are those 'with respect to whom there are *serious reasons* for considering' that they have committed a crime against peace, a war crime or a crime against humanity, which has been interpreted to require a lower standard of proof on matters of fact than a balance of probabilities.[97] Arguably also the crimes mentioned in article 1F(a) are necessarily extremely serious, to the extent that there is no room for any weighing of the severity of potential persecution against the gravity of the conduct which amounts to a war crime, a crime against peace or a crime against humanity. Being integral to the refugee definition, if the exclusion applies, the claimant cannot be a Convention refugee, whatever the other merits of his or her claim.[98]

4.1.2.1 Crimes against peace

Article VI of the IMT Charter provided for individual responsibility in the case of crimes against peace, defined to include 'planning, preparation, initiation or waging of a war of aggression or a war in violation of international treaties, agreements, or assurances or participation in a common plan or conspiracy for any of the foregoing'.[99] Control Council Law No. 10, from which the Allied

---

[93] Ibid., 16. The Canadian representative suggested that the working group might consider including a suitable reference to art. 30 of the Universal Declaration on Human Rights; in his view, one serious problem was that of refugees, or presumed refugees, who presented themselves and attempted then to subvert the country of refuge.

[94] A/CONF.2/SR.29, p. 9; A/CONF.2/92.

[95] In a commentary published after the 1951 Conference, the Israeli representative, Nehemiah Robinson, suggested that the agreed formulation of art. 1F(a) was broader than the corresponding reference to the London Charter in the UNHCR Statute, and took account of continuing work on the subject: Robinson, N., *Convention relating to the Status of Refugees: A Commentary*, (1953).

[96] 1946 London Agreement for the Establishment of an International Military Tribunal: 82 *UNTS* 279; confirmed by UNGA res. 3(I), 13 Feb. 1946 and 94(I), 11 Dec. 1946.

[97] *Moreno v. Minister of Employment and Immigration* 159 NR 210—the criteria are not satisfied if there are serious reasons for considering that an act *could* be classified as a crime against humanity, and so forth; it *must* be established that, in law, it definitely was. In another Canadian case, *Ramirez v. Canada (MEI)* [1992] FC 653, the Federal Court of Canada held that the words 'serious reasons for considering' in art. 1F imply a lower standard of proof than balance of probabilities.

[98] *Gonzalez v. Minister of Employment and Immigration* [1994] FCJ No. 765 (FCA)—the Court also held that it was not error of law for the first instance tribunal to apply the exclusion clause without making any explicit finding with respect to inclusion, that is, whether the claim to refugee status was well-founded.

[99] See Brownlie, I., *International Law and the Use of Force by States*, (1963), Ch. IX.

Military Tribunals in Germany derived their jurisdiction to try other war criminals, similarly provided that crimes against peace included the 'initiation of
invasions of other countries and wars of aggression in violation of international
law and treaties . . .' Here and in domestic war trials, as in the trials of the major
war criminals, those accused were 'almost exclusively leading members of the
governments and High Commands of the Axis States and those convicted on
such charges were principally the "policy-makers".'[100] Brownlie notes that neither the soldier in the field, nor the civilian who supported the war effort, were
intended to be punished under these provisions.[101]

Article 20 of the 1994 Draft Statute for an International Criminal Court
drawn up by the International Law Commission includes the 'crime of aggression' within those for which the Court has jurisdiction.

4.1.2.2 War crimes

'War crimes' are defined as violations of the laws or customs of war, including
'murder, ill-treatment or deportation to slave labour or for any other purpose of
civilian population of or in occupied territory, murder or ill-treatment of prisoners of war or persons on the seas, killing of hostages, plunder of public or private property, wanton destruction of cities, towns or villages, or devastation not
justified by military necessity'. Just as the International Military Tribunal succeeded to an existing body of law, so article 1F(a) today must be interpreted in
the light of more recent developments and the 'relevant international instruments' referred to have been considerably supplemented since 1951. The principles of the IMT Charter have been strengthened by the 1949 Geneva
Conventions and the 1977 Additional Protocols. 'War crimes' are thus considered to include the 'grave breaches' of the Geneva Conventions,[102] summarized
in the 1993 Statute of the International Tribunal on Yugoslavia to include any
of the following acts: wilful killing; torture or inhuman treatment, including bio-
logical experiments; wilfully causing great suffering or serious injury to body or
health; extensive destruction and appropriation of property, not justified by military necessity and carried out unlawfully and wantonly; compelling a prisoner
of war or a civilian to serve in the forces of a hostile power; wilfully depriving a
prisoner of war or a civilian or the rights of fair and regular trial; unlawful

---

[100] Brownlie, *Use of Force*, 176, 197.

[101] Ibid., 195.

[102] Art. 50, 1949 Geneva Convention for the Amelioration of the Condition of Wounded and
Sick in Armed Forces in the Field; see also arts. 50, 51, 1949 Geneva Convention for the
Amelioration of the Condition of Wounded, Sick and Shipwrecked Members of the Armed Forces
at Sea; arts. 129, 130, 1949 Geneva Convention relative to the Treatment of Prisoners of War; arts.
146, 147, 1949 Geneva Convention relative to the Protection of Civilian Persons in Time of War;
arts. 11, 85, Additional Protocol I. The term 'war crimes' is not used in the Conventions, but art.
85 of Additional Protocol I provides that grave breaches shall be considered as such: art. 85(5). See
generally, Rikhof, J., 'War Crimes, Crimes against Humanity and Immigration Law', 19 *Imm. L.R.*
(2d) 18.

deportation or transfer or unlawful confinement of a civilian; and taking civilians as hostages.[103]

Additional Protocol I also includes attack on or indiscriminate attack affecting the civilian population; attack on those known to be *hors de combat*; population transfers;[104] practices of *apartheid* and other inhuman and degrading practices involving outrages on personal dignity based on racial discrimination; and attacking non-defended localities and demilitarized zones.

4.1.2.3 Crimes against humanity

Crimes against humanity, as is clear from the definition provided by the IMT Charter, are akin to war crimes, save on a larger scale; the concept led directly to the Genocide Convention,[105] and inspired the 1973 International Convention on the Suppression and Punishment of the Crime of Apartheid.[106] The Statutes for the Tribunals on Yugoslavia and Rwanda each provide for jurisdiction with respect to crimes against humanity, defined to include murder, extermination, enslavement, deportation, imprisonment, torture, rape, persecutions on political, racial and religious grounds, and other inhumane acts.[107] The draft articles on

---

[103] Besides providing for jurisdiction to prosecute persons 'committing or ordering to be committed grave breaches of the Geneva Conventions' (art. 2), the 1993 Statute of the International Tribunal on Yugoslavia makes similar provision for persons 'violating the laws and customs of war' (art. 3): Text in *Report* of the Secretary-General pursuant to para. 2 of Security Council Resolution 808 (1993): UN doc. S/25704, 3 May 1993, Annex; see also Akhavan, P., 'Punishing War Crimes in the Former Yugoslavia: A Critical Juncture for the New World Order', 15 *HRQ* 262 (1993). The 1994 Statute of the International Tribunal on Rwanda provides for jurisdiction to prosecute 'persons committing or ordering to be committed serious violations of Article 3 common to the Geneva Conventions . . . and of Additional Protocol II thereto' (art. 4): Text in SC res. 955 (8 Nov. 1994), Annex. The 1994 Draft Statute of the International Criminal Court similarly provides for jurisdiction with respect to 'serious violations of the laws and customs applicable in armed conflict', as well as certain crimes established under treaty, including the 1949 Geneva Conventions, Additional Protocol I, and the 1984 UN Convention against Torture (art. 20 and Annex): Text in *Report of the International Law Commission*, (1994), UN GAOR, 49th Sess., Suppl. No. 10 (A/49/10). See UNHCR, *Handbook*, Annex VI, for an earlier list of the main international instruments relating to art. 1F(a).

[104] Either of the State's own population into occupied territory, or of the local population out of occupied territory: art. 85(4)(a).

[105] 78 *UNTS* 277.

[106] UNGA res. 3068(XXVIII), 30 Nov. 1973. Under art. 1, States parties declare apartheid to be a crime against humanity, undertake to adopt appropriate legislative and administrative measures to prosecute and punish those responsible, and agree that the acts constituting the crime shall not be considered political crimes. On the relation between war crimes, crimes against humanity, genocide, and apartheid, see generally Ruhashyankiko, N., 'Study of the Question of the Prevention and Punishment of the Crime of Genocide': UN doc. E/CN.4/Sub. 2/416, (1978), paras. 377–408.

[107] See art. 5, 1993 Statute of the International Tribunal on Yugoslavia, referring to crimes 'committed in armed conflict, whether international or internal in character, and directed against any civilian population'; art. 3, 1994 Statute of the International Tribunal on Rwanda, referring to crimes 'committed as part of a widespread or systematic attack against any civilian population on national, political, ethnic, racial or religious grounds'; cf. *Gonzalez* v. *Minister of Employment and Immigration* [1994] FCJ No. 765 (FCA)—killing of civilians during the course of armed action found not to be a war crime or crime against humanity; *Equizabal* v. *Minister of Employment and Immigration* [1994] FCJ No. 807 (FCA)—claimant, deserter from the Guatemalan army admitted torturing civilians; excluded on ground of crime against humanity and defence of superior orders not made out. See also Meron, T., 'Rape as a Crime under International Humanitarian Law', 87 *AJIL* 424 (1993).

State responsibility also establish a category of international crimes, in cases of 'a serious breach on a wide-spread scale of an international obligation of essential importance for safeguarding the human being, such as those prohibiting slavery, genocide and apartheid'.[108]

4.1.3 Individual responsibility

The International Military Tribunal had no hesitation on the issue of individual criminal responsibility; that a soldier was ordered to kill or torture in violation of the international law of war had never been recognized as a defence.[109] This responsibility derives ultimately from international law, whether it is established by an international tribunal, or by a domestic court whose competence itself is based on international law. The Tribunal rejected the argument that international law was concerned only with the actions of sovereign States, and that those who carried out such actions might be protected by the doctrine of State sovereignty:

individuals have international duties which transcend the national obligations of obedience imposed by the individual State. He who violates the laws of war cannot obtain immunity while acting in pursuance of the authority of the State, if the State in authorising action moves outside its competence under international law.[110]

The 1949 Geneva Conventions specifically provide for individual responsibility. Each Convention, for example, requires of each party that it search out persons, regardless of nationality, who are alleged to have committed, or ordered to be committed, a grave breach of a Convention, and to prosecute them.[111] The applicability of the principle of individual responsibility is widely recognized in the manuals of military law issued by States to their armed forces.[112] It is clarified further in the Statutes of the Tribunals on Yugoslavia and Rwanda, which

---

[108] Art. 19(3)(c): *Yrbk.*, International Law Commission, (1976), ii, (Pt. 2), 95–122. See also arts. 19 (genocide), 21 (systematic or mass violations of human rights), 22 (exceptionally serious war crimes): International Law Commission, Draft Articles on the Draft Code of Crimes against the Peace and Security of Mankind: UN doc. A/46/405, 11 Sept. 1991, Pt. IV. Cf. Preamble, 1994 Inter-American Convention on the Forced Disappearance of Persons, referring to the offence in question as a crime against humanity: Text in 33 *ILM* 1529 (1994).

[109] See generally *Attorney-General of Israel* v. *Eichmann* 36 *ILR* 277 (Supreme Court of Israel, 1962); *The Queen* v. *Imre Finta* [1994] SCJ No. 26; *In Matter of Demjanjuk*, 603 F. Supp. 1468; aff'd 776 F.2d 571; *Barbie* [1983] *Gaz. Pal. Jur.* 710 (Cass. crim., 6 Oct. 1983); *Barbie* (1988) *Sem. Jur. II*, 21149 (Cass. crim., 3 juin 1988). In *Barbie*, the court confirmed the non-applicability of any limitations period with respect to crimes against humanity.

[110] Judgment of the Nuremburg International Military Tribunal, 41 *AJIL* 172 (1947). In *Sivakumar* v. *Minister of Employment and Immigration* [1993] FCJ No. 1145; 163 NR 197, a senior member of the Sri Lankan LTTE was held excluded, the court ruling in a comprehensive judgment that non-governmental entities can commit crimes against humanity.

[111] See, for example, art. 49, 1949 Geneva Convention for the Amelioration of the Condition of the Wounded and Sick in Armed Forces in the Field.

[112] See, for example, the British *Manual of Military Law (Pt. III, The Law of War on Land)*. Grahl-Madsen is also of the view that it is reasonable to include within article 1F(a) anyone guilty of any of the grave breaches identified in the Geneva Conventions: *Status of Refugees*, vol. 1, 276.

stress that the 'official position of any accused person, whether as Head of State or Government or as a responsible Government official, shall not relieve such person of criminal responsibility nor mitigate punishment'.[113] A superior may also be responsible for the actions of a subordinate,[114] and while the subordinate will not be relieved of responsibility, superior orders may be considered in mitigation of punishment.[115]

A distinction must nevertheless be drawn between 'mere' membership of an organization which engages in international crimes, and actual complicity. The International Military Tribunal accepted that such membership was not sufficient to establish liability,[116] and recent jurisprudence has also required 'personal and knowing participation'.[117]

4.2 SERIOUS NON-POLITICAL CRIMES

4.2.1 *The drafting history of article 1F(b)*

Criminal and other undesirable refugees received little attention in the instruments and arrangements of the inter-war and immediate post-war period.[118] The IRO Constitution excluded refugees who were 'ordinary criminals . . . extraditable by treaty',[119] in terms to be recalled by the UNHCR Statute;[120] and article 14(2) of the Universal Declaration of Human Rights seems to rule out asylum 'in the case of prosecutions genuinely arising from non-political crimes'.

[113] Art. 7(2), 1993 Statute of the International Tribunal on Yugoslavia; art. 6(2), 1994 Statute of the International Tribunal on Rwanda.

[114] Ibid., arts. 7(3) and 6(3), respectively. Responsibility is contingent on the superior knowing or having reason to know that the subordinate was about to commit or had committed the crimes in question, and having failed to take reasons measures to prevent their commission or to punish the perpetrators.

[115] Art. 6(4), 1994 Statute of the International Tribunal on Rwanda. The 1993 Statute of the International Tribunal on Yugoslavia contains no equivalent provision; see art. 7.

[116] See Grahl-Madsen, *Status of Refugees*, vol. 1, 277.

[117] See *Ramirez* v. *Minister of Employment and Immigration* [1992] 2 FC 306—proposing a three-part test for complicity: (1) membership in an organization which committed international offences as a continuous and regular part of its operation; (2) personal and knowing participation; and (3) failure to disassociate from the organization at the earliest safe opportunity. Mere presence at the scene of crimes was insufficient, although being an associate of principal offenders may be. Although he had not personally tortured anyone, the applicant was excluded, as a participating and knowing member. Cf. *Moreno* v. *Minister of Employment and Immigration* 159 NR 210—witness of torture incident by forcible conscript in El Salvador not sufficient to exclude.

[118] The 1936 provisional agreement on German refugees, for example, proposed limiting expulsion to reasons of national security or public order: art. 4(2); text in 171 *LNTS* No. 3952; see also art. 5, 1938 Convention concerning the Status of Refugees coming from Germany: 192 *LNTS* No. 4461. The UK made a reservation to the effect that refugees subject to extradition proceedings commenced in the UK were not to be regarded as entitled to claim protection; and declared that 'public order' included matters relating to crime and morals.

[119] The IRO's *Eligibility Manual* included the following extradition crimes: murder, poisoning, rape, arson, forgery, issuing counterfeit money, perjury, theft, bankruptcy, receiving stolen goods, embezzlement, bigamy, assault, grave injury, and malicious destruction. Cf. Shearer, I.A., *Extradition in International Law*, (1971), ch. 5.

[120] Para. 7(d) excludes those whom there are serious reasons for considering have 'committed a crime covered by the provisions of treaties of extradition'.

Apart from the immediate concern of States with the exclusion of war criminals and their surrender to prosecution, the *travaux préparatoires* of the 1951 Convention disclose many unanswered questions relating to the general exclusion of criminals from the benefits of refugee status. The Convention finally uses the deceptively simple phrase, 'serious non-political crime', as the basis and limits such crimes to those committed 'outside the country of refuge prior to . . . admission . . . as a refugee'.[121]

As noted above, the British representative at the 1951 Conference objected to article 14(2) of the Universal Declaration as a reference for exclusion, arguing that it was arbitrary and unjust to place beyond protection all who might be caught by the notion of 'prosecutions genuinely arising from non-political crimes'.[122] France in turn objected that it was impossible to drop the limiting clause with respect to common law criminals, who should be eliminated from the definition.[123] The British concern remained not to prejudice those guilty of minor crimes; that of France, to retain discretion to grant asylum to minor criminals, but without being obliged to recognize refugee status; and that of other States, to avoid a clash of obligations between the Convention and extradition treaties.[124] One representative also suggested that it would be necessary to balance the seriousness of the crime against the degree of inconvenience or persecution feared.[125]

In later debate, the British representative reiterated that such a provision might be used to revoke the refugee status or asylum of one who committed a crime *after* entry, in circumstances in which the exceptional limitations on *non-refoulement* did not apply.[126] The Conference eventually agreed that crimes committed before entry were at issue, and that the word *crime* should be qualified by the word *serious*,[127] thus moving the exclusion clause nearer to the *non-refoulement* exception.[128]

---

[121] Cf. art. 32 regarding the circumstances in which lawfully resident refugees may be expelled, below, Ch. 4, s. 3.2.4, and Ch. 8, s. 1.2.3.

[122] See UN doc. A/CONF.2/SR.24, p. 4.   [123] Ibid., 5.

[124] Ibid., 9–16.   [125] Denmark: ibid., 13.

[126] UN doc. A/CONF.2/SR.29, pp. 11–12. The summary records reveal shared concerns, but little consensus. The Netherlands thought it illogical to exclude common criminals from the benefits of the Convention, but appropriate that they should not enjoy the right of asylum. Belgium thought there should be no denial of refugee status to a person simply because of conviction for a criminal offence, but that some reference to extradition was called for: UN doc. A/CONF.2/SR.29, pp. 11–12.

[127] UN doc. A/CONF.2/SR.29, pp. 17–24; cf. Tiberghien, F., 'La Commission des recours et l'article 1er, F de la Convention de Genève', *Doc. réf.* no. 169, 19 déc. 1991/1er janv. 1992, Suppl., JC, 1–8—criticizes CRR's abandonment of authorial intention, in favour of exclusion also for crimes committed within territory by one who has not yet obtained, or even applied for, refugee status; cf. CRR, 15 janv. 1991, *Saleh,* 130.181—exclusion for narcotics offences applies *a fortiori* to crimes committed in France by one who has not yet asked for or been granted refugee status; CRR, 8 fév. 1991, *Kacar,* 98.732—similarly, explosives offences.

[128] On art. 33(2), see further below, Ch. 4, s. 3.2.

4.2.1.1 The relation to extradition

What remains unclear is whether the drafters intended the exclusion clause to have more than an incidental role in the extradition process.[129] In addition, the *travaux préparatoires* do not reveal whether the commission of a serious crime outside the country of refuge was to be a permanent bar to refugee status; or whether the exclusion might be expunged by the lapse of time, by prosecution and conviction, by the serving of a sentence duly imposed, or by amnesty or pardon. The UNHCR *Handbook* notes:

In evaluating the nature of the crime presumed to have been committed, all the relevant factors—including any mitigating circumstances—must be taken into account. It is also necessary to have regard to any aggravating circumstances as, for example, the fact that the applicant may already have a criminal record. The fact that an applicant convicted of a serious non-political crime has already served his sentence or has been granted a pardon or has benefited from an amnesty is also relevant. In the latter case, there is a presumption that the exclusion clause is no longer applicable, unless it can be shown that, despite the pardon or amnesty, the applicant's criminal character still predominates.[130]

This statement of position leaves much to be desired. Its foundation on a principle of liberal interpretation is unexceptional in a commentary on a humanitarian instrument such as the 1951 Convention.[131] On the one hand, however, it seems to confirm that the role of article 1F(b) is not confined to extradition and prosecution as an immediate, or present process; on the other hand, it suggests that continuing exclusion may be justified by continuing criminal character, in a manner reminiscent of article 33(2).

Referring to the IRO Constitution, the Universal Declaration of Human Rights and the UNHCR Statute, Grahl-Madsen emphasized the objective of exclusion as ensuring that international instruments are not abused by 'fugitives from justice', and do not interfere with the law of extradition.[132] This led him

---

[129] Whatever may have been the legal situation in 1951, later developments in treaty law and the practice of States have confirmed that the principle of *non-refoulement* includes extradition; and that a refugee should not be extradited to a country in which he or she may be persecuted for Convention reasons. See Ch. 4, s. 3.3.3.

[130] UNHCR, *Handbook on Procedures and Criteria for Determining Refugee Status*, (1979), paras. 151–61, at 157.

[131] Cf. *Handbook*, para. 149: 'Considering the serious consequences of exclusion for the person concerned, . . . the interpretation of these exclusion clauses must be restrictive'. This position is determined by the overall approach to the refugee definition, which supposes that a person must first be found to satisfy the 'inclusion' provisions of art. 1A(2) (that is, to have a well-founded fear of persecution), before he or she can be considered as excluded under any of the subsequent provisions. In practice, the two issues frequently run together, and separation becomes quite arbitrary.

[132] A similar view is advanced by Tiberghien, *La protection des réfugiés en France*, (2e. éd., 1988), 103: 'L'article 1er F, b répond uniquement au désir des auteurs de la Convention d'exclure de son bénéfice les criminels qui cherchaient à obtenir le statut de réfugié dans un pays tiers pour échapper à une condamnation de droit commun dans leur pays d'origine.' The French representative at the 1951 Conference, however, seems to have been pressing for a wider discretion to deny refugee status to common criminals. In *Canada (Attorney-General)* v. *Ward* [1993] 2 SCR 689 the Supreme Court of Canada inclined to the view that art. 1F(b) was confined to accused persons who are fugitives from

to conclude that, given the non-applicability of extradition where the individual has already been convicted and punished, pardoned or amnestied, or has benefited from a statute of limitations, any such crimes as may have been committed 'should not be held against persons seeking recognition as refugees'.[133] He also took the view that war criminals are not excluded, provided that their fear of persecution is not related to the fear of repercussions for their criminal activity, and that their criminal character does not outweigh their character as refugees.

Although the *travaux préparatoires* provide no hard answers, a more principled approach may be justified. First, States were determined to limit the discretion to accord refugee status to war criminals.[134] Secondly, States have acted, both internationally and regionally,[135] to ensure that statutes of limitation shall not run in favour of war criminals. Thirdly, the notion of serious non-political crime, as understood in State extradition practice both before and after the conclusion of the 1951 Convention, reveals a striking similarity with many crimes against the laws of war. Finally, a principled basis justifying the continuing exclusion of serious non-political criminals is offered by the need to ensure the integrity of the international system of protection of refugees. The commission of a serious non-political crime may be sufficient reason for exclusion because it is indicative of some future danger to the community of the State of refuge; or because the very nature and circumstances of the crime render it a basis for exclusion in itself, regardless of extradition, prosecution, punishment or non-justiciability. In such cases, the principle of balancing crime against consequences becomes redundant.

4.2.1.2 'Serious' and 'non-political'

That the individual who had committed a political crime was to be distinguished from the 'common criminal'[136] is illustrated well by the equally authoritative French text of article 1F(b):

Les dispositions de cette convention ne seront pas applicables aux personnes dont on aura des raisons sérieuses de penser:

. . .

(b) Qu'elles ont commis *un crime grave de droit commun* en dehors du pays d'accueil avant d'y être admises comme réfugiés. (Emphasis supplied)

---

prosecution, as consistent with the *travaux préparatoires*. Rikhof doubts that this interpretation stands scrutiny, a reading of the *travaux* showing that they are nebulous at best: Rikhof, J., 'War Crimes, Crimes against Humanity and Immigration Law', 19 *Imm. L.R.* (2d) 18.

[133] Grahl-Madsen, *Status of Refugees*, vol. 1, (1966), 291f.

[134] See above, text to n. 81–90.

[135] See 1968 Convention on the Non-Applicability of Statutory Limitations of War Crimes and Crimes against Humanity: UNGA res. 2391 (XXIII), 26 Nov. 1968; in force Nov. 1970; also art. 1, 1975 Additional Protocol to the European Convention on Extradition: below, Annexe 2, No. 11.

[136] See, for example, UN docs. A/CONF.2/SR.24, pp. 5, 10 (France); SR.29, p. 12 (The Netherlands).

Each State must determine what constitutes a serious crime, according to its own standards, considered against the objectives of the 1951 Convention.[137] It thus has some discretion in determining whether the criminal character of the applicant for refugee status in fact outweighs his or her character as *bona fide* refugee, and so constitutes a threat to its internal order.[138] Just as the 1951 Conference rejected 'extradition crimes' as an excludable *category*, so *ad hoc* approaches founded on length of sentence are of little help,[139] unless related to the nature and circumstances of the offence.[140] Commentators and jurisprudence seem to agree, however, that serious crimes, above all, are those against physical integrity, life and liberty.[141]

The problem of determining whether a crime is political has already been considered.[142] The nature and purpose of the offence require examination, including whether it was committed out of genuine political motives or merely for personal reasons or gain, whether it was directed towards a modification of the political organization or the very structure of the State, and whether there is a close and direct causal link between the crime committed and its alleged political purpose and object. The political element should in principle outweigh the common law character of the offence, which may not be the case if the acts committed are grossly disproportionate to the objective, or are of an atrocious

---

[137] See *BVerwG* (Federal Administrative Court of the Federal Republic of Germany), 14.5.1962, cited in Kälin, *Das Prinzip des Non-refoulement*, (1982), 126. Elsewhere, Kälin has noted that 'unworthiness' as a ground for denial of asylum under art. 7 of the Swiss law is wider than exclusion under the Convention. Asylum can be denied to refugees who have committed crimes, who will benefit only from provisional admission, as will refugees who have become such because of activities following departure from their home country: Kälin, W., 'The Legal Condition of Refugees in Switzerland', 24 *Swiss Reports* presented at the XIVth International Congress of Comparative Law, (1994), 57, 59–60.

[138] At the Conference of Plenipotentiaries, the President, Mr Larsen, said that it would be 'for the country of refuge to strike a balance between the offences committed . . . and the extent to which [the] fear of persecution was well-founded': UN doc. A/CONF.2/SR.29, 23; cf. Weis, P., 'The concept of the refugee in international law', *Journal du dr. inter.* (1960), 1, 30. Cf. CRR, 20 fév. 1990, 108.387, *Sorubakanthan: Doc. réf.* no. 121, Suppl., JC, 6: the *Commission* maintained denial of refugee status to claimant who had been actively involved with the LTTE in Sri Lanka, including participation in combat and setting mines: '. . . des actes de terrorisme . . . (qui) . . . tombent sous le coup . . . de l'article 1er F b . . .' Also, Tiberghien, F., 'L'article 1er, F de la Convention de Geneve: Tendances récentes de la jurisprudence', *Doc. réf.* no. 43, 9/18 juill. 1988, Suppl., CJ, 1–4, commenting on *Urizar-Murgoitio* and meaning of 'serious non-political crime'.

[139] Cf. Grahl-Madsen, *Status of Refugees*, vol. 1, (1966), 294.

[140] Cf. Canadian *Immigration Act*, s. 48.01(e). Broadly, this excludes from the refugee status procedure convicted criminals and security risks, account being taken of conviction for an offence for which a term of imprisonment of ten years or more may be imposed, together with ministerial certification of danger to the public and the Minister's view of the public interest.

[141] Cf. Tiberghien, *La protection des réfugiés*, 104; Kälin, *Prinzip*, 124; Grahl-Madsen, *Status of Refugees*, vol. 1, 294ff; Köfner and Nicolaus, *Grundlagen des Asylrechts in der Bundesrepublik Deutschland*, 327; for examples of exclusion under art. 1F, see Tiberghien, F., 'La Commission des recours et l'article 1er, F de la Convention de Geneve', *Doc. réf.* no. 169, 19 dec. 1991/1er janv. 1992, Suppl., JC, 1–8, citing CRR, 5 fév. 1991, *Bahar*, 154.749—participation in terrorist activity including murders constitutes particularly serious crime; CRR, 29 janv. 1991, *Keles*, 136.526—bomb throwing, similarly.

[142] See Ch. 2, s. 4.2.2.3.

or barbarous nature.[143] The tendency to 'depoliticize' certain offences, such as hijacking, hostage-taking, offences against diplomats, and terrorism, is a potential source of difficulties[144] which are not entirely resolved by inclusion in certain of the conventions of the principle, *aut dedere aut judicare*. This may still leave open the option of *refoulement* to persecution and is considered further below.[145]

The political aspect apart, the phrase 'serious non-political crime' is not easy to define given the different connotations of the term 'crime' in different legal systems.[146] The standard finally to be applied is an international standard, in that a provision of a multilateral treaty is involved, but standards relating to criminal prosecution and treatment of offenders current in the potential country of asylum are also relevant. Each case will require examination on its merits, with regard paid to both mitigating and aggravating factors, and to the level of individual responsibility.[147]

Article 1F excludes 'persons', rather than 'refugees' from the benefits of the Convention, suggesting that the issue of a well-founded fear of persecution is irrelevant and need not be examined at all if there are 'serious reasons for considering' that an individual comes within its terms. In practice, the claim to be a refugee can rarely be ignored, for a balance must also be struck between the nature of the offence presumed to have been committed and the degree of persecution feared. A person with a well-founded fear of very severe persecution,

---

[143] The approach in the text was cited with approval by the Court of Appeals in *McMullen* v. *INS*, 788 F.2d 591, 597 (9th Cir. 1986). See also *Rodriguez Martinez Manuel* (1941) cited by Kiss, *Répertoire de la pratique français en matière de droit international public*, vol 2, (1966), 216; and *Morelli*, ibid., 217.

[144] See, for example, art. 16, 1963 Tokyo Convention on Offences and Certain other Acts committed on board Aircraft; art. 7, 1970 Hague Convention for the Suppression of Unlawful Seizure of Aircraft; art. 7, 1971 Montreal Convention for the Suppression of Unlawful Acts against the Safety of Civil Aviation; art. 7, 1973 Convention on the Prevention and Punishment of Crimes against Internationally Protected Persons, including Diplomatic Agents; art. 3, 1957 European Convention on Extradition; art. 5, 1977 European Convention on the Suppression of Terrorism; art. 9, 1979 United Nations Convention on the Taking of Hostages; art. 9, 1971 OAS Convention to prevent and punish Acts of Terrorism taking the form of Crimes against Persons and related Extortion that are of International Significance; art. 5, 1981 OAS Inter-American Convention on Extradition. Also, UNGA res. 40/61, 14 Jan. 1986, on measures to prevent international terrorism; SC res. 579 (1985), 18 Dec. 1985, condemning all acts of hostage-taking and abduction; Canada-US: Protocol amending the Treaty of Extradition, 11 Jan. 1988: 27 *ILM* 422 (1988)—listing offences that cannot be classified as 'political'; art. V, 1994 Inter-American Convention on the Forced Disappearance of Persons: 33 *ILM* 1529 (1994); art. 1, UK–US, Extradition Treaty Supplement limiting scope of political offences to exclude acts of terrorism, 25 Jun. 1985: 24 *ILM* 1104 (1985).

[145] See further below, Ch. 4, s. 3.2.

[146] Cf. Grahl-Madsen, *Status of Refugees*, vol. 1, 289–99.

[147] CRR, Section réunies, 20 juill. 1993, *Wilfred Karalasingham*, 233.673, *Doc. réf.* no. 239, 29 mars/11 avr. 1994, Suppl., CJ, 1—membership of organization some of whose members engage in activities falling within art. 1F(b) in Sri Lanka not alone sufficient to exclude; on individual examination, found that claimant, a Sri Lankan Tamil supporter of the LTTE, was arrested, detained and tortured, but that he had never participated in activities amounting to serious non-political crimes; CRR, Sections réunies, 20 juill. 1993, *Chahrour*, 231.390, ibid., 2—similarly, with respect to a member of the FIS in Algeria elected to post of deputy mayor.

such as would endanger life or freedom, should only be excluded for the most serious reasons. If the persecution feared is less, then the nature of the crime or crimes in question must be assessed to see whether criminal character in fact outweighs the applicant's character as a *bona fide* refugee.

In 1980, following the arrival of some 125,000 Cuban asylum seekers in the United States, UNHCR was requested by the authorities to advise on asylum applications which were likely to be refused on account of the applicants' criminal background.[148] The size of the influx made individual case-by-case assessment difficult, and it was later decided to accord the majority an interim status in anticipation of their situation being regularized by special legislation.[149] Suspected criminal cases, however, were examined in a joint UNHCR/State Department exercise, in which the author was closely involved during June and July 1980.

With a view to promoting consistent decisions, UNHCR proposed that, in the absence of any political factors, a presumption of serious crime might be considered as raised by evidence of commission of any of the following offences: homicide, rape, child molesting, wounding, arson, drugs trafficking, and armed robbery.[150] However, that presumption should be capable of rebuttal by evidence of mitigating factors, some of which are set out below. The following offences might also be considered to constitute serious crimes, provided other factors were present: breaking and entering (burglary); stealing (theft and simple robbery); receiving stolen property; embezzlement; possession of drugs in quantities exceeding that required for personal use; and assault. Factors to support a finding of seriousness included: use of weapons, injury to persons; value of property involved; type of drugs involved;[151] evidence of habitual criminal conduct. With respect to all cases, the following elements were suggested as tending to rebut a presumption or finding of serious crime: minority of the offender; parole; elapse of five years since conviction or completion of sentence; general good character (for example, one offence only); offender was merely accomplice; other circumstances surrounding commission of the offence (for example, provocation and self-defence).[152]

---

[148] The text of the US request for assistance is in 19 *ILM* 1296. The 1980 Refugee Act incorporates the substance of art. 1F(b) of the Convention as an exception to the prohibition on the deportation or return of an alien to a country in which his or her life or freedom may be threatened: s. 203(e), amending s. 243(h) of the Immigration and Nationality Act 1952.

[149] See 'Cuban-Haitian Arrivals in US', *Current Policy no. 193*, June 20, 1980, statement by Victor H. Palmieri, US Co-ordinator for Refugee Affairs.

[150] This list, of course, is by no means exclusive, but draws on the sorts of offences in fact admitted. The evidence in question was provided by the asylum seekers themselves, in interviews with US officials.

[151] Mere possession of marijuana for personal use was not considered to amount to a serious non-political crime.

[152] There was ample evidence in statements by convicts from different jails that an incentive to leave Cuba had been the threat by officials of a further term of imprisonment. Others, particularly former convicts, were threatened with up to four years' jail under Cuba's *Ley de Peligrosidad*, while some were issued with passports on simple production of their release certificates at local police

These criteria may still be of general value in the interpretation of the Convention and the Statute, bearing in mind that the objective of such provisions is to obtain a humanitarian balance between a potential threat to the community of refuge and the interests of the individual who has a well-founded fear of persecution.

4.3 ACTS CONTRARY TO THE PURPOSES AND PRINCIPLES OF THE UNITED NATIONS

4.3.1 *The drafting history of article 1F(c)*

The principle of exclusion from the Convention by reason of acts contrary to the purposes and principles of the United Nations appears in embryonic form in the IRO Constitution, which excluded those who, since the end of the Second World War, had participated in any organization seeking the overthrow by armed force of a government of a UN member State, or in any terrorist organization; or who were leaders of movements hostile to their government or sponsors of movements encouraging refugees not to return to their country of origin.[153]

The present text of article 1F(c) was adopted on the basis of a draft submitted by the Yugoslav representative,[154] notwithstanding doubts about using the terminology of article 14(2) of the Universal Declaration as a basis for exclusion. The British representative had in fact supposed that 'acts contrary to the purposes and principles of the United Nations' covered 'war crimes, genocide and the subversion or overthrow of democratic régimes', with other possibilities being suggested by various States.[155]

stations. During a period of some seven weeks, 1021 cases were examined and most provided few problems, in that the commission of serious crimes was clearly indicated. A number of cases, however, were discussed at length, resulting in general agreement on the serious or non-serious nature of the crime, or in deferral for further inquiries and reinterview regarding either the circumstances of the offence or political and refugee elements. In December 1984 the US and Cuba agreed on the return of some 2,746 inadmissible Cuban nationals and for the resumption of immigration processing in Havana by the US authorities: 24 *ILM* 32 (1985). Only a few had in fact been returned when Cuba suspended the agreements on commencement of broadcasting by a Florida-based station, Radio Marti, considered hostile to the government. It has not been possible to determine with certainty whether any of the cases considered non-serious in 1980 were in fact scheduled for deportation in 1984/85 and if so, on what grounds. For related litigation, see the various decisions entitled *Fernandez-Roque* v. *Smith* 535 F. Supp. 741 (1981); 671 F.2d 426 (1982); 539 F. Supp. 925 (1982); 557 F. Supp. 690 (1982); 567 F. Supp. 1115 (1983); 734 F.2d 576 (1984).

153 IRO Constitution, Annex I, Part II. See also Annex I, General Principles, para. 1 (d): 'It should be the concern of the Organization to ensure that its assistance is not exploited in order to encourage subversive or hostile activities directed against the Government of any of the United Nations.' IRO, *Manual for Eligibility Officers*, (s.d.), 39. IRGUN, for example, was classified as a terrorist organization: ibid., para. 64. With respect to the second category of excludables, the practice was to concentrate on leaders, not subordinates or followers: ibid., 40.

154 UN doc. A/CONF.2/SR.29, pp. 20–1, 27.

155 UN doc. A/CONF.2/SR.24, p. 5; SR.29, pp. 11–12. In debate in the Social Committee, the French representative also considered that those guilty of genocide were covered: UN doc. E/AC.7/SR.160, p. 15. He later added that the provision was not aimed at the ordinary individual, 'but at persons occupying government posts, such as heads of State, Ministers and high officials

4.3.2 The purposes and principles of the United Nations

The purposes and principles of the United Nations are set out in the Preamble and articles 1 and 2 of the United Nations Charter.[156] The main objectives are to prevent war, to reaffirm faith in fundamental human rights, to establish the conditions under which justice and respect for obligations can be maintained, and to promote social progress and better standards of life in larger freedom. To these ends, articles 1 and 2 set out the purposes and principles, including collective measures to prevent and remove threats to the peace and acts of aggression; the peaceful settlement of disputes; the development of friendly relations between States; respect for the equal rights and self-determination of peoples; international co-operation in economic, social, cultural, and humanitarian matters; and the promotion and encouragement of respect for human rights for all without distinction. Specifically, article 2 addresses both the Organization and its Members, laying down principles which should govern relations between them. These include recognition of the principle of sovereign equality of nations; the fulfilment in good faith of international obligations; the settlement of disputes by peaceful means; the obligation to refrain from the threat or use of force; and the duty of the United Nations not to intervene in the domestic jurisdiction of any State.

The statement of purposes and principles is essentially organizational, establishing what shall be done by States Members working together within the UN and how they should conduct relations between themselves. But like most constituent documents, the UN Charter also has a dynamic aspect, and in certain areas the practical content of the declared purposes and principles must be determined in the light of more general developments.

For example, the principle of respect for human rights has been developed through the Universal Declaration, the 1966 Covenants, regional treaty arrangements, and customary law. Thus, an individual who has denied or restricted the human rights of others arguably falls within the exception. Those who had persecuted others were indeed expressly excluded from the IRO's mandate, and a similar provision is found in the United States Refugee Act[157] and Canada's Immigration Act.[158] Also relevant are the individual's duties to the community,

. . .': SR.166, p. 6. The US representative mentioned collaborators: SR.160, p. 16; and the representative of the United Nations Secretariat was of opinion that it referred to those who violated human rights without committing a crime: SR.166, p. 9.

[156] Text in Brownlie, I., *Basic Documents in International Law*, (4th ed., 1995), 3–4.
[157] Refugee Act 1980, s. 203(e), amending INA s. 243(h). Tiberghien, *La protection des réfugiés*, 467.
[158] *Immigration Act*, (as amended 1992: Bill C-86), s. 19(1)(l) declares inadmissible for admission to Canada, 'persons who are or were senior members of or senior officials in the service of a government that is or was, in the opinion of the Minister, engaged in terrorism, systematic or gross human rights violations or war crimes or crimes against humanity . . . (1.1) For the purposes of paragraph (1)(l), "senior members of or senior officials in the service of a government" means persons who, by virtue of the position they hold or have held, are or were able to exert a significant influence on the exercise of government power and, without limiting its generality, includes (a) heads of state or government; (b) members of the cabinet or governing council; (c) senior advisors to persons described

and the limitations inherent in human rights.[159] Article 17 of the European Convention on Human Rights, for example, provides:

Nothing in this Convention may be interpreted as implying for any State, group or person any right to engage in any activity or perform any act aimed at the destruction of any of the rights and freedoms set forth herein or at their limitation to a greater extent than is provided for in the Convention.

Such a principle is sometimes incorporated or reflected in municipal law.[160]

4.3.2.1 Individuals and persons acting on behalf of the State

Although the purposes and principles focus on the conduct of, and the relations between, States, article 1F(c) clearly contemplates an area of individual responsibility. The question is, whether such responsibility is limited to those who control and implement the policies of States; or whether it also covers the relationship of one individual to another. The UNHCR *Handbook* sees article 1F(c) as overlapping with the preceding exclusion clauses, without introducing 'any specific new element'; it infers that for an individual to fall within this exclusion clause, he or she '*must* have been in a position of power . . . and instrumental' in the State's violation of the principles.[161]

Many commentators share a similar view, and would limit this exclusion clause to heads of State and high officials, while reserving its exceptional application to individuals not necessarily connected with government, such as torturers and others guilty of flagrant violation of human rights.[162] The jurisprudence developing in different countries, however, reveals two broad streams; one focuses almost exclusively on State officials and others similarly situated, while the other seeks to extend the scope of individual responsibility.

In two early cases, the French *Commission des recours* confirmed the denial of refugee status to individuals who, during the Second World War, denounced people to the occupation forces.[163] The individual dimension was also upheld in a 1972 German decision, in which the court held that bomb and terrorist attacks

---

in (a) or (b); (d) senior members of the public service; (e) senior members of the military and of the intelligence and internal security apparatus; (f) ambassadors and senior diplomatic officials; and (g) members of the judiciary.' This extensive application of an otherwise sound principle may well prove over-inclusive in practice, for example, when refuge is sought by moderates and certain good faith dissidents.

[159] Art. 29, Universal Declaration of Human Rights; see generally Daes, E.-I., 'Study of the Individual's Duties to the Community and the Limitations of Human Rights and Freedoms under Article 29 of the Universal Declaration of Human Rights': UN doc. E/CN.4/Sub.2/432/Rev.1 (1980).

[160] See, for example, art. 16, *Grundgesetz 1949* (Constitution of the Federal Republic of Germany); also the Irish cases cited above, Ch.2, n. 117.

[161] Paras. 162–3.

[162] Cf. Grahl-Madsen, *Status of Refugees*, vol. I, 282–3, 286; Kälin, *Prinzip*, 127–9; Köfner and Nicolaus, *Grundlagen*, 330.

[163] See *Milosek*, 304, 7 juill. 1954: Tiberghien, *La protection des réfugiés*, 470; *Kamykowski*, 858, 8 déc. 1955: ibid.

resulting in deaths in various countries were contrary to the purposes and principles of the United Nations.[164] In a 1973 case, the court found that continual terrorist and sabotage activities from Lebanese territory against Israel revealed a basis for exclusion under article 1F(c).[165] Decisions since 1975, however, have stressed that articles 1 and 2 of the UN Charter are concerned with international, not individual relations; and that only if inter-State peace or inter-State understanding is affected, will the exclusion clause apply.[166]

If German jurisprudence has tended to restrict the potential area of individual responsibility, decisions in France show a different emphasis. In *Shakeri Noori*, where the negative decision was ultimately based on the absence of a fear of persecution for Convention reasons, the *Commissaire du gouvernement*[167] argued that article 1F(c), 'ne pouvait viser que les agissements commis par les Etats et par les détenteurs du pouvoir au sein de l'Etat'.[168] That approach was exemplified in the *Duvalier* case, in which an application for refugee status by the former dictator of Haiti was rejected. The *Commission des recours* found that respect for human rights and fundamental freedoms was among the purposes and principles of the United Nations. It observed further that article 1F(c),

... se rapporte notamment à l'action contraire aux droits de l'homme et aux libertés fondamentales que la personne en cause a pu exercer dans son pays, ... que (M. Duvalier) a exercé ... les fonctions de président de la République de Haïti; ... que de graves violations des droits de l'homme ont été commises dans ce pays pendant ce période; ... que

[164] VG Ansbach, 17.10.1972, Nr. 2735–II/72, cited in Köfner and Nicolaus, *Grundlagen*, 330, n. 75. See also Grahl-Madsen, *Status of Refugees*, vol. I, 287–9 (criticizing a 1962 German decision excluding a former official in the Czech censor's office, notwithstanding his change of beliefs and later anti-government activities).

[165] VG Ansbach, 18.4.1973, Nr. 2907–II/72, cited in Köfner and Nicolaus, *Grundlagen*, 330f, n. 75. The applicant had been involved in transporting arms for the PFLP. In the view of the court, this had supported his organization in the escalation of the conflict with Israel. It found further that this organization was involved in terror and sabotage from Lebanon into Israel, and that this was contrary to the purposes and principles of the United Nations, specifically, peaceful co-existence and peaceful settlement of disputes. See also VG Ansbach, 31.10.1972, Nr. 7357–IV/71: ibid; the applicant had been involved in the private wars of exile groups, and in various incidents, including fighting and threats. In the view of the court, his conviction for possession of weapons excluded him under art. 1F(c).

[166] BVerwG, 1.7.1975, I C 44.68 ; cited in Marx, *Asylrecht*, Bd. 3, 1106-7. The applicant illegally purchased two loaded pistols for two fellow nationals; he ought to have known that they might have been used for political killings in Croatia. He was convicted and fined, and his application for asylum was initially refused on the ground that his offence had been contrary to the purposes and principles of the United Nations, in that it was likely to disturb German/Yugoslav relations. The Federal Administrative Court ruled, however, that art. 1F(c) did not apply. Art. 1 of the UN Charter was concerned with inter-State, that is, international relations; and art. 2 was directed to the UN Organization and its Members; neither of these areas was affected by the applicant's offence.

[167] The *Commissaire du gouvernement* is an official of the court, not a representative of the government as such, who reviews the dossier of each case, explores matters which the *rapporteur* may have overlooked, and then prepares a report or 'conclusions'. The purpose of the conclusions is to sum up the case as clearly as possible for the *Sous-section*, 'and to relate the proposed solution to the general pattern of the case-law and, if possible, to foreshadow its future development'. Brown and Garner, *French Administrative Law*, (3rd ed., 1983), 31, 64.

[168] Tiberghien, *La protection des réfugiés*, 106.

(M. Duvalier) était, en sa qualité de président . . . le chef des forces armées, de la police, et des volontaires de la sécurité nationale qui se sont livrés à de graves violations des droits de l'homme; *qu'alors même qu'il ne résulte pas de l'instruction que le requérant ait personnellement commis de tels agissements, il les a nécessairement couverts de son autorité* . . . [169] (emphasis supplied)

Other decisions have confirmed that personal involvement in human rights violations is not necessary, with respect to those occupying a certain level of office or responsibility, who knew or are deemed to have known what was going on. One commentator observes,

. . . la jurisprudence concordante de la Commission et du Conseil d'Etat considère que l'article 1er, F c vise les personnes qui ont exercé des fonctions d'autorité au sein d'un Etat où se sont produites de graves violations des droits de l'Homme.[170]

In *Aghel,* for example, the head of recruitment for the political police was excluded, on the ground that he must have known of the organization's various activities.[171] In *Nou,* a former member of the Democratic Kampuchean delegation to UNESCO in Paris was excluded:

. . . que même s'il n'a pas personnellement commis des agissements contraires aux buts et principes des Nations Unies, il a nécessairement, étant donné le caractère et les méthodes du régime Khmer Rouge, couvert leurs agissements en raison de ses responsabilités . . . [172]

This is an extreme interpretation of the jurisprudence, in the sense that the applicant was at some distance from the exercise of power, and was not personally guilty of violations of human rights. For while personal involvement is not required of the holders of power at the 'executive' level, it may be relevant in the exclusion of those further removed from political responsibility. The cases of *Pierre* and *Celestin,* for example, may be borderline; former members of the Tonton Macoutes in Haïti, they were excluded, apparently on the sole basis of their membership, 'eu égard à la nature des activités de cette force de police et à ses méthodes'.[173]

---

[169] *Duvalier,* 50.265, 19 juill. 1986: Tiberghien, *La protection des réfugiés,* 262–3. The Conseil d'Etat agreed: *Duvalier,* 31 juill. 1992, 81.963, *Doc. réf.* no. 211, 2/15 mars 1993, Suppl., CJ, 5; see also Conseil d'Etat, *Mme. Duvalier,* 31 juill. 1992, 81.962, ibid., 6—it was not error of law for CRR to find that the claimant's fear of persecution was the consequence of the serious human rights violations committed by security forces under the responsibility of her husband, and not to any political opinion of her own or to any other Convention reason.

[170] Tiberghien, F., *Doc. réf.* no. 43, 1988, Supp., p. 4.

[171] *Aghel,* Nos. 14.793 –14.795 and 14.909, 22 juin 1982; see also *Mohavedi,* No. 13.690, 4 fév. 1982; *Engabe,* No. 25.229, 31 août 1984; decisions of the *Commission des recours,* cited in Tiberghien, *La protection des réfugiés,* 470; *Padjuheshfar,* No. 19.679, 22 juin 1987, cited in *Doc. réf.* no. 43, juill. 1988, Supp., p. 7.

[172] *Doc. réf.* no. 55, nov. 1988, Supp., p. 5f.

[173] *Doc. réf.* no. 43, 9/18 juill. 1988, Supp., p. 8; Tiberghien, F., 'La Commission des recours et l'article 1er, F de la Convention de Genève', *Doc. réf.* no. 169, 19 dec. 1991/1er janv. 1992, Suppl., JC, 1–8, citing CRR, 14 fév. 1991, *Antoine,* 70.512—membership of 'Tontons Macoutes'; CRR, 26 fev. 1991, *Efekele Itela Bowole Zende,* 158.043—claimant with responsibilities in security services of Zairian president, had 'covered' acts of torture and other violations of human rights.

The formal exclusion of those who have persecuted others is justified, both historically and in the light of recent practice. In a 1982 Australian case, the Determination of Refugee Status Committee examined an application by an Iranian who had been present for some of the time at the occupation of the United States Embassy in Tehran, when diplomatic and consular staff were held hostage. In 1980, the International Court of Justice characterized the detention of the hostages as 'manifestly incompatible' with the purposes and principles of the United Nations.[174] Relying upon this, some members of the Committee argued that the mere fact of presence or involvement was sufficient to bring the applicant within article 1F(c). Others took the view that the Court's judgment was principally concerned with issues of State responsibility; its views on the initially independent actions of individuals[175] should not be taken as excluding an applicant for all time and all purposes from the benefits of refugee status. The nature and extent of the individual's role in the occupation should be examined, as well as his motives and intentions and current situation vis-à-vis his country of origin. A majority of the Committee recommended that the applicant be excluded by reason of the degree of his involvement in the hostages incident.[176]

In summary, article 1F(c) will generally exclude high officials of State responsible for the implementation of policies that violate human rights or are otherwise contrary to the purposes and principles of the United Nations. In appropriate circumstances, however, it also applies to individuals at some remove from political responsibility, who are party to human rights violations, either individually, or as members of organizations engaged in such activities. It remains open (in that there is no jurisprudence immediately in point), whether exclusion must be linked to the activities of a State or of State organizations, or whether it also extends to individuals acting on behalf of unrecognized entities,[177] belligerent groups, quasi-States, or on their own. The IRO's exclusion clauses were for the most part aimed specifically at individuals and members of non-State entities, such as terrorist organizations and other organizations seeking the overthrow of the government of a member State. In principle, there is no reason why such actions might not fall within article 1F(c), but the question may be somewhat academic; an individual whose actions outside the organization of a State give rise to the issue of exclusion will likely fall within article 1F(a) or (b).

---

[174] *United States Diplomatic and Consular Staff in Tehran* (USA v. Iran), ICJ *Rep.*, (1980), 3 at 42 (para. 91).

[175] Ibid., 35 (para. 74); 29–30 (paras. 58–9).

[176] *M.R.* The account of this case is drawn from the writer's involvement as UNHCR observer in the proceedings. In the event, the Minister for Immigration, who is finally responsible for decisions on refugee status, chose to disregard the DORS Committee recommendation, and accepted the applicant as a refugee. The principles relating to assessment of the degree of involvement, however, are considered to be generally valid.

[177] Cf. Köfner & Nicolaus, *Grundlagen*, 329, n. 69.

4.3.3 Article 1F(c) in brief

The legislative history of article 1F(c), considered together with the judicial and administrative decisions and the practice of States, establishes that the following general categories, in particular, may be excluded from benefits of the 1951 Convention: (1) policy-makers and those holding positions of political responsibility, in situations where, for example, violations of human rights or other activities contrary to the purposes and principles of the United Nations have occurred, and where they may be considered to have covered such activities with their authority; (2) the agents of implementation of such policies, including, for example, officials in government departments or agencies who knew or ought to have known what was going on; and the members of government and other organizations engaged in activities, such as persecution, contrary to the purposes and principles of the United Nations; and (3) individuals, whether members of organizations or not, who, for example, have personally participated in the persecution or denial of the human rights of others. In principle, exclusion under article 1F(c) may as well apply to State officials, as to others.

Article 1F(c) of the Convention is potentially very wide. Besides the examples mentioned above, the United Nations has also taken action to combat the narcotics traffic,[178] to promote democratic and representative forms of government, and to recognize the international standing of certain liberation movements. This may imply that those involved in the drugs trade, who displace or obstruct the democratic process, or who are responsible for maintaining colonial and colonial-style regimes should not subsequently be entitled to recognition of refugee status. Once rarely used, the exception is now frequently invoked; its interpretation and development are likely to vary, however, given the disparate interests of the sovereign States members of the United Nations.

---

[178] In *Pushpanathan (Velupillai)* v. *MEI*, FC-TD, IMM-240–93, 3 Sept. 1993 the Convention Refugee Determination Division excluded the claimant under art. 1F(c) on account of conviction *in Canada* of drug trafficking. UN initiatives in the field were considered sufficient to bring the subject within the scope of UN purposes and principles, and there was no reason to limit exclusion to acts outside the country of refuge. On appeal, the Federal Court, Trial Division, found no reason to interfere.

PART TWO

ASYLUM

Chapter 4

NON-REFOULEMENT

The principle of *non-refoulement* prescribes, broadly, that no refugee should be returned to any country where he or she is likely to face persecution or torture. In this chapter, the scope of the principle is examined against the background of a number of recurring issues: the question of 'risk'; the personal scope of the principle, including its application to certain categories of asylum seekers such as stowaways or those arriving directly by boat; exceptions to the principle; extraterritorial application; extradition; and the 'contingent' application of the principle in situations of mass influx. The possible application of *non-refoulement* or an analogous principle of refuge to those outside the 1951 Convention/1967 Protocol is also considered, as is the relationship between *non-refoulement* and asylum. The analysis takes account of the increasing number of references to *non-refoulement* in nominally non-refugee instruments, as well as the emerging jurisprudence of non-return in treaty-monitoring bodies such as the Committee against Torture, the Human Rights Committee and their regional counterparts.

1. Evolution of the principle

The term *non-refoulement* derives from the French *refouler*, which means to drive back or to repel, as of an enemy who fails to breach one's defences. In the context of immigration control in continental Europe, *refoulement* is a term of art covering, in particular, summary reconduction to the frontier of those discovered to have entered illegally and summary refusal of admission of those without valid papers.[1] *Refoulement* is thus to be distinguished from expulsion or deportation, the more formal process whereby a lawfully resident alien may be required to leave a State, or be forcibly removed.

The idea that a State ought not to return persons to other States in certain circumstances is of comparatively recent origin. Common in the past were formal agreements between sovereigns for the reciprocal surrender of subversives, dissidents, and traitors.[2] Only in the early- to mid-nineteenth century do the concept of asylum and the principle of non-extradition of political offenders

---

[1] Historically, many bilateral agreements have institutionalized the practice; see the '*conventions de prise en charge à la frontière*' discussed in Batiffol and Lagarde, *Droit international privé* (5th ed., 1970) i.198; and the '*Übernahme-*' or '*Schubabkommen*' discussed in Schiedermair, *Handbuch des Ausländerrechts der Bundesrepublik Deutschland*, 178, 227–30 (1968). For their more modern counterparts, see UNHCR, 'Overview of Re-Admission Agreements in Central Europe', (Sept. 1993); also Inter-Governmental Consultations, 'Working Paper on Readmission Agreements', (Aug. 1994).

[2] Goodwin-Gill, G. S., *International Law and the Movement of Persons between States*, (1978), 143, n. 2.

begin to concretize, in the sense of that protection which the territorial sovereign can, and perhaps should, accord. At that time, the principle of non-extradition reflected popular sentiment that those fleeing their own, generally despotic governments, were worthy of protection.[3] It was a period of political turmoil in Europe and South America, as well as of mass movements of populations occasioned by pogroms against Jewish and Christian minorities in Russia and the Ottoman Empire.

A sense of the need to protect the persecuted can be gathered from the United Kingdom's 1905 Aliens Act, where section 1 made an exception to refusal of entry for want of means in respect of those 'seeking to avoid prosecution or punishment on religious or political grounds or for an offence of a political character, or persecution involving danger of imprisonment or danger to life or limb on account of religious belief'. Not until after the First World War, however, did international practice begin to accept the notion of non-return, and only in 1933 does the first reference to the principle that refugees should not be returned to their country of origin occur in an international instrument.[4] In article 3 of the 1933 Convention relating to the International Status of Refugees, the contracting parties undertook not to remove resident refugees or keep them from their territory, 'by application of police measures, such as expulsions or non-admittance at the frontier (*refoulement*)', unless dictated by national security or public order.[5] Each State undertook, 'in any case not to refuse entry to refugees at the frontiers of their countries of origin'. Only eight States ratified this Convention, however; three of them, by reservations and declarations, emphasized their retention of sovereign competence in the matter of expulsion, while the United Kingdom expressly objected to the principle of non-rejection at the frontier.

Agreements regarding refugees from Germany in 1936 and 1938 also contained some limitation on expulsion or return.[6] They varied slightly: broadly, refugees required to leave a contracting State were to be allowed a suitable period to make arrangements; lawfully resident refugees were not to be expelled or sent back across the frontier[7] save 'for reasons of national security or public order'; and even in such cases, governments undertook not to return refugees to

---

[3] See, for example, 6 *British Digest of International Law*, 53–4, 64–5.

[4] Under a 1928 arrangement (89 *LNTS* No. 2005), States had adopted a recommendation (no. 7), 'that measures for expelling foreigners or for taking such other action against them be avoided or suspended in regard to Russian and Armenian refugees in cases where the person concerned is not in a position to enter a neighbouring country in a regular manner'. The recommendation was not to apply to a refugee who had entered a State in intentional violation of national law.

[5] 159 *LNTS* No. 3663; official text in French.

[6] Art. 4, Provisional Arrangement concerning the Status of Refugees coming from Germany, 1936: 171 *LNTS* No. 3952; official text in English and French. The arrangement was signed by seven States; the UK excluded refugees subject to extradition proceedings from the ambit of art. 4, and likewise, for most purposes, refugees admitted for a temporary visit or purpose. See also art. 5, Convention concerning the Status of Refugees coming from Germany, 1938: 192 *LNTS* No. 4461; official texts in English and French. The Convention was ratified by only three States; the UK repeated its 1936 reservations.

[7] The 1938 Convention substituted 'measures of expulsion or reconduction . . .'

the German Reich,[8] 'unless they have been warned and have refused to make the necessary arrangements to proceed to another country or to take advantage of the arrangements made for them with that object'.

Action in the inter-war period focused principally on improving administrative arrangements to facilitate resettlement and relieve the burden on countries of first asylum. The need for protective principles for refugees began to emerge, but limited ratifications of instruments containing equivocal and much qualified provisions effectively prevented the consolidation of a formal principle of *non-refoulement*. Nevertheless, the period was also remarkable for the very large numbers of refugees not in fact sent back to their countries of origin, whether they fled Russia after the revolution, Spain, Germany, or the Ottoman Empire.[9]

Following the Second World War, a new era began. In February 1946, the United Nations expressly accepted that 'refugees or displaced persons' who have expressed 'valid objections' to returning to their country of origin should not be compelled to do so.[10] The International Refugee Organization was established the same year, charged with resolving the problems of displacement left over from the war; some 1,620,000 refugees were assisted with resettlement and integration, while many others fleeing political developments in Eastern Europe were readily admitted to Western countries.[11]

In 1949, the United Nations Economic and Social Council (ECOSOC) appointed an *Ad hoc* committee to 'consider the desirability of preparing a revised and consolidated convention relating to the international status of refugees and stateless persons and, if they consider such a course desirable, draft the text of such a convention'.[12] The *Ad hoc* committee on Statelessness and Related Problems met twice in New York in January–February and August 1950,[13] and

---

[8] The 1936 arrangement read: 'refugees shall not be sent back across the frontier of the Reich'; the 1938 Convention provided that States parties 'undertake' not to reconduct refugees to German territory.

[9] Kiss notes, for example, that in 1939 France admitted 400,000 refugees from Spain in just ten days: *Répertoire de la pratique française en droit international public*, (1966), vol. 4, 433–5.

[10] UNGA res. 8(1), 12 Feb. 1946, para. (c)(ii).

[11] On IRO and post Second World War practice, see Marrus, M., *The Unwanted: European Refugees in the Twentieth Century*, (1985); Rystad, G., ed., *The Uprooted: Forced Migration as an International Problem in the Post-War Era*, (1990); Skran, C., *Refugees in Inter-War Europe: The Emergence of a Regime*, (1995). State practice of the immediate post-war period, however, is regrettably inconclusive. Writing in 1954, Weis found that *refoulement* was rare, save 'in the case of some Russians and Ukrainians covered by certain wartime agreements': Weis, P., 'The International Protection of Refugees', 48 *AJIL* 193 at 196 (1954). The release of relevant documents to public scrutiny thirty years later showed the full extent of a forcible repatriation policy which meant death or horrific treatment for well over two million, by no means all of them covered by those wartime agreements: see Tolstoy, N., *Victims of Yalta* (1977, rev. ed. 1979); Bethell, N., *The Last Secret* (1974).

[12] ECOSOC res. 248(IX)B, 8 Aug. 1949.

[13] The Committee decided to focus on the refugee, and duly produced a draft convention. In August 1950, ECOSOC returned the draft for further review, before consideration by the General Assembly, and finalized the Preamble and refugee definition. In Dec. 1950, the General Assembly decided to convene a Conference of Plenipotentiaries to complete the draft: UNGA res. 429(V), 14 Dec. 1950. See generally *Report* of the *Ad hoc* Committee on Refugees and Stateless Persons, Second Session: UN doc. E/1850. The Committee had been renamed in the interim. The

drew up the following provision, considered so fundamental that no exceptions were proposed:

No contracting State shall expel or return a refugee in any manner whatsoever to the frontiers of territories where his life or freedom would be threatened on account of his race, religion, nationality or political opinion.[14]

During this same period, however, States resisted inclusion of a right to be granted asylum, both in the 1948 Universal Declaration of Human Rights and in the 1951 Convention. The 1951 Conference of Plenipotentiaries also had concerns regarding the absoluteness of *non-refoulement*, adding the following paragraph to what was to become article 33:

The benefit of the present provision may not, however, be claimed by a refugee whom there are reasonable grounds for regarding as a danger to the security of the country in which he is, or who, having been convicted by a final judgment of a particularly serious crime, constitutes a danger to the community of that country.[15]

Apart from certain situations of exception, the drafters of the 1951 Convention clearly intended that refugees not be returned, either to their country of origin or to other countries in which they would be at risk.[16]

most important United Nations documents from this period are usefully collected in Takkenberg, A. and Tahbaz, C. C., *The Collected Travaux Préparatoires of the 1951 Convention relating to the Status of Refugees*, 3 volumes, Dutch Refugee Council/European Legal Network on Asylum, Amsterdam, 1988.

[14] UN doc. E/1850, para. 30. Cf. Louis Henkin, US delegation: 'Whether it was a question of closing the frontier to a refugee who asked admittance, or of turning him back after he had crossed the frontier, or even of expelling him after he had been admitted to residence in the territory, the problem was more or less the same . . . Whatever the case might be . . . he must not be turned back to a country where his life or freedom could be threatened. No consideration of public order should be allowed to overrule that guarantee, for if the State concerned wished to get rid of the refugee at all costs, it could send him to another country or place him in an internment camp': *Ad hoc* Committee on Statelessness and Related Problems: UN doc. E/AC.32/SR.20, paras. 54–5 (1950). The Israeli delegate reiterated that the prohibition on return 'must, in fact, apply to all refugees, whether or not they were admitted to residence; it must deal with both expulsion and non-admittance'; he concluded that '[t]he Committee had already settled the humanitarian question of sending any refugee whatever back to a territory where his life or liberty might be in danger.' Ibid., paras. 60–1. The British delegate also concluded from the discussion that the notion of *refoulement* 'could apply to . . . refugees seeking admission': UN doc. E/AC.32/SR.21, para. 16.

[15] The change in the international situation between the meeting of the *Ad Hoc* Committee in Aug. 1950 and the Conference in July 1951 is usually cited as the reason for the introduction of exceptions; see UN doc. A/CONF.2/SR.16, 8 (views of the UK).

[16] The *Ad hoc* Committee reported in its comments that the draft article referred 'not only to the country of origin but also to other countries where the life or freedom of the refugee would be threatened': see UN doc. E/AC.32/SR.20, p. 3, for the UK's proposal and views; UN doc. E/1618, E/AC.32/5, p. 61, for the *Ad hoc* Committee comment. Sweden proposed a more specific rule against the return of a refugee to a country 'where he would be exposed to the risk of being sent to a territory where his life or freedom' would be threatened, for example, by extradition or expulsion: see UN docs. A/CONF.2/70, A/CONF.2/SR.16, p. 9. This was withdrawn, on the assumption that art. 33 covered at least some of the ground. The Danish representative noted that a government expelling a refugee to an intermediate country could not foresee how that State might act. But if expulsion presented a threat of subsequent forcible return to the country of origin, then the life or liberty of the refugee would be endangered, contrary to the principle of *non-refoulement*: see UN doc. A/CONF.2/SR.16, p. 9f. In *Re Musisi* [1987] 2 WLR 606, at 620, the UK House of Lords

As expressed in article 33, the principle of *non-refoulement* raises questions as to its personal scope and relation to the issues of admission and non-rejection at the frontier. It is a rule clearly designed to benefit the refugee, the person who, in the sense of article 1 of the Convention, has a well-founded fear of being persecuted on grounds of race, religion, nationality, membership of a particular social group, or political opinion. In principle, its benefit ought not to be predicated upon formal recognition of refugee status which, indeed, may be impractical in the absence of effective procedures or in the case of a mass influx.[17] Likewise, it would scarcely be consonant with considerations of good faith for a State to seek to avoid the principle of *non-refoulement* by declining to make a determination of status.

From the point of general, as opposed to treaty-based international law, the issue is rendered more problematic by developments in the refugee definition, as well as by doubts as to the scope and standing of *non-refoulement* outside the relevant international instruments. Recent extensions of UNHCR's mandate might be purely functional, in that they authorize the channelling of material assistance but do not justify the exercise of protection. States have in turn argued that, in regard to the expanded class, their obligations are humanitarian rather than legal.[18] As shown below, however, State practice in cases of mass influx offers some support for the view that *non-refoulement*, or an analogous principle of refuge, applies both to the individual refugee with a well-founded fear of persecution, and to the frequently large groups of persons who do not in fact enjoy the protection of the government of their country of origin in certain fairly well-defined circumstances.

2. Relation of the principle of *non-refoulement* to particular issues

2.1 ADMISSION AND NON-REJECTION AT THE FRONTIER

Those who argue in favour of the restrictive view of the obligations of States under article 33 sometimes rely on comments made by the Swiss and Dutch delegates to the Conference of Plenipotentiaries in 1951. The Swiss interpretation of *non-refoulement* would have limited its application to those who have already entered State territory, but they spoke *only* about mass migrations, saying

struck down a decision to deny asylum to a Ugandan refugee and return him to Kenya, his country of first refuge. The reasons given by the Secretary of State indicated that he had failed to take into account, or to give sufficient weight to, a relevant consideration, namely, that on a number of occasions Kenya had handed over Ugandan refugees to the Ugandan authorities.

[17] Executive Committee Conclusion No. 6 (1977) reaffirms the principle of *non-refoulement*, irrespective of formal recognition of refugee status: para. (c). The 1979 Arusha Conference on the Situation of Refugees in Africa observed, among others, that refugee status procedures might be impractical in the case of large-scale movements of asylum seekers in Africa, and that special arrangements might be necessary. As a minimum, however, the conference recommended that the protection of individuals by virtue of the principle of *non-refoulement* be ensured: UN doc. A/AC.96/INF.158 at 9.

[18] See above, Ch. 1, s. 7.

nothing about the non-applicability of article 33 outside that context.[19] The Dutch delegate considered that the word 'return' related only to refugees already within the territory, and that mass migrations were not covered.[20] This narrow view did not fully square with the meaning of *refoulement* in European immigration law or with the letter of article 3 of the 1933 Convention, at least in their individual dimension. The words 'expel or return' in the English version of article 33 also have no precise meaning in general international law. The former may describe any measure, judicial, administrative, or police, which secures the departure of an alien, although article 32 possibly implies that measures of expulsion are reserved for lawfully resident aliens. The word 'return' is even vaguer; to the Danish representative it suggested such action as a State might take in response to a request for extradition.[21] The Dutch delegate's comments, however, primarily reflected concern that the draft article would require his government to grant *entry* in the case of a mass migration.[22]

Probably the most accurate assessment of States' views in 1951 is that there was no unanimity, perhaps deliberately so. At the same time, however, States were not prepared to include in the Convention any article on admission of refugees; *non-refoulement* in the sense of even a limited obligation to allow entry may well have been seen as coming too close to the unwished-for duty to grant asylum.

The views of commentators on the scope of article 33 have varied,[23] and lit-

---

[19] UN doc. A/CONF.2/SR.16, p. 6; see also Weis, P., 'Legal Aspects of the Convention of 28 July 1951 relating to the Status of Refugees,' 30 *BYIL* 478, at 482 (1953).

[20] See below, n. 22.

[21] UN doc. A/CONF.2/SR.16, p. 10. On extradition and *non-refoulement*, see below, s. 3.3.3.

[22] For the Dutch delegate's comments, see UN doc. A/CONF.2/SR.35 at 21: Baron van Boetzelaer of the Netherlands, 'recalled that at the first reading the Swiss representative had expressed the opinion that the word "expulsion" related to a refugee already admitted into a country, whereas the word "return" ("refoulement") related to a refugee already within the territory but not yet resident there ... At the first reading the representatives of Belgium, the Federal Republic of Germany, Italy, the Netherlands and Sweden had supported the Swiss interpretation ... In order to dispel any possible ambiguity and to reassure his Government, he wished to have it placed on record that the Conference was in agreement with the interpretation that the possibility of mass migrations across frontiers or of attempted mass migrations was not covered by article 33 . . . .There being no objection, the PRESIDENT ruled that the interpretation given by the Netherlands representative should be *placed on the record*.' (Emphasis added). Earlier, the Dutch delegate explained that his concern was that of 'a country bordering on others . . . about assuming unconditional obligations as far as mass influxes of refugees were concerned ... *unless international collaboration was sufficiently organized to deal with such a situation*': UN doc. A/CONF.2/SR.16 at 11 (emphasis added). The Dutch comments are thus neither an 'official' interpretation of the Convention, nor a binding limitation on the plain language.

[23] Cf. Robinson: *Commentary*, (1953), 163—art. 33 'concerns refugees who have gained entry into the territory of a contracting State, legally or illegally, but not refugees who seek entrance into this territory'; Weis: 30 *BYIL* (1953) at 482–3—*non-refoulement* 'leads the way to the adoption of the principle that a State shall not refuse admission to a refugee, i.e. it shall grant him at least temporary asylum ... if non-admission is tantamount to surrender to the country of persecution'; (High Commissioner for Refugees) Schnyder, F., 'Les aspects juridiques actuels du problème des réfugiés', Hague *Recueil* (1965–I) 339, at 381—the principles of non-rejection and temporary asylum are becoming more and more recognized; (High Commissioner for Refugees) Sadruddin Aga Khan,

tle is to be gained today by further analysis of the motives of States or the meaning of words in 1951. Likewise, it is fruitless to pay too much attention to moments of entry or presence, legal or physical. As a matter of fact, anyone presenting themselves at a frontier post, port, or airport will already be within State territory and jurisdiction; for this reason, and the better to retain sovereign control, States have devised fictions to keep even the physically present alien technically, legally, unadmitted.[24] Similarly, no consequence of significance can be derived from repeated reliance on the proposition that States have no duty to admit refugees, or indeed, any other aliens. 'No duty to admit' begs many questions; in particular, whether States are obliged to protect refugees to the extent of not adopting measures which will result in their persecution or exposure to danger. State practice in fact attributes little weight to the precise issue of admission, but far more to the necessity for *non-refoulement* through time, pending the obtaining of durable solutions.

Let it be assumed that, in 1951, the principle of *non-refoulement* was binding solely on the conventional level, and that it did not encompass non-rejection at the frontier. Analysis today requires full account of State practice since that date,[25] as well as that of international organizations. Over the last forty-five or so years, the broader interpretation of *non-refoulement* has established itself. States have allowed large numbers of asylum seekers not only to cross their frontiers, for example, in Africa, Europe and South East Asia, but also to remain pending a solution.[26] State practice, individually and within international organizations, has contributed to further progressive development of the law. By and large, States in their practice and in their recorded views, have recognized that

'Legal problems relating to refugees and displaced persons', Hague *Recueil* (1976–I) 287, at 318–22—concluding that States do not accept the rule of non-rejection. See also Weis, P., 'Territorial Asylum', 6 *Indian Journal of International Law* (1966) 173, at 183—arguing for extension of the principle to non-rejection at the frontier, otherwise protection becomes dependent on 'the fortuitous circumstance' that the refugee has successfully entered State territory. Grahl-Madsen consistently argued that art. 33 is limited to those present, lawfully or unlawfully, in the territory of contracting States, that protection depends upon having 'set foot' in that territory: *The Status of Refugees in International Law*, (1966), vol. 2, 94–9; *Territorial Asylum*, (1980), 40ff.

[24] See, for example, the elaborations of Lord Denning in *R.* v. *Governor of Brixton Prison, ex parte Soblen* [1963] 2 QB 243; also the US decisions cited by Pugash, 'The Dilemma of the Sea Refugee: Rescue without Refuge,' 18 *Harv. ILJ* (1977) 577, at 592ff; *A Study on Statelessness* (UN doc. E/1112 and Add. 1, 1949, at 60) defines *reconduction* as 'the mere physical act of ejecting from the national territory a person who has gained entry or is residing therein irregularly' and *expulsion* as 'the juridical decision taken by the judicial or administrative authorities whereby an individual is ordered to leave the territory of the country'. The study observes that terminology varies, but for its purposes the term *refoulement* (reconduction) was not used to signify the act of preventing a foreigner present at the frontier from entering the national territory.

[25] Note Vienna Convention on the Law of Treaties, art. 31(1), (2) and further below, Ch. 9, s. 3.3.

[26] In 1953 the French Minister of the Interior, advising the Parliament that asylum seekers from Spain were still arriving, gave assurances that none was refused admission; all were allowed to remain pending determination of refugee status, when those not recognized were invited to return to their country: Kiss, *Répertoire de la pratique française*, vol. 4, 434–5. In 1956, following the Hungarian crisis, some 180,000 were granted immediate first asylum in Austria, and a further 20,000 in Yugoslavia: UNHCR, *A Mandate to Protect and Assist Refugees*, (1971), 67–77.

non-refoulement applies to the moment at which asylum seekers present themselves for entry. Certain factual elements may be necessary (such as human rights violations in the country of origin) before the principle is triggered, but the concept now encompasses both non-return and non-rejection. A realistic appraisal of the normative aspect of *non-refoulement* in turn requires that the rule be examined not in isolation, but in its dynamic sense and in relation to the concept of asylum and the pursuit of durable solutions.

2.2 CONVENTIONS AND AGREEMENTS

In addition to the 1951 Convention/1967 Protocol, the principle of *non-refoulement* is powerfully expressed in article 3 of the 1984 UN Convention against Torture:

1. No State Party shall expel, return ('refouler') or extradite a person to another State where there are substantial grounds for believing that he would be in danger of being subjected to torture.
2. For the purpose of determining whether there are such grounds, the competent authorities shall take into account all relevant considerations including, where applicable, the existence in the State concerned of a consistent pattern of gross, flagrant or mass violations of human rights.

International humanitarian law provides additional support. The 1949 Geneva Convention relative to the Protection of Civilian Persons in Time of War define 'protected persons' as 'those who, at a given moment and in any manner whatsoever, find themselves, in case of a conflict or occupation, in the hands of a Party to the conflict or Occupying Power of which they are not nationals'.[27] Article 45 provides in part:

Protected persons shall not be transferred to a Power which is not a party to the Convention . . . In no circumstances shall a protected person be transferred to a country *where he or she may have reason to fear persecution for his or her political opinions or religious beliefs.* (Emphasis added).

Non-refoulement is also embodied in regional instruments. Article II(3) of the 1969 OAU Convention Governing the Specific Aspects of Refugees Problems in Africa[28] declares that,

[n]o person shall be subjected . . . to measures such as rejection at the frontier, return or expulsion, which would compel him to return to or remain in a territory where his life, physical integrity or liberty would be threatened.

Article 12(3) of the 1981 African [Banjul] Charter of Human and Peoples' Rights focuses specifically on asylum:

---

[27] Art. 4, Geneva Convention Relative to the Protection of Civilian Persons in Time of War (Fourth Convention of 12 Aug. 1949).
[28] 1001 *UNTS* 45; below Annexe 2, No. 1.

Every individual shall have the right, when persecuted, to seek and obtain asylum in other countries in accordance with the law of those countries and international conventions.

The central features of *non-refoulement* are present in article 22(8) the 1969 American Convention on Human Rights:

In no case may an alien be deported or returned to a country, regardless of whether or not it is his country of origin, if in that country his right to life or personal freedom is in danger of being violated because of his race, nationality, religion, social status, or political opinions.[29]

In the Americas, regional protection of asylees goes back to the 1889 Montevideo Treaty on International Penal Law;[30] article 16 proclaims that 'Political refugees shall be afforded an inviolable asylum', and article 20 excludes extradition for political crimes.[31] Each of these regional instruments has been widely accepted, with no reservations recorded or attempted with respect to the basic principle of non-return.

Non-refoulement is covered, at least in part, by article 3 of the 1950 European Convention on Human Rights, prohibiting torture, or cruel, inhuman or degrading treatment or punishment. In the view of the European Commission on Human Rights,

If conditions in a country are such that the risk of serious treatment and the severity of that treatment fall within the scope of article 3, a decision to deport, extradite or expel an individual to face such conditions incurs the responsibility . . . of the contracting State which so decides.[32]

This illustrates the general issue of State responsibility in regard to the removal of persons from State territory, and is founded on the unqualified terms of article 3, read in conjunction with article 1, requiring Contracting States to protect everyone within their jurisdiction from the real risk of such treatment, in the light of its irremediable nature.[33]

---

[29] *OAS Official Records*, OEA/Ser.K/XVI/1.1.

[30] *OAS Official Records*, OEA/Ser.X/1. Treaty Series 34. See also art. 20, 1940 Montevideo Treaty on International Penal Law; art. 3, 1954 Caracas Convention on Territorial Asylum ('No State is under the obligation to surrender to another State, or to expel from its own territory, persons persecuted for political reasons or offenses'); below, Annexe 2, No. 3.

[31] Other relevant provisions include art. 4(5), 1981 Inter-American Convention on Extradition; art. 3(2), 1957 European Convention on Extradition; below, Annexe 2, No. 10.

[32] *Kirkwood* v. *United Kingdom* (10479/83), 37 *D & R* 158; *The Chahal Family* v. *United Kingdom* (22414/93), 27 June 1995: according to the European Commission on Human Rights, art. 3 guarantees 'are of an absolute character, permitting no exception', and '[t]o this extent the Convention provides wider guarantees than Articles 32 and 33' of the 1951 Convention (paras. 103–4). See further below, Ch. 8, s. 2.2.1, for an assessment of the practical protection that may, or may not, be due under the regional system.

[33] Art. 3 of the European Convention has been interpreted as an obligation to afford humanitarian assistance in cases of gross violation of human rights by other States, although it has been argued that this gives rise to no general right of 'temporary refuge', and that the article's focus on conduct of particular gravity attracts a heavy evidential burden ('substantial grounds to fear', 'actual concrete danger'): Hailbronner, K., '*Non-refoulement* and "Humanitarian" Refugees: Customary

2.3 DECLARATIONS AND RESOLUTIONS

Besides the range of obligations formally undertaken by States, the standing of the principle of *non-refoulement* in international law must also be assessed by reference to formally non-binding declarations and resolutions. States are able to express their views and policies in a variety of international fora; if their practice in turn conforms to such statements, this may give further support to the concretization of a norm of customary international law.

Thus, the 1967 Declaration on Territorial Asylum, adopted unanimously by the General Assembly, recommends that States be guided by the principle that no one entitled to seek asylum 'shall be subjected to measures such as rejection at the frontier or, if he has already entered the territory in which he seeks asylum, expulsion or compulsory return to any State where he may be subjected to persecution'.[34]

Very similar language was used in article III(3) of the Principles concerning Treatment of Refugees, adopted by the Asian–African Legal Consultative Committee in Bangkok in 1966.[35] A resolution adopted by the Committee of Ministers of the Council of Europe the following year acknowledged that member States should 'ensure that no one shall be subjected to refusal of admission at the frontier, rejection, expulsion or any other measure which would have the result of compelling him to return to, or remain in, a territory where he would be in danger of persecution . . .'[36] The Committee of Ministers reiterated this principle in 1984, 'regardless of whether [the] person has been recognized as a refugee . . .'[37] The 1984 Cartagena Declaration is yet more categoric, not only endorsing a broader, regional-specific refugee definition, but also reiterating the importance of *non-refoulement* and non-rejection at the frontier as a 'corner-stone' of international protection, having the status of *jus cogens*.[38]

The United Nations has lately recognized the relationship between *non-refoulement* and the protection of human rights. For example, the Principles on

International Law or Wishful Legal Thinking?' 26 *Virg JIL* 857 (1986); also published in Martin, D., *The New Asylum-Seekers*, (1988). So far as this is indeed borne out by the case law, art. 3 may fail to offer any *additional* protection to the refugee, while it nevertheless strengthens the basic principle of non-return to certain specifically threatening situations. See further below.

[34] Art. 3(1); below, Annexe 1, No. 6. Note that art. 3(2) provides that an exception may be made to the basic principle, 'only for overriding reasons of national security or in order to safeguard the population, as in the case of a mass influx of persons'. In such circumstances, the State contemplating such exception, 'shall consider the possibility of granting to the person concerned, under such conditions as it may deem appropriate, an opportunity, whether by way of provisional asylum or otherwise, of going to another State': art. 3(3).

[35] *Report of the Eighth Session of the Asian–African Legal Consultative Committee*, Bangkok, 8–17 Aug. 1966, 355; below, Annexe 4, No. 8. The Bangkok Principles also make provision for provisional asylum in cases of exception; see art. III(4).

[36] Res. (67) 14 on Asylum to Persons in Danger of Persecution, adopted 29 June 1967; below, Annexe 4, No. 5. Compare the formulation adopted in art. II(3) of the 1969 OAU Convention.

[37] Rec. No. R (84) 1, Recommendation on the Protection of Persons satisfying the Criteria in the Geneva Convention who are not Formally Recognized as Refugees.

[38] Cartagena Declaration, Conclusions and Recommendations, III, 5; below, Annexe 2, No. 7.

the Effective Prevention and Investigation of Extra-Legal, Arbitrary and Summary Executions, endorsed by the General Assembly in 1989, provide that 'no one shall be involuntarily returned or extradited to a country where there are substantial grounds for believing that he or she may become a victim of extra-legal, arbitrary or summary execution in that country'.[39] In 1992, the General Assembly adopted the Declaration on the Protection of All Persons from Enforced Disappearance, article 8(1) of which declares that 'No State shall expel, return (*refouler*) or extradite a person to another State where there are substantial grounds to believe that he would be in danger of enforced disappearance'.[40] Both of these provisions contribute to and confirm the meaning of persecution, and even if they do not expand the substantive scope of protection, nevertheless consolidate the legal standing of the principle of *non-refoulement* in general international law.

2.4 THE UNHCR EXECUTIVE COMMITTEE CONCLUSIONS ON INTERNATIONAL PROTECTION

The UNHCR Executive Committee[41] has consistently endorsed the fundamental character of the principle of *non-refoulement*, in its annual general and specific conclusions. In 1977, for example, the Executive Committee noted that the principle was 'generally accepted by States', expressed concern at its disregard in certain cases, and reaffirmed,

the fundamental importance of the observance of the principle of *non-refoulement*—both at the border and within the territory of a State—of persons who may be subjected to persecution if returned to their country of origin irrespective of whether or not they have been formally recognized as refugees.[42]

Non-refoulement as a paramount consideration has also been reiterated in specific contexts. For example, 'in the case of large-scale influx, persons seeking asylum should always receive at least temporary refuge';[43] similarly, 'in situations of large-scale influx, asylum seekers should be admitted to the State in which they first seek refuge ... In all cases the fundamental principle of *non-refoulement*— including non-rejection at the frontier—must be scrupulously observed'.[44]

In its 1982 general conclusion on protection, the Executive Committee expressed the view that the principle 'was progressively acquiring the character of a peremptory rule of international law'.[45] Reported instances of breach of the

---

[39] UNGA res. 44/162, 15 Dec. 1989, para. 5; below, Annexe 4, No. 3. See also ECOSOC res. 1989/65, 24 May 1989, recommending that the principles annexed to the resolution be taken into account and respected by governments.

[40] UNGA res. 47/133, 18 Dec. 1992, adopted without a vote; below, Annexe 4, No. 4. Art. 8(2) reproduces art. 3(2), 1984 Convention Against Torture.

[41] On which see further below, Ch. 6, s. 1.1.1.

[42] Executive Committee Conclusion No. 6 (1977)

[43] Executive Committee Conclusion No. 19 (1980).

[44] Executive Committee Conclusion No. 22 (1981).

[45] *Report* of the 33rd Session: UN doc. A/AC.96/614, para. 70.

principle have been consistently deplored,[46] and in 1989, after the matter was raised expressly by UNHCR in its annual *Note on International Protection*,[47] the Executive Committee expressed its deep concern 'that refugee protection is seriously jeopardized in some States by expulsion and *refoulement* of refugees or by measures which do not recognize the special situation of refugees'.[48] The same year, when dealing with the problem of irregular movements, the Executive Committee affirmed that 'refugees and asylum seekers [who] move in an irregular manner from a country where they have already found protection . . . may be returned to that country if . . . they are protected there against *refoulement* . . .'; but if, in exceptional circumstances, the physical safety or freedom of such refugee or asylum seeker may be at risk, or he or she has good reason to fear persecution there, then their cases should be considered favourably.[49]

Similar language occurs in later conclusions. In 1991, the Executive Committee emphasized 'the primary importance of *non-refoulement* and asylum as cardinal principles of refugee protection', while indirectly stressing the protective purpose of the principle by reference to the need for refugees to be able to 'return in safety and dignity to their homes without harassment, arbitrary detention or physical threats during or after return'.[50]

In 1992, the Executive Committee maintained this traditional language, but emphasized also that UNHCR's involvement with internally displaced persons and related approaches, 'should not undermine the institution of asylum, as well as other basic protection principles, notably the principle of *non-refoulement*.'[51]

The conclusions adopted by the UNHCR Executive Committee do not have force of law and do not, of themselves, create binding obligations. They may contribute, however, to the formulation of *opinio juris*—the sense of legal obligation with which States may or may not approach the problems of refugees. Some conclusions seek to lay down standards of treatment, or to resolve differences of interpretation between States or between States and UNHCR, while others are more hortatory, repeating and reaffirming basic principles without seeking either to expand their field of application.[52] They must therefore be reviewed in

[46] See, for example, Executive Committee Conclusions No. 46 (1987), *Report* of the 38th Session: UN doc. A/AC.96/702, para. 204; No. 50 (1988), *Report* of the 39th Session: UN doc. A/AC.96/721, para. 23.

[47] UN doc. A/AC.96/728 (2 Aug. 1989), para. 19.

[48] Executive Committee Conclusion No. 55, *Report* of the 40th Session: UN doc. A/AC.96/737 (19 Oct. 1989), para. 22(d).

[49] Executive Committee Conclusion No. 58 (1989), paras. (f), (g).

[50] Executive Committee Conclusion No. 65 (1991), *Report* of the 42nd Session: UN doc. A/AC.96/783 (21 Oct. 1991), para. 21(c), (j).

[51] Executive Committee Conclusion No. 68 (1992), *Report* of the 43rd Session: UN doc. A/AC.96/804, (15 Oct. 1992), para. 21(e), (f), (r). See also Executive Committee Conclusions No. 71 (1993); No. 74 (1994), *Report* of the 45th Session: UN doc. A/AC.96/839, para. 19; No. 77, *Report* of the 46th Session: UN doc. A/AC.96/860, para. 19 (1995).

[52] See Sztucki, J., 'The Conclusions on the International Protection of Refugees Adopted by the Executive Committee of the UNHCR Programme', 1 *IJRL* 285 (1989).

the context of States' expressed opinions, and in light of what they do in practice.

2.5 STATE VIEWS AND STATE PRACTICE

2.5.1 State views

The views and comments of States in the Executive Committee fall into two broad categories: first, general endorsements of the principle of *non-refoulement*, which usually say little about content or scope; and secondly, more focused comments, by which States seek to show where, in their opinion or practice, the limits to obligation lie.

One of the clearest general statements in support of the principle of *non-refoulement* was made by Ambassador Jonathan Moore, United States Coordinator for Refugee Affairs, at the Executive Committee in 1987.

Forced repatriation had occurred in almost every region of the world during the past year, resulting in death, serious injury and imprisonment. Considering that the most important element of a refugee's protection was the obligation of *non-refoulement*, it was tragic that refugees had been forced to return to their countries against their will and without assurances that they would not face persecution on their return, especially when such violations were committed by, or with the concurrence of, States parties to international instruments prohibiting such acts. The threat to a country posed by influxes of economic migrants should not serve as an excuse for refusing asylum.[53]

Other comments in the years since 1987 have ranged from support for the idea that *non-refoulement* was a rule of *jus cogens*,[54] to regret at reported instances of non-observance of fundamental obligations,[55] to concern at current challenges to the related 'principle of first asylum',[56] to the need, before implementing any form of compulsory return, to define objective criteria 'to determine whether security concerns had been fully met', and further, with respect to the cessation clauses, 'to ensure that refugees were not forced to return to unsafe countries'.[57]

More focused comments have raised issues of specific application. In 1987, the Turkish representative raised a particularly serious question:

The principle of *non-refoulement* . . . had to be scrupulously observed. Nevertheless, . . . countries of first asylum or transit . . . , faced with the difficulties of repatriation and the progressively more restrictive practices of host countries, might find themselves unable to continue bearing the burden and, for want of any other solution, come to regard *refoulement* as the only possible way out. If that should occur, they would not be

---

[53] UN doc. A/AC.96/SR.415, para. 16 (1987).

[54] Mr Mponda (Observer for Malawi): UN doc. A/AC.96/SR.431, para. 32 (1988).

[55] 'The *refoulement* of refugees must not be allowed to occur under any circumstances.' Mr Ceska (Austria): UN doc. A/AC.96/SR.439, para. 9 (1989).

[56] Mrs Lafontant (USA): UN doc. A/AC.96/SR.437, para. 49 (1989). Mrs Lafontant had succeeded Jonathan Moore, and was Ambassador-at-Large and US Co-ordinator for Refugee Affairs.

[57] Mr de Sa Barbuda (Brazil): UN doc. A/AC.96/SR.475, para. 83 (1992), commenting on temporary protection and its eventual termination as a possible alternative to the right of asylum in mass influx situations.

the only ones at fault, since the responsibility for ensuring the conditions necessary for observance of the *non-refoulement* principle rested with the international community as a whole.[58]

This precise point emerged again in 1989, when the Turkish representative remarked that the refugee problem, 'was such that it was no longer possible to disassociate international protection from international co-operation and assistance'.[59] Commenting on developments in Iraq in April 1991 and the arrival on the border of some half million Kurdish asylum seekers, the Turkish representative noted that while his country had tried to meet the needs of those concerned, '[t]he scale of the operation had . . . been prohibitive, and Turkey had been compelled to call for urgent international assistance . . . As a result of the subsequent international co-operation, virtually all those displaced persons had now been resettled in the security zone established in the north of Iraq.'[60] If the reference to 'security' can be taken as controlling, then the rather unique situation of the Kurdish people in search of refuge might still be interpreted consistently with a variant of *non-refoulement* that permits only limited exceptions, conditioning return or rejection in situations of mass influx on the availability of alternative forms of safety. This is not particularly persuasive, but the 'solution' imposed on northern Iraq remains unique.[61] In cases not involving 'mass migrations', no such exception could apply.[62]

Since 1985, a number of States have stressed that *non-refoulement* does not apply to non-Convention refugees, although many accept that protection needs are involved. In 1988, the Swiss representative was apprehensive that the 'dilution' of the refugee concept 'would . . . weaken the basic principle of *non-refoulement.*' While others might be allowed to remain for humanitarian reasons, this would not be based on a Convention obligation, so much as on 'considerations of humanitarian law or international solidarity, in other words, on a free decision by the State concerned'.[63] In 1990, several States called attention to the fact that they were parties to the 1984 United Nations Convention against Torture, and consequently also bound by that treaty's provision prohibiting return to situations of torture even of persons not technically within the refugee definition.

[58] Mr Yavuzalp (Turkey): UN doc. A/AC.96/SR.418, para. 74 (1987).

[59] Mr Demiralp (Turkey): UN doc. A/AC.96/SR.442, para. 92 (1989); see also Mr Cem Duna (Turkey): UN doc. A/AC.96/SR.456, para. 7 (1991). On several occasions, the Turkish representatives have both upheld the fundamental character of *non-refoulement* while simultaneously supporting the right of the asylum seeker to choose in which country to seek asylum, thereby staking a claim for a form of 'natural' burden-sharing. See further below, s. 3.2 on mass influx as exception.

[60] Mr Atkan (Turkey): UN doc. A/AC.96/SR.468, para. 18 (1991).

[61] See generally, Adelman, H., 'Humanitarian Intervention: The Case of the Kurds', 4 *IJRL* 4 (1992).

[62] Although Turkey's formal reservations have focused on mass influx, its record on individual cases has not always been perfect; see Amnesty International, 'Turkey: Selective Protection. Discriminatory treatment of non-European refugees and asylum seekers' (1994); Kirişçi, K., 'Asylum seekers and Human Rights in Turkey', 10 *Neth. Q.H.R.* 447 (1992). Note however that Turkey maintains the geographical limitation to its obligations under the 1951 Convention/1967 Protocol.

[63] Mr Hadorn (Switzerland): UN doc. A/AC.96/SR.430, para. 42, (1988).

Two delegations commented that 'any responsibility not to return non-refugees was far less clear-cut in situations that do not involve torture.'[64]

In the Sub-Committee of the Whole on International Protection in 1992, a number of delegations warned against 'borrowing terminology and approaches from the Convention for new refugee situations, to which these instruments were not intended to apply'. Several also did not accept that there was 'a legal right of *non-refoulement* for non-1951 Convention refugees'; nevertheless, 'minimum standards of protection' were due, 'including non-discrimination and other fair and humane treatment, as well as respect for the integrity of the family unit'.[65] While the 'central importance' of basic principles such as *non-refoulement* was reaffirmed, one delegation stated its belief that there was no 'rule of customary international law preventing repatriation because of generalized conditions of unrest or violence'.[66] The year before, on the other hand, the Swedish representative, while conscious that legal solutions did not suffice and that prevention must also be considered, was of the view that protection should be extended not only to Convention refugees, 'but also to people fleeing . . . armed conflict or other forms of violence and to victims of natural or ecological disasters and extreme poverty. It was often far from easy to differentiate between such categories and asylum seekers motivated by purely economic considerations'.[67]

On other occasions, States have described practices which, in their view, did not amount to *refoulement*, such as normal immigration controls, visa policies and carrier sanctions. In 1988 again, the United Kingdom representative declared his country's intention to abide fully by the principle, but this did not prevent the return of 'failed asylum seekers', or returns to 'safe third countries'.[68] The representative for Argentina, on the other hand, was careful to stress that practices such as 'the refusal of admission at a border for purely administrative reasons vitiated the principle of *non-refoulement*.'[69]

Discussion of the 'safe country/safe country of asylum' question has also led States to consider its relation to *non-refoulement*, with several delegations emphasizing that 'the fundamental criterion when considering resort to the notion, was protection against *refoulement*'.[70] Similarly, only a change of circumstances 'of a fundamental character' in the country of origin would justify the termination of protection against *refoulement*.[71]

[64] *Report* of the Sub-Committee of the Whole on International Protection: UN doc. A/AC.96/758, 2 Oct. 1990, para. 29.
[65] *Report* of the Sub-Committee: UN doc. A/AC.96/802, 6 Oct. 1992, paras. 16–17.
[66] Ibid., para. 17.
[67] Mr Willen (Sweden): UN doc. A/AC.96/SR.464, para. 31 (1991).
[68] Mr Wrench (UK): UN doc. A/AC.96/SR.430, para. 53, (1988). This interpretation was reiterated the following year; see UN doc. A/AC.96/SR.442, para. 51 (1989).
[69] Mr Strassera (Argentina): UN doc. A/AC.96/SR. 442, para. 46 (1989).
[70] *Report* of the Sub-Committee of the Whole on International Protection: UN doc. A/AC.96/781, 9 Oct. 1991, para. 34.
[71] *Report* of the Inter-Sessional Meeting of the Sub-Committee of the Whole on International Protection (23 Jan. 1992): UN doc. EC/SCP/70, 7 Jul. 1992.

Perhaps the most significant attack on the principle occurred in the Sub-Committee of the Whole on International Protection in 1989, when the United States representative attempted to establish some of the groundwork for its domestic litigation strategy in support of Haitian interdiction. Despite earlier US declarations of support for the principle of 'first asylum',[72] the United States delegate sought to distinguish between legally binding obligations and non-binding 'generally-accepted moral and political principles of refugee protection'.[73] The United States, he said, did not believe that States were under a legal obligation 'to admit persons seeking asylum':

As a matter of practice, the United States authorities did not return persons who were likely to be persecuted in their countries of origin . . . That was the practice, and . . . the policy of the United States, and not a principle of international law with which it conformed . . . It did not consider that the *non-refoulement* obligation under article 33 of the Convention included an obligation to admit an asylum seeker. The obligation . . . pertained only to persons already in the country and not to those who arrived at the frontier or who were travelling with the intention of entering the country but had not yet arrived at their destination. Furthermore, there was nothing to suggest that an obligation to admit asylum seekers had ripened into a rule of customary international law.[74]

The intervention, which attracted no support or comment from other States, was clearly drafted with the Haitian interdiction programme in mind; equally clearly, it failed to notice that *non-refoulement* is not so much about *admission* to a State, as about not returning refugees to where their lives or freedom may be endangered. It was also inconsistent with US support for the principle of first asylum, declared earlier in the same session, and even repeated in the same intervention.[75] Ultimately, however, this strategic departure from the accepted meaning of *non-refoulement* came too late to alter the obligations of the United States under international law.[76]

2.5.2 *State practice: some aspects*

The views of States and to some extent their practice also indicate a contingent dimension to the principle of *non-refoulement*. Reservations with respect to the security aspects of mass influxes have not died away since they were formally recognized in the 1967 UN Declaration on Territorial Asylum. On the contrary, they continue to surface in the discourse of many 'frontline' States, such as Turkey, Thailand, Zaire, or Tanzania. Clearly, from 1979 onwards resettlement guarantees and substantial financial contributions were a major factor in preserving the so-called principle of first asylum. In October 1979, for example,

---

[72] See above, n. 56 and text. US concern to defend the principle of first asylum was motivated in particular by practices in South East Asia, where Indo-Chinese boat people were not infrequently denied access to coastal States, placed back on board ships returning to their country of origin, or towed out to sea, often with resulting loss of life.

[73] Mr Kelley (USA): UN doc. A/AC.96/SR.442, paras. 78–9 (1989).

[74] Ibid., paras. 80, 82.   [75] Ibid., para. 81.

[76] See further below, s. 3.2.1.

Thailand announced the reversal of a policy which had earlier led to the forcible return of some 40,000 Kampucheans; henceforth, all asylum seekers were to allowed to enter.[77] Likewise, the unnerving prospect of a repeat operation on behalf of Kurdish refugees imminently leaving northern Iraq for Turkey was a factor in the decision to establish a security zone, thereby removing or attenuating the factor of risk that would otherwise have triggered the principle of *non-refoulement*, if not its application in the particular circumstances.[78]

It is therefore important to distinguish carefully between situations of mass influx and other situations where the failure to apply the principle has led to protest. For example, bilateral agreements between East African States which led to *refoulement* and a mutual exchange of refugees were the subject of protest in 1983–4, followed by appeals for clemency on behalf of those tried and sentenced to death.[79] In 1987, the United States and UNHCR also protested the action of the Singapore authorities in placing two Vietnamese stowaways back on board a ship returning to Vietnam, despite the offer of resettlement guarantees. In another case in 1988, the High Commissioner intervened directly with the Prime Minister of Singapore, and the stowaways were allowed to disembark from the vessel on condition that they went straight to the airport and left Singapore.

In 1989, UNHCR welcomed the inclusion of *non-refoulement* in a new Italian decree, particularly given its broadening of criteria to cover those who could be persecuted for reasons of sex, language, personal or social conditions, or who risked being returned to another country in which they might run such risk. It expressed concern, however, at the limitation of protection to expulsion proceedings, so that rejection at the frontier was not covered. When the decree was 'converted' to a law the following year, protection was also extended to certain categories of asylum seekers, although the risk of frontier rejections and possible *refoulement* was increased, as in other European countries, by summary exclusions based on assumptions of 'protection elsewhere'. In June 1991, the Italian authorities sent back some 800–1,000 Albanian 'boat people', against guarantees from the country of origin. The non-penalization of the group led the authorities summarily to reject all of the 18,000 or so Albanians who arrived in early August that year. UNHCR did not intervene, on the basis that the Albanians were not of concern to the Office. Those fleeing the conflict in former Yugoslavia were admitted and protected during the same period, however.

Also in 1991, the United States revised its policy and practice with respect to Haitians intercepted on the high seas, electing to abandon the procedure of

---

[77] See *Report* of the Secretary-General: UN doc. A/34/627, para. 48; annex 1, para. 8.

[78] Both art. II(4), 1969 OAU Convention and paras. 3 and 4 of Council of Europe Resolution 67 (14) acknowledge that States may have difficulty in fulfilling their obligations without international co-operation. Cf. Fonteyne, J.-P., 'Burden-Sharing: An Analysis of the Nature and Function of International Solidarity in Cases of Mass Influx of Refugees', 8 *Aust. YB Int'l Law* 162 (1983).

[79] See *Report* of the 35th Session of the Executive Committee (1984): UN docs. A/AC. 96/651, para. 24; A/AC.96/SR.369, para. 60 (The Netherlands).

screening for 'colorable claims' to asylum that had been applied over the previous ten years. The legality of this action is considered in more detail below.

The recent practice of States has frequently included the protection of persons fleeing situations of grave and urgent necessity, even as States resist formally classifying such persons as *refugees* when outside the terms of the 1951 Convention/1967 Protocol, and do not accept any obligation to grant them asylum or provide any particular durable solution.[80] The practice shows that States commonly accord refuge in such cases, and thereby confirm essential humanitarian principles deriving from a variety of sources, including the duties owed to the victims of armed conflict and to civilians caught up in or fleeing war; the obligation to protect those in danger of torture, as required by customary international law, now re-stated in article 3 of the 1984 United Nations Convention; and even the traditional practice whereby ships under *force majeure* or stress of weather are considered immune from the exercise of jurisdiction when entering a State, on the basis of urgent distress and grave necessity.

2.6 THE PRINCIPLE AND THE COMMENTATORS

While there is little difficulty in showing the extent of *treaty* obligations of *non-refoulement*, establishing the status of the principle in general on customary international law presents greater problems. In 1954, twenty-seven States participating in the UN Conference on the Status of Stateless Persons unanimously expressed the view that the *non-refoulement* provision of the 1951 Refugee Convention was 'an expression of the generally accepted principle' of non-return; for that reason, it was considered unnecessary to include an equivalent article for stateless persons.[81] That assessment was premature, but, as shown above, the principle of *non-refoulement* has since been reiterated and refined, included in a range of regional refugee, human rights and extradition treaties, repeatedly endorsed in a variety of international fora, and its violation protested by UNHCR and States.

Both article 33 of the 1951 Convention and article 3 of the 1984 Convention against Torture are of a 'fundamentally norm-creating character such as could be regarded as forming the basis of a general rule of law', as that phrase was used by the International Court of Justice in the *North Sea Continental Shelf* cases.[82] So far as both Convention provisions are formally addressed to the contracting Parties, the universality of the principle of *non-refoulement* has nevertheless been a constant emphasis of other instruments, including declarations, recommendations and resolutions at both international and regional levels. The proof of international customary law requires consistency and generality of practice, but

---

[80] A cogent account and analysis of State practice is given in Perluss, D. and Hartman, J., 'Temporary Refuge: Emergence of a Customary International Norm,' 26 *Virg. JIL* 551 (1986); see also Meron, T., *Human Rights and Humanitarian Norms as Customary Law*, (1989); Goodwin-Gill, G. S., '*Non-refoulement* and the New Asylum-Seekers,' 26 *Virg. JIL* 897 (1986).

[81] Final Act, UN Conference on the Status of Stateless Persons: 360 UNTS 117.

[82] ICJ *Rep.*, 1969, 3 at 42.

no particular duration; universality and complete uniformity are not required, but the practice must be accepted as law. In many cases, this *opinio juris* may be inferred from the evidence of a general practice, or a consensus in the literature.[83]

Writing separately in 1982, Feliciano, Hyndman and Kälin all expressed degrees of cautious reservation with respect to the scope of any customary international law rule prohibiting the return of refugees to countries in which they might be persecuted. Feliciano considered that, with one material qualification, 'the *non-refoulement* principle may properly be regarded as having matured into a norm of customary international law'. That qualification concerned the position of the 'socialist' countries: '[t]hus it appears that *non-refoulement* is a principle not of *general* customary law but of *regional* or *hemispherical* customary law, being widely or generally acknowledged in the non-socialist part of the globe'.[84]

Hyndman also thought that a good case could be made for a customary rule, but recognized that many States had reservations in the case of threats to national security, or in situations of mass influx: '. . . the oft-repeated . . . exceptions cannot be ignored and may be indicative that if *non-refoulement* has become a binding principle it has become so with these limitations'.[85] Kälin was of the view that while the principle was customary law in the making, it was acknowledged as regional custom only in Europe, the Americas and Africa. In particular, he found significant the fact that in discussions on the UN Declaration on Territorial Asylum in the Sixth (Legal) Committee of the General Assembly, 'the great majority of delegations stressed that the draft . . . was not intended to propound legal norms, but to lay down broad humanitarian and moral principles upon which States might rely in seeking to unify their practices relating to asylum'.[86] Kälin was also concerned by the inconsistency and divergencies in State practice, including application of the refugee definition and its exceptions, which further narrowed the reach of the principle itself.[87]

A monograph on non-expulsion and *non-refoulement* published in 1989 took

---

[83] See Brownlie, I., *Principles of Public International Law*, (4th ed., 1990), 4–11.

[84] Feliciano, F. P., 'The Principle of *Non-Refoulement*: A Note on International Legal Protection of Refugees and Displaced Persons,' 57 *Philippine L.J.* 598, 608–9 (1982). (Emphasis in original).

[85] Hyndman, P., 'Asylum and *Non-Refoulement*—Are these Obligations owed to Refugees under International Law?' 57 *Philippine L.J.* 43, 68–9 (1982). Grahl-Madsen thought the exception relating to mass influx 'may be acceptable': *Territorial Asylum*, (1980), 65–6. See also Martin, D. A., 'Large Scale Migrations of Asylum Seekers,' 76 *AJIL* 598 (1982).

[86] UN doc. A/6912, para. 13, quoted in Kälin, W., *Das Prinzip des Non-Refoulement*, (1982), 71. Grahl-Madsen, writing in 1980, commented that by 'being adopted by the General Assembly . . . the principle of *non-refoulement* has most certainly acquired a high degree of general acceptance,' but he accorded it no greater legal status: *Territorial Asylum*, (1980), 42.

[87] 'Zusammenfassend ist festzustellen, dass das refoulement-Verbot heute noch nicht den Rang von universellem Völkergewohnheitsrecht erlangt hat, dass aber eine deutliche Entwicklung in diese Richtung besteht. Insofer lässt sich sagen, das non-refoulement-Prinzip sei in Entstehung begriffenes universelles Völkergewohnheitsrecht . . . Die Bedeutung dieser Aussage darf nicht überschätzt werden. Ein Blick auf die heutige Staatenpraxis zeigt nämlich, dass der Inhalt und die Tragweite eines solchen gewohnheitsrechtlichen Rückschiebungsverbotes sehr begrenzt wären.' Kälin, W., *Das Prinzip des Non-Refoulement*, (1982), 80–1.

issue with Kälin's thesis of lack of generality of practice sufficient to found a rule of customary international law. Stenberg argued that 'there is at least persuasive evidence that Article 33 . . . satisfies the criterion of generality. Moreover, the weightiest reason for the "persistent objection" by the South East Asian States does not seem to stem from a disregard of the principle of *non-refoulement* as such, but from the fear that these States may be left . . . with a large backlog of persons who they feel they cannot admit on a permanent basis because of dangerous political, economic and social strains'.[88] Kälin also seems to have moved in the direction of customary international law, both as regards *non-refoulement* in its narrow, Convention-refugee sense,[89] and as a concept that includes protection against torture, inhuman treatment or other serious violations of human rights.[90]

Where those in flight have 'valid reasons' to seek refuge, but do not otherwise fall within the terms of the 1951 Convention/1967 Protocol, the responsibilities of States in general international law remain controversial. Differing approaches are evident in the UNHCR Executive Committee, with some States concerned to emphasize protection needs, and others to stress their sovereign discretion. In a 1986 paper somewhat ill-advisedly titled '*Non-refoulement* and the new asylum seekers', the present writer argued that while customary international law had incorporated the core meaning of article 33, it had also 'extend[ed] the principle of *non-refoulement* to include displaced persons who do not enjoy the protection of the government of their country of origin'.[91] Although framed with specific reference to danger caused by civil disorder, internal conflicts or human rights violations, the argument in terms of *non-refoulement* was not well chosen, particularly given States' perceptions linking the principle closely to Convention refugees and asylum. Rather, the impact on State competence of the broader developments relating to human rights and displacement would have been better served by characterizing State responsibilities in terms of a general principle of *refuge*.

Hailbronner has criticized the arguments for extended application of the *non-refoulement* principle as 'wishful legal thinking'.[92] His critique focuses on article 3 of the European Convention on Human Rights, rather than on international responses to a somewhat loosely defined category of 'humanitarian refugees'.

---

[88] Stenberg, G., *Non-expulsion and Non-Refoulement*, (1989), 275; on uniformity and consistency of practice and *opinio juris*, see also at 275–9.

[89] Kälin, W., *Grundriss des Asylverfahrens*, (1990), 210–11: 'Das Prinzip des non-refoulement *im engeren Sinn* ist ein Institut des *Flüchtlingsrechtes*: Es schützt Flüchtlinge vor Rückschiebung in einen Staat, in welchen ihnen Verfolgung im flüchtlingsrechtlichen Sinn droht. Dieses Prinzip gilt nicht nur kraft Vertragsrecht, sondern . . . auch kraft Völkergewohnheitsrecht.' (Footnotes omitted).

[90] 'Das Prinzip des non-refoulement bezeichnet das *Verbot, Personen zwangsweise in einen Staat zurückzuschieben, in welchem sie in flüchtlingsrechtlich relevanter Weise verfolgt oder Folter, unmenschlicher Behandlung oder anderen besonders schwerwiegenden Menschenrechtsverletzungen ausgestzt würden*': ibid., 210.

[91] Goodwin-Gill, G. S., '*Non-Refoulement* and the New Asylum-Seekers', 26 *Virg. JIL* 897, 902.

[92] Hailbronner, K., '*Non-Refoulement* and "Humanitarian" Refugees: Customary International Law or Wishful Legal Thinking?' 26 *Virg. JIL* 857 (1986).

Hailbronner accepts that article 3 has been interpreted as an obligation to afford humanitarian assistance in cases of gross violation of human rights by other States, but concludes that neither this nor State practice at large gives rise to a general right of 'temporary refuge'.[93] Such a reverse individualistic approach to international obligations, which is also common to States[94] and in the works of a number of commentators, unfortunately diverts attention from the human rights dimension: so far as a State's actions may expose an individual to risk of violation of fundamental human rights, its responsibility is duty-driven, rather than strictly correlative to any individual 'right'.[95]

3. The scope of the principle of *non-refoulement*

3.1 PERSONAL SCOPE

The principle of *non-refoulement*, as it appears in article 33 of the 1951 Convention, applies clearly and categorically to refugees within the meaning of article 1. It also applies to *asylum seekers*, at least during an initial period and in appropriate circumstances, for otherwise there would be no effective protection. Those with a presumptive or prima facie claim to refugee status are therefore entitled to protection, as the UNHCR Executive Committee has stressed, for example, in Conclusion No. 6 (1977), reaffirming 'the fundamental importance of the principle of *non-refoulement* . . . irrespective of whether or not individuals have been formally recognized as refugees'.

Equally irrelevant is the legal or migration status of the asylum seeker. It does not matter *how* the asylum seeker comes within the territory or jurisdiction of the State; what counts is what results from the actions of State agents. If the asylum seeker is forcibly repatriated to a country in which he or she has a well-founded fear of persecution or faces a substantial risk of torture, then that is *refoulement* contrary to international law.

The status or personal circumstances of the asylum seeker, however, may control the options open to the receiving State. In the case of a stowaway asylum seeker, for example, the port of call State may require the ship's master to keep him or her on board and travel on to the next port of call; or it may call upon the flag State to assume responsibility where the next port of call is unaccept-

---

[93] Ibid., 875f. Hailbronner rightly notes that art. 3 focuses on conduct of particular gravity and that this has attracted a heavy evidential burden ('substantial grounds to fear', 'actual concrete danger'); the victims of generalized violence or terror which is not specifically directed at them are thus unable to invoke its protection. For an alternative view, see Einarsen, T., 'The European Convention on Human Rights and the Notion of an Implied Right to *de facto* Asylum,' 2 *IJRL* 361 (1990); and for an assessment, see further below, Ch. 8, s. 2.2.1.

[94] See above, n. 72–6 and accompanying text, remarking the confusion between 'admission' and not returning a refugee to persecution.

[95] See also Kälin, W., *Grundriss des Asylverfahrens*, (1990), 211: 'In seinem *weiteren, menschenrechtlichen Sinn* schützt [das Prinzip des non-refoulement] vor Aushändigung an einen Staat, welcher aus irgend welchen Motiven den betroffenen Ausländer Folter oder bestimmten anderen schwerwiegenden Menschenrechtsverletzungen aussetzen würde.'

able; or it may allow temporary disembarkation pending resettlement elsewhere. Thus, by itself, a categorical refusal of disembarkation can only be equated with *refoulement,* if it actually results in the return of refugees to persecution. Similar considerations apply also to rescue at sea cases seeking disembarkation, and even to boats of asylum seekers arriving directly. From a practical perspective, however, a refusal to take account of their claims to be refugees would not suffice to avoid liability for breach of the principle of *non-refoulement.*[96]

3.1.1 *The question of risk*

The legal, and to some extent logical, relationship between article 33(1) and article 1 of the 1951 Convention/1967 Protocol is evident in the correlation established in State practice, where entitlement to the protection of *non-refoulement* is conditioned simply upon satisfying the well-founded fear criterion. So far as the drafters of the 1951 Convention were aware of a divergence between the words defining refugee status and those requiring *non-refoulement,* they gave little thought to the consequences. Mr Rochefort, the French representative, suggested that article 1 referred to examination at the frontier of those wishing to enter a contracting State, whereas article 33 was concerned with provisions applicable at a later stage. The co-existence of these two possibilities was perfectly feasible, though he detected a distinct and somewhat uncomfortable inconsistency between article 33(1) and article 1.[97] This related not to the presence of conflicting standards of proof, however, or to issues of extraterritorial application, but to the class and extent of those, principally criminals, who were to be excluded from refugee status and/or denied the benefit of *non-refoulement.*

The intimate link between articles 1 and 33 was nevertheless recognized;[98] in both, the status of 'refugee' was to be governed by the criterion of well-founded fear, and withdrawal of status or *refoulement* would always be exceptional and restricted.[99] The *travaux préparatoires* do not explain the different wording chosen for the formulations respectively of refugee status and *non-refoulement;* but neither do they give any indication that a different standard of proof was intended to be applied in one case, rather than in the other. In practice, the same standard is accepted at both national and international levels, reflecting the sufficiency of serious risk, rather than any more onerous standard of proof, such as the clear probability of persecution.[100]

At the international level, no distinction is recognized between refugee status and entitlement to *non-refoulement.* In only one instance were articles 1 and 33, as a coherent structure of protection, severed by a judicial ruling on literal meaning; and on that occasion, the executive branch of government took steps by

---

[96] See further below, s. 4.1.

[97] United Nations Conference of Plenipotentiaries, *Summary Records:* UN doc. A/CONF.2/SR.35, p. 23.

[98] UN doc. A/CONF.2/SR.35, p. 22.   [99] UN doc. A/CONF.2/SR.16, pp. 4, 8.

[100] Support for the principle of serious risk as the determinant for refugee status and consequently also for *non-refoulement,* can be found in numerous national decisions; see above, Ch. 2, s. 3.

regulation to bridge the gap between the refugee eligible for the discretionary grant of asylum and the refugee with a right to the benefit of *non-refoulement*.[101] The relation of refugee status and *non-refoulement* was described more coherently by the United Kingdom House of Lords in 1987, in *R* v. *Secretary of State for the Home Department, ex parte Sivakumaran:*

It is . . . plain, as indeed was reinforced in argument . . . with reference to the travaux préparatoires, that the *non-refoulement* provision in article 33 was intended to apply to all persons determined to be refugees under article 1 of the Convention.[102]

Non-refoulement extends in principle, therefore, to every individual who has a well-founded fear of persecution, or where there are substantial grounds for believing that he or she would be in danger of torture if returned to a particular country.

3.2 EXCEPTIONS TO THE PRINCIPLE OF *NON-REFOULEMENT*

The Convention refugee definition is not an absolute guarantee of protection, and *non-refoulement* is not an absolute principle. 'National security' and 'public order', for example, have long been recognized as potential justifications for derogation.[103] Article 33(2) expressly provides that the benefit of *non-refoulement* may not be claimed by a refugee, 'whom there are reasonable grounds for regarding as a danger to the security of the country . . . or who, having been convicted by a final judgment of a particularly serious crime, constitutes a danger to the community of that country'. The exceptions to *non-refoulement* are thus framed in terms of the individual, but whether he or she may be considered a security risk appears to be left very much to the judgment of the State authorities.[104] This, at least, was the intention of the British representative at the 1951 Conference, who proposed the inclusion of article 33(2), and such an approach

---

[101] See the US Supreme Court decisions in *INS* v. *Stevic*, 467 US 407 (1984) and *INS* v. *Cardoza-Fonseca* 480 US 421 (1987); for comment, see 2 *IJRL* 461–7 (1990). The remedy was provided by the *Final Rule on Asylum and Withholding of Deportation Procedures*, issued by the US Department of Justice Immigration and Naturalization Service in July 1990.

[102] [1988] 1 All ER 193. UNHCR submitted an intervenor brief.

[103] See, for example, art. 3, 1933 Convention relating to the International Status of Refugees: 159 *LNTS* 199; art. 5(2), 1938 Convention concerning the Status of Refugees coming from Germany: 192 *LNTS* 59. At the first session of the *Ad hoc* Committee, the British delegate suggested that *non-refoulement* should not apply when national security was involved: UN doc. E/AC.32/SR.20, paras. 10–12. The French representative had suggested limiting 'protected opinions' to those not contrary to the purposes and principles of the United Nations: ibid., paras. 8, 19. Several States thought this a too drastic qualification: Belgium, Israel and the US: ibid., paras. 13, 15, 16, and generally, while others remained concerned to protect public order, even if the concept were somewhat ambiguous: cf. Venezuela: ibid., paras. 38–43. The concept of public order was discussed further at the second session; see UN doc. E/AC.32/SR.40, pp.10–30; *Report* of the *Ad hoc* Committee: UN doc. E/AC.32/8, para. 29; also Goodwin-Gill, below n. 109.

[104] The reference to 'reasonable grounds' was interpreted by one representative at the 1951 Conference as allowing States to determine whether there were sufficient grounds for regarding the refugee as a danger and whether the danger likely to be encountered by the refugee on *refoulement* was outweighed by the threat to the community: UN doc. A/CONF.2/SR.16, 8.

to security cases is supported both by article 32(2) of the Convention and by immigration law and practice generally.[105]

It is unclear to what extent, if at all, one convicted of a particularly serious crime must also be shown to constitute a danger to the community. The jurisprudence is relatively sparse and the notion of 'particularly serious crime' is not a term of art,[106] but principles of natural justice and due process of law require something more than mere mechanical application of the exception. An approach in terms of the penalty imposed alone will be somewhat arbitrary, and the application of article 33(2) ought always to involve the question of proportionality, with account taken of the nature of the consequences likely to befall the refugee on return.[107] The offence in question and the perceived threat to the community would need to be extremely grave if danger to the life of the refugee were to be disregarded, although a less serious offence and a lesser threat might justify the return of an individual likely to face only some harassment or discrimination. This approach has not always been understood or endorsed by national tribunals, although practice overall appears compatible with such an interpretation.

In contrast to the 1951 Convention, the 1969 OAU Convention declares the principle of *non-refoulement* without exception. No formal concession is made to overriding considerations of national security, although in cases of difficulty 'in continuing to grant asylum' appeal may be made directly to other member States and through the OAU. Provision is then made for temporary residence pending resettlement, although its grant is not mandatory.[108] The absence of any formal exception is the more remarkable in view of the dimensions of the refugee problems which have faced individual African States.

Article 3 of the Declaration on Territorial Asylum, adopted by the General Assembly only two years before the OAU Convention, not only acknowledges the national security exception, but also appears to authorize further exceptions 'in order to safeguard the population, as in the case of a mass influx of persons'.[109] The latter reappeared at the 1977 Conference on Territorial Asylum

---

[105] See Goodwin-Gill, *Movement of Persons*, 241–2, 247–50.

[106] With respect to the analogous terms of art. 1F(b), see above Ch. 3, s. 4.2.

[107] See among others, *Toboso-Alfonso*, Board of Immigration Appeals, 12 Mar. 1990—burglary and possession of cocaine not 'particularly serious'; *Hung Duyet*, Board of Immigration Appeals, 30 Dec. 1988—armed robbery a 'particularly serious crime', amounting to criminal behaviour which 'contributes a danger to the community of the United States'; *Ipina* v. *INS* 868 F.2d 511 (1st Cir. 1989)—possession of cocaine with intent to distribute makes applicant ineligible for asylum; *O.V.*, Federal Council *(Bundesrat)*, Switzerland, 23 Aug. 1989; 4 *Asyl* 1—applicant responsible for killing but acquitted by reason of insanity. Notwithstanding absence of conviction 'by a final judgment', not entitled to *non-refoulement* because underlying purpose is to protect community from dangerous refugees.

[108] Art. II.

[109] For criticism of the terms, see Weis, P., 'The United Nations Declaration on Territorial Asylum' 7 *Can. YIL* 92, 113, 142–3 (1969). Weis nevertheless applauds rejection of the 'public order' exception, which he sees as too wide and susceptible of different connotations in civil and common law countries. For an examination of the *ordre public* concept in the context of entry and expulsion generally, see Goodwin-Gill, *Movement of Persons*, 168–9, 229–37, 298–9.

when Turkey, in a prescient move, proposed an amendment whereby *non-refoulement* might not be claimed 'in exceptional cases, by a great number of persons whose massive influx may constitute a serious problem to the security of a Contracting State'.[110] It can be argued that a mass influx is not itself sufficient to justify *refoulement*, given the likelihood of an international response to offset any potential threat to national security. Turkey's decision to close its border to Kurdish refugees, and the support or non-objection of a substantial number of members of the international community, if it did not breach *non-refoulement* (understood as a general principle of international law that includes the dimension of non-rejection at the frontier), certainly consolidated the exception.[111] In the instant case, the international response was part of the problem, so far as the creation of a safe zone for Kurds in Iraq arguably removed the (legal) basis for departure in search of asylum. The uniqueness of the circumstances, however, might suggest that they have little precedential value, and that the principle of *non-refoulement* has emerged relatively unscathed. Nevertheless, it must be admitted that the prospect of a massive influx of refugees and asylum seekers exposes the limits of the State's obligation otherwise not to return or refuse admission to refugees.

3.3 TIME AND PLACE, WAYS AND MEANS

The recognition of refugee status under international law is essentially declaratory in nature.[112] The duty to protect refugees arises as soon as the individuals or group concerned satisfy the criteria for refugee status set out in the definition (flight from the State territory for relevant reasons) and come within the territory or jurisdiction of another State, regardless of whether refugee status has been formally determined. Under general principles of international law, State responsibility may arise directly from the acts and omissions of its government officials and agents, or indirectly where the domestic legal and administrative systems fail to enforce or guarantee the observance of international standards.[113] The fact that the harm caused by State action may be inflicted outside the territory of the actor, or in an area identified by municipal law as an international zone, in no way diminishes the responsibility of the State.[114]

3.3.1 Extraterritorial application

A State's obligations under international law extend beyond its physical territory. The United Nations Human Rights Committee has held that a State party

[110] UN doc. A/CONF.78/C.1/L.28/Rev.1, adopted in the committee of the Whole by 24 votes to 20, with 40 abstentions, in a vote to put in context with premature efforts to secure the agreement of States on a 'right to asylum'. See further below, Ch. 5, s. 3.

[111] Turkey maintains the geographical limitation to its obligations under the 1951 Convention, and is thus not bound by treaty towards non-European refugees arriving on its territory or at its borders.

[112] See UNHCR, *Handbook on Procedures and Criteria for Determining Refugee Status*, (1979), para. 28.

[113] Brownlie, I., *System of the Law of Nations: State Responsibility, Part I*, (1983), 150–1.

[114] Ibid., at 135–7, 159–66.

may be accountable under article 2(1) of the 1966 Covenant on Civil and Political Rights for violation of protected rights committed by its agents in the territory of another State, whether or not that State acquiesced. In the view of the Committee, the phrase 'within its territory *and subject to its jurisdiction*' refers not to the place where the violation occurred, but to the relationship between the individual and the State concerned.[115] Similarly, the European Commission on Human Rights has taken the position that the obligations of States under the European Convention extend to 'all persons under their actual authority and responsibility, whether that authority is exercised within their own territory or abroad'.[116] Unlike other provisions in the 1951 Convention, which condition rights and benefits on degrees of presence and lawful residence, article 33(1) contains no such restriction. On the contrary, it prohibits the return of refugees *'in any manner whatsoever.'*

In domestic litigation arising out of the Haitian interdiction programme, the US government argued that the prohibition against *non-refoulement* applies only to refugees within State territory. Beginning with a September 1981 Presidential Proclamation and Executive Order, the US Coast Guard regularly 'interdicted' Haitians and returned them to their country of origin, initially with a form of screening and guarantees for the non-return of those found to be refugees. The US government informed the Haitian government that it would not return any individual whom it determined to qualify for refugee status, and President Reagan's Executive Order likewise confirmed, 'that no person who is a refugee will be returned without his consent.' US officials made similar statements on other occasions in different fora.

Following the September 1991 military coup against the democratically elected government of Haiti and President Jean Bertrand Aristide, repatriations were first suspended but then resumed after some six weeks. In May 1992, President Bush decided to continue interdiction and repatriation, but without offering the possibility of screening in for those who might qualify as refugees.[117] President Clinton elected to maintain the practice, which continued until May 1994 when full refugee status determination interviews on board ships were announced.[118] Local court challenges were commenced, but in its 1993 decision in *Sale, Acting Commissioner, INS* v. *Haitian Centers Council*, the US Supreme Court ruled that neither domestic law nor article 33 of the 1951 Convention limited

---

[115] *De Lopez* v. *Uruguay* (52/1979), HRC, *Selected Decisions under the Optional Protocol*: UN doc. CCPR/C/OR/1 (1985), 88–92, para, 12; *de Casanego* v. *Uruguay*, ibid., 92–4, para. 10. See also Inter-American Human Rights Commission, *Haitian Refugee Cases*, Case No. 10.675, Inter-Am. C.H.R. 334, OEA/Ser.L/V/II.85, doc. 9 rev (1994)—ruling on the issue of admissibility that US interdiction policies appeared to violate, among others, the American Declaration of Human Rights and the American Convention on Human Rights.

[116] *Cyprus* v. *Turkey* (6780/74; 6950/75), *Report*: 10 July 1976.

[117] See Executive Order No. 12,807: 57 *Fed. Reg.* 23133.

[118] 16 *Refugee Reports*, 28 Feb. 1995, 11.

the power of the President to order the Coast Guard to repatriate undocumented aliens, including refugees, on the high seas.[119]

The Supreme Court decision, by an 8–1 majority, held first that domestic law provisions applied only in immigration proceedings for exclusion or deportation. As such proceedings do not operate outside the US, neither the President nor the Coast Guard were under any statutory limitation in dealing with those, such as Haitians, found on the high seas while in flight from persecution. The international law dimensions to the interdiction practice, not surprisingly, received little substantive attention. Although the Court made passing reference to the *travaux préparatoires* of the 1951 Convention, its essentially *policy* decision to deny a remedy to individuals beyond territorial jurisdiction relied mostly on the language of 'congressional intent' at the time of enactment.[120]

The judgment of the Supreme Court attempts to confer domestic 'legality' on a practice of returning individuals to their country of origin, irrespective of claims to have a well founded fear of persecution. That decision could not and did not alter the State's international obligations.[121] The principle of *non-refoulement* has crystallized into a rule of customary international law, the core element of which is the prohibition of *return in any manner whatsoever* of refugees to countries where they may face persecution. The scope and application of the rule are determined by this essential purpose, thus regulating State action *wherever* it takes place, whether internally, at the border, or through its agents outside territorial jurisdiction. This development is amply confirmed in instruments subsequent to the 1951 Convention, including declarations in different fora and treaties such as the 1984 UN Convention against Torture, by the will of States expressed in successive resolutions in the UN General Assembly or the Executive Committee of the UNHCR Programme, in the laws and practice of States, and especially in unilateral declarations by the United States government.

During the first ten years of the Haitian interdiction programme, senior United States officials publicly and repeatedly affirmed the principle of *non-refoulement*, not only in the broad general sense,[122] but also in the specific context of Haitian operations. Moreover, the relevant Executive Order stated quite clearly that '[t]he Attorney General shall . . . take whatever steps are necessary to ensure . . . the strict observance of our international obligations concerning those who genuinely flee persecution in their homeland'.[123] In his 16 February 1982 letter to the UNHCR Chief of Mission in Washington, DC, US Attorney

---

[119] 113 S.Ct 2549 (1993); see also *Haitian Refugee Center* v. *Christopher*, 5 Jan 1995, in which the Court of Appeals for the 11th Circuit ruled that refugees in safe haven camps outside the US do not enjoy constitutional due process and are not protected by art. 33 or the Immigration and Nationality Act from forced return.

[120] For further views, see the dissenting judgment of Blackmun J. and this author's 'Comment' in 6 *IJRL* 71, 103 (1994).

[121] Cf. UNHCR, Brief *amicus curiae*, 6 *IJRL* 85 (1994).

[122] See above n. 53, 56 and accompanying text.

[123] Executive Order 12324, 29 Sept. 1981, s. 3.

General William French Smith extended unqualified recognition to international obligations.[124]

These substantial undertakings by US government officials were applied in practice for at least ten years, until the President decided to return even Haitians who might have a 'colorable claim' to be refugees. The combination of declarations in the sense of an international obligation with practice confirming that obligation is conclusive evidence of the applicability of the principle of *non-refoulement* to the extraterritorial activities of United States agents. This conclusion is further strengthened by the fact that even though the United States authorities considered that the vast majority of Haitians were leaving for economic reasons, they were still prepared, against interest, to take steps to ensure that no refugees among them were returned contrary to international obligations.

In its judgment in the *Nuclear Tests* Cases, the International Court of Justice observed that,

... declarations made by way of unilateral acts, concerning legal or factual situations, may have the effect of creating legal obligations ... [N]othing in the nature of a *quid quo pro* nor any subsequent acceptance of the declaration, nor even any reply or reaction from other States, is required for the declaration to take effect, since such a requirement would be inconsistent with the strictly unilateral nature of the juridical act by which the pronouncement of the State was made ... [125]

The Court further emphasized the central value of good faith in this context:

Just as the very rule of *pacta sunt servanda* in the law of treaties is based on good faith, so also is the binding character of an international obligation assumed by unilateral declaration. Thus interested States may take cognizance of unilateral declarations and place confidence in them, and are entitled to require that the obligation thus created be respected.[126]

UNHCR has been entrusted by the United Nations General Assembly with the international protection of refugees, and States in turn have formally undertaken

---

[124] '... the Administration is firmly committed to the full observance of our international obligations and traditions regarding refugees, including ... the principle of non-refoulement ... If there were an indication of a colorable claim of asylum, the individual would be brought to the United States where a formal application for asylum would be filed ... these procedures will insure that nobody with a well-founded fear of persecution is mistakenly returned to Haiti.' The relevant correspondence and statements are cited in UNHCR's *amicus curiae* brief: 6 *IJRL* 85. See also (1994) Memorandum to all INS employees assigned to duties related to interdiction at sea, revised 26 August 1982 under signature of the INS Associate Commissioner Examinations: 'The only function INS officers are responsible for is to ensure that the United States is in compliance with its obligations regarding actions towards refugees, including the necessity to be keenly attuned ... to any evidence which may reflect an individual's well-founded fear of persecution.' The list of authorities expressly cited for this memorandum included not only the Presidential Proclamation and Executive Order of 29 Sept. 1981, but also art. 33 of the 1951 Convention. INS Acting Commissioner Doris M. Meissner's letter of 29 Dec. 1981 to the UNHCR Chief of Mission: 'These *procedures* fully comply with our responsibilities under the UN Convention and Protocol'. (Emphasis supplied). Similar statements are cited by Blackmun, J., dissenting in *Sale* v. *Haitian Centers Council, Inc.*: 6 *IJRL* 71 (1994)

[125] *Nuclear Tests Case* (Australia v. France), ICJ *Rep.*, 1974, 253 at 267.

[126] Ibid., para. 46.

to co-operate with UNHCR, 'in the exercise of its functions, and shall in particular facilitate its duty of supervising the application of the provisions' of the
1951 Convention/1967 Protocol.[127] UNHCR's legal interests are equivalent to
those of States in the circumstances described by the International Court of
Justice; it was entitled to take notice of and place confidence in the declarations
of the United States.

In fact, UNHCR appears to have done just this. At no time did the Office
challenge the exercise of jurisdiction on the high seas. Rather, it focused its interventions on the *adequacy* of the on-board procedures, to sift out effectively those
Haitians who might have a 'colourable claim' to asylum.[128] The declaration of
intent to abide by article 33, substantiated by ten years of practice in which all
interdicted Haitians were screened, sufficiently confirms the 'extraterritorial'
obligations of the United States, which are implicit in the words of the
Convention.

3.3.2 *'International zones'*

Whereas State activities beyond territorial jurisdiction are sometimes said to be
outside the scope of the *non-refoulement* obligation, in other circumstances international obligations are claimed to have limited effect even within the State. Any
argument for the non-application of international obligations in State territory
(for example, in transit or international zones, whether in the matter of refugees,
asylum seekers, stowaways or any other subject) faces substantial objections,
however. It is a fundamental principle of international law that every State
enjoys prima facie exclusive authority over its territory and persons within its
territory, and with that authority or jurisdiction goes responsibility. Thus, a State
could hardly argue that it is not bound by international duties of protection with
respect to diplomatic personnel, merely by reason of the fact of their location
within an 'international' or transit area of an airport.

Many States, of course, do choose to accord lesser rights in their municipal
law to those awaiting formal admission, than to those who have entered. The
United States is a typical example, where *physical* presence is not necessarily syn-
onymous with *legal* presence for the purpose of determining constitutional guarantees. Other States make similar distinctions, for example, in the case of
stowaways or illegal entrants, who are often deemed not to have entered the
country. The purpose of such provisions is usually to facilitate summary or

[127] Art. 35, 1951 Convention; art. II, 1967 Protocol.
[128] For example, in its *amicus curiae* brief in *Haitian Refugee Center, Inc.* v. *Gracey*, UNHCR argued
that, '[g]iven the applicability of the principle of *non-refoulement* to the broad field of State action or
omission, the secondary principle of effectiveness of obligations itself obliges a State to establish procedures adequate and sufficient to ensure fulfilment of the primary duty . . . [W]here . . . a State of
its own volition, elects to intercept asylum-seekers on the high seas and outside their own or any
State's territory, particularly high standards must apply and be scrupulously implemented'. Motion
for Leave to file Brief *Amicus Curiae* and Brief *Amicus Curiae* of the United Nations High Commissioner
for Refugees in support of Haitian Refugee Center, Inc., et al, 8 Jul. 1985, Section III, 19–24.

discretionary treatment, but from the perspective of international law, what counts is not the status or non-status conferred by municipal law, but the treatment in fact accorded. For international law purposes, *presence within State territory* is a juridically relevant fact sufficient in most cases to establish the necessary link with the authorities whose actions may be imputable to the State in circumstances giving rise to State responsibility. General principles of State responsibility will govern, flowing from the fact of control over territory including, with respect to human rights, the obligation of the State to ensure and to protect the human rights of everyone within its territory or subject to its jurisdiction.[129] Municipal courts, too, have rarely doubted their authority to extend their jurisdiction and protection into so-called international zones.[130]

In examining the legality and implications of such zones, the point of departure is the State's sovereign and prima facie exclusive authority or jurisdiction over all its territory, and the concomitant international legal responsibilities flowing from the fact of control and the activities of its agents. This authority or jurisdiction, with its basis in customary international law, is amply confirmed by international treaties, such as the 1944 Chicago Convention and the 1982 Convention on the Law of the Sea. No State, by treaty or practice, appears to have abandoned the territory comprised by its ports of entry; the extent of

---

[129] See art. 2(1), 1966 Covenant on Civil and Political Rights; art. 1, 1950 European Convention on Human Rights; art. 1, 1969 American Convention on Human Rights. Although the 1966 Covenant employs the phrase, '*and* subject to its jurisdiction', the Human Rights Committee has interpreted it to mean, 'or'; see above, n. 115 and text. The judgment of the Supreme Court in *Singh* is premised on the fact that those seeking Charter protection were physically present in Canada, and 'by virtue of that presence, amenable to Canadian law': *Re Singh and Minister of Employment and Immigration* [1985] 1 SCR 177. Cf. *habeas corpus* jurisprudence: *Re Harding* (1929) 63 OLR 518 (Ontario Appeal Division); *Barnard* v. *Ford* [1892] AC 326; Cf. Habeas Corpus Act 1679, s. 10; Habeas Corpus Act 1816, s. 5; Habeas Corpus Act 1862; *The Sitka* (1855), 7 *Opinions of the Attorney General*, 122; *Calvin's Case* (1609) 7 Co. Rep. 1; cited by Sharpe, R. J., *The Law of Habeas Corpus*, (1976), 182. See also *Ramirez* v. *Weinberger* 745 F. 2d 1500 (DC Cir., 1984), where the court considered that US Constitutional guarantees of due process could be invoked by citizens whose property overseas is affected by US governmental action: 'Where . . . the court . . . has personal jurisdiction over the defendants, the extra-territorial nature of the property involved in the litigation is no bar to equitable relief.' So far as the power to expel and deport implicitly authorizes such extra-territorial constraint as is necessary to effect execution: *Attorney-General for Canada* v. *Cain* [1906] AC 542, 546–7, then the legality of such constraint remains reviewable so long as it continues: Cf. *R.* v. *Secretary of State, ex p. Greenberg* [1947] 2 All ER 550. Note also s. 6, UK Consular Relations Act 1968, which provides that a crew member on board a ship flying the flag of a designated State who is detained for a disciplinary offence shall not be deemed to be unlawfully detained unless (a) his detention is unlawful under the laws of that State or the conditions of detention are inhumane or unjustifiably severe; *or* (b) there is reasonable cause to believe that his life or liberty will be endangered for reasons of race, nationality, political opinion or religion, in any country to which the ship is likely to go.

[130] See Hamerslag, R. J., 'The Schiphol Refugee Centre Case,' 1 *IJRL* 395 (1989). Earlier cases dealt, for example, with habeas corpus and false imprisonment. See *Küchenmeister* v. *Home Office* [1958] 1 QB 496, in which a non-citizen in transit at London Airport succeeded in an action for false imprisonment, when immigration officers prevented him from joining his connecting flight after he had been refused permission to enter. On art. 1, European Convention on Human Rights, see further below, Ch. 8, s. 2.2.1.

national control exercised therein sufficiently contradicts any assertion of their purely *international* character.

Obligations relating to *non-refoulement* and the protection of human rights come into play by reason of the juridically relevant facts of presence within State territory and jurisdiction. Whether responsibility for breach of international obligations results will in turn depend upon whether the actions taken with respect to an individual, such as removal, are imputable in the State (more than likely in the case of 'immigration action'), and whether they result in harm to an internationally protected interest. At the same time, however, the State retains choice of means as to the methods of implementation of these obligations. To apply different procedures and standards in such zones will not necessarily result in the breach of an international obligation. The underlying practical issue is one of monitoring and compliance, but experience unfortunately confirms that errors of *refoulement* are more likely when procedural shortcuts are taken in zones of restricted guarantees and limited access.[131]

3.3.3 'Non-refoulement' and extradition

The 1951 Convention says nothing about the extradition of refugees. In principle, *non-refoulement* should also apply in this context, for other provisions of the Convention already recognize the interests of the State of refuge in not committing itself to the reception of serious criminals. In 1951, however, a number of States were of the view that article 33 did not prejudice extradition.[132] One suspected of a serious non-political crime would in any event be excluded from the benefits of refugee status;[133] but one suspected or guilty of a non-serious non-political crime would remain liable to extradition, even to the State in which he or she had a well-founded fear of persecution. Any conflict of treaty obligations might be further dependent upon which obligation was contracted first.

This issue today again requires analysis of State practice since 1951, in light of the object and purpose of the Convention and the principle of *non-refoulement*. If States had reservations about the relationship between extradition and article 33 in 1951, these have been displaced by subsequent regional, bilateral and multilateral State practice. The 1957 European Convention on Extradition, for

---

[131] Cf. loi no. 92–625, 6 juill. 1992, sur la zone d'attente des ports et des aeroports: *J.O.*, 9 juill. 1992, 9185; Julien-Laferrière, F., 'Droit d'asile et politique d'asile en France', *Asyl*, 1993/4, 75–80— detention after four days can be continued only by decision of the president of the *tribunal de grande instance*, and entry can only be refused if the application is manifestly unfounded. However, a claimant detained in the zone does not have access to OFPRA to lodge application for asylum, so that the holding allows has a filter effect, infringing OFPRA's exclusive competence (at 78).

[132] See UN doc. A/CONF.2/SR.24, 10 (UK); ibid., SR.35, 21 (France). At the abortive 1977 United Nations Conference on Territorial Asylum, one article proposed would have protected refugees against extradition to a country in which they might face persecution. The German Democratic Republic and the USSR, however, both prepared amendments reiterating the paramountcy of States' extradition obligations. These conflicting approaches were not resolved at the Conference, but have been overtaken by consolidating State practice.

[133] See above, Ch. 3.

example, prohibits extradition, 'if the requested Party has substantial grounds for believing that a request for extradition for an ordinary criminal offence has been made for the purpose of prosecuting or punishing a person on account of his race, religion, nationality or political opinion, *or that that person's position may be prejudiced for any of those reasons.*'[134] The Committee of Experts of the Council of Europe expanded this article expressly to include the basic elements of the refugee definition, although declining to write in 'membership of a particular social group' on the ground that it might be interpreted too freely. That apart, every indication is that the Committee intended to close the gap between the political offender and the refugee. It further proposed that the transit of those extradited be excluded through any territory where the life or freedom of the person claimed could be threatened for any of the stated reasons, and this was included in article 21.[135]

Article 3 of the European Convention now serves as a model for bilateral treaties and municipal laws.[136] It clearly influenced the Scheme for the Rendition of Fugitive Offenders adopted in 1966 by the Meeting of Commonwealth Law Ministers,[137] and implemented in many Commonwealth countries since then,[138] and is likewise reflected in a number of other multilateral agreements.[139]

[134] Art. 3(2), emphasis supplied; *ETS*, No. 24; see below, Annexe 2, No. 10.

[135] See generally *Supplementary Report of the Committee of Experts on Extradition to the Committee of Ministers*, Council of Europe doc. CM(57)52.

[136] See, for example, art. 19, 1979 Austrian Extradition Law (*Auslieferungs und Rechtshilfegesetz: BGBl Nr.* 529/1979), which provides for non-extradition where the proceedings in the requesting State are likely to offend arts. 3 and 6 of the European Convention on Human Rights; where the likely punishment is likely to offend art. 3 of that Convention; or where the requested person may face persecution or other serious consequences on grounds akin to those in art. 1 of the 1951 Convention. Art. 3 of the 1976 Austria-Hungary Extradition Treaty (*BGBl Nr.* 340/1976) likewise provides for non-extradition (1) in respect of political offences; (2) when the person sought enjoys asylum in the requested State; and (3) when it is not in accord with other international obligations of the requested State. Art. 4 of the 1980 Austria-Poland Extradition Treaty (*BGBl Nr.* 146/1976) is to similar effect.

[137] Cmn. 3008. The UK has not ratified the European Convention on Extradition, but contributed two experts to the discussion described in the text.

[138] For example UK Fugitive Offenders Act 1967, s. 4; Barbados Extradition Act 1979, s. 7; Kenya Extradition (Commonwealth) Countries Act 1968, s. 6; Papua New Guinea Extradition Act 1975, s. 8; Sierra Leone Extradition Act 1974, s. 15; Singapore Extradition Act 1968, ss. 8, 21; Zambia Extradition Act 1968, s. 31.

[139] Cf. art. 4, 1981 Inter-American Convention on Extradition, calling for non-extradition, 'when, from the circumstances of the case, it can be inferred that persecution for reasons of race, religion or nationality is invoked, or that the position of the person sought may be prejudiced for any of these reasons'. See also art. 5, 1977 European Convention on the Suppression of Terrorism, in which non-extradition is optional ('Nothing in this Convention shall be interpreted as imposing an obligation to extradite if . . .'); art. 9, 1979 International Convention against the Taking of Hostages: UNGA res. 34/146, 17 Dec. 1979, which employs the 'extradition shall not be granted' formula, includes ethnic origin within the list of relevant grounds, and adds one further likely cause of prejudice: 'the reason that communication with [the person requested] by the appropriate authorities of the State entitled to exercise rights of protection cannot be effected'. Where extradition is not granted, art. 8 provides that the State in which the alleged offender is found 'shall . . . be obliged, without exception whatsoever and whether or not the offence was committed in its territory' to submit the case for prosecution.

The inclusion of the principle *aut dedere aut judicare* in instruments aimed at suppressing certain crimes with an international dimension[140] is further acknowledgement that even the serious criminal may deserve protection against persecution or prejudice, while not escaping trial or punishment. Where non-extradition in such cases is prescribed as an *obligation*, the discretion of the State is significantly confined. *Non-refoulement* becomes obligatory[141] in respect of a class of alleged serious offenders, and no less should be required for the non-serious criminal who would otherwise fall within the exception.

The extradition of refugees was examined in 1980 by the Executive Committee, which reaffirmed the fundamental character of the principle of *non-refoulement*, and recognized that 'refugees should be protected in regard to extradition *to a country where they have well-founded reasons to fear persecution on the grounds enumerated in Article 1(A)(2)* of the 1951 Convention'.[142] Anxious to ensure not only the protection of refugees, but also the prosecution and punishment of serious offences, the Executive Committee stressed 'that protection in regard to extradition applies to persons who fulfil the criteria of the refugee definition and who are not excluded by virtue of Article 1(F)(b)' of the Convention.[143]

Judicial decisions from different jurisdictions support this approach. In the United Kingdom, a serious risk of prejudice has been considered sufficient to justify protection in extradition and refugee cases, certainly since the decision of the House of Lords in *Fernandez* v. *Government of Singapore*.[144] Courts in other States have also consolidated the basic principle of protection against extradition in favour of the refugee. In *Bereciartua-Echarri*, for example, the French

[140] Art. 16, 1963 Tokyo Convention on Offences and certain Other Acts Committed on board Aircraft; art, 7, 1970 Hague Convention for the Suppression of Unlawful Seizure of Aircraft; art. 7, 1971 Montreal Convention for the Suppression of Unlawful Acts against the Safety of Civil Aircraft; art. 7, 1973 Convention on the Prevention and Punishment of Crimes against Internationally Protected Persons, including Diplomatic Agents.

[141] Given that the 'obligation' only arises where the State 'has substantial grounds' (that is, it has a discretion), it must be considered imperfect. That *non-refoulement* is obligatory does not entail either a duty to grant asylum or a duty to expel; see further below, and Ch. 5.

[142] See Executive Committee Conclusion No. 17 (1980)—emphasis supplied; *Report* of the Sub-Committee of the Whole on International Protection: UN doc. A/AC.96/586, para. 16. The Sub-Committee's recommendations regarding the refugee, recognized in one State, whose extradition is then sought from another State in which he or she is temporarily visiting (UN doc. A/AC.96/586, para. 16, conclusions 8 and 9) were not adopted by the Executive Committee.

[143] As the Argentine delegate reiterated at the Executive Committee in 1989, 'While extradition was a legitimate practice in combating crime, it was inadmissible in international law in the case of a refugee': UN doc. A/AC.96/SR.442, para. 46. Later in the same session, the US delegate appeared to qualify his country's position: 'Concerning the extradition of refugees, the US government reserved its position on the application of the 1951 Convention and the 1967 Protocol to persons against whom extradition proceedings had been initiated until the courts hearing their cases had taken a formal position on them': UN doc. A/AC.96/SR.442, para. 84. Given the ambiguity and general lack of clarity, one cannot be certain whether, in the context of extradition proceedings (which involve both a judicial process and an executive decision), the US will or will not take refugee status into account. If it chooses to ignore status in the case of one who is not excluded or otherwise within the exceptions to *non-refoulement*, then violation of international obligations will result.

[144] [1971] 1 WLR 987.

Conseil d'Etat ruled in 1988 that the appellant could not be extradited so long as he retained the status of refugee, save in the serious cases contemplated by article 33(2) of the Convention. This was part of the general principles of refugee law, and to permit extradition would render the concept of protection ineffective.[145] In a 1990 decision, the *Schweizerisches Bundesgericht* (Swiss Federal Court) also ruled that a refugee could not be returned to his or her country of origin. Most States, said the Court, consider that article 33 is a legal bar to extradition; the article's purpose is to guarantee refugees against the loss of protection in the asylum State, and it would be unjust if a refugee who could not lawfully be expelled to the country of origin, could nevertheless be extradited.[146] In both the French and the Swiss cases it was implicitly accepted that extradition might proceed, once or if asylum or refugee status were revoked in accordance with the Convention.

In the *Altun* case, the European Commission considered that even though extradition for a political offence did not necessarily raise an issue under article 3, the facts might nevertheless oblige it 'to determine whether . . . there is a certain risk of prosecution for political reasons which could lead to an unjustified or disproportionate sentence being passed on the applicant and as a result inhuman treatment'. The Commission took account of the applicant's political past, the political background to the extradition request, and occurrences of torture in Turkey. It was unable to rule out 'with sufficient certainty that the criminal proceedings . . . had been falsely inspired', or dismiss the fact that the applicant 'is not someone who may be considered protected from all danger'.[147]

State practice, and the greater body of opinion, representing those most active in the protection of refugees and the development of refugee law, regards the principle of *non-refoulement* as likewise protecting the refugee from extradition.[148]

---

[145] *Bereciartua-Echarri*, No. 85.234, *Recueil Lebon*, 1 Apr. 1988; Iogna-Prat, M., 'L'Affaire Bereciartua-Echarri,' 1 *IJRL* 403 (1989).

[146] *Schweizerisches Bundesgericht*, Ref. 1A.127/1990/tg, 18 Dec. 1990; abstracted as Case Abstract No. *IJRL/0152*: 5 *IJRL* 271 (1993). In its 1980 paper on extradition submitted to the Sub-Committee (UN doc. EC/SCP/14, 27 Aug. 1980), UNHCR stressed that the principle of speciality offered no defence against excessive punishment or prejudicial treatment. The Court agreed, and remarked that it was no alternative to protection by non-extradition. The Court further took into account art. 3 of the European Convention on Extradition, which it characterized as the concrete expression of *non-refoulement* in extradition law, additionally capable of protecting persons who had committed serious non-political crimes, and so might be denied protection under the 1951 Convention.

[147] *Altun* v. *Federal Republic of Germany* (10308/83), 36 *D & R* 201. See also *Kirkwood* v. *United Kingdom* (10479/83), 37 *D & R* 158; Van den Wyngaert, C., 'Applying the European Convention on Human Rights to Extradition: Opening Pandora's Box?' 39 *ICLQ* 757 (1990).

[148] See Recommendation no. R(80)9 of the Committee of Ministers of the Council of Europe to the effect that governments should not allow extradition to States not party to the European Convention on Human Rights where there are substantial grounds to believe that art. 3(2) of the European Convention on Extradition would otherwise be applicable.

[149] Generally on States' power of expulsion, see Goodwin-Gill, *Movement of Persons*, 201–310; and on expulsion to a particular State, 218–28.

3.2.4 'Non-refoulement' and expulsion[149]

While States may be bound by the principle of *non-refoulement*, they as yet retain discretion as regards both the grant of 'durable asylum' and the conditions under which it may be enjoyed or terminated. States parties to the Convention and Protocol, however, have acknowledged that the expulsion of refugees raises special problems and under article 32 they undertake not to 'expel a refugee lawfully in their territory save on grounds of national security or public order'. Decisions to expel are further required to be in accordance with due process of law and 'except where compelling reasons of national security otherwise require', refugees shall be accorded the right of appeal.[150] Moreover, refugees under order of expulsion are to be allowed a reasonable period within which to seek legal admission into another country, though States retain discretion to apply 'such internal measures as they may deem necessary'.

The restricted grounds of expulsion have been adopted in the laws of many States,[151] and have been taken into account in a number of judicial decisions.[152] The benefit is limited to refugees who enjoy what might loosely be called 'resident status' in the State in question, and one admitted temporarily remains liable to removal in the same way as any other alien.[153] The permitted power of expulsion, however, does not include the power to return the individual to the country in which his or her life or freedom may be threatened, unless the further exacting provisions which regulate exceptions to the principle of *non-refoulement* are also met.[154]

Article 32 may yet have both advantages and disadvantages for the refugee. Thus, one expelled for the serious reasons stated in article 32(1) is likely to face

[150] See also art. 13, 1966 Covenant on Civil and Political Rights; Clark, T., 'Human Rights and Expulsion: Giving Content to the Concept of Asylum', 4 *IJRL* 189 (1992); Tiberghien, F., 'L'expulsion des réfugiés: Problèmes legislatifs et jurisprudenticls', *Doc. réf.*, no. 73, 5/14 mars 1989, Suppl., CJ, 1–8.

[151] See, for example, the Aliens Law 1990 of the Federal Republic of Germany (*Ausländergesetz: BGBl.* I, S.1354, 9 Juli 1990), art. 48(1): 'Ein Ausländer, der . . . 5. als Asylberechtigter anerkannt ist, im Bundesgebiet die Rechtstellung eines ausländischen Flüchtlings genießt oder einen von einer Behörde der Bundesrepublik Deutschland ausgestellten Reiseausweis nach dem Abkommen über die Rechtstellung für Flüchtlinge vom 28. Juli 1951 . . . besitzt, kann nur aus schwerwiegenden Gründen der öffentlichen Sicherheit und Ordnung ausgewiesen werden'; Asylum Law 1979 (*loi sur l'asile*) of Switzerland. art. 43(1): 'Un réfugié auquel la Suisse a accordé l'asile ne peut être expulsé que s'il compromet la sureté intérieure ou extérieure de la Suisse ou s'il a porté gravement atteinte à l'ordre public. (2) L'asile prend fin par l'exécution de l'expulsion administrative ou judiciaire.'

[152] See, for example, *Yugoslav Refugee (Germany)* case: 26 *ILR* 496; *Homeless Alien (Germany)* case: 26 *ILR* 503; *Refugee (Germany)* case: 28 *ILR* 297; *Expulsion of an Alien (Austria)* case: 28 *ILR* 310. But see also Henckaerts, J. -M., *Mass Expulsion in Modern International Law and Practice*, (1995), 99–107.

[153] Robinson, *Commentary*, 157.

[154] In the *Refugee (Germany)* case (above n. 152) the Federal Administrative Court held that a refugee unlawfully in the country could be expelled, provided he or she was not returned to the country in which life or freedom would be threatened. An almost identical conclusion was reached in a 1974 US decision, *Chim Ming v. Marks* 505 F.2d 1170 (2nd Cir.). In the *Expulsion of an Alien (Austria)* case (above n. 152), the Austrian Supreme Court observed when upholding an expulsion order that it merely required a person to leave the State, but did not render him or her liable to be returned to a specific foreign country.

major difficulties in securing admission into any other country. Return to the country of origin being ruled out, the refugee may be exposed to prosecution and detention for failure to depart. As only the State of nationality is obliged to admit the refugee,[155] the expelling country may find itself frustrated in its attempts at removal. For these reasons, in 1977, the Executive Committee recommended that expulsion should be employed only in very exceptional cases. Where execution of the order was impracticable, it further recommended that States consider giving refugee delinquents the same treatment as national delinquents, and that the refugee be detained only if absolutely necessary for reasons of national security or public order.[156]

3.2.5 'Non-refoulement' and illegal entry

In view of the normative quality of *non-refoulement* in international law, the precise legal status of refugees under the immigration or aliens law of the State of refuge is irrelevant, although a State seeking to avoid responsibility will often classify them as prohibited or illegal immigrants. Refugees who flee frequently have no time for immigration formalities, and allowance for this is contained in article 31 of the Convention, which of all articles comes closest to dealing with the controversial question of admission. This is not formally required, instead, penalties on account of illegal entry or presence shall not be imposed on refugees 'coming directly from a territory where their life or freedom was threatened . . . provided they present themselves without delay . . . and show good cause for their illegal entry or presence'. Refugees are not required to have come directly from their *country of origin*, but other countries or territories passed through should also have constituted actual or potential threats to life or freedom. What remains unclear is whether the refugee is entitled to invoke article 31 when continued flight has been dictated more by the refusal of other countries to grant asylum, or by the operation of exclusionary provisions such as those on safe third country, safe country of origin or time limits. Whether these constitute 'good cause' for illegal entry would seem to rest with the State authorities, subject however to the controlling impact of *non-refoulement*.[157]

At the 1951 Conference, several representatives considered that the undertaking not to impose penalties did not exclude the possibility of resort to expulsion.[158] Article 31 does not require that refugees be permitted to remain, and paragraph 2 emphasizes this point indirectly, by providing:

The Contracting States shall not apply to the movements of such refugees restrictions other than those which are necessary and . . . [they] shall only be applied *until their status*

---

[155] See Goodwin-Gill, *Movement of Persons*, 20–1, 44–6. 136–7.

[156] Executive Committee Conclusion No. 7 (1977). In France, under art. 28 of the ordinnance no. 45–2658 of 2 Nov. 1946, '*assignation à résidence*' may be the consequence for the alien who finds it impossible to leave.

[157] See further below Ch. 9, s. 2.1.

[158] UN doc. A/CONF.2/SR.13, 12–14 (Canada, UK). Cf. art. 5, 1954 Caracas Convention on Territorial Asylum; see below, Annexe 2, No. 3.

in the country is regularized or they obtain admission into another country. The Contracting States shall allow such refugees a reasonable period and all the necessary facilities to obtain admission into another country. (Emphasis supplied)

Given that the principle of *non-refoulement* remains applicable, the freedom of the State finally to refuse regularization of status can well be circumscribed in practice. As a matter of law, however, the State may continue to keep the unresettled refugee under a regime of restricted movement, either in prison or a refugee camp.[159]

3.2.6 'Non-refoulement' and the Committee against Torture[160]

States which have ratified the 1984 UN Convention against Torture may also opt to recognize the right of individual petition. Article 3 thus offers an alternative or additional measure of protection against *refoulement* for individuals facing removal to their own country.

The *Khan* case concerned a citizen of Pakistan of Kashmiri origin, who claimed refugee status in Canada in 1990.[161] His application was rejected by the Immigration and Refugee Board (IRB), and a motion for judicial review was also refused. His claim was based, among others, on political activities and earlier arrest and detention during which he stated that he had been tortured.[162] Following rejection of the refugee claim and various intervening events, a 'post-claim risk-assessment' conducted by the Canadian authorities concluded that he would not face danger to life or inhumane treatment if returned.[163]

Before the Committee, Canada noted that the claimant had made many requests for exceptional grant of residence status on humanitarian and compassionate grounds, but had produced no materials indicating a personal risk of torture until 1994.[164] Canada also called attention to many inconsistencies in the claimant's story, and to the fact that the IRB, after benefit of an oral hearing, had concluded that his testimony was largely fabricated.[165] The Committee, on the other hand, noted that the claimant had presented 'a medical report which

---

[159] See further below, Ch. 5, ss. 5.1, 5.2, on the implications of *non-refoulement* through time; see also below, Ch. 7, s. 1.1 on detention.

[160] See below, Ch. 8, s. 2.1. Gorlick, B., 'Refugee Protection and the Committee against Torture', 7 *IJRL* 504 (1995); also Clark, T., 'Human Rights and Expulsion: Giving Content to the Concept of Expulsion', 4 *IJRL* 189 (1992).

[161] Committee against Torture, Communication No. 15/1994, *Khan* v. *Canada,* 15 Nov. 1994: UN doc. CAT/C/13/D/15/1994 (18 Nov. 1994).

[162] Ibid., para. 3.2.

[163] Amendments to the *Immigration Act*, in force 1 Feb. 1993, provide for a post-claim risk-assessment for individuals found not to be Convention refugees but who may face some risk of serious harm if returned to their country of origin. The individual will be allowed to remain if, on removal, he or she would be subjected to an objectively identifiable risk to life, extreme sanctions, or inhumane treatment. Claimants may make submissions in writing, and other material will also be examined, including the immigration file, the refugee division hearing and country-specific information. Negative decisions are subject to judicial review with leave.

[164] *Khan* v. *Canada:* UN doc. CAT/C/13/D/15/1994 (18 Nov. 1994), para. 7.6.

[165] Ibid., paras. 8.3, 8.4.

does not contradict his allegations', that the late submission of claims and corroboration was 'not uncommon for victims of torture', and concluded that, 'even
if there could be some doubts about the facts adduced by the author, it must
ensure that his security is not endangered'.[166] It took account of evidence that
torture is widely practised in Pakistan against political dissenters as well as
against common detainees, but did not find, as it had with respect to Zaire in
the case of *Mutombo*,[167] 'a consistent pattern of gross, flagrant or mass violations'
of human rights.

The *Khan* case contrasts markedly with that of *Mutombo*, particularly with
respect to the evidence and (apparent) standard of proof. In the latter case, a
considerable body of cogent evidence of country conditions existed, together
with substantial *uncontradicted* elements relating to the claimant's individual circumstances.[168] In both cases, the Committee described its function of determining whether there are substantial grounds for believing that the claimant
would be in danger of being subject to torture as follows:

> ... the Committee must take into account all relevant considerations, pursuant to para-
> graph 2 of article 3, including the existence of a consistent pattern of gross, flagrant or
> mass violations of human rights. The aim of the determination, however, is to establish
> whether the individual concerned would be personally at risk of being subjected to tor-
> ture in the country to which he would return. It follows that the existence of a consistent
> pattern of gross, flagrant or mass violations of human rights in a country does not as such
> constitute a sufficient ground for determining that a person would be in danger of being
> subjected to torture upon his return to that country; additional grounds must exist that
> indicate that the individual concerned would be personally at risk. Similarly, the absence
> of a consistent pattern of gross violations of human rights does not mean that a person
> cannot be considered to be in danger of being subjected to torture in his specific cir-
> cumstances.[169]

It is difficult to infer from the few decisions so far handed down by the
Committee against Torture how precisely it interprets the 'substantial grounds'
requirement of article 3 of the Convention, especially in relation to the evidence
submitted by both claimant and government. In *Mutombo* it placed great reliance
on uncontradicted testimony, whereas in *Khan* it did the same with respect to
testimony, the truth of which had indeed been disputed.[170] Negative decisions

---

[166] Ibid., para. 12.3; this phrase was also used in *Mutombo*, below. The Committee also relied on
a copy of an arrest warrant and a letter advising against return.

[167] Committee against Torture, Communication No. 13/1993, *Mutombo* v. *Switzerland*, 27 Apr.
1994: UN doc. CAT/C/12/D/13/1993 (27 Apr. 1994); also published in 7 *IJRL* 322 (1995). The
claimant here had deserted from the Zaire armed forces, and provided a history of detention and
torture.

[168] For example, the government relied on an anonymous informant whose testimony could not
be checked, rejected a medical report indicating that the claimant's injuries corresponded with the
alleged torture without conducting a re-examination, and did not dispute that he had deserted and
left Zaire clandestinely: ibid., paras. 7.3, 7.5, 9.4.

[169] *Mutombo*, para. 9.3; *Khan*, para. 12.2.

[170] In each case also, it stated clearly that it would not allow doubts about the facts to prevent it
from ensuring the security of the applicant: *Mutombo*, para. 9.2; *Khan*, para. 12.3.

by the Committee provide little additional help, being confined to a brief account of the facts alleged, followed by the formulaic conclusion that the account 'lacks the minimum substantiation that would render the communication compatible with article 22 of the Convention against Torture . . .'[171] How the evidence is tested, and against what standards of authority and corroboration, remains unclear, which is likely to be a matter of some concern, especially among States parties that have reasonably well-developed refugee determination procedures.

4. Measures not amounting to *refoulement*

The core of meaning of *non-refoulement* requires States not to return refugees in any manner whatsoever to territories in which they face the possibility of persecution. But States may deny admission in ways not obviously amounting to breach of the principle. For example, stowaways and refugees rescued at sea may be refused entry; refugee boats may be towed back out to sea and advised to sail on; and asylum applicants can be sent back to transit or 'safe third countries'. State authorities can also induce expulsion through various forms of threat and coercion.[172]

4.1 STOWAWAYS

Without breaching the principle of *non-refoulement*, the State where a stowaway asylum seeker arrives may require the ship's master to keep the stowaway on board and travel on to the next port of call; or it may call upon the flag State to assume responsibility where the next port of call is unacceptable; or it may allow temporary disembarkation pending resettlement elsewhere. In the absence of rules regulating the appropriate State to consider the asylum claim, the situation is comparable to that of refugees in orbit, while practical solutions are made more difficult to obtain by the tendency of States' immigration laws to deal summarily with stowaways.[173]

On several occasions during the Indo-China exodus, port of call States sought to make stowaways' disembarkation conditional on guarantees of resettlement

[171] Committee against Torture, Communication No. 17/1994, *X* v. *Switzerland*, 17 Nov. 1994: UN doc. CAT/C/13/D/17/1994, para. 4.2; Communication No. 18/1994, *X* v. *Switzerland*, 17 Nov. 1994: UN doc. CAT/C/13/D/18/1994, para. 4.2.

[172] In *Orantes-Hernandez* v. *Meese* 685 F. Supp. 1488 (C.D.Cor. 1988) the court found that substantial numbers of Salvadoran asylum seekers were signing 'voluntary departure' forms under coercion, including threats of detention, deportation, relocation to a remote place and communication of personal details to their government. See also Amnesty International British Section *Playing Human Pinball*, (1995), 59–61 (coercion to effect 'voluntary departure' to 'safe third country').

[173] See, for example, the US Immigration and Nationality Act 1952, 8 USC s. 1182(a) (18).

from flag States, by analogy with the then developing practice for rescue at sea cases in South East Asia.[174]

The issue of stowaway asylum seekers was first briefly examined by an Executive Committee working group during a rescue-at-sea meeting in Geneva in July 1982. While it was agreed that the principle of *non-refoulement* should be maintained, there were widely diverging views on how problems should be solved and the recommendations on stowaways were not adopted.[175] Although there was more success in 1988, the debate was not all plain sailing. Executive Committee Conclusion No. 53 (1988) emphasized that like other asylum seekers, stowaway asylum seekers 'must be protected against forcible return to their country of origin'. Without prejudice to any flag State responsibilities, it also recommended that they 'should, whenever possible, be allowed to disembark at the first port of call', with the opportunity to have their refugee claim determined, 'provided that this does not necessarily imply durable solution in the country of the port of disembarkation'.[176]

State practice has so far given rise to no rule on the treatment of stowaway asylum seekers. In reality, however, the discretion of the coastal State may be limited by the particular facts of the case. If the flag State refuses to accept any responsibility for resettlement and if the ship's next port of call is in a country in which the stowaway asylum seeker's life or freedom may be threatened, then the practical effect of refusing disembarkation is *refoulement*. The nominal authority of the flag State to require diversion to a safe port, which would anyway be controversial where a charter party was involved, can hardly be considered a practical alternative, or 'last opportunity', to avoid *refoulement*. The paramount consideration remains the refugee status of those on board; a refusal to take

[174] As a port-of-call State, Australia had only limited success in arguing for this proviso with respect to flag States Greece, Italy, and Denmark. Most stowaways in the period 1979–82 were ultimately allowed to disembark and to lodge claims for refugee status; a few were resettled with relatives in third States. None of the States involved had ratified the 1957 Brussels Convention on Stowaways, which still awaits entry into force. Art. 5(2) provides that in considering application of the Convention, 'the Master and the appropriate authorities of the port of disembarkation will take into account the reasons which may be put forward by the stowaway for not being disembarked at or returned to' various ports or States. Art. 5(3) declares that 'The provisions of [the] Convention shall not in any way affect the power or obligation [*sic*] of a Contracting State to grant political asylum.' Art. 3 provides, that where a stowaway is otherwise unreturnable to any other State, he may be returned to 'the Contracting State whose flag was flown by the ship in which he was found', unless subject to 'a previous individual order of deportation or prohibition from entry'. For text, see *Conférence diplomatique de droit maritime, 10ème session, Bruxelles*, 491–503, (1958). Both the UK and the Netherlands opposed these aspects of the Convention on the ground that they made too many inroads on national immigration control: ibid., 200, 436–7, 441–3, and 632–3.

[175] *Report* of the Working Group on problems related to the rescue of asylum seekers in distress at sea: UN doc. EC/SCP/21, (1982) paras. 22ff.

[176] For full text see below, Annexe 3; *Report* of the 39th Session: UN doc. A/AC.96/721 (13 Oct. 1988), para. 25. Greece proposed deletion of the words 'whenever possible', and the phrase beginning, 'provided that this does not necessarily imply . . .': ibid., para. 36.2. See also UNHCR, *Note on Stowaway Asylum-Seekers*: UN doc. EC/SCP/51 (22 Jul. 1988); *Report* of the Sub-Committee of the Whole on International Protection: UN doc. A/AC.96/717 (3 Oct. 1988), paras. 36–42; Venezuela: UN doc. A/AC.96/SR.431, para. 7; Australia: ibid., para. 9 (1988).

account of their claims, either on the specious basis that they have not 'entered' State territory or on the (disputed) ground that they are the responsibility of the flag or any other State, would not suffice to avoid liability for breach of the principle of *non-refoulement*.[177]

4.2 RESCUE-AT-SEA

Asylum seekers have been escaping by sea for years, only the most recent examples being Cubans, Haitians, and Indo-Chinese. As with stowaways, several options are open to the State where those rescued arrive; it may refuse disembarkation absolutely and require ships' masters to remove them from the jurisdiction, or it may make disembarkation conditional upon satisfactory guarantees as to resettlement, care and maintenance, to be provided by flag or other States, or by international organizations. Once again, a categorical refusal of disembarkation cannot be equated with breach of the principle of *non-refoulement*, even though it may result in serious consequences for asylum seekers.

The duty to rescue those in distress at sea is firmly established in both treaty[178] and general international law.[179] No provision has been made, however, in respect of the rescue of those who do not in fact enjoy the protection of their country of origin.[180] During the Indo-China exodus, given the expense and delay which often resulted from attempting to disembark those rescued at sea, many in distress were ignored by ship's masters and left to their fate. The problem was recognized as early as 1975[181] and the following year the Executive

---

[177] Cf. *Yiu Sing Chun* v. *Sava* 708 F.2d 869 (2nd Cir., 1983), holding that under the 1980 US Refugee Act, alien stowaways are entitled to an evidentiary hearing on their asylum applications. Such proceeding is now provided in the asylum regulations: 8 *CFR* 8253.1(F).

[178] See, for example, art. 11, 1910 Brussels International Convention with respect to Assistance and Salvage at Sea: 1 *Bevans* 780 (1968); art. 45 (1), 1929 International Convention on the Safety of Life at Sea: 136 *LNTS* 82; ch. V, Reg. 10a, 1960 International Convention on the Safety of Life at Sea; art. 12, 1958 Convention on the High Seas; art. 98, 1982 Convention on the Law of the Sea.

[179] This view was expressed by the International Law Commission with regard to its proposed draft of art. 12 of the 1958 Convention on the High Seas; see UN doc. A/3179 (1956).

[180] See generally, Grant, B., *The Boat People*, (1980), 68–72; Grahl-Madsen, *Status of Refugees*, vol. 2, 271–2; Pugash, J. Z., 'The Dilemma of the Sea Refugee: Rescue without Refuge', 18 *Harv. ILJ* 577 (1977). Art. 11 of the 1951 Convention requires contracting States to give 'sympathetic consideration' to the establishment within their territory of 'refugees regularly serving as crew members' on ships flying their flag. At the 1951 Conference, it was stated that this provision was intended to benefit genuine seamen, not those escaping by sea: UN doc. A/CONF.2/SR.12, p. 5. Likewise, the 1957 agreement relating to refugee seamen (updated by the 1973 protocol thereto) offers little solace to the asylum seeker at sea. Art. 1 defines a 'refugee seaman' as a refugee within the meaning of the Convention and Protocol, who 'is serving as a seafarer in any capacity on a mercantile ship, or habitually earns his living as a seafarer on such ship'. The objective is to determine the links which a refugee seaman may have with contracting States, with a view to establishing entitlement to residence and/or the issue of travel documents. The qualifying links are such as generally to exclude the seafaring asylum seeker; for example, 600 days service under the flag of a contracting State, previous lawful residence in a contracting State, or travel documents previously issued by a contracting State: arts. 2, 3. 'Sympathetic consideration' is to be given to extending the agreement's benefits to those not otherwise a qualifying: art. 5.

[181] *Report* of the 26th Session of the Executive Committee: UN doc. A/AC.96/516/Add.I, para. 92.

Committee stressed the obligations of ships' masters and States under the 1910 Brussels and 1958 Geneva Conventions, and called for the grant of first asylum.[182] The situation continued to worsen, and in October 1977 UNHCR appealed jointly with the Inter-governmental Maritime Consultative Organization (IMCO) to the shipping community directly, through the London-based International Chamber of Shipping, requesting owners to instruct ships' masters of the need for scrupulous observance of obligations relating to rescue at sea.[183]

The fears of first-port-of-call countries had also to be allayed by developing the practice of resettlement guarantees. In October 1978, the Executive Committee called for at least temporary admission to be granted, and appealed to the international community to support efforts to obtain the resettlement assurances that would facilitate disembarkation.[184] The general situation regarding Indo-Chinese refugees in South East Asia deteriorated rapidly in the first half of 1979, with the escalation in numbers leading to forcible measures against asylum seekers in various countries. A United Nations meeting convened in Geneva in July resulted in substantially increased resettlement offers, financial aid, and a number of practical proposals regarding rescue at sea.[185] A follow-up meeting of experts[186] in August 1979 took note of the principle of flag State responsibility and also proposed for consideration a further principle of responsibility for nationally-owned vessels sailing under a flag of convenience. A pool of resettlement places was suggested for difficult cases, to be available to UNHCR in its efforts to secure disembarkation where the flag State was unable to provide a guarantee or where it was unreasonable to expect that State to offer resettlement. Practical protection and a realistic appraisal of the various competing interests were combined in a resettlement places scheme known as DISERO (Disembarkation Resettlement Offers), which operated principally in Singapore.[187] By institutionalizing resettlement guarantees and disembarkation procedures (and thus by linking flight to solution), the scheme effectively made international co-operation concrete, and enhanced the protection of those in flight.[188]

[182] *Report* of the 27th Session of the Executive Committee: UN doc. A/AC.96/534, para. 87(f), (g), (h).

[183] Cf. *Report* of the 28th Session of the Executive Committee: UN doc. A/AC.86/549, paras. 21, 36.B(d), (e); also UN doc. E/1978/75, para. 9. The appeal was renewed in Dec. 1978. At the 29th Session, the Executive Committee recommended that UNHCR advise IMCO of the names of ships which ignored distress signals, with a view to their being reported to countries of ownership or registration: UN doc. A/AC.96/559, para. 38.E. IMCO was later renamed the International Maritime Organization (IMO).

[184] *Report* of the 29th Session of the Executive Committee: UN doc. A/AC.96/559, para. 38.E.

[185] See UN doc. A/34/627, paras. 31–6; annexe I.

[186] The meeting was attended by representatives of Australia, Canada, France, Federal Republic of Germany, Italy, Japan, the Netherlands, the UK and the US.

[187] Participating States in 1985 were Australia, Canada, France, Federal Republic of Germany, New Zealand, Sweden, Switzerland and the US: see UN doc. EC/SCP/42 (July 1985), para. 3. Executive Committee Conclusion No. 38 (1985), *Report* of the 36th Session: UN doc. A/AC.96/673, para. 115(3).

[188] UNHCR's *Guidelines for the Disembarkation of Refugees*, (1983), and later development of the RASRO (Rescue at Sea Resettlement Offers) scheme refined and rationalized related aspects of the

Despite the significant numbers rescued and disembarked under this scheme,[189] the principle of flag State responsibility was soon called into question. Doubt as to its general applicability had emerged with the rescue in November 1979 of some 150 Vietnamese by the British registered vessel *Entalina* which was then heading for Darwin. The Australian government requested a resettlement guarantee as a pre-condition to disembarkation, but the British government appears initially to have considered the practice to be geographically limited to South East Asia, where all possibility of local settlement was ruled out; in other cases in other regions the principle of first-port-of-call responsibility should apply. In the event, the British government did accept for ultimate settlement in the United Kingdom any refugees not resettled in other countries. The Australian government in turn announced that it would consider accepting any who met Australian requirements, and who had relatives in the country or other special reasons to support their applications.[190]

At the 1980 Executive Committee Meeting, the United Kingdom representative called for a special approach to the problem of rescue cases.[191] He was supported by the Netherlands representative who pointed out that, while numerous guarantees had been given by his country, the growth in numbers was becoming more difficult to handle. With the overall decline in refugee arrivals, he hoped that first-port-of-call States would reconsider their policy of requiring time-limited guarantees from flag States.[192] The representative for Greece was more direct. In his view, the rescue of refugees at sea should not impose flag State responsibility; that responsibility rested with all signatories of the Convention and Protocol and the problem should be thoroughly re-examined with a view to an equitable sharing of the burden.[193]

basic problem (rescue-disembarkation-solution). In particular, UNHCR developed a scheme for reimbursement of expenses, while States within the RASRO scheme collaborated to share out the rescue caseload more evenly.

[189] In 1979, after rescue by 128 ships, 8,624 individuals known to UNHCR were disembarked, mostly in Hong Kong, the Philippines, Singapore, Thailand, and Japan, most of them against flag-State guarantees. In 1980, the numbers rose to 15,563 from 217 ships, and in 1981 to 14,589 from 213 ships.

[190] Department of Immigration and Ethnic Affairs, Press Releases 173/79(a), 30 Nov. 1979; 176/79, 4 Dec. 1979; 177/79, 5 Dec. 1979; and 180/79, 6 Dec. 1979. In June 1980, Australia announced that it accepted responsibility for some 70 refugees rescued by one of its *naval* vessels, referring to 'accepted international practice': Press Release 64/80, 17 June 1980. The following month the British government gave a further guarantee in respect of 51 Vietnamese rescued by the bulk carrier *Glenpark*: Press Release 78/80, 3 July 1980.

[191] UN doc. A/AC.96/SR.317, para. 47.

[192] UN doc. A/AC.96/SR.319, para. 27; see also the views of the Netherlands and others at the July 1982 working group of government representatives on rescue at sea: UN doc. EC/SCP/21, paras. 11, 12, 16.

[193] UN doc. A/AC.96/SR.319, para. 4; the representative cited Colombos, *The International Law of the Sea*, (6th ed., 1967), 285, and Simonet, *La Convention sur la haute mer* (1966), 78, in support of the argument against obligation. In 1979/80, British, Dutch, and Greek ships rescued 6,223 persons, or 27.5% of the total. Representatives of maritime nations reiterated their concern at the 1981 Executive Committee meeting; see UN doc. A/AC.96/SR.322, para. 3; UN doc. A/AC.96/601, para. 52.

A working group on problems related to rescue at sea was duly set up, composed of the representatives of the maritime and coastal States most concerned, of the potential resettlement countries and competent international bodies. It met in July 1982 and its report was considered by the Executive Committee later that year.[194] The fundamental character of the duty to rescue was reiterated and it was generally acknowledged that the problem of refugees at sea entailed a division of responsibilities between flag States, coastal States and resettlement States. The question was how to delimit more precisely their scope and content.

As a matter of law, the responsibilities of flag States *after* disembarkation were also uncertain. Some saw legal responsibility as limited to rescue, with any resettlement obligations thereafter deriving from flag States' membership of the international community. The issue of disembarkation was also unclear. The IMO representative observed that there existed no 'formal, multilateral agreement' embodying a principle of disembarkation at the next scheduled port of call. Port of call States in the region indicated that they were prepared to continue to allow disembarkation, but only where resettlement guarantees were given and those disembarked were rapidly moved out. The solutions proposed by the Executive Committee in 1982 consequently relied more on practical arrangements than legal norms.[195]

In light of the practice and views summarized above, the principle of flag State responsibility cannot be said to have established itself as 'international custom, as evidence of a general practice accepted as law'. The special circumstances which affected the finding of solutions to the South East Asia refugee problem dictated the emergence of a particular usage, limited also in time and place. In other situations it may be appropriate to emphasize the responsibility of the first port of call, given the inescapable but internationally relevant fact of the refugees' presence within the territory of the State. As with stowaways, effective solutions ought in principle to be attainable through a weighing of competing interests, taking account not only of the prospects, if any, of local integration, but also of notions of international solidarity and burden-sharing,[196] as well as the extent to which refusal of disembarkation may lead in fact to *refoulement*, or to other serious harm for the asylum seekers.

---

[194] See *Report* of the Working Group on problems related to the rescue of asylum-seekers in distress at sea: UN docs. EC/SCP/21 and EC/SCP/24; *Report* of the Meeting of the Sub-Committee of the Whole on International Protection: UN doc. A/AC.96/613, paras. 3–12; *Report* on the 33rd Session of the Executive Committee: UN doc. A/AC.96/614, paras. 61, 70(2).

[195] *Report* on the 33rd Session: UN doc. A/AC.96/614, paras. 61, 70(2). The Working Group suggested further contributions to DISERO, which was generally favoured, as was the idea of expanding the scheme to include a funding element to meet costs related to rescue, disembarkation and temporary admission: UN doc. EC/SCP/21, para. 18.

[196] At the 1981 Executive Committee meeting, one speaker suggested that arrangements relating to rescue and resettlement 'already reflected the principle of burden-sharing between maritime and coastal States and should therefore be maintained': UN doc. A/AC.96/601, para. 52.

4.3 ARRIVAL OF ASYLUM SEEKERS BY BOAT

The arrival of asylum seekers by boat puts at issue not only the interpretation of *non-refoulement*, but also the extent of freedom of navigation and of coastal States' right of police and control. In South East Asia during the Indo-China exodus, States several times prevented boats landing, and towed back to the high seas many which had penetrated the territorial sea and internal waters. In 1981, the United States announced a policy of 'interdiction' on the high seas of boats which were believed to be bringing illegal aliens to the United States.

The high seas,[197] of course, are not subject to the exercise of sovereignty by any State, and ships are liable to the exclusive jurisdiction of the flag State, save in exceptional cases provided for by treaty or under general international law. The freedom of the high seas, however, is generally expressed as a freedom common to States,[198] while the boats of asylum seekers, like their passengers, will most usually be denied flag State protection. Similarly, the right of innocent passage for the purpose of traversing the territorial sea or entering internal waters is framed with normal circumstances in mind. A coastal State may argue, first, that boats of asylum seekers are to be assimilated to ships without nationality[199] and are subject to boarding and other measures on the high seas. Additionally, it may argue that existing exceptions to the principle of freedom of navigation, applying within the territorial sea and the contiguous zone,[200] justify such preventive measures as the coastal State deems necessary to avoid landings on its shores.

Under general international law, ships on the high seas may be boarded only in very limited circumstances, namely, suspicion of piracy or slave trading, where the ship has no nationality or has the same nationality as the warship purporting to exercise authority, and where the ship is engaged in unauthorized broadcasting.[201] Somewhat different considerations arise where, under a bilateral agreement, a flag State agrees to permit the authorities of another State to intercept its vessels. Precedents have existed for many years in regard to

[197] Art. 1, 1958 Geneva Convention on the High Seas; art. 86, 1982 UN Convention on the Law of the Sea.

[198] Art. 2, 1958 Geneva Convention; art. 87, 1982 UN Convention.

[199] Art. 6, 1958 Geneva Convention; arts. 91, 92, 1982 UN Convention.

[200] See arts. 14–20, 24, 1958 Geneva Convention on the Territorial Sea and the Contiguous Zone; arts. 17–26, 33, 1982 UN Convention.

[201] Art. 22, 1958 Geneva Convention on the High Seas; art. 110, 1982 UN Convention. Because of doubts as to the obligation, if any, to submit to visit and search, O'Connell suggests that 'the only safe course to assume is that a right of boarding exists only under the law of the flag': O'Connell, D. P., *The International Law of the Sea*, vol. II, 801–2. Cf. *Molvan* v. *Attorney-General for Palestine* [1948] AC 351, which is some authority for the view that even the 'freedom of the open sea' may be qualified by place or circumstance. In that case, the Privy Council found that no breach of international law resulted when a ship carrying illegal immigrants bound for Palestine was intercepted on the high seas by a British destroyer, and escorted into port where the vessel was forfeited. The Board nevertheless considered relevant the fact that the ship in question flew no flag, and could not therefore claim the protection of any State.

smuggling, slaving, and fisheries conservation. Under the Haitian interdiction programme, the US Coast Guard was instructed to stop and board specified vessels, including those of US nationality, or no nationality, or possessing the nationality of a State which had agreed to such measures. Those on board were to be examined and returned to their country of origin, 'when there is reason to believe that an offence is being committed against the United States immigration laws . . .'[202]

The lack of nationality perhaps most closely approximates the situation of asylum seekers, but even if their boats are without the effective protection of the country of origin, it is doubtful whether they can be assimilated to ships without nationality. No boat is ever entirely without the protection of the law. Obligations with regard to the rescue of those in distress at sea will circumscribe a State's freedom of action in certain cases. In others, elementary considerations of humanity[203] require that account be taken of the rights to life, liberty, and security of the person, and to freedom from torture, cruel, inhuman, and degrading treatment; with respect to many such rights no derogation is permitted, even in time of public emergency threatening the life of the nation.

In the absence of an armed attack, the use of force against asylum seekers cannot be justified on the ground of self-defence.[204] Notions of necessity[205] or self-preservation,[206] as well as exceptions relating to the 'peace, good order or security' of the coastal State[207] are subject to the limitations just set out. While a State necessarily enjoys a margin of appreciation in determining whether an influx of asylum seekers constitutes a threat, the lawfulness of measures taken to meet it will depend on there being some relationship of proportionality between the means and the end. International procedures for assistance and for finding solutions to refugee problems exist and it is highly doubtful whether the use of such force as is reasonably likely to result in injury or death can ever be justified.[208]

4.3.1 Internal waters and the territorial sea

Internal waters, lying behind the baselines used to delimit territorial waters, are completely within the jurisdiction of the State. The territorial sea also is an area

---

[202] Executive Order no. 12324, *Interdiction of Illegal Aliens*, s. 2(c) (3), which continued: '. . . or appropriate laws of a foreign country [with which an agreement exists]; provided, however, that no person who is a refugee will be returned without his consent'. See further above, s. 3.3.1.

[203] *Corfu Channel* case, ICJ *Rep.*, 1949, 4, at 22; Brownlie, *Principles of Public International Law*, (4th ed., 1990), 28.

[204] Brownlie, I., *International Law and the Use of Force by States*, (1963), 264ff., 278–9. Schwarzenberger, G. and Brown, L., *A Manual of International Law*, (6th ed.), 150. On the distinction between self-defence and self-help, see Bowett, D., *Self-Defence in International Law*, (1958), 11–12.

[205] Brownlie, *Principles*, 465–6.

[206] Cf. Johnson, D. H. N. 'Refugees, Departees and Illegal Migrants' 9 *Sydney LR* 11, at 30–1; Bowett, *Self-Defence*, 22.

[207] See arts. 14, 19 and 24, 1958 Geneva Convention on the Territorial Sea and the Contiguous Zone; arts. 17–20, 27, 33, 1982 UN Convention Brownlie points out, coastal States' powers are essentially powers of police and control: *Principles*, 205

[208] Cf. Johnson, below n. 220 and accompanying text.

over which the coastal State exercises full sovereignty and in which, subject to the requirements of innocent passage, all the laws of the coastal State may be made applicable. The sovereignty here exercised is no different in kind from that over State territory.

Under international law, States are entitled to regulate innocent passage through the territorial sea,[209] for example, to prevent the infringement of immigration provisions. Non-compliance with such regulations may make passage non-innocent. Articles 25 and 19(2)(g) of the 1982 UN Law of the Sea Convention are probably declaratory of customary international law. Article 19(2)(g) provides:

Passage of a foreign ship shall be considered to be prejudicial to the peace, good order or security of the coastal State if in the territorial sea it engages in any of the following activities:

. . .

(g) the loading or unloading of any commodity, currency or person contrary to the customs, fiscal, immigration or sanitary laws and regulations of the coastal State . . .

Article 25 of the 1982 Convention, and article 16 of the 1958 Geneva Convention before it, provides expressly that, 'The coastal State may take the necessary steps in its territorial sea to prevent passage which is not innocent'.

Although the territorial limits of a State run to the boundaries of its territorial sea, it does not follow that entry within the latter constitutes entry within the State, where 'entry' is the juridical fact necessary and sufficient to trigger the application of a particular system of international rules, such as those relating to landings in distress or immunity for illegal entry.[210] States generally apply their immigration laws, not within territorial waters, but within internal waters, even though it may be argued that 'entry' occurs at the moment when the outer limit of the territorial sea is crossed. Under article 31 of the 1951 Convention, refugees who cross into territorial waters and who otherwise satisfy the requirements of that provision, could be said to have entered illegally and to be

---

[209] 'Regulation' does not necessarily imply the exercise of control; in principle, the law of the flag State governs the internal affairs of a ship, while neither civil nor criminal jurisdiction should be exercised, absent any actions prejudicial to the peace, good order, or security of the coastal State: art. 16, 1958 Geneva Convention on the Territorial Sea and the Contiguous Zone; cf. art. 21, 1982 UN Convention. Moreover, the power to suspend innocent passage temporarily in certain areas is qualified by the requirement that this be essential for the protection of security: art. 16(3), 1958 Geneva Convention; art. 25(3), 1982 UN Convention, and it is arguably not intended to be used against specific vessels, or for unrelated reasons.

[210] O'Connell, D. P., *The International Law of the Sea*, vol. 1, (Shearer, I., ed.), (1982), 80–1, observes that art. 1 of the 1958 Geneva Convention on the Territorial Sea and the Contiguous Zone 'allows for the maximum implications that may be drawn from the concept of sovereignty, but it does not impose those implications on the coastal State; it leaves them to be drawn in municipal law'. He notes further that ratification '. . . does not necessarily and automatically have the effect of altering the natural boundary. If that boundary encompasses the territorial sea, the Convention endorsed this by securing the recognition of the maximum implications on the part of all other States. If that boundary does not already encompass it, ratification by itself would not seem to affect the situation . . . .'

entitled to exemption from penalties. Entry within territorial waters may be an 'entry' for certain purposes,[211] but it is incorrect to generalize from these particulars. The notion of distress, or *force majeure*, reflects not so much a right of entry, as a limited immunity for having so entered in fairly well-defined circumstances.[212] Similarly, article 31 of the 1951 Convention, within its restricted area of application, operates as a defence to prosecution and penalty, but neither *force majeure* nor article 31 come into operation unless and until a measure of enforcement action is taken.

The coastal State may elect to exercise jurisdiction, and prosecute and punish, or simply prohibit and prevent the passage in question.[213] The fact that a vessel may be carrying refugees or asylum seekers who intend to request the protection of the coastal State arguably removes that vessel from the category of innocent passage, even though the status of the passengers may entitle them to claim immunity from penalties under article 31 of the 1951 Convention. Even if the refugee character of those on board were compatible with innocent passage, this would not alone entail a right of entry into any port, although other rules of international law may affect or control the discretionary decision as to what is to be done with respect to any particular vessel. International law nevertheless allows States to take all reasonable measures in the territorial sea to prevent the entry into port of a vessel carrying illegal immigrants, and to require such vessel to leave the territorial sea.

4.3.2 *The contiguous zone*

In the law of the sea, the term 'contiguous zone' describes the area of seas between twelve and twenty-four miles from the baselines employed to delimit the boundaries of the territorial sea.[214] In this zone, or equivalent areas, international law has long limited the range of permissible enforcement measures.[215]

Article 24 of the 1958 Geneva Convention on the Territorial Sea and the Contiguous Zone acknowledges a power of control, 'to prevent infringement within its territory or territorial sea'. O'Connell observes, however:

It is also arguable that necessary power to control does not include the right to arrest, because at this stage (i.e. that of a ship coming into the contiguous zone) the ship cannot have committed an offence. Enforced direction into port may not be arrest, in a techni-

---

211   *The Ship 'May'* v. *R.* [1931] SCR 374.

212   O'Connell, *Law of the Sea,* vol. 2, (1984), 853–8, at 856, citing authority for the proposition that if a ship incurs trouble while engaged in an illegal enterprise against the State in whose waters it takes refuge, it cannot claim immunity from the local jurisdiction, even if entry was indeed occasioned by distress.

213   Arts. 19, 25, 1982 UN Convention; McDougal and Burke, *The Public Order of the Oceans,* (1962), 187–92, 272.

214   Art. 24, 1958 Geneva Convention on the Territorial Sea and the Contiguous Zone, now extended by art. 33, 1982 UN Convention.

215   In *Croft* v. *Dunphy* [1933] AC 156, 164–5, for example, the Privy Council, upholding Canadian Customs Act provisions on 'hovering', took account of the fact that they did not apply to foreign vessels in the area of extended jurisdiction.

cal sense, but it is tantamount to it and therefore is in principle excluded. The necessary examination should take place at sea, while the ship to be examined is in the zone.[216]

He further suggests that 'additional powers of seizure for the purpose of punishment' would come into operation where illegal immigrants have been landed, but this would be because the infringement of protected interests has already occurred in national territory.

The contiguous zone exists for the protection of the coastal State's customs, fiscal, sanitation and immigration interests. Even before the crystallization of State competence in the 1958 Geneva Convention on the Territorial Sea and the Contiguous Zone, it was widely recognized that jurisdiction might be exercised beyond the 'exact boundaries' of a State's territory, for law enforcement purposes, or in order to preserve national safety.[217] The question is, whether 'the interest sought to be protected warrants the authority asserted for the time projected in the area specified'.[218] By comparison with those which run in the territorial sea, the special jurisdictional rights which a State can exercise in the adjacent area of the contiguous zone do not clearly include the interception of vessels believed to be carrying asylum seekers.[219] One authority argues that 'such force and only such force may be used as will prevent the attempted incursion of illegal immigrants from becoming a danger to the preservation of the State'.[220] Although the basic principle of control is undisputed, this proposition begs the question, what is permissible in less extreme cases. The degree of force which might be used would need to be determined in light of all the circumstances, in the same way that the initial exercise of discretion would need to take into account the safety of passengers, the status of those on board, and the likely consequences of interdiction.[221]

If there are reasonable and probable grounds to believe that a vessel's intended purpose is to enter the territorial sea in breach of the immigration law,

[216] O'Connell, *Law of the Sea*, vol. 1, (1982), 1058.
[217] See McNair, *International Law Opinions*, vol. 2, (1956), 186 (enforcement of revenue laws in respect to vessels not yet within maritime jurisdiction); Jessup, P., *The Law of Territorial Waters and Maritime Jurisdiction*, (1927), 75–6, 242ff. O'Connell, *Law of the Sea*, vol. 2, (1984), 1045–7, identifying Canada as the first State in modern times to assert a revenue jurisdiction independent of the territorial sea.
[218] McDougal and Burke, *Public Order of the Oceans*, 584, 585 ff. See also O'Connell, *Law of the Sea*, vol. 2, (1984), 1057–61, noting the 'anticipatory' nature of contiguous zone powers.
[219] The powers allowed in the contiguous zone are only those permitted by international law: O'Connell, *Law of the Sea*, vol. 1, (1982) 1058–9; also Morin, 'La zone de pêche exclusive du Canada', 2 *Can. YBIL* (1964), 77, 86: 'la notion de zone contigue ... est très stricte et ne comporte aucune extension de la compétence de l'Etat côtier sur les eaux situées au delà de sa mer territoriale ...' He identifies the contiguous zone as forming part of the high seas, and as defined, 'précisement par l'absence de toute souveraineté étatique. Il n'est pas douteux que, dans la pratique, certains Etats voient dans la zone contigue le prolongement de leur mer territoriale et prétendent y exercer les mêmes compétences douanières ou fiscales, mais nous convenons ... que ces Etats sont en opposition avec le droit international tel qu'établi par les conventions sur le droit de la mer.'
[220] Johnson, D. H. N., 'Refugees, Departees and Illegal Migrants', 9 *Sydney L.R.* (1979–82), 11, 32.
[221] Some attention would always need to be given to a vessel's next likely port of call, if all information available indicated that refugees, rather than migrants, were on board.

the coastal State may have the right to stop and board the vessel. However, action taken under those powers, including inspection and redirection, might be objected to by flag States.[222] In certain circumstances, the Office of the United Nations High Commissioner for Refugees might be expected to make representations, in the absence of the flag State.[223]

In summary, the exercise and enforcement of jurisdiction over ships in the contiguous zone may violate international law where it is inconsistent with the purposes for which the contiguous zone exists and the limited authority allowed to coastal States; or because the exercise of enforcement powers (surveillance, identification, interception and arrest) exceed what is permissible under that law.[224]

4.3.3 *The consequences of enforcement action*

The simple denial of entry of ships to territorial waters cannot be equated with breach of the principle of *non-refoulement*, which requires that State action have the effect or result of returning refugees to territories where their lives or freedom would be threatened. In its comments in 1950 on the draft convention, the *Ad hoc* Committee observed:

> ... the obligation not to return a refugee to a country where he was persecuted did not imply an obligation to admit him to the country where he seeks refuge. The return of a refugee-ship, for example, to the high seas could not be construed as a violation of this obligation.[225]

Denial of entry to internal or territorial waters must therefore be distinguished from programmes of interdiction of boats which are accompanied by the actual, physical return of passengers to their country of origin. Even in the latter situation, the principle of *non-refoulement* would come into play only in the presence of certain objective conditions indicating the possibility of danger befalling those returned.[226]

---

[222] See above, n. 201. Obviously, all will turn on whether the flag State, if any, decides to object. The interdiction programme was based upon the Haitian government's agreement thereto. The US–Great Britain Treaty of 1924 (concluded in the context of prohibition) included express agreement by the British to raise no objections to the boarding of private vessels flying the British flag and outside US territorial waters. Enquiries might be undertaken to determine whether the vessel was endeavouring to violate US laws, and vessels might be seized on reasonable cause: Jessup, *Territorial Waters*, 289–93.

[223] Such representations were indeed made when the use of force (such as towing out to sea at high speed) resulted in sinking and loss of life of asylum seekers arriving directly from Vietnam in Singapore and Malaysia in 1979.

[224] See O'Connell on practical intervention and enforcement problems, which flow from international law restrictions on the use of force, and on the overall requirements of the necessary vessels: *Law of the Sea*, vol. 2, 1064 and n. 25. See also at 1071ff. on the degree of force which may be used.

[225] See UN doc. E/AC.32/L.32/Add.1 (10 Feb. 1950), comment on draft article 28 (expulsion to country of persecution).

[226] Goodwin-Gill, G. S, '*Non-refoulement* and the new asylum seekers', 26 *Virg. JIL* 897, 902 (1986).

It does not follow that States enjoy complete freedom of action over arriving boats, even if they come in substantial numbers and without nationality. The range of permissible measures is limited by obligations relating to rescue at sea and arising from elementary considerations of humanity, while action which would directly effect the return of refugees is prohibited by the principle of *non-refoulement*. Whether on the high seas or in waters subject to the jurisdiction of any State, refugees may also be protected by UNHCR in the exercise of its functional protection role.[227]

5. *Non-refoulement*, access to procedures and 'safe' countries

The practice of restricting access to State territory and/or refugee status procedures through the use of various admissibility thresholds is examined in Chapter 9, s. 2.1, with reference also to the principle of *non-refoulement*.

6. The principle of *non-refoulement* in general international law

The evidence relating to the meaning and scope of *non-refoulement* in its treaty sense also amply supports the conclusion that today the principle forms part of general international law. There is substantial, if not conclusive, authority that the principle is binding on all States, independently of specific assent. State practice before 1951 is, at the least, equivocal as to whether, in that year, article 33 of the Convention reflected or crystallized a rule of customary international law.[228] State practice since then, however, is persuasive evidence of the concretization of a customary rule, even in the absence of any formal judicial pronouncement.[229] In this context, special regard should also be paid to the practice of international organizations, such as the United Nations General Assembly and the United Nations High Commissioner for Refugees. General Assembly resolutions dealing with the report of the High Commissioner and consistently endorsing the principle of *non-refoulement* tend to be adopted by consensus. While consensus decision-making denotes the absence of formal dissent,[230] it still allows

---

[227] Ibid.

[228] This conclusion represents a modification of views first set out in Goodwin-Gill, *Movement of Persons*, 141.

[229] See *United States Diplomatic and Consular Staff in Tehran*, ICJ *Rep.*, 1980, 3, at 41 (para. 88), in which the Court hints at the 'legal difficulties, in internal and international law' which might have resulted from the United States acceding to Iran's request for the extradition of the former Shah.

[230] The Special Committee on the Rationalization of the Procedures and Organization of the General Assembly concluded that 'the adoption of decisions and resolutions by consensus is desirable when it contributes to the effective and lasting settlement of differences, thus strengthening the authority of the United Nations'. The Committee emphasized, however, 'that the right of every Member State to set forth its views in full must not be prejudiced by this procedure': *Report* of the Special Committee, *GAOR*, 26th Sess., Supp. no. 26 (A/8426), 1971, paras, 28–9; Rules of Procedure of the General Assembly, A/520/Rev.12 (1974), annexe V, para. 104. See D'Amato, A., 'On Consensus', 8 *Can. YIL* 104 (1970); Buzan, B., 'Negotiating by Consensus: Developments in Techniques at the United Nations Conference on the Law of the Sea', 75 *AJIL* 324 (1981).

States the opportunity to express opposing views in debate and in summary records.[231] No formal or informal opposition to the principle of *non-refoulement* is to be found, and where objection has been made on occasion to the protection and assistance activities of UNHCR, it has been founded on a challenge to the status as refugees of the individual involved. Moreover, while a number of commentators have disagreed as to the legal inferences to be drawn from the practice of States, none has been able to dispute the factual record.[232]

Article 33 of the 1951 Convention is of a 'fundamentally norm-creating character' in the sense in which that phrase was used by the International Court of Justice in the *North Sea Continental Shelf* cases.[233] That *refoulement* may be permitted in exceptional circumstances does not deny this premise, but rather indicates the boundaries of discretion.[234]

The practice examined hitherto has necessarily been selective and far from embracing the views of all States. The position of certain countries remains ambivalent, even though no State today claims any general right to return refugees or bona fide asylum seekers to a territory in which they may face persecution or danger to life or limb. Where States do claim not to be bound by

[231] On 16 Dec. 1981, the General Assembly adopted without a vote res. 36/148 on International Co-operation to Avert New Flows of Refugees, on the recommendations of the Special Political Committee (*Report:* UN doc. A/36/790). In the course of debate in the Committee, a number of delegates made statements in explanation which included substantial reservations regarding the draft resolution; other delegates expressly stated that they would have abstained, had the draft been put to the vote: UN doc. A/SPC/36/SR.45, paras. 49ff.

[232] For a detailed and cogent account of State practice, see Perluss and Hartman, 'Temporary Refuge: Emergence of a Customary International Norm', 26 *Virg. JIL* 551 (1986). For an example of failure to address either the facts or the legal issues, see Martin, D. A., 'Effects of International Law on Migration Policy and Practice', 23 *Int. Mig. Rev.* 547 (1989), who asserts (at 567) that Perluss and Hartmann (and the present author) 'essentially' propound the idea, 'hardly credible to the average citizen or to politicians and government officials', that international law forbids return if there is danger in the homeland. Perluss and Hartman and the present author in fact are somewhat more subtle. Martin further asserts (ibid., n. 62) that Hailbronner in 26 *Virg. JIL* 857 (1986) 'offered a detailed examination of the evidence used', to conclude that practice does not support a norm of customary international law. In fact, Hailbronner scarcely comments at all on the extensive examples offered by Hartman and Perluss, concentrating mostly on *municipal* law, limiting himself to disagreeing with their conclusions while dealing principally with an interesting, but peripheral issue, namely, the extent to which art. 3 of the European Convention on Human Rights has not been of use to refugees; on which, see below, Ch. 8, s. 2.2.1.

[233] ICJ *Rep.*, 1969, 3 at 42. No reservations may be made to art. 33; see art. 42.

[234] In 1984, the Cartagena Declaration included a reference to the actual or imminent *jus cogens* status of the principle of *non-refoulement*; see Conclusions and Recommendations, III, 5; below Annexe 2. In 1985, the High Commissioner observed in his report to the General Assembly that the principle of non-return had crystallized to the status of a peremptory norm of international law, unrestricted by geographical or territorial limitations: *Report* of the United Nations High Commissioner for Refugees: UN E/1985/62 (1985), paras. 22–3. A peremptory norm is one 'accepted and recognized by the international community of States as a whole as a norm from which no derogation is permitted and which can be modified only by a subsequent norm of general international law having the same character': art. 53, 1969 Vienna Convention on the Law of Treaties. Although a sound case can be made for the customary international law status of the principle of *non-refoulement*, its claim to be part of *jus cogens* is far less certain, and little is likely to be achieved by insisting on its status as such.

any obligation, their arguments either dispute the status of the individuals in question, or invoke exceptions to the principle of *non-refoulement*, particularly on the basis of threats to national security. Such considerations were dominant in the March/April 1995 decision by Tanzania to close its border to Rwandan refugees,[235] in the *refoulement* of Rwandans carried out by Zaire in the following September, and in Turkey's response to Kurdish refugees in the aftermath of the Gulf War.[236] The principle of *non-refoulement* applies to all States, whether or not they have ratified the 1951 Convention or the 1967 Protocol. However, the practice of States indicates that a significant element of *contingency* attaches to the obligation, particularly in cases of mass influx that may constitute a threat to the security of the receiving State.[237]

One further possible objection to including *non-refoulement* within the corpus of general international law lies in the so-called 'right of unilateral qualification'. Article 1(3) of the 1967 Declaration on Territorial Asylum declares that, '[i]t shall rest with the State granting asylum to evaluate the grounds for the grant of asylum'.[238] This provision, which Poland introduced during discussions in the Third Committee, is of uncertain scope. So far as the grant of *asylum* remains discretionary and a manifestation of sovereignty by the territorial State, it is redundant. Some commentators fear, however, that, rather than facilitate liberal policies, such a provision might be invoked to justify decisions to *refoule* refugees.[239] The disparate interpretations of 'political offence' in extradition, and its tendency to become dominated by political considerations, emphasize how, in the absence of directly applicable international standards, States' discretion can remain paramount.

If each State remains absolutely free to determine the status of asylum seekers and either to abide by or ignore the principle of *non-refoulement*, then the refugee's status in international law is denied and the standing, authority, and effectiveness of the principles and institutions of protection are seriously undermined. Despite instances of negative practice, particularly during the 1990s, the weight of the evidence still favours limits to discretion flowing, first, from an international legal definition of the refugee; and secondly, from general

---

[235] Kiley, Sam, 'Tanzania closes border to 100,000 Rwanda refugees', *The Times*, 1 Apr. 1995.

[236] See above, s. 3.2.

[237] The practical necessity for UNHCR to involve other States in the provision of material and political support for countries of first asylum has clear implications for the manner in which UNHCR can seek to uphold the basic principle.

[238] The 1975 Group of Experts' text (UN doc. A/10177) proposed the following article for inclusion in a convention on territorial asylum: 'Qualification of the grounds for granting asylum *or applying the provisions of this Convention* appertains to the Contracting State whose territory the person concerned has entered or seeks to enter and seeks asylum' (art. 9, emphasis supplied). Various amendments were proposed, including deletion of the article, but none was considered by the Committee of the Whole: UN doc. A/CONF.78/12, 63.

[239] Grahl-Madsen, A., *Territorial Asylum* (1980) 46, 88. See also provisions on the right of qualification in Latin American treaties, for example, art. 23, 1889 Montevideo Treaty on International Penal Law; art. 3, 1933 Montevideo Convention on Political Asylum; arts. 20, 23, 1940 Montevideo Treaty on International Penal Law; art. 4, 1954 Caracas Convention on Diplomatic Asylum.

recognition of the principle of *non-refoulement*. Security considerations and the practical dimensions of large-scale movements pose challenges to the continuing vitality of the principle, as well as to its precise scope and content. That certain grey areas continue to persist in the formulation of *non-refoulement* hardly confirms its lack of status in general international law, however. As Brierly noted some fifty-six years ago, 'the principles of international law are not susceptible of precise formulation . . . [the] rules are . . . constantly changing and modelling themselves on the ever-changing needs of international life.'[240]

6.1 *NON-REFOULEMENT* OR REFUGE BEYOND THE 1951 CONVENTION/1967 PROTOCOL

While the formal requirements of *non-refoulement* may be limited to Convention refugees, the *principle of refuge* is located within the body of general international law. It encompasses those with a well-founded fear of being persecuted, or who face a substantial risk of torture; it equally includes those who would face other 'relevant harm'. The limited protection due springs from objective conditions, wherever the facts are such as to indicate a serious risk of harm befalling those compelled to flee for *valid reasons* including war, violence, conflict, violations of human rights or other serious disturbance of public order.[241]

The juridically relevant situation of need flows from objectively verifiable evidence confirming the causes for flight, and the circumstance of danger facing specific groups or individuals. This essential factual base makes individualized inquiries into persecution or harm redundant. At the same time, host community interests are protected, within the principle of refuge, by the exclusion of, for example, those who have persecuted others, who are serious criminals or threats to *ordre public*, or who, on their own admission, are motivated by reasons of purely personal convenience.[242]

A combination of legal and humanitarian principle imposes significant limitations on the return of individuals to countries in which they may face inhumane or degrading treatment, or where their readmission is uncertain and their

---

[240] 'The Shortcomings of International Law', in Brierly, *The Basis of Obligation in International Law*, (1958, ed. Lauterpacht and Waldock) 68, 74.

[241] This characterization does not exclude, but neither does it determine, the solution that may be ultimately due. The phrase 'relevant harm' is used in this context to signify the validity of the reasons lying behind the claim for protection, and includes but is not limited to the risk of extralegal, arbitrary and summary executions, and to enforced disappearance: above, s. 2.4.

[242] Unlike other responses which generally call for once only determinations and once for all solutions, the principle of refuge permits the reasons for flight and the conditions producing distress to be regularly re-examined. It also allows complementary policies aimed at remedying the situation at source or otherwise promoting solutions to be pursued, through bilateral and multilateral means, and through the United Nations system. The conditions of refuge will require to be moderated and improved over time, however, as other human rights interests begin to predominate, for example, through lapse of time or the establishment of effective links. The western European response to the exodus from former Yugoslavia, though couched in the language of temporary protection (see below, section Ch. 5, s. 5.2), essentially reflected the principle of refuge described here, although not always with adequate reference to other complementary human rights, such as that to family reunion.

security precarious. Notwithstanding some of the rhetoric and recent exceptions, particularly in Europe with regard to asylum seekers from countries beyond the region, such as Iran and Sri Lanka, practice reveals a significant level of general agreement not to return to danger those fleeing severe internal upheavals or armed conflict in their own countries. What is disputed is the extent to which, if at all, any international legal obligation is involved.[243]

Despite the concerns of States and various exceptions in recent years, nearly four decades of practice contain ample recognition of a humanitarian response to refugees falling outside the 1951 Convention. Whether practice has been sufficiently consistent over time, and accompanied by the *opinio juris* essential to the emergence of a customary rule of refuge, is possibly less certain, even at the regional level.

In part, a strictly normative approach[244] is misconceived, for international legal obligations deriving from human rights treaties, among others, have clearly influenced the practice, and have constrained States' freedom of action. In that process, the obligations themselves have developed, even if what emerges at the present time is an incomplete relation of rights and duties. The primary responsibility for the protection of human rights rests on the territorial State; other States do not automatically assume or share in that responsibility when they remove non-nationals to their own country. So far as a State's actions may forcibly return an individual to the risk of violation of basic human rights, however, its responsibility is duty-driven, rather than strictly correlative to any individual 'right'. What exactly this entails in terms of policies, practices, State conduct and international responsibility still needs to be worked out, especially in the relation of States to UNHCR and its institutional role.[245]

---

[243] See above, Ch. 1, s. 7.
[244] That is, an approach in search of a set of correlative rights and duties.
[245] See further below, Ch. 6.

Chapter 5

THE CONCEPT OF ASYLUM

1. Introduction

The meaning of the word 'asylum' tends to be assumed by those who use it, but its content is rarely explained. The Universal Declaration of Human Rights refers to 'asylum from persecution', the UN General Assembly urges the grant of asylum and observance of the principle of asylum, and States' constitutions and laws offer the promise of asylum, yet nowhere is this act of States defined. The word itself and the phrase 'right of asylum' have lost much of their pristine simplicity.[1] With the growth of nation States and the corresponding development of notions of territorial jurisdiction and supremacy, the institution of asylum underwent a radical change. It came to imply not only a place of refuge, but also the right to give protection, not so much to the ordinary criminal, as to the one class previously excluded, namely, exiles and refugees.[2] The anomalous position of exiles had already been noted by the jurist Wolff who, writing in 1764, observed that 'exiles do not cease to be men . . . [By] nature the right belongs to them to dwell in any place in the world which is subject to some other nation'.[3] But this was a 'right' which even Wolff tempered with recognition of the fact of sovereignty. Compassion ought to be shown to those in flight, but admission might be refused for good reasons.[4] The interest of the State in admission or non-admission continued to predominate.[5] Moore, in 1908, noted that the right to grant asylum 'is to be exercised by the government in the light of

---

[1] See generally Reale, E., 'Le droit d'asile', Hague *Recueil* (1938–I), 473; Koziebrodski, L. B., *Le droit d'asile* (1962); Reville, *'L'abjuratio regni*: histoire d'une institution anglaise', *Revue historique*, (1892), 1; Trenholme, N. M., 'The Right of Sanctuary in England', 1 *Univ. Missouri Studies*, No. 5 (1903); Kimminich, O., *Der internationale Rechtsstatus des Flüchtlings*, (1962) 65–98; Sinha, S. P., *Asylum and International Law*, (1971); Grahl-Madsen, A., *The Status of Refugees in International Law*, vol. 2, (1972); Garcia-Mora, M. R., *International Law and Asylum as a Human Right*, (1956); Bau, I., *This Ground is Holy*, (1985), 124–71. For some alternative perspectives, see the articles by Gorman, R., 'Poets, Playwrights, and the Politics of Exile and Asylum in Ancient Greece and Rome', 6 *IJRL* 402 (1994); and 'Revenge and Reconciliation: Shakespearean Models of Exile and Banishment', 2 *IJRL* 211 (1990).

[2] Reale, Hague *Recueil* (1938–I), 499–550, 544–54, locates the beginning of this development in the mid-eighteenth century, with its hardening into an institution after the events in Europe of 1848–9.

[3] *Jus Gentium Methodo Scientifica Pertractatum*, (1764), s. 147.

[4] Ibid. s. 148; see also Vattel, ed. Chitty, (1834), I. 19. 229–30; Grotius, *De Jure Belli et Pacis*, (1646), iii. 20. xli.

[5] Generally on States' powers over entry and exclusion, see Goodwin-Gill, G. S., *International Law and the Movement of Persons between States*, (1978); also, Hailbronner, K., 'The Right to Asylum and the Future of Asylum Procedures in the European Community', 2 *IJRL* 341.

its own interests, and of its obligations as a representative of social order'.[6] Hackworth similarly observed the freedom of each sovereign State to deal with refugees 'as its domestic policy or its international obligations may seem to dictate'.[7] In 1949, Morgenstern settled the competence of States to grant asylum upon 'the undisputed rule of international law' that every State has exclusive control over the individuals in its territory, including all matters relating to exclusion, admission, expulsion, and protection against the exercise of jurisdiction by other States.[8]

This element, protection granted to a foreign national against the exercise of jurisdiction by another State, lies at the heart of the institution of asylum,[9] even if today some reference is also required to the goal of *solution*. Protection must nevertheless be distinguished in its international law and municipal law aspects. In international law, protection is founded either in an exercise of territorial jurisdiction or on treaty or some regional or local custom. The latter bases are particularly relevant to the institution of 'diplomatic asylum', understood in the sense of protection against *local* jurisdiction granted in embassies and consulates and on warships.[10] Although the notion of extraterritoriality has been adduced in support of the practice, regional treaty and custom appear to be its surer foundations.[11] In the *Asylum* case in 1950 the International Court of Justice described the practice as involving,

a derogation from the sovereignty of [the local] State. It withdraws the offender from the jurisdiction of the territorial State and constitutes an intervention in matters which are exclusively within the competence of that State . . . In the case of extradition, the refugee

---

[6] Moore, *Digest*, ii, 757.

[7] Hackworth, *Digest*, ii, 622.

[8] 'The Right of Asylum', 26 *BYIL* 327 (1949). See also Koziebrodski, *Droit d'asile*, 24, 79–81; Simpson, *The Refugee Problem*, (1939), 230: 'Asylum is a privilege conferred by the State. It is not a condition inherent in the individual'; Arboleda, E. and Hoy, I., 'The Convention Refugee Definition in the West: Disharmony of Interpretation and Application', 5 *IJRL* 66 (1993).

[9] Cf. the definition adopted by the Institute of International Law at its 1950 Bath Session: 'Asylum is the protection which a State grants on its territory or in some other place under the control of its organs to a person who comes to seek it': 1 *Annuaire*, (1950), 167, art. 1.

[10] Note also the recognition given after the 1973 coup in Chile to UNHCR 'safe havens', that is, refuges for foreign refugees granted asylum under the Allende government; see UN doc. A/AC.96/508, 5. Cited also by the Chilean representative to the UNHCR Executive Committee in 1992: UN doc. A/AC.96/SR.477, para. 51.

[11] Many States do not accept the institution of diplomatic asylum, or do so only in very limited cases; see debate in the International Law Commission in 1949: *Yearbook of the ILC*, paras. 49, 87–8; debate on the draft Declaration on the Right of Asylum in 1966: UN doc. A/6570, para. 11; Moore, *Digest*, ii, 755ff.; Hackworth, *Digest*, ii, 623ff.; Whiteman, *Digest*, vi, 445ff.; McNair, 'Extradition and Exterritorial Asylum', 28 *BYIL* 172 (1951); 7 *British Digest of International Law*, 905–23. In 1974, on an Australian initiative, the General Assembly requested the Secretary-General to prepare and circulate a report on the practice of diplomatic asylum and invited member States to make known their views: UNGA res. 3321 (XXIX), 14 Dec. 1974. The report (UN doc. A/10139) confirmed the regional nature of the practice; of 25 States which made known their views, only seven favoured drawing up an international convention on the matter. Further consideration of the subject was postponed indefinitely: UNGA res. 3497(XXX), 15 Dec. 1975. Cf. Riveles, S., 'Diplomatic Asylum as a Human Right: The Case of the Durban Six', 11 *HRQ* 139 (1989).

is within the territory of the State of refuge. A decision with regard to extradition implies only the normal exercise of territorial sovereignty. The refugee is outside the territory of the State where the offence was committed, and a decision to grant him asylum in no way derogates from the sovereignty of that State.[12]

The generality of these last dicta can be misleading unless the normative effect of extradition treaties is taken into account, as well as more recent developments which limit or qualify the 'normal exercise' of sovereignty.[13] From the point of view of international law, therefore, the grant of protection in its territory derives from the State's sovereign competence, a statement of the obvious. The content of that grant of protection—whether it embraces permanent or temporary residence, freedom of movement and integration or confinement in camps, freedom to work and attain self-sufficiency or dependence on national and international charity—is less easy to determine. What cannot be ignored, however, is the close relationship existing between the issue of refugee status and the principle of *non-refoulement*, on the one hand, and the concept of asylum, on the other hand. These three elements are, as it were, all links in the chain between the refugee's flight and his or her attainment of a durable solution.

Certain legal consequences flow from the existence of a class of refugees known to and defined by general international law and, in particular, from the principle of *non-refoulement*. In regard to asylum, however, it will be seen that the argument for obligation fails, both on account of the vagueness of the institution and of the continuing reluctance of States formally to accept such obligation and to accord a right of asylum enforceable at the instance of the individual.

2. Asylum in international conventions, other instruments and acts: 1945–70

The refusal of States to accept an obligation to grant asylum, in the sense of admission to residence and lasting protection against the jurisdiction of another State, is amply evidenced by the history of international conventions and other instruments. Measures taken between the two world wars related, initially, to arrangements for the issue of travel documents which would facilitate the resettlement of refugees, but no obligations to resettle were assumed. The 1933 Convention, which proposed non-rejection of refugees at the frontier, was rati-

[12] ICJ *Rep.*, 1950, 266, at 274. In this and the *Haya de la Torre* case, ICJ *Rep.*, 1951, 71, the Court was concerned, among others, with interpretation of the 1928 Havana Convention on Asylum, in force betweem Colombia and Peru, which embodied the right to grant asylum in embassies to political offenders in urgent cases. Colombia's claim that it was entitled to qualify the offence in question as political and also to determine the urgency of the case was rejected by the Court, as was its further claim that the territorial State was bound to allow the asylee to leave. Nevertheless, the Court agreed that the offence was political, but disagreed on the issue of urgency. The resulting stalemate, in which Colombia was not bound to hand over the fugitive, notwithstanding the improper grant of asylum, and Peru was not bound to allow safe passage, was not covered by the Convention or by any regional custom; the parties were urged to reach a friendly settlement.
[13] On which, see above Ch. 3, s. 4.2.1.1.

fied by only a few States, while it, too, made no provision in respect of permanent asylum. Likewise, those States which subscribed to the Constitution of the IRO, though urged to co-operate in its function of resettling refugees, accepted no obligations to that end. Little progress was achieved by the statement in article 14(1) of the Universal Declaration of Human Rights that 'everyone has the right to seek and to enjoy ... asylum from persecution'. Lauterpacht rightly noted that there was no intention among States to assume even a moral obligation in the matter.[14] The proposal to substitute 'to be granted' for 'to enjoy' was vigorously opposed, as was the suggestion that the United Nations itself should be empowered to secure asylum.[15] Contemporary opinion held that to grant asylum to refugees within its territory was the sovereign right of every State, while the corresponding duty was respect for that asylum by all other States.

This approach was substantially reiterated in the UN General Assembly resolution establishing UNHCR, which merely urged States to co-operate with the High Commissioner by, among other matters, admitting refugees.[16] Draft conventions submitted by France and the UN Secretariat in the course of debate on the 1951 Convention both contained an article on admission of refugees,[17] but the Conference of Plenipotentiaries preferred to leave asylum and admission to be covered by exhortatory statements in the Final Act.[18] Nevertheless, efforts continued in other fora. In 1957, France proposed a declaration on the right of

[14] Lauterpacht, H., *International Law and Human Rights*, (1950), 421. As Kimminich succinctly puts it: 'Das Recht, Asyl zu suchen, bedeutet nichts anderes als das Recht, sich auf die Flucht zu begeben': *Internationale Rechtsstatus des Flüchtlings*, 81.

[15] See the original draft of art. 14: UN doc. A/C.3/285/Rev. 1; the objections raised, particularly by the UK: UN doc. A/C.3/SR.121, 4–6; and the French proposal for a United Nations role, which was rejected: UN doc. A/C.3/244.

[16] UNGA res. 428(V), 14 Dec. 1950; see also UNGA res. 430(V) of the same date, urgently appealing to States to assist the IRO in its resettlement efforts.

[17] *Ad Hoc* Committee on Statelessness and Related Problems, Memorandum by the Secretary-General: UN doc. E/AC.32/2, (3 Jan. 1950), 22, preliminary draft convention, art. 3: '1. In pursuance of Article 14 of the Universal Declaration ... , the High Contracting Parties shall give favourable consideration to the position of refugees seeking asylum from persecution or the threat of persecution ... 2. [They] shall to the fullest possible extent relieve the burden assumed by initial reception countries which have afforded asylum ... They shall do so, *inter alia*, by agreeing to receive a certain number of refugees in their territory'. The Committee decided that the convention should not deal with the right of asylum; see comments by the US delegate, Louis Henkin, in the first session of the *Ad hoc* Committee: UN doc. E/AC.32/SR.20 (10 Feb. 1950), paras. 15, 44, 54–6; also UN doc. E/AC.32/SR.21, paras. 12, 16, 26. See Weis, P., 'Legal Aspects of the Convention of 28 July 1951 relating to the Status of Refugees', 30 *BYIL* 478, 481 (1953). Generally for the preparatory works, see Takkenberg, A. and Tahbaz, C., *The Collected travaux préparatoires of the 1951 Convention relating to the Status of Refugees*, 3 vols., Dutch Refugee Council/European Legal Network on Asylum, (1988).

[18] For discussion in the 1951 Conference on asylum as a right and not a duty of the State, see Colombia: A/CONF.2/SR.13, p. 12; UK, ibid., 14. Cf. France, 'the right of asylum was implicit in the Convention, even if it was not explicitly proclaimed therein, for the very existence of refugees depended on it': ibid., 13.

asylum to the Economic and Social Council,[19] and in 1959, the General Assembly called on the International Law Commission to work on its codification.[20] The subject was included in the Commission's future work programme in 1962,[21] but in the absence of progress generally it fell to the Commission on Human Rights and to the Third and Sixth Committees to take up the cause, culminating in the Declaration on Territorial Asylum, adopted unanimously by the General Assembly in 1967.[22]

The Declaration recommends that States should base their asylum practice upon the principles declared, but it stresses throughout the sovereign competence aspect of territorial asylum and reaffirms the position of each State as sole judge of the grounds upon which it will extend such protection.[23] Article 2, however, acknowledges that the plight of refugees remains of concern to the international community, and that where a State finds difficulty in granting or continuing to grant asylum, other States 'shall consider', in a spirit of international solidarity, measures to lighten the burden. Article 3 declares the principle of *non-refoulement* and States contemplating derogation, once again, 'shall consider' the possibility of according those affected the opportunity, 'by way of provisional asylum or otherwise', of going to another State.

The 1967 Protocol relating to the Status of Refugees is limited to updating the refugee definition and no other instruments of a universal character have specifically strengthened the institution of asylum. On a regional level, however, some slight progress can be discerned. Thus, the European Convention on Human Rights has facilitated an overall improvement in the situation of individuals at large, whether citizens, non-nationals or refugees, although not to the extent that might be expected.[24] Under treaty arrangements generally, the obligation to provide a remedy to victims of human rights violations is usually predicated on two conditions: (a) recognition of the specific right violated as a protected right within the system in question; and (b) the existence of a sufficient link between the actual or putative victim and the State from which a remedy is sought. For all its intrinsic value, article 3 of the European Convention on Human Rights, which prohibits torture and cruel, inhuman or degrading treatment or punishment, is neither a right to enter a State, nor a right to asylum.

---

[19] ECOSOC, *Official Records*, 22nd Sess., Supp., paras. 109–12. Other States objected, citing issues of sovereignty and domestic jurisdiction; see UN doc. E/CN.4/781, 3 (Czechoslovakia); ibid., 10–11 (UK).

[20] UNGA res. 1400(XIV), 21 Sept. 1959. The ILC had been tentatively involved with the issue some ten years previously, in debate on an article proposed for inclusion in a draft declaration on the rights and duties of States: *Yearbook of the ILC*, (1949), 125, paras. 49ff.

[21] UN doc. A/CN.4/245.

[22] UNGA res. 2312(XXII), 14 Dec. 1967. For text, see below, Annexe 1, No. 6. For a detailed account of the background, see Weis, P., 'The United Nations Declaration on Territorial Asylum', 7 *Can. YIL* 92 (1969).

[23] Art. 1(1), (2).

[24] Cf. Einarsen, T., 'The European Convention on Human Rights and the Notion of an Implied Right to *de facto* Asylum', 2 *IJRL* 361 (1990).

This has been clearly recognized in the jurisprudence of the European Court and Commission, even as they marked out the boundaries beyond which exclusion or expulsion might infringe that provision.[25] In the *Altun* case, where particularly cogent evidence of risk to the applicant was considered sufficient to declare the application admissible, the European Commission nevertheless noted that its role in relation to article 3 was not to ensure the correct application of extradition law at large. Rather, it was called upon to ensure observance of those obligations which flowed from ratification of the European Convention on Human Rights. This did not prohibit extradition for political offences, and such extradition would not, without more, be considered as prohibited by article 3.[26] Much the same reasoning applies in asylum and refugee status cases.[27]

The 1957 European Convention on Extradition, on the other hand, formulates the principle of non-extradition for political offences in the form of an obligation ('extradition shall not be granted') and applies the same principle where the request is made for the purpose of prosecuting or punishing a person on account of race, religion, nationality, or political opinion, or where a person's position may be prejudiced for any of these reasons.[28] In a 1967 resolution, the Committee of Ministers of the Council of Europe recommended that member governments 'should act in a particularly liberal and humanitarian spirit in relation to persons who seek asylum in their territory', but also recognized 'the necessity of safeguarding national security and of protecting the community from serious danger'.[29] Observance of the principle of *non-refoulement* was called for and, where exceptions were contemplated, the individual should 'as far as possible and under such conditions as [were considered] appropriate' be accorded the opportunity of going to another State.

Within Latin America, the 1954 Caracas Convention on Territorial Asylum reaffirmed the territorial State's sovereign right to grant asylum, the duty of other States to respect such asylum, and the exemption from any obligations to surrender or expel persons 'sought for political offences' or 'persecuted for

---

[25] See *Becker* v. *Denmark* (7011/75), 4 *D & R* 215, in which the European Commission took the view that it was not within the government's power to give guarantees as to what would happen to children whom it proposed to repatriate to South Vietnam, and that it was neither reasonable nor feasible to require guarantees. Most cases alleging breach of art. 3 in the present context have failed on the facts, that is, the applicant was unable to satisfy the European Commission that his or her life or liberty was sufficiently at risk.

[26] *Altun* v. *Federal Republic of Germany* (10308/83), 36 *D & R* 201, 209. In a simple sense, rights depend upon facts. See further *X* v. *United Kingdom* (9856/82), Decision of the European Commission, 14 May 1987.

[27] See further below, Ch. 8, s. 2.2.1.   [28] *ETS* no. 24, art. 3(2).

[29] Res. (67) 14 of 29 June 1967 on Asylum to Persons in Danger of Persecution, Preamble and para. 1. See also the earlier Recommendation 293 of 26 Sept. 1961 of the Consultative Assembly of the Council of Europe, proposing that the Committee of Experts be instructed to include an article on asylum in a protocol to the European Convention on Human Rights; this was rejected by the Committee of Experts, which favoured either a separate convention or a resolution. The principles of the 1967 resolution were reaffirmed in the Declaration on Territorial Asylum adopted by the Committee on Ministers on 18 Nov. 1977. For texts, see below Annexe 4, Nos. 5 and 6.

political reasons or offences'.[30] As regards diplomatic asylum,[31] another Caracas Convention of the same year stressed that while 'every State has the right to grant asylum ... it is not obligated to do so or state its reasons for refusing it'; and that it rested with 'the State granting asylum to determine the nature of the offence or the motives for the persecution'.[32] The Convention provides further that 'the State granting asylum is not bound to settle him in its territory, but it may not return him to his country of origin, unless this is the express wish of the asylee'.[33]

The 1969 OAU Convention, by contrast, besides broadening the refugee definition, also strengthens the institution of asylum. Member States of the OAU, proclaims Article II, 'shall use their best endeavours ... to receive refugees and to secure the settlement' of those unable or unwilling to be repatriated. The principle of *non-refoulement* is declared without exception, although once again a call is made to lighten the burden on countries of first refuge.[34] A further provision, dealing with the refugee who has not received the right to reside in any country, merely acknowledges that he or she 'may' be granted temporary residence pending resettlement. On asylum at large, the Convention affirms that its grant is a peaceful and humanitarian act, and thus not to be regarded as unfriendly. It also emphasizes the duty of refugees to abide by the laws of the country in which they find themselves and to refrain from subversive activities against any member State.

Despite the encouraging tone of the OAU Convention, neither this instrument nor any other permits the conclusion that States have accepted an international obligation to grant asylum to refugees, in the sense of admission to residence and lasting protection against persecution and/or the exercise of jurisdiction by another State. The period under review, however, is replete with examples of asylum given; the humanitarian practice exists, but the sense of obligation is missing.

The practice of international organizations tends to support this view, while simultaneously revealing an awareness of the need for pragmatic, flexible responses. In the years after the Second World War, for example, many thousands of refugees had the benefit, at least, of asylum in the refugee camps of Europe.[35] Their principal need was for resettlement, and the General Assembly repeatedly called upon immigration countries to allow refugees access to their programmes.[36] On other occasions, the General Assembly reiterated that permanent solutions should be sought in voluntary repatriation and assimilation

[30] Arts. 1–4, see below, Annexe 2, No. 3.

[31] That is, asylum granted 'in legations, war vessels, and military camps or aircraft, to persons being sought for political offences': art. 1, 1954 Caracas Convention on Diplomatic Asylum; see below, Annexe 2, No. 4.

[32] Ibid., arts. 2, 4.   [33] Ibid., art. 17.   [34] Art. II(4); see below, Annexe 2, No. 1.

[35] See generally, Vernant, J., *The Refugee in the Post-War World*, (1953); Holborn, L., *The International Refugee Organization*, (1956).

[36] See, for example, UNGA res. 430(V), 14 Dec. 1950, urgently appealing to all States to assist the IRO with resettlement; UNGA res. 538(VI), 2 Feb. 1952, appealing specially to States interested in migration.

within new national communities, either locally in countries of first refuge or in countries of immigration.[37] The initial burden may fall in fact upon the receiving country,[38] but solutions are the responsibility of the international community at large.[39]

General Assembly resolutions are not the most consistent of sources from which to extract the views of States. Those adopted in the period under review are significant for the extent to which the notion of asylum is left unexplained and unexplored. There is, as it were, implicit recognition of the plight of the refugee as a situation of exception, in which no assumptions can be made as to the appropriateness of any particular solution. Thus, in the case of refugees in European camps in the 1950s, the international community acknowledged that resettlement or aid with local integration were the most suitable courses.[40] In the case of refugees from Algeria in Morocco and Tunisia fleeing the struggle for independence, the temporary nature of the problem was recognized; living conditions required improvement until the refugees were able to return home.[41] Angolan refugees in the Congo[42] and refugees in Africa generally, met with much the same response.[43] Although no *a priori* assumptions may be possible as to the appropriateness of particular solutions, in the hierarchy of voluntary repatriation, local integration, and resettlement in third countries, the first mentioned is seen as the most desirable. Voluntary repatriation puts an end to the situation of exception; asylum is a link in the chain between the refugees' flight and re-establishment in their old communities.

3. A decade of drafts and more: 1971–85

The 1970s were characterized by wide ranging activity. In many respects, it was a high point for refugee status determination procedures, with the UNHCR

[37] UNGA res. 1166(XII), 26 Nov. 1957, para. 2, reaffirming the basic approach set out in para. 1 of the UNHCR Statute; also UNGA res. 1285(XIII), 5 Dec. 1958, on special efforts to be made in the context of World Refugee Year.

[38] UNGA res. 832(IX), 21 Oct. 1954, '*Considering* that, while the ultimate responsibility for . . . refugees . . . falls in fact upon the countries of residence, certain of these countries have to face particularly heavy burdens as a result of their geographical situation, and some complementary aid has been shown to be necessary . . .'

[39] UNGA res. 1167(XII), 26 Nov. 1957, recognizing the heavy burden placed on the government of Hong Kong by the massive influx of Chinese refugees, and noting that the problem is such 'as to be of concern to the international community'.

[40] UNGA resolutions 538(VI), 2 Feb. 1952; 638(VII), 20 Dec. 1952; 639(VII), 20 Dec. 1952; 832(IX), 21 Oct. 1954; 1166(XII), 26 Nov. 1957; 1284(XIII), 5 Dec. 1958; 1388(XIV), 20 Nov. 1959. Note also UNGA resolutions 1039(XI), 23 Jan. 1957; 1129(XI), 21 Nov. 1956 and 1006(ES-II), 9 Nov. 1956 on the situation of Hungarian refugees 'obliged . . . to seek asylum in neighbouring countries'.

[41] UNGA res. 1500(XV), 5 Dec. 1960, and 1672(XVI), 18 Dec. 1961.

[42] UNGA res. 1671(XVI), 18 Dec. 1961, noting efforts to provide immediate assistance and to help the refugees become self-supporting until they can return home; also recognizing that the needs of the refugees may not be separable from those of the local population.

[43] UNGA res. 2040(XX), 7 Dec. 1965.

Executive Committee's recommended minimum standards being adopted in many States.[44] Despite the progress at the level of individual protection and the resolution of a number of major refugee problems through repatriation and resettlement, hopes centring on asylum were dashed by the failure of the 1977 United Nations conference. Efforts to promote a convention and States' responses to refugee crises showed, on the one hand, continuing reluctance to do more than recognize the humanitarian aspects of refugees in need; and, on the other hand, increasing recognition of the normative quality of the principle of *non-refoulement* and of the responsibility of the international community to find solutions. Contemporaneously with these developments, and perhaps anticipating the persistence of large-scale movements, some States began to enquire into the root causes of refugee problems, particularly those producing a massive exodus of refugees.[45]

Discussions in the UN Sixth Committee shortly before adoption of the 1967 Declaration on Territorial Asylum had revealed some expectation that that instrument would be the precursor to a universal convention.[46] The first draft was in fact proposed, not by the International Law Commission (as General Assembly resolutions might have anticipated), but by a group of experts meeting in 1971 and 1972 under the auspices of the Carnegie Endowment for International Peace, in consultation with UNHCR. Article 1 of their text proposed that contracting States 'acting in an international and humanitarian spirit, *shall use [their] best endeavours to grant asylum* in [their] territory, which . . . includes permission to remain in that territory'.[47] The draft was discussed in the Third Committee later in 1972, where it was decided that the High Commissioner should consult governments, with a view to the eventual convening of an international conference.[48] When governments were canvassed, many appeared to favour a convention,[49] and the General Assembly decided that the text should be reviewed.[50]

The UN Group of Experts' revision indicated continuing adherence to the discretionary aspect of asylum practice.[51] Article 1 proposed that '[e]ach Contracting State, *acting in the exercise of its sovereign rights, shall use its best endeavours in a humanitarian spirit to grant asylum in its territory* . . .'[52] The same 'best

---

[44] See further below, Ch. 9.   [45] See further below, Ch. 7, s. 3.5.

[46] See UN docs. A/C.6/SR. 983–9; A/6912, *Report* of the Sixth Committee, paras. 64–5; also the Preamble to the 1967 Declaration, adopted by UNGA res. 2312(XXII), 14 Dec. 1967.

[47] UN doc. A/8712 appx., annexe 1. This and other drafts are collected in Grahl-Madsen, A., *Territorial Asylum,* (1980), annexes KK and following.

[48] UN docs. A/C.3/SR.1956 and 1957, paras. 25, 32.

[49] UN doc. A/9612/Add.3, annexe (1974). Of 91 states which made known their views, 76 favoured elaboration of a convention on territorial asylum. See also UN doc. A/C.3/SR.2098–2101; and SR.2103, paras. 44–60. (1974).

[50] UNGA res. 3272(XXIX), 9 Jan. 1975.

[51] UN doc. A/10177 and Corr. 1 (1975); Grahl-Madsen, *Territorial Asylum,* annexe RR; also UN doc. A/C.3/SR.2161–4.

[52] Cf. the draft prepared by the International Law Association at its 55th Conference in 1972, under which States would 'undertake to grant refuge in their territories to all those who are seeking

endeavours' formula was again introduced in article 3 where, following a statement of the principle of *non-refoulement* on behalf of those 'in the territory of a
contracting State', it would have operated to reduce the level of obligation in
relation to rejection at the frontier from that previously adopted in both the 1967
Declaration and the 1969 OAU Convention.[53] Acting on the Group of Experts'
report, the General Assembly requested the Secretary-General, in consultation
with the High Commissioner, to convene a conference on territorial asylum in
early 1977.[54]

Dissatisfaction with much of the proposed texts inspired a working group of
non-governmental organizations to suggest an alternative version,[55] the asylum
provisions of which were largely supported by consensus at a Nansen
Symposium held in 1976.[56] In both cases, the proposals favoured an obligation
to grant asylum, subject to certain exceptions; confirmation of the notion of non-
rejection at the frontier within the principle of *non-refoulement*, and general recognition of the principle of provisional admission as a minimum requirement.

The 1977 United Nations Conference on Territorial Asylum was an abject
failure, with close voting on major issues apparently heralding emerging divisions between States and on matters of principle.[57] One article only, that on asylum, was considered by the drafting committee, which reduced the 'best
endeavours' formula of the Group of Experts draft to that of 'shall endeavour
. . . to grant asylum'.[58] On the other hand, non-rejection at the frontier was
endorsed overall within the principle of *non-refoulement*, though the latter generally would have been qualified by States' preoccupation with numbers and security. Recognizing that little of substance had been achieved, the Conference at
its final session recommended that the General Assembly consider its reconvening at a suitable time.[59] Later that year, however, the Third Committee declined
to submit any formal proposal to that effect, and it was thought more appropriate that the High Commissioner continue consultations with governments.[60]

---

asylum . . .', save where danger to the security of the country or to the safety and welfare of the
community was apprehended (art. 1(b)). Art. 3, however, proposed that '[a] grant of asylum does
not imply any right of permanent immigration'. ILA, *Report of 55th Session*, (1972); text also in Grahl-
Madsen, *Territorial Asylum*, annexe LL.

[53] Art. 4 did provide for provisional admission pending consideration of a request for asylum, but
meeting the qualifications still gave no entitlement to the grant of asylum.

[54] UNGA res. 3456(XXX), 9 Dec. 1975.

[55] Text in Grahl-Madsen, *Territorial Asylum*, annexe TT.

[56] 'Towards an Asylum Convention', Report of the Nansen Symposium (1977); text of draft convention proposed by Grahl-Madsen and Melander also in Grahl-Madsen, *Territorial Asylum*, annexe
UU.

[57] See generally, Grahl-Madsen, *Territorial Asylum*; Weis, P., 'The Draft Convention on Territorial
Asylum', 50 *BYIL* 176 (1979).

[58] For full text of the articles considered by the Committee of the Whole and by the Drafting
Committee, see below, Annexe 4, No.1.

[59] See *Report* of the Conference: UN doc. A/CONF.78/12, para. 25; also *Report* of the UNHCR
to ECOSOC: doc. E/5987, paras. 10–16 (June 1977).

[60] UN doc. A/C.3732/SR.49, paras. 16–19 (Nov. 1977).

Since 1977, there has been no further progress towards reconvening the Conference; on the contrary, refugee problems, including aspects of asylum, status, *non-refoulement* and solutions have responded more to regional initiatives, such as the comprehensive programmes implemented for Central America (CIREFCA) and Indo-China (CPA).[61]

3.1 FLIGHT AND RESPONSE

The experience of these fifteen years must be assessed not only on its own terms, but in the light of the events and responses of the period. The years 1971–1985 were remarkable for the magnitude and frequency of refugee crises and for the increasing attention paid to them within international organizations. With the events leading to the partition of Pakistan in 1971–2, India underwent a massive influx of refugees, principally from East Bengal.[62] By December 1971, they numbered 10 million, and the only acceptable solution was voluntary repatriation. The Indian government insisted on a maximum stay of six months, the General Assembly endorsed repatriation,[63] and by February 1972 over ninety per cent of the refugees had returned to the newly independent State of Bangladesh. That political development and the acceptance by all parties concerned of the principle of voluntary repatriation, were clearly the controlling conditions for the ultimate solution.

Similar factors were present in refugee problems resulting from the struggle for liberation from colonial rule, particularly in Africa. Their provisional nature was acknowledged in anticipation of repatriation on independence, with appropriate, international assistance in rehabilitation being given to those returning.[64] Where this preferred solution was more remote in time, attention focused on the need for the international community to relieve the pressure on countries of first refuge. Thus, in 1976, the General Assembly formally recognized the heavy burden placed on Botswana, Lesotho, and Swaziland by the influx after Soweto of large numbers of South African student refugees.[65] In succeeding years, it urged other governments to assist by providing opportunities for settlement, education, and vocational training.[66] Where the attainment of the political conditions essential to voluntary repatriation is uncertain, interim and long-term self-sufficiency

[61] Generally see UNHCR, *The State of the World's Refugees*, (1993), 26–9, 117–20; 'Focus on the Comprehensive Plan of Action', 5 *IJRL* 507 (1993).
[62] See International Commission of Jurists, *The Events in East Pakistan, 1971*, (1972).
[63] UNGA res. 2790(XXVI), 6 Dec. 1971.
[64] For example, in 1974 the General Assembly requested the High Commissioner 'to take appropriate measures in agreement with the Governments concerned, to facilitate the voluntary repatriation of refugees from territories emerging from colonial rule and, in co-ordination with other competent bodies of the United Nations, their rehabilitation in their countries of origin': UNGA res. 3271(XXIX), 10 Dec. 1974.
[65] UNGA res. 31/126, 16 Dec. 1976.
[66] UNGA resolutions 32/70, 8 Dec. 1977; 32/119, 16 Dec. 1977; 33/164, 20 Dec. 1978; 34/174, 17 Dec. 1979; 35/184, 15 Dec. 1980; 36/170, 16 Dec. 1981; 37/177, 17 Dec. 1982; 28/88, 16 Dec. 1983; 38/95, 16 Dec. 1984; 38/120, 16 Dec. 1983 (ICARA II); 39/109, 14 Dec. 1984; 39/139, 14 Dec. 1984 (ICARA II); 40/117, 13 Dec. 1985 (ICARA II); 40/138, 13 Dec. 1985.

programmes may be called for. African States generally were prepared in these situations to allow refugees to remain, and internationally funded schemes contributed to a degree of local integration.[67] Where repatriation was altogether excluded, the local integration process was sometimes completed by naturalization.[68]

In Latin America, solutions to refugee problems were more problematic. Following the *coup d'état* in Chile in 1973, large numbers of Chileans and resident foreign refugees fled to neighbouring countries. Some States, for example, Peru, indicated that they were only prepared to allow a transit facility. In Argentina, a certain proportion was allowed to remain, but resettlement was demanded of others and the personal security of many was so severely threatened by the activities of paramilitary groups that a solution beyond the region was urgently called for. As a result of numerous appeals by UNHCR, some 14,000 refugees were resettled by other countries in the period 1973–80.[69]

In Asia, apart from limited exceptions, opportunities for voluntary repatriation or local integration in countries of first refuge were minimal.[70] Even temporary admission pending other solutions was difficult to obtain; in May 1975, for example, Singapore refused to admit some 8,000 Vietnamese who arrived in sixty ships.[71] Subsequently, even the disembarkation of refugees rescued at sea became problematic, notwithstanding resettlement guarantees by flag or other States. In succeeding years, the Indo-Chinese refugee problem developed into one of the largest and most intractable. Over one and a half million people fled Cambodia, Laos, and Vietnam, and almost without exception the countries of first refuge declined to allow refugees to settle locally.[72] Their repeated calls for more assistance were interspersed with threatened and actual forcible action

[67] Details of various programmes can be found in UNHCR reports on assistance activities, submitted each year to the Executive Committee of the High Commissioner's Programme.

[68] In 1980, for example, Tanzania naturalized a group of Rwandese refugees; see generally Gasarasi, C. P., 'The Mass Naturalization and further Integration of Rwandese Refugees in Tanzania: Process, Problems and Prospects', 3 *JRS* 88 (1990).

[69] See 'Human Rights, War and Mass Exodus', *Transnational Perspectives*, (1982), 8–9.

[70] Generally, see Muntarbhorn, V., *The Status of Refugees in Asia*, (1992). In 1981, there were small scale returns of Laotian refugees from Thailand: UN doc. A/AC.96/594, para. 552, but the main voluntary repatriation movement was the return of Burmese Moslem refugees from Bangladesh in 1978–9: UN doc. A/AC.96/564, paras. 392ff. This problem re-emerged in the 1990s, however; see Piper, T., 'Myanmar: Exodus and Return of Muslims from Rakhine State', 13 *RSQ* No. 1, 11 (1994). The principal exception as regards local integration was the settlement of some 267,000 refugees who entered the People's Republic of China from Vietnam in 1979: UN doc. A/AC.96/594, paras. 505ff. Malaysia admitted some 90,000 refugees from the southern Philippines during 1979/80: ibid., paras. 582ff., and resettled several thousand Cambodian Muslims from Thailand.

[71] The asylum seekers eventually made their way to the US territory of Guam.

[72] Indonesia, Malaysia, the Philippines, Singapore, and Thailand each adduced various objections to local integration, including racial, religious, cultural, financial, and security grounds. The exceptions were Australia, which was prepared to grant asylum to those arriving directly who were recognized as refugees by the Determination of Refugee Status Committee (the small number of direct arrivals—just over 2,000 from 1975–81—was clearly an important factor in this policy); Hong Kong, which granted residence to some 14,500 Vietnamese, though calling on the international community to resettle many thousands of others; and the People's Republic of China.

against asylum seekers.[73] The international community finally responded with increased financial aid and more resettlement offers, while calling upon receiving countries to respect the principles of first asylum and *non-refoulement*.[74] Following a major international conference in July 1979, the resettlement rate rose dramatically. Vietnam announced efforts to curb illegal departures and declared that it would co-operate with UNHCR in expanding and implementing a programme for 'orderly departures'.[75] Refugee processing centres were established in Indonesia and the Philippines,[76] and first refuge countries modified their threats of forcible measures. Thereafter, with a few exceptions, States in the region continued to allow admission on a temporary basis pending a solution elsewhere, but their practice must be seen in the context of other States' preparedness to shoulder financial and resettlement costs, and ultimately judged in light also of the Comprehensive Plan of Action initiated in 1989.[77]

By contrast, Pakistan in this period was much more ready to admit refugees, and by 1985 had accepted nearly 3 million from Afghanistan. Resettlement was recognized as inappropriate, while the weight of numbers likewise militated against long-term local integration, despite common aspects of language and culture. Voluntary repatriation was expected to be the eventual solution, but a realistic appreciation of political realities required that provision be made for accommodation and for measures to assist the refugees to attain a degree of self-sufficiency.[78]

---

[73] Thus, Malaysia in Jan. and Mar. 1979 announced it would permit no more landings; Thailand in May 1979 ordered an (ineffective) blockade of its coast and later forcibly repatriated some 40,000 Cambodians. In June 1979, Indonesia announced it could accept no more and Malaysia threatened to tow boats out to sea and to shoot asylum seekers on sight. The threat to shoot was subsequently withdrawn, but numerous boats were turned away or towed out to sea, with resulting loss of life. See generally, Grant, B., *The Boat People*, (1980); Wain, B., *The Refused: The Agony of the Indochina Refugee*, (1982). For arrivals statistics, see UNHCR, *The State of the World's Refugees*, (1993), 26; McNamara, D., 'The Origins and Effects of "Humane Deterrence" Policies in South-east Asia', in Loescher, G. and Monahan, L., eds., *Refugees and International Relations*, (1989), 123.

[74] UNGA res. 33/26, 29 Nov. 1978.

[75] *Report* of the Secretary-General on the Meeting on Refugees and Displaced Persons in South-east Asia, Geneva, 20, 1 July 1979, and subsequent developments: UN doc. A/34/627. In Jan. 1979, Vietnam announced that it would permit the emigration of those who wished to leave, subject to certain exceptions. UNHCR missions to Vietnam in March and May led to a Memorandum of Understanding whereby the legal emigration of family reunion and 'other humanitarian cases' was to be facilitated; so began the 'Orderly Departure Programme'. For statistics in the period 1979–82, see UNHCR, *The State of the World's Refugees*, (1993), 26.

[76] See UN docs. A/AC.96/577, paras. 541, 638–41; A/AC.96/594; paras. 548–9, 632. In proposing such centres in Dec. 1978, the ASEAN States had insisted on guarantees that they would face 'no residual problem'. In Bangkok in Feb. 1979, ASEAN foreign Ministers announced the terms for the centres: refugees would be admitted only on the basis of firm commitments from third countries that they would be resettled within a reasonable time; the country providing the site would be entitled to limit numbers, would retain sovereignty, administrative control and responsibility for security, and should not bear the cost.

[77] See further below, Ch. 7, s. 4.

[78] See UN doc. A/AC.96/594, paras. 595ff., and subsequent UNHCR reports. The situation of Iranian refugees and asylum seekers, however, was far less secure.

4. A Decade of Disillusion: 1986–95

According to world refugee statistics published by the United States Committee for Refugees (USCR), there were over 13.2 million refugees and asylum seekers in need of protection and/or assistance at the end of 1987, up from some 8.2 million in 1980.[79] By the end of 1994, USCR estimated the number at 16.2 million, while UNHCR listed a total of 27.4 million 'persons of concern', including refugees, returnees, others of concern and internally displaced.[80] USCR also estimated that there were more than 26 million internally displaced persons without international protection.[81]

The reasons for exodus were various, often the direct consequence of persecution, discrimination or massive violations of human rights; or resulting from the more indirect loss of State protection as a consequence of conflicts, or radical political, social or economic changes, with root or structural causes often mixed in.[82] For example, many Afghans fled to Iran and Pakistan from the devastating effects of modern warfare, behind which lay the 1979 Soviet invasion. But when Soviet troops withdrew in February 1989, fighting continued, both between government and mujahedeen, and between different tribal elements among the opposition; the structural bases for future conflict remained unreconciled, namely, tribal divisions, ideology, and power.

What began in 1983 in Sri Lanka as a largely ethnic struggle between Hindu Tamils in the north and east and the Buddhist Sinhalese community in the south deteriorated into a violent nation-wide war. The July 1987 Indo-Sri Lankan Peace Accord, under which the Tamils acquired some regional autonomy in exchange for an Indian pledge to disarm the guerrillas,[83] failed to bring a

[79] USCR, *World Refugee Survey: 1989 in Review*, (1990), 30–4. This total did not include some 450,000 estimated to be in procedural backlogs in Europe and North America; some 720,000 ethnic Germans who entered the German Federal Republic as immigrants; or some 250,000 ethnic Turks from Bulgaria in Turkey. The USCR figures, which draw on data provided by UNHCR, governments and other sources, are widely accepted as reliable, particularly as they are unconstrained by institutional mandates or formal, legal definitions. For a list of sources, see USCR, *World Refugee Survey—1995*, 41.

[80] Refugees—14,488,700; returnees—3,983,200; others of concern—3,524,100; internally displaced—5,423,000: UNHCR, 'Populations of Concern to UNHCR: A Statistical Overview-1994', Geneva, (1995).

[81] USCR in fact offers only estimates for the internally displaced, given the fragmentary information available: *World Refugee Survey—1995*, (1995), 44. Other analysts suggest higher numbers.

[82] On causes and the reasons for displacement, particularly across borders, see generally Zolberg, A. R., Suhrke, A. and Aguayo, S., *Escape from Violence: Conflict and the Refugee Crisis in the Developing World*, (1989); also, Rizvi, Z., 'Causes of the Refugee Problem and the International Response', in Nash, A. E., ed., *Human Rights and the Protection of Refugees under International Law*, (1988), 107; Allen, R. and Hiller, H. H., 'Social Organization of Migration: An Analysis of the Uprooting and Flight of Vietnamese Refugees', 23 *Int. Mig.* 439 (1985); Menjivar, C., 'Salvadorian Migration to the United States in the 1980s: What can we learn *about* it and *from* it?' 32 *Int. Mig.* 371 (1994).

[83] In Dec. 1988, Parliament unanimously approved a constitutional amendment making Tamil one of the country's two official languages, together with Sinhala. In April 1989, the government granted voting rights to 320,000 Indian Tamils, whose ancestors were brought to Sri Lanka during the British colonial period: *The Europa World Year Book 1989*, vol. 2 (1989), 2371. Peace negotiations in 1995, which at one time seemed close to producing a settlement, were abandoned by the Tamils and fighting resumed.

lasting settlement. Over the years, hundreds of civilians in the north and east were killed in the armed conflict between the Liberation Tigers of Tamil Eelam (LTTE) and the Indian Peace Keeping Forces (IPKF), as a result of clashes between rival Tamil groups and reprisal killings by all sides.[84] Inter-communal violence continued during the late 1980s. In pursuit of the government's military objective to destroy the LTTE, many hundreds of Tamils, mostly young males, were detained. Reports increased of disappearances, ill-treatment and death in detention. By the end of 1994, some 104,000 were estimated to have found refuge in India, while many others continued to make their way to the industrialized world, particularly to Europe and North America.[85]

In 1989, more than 70,000 Vietnamese fled their country, the largest number for ten years, with more than half coming from the northern and central region.[86] With the introduction that year of the Comprehensive Plan of Action and the practice of refugee determination in each case, arrivals fell away almost completely. In Hong Kong, where the majority of Vietnamese arrived by boat, screening procedures were introduced in late 1988.[87] According to the Hong Kong government, almost all arrivals after 1980 were ethnic Vietnamese (98 per cent) and the proportion of northerners also steadily increased, reaching 86 per cent in 1989; this contrasted with the predominantly ethnic Chinese character of the exodus in 1978–80, when 'economic restructuring' was underway in Vietnam. The Hong Kong government considered that thereafter most left for economic reasons,[88] although other commentators doubted the answer was so simple.[89]

In Africa, conflict within Ethiopia lasted for more than thirty years, initially as a reflection of Eritrea's long-standing struggle for independence;[90] then as a part of the revolution and overthrow of Haile Selassie; and finally as a conse-

---

[84] See, for example, Amnesty International, *Sri Lanka: Continuing Human Rights Violations*: AI Index: ASA 37/04/89, May 1989, 20.

[85] Between 1987–1994, an estimated 114,830 Sri Lankans applied for asylum in Europe, particularly Germany, France and Switzerland, and many thousands more in North America: *World Refugee Survey—1995*, 107.

[86] *World Refugee Survey—1989 in Review*, 57.

[87] All boat people who arrived in Hong Kong were thereafter presumed to be illegal immigrants, unless screened in as refugees. For earlier practice, see Mushkat, R., 'Refuge in Hong Kong', 1 *IJRL* 449 (1989). 'Refugees' were permitted to reside in open centres and were eligible for resettlement. 'Illegal immigrants' were detained, in conditions which incited controversy and violent disturbances, pending repatriation or removal to Vietnam. In the period March 1989–December 1994, a total of 68,065 returned voluntarily to Vietnam, and a further 1,174 were deported: *World Refugee Survey—1995*, 87–9, 97–8. For text of the CPA, see Annexe 5, No. 1.

[88] Hong Kong Government, *Fact Sheet: Vietnamese Boat People in Hong Kong*, (May 1990), annexed to Fan, R., 'Hong Kong and the Vietnamese Boat People: A Hong Kong Perspective', 2 *IJRL, Special Issue* (1990), 144, 153.

[89] See Amnesty International, *Memorandum to the Governments of Hong Kong and the United Kingdom regarding the protection of Vietnamese Asylum-seekers in Hong Kong*, (Jan. 1990). Also, Le Xuan Khoa, 'Forced Repatriation of Asylum Seekers: The Case of Hong Kong', 2 *IJRL, Special Issue*, 137 (1990); Wolf, Daniel, 'A Subtle Form of Inhumanity: Screening of the Boat People in Hong Kong', ibid., 161.

[90] The war ended in 1991, and Eritrea became a sovereign State in May 1993.

quence of other secessionist movements, for example, in Tigray. Drought in
Ethiopia added to the intense armed conflict between government forces and
insurgents;[91] more than one million Ethiopians were in exile in neighbouring
countries at the end of 1989, although that number had fallen to some 190,000
by the end of 1994.[92]

Refugee numbers in the region were significantly affected by continuing hostilities between Somalia and Ethiopia throughout the 1980s. In April 1988, the two
countries reached a peace settlement over the long-disputed Ogaden region and
each government agreed to end its support of the insurgent groups operating from
its territory. Within a month of the Somali-Ethiopian border agreement, however,
Somali National Movement (SNM) guerrillas entered from Ethiopia and launched
attacks on several northern cities and small towns. The government's response
spurred a massive exodus. Artillery and aerial shelling killed as many as 50,000
civilians, and left Hargheisa a 'ghost town'; over 400,000 people fled the war to
become refugees in Ethiopia, and some 1.5 million were internally displaced.[93]
The eventual overthrow of Siad Barre was closely followed by internecine conflict, anarchy and famine, with some one million Somalis leaving the country and
a further 2 million being internally displaced. Armed intervention by the United
States and United Nations troops brought a measure of humanitarian relief, but
was not able to secure a political settlement.[94]

The conflict between the government of Mozambique and RENAMO
(Mozambican National Resistance) lasted for sixteen years, coming finally to an
end in late 1992. Nearly one and half million Mozambicans fled to neighbouring countries, and a further 2 million were internally displaced.[95] With the peace
accord and elections in 1994, the vast majority began to repatriate or to return
to their homes.

Eleven years of 'the current phase of Sudan's civil war', the continuation of a
north/south autonomy struggle exacerbated by ethnic/religious conflict and

[91] For related details and background, see Ruiz, H. A., 'Early Warning is Not Enough: The
Failure to Prevent Starvation in Ethiopia, 1990', 2 *IJRL, Special Issue*, 83 (1990).

[92] US Department of State, *Country Reports for 1988*, 111; *World Refugee Survey—1989 in Review*, 32;
World Refugee Survey—1995, 57; cf. *World Refugee Survey—1993*, 60–2.

[93] See US General Accounting Office, *Somalia: Observations Regarding the Northern Conflict and Resulting
Conditions*, (May 1989), 4–6; Amnesty International, *Somalia: The Imprisonment of Members of the Issak
Clan since Mid-1988*, (AI Index: AFR 52/41/88, Dec. 1988), 2; Gersony, R., 'Why Somalis flee,' 2
IJRL 4 (1990). Years of authoritarian rule, as well as a political system based on family and clan loy-
alties, also contributed to the internal conflict: Amnesty International, *Somalia: A Long-Term Human
Rights Crisis*, (Sept. 1988), 1-52; Lawyers Committee for Human Rights, Testimony of Michael H.
Posner to the Subcommittee on African Affairs, House Committee on Foreign Affairs (Washington,
10 Mar. 1987), 21–7; US Department of State, *Country Reports on Human Rights Practices for 1988*,
(1989), 308–18.

[94] *World Refugee Survey—1994*, 66–7; *World Refugee Survey—1995*, 74–5.

[95] An estimated 1 million were killed or died as a result of the hostilities, where the level of atrocities had few precedents. See Gersony, R., Consultant, Bureau for Refugee Programs, Department
of State, Washington, DC, *Summary of Mozambican Refugee Accounts of Principally Conflict-Related Experience
in Mozambique*, (Apr. 1988); *World Refugee Survey—1993*, 67–8; *World Refugee Survey—1994*, 61–3; *World
Refugee Survey—1995*, 68–9.

human rights violations that have attracted the condemnation of the UN Commission on Human Rights and the General Assembly, had caused an estimated 510,000 persons to seek refuge in neighbouring countries by the end of 1994, with as many as 4 million internally displaced.[96]

Civil wars in other parts of Africa also took their toll. Some 345,000 Angolans were refugees at the end of 1994, and a further 2 million internally displaced. A similar number of Burundians had also fled, and more joined them during 1995, fearing a resurgence of political and ethnic violence. Some 1.7 million refugees from neighbouring Rwanda were in exile following the genocide that racked the country in April 1994 and the ensuing civil war.[97] Over 750,000 Liberians had found refuge in Guinea, Côte d'Ivoire, Ghana, Sierra Leone[98] and other countries.

During the 1980s, Iraq pursued an aggressive campaign against the Kurdish population in the north of the country. Chemical weapons, including poison gas,[99] caused tens of thousands of Kurds to flee, many to an uncertain reception in Turkey, and others to western Europe. After the unsuccessful uprising that followed the Gulf War, some 1.5 million Kurds sought refuge along the border with Turkey and in Iran. Most returned after the United States, British and French forces established a security zone in northern Iraq in April 1991; although Iraqi Kurdistan secured a measure of autonomy, security and stability remained precarious in face of internal conflict, cross-border military operations by Turkey, and pressure from the Iraqi authorities.

The Lebanese conflict began in 1975,[100] and in its 1989 report, the United States Committee for Refugees estimated that between 500,000 and 1 million people had been displaced. The violence had a devastating effect on a once prosperous economy,[101] and the division of the country into zones controlled by militia and foreign armies disrupted trade, leading to serious economic hardship. In addition, the Lebanese government and the Lebanese Army were implicated in a variety of human rights abuses, including abductions, disappearances and incommunicado detention.[102] The army in fact controlled little territory, and offered even less protection against non-government militia, whose complex organization was determined by a variety of ethnic, religious and political factors.

---

[96] *World Refugee Survey—1995*, 76–7.

[97] *World Refugee Survey—1995*, 69–72, 80–81 (Rwandese in Zaire); USCR, 'Genocide in Rwanda: Documentation of two Massacres during April 1994', (1994).

[98] As many as 150,000 Sierra Leonians found refuge from conflict in Liberia and another 100,000 in other countries. USCR, 'The Usual People: Refugees and Internally Displaced Persons from Sierra Leone', (Feb. 1995).

[99] See Physicians for Human Rights, *Winds of Death: Iraq's use of Poisonous Gas against its Kurdish Population*, (1989).

[100] For a useful summary account, see Immigration and Refugee Board Documentation Centre, 'Lebanon: Country Profile', 1 *IJRL* 331 (1989).

[101] Odeh, B. J., *Lebanon: Dynamics of Conflict*, (1985), 105; *Encyclopedia of the Third World*, 1154;

[102] Amnesty International, *Concerns in Lebanon*, (Dec. 1985), 1–14.

Arrivals in western Europe of asylum seekers from eastern Europe rose steadily during the late 1980s, as well as those from Turkey, where political violence and human rights violations were common, and where the Kurdish minority faced particularly serious problems.[103] In 1989, some 320,000 Bulgarians of Turkish ethnic origin headed for Turkey after a period of aggressive assimilation; about 125,000 returned voluntarily, and those who remained were granted Turkish citizenship. Successive departures from Albania in 1991 led to summary return from Italy and a naval interdiction programme in the Adriatic.[104] The break-up of Yugoslavia was accompanied by savage fighting, and by genocide-like policies of 'ethnic cleansing', particularly in Bosnia and Herzegovina.[105] More than 1 million fled, mostly to neighbouring countries,[106] but also further afield throughout Europe, where their refugee and protection needs were the subject of *ad hoc* and not always generous responses.

The number of Central Americans who fled their country during the 1980s may have been as high as 500,000, or even a million, but the total and extent of dispersal were never very clear. By the end of 1994, Guatemala was still producing the most refugees in the region, but the end of the conflicts in El Salvador and Nicaragua led many to return. Other countries, including Peru and Colombia underwent massive internal displacement, as a result of civil conflict, human rights violations and the campaign against the drug trade. Political violence in Cuba and Haiti contributed to increased departures, leading also to the extension of the United States policy and practice of interdiction at sea.

4.1 A SUMMARY OF CAUSES

Reasons for flight during this period are clear even from the above very cursory overview. Civil war as political or ethnic conflict, with or without external involvement or support, is the cause of the largest outflows, such as Afghanistan, Angola, Bosnia and Herzegovina, El Salvador, Nicaragua, Ethiopia, Mozambique, Somalia and Sri Lanka. The most intractable situations are the secessionist and liberation struggles, as in Bosnia and Herzegovina, Ethiopia, or in Sudan and Sri Lanka, where autonomy and ethnicity are integral to the

[103] Migration has also long been a major feature in Turkey's economy. In 1982, there were two and a half million expatriate Turkish citizens, and the outwards migratory movement was fuelled by rural depopulation, as whole villages moved to the major cities, often to overcrowded slums. During the first eight months of 1983, Turkish workers abroad sent back some US$1.046 billion in remittances: 'Turken raus?', *Le Monde diplomatique*, déc. 1983, 13. While the majority of asylum seekers from Turkey were no doubt motivated by economic reasons, consistent human rights reporting confirmed other, refugee related factors.

[104] The first wave of some 28,000 were admitted and allowed to lodge applications for asylum; the second wave of some 17,000 were summarily removed and a naval interdiction policy implemented in the Adriatic; Nascimbene, B., 'The Case of Albanians in Italy: Is the Right of Asylum under Attack?' 3 *IJRL* 714 (1991).

[105] USCR, 'Croatia's Crucible: Providing Asylum for Refugees from Bosnia and Herzegovina', (Oct. 1992); *World Refugee Survey—1995*, 114–8.

[106] Croatia, Slovenia and Macedonia officially closed their borders to further refugee arrivals: *World Refugee Survey—1993*, 115.

conflict. The reverse of the coin is the assimilationist and centralist policies of certain States, often themselves reflecting efforts to maintain or consolidate a power-base by a dominant ethnic or political group, as for example with Tamils in Sri Lanka, Kurds in Iraq, or Issaks in Somalia.

The Group of Governmental Experts on International Co-operation to Avert New Flows of Refugees separated man-made causes and factors, sub-divided into political causes and socio-economic factors, from natural causes. Within the man-made category were wars, colonialism, the treatment of minorities (for example, under apartheid), discrimination and internal conflict, violation of human rights and fundamental freedoms, and expulsions. Relevant socio-economic factors were those that threatened the physical integrity and survival of individuals and groups, underdevelopment, particularly the legacy of colonialism, the absence of adequate economic infra-structures, and the declining world economy.[107] An alternative, non-hierarchical model of causes, incorporating primary, secondary and auxiliary factors was proposed by Rizvi in 1989. He identified *primary* factors as the racial, religious, political and social elements enumerated in the 1951 Convention, and *secondary* factors as those reflected partly in the 1969 OAU Convention and partly in the practice of States, such as military, ideological and ethnic/cultural considerations. Increasingly important economic, ecological and demographic factors, however, are often seen as *auxiliary*, and unrealistically placed outside refugee discourse.[108]

At a certain level of abstraction, some comparisons can be drawn between the causes of exodus at different periods of time. The secessionist struggles in Ethiopia and Sri Lanka recall earlier conflicts in Nigeria and Pakistan, or the liberation struggles of the post-colonial period. The political and economic flight from Vietnam parallels that from eastern Europe in the 1940s and 1950s, when somewhat equivalent processes of social restructuring were underway. The ethnic strife in Sri Lanka, Somalia and Iraq, while also containing elements of nation-formation, has been seen too often, for example, in Rwanda, Burundi, Burma and Indonesia.[109]

[107] *Report* of the Group of Governmental Experts on International Co-operation to Avert New Flows of Refugees: UN doc. A/41/324 (May 1986).

[108] See Rizvi, Z., 'Causes of the Refugee Problem and the International Response', in Nash, A., *Human Rights and the Protection of Refugees under International Law*, (1989), 107, who rightly notes the inadvisability of attempting to attribute any refugee situation to one factor alone; such superficial characterizations tend rapidly to rigidify, constraining options and imagination in solution. See also Independent Commission on International Humanitarian Issues, *Refugees: The Dynamics of Displacement*, (1986), 10–15, 130–2.

[109] A central, well-documented theme in Zolberg's analyses, is that refugee displacements result from, 'two major historical processes, the formation of new States out of colonial empires, and confrontations over the social order in both old and new States'. These processes are frequently combined, and just as frequently fuelled by external forces. By their very nature, revolution and new-State formation tend to engage the interests of other States, and not just those nearby. See Zolberg, A., 'The Refugee Crisis in the Developing World: A Close Look at Africa', in Rystad, G., *The Uprooted: Forced Migration as an International Problem in the Post-War Era*, (1990), 87, 93. See also Zolberg, A., Suhrke, A., and Aguayo, S., *Escape from Violence: Conflict and the Refugee Crisis in the Developing World*, (1989).

4.2 A SUMMARY OF RESPONSES

The policies and practices of selected west European countries[110] during the 1980s and 1990s illustrate not just a 'restrictive trend', but also an overall failure to find solutions, to deal directly with underlying causes, or even to model responses on the basis of principles of international co-operation and solidarity. Visa requirements, restrictive admissibility criteria, safe third country removals, carrier sanctions and the introduction or resumption of removals during the years 1985–90 appear to have had a short-term impact on arrivals, as the following illustrative and somewhat impressionistic account suggests.[111]

For example, France introduced a general visa requirement[112] for all foreign nationals in September 1986; only European Community and Swiss citizens were exempt. Arrivals of asylum seekers for 1987 were held to more or less the 1986 level (24,800 as against 23,400). In the same period, Italy's 'share' increased from 6,500 to 11,050; and Austria's from 8,650 to 11,400. In December 1985, Denmark reached agreement with the German Democratic Republic, under which the latter undertook to restrict the transit of Sri Lankans. Denmark also lifted its ban on removals to Lebanon in August 1986, and amended its asylum law three times between 1985–6 to permit the summary removal of arrivals from western Europe, Canada or the United States, and to authorize expedited border procedures, particularly with respect to the undocumented. Arrivals fell from 9,300 in 1986 to 2,750 in 1987, with the number of Middle East applicants dropping from 5,106 to 1,313, and applicants from Asia, from 2,824 to 548.[113] The effect was relatively short-term, however, and applications rose again in 1988 and 1989, even with the introduction of carrier sanctions in January 1989.[114]

Similarly, in the Netherlands, despite the introduction of a transit visa requirement in July 1985 (applicable to certain classes of Afghans, Iranians, Iraqis, Turks and Sri Lankans), an initial small decrease in 1986 (from an estimated 2,000 asylum seekers from Asia in 1985, to 1,448 in 1986; and from an

---

[110] Austria, France, Federal Republic of Germany, the Netherlands, Sweden, Switzerland, Turkey and the UK. See also US Committee for Refugees Issue papers, 'Refugees at our Borders: The US Response to Asylum Seekers', Sept. 1989; 'Uncertain Harbors: The Plight of Vietnamese Boat People', Oct. 1987; 'Despite a Generous Spirit: Denying Asylum in the United States', Dec. 1986; 'The Asylum Challenge to Western Nations', Dec. 1984.

[111] The figures used below were provided by governments and UNHCR at a time when statistical standards were still at a relatively primitive stage and common methods of counting were almost entirely absent. Cf. UNHCR, *The State of the World's Refugees*, (1993), Annex 1, 'Refugee Statistics', at 145–60.

[112] The visa requirement was in fact driven by security, rather than refugee related considerations.

[113] The corresponding numbers of applications in the three previous years were: 800 (1983); 4,300 (1984); 8,700 (1985).

[114] Applications from Asia remained relatively steady (700 in 1988; 515 in 1989), but increased from the Middle East (2,669 in 1988; 2,816 in 1989). Visas for Romanians and an expedited procedure for Poles appear to have reduced numbers in 1989: USCR, *World Refugee Survey—1989 in Review*, 61f.

estimated 1,000 Middle Eastern applicants in 1985, to 968 in 1986), numbers from these two regions rose again in 1987.[115] Compulsory special accommodation introduced in April 1985 for Sri Lankan Tamils seems to have led immediately to the diversion of some 2,000 claimants to the United Kingdom.

The United Kingdom itself introduced a visa requirement for Sri Lankans in May 1985; the flow stopped or, as one commentator has observed, 'rather, it was deflected for another friendly State to cope with'.[116] Visas were also brought in for Ghana, Nigeria, Pakistan, India and Bangladesh in September 1986, but overall arrivals increased from 4,000 in 1986 (1,773 from Asia; 1,270 from Africa), to 5,150 in 1987 (1,438 from Asia; 1,764 from Africa). Carrier sanctions came into force in May 1987, retroactive to March, and a considerable number of fines were imposed.[117] After holding steady for two years (5,150 in 1987; 5,100 in 1988), however, arrivals leapt to some 13,500 in 1989. Early the same year, the number of Kurdish asylum seekers from Turkey increased substantially, numbering some 1,500 in May alone.

The Federal Republic of Germany concluded an agreement with the German Democratic Republic on Sri Lankans in August 1985, and imposed a transit visa requirement for nationals of Lebanon, Syria, Ghana, Pakistan and Bangladesh a year later. Substantial revisions to its asylum laws and procedures were made in January 1987,[118] including provision for border refusals, restrictions on the grounds for asylum; the exclusion of those considered to have found 'security elsewhere'; carrier sanctions; and restrictions on the grant of work authorizations. A general ban on removals to Lebanon was also lifted in September 1986. Arrivals fell in 1987 to 57,400 (as against 99,650 in 1986), but returned to previous levels the following year (to 103,100 in 1988, and to 121,300 in 1989). Asylum seekers from Asia dropped from 29,866 in 1985 to 20,571 in 1986, 6,962 in 1987, rising to 9,514 in 1988; they then rose to 18,881 in 1989. Middle Eastern applicants rose from 14,432 in 1985 to 36,004 in 1986, fell to 9,926 in 1987, before beginning to rise again to 15,197 in 1988 and 16,154 in 1989. On 9 November 1989, the Berlin Wall was breached, contributing to the immigration of some 720,000 ethnic Germans.[119] Two-thirds of the 121,300 asylum applications lodged in 1989, however, came from non-German Europeans, with

---

[115] In 1988, the number of applicants from Asia fell substantially (1,415), beginning to rise again in 1989 (1,918).

[116] McDowall, R., 'Co-ordination of Refugee Policy in Europe', in Loescher, G. and Monahan, L., *Refugees and International Relations*, (1989), 179, 182.

[117] See Ruff, A., 'The United Kingdom Immigration (Carriers' Liability) Act 1987: Implications for Refugees and Airlines', 1 *IJRL* 481, 498 (1989).

[118] *Gesetz zur Änderung asylverfahrensrechtlicher, arbeitserlaubnisrechtlicher und ausländerrechtlicher Vorschriften vom 6 Januar 1987*: 1987 *BGBl.* I, 89.

[119] Under art. 116 of the *Grundgesetz* (Basic Law of the Federal Republic of Germany), those born in the territory of the Germany Democratic Republic were considered German nationals, while other ethnic Germans (*deutscher Volkszugehöriger*) may claim German nationality once established in the Federal Republic. Neither category therefore fell or falls within the international law concept of refugee, even though the motives for flight, particularly before the fall of communism, might sometimes be similar.

Poland, Yugoslavia and Turkey predominant. A visa requirement for the nationals of a further sixteen countries, including Yugoslavia, was brought in on 1 May 1989. Arrivals of Yugoslav asylum seekers during January and February 1990 were down by comparison with the same period in 1989 (4,876 as against 5,798); but went up in Switzerland (802 as against 320).[120]

Sweden, long considered one of the most liberal receiving countries, also revised its laws and practices during 1989. A visa was introduced for Chileans, and arrivals in January and February totalled 43, by comparison with 494 in the same period in 1988.[121] Arrivals in the first half of 1989 (January–June) were relatively moderate, but in the last half of the year they exceeded 21,000, including some 5,000 Bulgarians of ethnic Turkish origin.[122] When the policy of drawing negative inferences as to credibility in undocumented cases had little effect on numbers, in December 1989 it was decided to limit eligibility for asylum to Convention refugees or others who had a specially strong need for protection.[123]

4.3 A SUMMARY ANALYSIS OF EFFECTS

Taking 1985 as the year in which restrictive measures began to be introduced with some frequency, arrivals in the eight selected receiving countries show considerable fluctuations. Applicants from Africa increased steadily, showing only a slight decrease in 1987; applicants from the Americas increased from 1985 to 1987, when they fell;[124] asylum seekers from Asia, whose numbers had risen dramatically between 1984 and 1985 (from 22,386 to 48,041), fell almost as dramatically until they surged again in 1988–9, from 20,905 to 40,792. The greatest fluctuation was in the numbers of applicants from Middle Eastern countries; they rose between 1985–6 from 29,059 to 53,070, fell between 1986–7 by an almost equal amount to 28,408, before rising substantially to 83,628 in 1988 and falling again in 1989, to 33,417.[125]

Ironically, the one region of origin in this period that showed no signs of falling, at least in terms of western European arrivals, was Europe, with or without Turkey. For example, of the 11,760 asylum applications lodged in Switzerland in 1989, 9,395 were by Turkish applicants. East European asylum

---

[120] Yugoslavia itself also began to deny passports to gypsies and ethnic Albanians, both groups having generally higher than average potential for successful refugee claims.

[121] Sweden was long a favoured destination for Chileans, and the visa decision undoubtedly contributed to the downturn in arrivals from the Americas, (from 3,384 in 1988 to 140 in 1989); they rose slightly in the Netherlands (from 397 to 526), and considerably more in France (from 2,236 to 3,352).

[122] Apart from Turkey itself, Sweden was the only other west European country to receive significant numbers of ethnic Turkish Bulgarians, who arrived mostly by car and train.

[123] See Nobel, P., 'What Happened with Sweden's Refugee Policies?' 2 *IJRL* 265 (1990).

[124] 3,260 (1985); 4,432 (1986); 7,245 (1987); 6,602 (1988); 4,521 (1989).

[125] As arrivals from Asia and the Middle East fell or held steady in certain European countries between 1985–89, they increased in Canada, rising from 8,400 in 1985 to 18,000 in 1986, 25,950 in 1987 and 40,000 in 1988, with growing numbers of Sri Lankans, Iranians and Lebanese. The increase in 1988 was undoubtedly influenced by anticipation of the new refugee law, which came into force on 1 January 1989.

seekers constituted an increasing proportion of arrivals during the 1980s, and if the 27,000 ethnic Hungarians from Romania are taken into account, Europeans constituted some 58 per cent of arrivals in 1989.[126] Between 1985 and 1989, and leaving aside arrivals in Hungary and Turkey, asylum applications by eastern European nationals in the eight selected countries grew from 21,378 to 87,950 in 1989. Although the causes varied, the background was often a period of liberalization, failing or faltering economies, and the emergence of ethnic strife; movements were also facilitated by geographical contiguity. In May 1989, the border between Austria and Hungary was 'liberalized', followed in December by that with Czechoslovakia. Many East Germans chose that way to the west, before the fall of the Berlin Wall. The easing of travel restrictions in Poland and Hungary led to a four-fold increase of asylum applications in Austria, which introduced a summary procedure for nationals of those countries, later extended to Romanians and Yugoslavs.[127] Although the refugee claims often appeared to have little or no foundation, the general response was far more accommodating than with respect to extra-regional nationalities.[128]

The somewhat crude data summarized above, drawn from States, UNHCR and NGO sources, allow a number of inferences with respect to ebb and flow. First, restrictive measures, particularly visa and transit visa requirements do curb asylum seeker movements in the short-term, and tend to be most effective when applied to countries which do not produce refugees, either at all or in large numbers.[129] Other measures, such as detention, designated accommodation, employment restrictions, summary process, removals, carrier sanctions, and restrictive interpretations of asylum criteria, may also have a dampening effect, but appear to be of more limited duration.

Secondly, restrictive measures almost always have a 'sideways' effect: no exact correlation is possible, and overall numbers are not necessarily comparable, but while the flow of asylum seekers from the Asia region into Denmark and the Federal Republic of Germany fell by 80 per cent and 60 per cent respectively between 1986–7, that into Greece, the Netherlands and Norway increased by 450 per cent, 144 per cent and 629 per cent, respectively. Similarly, while the flow from the Middle East into Denmark and the Federal Republic of Germany

---

[126] Hungary ratified the 1951 Convention on 14 March 1989. Already in 1988, some 10,000 Romanians had arrived, the majority ethnic Hungarians in flight from cultural and linguistic discrimination. During the following months, the profile of the asylum seekers changed, with the proportion of ethnic Romanians increasing from 9% to 21%, and including some 9% ethnic Germans. See *World Refugee Survey—1988 in Review*, 57; *World Refugee Survey—1989 in Review*, 64f; Refugee Policy Group, *East to East: Refugees from Rumania in Hungary*, (1989).

[127] *World Refugee Survey—1989 in Review*, (1990), 60.

[128] This also constituted a pull factor, a gateway of opportunity, in a historical process that rapidly converted a refugee flow into a migratory movement. Cf. Goodwin-Gill, G. S., 'Different Types of Forced Migration as an International and National Problem', in Rystad, G., *The Uprooted: Forced Migration as an International Problem in the Post-War Era*, (1990), 15, 34–6.

[129] After Canada introduced visa requirements for Portugal (1986) and Turkey (1987), asylum applications fell to nearly zero: Malarek, V., *Haven's Gate*, (1987), Ch. 9, 'The Portuguese Scam'.

fell by 74 per cent and 72 per cent, it rose by 93 per cent in Greece, 18.6 per cent in the Netherlands, 116 per cent in Norway and 62 per cent in Turkey.[130] The impact of restrictions on regional neighbours may also be amplified by incidents such as the introduction of new, or more liberal, procedures;[131] or by the administrative collapse of national systems.[132] Regional co-operation clearly has a role to play, but if the directly causative factors are not dealt with the pressure to move and actual movements will persist.[133] This is confirmed also by the patterns of violence[134] in selected areas at certain times, during which asylum seekers from these regions have managed to arrive or secure admission, notwithstanding the variety of obstructions opposed to them.

The experience of the late 1980s, and the inability of States to deal with causes sufficiently to reduce the pressure on national asylum procedures, doubtless accounts for the 'unique' measures adopted when a further massive outflow from Iraq seemed likely after the Gulf War. Policies of containment, temporary protection at discretion, and the promotion of regional solutions have joined with procedural devices in a continuing attempt to maintain distance between the problem and its solution. By contrast with the level of co-operation in Central America and even in South East Asia, Europe has long seemed unable to agree on a co-ordinated regional response.

5. *Non-refoulement* and asylum in cases of mass influx

Large-scale population movements are the source of many of the most intractable refugee-related problems. In some cases, ethnic similarities encourage reception and hospitality, but where the flow is cross-cultural, serious political issues arise, in addition to the usual logistical and economic ones. Even assistance to refugees can be problematic, as where the local, often displaced, population perceives refugees receiving benefits hitherto denied to them.

---

[130] By 1988 and 1989, arrivals in Denmark and Germany had again risen significantly.

[131] Denmark undoubtedly drew asylum seekers from other possible European destinations when it introduced a law and process more liberal than its neighbours in 1983.

[132] This seems to have happened in Sweden in 1989.

[133] See generally Jaeger, G., *Study on Irregular Movements of Asylum Seekers and Refugees*, Working Group on Irregular Movements of Asylum Seekers and Refugees, (Geneva, 1985). Jaeger queried in 1985 whether large-scale influxes into industrialized countries could or should be characterized as 'irregular', having found that there was little evidence of 'genuine abuse'. In his view, movements were more often 'the consequences of deficient legal, economic and social conditions in countries adjacent to the countries of origin of refugees'. See UNHCR Executive Committee Conclusion No. 58 (1989); also UNHCR, *Note* on the Consultation on the Arrivals of Asylum-seekers and Refugees in Europe: UN doc. A/AC.96/INF. 174; Swart, A., 'The problems connected with the admission of asylum-seekers to the territory of member States', in *The Law of Asylum and Refugees: Present Tendencies and Future Perspectives*, Proceedings of the 16th Colloquy on European Law, Lund, 15 –17 Sept. 1986, (Council of Europe, Strasbourg, 1987), 65.

[134] Considered as including civil and international conflict, human rights violations, and repression, whether or not exacerbated by natural disasters that are often perpetuated or not averted for political reasons.

The 1951 Convention was drawn up very much with the individual asylum seeker in mind, and yet it contains no provision on admission. Article 31 gives some protection to refugees entering illegally, but at the same time acknowledges that no refugee can expect, as a matter of right, to regularize his or her stay in the State of first refuge.[135] The refugee unable to secure entry to another State, denied local settlement and yet benefiting from *non-refoulement* thus falls into limbo. This indeed was the condition of many refugees in European camps in the 1950s and of others in South East Asia and Africa in the 1970s, the 1980s, and the 1990s. The principle of *non-refoulement* has developed to include non-rejection at the frontier, thus promoting admission, but there has been no corresponding development with regard to the concept of asylum, understood in the sense of a duty upon States to accord a lasting solution. *Non-refoulement* is to that extent divorced from the notion of asylum, this being the price demanded by States in otherwise accepting the obligation to allow the entry to their territories of large numbers of refugees and asylum seekers.

Traditional notions of asylum still help us to understand the past and may equally be part of some future promotion of the rights of the individual in the municipal laws of States, but it is doubtful whether they are consistent or appropriate enough for application to the political and humanitarian problems of today. This was especially apparent in the discussion in the Executive Committee of the notion of 'temporary refuge' in 1980 and 1981. Temporary refuge, it was claimed, would erode present practices on asylum and undermine the principle of *non-refoulement*; it was a 'new concept', and States had no need of it. Ten years later, and slightly reworked as 'temporary protection', the broad outlines of such a concept are well-established in the armoury of State responses.

5.1 TEMPORARY REFUGE: THE BACKGROUND

The practice of temporary refuge, of admission and protection, that is, asylum, on a temporary basis, has a long history, even if the attempt at conceptualization was relatively novel in the early 1980s. Finding durable solutions to refugee problems has long been seen as the responsibility of the international community. The Preamble to the 1951 Convention notes expressly 'that the grant of asylum may place unduly heavy burdens on certain countries', and that satisfactory solutions to problems international in scope depend upon international co-operation. These sentiments were repeated in Recommendation D of the Final Act, calling upon governments to continue to receive refugees and to act in concert that such refugees 'may find asylum and the possibility of resettlement'. In this context, 'asylum' is used broadly, to mean the protection given by the State of first refuge, which may be continued or which may be taken over by another State in the spirit of international co-operation. Such an approach well describes the situation in Europe in the 1950s. The thousands who fled

---

[135] See further below, Ch. 8, s. 1.2.2.

Hungary in 1956, for example, were granted what turned out to be relatively temporary 'asylum' in Austria and Yugoslavia, prior to onward movement (some 170,000 being resettled within eighteen months). Then as now, generous admission policies were dependent on, if not conditioned by, generous resettlement policies maintained by other countries. For many years, Australia, Canada, and the United States, among others, ran extensive resettlement programmes for east European asylum seekers admitted to west European countries, and western Europe itself joined the international response to the needs of Latin American and Indo-Chinese refugees in the 1970s and 1980s.

The idea of 'temporary' or 'provisional' asylum or admission, or residence pending movement to another country has also figured in a number of international instruments, as an alternative to *refoulement*.[136] Some provisions encompass the individual who is considered a security or equally serious threat to the State of refuge; others cover groups of persons who, by reason of their numbers, are thereby considered a danger to the community of the State. There is nevertheless not only a quantitative, but also a qualitative difference between the two types of case. In that of the individual, the fact of being a refugee in the sense of the 1951 Convention/1967 Protocol may properly give rise to a presumption or expectation that asylum in the sense of a local, lasting solution will be forthcoming.[137] As a matter of principle, that presumption should only be rebutted by evidence clearly indicating the personal unacceptability of the refugee. In the case of the mass influx, however, formal determination of status may be impracticable in view of the numbers or the absence of appropriate machinery; or impossible in strict terms owing to the mixed motives of those fleeing, for example, from a combination of civil disorder, hostilities, and famine. In addition, any expectation or presumption of a local solution may be redundant in face of evidence of cross-cultural, ethnic, or religious conflict, or for other demographic, resource and costs-related reasons.[138]

The search for solutions must often distinguish between refugees in the strict sense, who have a well-founded fear of persecution, and refugees in the broader sense. Causes cannot be ignored; they condition the protection which is required in the short and medium term and bear on the solutions which are possible. The

---

[136] Art. 3(3), 1967 Declaration on Territorial Asylum; art. II(5), 1969 OAU Convention; para. 3, Council of Europe Res. 14(1967); art. 3(3), adopted by the Committee of the Whole of the 1977 United Nations Conference on Territorial Asylum.

[137] That expectation may be held not only by the individual, but also by other States parties to the international system of refugee protection, which commonly attribute primary responsibility for the asylum solution to the State in which the refugee is first received.

[138] At the Executive Committee in 1982, the Sub-Committee of the Whole on International Protection emphasized, with good reason, the importance of distinguishing on the occasion of a mass influx between the decision that a group should receive protection and assistance, or be admitted temporarily, and later individual determinations of status. To determine a *group* to be refugees obscures too many difficulties and may additionally generate unwarranted expectations: *Report* of the Sub-Committee: UN doc. A/AC.96/613, para. 33.

immediate need is for admission to a State of refuge, without which there can be no solutions, but ultimately asylum is relative to circumstance.[139]

At its 1979 Session, the Executive Committee stressed the humanitarian obligation of coastal States 'to allow vessels in distress to seek haven in their waters and to grant asylum, or at least temporary refuge' to those on board seeking it. Similarly, it noted that in 'cases of large-scale influx, persons seeking asylum should always receive at least temporary refuge', and that States 'faced with a large-scale influx, should as necessary and at the request of the State concerned receive immediate assistance from other States in accordance with the principle of equitable burden-sharing'.[140]

The notion of temporary refuge prompted differing responses, with some States apprehensive lest it upset established principles.[141] In 1980, on an Australian initiative, the Executive Committee requested the High Commissioner to convene a group of experts 'to examine temporary refuge in all its aspects within the framework of the problems raised by large-scale influx'.[142] The Group of Experts met in Geneva in April 1981, and discussions focused on a working paper that referred to many refugee situations clearly illustrating that receiving States were often not in a position to offer permanent settlement at the time of admission. The debate and conclusions were inconclusive and remarkable chiefly for the imprecise and inconsistent use of terminology, as well as for the adherence of many participants to a methodology appropriate to the individual asylum seeker, but not necessarily to the situation of mass influx. 'Asylum' itself, though often invoked, was never defined in the report that emerged; it was recognized that there might be asylum on a permanent basis and asylum on a temporary basis, but the consequences of that distinction were not pursued. It was said that asylum was not necessarily linked to the grant of a durable solution; that the grant of asylum was the prerogative of States, but that where life was in danger, States 'should give at least temporary asylum'.[143]

The conclusions of the Group of Experts on international solidarity, burden-sharing and minimum standards of treatment were endorsed by the Executive

---

[139] The difficulties in obtaining even temporary asylum in South-east Asia were noted several times by the Executive Committee; see *Report* of the 28th Session (1977): UN doc. A/AC.96/549, para. 53.3(b); *Report* of the 29th Session (1978): UN doc. A/AC.96/559, para. 68.1(d).

[140] *Report* of the 30th Session (1979): UN doc. A/AC.96/572, para. 72(2)(c),(f). The Executive Committee urgently appealed to governments 'to grant at least temporary *asylum* to those seeking refuge pending alternative solutions being found for them': ibid., para. 43C(c) (emphasis supplied).

[141] See UN doc. A/AC.96/SR.309, paras. 22–3, 26, 33, 43–4, 59, 60. The Australian representative had earlier expressed the view that solidarity and assistance would enable States of first asylum or refuge to meet fundamental humanitarian obligations: ibid., paras. 18–19; also UN doc. A/AC.96/SR.322, paras. 24, 34, 41, 46, and 48.

[142] UN doc. A/AC.96/588, para. 48(4) (e).

[143] One expert even claimed, though without adducing evidence in support, that it was 'generally recognized that the country of asylum [*sic*] should be obliged to regularise the situation of an asylum seeker if, after a certain period, a durable solution was not forthcoming': UN doc. EC/SCP/16, para. 21. While this sentiment may be appropriate in individual cases, it is hardly a candidate for the status of general principle.

Committee at its 32nd Session in October 1981, and further confirmed in UN General Assembly resolution 36/125 (14 December 1981). On the whole, however, the Executive Committee preferred the language of *admission* to that of asylum as used by the Group of Experts:

1. In situations of large-scale influx, asylum seekers should be *admitted* to the State in which they first seek refuge and if that State is unable to *admit* them on a durable basis, it should always *admit* them at least on a temporary basis and provide them with protection according to the principles set out below. They should be *admitted* without any discrimination as to race, religion, political opinion, nationality, country of origin or physical incapacity.
2. In all cases the fundamental principle of *non-refoulement*—including non-rejection at the frontier—must be scrupulously observed.[144]

The references to 'asylum seekers' in this context must be interpreted as presupposing refugee status (in the broad sense), or at least a presumptively sound claim to international protection as the necessary condition of entitlement, if the relevant principles and concepts are not to lose all meaning. Admission on a temporary basis, especially in situations of large-scale influx, remains an inescapable fact of life, practised or tolerated by States throughout the world. Conceptualization nonetheless offers significant practical advantages as a tool for securing the entry of large groups, in improving their protection, and in working towards durable solutions.[145]

5.2 FROM TEMPORARY REFUGE TO TEMPORARY PROTECTION

Experience shows that solutions will vary in complexity, duration, and attainability. In the case of Indo-China, cultural and political factors ruled out repatriation and local integration; *non-refoulement* through time allowed eventual resettlement. For Afghan refugees, resettlement was considered inappropriate and repatriation hoped for, but remote; *non-refoulement* through time facilitated international aid and assistance and the establishment of a degree of interim self-sufficiency. For Salvadoran refugees in Honduras, both local integration and resettlement were also ruled out; refuge in closed camps, though in far from ideal conditions, provided a measure of protection pending return. In no case could the condition of temporary refuge be considered a satisfactory durable solution in itself; that was an objective which remained to be pursued.

The practice of 'temporary protection', at least in Europe, is explicitly premised on (eventual) return, by contrast with the South East Asia model of temporary refuge, which was initially premised on third country resettlement, and only later joined by voluntary or involuntary repatriation in the aftermath of the CPA. The European version of temporary protection also distinguishes itself by being linked to admission to State territory, rather than to camps, while

---

[144] Executive Committee Conclusion No. 22 (1981), para. II, A (emphasis supplied).
[145] For an alternative view, see Kennedy, D., 'International Refugee Protection', 8 *HRQ* 1, 65–9 (1986).

temporary refuge was contingent on guarantees by others that the State providing refuge would not pay the costs, and would not bear any residual burden.[146] The language of 'temporary protection' emerged in the discourse of reaction to the crisis in former Yugoslavia,[147] where, as part of the 'comprehensive response', it was considered a 'flexible and pragmatic means of affording needed protection to large numbers of people fleeing human rights abuses and armed conflict . . . , who might otherwise have overwhelmed asylum procedures.'.[148] Some States considered that such a response should be linked to burden-sharing at the regional level,[149] while others emphasized the necessity for certain minimum conditions of enjoyment.[150] In general, the beneficiaries of temporary protection have included at least those who would come within the Cartagena and OAU refugee definitions, although many would also be Convention refugees in the strict sense.[151] While force of circumstance certainly dictated a response in line with the principle of *non-refoulement* or an equivalent principle of refuge, European regional practice provides little evidence of a coherent reception policy. During 1994–5, for example, States displayed continuing reluctance to move ahead formally on a set of practical, non-binding guidelines,[152] and seemed even less enthusiastic about committing themselves to basic standards of treatment after admission.

However labelled, the concept of temporary refuge/temporary protection as the practical consequence of *non-refoulement* through time provides, first, the necessary theoretical nexus between the admission of refugees and the attainment of a lasting solution. It establishes, *a priori*, no hierarchy in the field of solutions, but allows a pragmatic, flexible, yet principled approach to the idiosyncrasies of each situation. So, for example, it does not rule out the eventual local integration or third country resettlement of all or a proportion of a mass influx in the

[146] In effect, temporary refuge for Indochinese refugees was bought and paid for by (mostly) western countries, on terms which kept the majority of asylum seekers away from their frontiers while leaving them able to pick and choose among candidates for permanent settlement.

[147] See generally Marx, R., 'Temporary Protection—Refugees from Former Yugoslavia: International Protection or Solution Orientated Approach?', ECRE, June 1994; Kjaerum, M., 'Temporary Protection in Europe in the 1990s', 6 *IJRL* 444 (1994); Luca, D., 'Questioning Temporary Protection, together with a Selected Bibliography on Temporary Refuge/Temporary Protection', 6 *IJRL* 535 (1994); Thorburn, J., 'Transcending Boundaries: Temporary Protection and Burden-Sharing in Europe', 7 *IJRL* 459 (1995).

[148] UNHCR, 'Note on International Protection': UN doc. A/AC.96/815 (1993), para. 25; 'Note on International Protection': UN doc. A/AC.96/830 (1994), paras. 45–51.

[149] UN doc. A/AC.96/SR.474 (1992), para. 20 (Switzerland).

[150] UN doc. A/AC.96/SR.483 (1993), para. 73 (Holy See, arguing for decent living conditions, a family life, a job and the possibility of educating children). See also 'Temporary Protection: Summary and Recommendations from the Report of the Inter-Ministerial Working Group, Norway, April 1993', 5 *IJRL* 477 (1993).

[151] UNHCR, for example, considered that most Bosnians taking refuge outside former Yugoslavia fell within the 1951 Convention: UNHCR Information Note, 'Temporary Protection', 20 Apr. 1995, para. 11.

[152] See *Report* of the Sub-Committee: UN doc. A/AC.96/858 (11 Oct. 1995), paras. 11–12, 16–17; Executive Committee General Conclusion on International Protection (1995), *Report* of the 46th Session: UN doc. A/AC.96/860, para. 19(f).

State of first refuge, acting in concert with others and pursuant to principles of international solidarity and equitable burden-sharing.[153] Secondly, the concept provides a platform upon which to build principles of protection for refugees pending a durable solution, whereby minimum rights and standards of treatment may be secured.

This is not to say, however, that the principles have been satisfactorily applied in all cases; to the contrary. When international solidarity falters, then the practical consequence may be forcible repatriation, as happened with Rwandese refugees in Zaire in August 1995. Similarly, the challenge failed to find a coherent, regional response in Europe to the protection needs of many in flight from former Yugoslavia. Burden-sharing was rejected and standards of treatment of those in fact admitted often fell short of human rights requirements.

Without underestimating the necessity to ensure that regimes for the reception and treatment of refugees and asylum seekers conform with the requirements of international law, words such as 'refuge' and 'protection' may offer some advantages over any comparable use of the word 'asylum' in situations of mass influx. Asylum is undefined; it can be used broadly to signify protection of refugees, or it can be used in the narrow sense of a durable or permanent solution, involving residence and lasting protection against the exercise of jurisdiction by the State of origin. A receiving State called upon to grant 'asylum' to large numbers may well demur; admission is more likely to be facilitated by reference to the norm of *non-refoulement* and to its manifestation as refuge or protection in the dynamic sense, through time, pending arrangements for whatever solution is appropriate to the particular problem. The peremptory character of *non-refoulement* makes it independent of principles of solidarity and burden-sharing, but these cannot be ignored in a society of inter-dependent States.[154] In situations of large-scale influx, protection cannot cease with the fact of admission; on the contrary, it must move towards solutions in full knowledge of the political and practical consequences which result from a State abiding by *non-refoulement*.

The political and legal reality is that States generally have not undertaken, and foreseeably will not undertake, an obligation to grant asylum in the sense

---

[153] These principles may find expression not just in offers of resettlement, but also in financial and material assistance, moral and political support.

[154] Note, however, that in the debate on international solidarity in 1988, the Sub-Committee left for further discussion in plenary the following proposed operative paragraph, in which the Executive Committee would have underlined, 'that, while international solidarity is important for the satisfactory resolution of refugee problems, *the absence of solidarity cannot serve as the pretext for failing to respect basic humanitarian principles*': *Report* of the Sub-Committee of the Whole on International Protection: UN doc. A/AC.96/717 (3 Oct. 1988), para. 35, (emphasis added). As finally adopted, para. 4 of Executive Committee Conclusion No. 52 (1988) merely, recalled that 'the respect for fundamental humanitarian principles is an obligation for all members of the international community, it being understood that the principle of international solidarity is of utmost importance to the satisfactory implementation of these principles'.

of a lasting solution.[155] The peremptory norm of *non-refoulement* secures admission and, in the individual case, may raise the presumption or at least a reasonable expectation that a local durable solution will be forthcoming. In the case of large-scale movements, however, no such presumption is raised. In attaining its present universal and peremptory character, *non-refoulement* has separated itself from asylum in the sense of a lasting solution. *Non-refoulement* through time is nonetheless the core element both promoting admission and protection, and simultaneously emphasizing the responsibility of nations at large to find the solutions. Thus, in admitting large numbers of persons in need of protection and in scrupulously observing *non-refoulement*, the State of first admission can be seen as acting on behalf of the international community.

The concept of temporary refuge/temporary protection, in the context of large movements, thus stands paradoxically as both the link and the line between the peremptory, normative aspects of *non-refoulement* and the continuing discretionary aspect of a State's right in the matter of asylum as a permanent or lasting solution, and in the treatment to be accorded to those in fact admitted.

6. Conclusions

The plight of the refugee in search of asylum has been a dominant theme on the international agenda since the late 1970s, as is evident from repeated appeals of the Executive Committee, the General Assembly, intergovernmental organizations and other concerned bodies.[156] At one level, State practice nevertheless permits only one conclusion: the individual still has no right to be granted asylum. The right appertains to States and the correlative duty, if any, is that which obliges other States to respect the grant of asylum, as any other exercise of territorial jurisdiction. The right itself is in the form of a discretionary power—the State has discretion whether to exercise its right, as to whom it will favour, as to the form and content of the asylum to be granted.[157] Save in so far as treaty or other rules confine its discretion, for example, by requiring the extradition of war criminals, the State remains free to grant asylum to refugees as defined by international law or to any other person or group it deems fit. It is likewise free to prescribe the conditions under which asylum is to be enjoyed.[158] It may thus

---

[155] Hailbronner attributes refusal to accept a treaty-based asylum obligation to fear of 'restriction of political decision-making through the concept of an individual right': Hailbronner, K., 'The Right to Asylum and the Future of Asylum Procedures in the European Community', 2 *IJRL* 341, 347 (1990).

[156] See, for example, the annual reports of the UNHCR Executive Committee, the yearly resolutions of the UN General Assembly on UNHCR and related issues, and reviews by non-governmental organizations, such as the *World Refugee Survey* published each year by the US Committee for Refugees.

[157] For a view of asylum as contingent on the existence of States having 'different socio-economic systems and pursuing different objectives and contradictory interests', see Wierzbicki, B., 'Political Asylum in International Law', *Revue héllenique de droit international*, 1985–6, 11, 15 (1988); for other aspects of discretion in the grant of asylum, see Fitzpatrick, J. and Pauw, R., 'Foreign Policy, Asylum and Discretion', 28 *Willamette L.R.* 751 (1992); Anker, D.E., 'Discretionary Asylum: A Protection Remedy for Refugees under the Refugee Act of 1980', 28 *Virg. JIL* 1 (1987);

accord the refugee the right to permanent or temporary residence, it may permit or decline the right to work, or confine refugees to camps, dependent on international assistance pending some future solution, such as repatriation or resettlement. Refugees may also be subject to measures falling short of *refoulement*, which nevertheless prevent them from effectively making a claim to status or asylum, or in securing admission to a particular country.

Since 1951, many States in fact have adopted the refugee definition as the criterion for the grant of asylum, and as the sole criterion for the grant of the specific, limited, but fundamental protection of *non-refoulement*. Likewise, in the practice of many States party to the 1951 Convention/1967 Protocol, the recognized refugee, the person with a well-founded fear of persecution, is not only effectively entitled to asylum in the sense of residence, but is also protected against return to the country in which he or she runs the risk of persecution or other relevant harm.

There is nevertheless a certain discontinuity in the protection regime established by the 1951 Convention/1967 Protocol and general international law, and between the status of refugee and a solution to the problem of the refugee. Refugees benefit from *non-refoulement* and refugee status is often, but not necessarily, the sufficient condition for the grant of permanent or durable asylum. But there is no *necessary* connection between *non-refoulement* and admission or asylum. In international law as well as in national practice, the discretion to grant asylum and the obligation to abide by *non-refoulement* remain divided, even as they are linked by the common definitional standards of well-founded fear or risk of torture or other relevant harm.

To pursue an ideal of asylum in the sense of an obligation imposed on States to accord lasting solutions, with or without a correlative right of the individual, is currently a vain task. Asylum remains an institution which operates between subjects of international law. Moreover, in an era of mass exodus, of actual or perceived threats to national security, States are not prepared to accept an obligation without determinable content or dimension. Experience shows that efforts to secure agreement on such a divisive issue are more likely to produce equivocation, qualification, and exception, that can tend only to dilute the rules and principles already established in State practice.[159] But asylum as lasting

---

[158] For a detailed account of what the grant of asylum entails in Switzerland, see Kälin, W., 'The Legal Condition of Refugees in Switzerland', 24 *Swiss Reports presented at the XIVth International Congress of Comparative Law*, 57–73 (1994).

[159] This is not to say the individual's right to asylum may not have some future; merely that progress is more likely to be achieved through the development of regional instruments and the promotion of effective municipal laws, particularly to ensure the integrity of the principle of *non-refoulement*. Note, however, the 1991 decision of the *Conseil constitutionnel* of France on the right of asylum and the Schengen Convention. Referring to the Preamble of the 1946 Constitution ('Tout homme persécuté en raison de son action en faveur de la liberté a droit d'asile sur les territoires de la République'), the court decided that the Schengen Convention might be ratified without infringing this right, because it expressly reserved to States the entitlement to consider an asylum claim *even though it was properly the responsibility of another State party*. Julien-Laferrière, F., *Doc. réf.* No. 163, Supp.,

solution, though a preferred sense, represents one aspect only. State practice is not solely concerned with permanent protection, and the concept of asylum at large cannot be analysed adequately apart from the concept of refuge and the normative principle of *non-refoulement*. States *are* obliged to protect refugees, and consequently they are obliged to abide by *non-refoulement* through time. That time is not and cannot be determined by any principle of international law, but likewise the duty to accord *non-refoulement* through time cannot be separated in practice from that other complex duty which recognizes the responsibility of the community of States in finding durable solutions.[160]

So far as a State's actions may expose an individual to the risk of violation of his or her human rights, its responsibility is duty-driven, rather then strictly correlative to any individual right. The duty not to return refugees to persecution or to a situation of danger to life or limb is owed to the international community of States which, for many purposes, is represented by UNHCR. The international community is likewise entitled to require of individual States, not only that they accord to refugees the benefit of *non-refoulement* through time, but also the opportunity of finding a lasting solution to their plight. The degree of protection required is that commensurate with the occasion, and given the present level of development of international law, certain exceptions in favour of the State remain. The area continues to be governed by discretion, rather than duty, but analysis reveals that discretion to be not only confined by principle, but also structured in the light of other legally relevant considerations, including international solidarity, burden-sharing, and the right of functional protection enjoyed by UNHCR.

Freedom to grant or to refuse permanent asylum remains, but save in exceptional circumstances; States do not enjoy the right to return refugees to persecution or relevant situation of danger. Protection against the immediate eventuality is the responsibility of the country of first refuge. So far as a State is required to grant that protection, the minimum content of which is *non-refoulement* through time, it is required also to treat the refugee in accordance with such standards as will permit an appropriate solution, whether voluntary repatriation, local integration, or resettlement in another country. There was some support in the past for the overall primary responsibility in fact falling on the first country of refuge,[161] but experience in South East Asia, Central America, Western Asia, Africa and Europe, where so many States declined to allow refugees to regularize their status or otherwise to remain within their borders, has served to emphasize the international dimension to burden-sharing.

25 oct./8 nov. 1991, 3; Oliver, P., 'The French Constitution and the Treaty of Maastricht', 43 *ICLQ* 1 (1994).

[160] See further below, Ch. 7, s. 4.

[161] Cf. UNGA resolutions 832(LX), 21 Oct. 1954, and 1166(XII), 26 Nov. 1957.

PART THREE

PROTECTION

Chapter 6

INTERNATIONAL PROTECTION

The lack or denial of protection is a principal feature of refugee character, and it is for international law, in turn, to substitute its own protection for that which the country of origin cannot or will not provide. *Non-refoulement* is the foundation-stone of international protection, and in this and the following two chapters the content of that protection is examined in more detail, with attention specifically to international institutions, treaties, the incorporation of international standards in municipal law, and emergent problems in the field of law and practice that illustrate the role of State responsibility.

1. International institutions

The first intergovernmental arrangements on behalf of refugees were contemporaneous with the establishment of various institutions charged with their implementation.[1] In 1921, Gustave Ador, President of the International Committee of the Red Cross, addressed the Council of the League of Nations on behalf of an estimated 800,000 Russians scattered throughout Europe, without protection or status.[2] So it was that in June 1921 the Council decided to appoint a High Commissioner for Russian Refugees, naming Dr Fridtjof Nansen to the post some two months later.[3] The tasks of the High Commissioner included defining the legal status of refugees; organizing their repatriation or 'allocation' to potential resettlement countries and, together with private organizations, providing relief.[4] In this period, the League also acted for many other

---

[1] On the inter-war years generally, see Simpson, J. H., *The Refugee Problem*, (1939); Reale, E., 'Le problème des passeports', 50 Hague *Recueil*, (1934–IV), 89; *A Study of Statelessness*, (1949): UN doc. E/1112 and Add. 1, 34–8; Sjöberg, T., *The Powers and the Persecuted: The Refugee Problem and the Intergovernmental Committee on Refugees*, (1991), Ch. 1.

[2] (1921) 2(2) *LNOJ* 227. They included some 50,000 former prisoners of war unwilling to return, civilians who had fled the Bolshevik revolution, as well as members of the various defeated armies which had opposed the revolutionaries during the first years. The *de facto* unprotected status of many was further compounded by two decrees of Oct. and Dec. 1921, under which Soviet citizenship was forfeited by certain groups residing abroad; see generally Fisher Williams, J., 'Denationalization', 8 *BYIL* 45 (1927).

[3] See generally Reynolds, E. E., *Nansen* (1932, rev. ed. 1949).

[4] Annexe 224, Minutes of the 13th Session of the Council of the League of Nations, Geneva, 17–28 June 1921; cited by Weis, P., 'The International Protection of Refugees', 48 *AJIL* 193, 207–8 (1954). During the 1920s, large-scale relief operations were undertaken by private organizations for the multitudes displaced by the First World War and its aftermath: Marrus, M., *The Unwanted—European Refugees in the Twentieth Century*, (1985), 82–6. In the same period, considerable international attention and assistance focused also on spontaneous, coerced and agreed population exchanges in

groups; they included Armenians, whose exodus from Turkey to various neighbouring countries had begun in 1915, and began again in 1921;[5] Assyrians and Assyro-Chaldeans; and a group of one hundred and fifty persons of Turkish origin who, under the terms of the Protocol of Lausanne of 24 July 1923, were expressly barred from returning to their country of origin.[6] Also beginning in the 1920s came the flight from fascism, first from Italy, then from Spain, and finally from Germany and its conquered or incorporated territories in the 1930s.

A 1928 arrangement[7] recommended that the services normally rendered to nationals abroad by consular authorities should be discharged on behalf of refugees by representatives of the High Commissioner. Unless within the exclusive competence of national authorities, such services were to include: certifying the identity and position of refugees; certifying their family position and civil status, so far as that was based on documents issued or action taken in the refugees' country of origin; testifying to the regularity, validity, and conformity with the previous law of their country of origin of documents issued in that country; certifying the signature of refugees and copies and translations of documents drawn up in their own language; testifying before the authorities of the country to the good character and conduct of individual refugees, their previous record, professional qualifications, and university or academic standing; and recommending individual refugees to the competent authorities with a view to obtaining visas, residence permits, admission to schools, libraries, and so forth.[8] In order to give legal effect to these recommendations two States, France and Belgium, concluded an agreement authorizing the High Commissioner's representatives to issue the documents in question.[9]

In the period 1923–9, certain 'technical services' principally relating to assistance, were entrusted to the International Labour Organization, leaving the High Commissioner responsible for the political and legal protection of refugees. With Nansen's death in 1930, the Assembly of the League of Nations established the Nansen Office to undertake humanitarian activities on behalf of refugees,

the Balkans; on the exchanges between Greece and Turkey and Greece and Bulgaria: Marrus, *The Unwanted*, 96–109.

[5] Marrus, *The Unwanted*, 74–81, 119–21. Arrangement relating to the Issue of Identity Certificates to Russian and Armenian Refugees of 12 May 1926: 84 *LNTS* No. 2006.

[6] Arrangement concerning the Extension to other Categories of Refugees of certain Measures taken in favour of Russian and Armenian Refugees of 30 June 1928: 89 *LNTS* No. 2006.

[7] Arrangement relating to the legal status of Russian and Armenian refugees, 30 June 1928: 89 *LNTS* No. 2005. It came into force between 10 States.

[8] Ibid., res. (1). Other resolutions made recommendations, among others, in respect of choice of law in matters of marriage and divorce; that refugees not be denied certain rights and privileges on the basis of lack of reciprocity; that they be exempt from the *cautio judicatum solvi* (security for costs in legal proceedings); that they be accorded national treatment in matters of taxation.

[9] Agreement concerning the functions of the representatives of the League of Nations High Commissioner for Refugees: 93 *LNTS* No. 2126. In France, this function was taken over by the IRO (agreement cited by Weis, P., 'Legal Aspects of the Convention of 28 July 1951 relating to the Status of Refugees', 30 *BYIL* 478, 484 (1953), and subsequently by the *Office français de protection des réfugiés et apatrides (OFPRA): loi no. 52–893 du 25 juill. 1952, art. 4 décret no. 53–377 du 2 mai 1953, art. 5.

and entrusted protection to the Secretary-General. A succession of other bodies followed: first, the High Commissioner's Office for Refugees Coming from Germany was established in 1933;[10] then, in 1938, came the High Commissioner's office for all refugees, charged with providing political and legal protection, superintending the entry into force of the relevant conventions, co-ordinating humanitarian assistance, and assisting governments and private organizations in their efforts to promote emigration and permanent settlement.[11] The same year, following the thirty-two nation Evian Conference convened on the initiative of the United States to deal with 'the question of involuntary emigration', the Intergovernmental Committee on Refugees (IGCR) was created.[12] At this time of a continuing outflow from Germany and Austria, the answer was thought to lie in co-ordinating involuntary emigration with existing immigration laws and practices, in collaboration with the country of origin.

From October 1939, the IGCR was essentially non-functional, although it was substantially reorganized following an Anglo–American meeting in Bermuda in April 1943.[13] In November of that year, the Allies also set up the United Nations Relief and Rehabilitation Administration (UNRRA); as the name and time imply, its role was to provide relief to the millions displaced by the Second World War and, in particular, to assist those wishing to repatriate.[14] UNRRA was conceived as a temporary institution, and its only concern with refugees arose from its relief responsibilities. Notwithstanding some remarkable success in

---

[10] This office was initially set up outside the League, owing to German government opposition. Two years later, the High Commissioner, James G. McDonald, resigned, observing in a letter of 27 Dec. 1935 to the Secretary-General of the League, that private and international organizations could only mitigate an increasingly grave and complex situation. Given the condition of the world economy, resettlement opportunities were few and the problem had to be tackled at source. An annexe to his letter called attention to human rights in Germany, to that country's international obligations towards minorities, and the violation of the rights and territorial sovereignty of other States that was involved by forced migration, denationalization, and withdrawal of protection: see Marrus, *The Unwanted*, 161–6; Jennings, R. Y., 'Some International Law Aspects of the Refugee Question', 20 *BYIL* 98 (1939).

[11] League of Nations, *OJ* Special Supp., no. 189, (1938) 86; see also Provisional Arrangement concerning the Status of Refugees coming from Germany of 4 July 1936: 171 *LNTS* No. 3952.

[12] The functions of the Committee were defined in a resolution adopted on 14 July 1938; text in *A Study of Statelessness*, (above, n. 1), 116–18. For a full account, see Sjöberg, T., *The Powers and the Persecuted: The Refugee Problem and the Intergovernmental Committee on Refugees (IGCR), 1938–1947*, (1991). And for later developments, Salomon, K., *Refugees in the Cold War: Toward a New International Refugee Regime in the Early Postwar Era*, (1991).

[13] Sjöberg, *The Powers and the Persecuted*, Ch. 4. Issues discussed included a British proposal to provide temporary asylum to refugees 'as near as possible to the areas in which the people find themselves at the present time and from which they may be returned to their homelands with the greatest expediency on the termination of hostilities': ibid., 135.

[14] See generally Woodbridge, G., *UNRRA: The History of the United Nations Relief and Rehabilitation Administration*, 3 vols., (1950); Salomon, K., *Refugees in the Cold War*, (1991), 46–54, 57–61 and generally; Salomon, K., 'UNRRA and the IRO as Predecessors of UNHCR', in Rystad, G., ed., *The Uprooted: Forced Migration as an International Problem in the Post-War Era*, (1990), 157; Hathaway, J., 'The Evolution of Refugee Status in International Law: 1920–1950', 33 *ICLQ* 348 (1984).

overseeing the return movements of the displaced,[15] by June 1947 nearly 650,000 still remained without solutions, most of them east Europeans and many of them refugees from the events of the post-war. In 1946, however, the United Nations recognized the fundamental principle that no refugees with valid objections to returning to their countries of origin should be compelled to do so.[16] Following the recommendation of ECOSOC, it also created the International Refugee Organization (IRO)[17] and defined those within its mandate.[18] While there was general agreement on the necessity to assist the victims of nazi, fascist and similar regimes, many countries remained adamantly opposed to providing international protection to so-called political dissidents. These same countries argued that the number of 'non-repatriables' would be considerably reduced if hostile propaganda ceased in the camps, and if the activities of war criminals and the like were curbed. This opposition extended to a refusal to contribute to the financing of large scale resettlement operations.[19]

The IRO operated until 28 February 1952,[20] its functions defined in its Constitution to include: repatriation; identification; registration and classification; care and assistance; legal and political protection; and transport, resettlement, and re-establishment of persons of concern to the Organization.[21] Throughout its life, the IRO and particularly its resettlement work, were sharply attacked in the United Nations, both directly and indirectly.[22] Direct attacks concentrated on the IRO's 'complicity' in resettlement activities designed to meet labour demands and to provide shelter for expatriate organizations hatching plots and threatening world peace.[23] The responses were generally muted,

[15] By the beginning of 1946, an estimated three-quarters of the displaced in Europe had been sent home: Marrus, *The Unwanted*, 320.

[16] UNGA res. 8(I), 12 Feb. 1946.

[17] The IRO Constitution was adopted by thirty votes to five, with eighteen abstentions: UNGA res. 62(I), 15 Dec. 1946. A Preparatory Commission (PCIRO) was set up to ensure continuity between UNRRA and the IGCR (both of which were wound up on 30 June 1947) and the IRO, pending sufficient ratifications to bring the latter's Constitution into force. This became effective 20 Aug. 1948.

[18] See generally GAOR, 1st Sess., 2nd Part, Supplement No. 2, *Report* of ECOSOC to the General Assembly, 53–62; UN doc. A/265, *Report* of the Third Committee, Summary Records, 1420–54; UN doc. A/275, Budget of the IRO. The budget was based on an estimated total of 844,525 European refugees and displaced persons at 1 January 1947. For background (and highly political) debate in the Third Committee, see GAOR, Third Committee, 1st Sess., 1st Part, Summary Records: UN doc. A/C.3/SR.4, SR.5, SR.6, SR.7 and SR.8.

[19] Under art. 10, IRO Constitution, as amended by the Fifth Committee, contributions to large-scale resettlement operations were to be made on a voluntary basis: UN doc. A/275, para. 7 and Annex I.

[20] See generally Holborn, L., *The International Refugee Organization*, (1956).

[21] Art. 2, Constitution of the IRO.

[22] See GAOR, 2nd Sess., (1947), Plenary, Summary Records, 1025-31; Annex 12, pp. 257–66. Also, GAOR, 4th Sess., (1949), Third Committee, Summary Records, 72–89; Plenary, Summary Records, 212–25.

[23] See, for example, GAOR, 3rd Sess., 2nd Part, Third Committee, Summary Records, 434 (Poland); 446 (Yugoslavia); 451 (Ukrainian SSR); also, GAOR, 3rd Sess., 2nd Part, Plenary, Summary Records, 504–18.

relying more on statements of principle—the freedom to return or not to return—and only rarely charging east European countries with direct responsibility for the exodus.[24] IRO operations continued in a period of heightening east-west tension. It remained funded by only eighteen of the fifty-four governments then members of the United Nations, and it is hardly surprising, either that its policies should be caught up in the politics of the day, or that there may not have been some truth behind the 'immigration bureau' charge.

Many tens of thousands of refugees and displaced persons were resettled under IRO auspices.[25] The self-interest of States was at work, and refugee resettlement policies also served broader political interests.[26] And yet at the same time, there was a vast humanitarian problem then facing individual States and the international community. Refugee situations can and do lead to instability; if left unresolved, they may breed refugee discontent, leading to political tensions at the local, regional or universal level. Solutions had to be found; given the relations then prevailing between east and west, given the west's popular endorsement of human rights and freedom of choice, and given population pressures in much of Europe, third country resettlement was the single most attractive option available to those States committed to resolving the problem.

The IRO existed to deal with the aftermath of the Second World War and the immediate consequences of political change. Even during its lifetime, however, the General Assembly acknowledged the need for a successor organization, and in the days of the IRO's demise, the major questions debated were *definitional*—just who should benefit from international action; and *functional*—what should be done for refugees, who should do it, and who should pay. Eastern European countries continued to voice their suspicions, but there was also a significant change in the policy of the United States, the major donor. The IRO had been expensive, and increasingly the US authorities came to rely on their own refugee schemes (such as the escapee programme), on bilateral and regional arrangements, and on the Intergovernmental Committee for European Migration, set up in 1951 outside the United Nations system.[27] While these developments were yet to come, the General Assembly decided in 1949 to establish a High Commissioner's Office for Refugees.[28]

---

[24] See GAOR, 4th Sess., Third Committee, Summary Records, 82-3 for an exception, the UK representative referring to instances of forced migration and deportation in the USSR.

[25] Holborn, L., *Refugees: A Problem of our Time,* (1975), 31.

[26] See Loescher, G. and Scanlan, J., *Calculated Kindness,* (1986), 15–24.

[27] See further below, s. 1.4.1.

[28] UNGA res. 319(IV), 3 Dec. 1949. For completeness sake, mention should also be made of the United Nations Relief and Works Agency for Palestine Refugees in the Near East (UNRWA), established by UNGA res. 302(IV), 8 Dec. 1949, and on which see further below s. 1.2; and the United Nations Korean Reconstruction Agency established by UNGA res. 401A and B(V), 1 Dec. 1950, which was principally concerned with relief and economic reconstruction, and concluded its activities in 1958.

1.1 THE OFFICE OF THE UNITED NATIONS HIGH COMMISSIONER FOR REFUGEES (UNHCR)

At its 1950 session, the General Assembly formally adopted the Statute of UNHCR as an annexe to resolution 428(V),[29] in which it also called upon governments to co-operate with the Office. The functions of UNHCR encompass 'providing international protection' and 'seeking permanent solutions' to the problems of refugees by way of voluntary repatriation or assimilation in new national communities.[30] The Statute expressly provides that 'the work of the High Commissioner shall be of an entirely non-political character; it shall be humanitarian and social and shall relate, as a rule, to groups and categories of refugees'.[31] Of the two functions, the provision of international protection is of primary importance, for without protection, such as intervention to secure admission and *non-refoulement* of refugees, there can be no possibility of finding lasting solutions.[32]

Besides defining refugees, the UNHCR Statute prescribes the relationship of the High Commissioner with the General Assembly and the Economic and Social Council (ECOSOC), makes provision for organization and finance, and identifies ways in which the High Commissioner is to provide for protection.[33] These develop the functions engaged in by predecessor organizations and include: (1) promoting the conclusion of international conventions for the protection of refugees, supervising their application and proposing amendments thereto; (2) promoting through special agreements with governments the execution of any measures calculated to improve the situation of refugees and to reduce the number requiring protection; and (3) promoting the admission of refugees.[34]

Notwithstanding the statutory injunction that the work of the Office shall relate, as a rule, to groups and categories of refugees, a major part of UNHCR's

---

[29] For full text of resolution and Statute, see Annexe 1, No. 3. Adopted by thirty-six votes to five, with eleven abstentions. The UK abstained, principally because of concerns over the refugee definition in the Statute, including the fact that, in a remarkably prescient observation, the High Commissioner was likely to have difficulty in practice in determining the persons whom he was competent to protect: GAOR, 5th Sess., Plenary, Summary records, 669-80, paras. 66-8, 14 Dec. 1950.

[30] Statute, para. 1.

[31] Ibid., para. 2. The 'non-political' qualification was introduced on the proposal of Yugoslavia. Para. 3, however, obliges the High Commissioner to follow policy directives of the General Assembly and the Economic and Social Council.

[32] The protection of refugees has its origins in a human rights context, and the General Assembly has reaffirmed international protection as a principal function of UNHCR since at least 1974: UNGA res. 3272(XXIX), 10 Dec. 1974.

[33] Statute, para. 8.

[34] Besides the declared functions, UNHCR's indirect or promotional activities encompass the application of national laws and regulations benefiting refugees, the development and adoption of appropriate national laws, regulations, and procedures, promotion of accession to international instruments, and the development of new legal instruments. Latterly, the Executive Committee has also approved the dissemination and promotion of refugee law, training and information; see, for example, *Report* of the 31st Session (1980): UN doc. A/AC.96/588, para. 48(1)(k).

protection work has long been concerned with individual cases, as was that of its predecessor organizations. No State has objected to UNHCR taking up individual cases as such,[35] although States may, and do, question whether an individual is indeed a refugee.[36] Nevertheless, the individual dimension to the protection function is a natural corollary to the declared task of supervising the application of international conventions. Such instruments define refugees in essentially individualistic terms and provide rights on behalf of refugees which can only be understood in the sense of the particular. The acquiescence of States in the individual protection function of UNHCR, however, significantly delineates both the competence of the Office and the status of the individual refugee in international law.

Today, most States clearly want the United Nations to assume responsibilities for a broad category of persons obliged to flee their countries for a variety of reasons.[37] The General Assembly has endorsed UNHCR activities for humanitarian reasons, but also essentially because the lack of protection creates a vacuum.[38] This in turn may be due to the legal consequences of statelessness;[39] or it may be a matter of fact, where an individual is unable or unwilling to avail

---

[35] Sadruddin Aga Khan, 'Legal problems relating to refugees and displaced persons', Hague *Recueil* (1976–I) 331–2; Schynder, F., 'Les aspects juridiques actuels du problème des réfugiés', Hague *Recueil* (1965–I) 319, 416.

[36] See above, Ch. 1, s. 3.2.

[37] In 1980, for example, the UNHCR Executive Committee 'emphasized . . . the leading responsibility of (UNHCR) in emergency situations which involve refugees in the sense of its Statute or of General Assembly resolution 1388(XIV) and its subsequent resolutions': *Report* of the 31st Session (1980): UN doc. A/AC.96/588, paras. 29.A(c), 29.B(c)(e)(f)). Those 'subsequent resolutions' in turn tracked the UNHCR's good offices work in securing contributions for assistance to refugees not within the competence of the UN, its development to include protection and assistance activities, and eventual recognition of a general responsibility to seek solutions to the problems of refugees and displaced persons of concern to UNHCR, wherever they occur; see UNGA resolutions 1499(XV), 5 Dec. 1960; 1673(XVI), 18 Dec. 1961; 1959(XVIII), 12 Dec. 1963; 2294(XXII), 11 Dec. 1967; 3143(XXVIII), 14 Dec. 1973; 34/60, 29 Nov. 1979. For indications of a further qualitative change in UNHCR's protection function, see the High Commissioner's speech to the UN Third Committee in Nov. 1992, where she described UNHCR's 'direct engagement in situations of acute crisis or open conflict', 'extending protection and assistance to internally displaced and other victims of conflict in an effort to limit, to the extent possible, the impetus to flight', and 'creating time and space for the political process'; text in 4 *IJRL* 541 (1992). On 'preventive protection', see further below Ch. 7.

[38] During debate on the Statute, one representative suggested that the lack of protection should be the sole criterion for determining UNHCR's competence: GAOR, 5th Session, Third Committee, Summary Records, 324th Meeting, 22 Nov. 1950, para. 40f (UK); see also ibid., 325th Meeting, 24 Nov. 1950, para. 36 (Chile—protection should be extended to anyone who, for reasons beyond their control, could no longer live in the country of their birth); 329th Meeting, 29 Nov. 1950, paras. 3, 8f (Turkey—those needing protection included fugitives from war or persecution, or for political reasons). While in 1950 the debate was premised on the assumption that those needing protection would have left their country of origin, UNHCR has been increasingly called on to provide protection and humanitarian assistance to persons displaced within their own countries. See below, Ch. 7, s. 2.

[39] In resolutions 3274(XXIX), 10 Dec. 1974, and 31/36, 30 Nov. 1976, the General Assembly entrusted UNHCR with responsibilities under arts. 11 and 20 of the 1961 Convention on the Reduction of Statelessness (examination of claims and assistance in their presentation to the appropriate authorities). See also Executive Committee Conclusion No. 78 (1995), below, Annexe 3.

him or herself of the protection of the government of their country, either because of a well-founded fear of persecution, or because of some man-made disaster, such as violence resulting from a variety of sources.[40]

The underlying rationale for international protection is thus that humanitarian necessity which derives from valid reasons involving elements of coercion and compulsion. The refugee in flight from persecution and the refugee in flight from the violence of a 'man-made disaster' are alike the responsibility of the United Nations, even as the present system of duty and co-operation falls short of demanding durable solutions from sovereign States. General Assembly resolutions can extend the functional responsibilities of UNHCR, its subsidiary organ, but they do not thereby directly impose obligations on States.

1.1.1 Relation of UNHCR to the General Assembly and its standing in general international law

UNHCR was established by the General Assembly as a subsidiary organ under article 22 of the UN Charter,[41] and the parent body has continued its role in expanding or approving extensions of the mandate of the Office.[42] The relationship of the two organizations is laid down in the Statute, which declares that UNHCR acts, not at the direction of the UN Secretary-General, but 'under the authority of the General Assembly',[43] that it shall 'follow policy directives given by [that body] or the Economic and Social Council',[44] and that it 'shall engage in such additional activities, including repatriation and resettlement, as the General Assembly may determine'.[45]

---

[40] Man-made disasters have never been precisely defined, but General Assembly resolutions have indicated typical instances; see, for example, on refugees from Algeria: UNGA resolutions 1286(XIII), 5 Dec. 1958; 1389(XIV), 20 Nov. 1959; 1500(XV), 5 Dec. 1960 and 1672(XVI), 18 Dec. 1961. See also UNGA resolutions 1671(XVI), 18 Dec. 1961 (Angolan refugees in the Congo); 2790(XXVI), 6 Dec. 1971 (East Pakistan refugees in India); 3271(XXIX), 10 Dec. 1974 (voluntary repatriation of refugees from territories emerging from colonial rule).

[41] 'The General Assembly may establish such subsidiary organs as it deems necessary for the performance of its functions'. UNHCR was originally set up for three years; its mandate is now subject to renewal every five years and was recently renewed in 1992 for a further five years from 1 Jan. 1994: UNGA res. 47/104, 16 Dec. 1992.

[42] From the beginning, the General Assembly acknowledged that refugees were an international responsibility, and that it would be necessary and desirable to modify and extend the competence of UNHCR to new groups of refugees and to new fields of activity: see UNGA res. 319(IV), 3 Dec. 1949, Annex, para. 3.

[43] Statute, para. 3. The High Commissioner is elected by the General Assembly, on the nomination of the Secretary-General: ibid. para. 13. This (compromise) solution was adopted precisely in order to shelter the High Commissioner from the highly political work of the UN Secretariat, and to ensure that UNHCR enjoyed the necessary independence, authority and impartiality to carry out its humanitarian work. On background and one Secretary-General's attempt to pre-empt established consultative procedures, see 'Sadako Ogata elected as UN High Commissioner for Refugees', 3 *IJRL* 120 (1991).

[44] Statute, para. 4.

[45] Ibid., para. 9. Since 1972, at least, such additional activities have also included assistance and *de facto* protection to repatriating refugees and internally displaced persons, or assistance to local populations affected by a refugee influx. To these specific or implied mandate responsibilities must now also be added the special humanitarian tasks entrusted to UNHCR, for example, in former

The High Commissioner is further required to report annually to the General Assembly, through the Economic and Social Council, and the report is to be considered as a separate agenda item.[46] Finally, the Statute calls upon the High Commissioner, particularly where difficulties arise, to request the opinion of the advisory committee on refugees, if it is created.[47] Such a committee was first established in 1951,[48] and was replaced four years later by the UN Refugee Fund Executive Committee,[49] whose functions included supervision of material assistance programmes financed by the fund. The General Assembly called for its replacement in turn by the Executive Committee of the High Commissioner's Programme, which was set up by the Economic and Social Council in 1958.[50] Originally comprising twenty-four States, it has been progressively enlarged to its present (1997) membership of fifty-three.[51] The Committee's original terms of reference include advising the High Commissioner, on request, in the exercise of the Office's statutory functions; and advising on the appropriateness of providing international assistance through the Office in order to solve any specific refugee problems. In 1975, the Executive Committee set up a Sub-Committee of the Whole on International Protection,[52] which has regularly reviewed situations of concern, and whose conclusions, when adopted in Plenary, constitute some of the 'soft law' background to refugee protection.[53] At its 1995 session, the Executive Committee decided to reorganize its meetings schedule around one annual plenary session and a number of inter-sessional meetings of a new Standing Committee of the Whole, to replace the Sub-Committees and to have general competence over protection, programme and financial issues.[54] Notwithstanding the apparently limited role anticipated by the Executive Committee's initial terms of reference, it has come to exercise considerably more influence on the day-to-day management of UNHCR, as well as in the development of policy.[55]

Yugoslavia, including assistance and, within difficult limits, protection of populations at risk in their own land. See further below, Ch. 7, s. 2.

[46] Ibid., para. 11. As a corollary, the same paragraph entitles the High Commissioner to present his or her views before the General Assembly and ECOSOC and their subsidiary bodies. Sine 1969, the practice has been to transmit the report without debate to the General Assembly, unless one or more ECOSOC members or the High Commissioner so request: Decision on Item 9, ECOSOC, *OR*, Resumed 47th Session: UN doc. E/4735/Add.1.

[47] Statute, para. 1. By para. 4 ECOSOC was empowered to establish such a committee.

[48] ECOSOC res. 393B(XIII), 10 Sept. 1951.

[49] ECOSOC res. 565(XIX), 31 Mar. 1955, further to UNGA res. 832(IX), 21 Oct. 1954.

[50] UNGA res. 1166(XII), 26 Nov. 1957, and ECOSOC res. 672(XXV), 30 Apr. 1958.

[51] For membership, see below, Annexe 6.

[52] *Report* of the 26th Session (1975): UN doc. A/AC.96/521, para. 69(h).

[53] For text of selected conclusions, see below Annexe 3; also Sztucki, J., 'The Conclusions on the International Protection of Refugees adopted by the Executive Committee of the UNHCR Programme', 1 *IJRL* 285 (1989).

[54] The penultimate annual meeting of the Standing Committee will deal with international protection; see *Report* of the 46th Session: UN doc. A/AC.96/860 (23 Oct. 1995), para. 32. The proposed meetings cycle will be reviewed after one year, in Oct. 1996.

[55] Cf. Morris, N., 'Refugees: Facing Crisis in the 1990s—A Personal View from within UNHCR', 2 *IJRL, Special Issue—September 1990*, 38.

Each of the above elements involves the participation of States, at varying levels, in the principal international institutions concerned with the protection of refugees. The practice of such organizations is therefore relevant in assessing both the standing of UNHCR and the legal status of the rules benefiting refugees in general international law. UNHCR is not only a forum in which the views of States may be represented; it is also, as a subject of international law, an actor in the relevant field whose actions count in the process of law formation. Specific authority to involve itself in the protection of refugees has been accorded to the Office by States parties to the 1951 Convention and/or the 1967 Protocol relating to the Status of Refugees. Article 35 of the Convention, for example, provides: 'The contracting States undertake to co-operate with the Office of the United Nations High Commissioner for Refugees . . . in the exercise of its functions, and shall in particular facilitate its duty of supervising the application of the provisions of this Convention'.[56] The 1969 OAU Convention requires member States to co-operate similarly, while declaring itself to be the 'effective regional complement in Africa' of the 1951 Convention.[57] UNHCR, however, is not itself a party to those instruments, and its standing must be located in more general principles and in relevant practice, including its formal participation in the drafting and implementation of comprehensive approaches to refugee problems, such as CIREFCA and the CPA.[58]

Clearly, by derivation and intention, UNHCR does enjoy international personality. As a subsidiary organ of the General Assembly, its 'personality' (its capacity to possess international rights and duties) can be traced to the United Nations at large.[59] Moreover, its Statute shows that the Office was intended by the General Assembly to act on the international plane.[60] Its standing in regard to protection has been further reinforced by successive General Assembly resolutions urging all States to support the High Commissioner's activities, for example, by granting asylum, observing the principle of *non-refoulement* and acceding to the relevant international treaties. While it is trite knowledge that General Assembly resolutions are not legally binding, 'it is another thing', as Judge Lauterpacht noted in the *Voting Procedure* case, 'to give currency to the view that they have no force at all, whether legal or other, and that therefore they cannot be regarded as forming in any sense part of a legal system of supervision'.[61] On

---

[56] Art. II of the 1967 Protocol is to similar effect.
[57] Art. VIII; Cartagena Declaration on Refugees, Conclusion and Recommendations, II.
[58] See Annexe 5.
[59] See generally, *Reparations* case, ICJ *Rep.*, 1949, 174 at 178–9.
[60] For example, the Statute refers to the High Commissioner supervising the application of international conventions, promoting certain measures through special agreements with governments, and consulting governments on the need to appoint local representatives: paras. 8(a), (b), 16.
[61] See generally, *South West Africa, Voting Procedure*, advisory opinion, ICJ *Rep.*, 1955, 67, at 120–2—separate opinion of Judge Lauterpacht, noting that General Assembly resolutions are 'one of the principal instrumentalities of the formation of the collective will and judgment of the community of nations represented by the United Nations'. Cf. Brownlie, I., *Principles of Public International Law*, (4th ed., 1990), 14, 699.

this occasion, the 'legal system of supervision' was the mandate in respect of South West Africa. In his separate opinion, Judge Lauterpacht noted that, while the mandatory had the right not to accept a recommendation of the supervising body, it was nevertheless bound to give it due consideration in good faith, which in turn entailed giving reasons for non-acceptance.

Admittedly, General Assembly resolutions with regard to refugees and to UNHCR do not have the same degree of particularity as a recommendation relating to the administration of a mandate. Nevertheless, against the background of the UN Charter and general international law, UNHCR, with its principal function of providing 'international protection' to refugees, can be seen to occupy the central role in an analogous legal system of supervision. Indeed, though discretions continue to favour States in certain of their dealings with refugees, the peremptory character of the principle of *non-refoulement* puts it in a higher class than the 'intangible and almost nominal' obligation to consider in good faith a recommendation of a supervisory body, such as Judge Lauterpacht discerned in the *Voting Procedure* case.[62] The entitlement of UNHCR to exercise protection on the basis of a universal jurisdiction receives additional support from the decision of the International Court of Justice in the *Reparations* case. There, the Court read into the rights and duties of the United Nations Organization, as a 'necessary intendment', the capacity to exercise a measure of functional protection on behalf of its agents.[63] UNHCR, by comparison, is *expressly* ascribed the function of providing international protection to refugees; State practice reflects 'recognition or acquiescence in the assumption of such jurisdiction'[64] universally, and without regard to any requirement of treaty ratification. The 'effective discharge'[65] of this function evidently requires capacity to assert claims on behalf of individuals and groups falling within the competence of the Office.

Given States' obligations with regard to refugees, to whom are they owed? The individual is still not considered to be a subject of international law, capable of enforcing his or her rights on the international plane,[66] while the problems faced by refugees (such as interdiction on the high seas, or violations of

---

[62] *Voting Procedure* case, ICJ *Rep.*, 1955, 67, at 119. See also Judge Lauterpacht's remarks generally in regard to good faith in the exercise of discretion: ibid., 120.

[63] *Reparations* case, ICJ *Rep.*, 1949, 174, at 184.

[64] Cf. Schwarzenberger and Brown, *A Manual of International Law*, (6th ed., 1976), 115, commenting on the movement of an implied consensual right or exercise of functional protection from its basis in consent to its acquisition of 'an increasingly absolute validity'.

[65] *Reparations* case, ICJ *Rep.*, 1949, 174, at 180.

[66] In Schwarzenberger and Brown, *Manual*, at 64, the traditional view was stated thus: 'Whether [the individual] is entitled to benefit from customary or consensual rules of international law depends on his own link—primarily through nationality—with a subject of international law which, on the international level, is alone competent to assert his rights against another subject of international law'. Later, the authors noted that, '[b]y means of conventions, attempts have been made to alleviate the position of refugees and stateless persons. Otherwise, they are objects of international law for whom no subject of international law is internationally responsible—a notable twentieth-century contribution to the category of *res nullius*.': 114–5. This was questionable, even in 1976.

human rights), are not such as would prompt exercise of the right of diplomatic
protection on the part of the State of nationality. In the case of States parties to
the 1951 Convention and the 1967 Protocol, the existence of obligations *inter se*
is established. Both instruments expressly provide for the settlement of disputes
relating to their interpretation or application, and for reference to the
International Court of Justice at the request of any of the parties to the dispute,
should other means of settlement fail.[67] No litigation has resulted, and, in the
absence of injury to an individual related to a claimant State by the link of
nationality, the results of any such litigation are likely to be without practical
consequence.[68] There are precedents, however, by which States may yet have
legal interests in matters other than those which affect directly their material
interests.[69]

Under article 24 of the European Convention on Human Rights, for example, any contracting State may refer to the European Commission an alleged
breach of the Convention by another party. The instrument itself thus provides
for a 'European public order', a regime in which all States parties have a sufficient interest in the observance of the European Convention's provisions to
allow for the assertion of claims. While there are similarities in the objectives of
the European Convention and the refugee conventions—both call for certain
standards of treatment to be accorded to certain groups of persons—the refugee
conventions lack effective investigation, adjudication, and enforcement procedures; they can hardly be considered to offer the same opportunity for judicial
or quasi-judicial solutions. Nonetheless, in view of the importance of the rights
involved, all States have an interest in their protection;[70] and UNHCR, by
express agreement of some States and by the acquiescence of others, is the qualified representative of the 'international public order' in such matters. A cogent
theory of responsibility remains to be developed to cover this situation, however,
and the legal consequences that may flow from a breach of the international
obligations in question are still unclear.

International claims can take the form of protest, a call for an inquiry, negotiation, or a request for submission to arbitration or to the International Court
of Justice. Both the nature of breaches of obligation affecting refugees and the

---

[67] 1951 Convention, art. 38; 1967 Protocol, art IV. Under the Protocol, but not under the
Convention, States are entitled to make reservations to the article on settlement of disputes, and
many have; see below, Ch. 8, s. 1.

[68] See *Northern Cameroons case, Preliminary Objections*, ICJ *Rep.*, 1963, 15, at 34–5.

[69] See *South West Africa* cases, preliminary objections, ICJ *Rep.*, 1962, 319, at 424–33 (separate
opinion of Judge Jessup). But cf. *South West Africa* cases, second phase, ICJ *Rep.*, 1966, 6 at 32–3, 47
(holding that individual States do not have a legal right to require the performance of South Africa's
mandate over South West Africa).

[70] *Barcelona Traction* case, ICJ *Rep.*, 1970, 3 at 32; also 1967 Declaration on Territorial Asylum,
art. 2(1). An inter-State procedure also exists under other regional arrangements, such as the 1969
American Convention on Human Rights (arts. 45, 62), the 1981 African Charter on Human and
Peoples' Rights (art. 47), and the 1966 Covenant on Civil and Political Rights, art. 41; the last-mentioned has not so far been used.

nature of the protecting organization rule out certain types of claims, such as arbitration,[71] while strictly legal considerations might exclude, for example, recourse to the International Court of Justice.[72] The possibility of interim measures ordered by the Court under article 41 of the Statute should not be discounted, however.[73] In *United States Diplomatic and Consular Staff in Tehran (Request for the Indication of Provisional Measures)*,[74] the Court noted that the object of its power to indicate such measures is to preserve the respective rights of the parties pending the decision of the Court, and presupposes that irreparable prejudice should not be caused to rights which are the subject of dispute in judicial proceedings. The rights of the United States to which the Court referred included the rights of its nationals to life, liberty, protection, and security. It held that continuation of the situation exposed those individuals to privation, hardship, anguish, and even danger to health and life and thus to a serious possibility of irreparable harm. The government of the Islamic Republic of Iran was ordered, among others, to ensure the immediate release of those held.[75] In its judgment on the merits, the Court noted that, 'Wrongfully to deprive human beings of their freedom and to subject them to physical constraint in conditions of hardship is in itself manifestly incompatible with the principles of the Charter of the United Nations, as well as with the fundamental principles enunciated in the Universal Declaration of Human Rights'.[76]

The potential for further development of a limited protection competence is also implicit in the Court's rulings on the requests by Bosnia and Herzegovina for interim measures to prevent genocide, and in its finding that a human rights instrument, the 1948 Genocide Convention, was a sufficient basis for the exercise of jurisdiction, so far as the subject-matter of the dispute related to the 'interpretation, application or fulfilment' of that treaty.[77] As Merrills points out, however, the function of interim measures is to protect the *rights* of both sides pending a decision on the merits, and many of those for which the applicant sought protection were outside the scope of the Convention.[78]

[71] But see Ch. 7.

[72] For example, only the General Assembly or the Security Council may request advisory opinions; 'other organs' of the UN and specialized agencies may be authorized by the General Assembly to request such opinions, 'on legal questions arising within the scope of their activities': art. 96, UN Charter; art. 65, Charter of the ICJ.

[73] Art. 41 provides: 'The Court shall have the power to indicate, if it considers that circumstances so require, any provisional measures which ought to be taken to preserve the rights of either party.' See Merrills, J. G., 'Interim Measures of Protection in the Recent Jurisprudence of the International Court of Justice', 44 *ICLQ* 90 (1995). On the possibility of 'anticipatory provisional measures', see also *Hugo Bustios Saavedra* v. *Peru*, Case no. 10548, Inter-American Commission on Human Rights, 16 May 1990, calling on the government to take whatever measures may be necessary to protect the life of the widow of the applicant, a murdered journalist.

[74] ICJ *Rep.*, 1979, 7.   [75] Ibid., paras. 36, 37, 42, 91.

[76] ICJ *Rep.*, 1980, 3 at 42 (para. 91).   [77] See *Genocide Convention Case*, ICJ *Rep.*, 1993, 16.

[78] Merrills, above n. 73, 103. Thus, the Court rejected claims relating to the territorial integrity of the applicant, as genocide concerns 'the intended destruction of "a national, ethnic, racial or religious group" and not the disappearance of a State as a subject of international law': ICJ *Rep.*, 1993, 345, para. 42; Merrills, ibid., 105.

In most other cases, the simple existence of obligations owed at large may provide sufficient justification, not just for 'expressions of international concern',[79] but also for formal protest on the part of UNHCR. The significance of this development for the individual's standing in general international law should not be underestimated.

1.2 THE UNITED NATIONS RELIEF AND WORKS AGENCY FOR PALESTINIAN REFUGEES IN THE NEAR EAST (UNRWA)

On 29 November 1947, the United Nations General Assembly voted in favour of a plan to partition Palestine into two separate States, one Arab and one Jewish;[80] fighting between the two communities commenced almost at once. The British mandate terminated on 14 May 1948, and the next day the Jewish community proclaimed the State of Israel. The first Arab–Israel war followed, with many thousands of Palestinian Arabs fleeing into neighbouring countries. On 11 December 1948, the General Assembly established a Conciliation Commission for Palestine (UNCCP), charged with taking steps to achieve a final settlement.[81] A year later, in December 1949, the United Nations Relief and Works Agency for Palestine Refugees in the Near East (UNRWA) was set up as a subsidiary organ of the General Assembly, to assist those who had left Palestine as a result of the conflict.[82] That assistance is mainly in the fields of relief, health and education, for which purposes a refugee is defined by UNRWA as 'a person whose normal residence was Palestine for a minimum of two years immediately preceding the outbreak of conflict in 1948, and who, as a result of that conflict, lost both . . . home and . . . means of livelihood, and who is in need'.

This definition has been extended to the children of such persons, and by resolution 2252(ES-V) of 4 July 1967 the General Assembly authorised UNRWA to assist others in the area, displaced by the latest hostilities, as a matter of urgency and on a temporary basis.[83] UNRWA assistance has always been limited as to locality, being restricted to Lebanon, Syria, Jordan, the Gaza Strip and, after the 1967 displacements, Egypt; and limited also as to refugees registered and actually residing in those host countries. Registration, which initially facilitated ration distribution, acquired greater significance in the countries of refuge, where it was increasingly equated with acceptance as a refugee and prima facie entitlement to remain.[84]

---

[79] See Goodwin-Gill, *Movement of Persons*, 23.   [80] UNGA res. 181(II) A, 29 Nov. 1947.
[81] UNGA res. 194(III), 11 Dec. 1948.
[82] The Agency succeeded the Special Fund for Relief of Palestine Refugees, set up by UNGA res. 212(III), 19 Nov 1948.
[83] Confirmed by UNGA res. 2341 B(XXII), 19 Dec. 1967.
[84] In Lebanon, UNRWA-registered Palestinian refugees are entitled to residence permits; those not registered have no right to reside in the country, and neither do the children of unregistered Palestinian parents: McDowall, D., *Lebanon: A Conflict of Minorities*, (1986), 8; Buehrig, E., *The UN and the Palestinian Refugees—A Study in Non-Territorial Administration*, (1971), 43. See also Cervenak, C. M., 'Promoting Inequality: Gender-Based Discrimination in UNRWA's Approach to Palestine Refugee Status', 16 *HRQ* 300 (1994).

Palestinian refugees were excluded from the competence of UNHCR, and later also from the 1951 Convention relating to the Status of Refugees. Political reasons were partly responsible, as was the desirability to delimit formally the mandates of UNHCR, the United Nations Relief and Works Agency (UNRWA), and the United Nations Conciliation Commission for Palestine (UNCCP).[85] At the time, both protection and assistance for Palestinian refugees fell within institutional arrangements that included UNCCP and UNRWA. Solutions, repatriation or compensation, were also expected to eventuate; the General Assembly, for example, intended UNCCP to take on, 'in so far as it considers necessary in existing circumstances, the functions given to the United Nations Mediator on Palestine by resolution 186(S-2) . . .'[86] Those functions had in turn been defined to include the use of,

. . . good offices with the local and community authorities in Palestine to (i) Arrange for the operation of common services necessary to the safety and well-being of the population of Palestine; . . . (iii) Promote a peaceful adjustment of the future situation of Palestine.[87]

The UN Conciliation Commission was instructed to 'facilitate the repatriation, resettlement and economic and social rehabilitation of the refugees and the payment of compensation', and by resolution 394(V) of 14 December 1950, to 'continue consultations with the parties concerned regarding measures for the protection of the rights, property and interests of the refugees'. But already the effectiveness of UNCCP, contingent upon the co-operation and political will of the States concerned, was in doubt; the summary of debate in the General Assembly is brief but eloquent testimony to the fundamental differences between the parties, upon whom depended a solution to the refugee problem. To one side, the objective of a peaceful settlement required direct negotiations; to the other, direct negotiations were contingent on full recognition of the rights of the Arabs to Palestine and to their own homes.[88] With the passing of the years, the General Assembly's repeated requests to the Conciliation Commission to continue its efforts became increasingly formal, almost ritualistic. The prospects for repatriation, resettlement, rehabilitation and compensation waned, UNCCP became irrelevant to the protection needs of Palestinian refugees, and UN institutional mechanisms were unable to bridge the gap.

[85] Statute, para. 7(1); Convention, article 1D; see above, Ch. 3, s. 3.2.

[86] UNGA res. 194(III), 11 Dec. 1948.

[87] Ibid., para. 11: 'the refugees wishing to return to their homes and live at peace with their neighbours should be permitted to do so at the earliest practicable date, and . . . compensation should be paid for the property of those choosing not to return and for loss of or damage to property which, under principles of international law or in equity, should be made good by the Governments or authorities responsible.'

[88] Cf. GAOR, 5th Sess., Plenary, Summary Records, 325th Meeting, 14 Dec. 1950, paras. 170–211. In his 1948 report to the General Assembly, the Mediator for Palestine, Count Bernadotte, referred to the misgivings of the provisional government in Israel regarding the return of Palestinian refugees; these derived from security, as well as from economic and political conditions. At that time, the Mediator doubted whether the security fears were in fact well-founded.

UNRWA's role continued as the provider of international assistance to Palestinian refugees, save that with the beginnings of the *intifada* movement in 1989, it came in practice also to exercise a significant, if limited, protection role on behalf of Palestinians against the occupying forces.[89] The perception of the Palestinian refugee problem as 'temporary', however, accounts in part for the fact that the nationality status of many individual Palestinians remains unresolved.[90]

1.3 THE COMPLEMENTARY ROLE OF UN AGENCIES

In dealing with the crises of forcible displacement, many United Nations agencies become involved. For example, the original mandate of UNICEF, the United Nations Children's Fund established in 1946, was to provide assistance to children in countries which were the victims of aggression; now it provides both emergency and long-term assistance to mothers and children in need throughout the world. UNICEF's work with children frequently extends into refugee situations, providing assistance to unaccompanied children, for example, or establishing safe water supplies and therapeutic feeding. UNICEF also acted as lead agency to co-ordinate UN relief operations along the Thai–Kampuchean border from 1979–82 (before the establishment of UNBRO—the United Nations Border Relief Operation), and in 1994 provided assistance both in the camps for Rwandese refugees in Zaire and Tanzania, and to those displaced within Rwanda itself.

The FAO (Food and Agriculture Organization) also has long been involved in disaster assistance, and the UN's capacity to respond was strengthened in the 1960s with the creation of WFP (World Food Programme),[91] responsible for disposing of surplus food and channelling aid to meet food needs and emergencies inherent in chronic malnutrition.[92] WFP has its own staff in many countries, and the UNDP (United Nations Development Programme) Resident Representative also acts on its behalf.

Article 2(d) of the Constitution of WHO (World Health Organization) empowers it to furnish appropriate technical assistance and, in emergencies, necessary aid upon the request or acceptance of governments. WHO is strongly represented throughout the world, with Programme Co-ordinators or National Programme Co-ordinators working in almost every country. Obviously, mass

[89] See Takkenberg, L., 'The Protection of Palestine Refugees in the Territories Occupied by Israel', 3 *IJRL* 414 (1991).

[90] To the policies of States of refuge must be added the aspirations of the Palestinian people to self-determination and statehood. See further below, s. 3.

[91] UNGA res. 1714 (XVI), 19 Dec. 1961; Stephens, T., *The United Nations Disaster Relief Office: The Politics and Administration of International Relief Assistance*, (1978), 39ff; Brown, B. J., *Disaster Preparedness and the United Nations*, (1979), 54ff.

[92] The WFP definition of emergency includes 'urgent situations in which there is clear evidence that an event has occurred which causes human suffering or loss of livestock and which the Government concerned has not the means to remedy; and it is a demonstrably abnormal event which produced dislocation in the life of the community on an exceptional scale'.

displacements across borders can contribute to the incidence and spread of disease, particularly where large numbers are crowded into makeshift camps with poor sanitation. In emergencies, WHO can provide advice and the services of specialists, as well as urgently needed medicaments from its Geneva and regional stocks.[93]

1.3.1 Strengthening the co-ordination of UN humanitarian emergency assistance

'Root causes', 'early warning' and 'measures to avert refugee flows' are now part of international discourse. Following the 1986 Report of the Group of Government Experts, some initial steps were taken to improve the UN's capacity to respond to forcible displacement, in particular, by the establishment of the Office for Research and Collection of Information (ORCI) in an attempt to provide the UN system with some form of early warning of impending mass movements.[94] Dissatisfaction with the effectiveness of these first measures led to the proposal for the designation by the United Nations Secretary-General of 'a high level official . . . as emergency relief co-ordinator'.

On 19 December 1991, the General Assembly adopted resolution 46/182 on strengthening the co-ordination of United Nations humanitarian emergency assistance.[95] Annexed to that resolution was a set of guidelines, principles and proposals, which included the standards of humanity, neutrality and impartiality as the essential basis for the provision of humanitarian assistance;[96] but also respect for 'the sovereignty, territorial integrity and national unity of States', and recognition of the responsibility of each State, 'first and foremost to take care of

[93] For a summary account of humanitarian assistance activities, see *Report* of the Secretary-General. Strengthening of the Coordination of Humanitarian and Disaster Relief Activities, etc.: UN doc. A/50/203; E/1995/79 (14 June 1995); also Add.1 (27 June 1995); ECOSOC res. 1995/56 (28 July 1995).

[94] See Ramcharan, B. G., 'Early Warning at the United Nations: The First Experiment', 1 *IJRL* 379 (1989); Beyer, G. A., 'Human Rights Monitoring and the Failure of Early Warning: A Practitioner's View', 2 *IJRL* 56 (1990)—the relevant recommendations of the Group of Governmental Experts and an extract from the United Nations *Organization Manual* describing the functions and organization of ORCI appear at 75–81; Beyer, G. A., 'Monitoring Root Causes of Refugee Flows and Early Warning: The Need for Substance', 2 *IJRL Special Issue—September 1990* 71; Rusu, S., 'The Role of the Collector in Early Warning', 2 *IJRL Special Issue—September 1990* 65; Ruiz, H. A., 'Early Warning Is Not Enough: The Failure to Prevent Starvation in Ethiopia, 1990', 2 *IJRL Special Issue—September 1990* 83; Dimitrichev, T. F., 'Conceptual Approaches to Early Warning: Mechanisms and Methods—A View from the United Nations', 3 *IJRL* 264 (1991); Centre for Refugee Studies, York University, Toronto, 'Towards Practical Early Warning Capabilities concerning Refugees and Displaced Persons', 4 *IJRL* 84 (1992); Refugee Policy Group, *Improving International Response to Humanitarian Situations*, (1989); Clark, L., *Early Warning of Refugee Flows*, Refugee Policy Group, (1989); Gordenker, L., *Refugees in International Politics*, (1987), ch. 7; Gordenker, L., 'Early Warning of Disastrous Population Movements', 20 *Int. Mig. Rev.* 170 (1986); Drüke, L., *Preventive Action for Refugee Producing Situations*, (1990).

[95] See UN doc. A/46/L.55, 17 Dec. 1991 (Sweden); *Report* of the Secretary-General on the review of the capacity, experience and coordination arrangements in the United Nations system for humanitarian assistance: UN doc. A/46/568.

[96] These principles in the provision of humanitarian assistance derive directly from ICRC doctrine. See also *Report* of the Third Committee, Draft resolution I, Promotion of international cooperation in the humanitarian field: UN doc. A/45/751 (21 Nov. 1990).

the victims of natural disasters and other emergencies occurring on its terri-tory'.[97]

States with populations in need of humanitarian assistance are called upon to facilitate the work of appropriate intergovernmental and non-governmental organizations, while neighbouring States are urged to participate closely with affected countries. The nexus between disaster prevention and preparedness, and economic growth and sustainable development, is also acknowledged.[98]

The role of the Emergency Relief Co-ordinator and of the Department of Humanitarian Affairs (DHA) is, in principle, wide enough to allow the promo-tion of significantly higher levels of inter-State and inter-organization co-operation than have been seen so far.[99] The Co-ordinator is responsible not only for processing requests from States for emergency assistance, but also oversee-ing all emergencies through 'the systematic pooling and analysis of early-warning information'.[100] While expected to organize needs assessment missions 'in consultation with the Government of the affected country', the Co-ordinator is also authorized to facilitate the provision of emergency assistance 'by obtain-ing the consent of all the parties,'[101] for example, in a situation of internal con-flict, or where no effective governmental authority exists. In addition, the Co-ordinator acts as a central focal point on UN emergency relief operations,[102] and is expected to work closely not only with agencies in the UN system, but also with the ICRC, the International Federation of Red Cross and Red Crescent Societies, IOM, and 'relevant non-governmental organizations'.

Inter-agency co-operation may be pursued through other mechanisms, how-ever, as was the case with respect to UN operations in former Yugoslavia. In November 1991, UNHCR was mandated by the United Nations Secretary-General to act as *lead agency* within the UN system, and to provide protection and assistance to those affected by the conflict in former Yugoslavia. When fight-ing and displacement increased, the High Commissioner convened the

[97] UNGA res. 46/182, 19 Dec. 1991, Annex, paras. 2–4.
[98] Ibid., para. 10; see also paras. 13–17 (Prevention); 18–20 (Preparedness, including early warn-ing); 35(h) (Co-ordinator to promote transition from relief to rehabilitation and reconstruction); 40–2 (Continuum from relief to rehabilitation and development). A $50 million central emergency revolv-ing fund, financed by voluntary contributions, is called for, together with additional measures for rapid response, including a central register of specialized personnel and technical experts: ibid., paras. 21–30; also paras. 31–2 (Consolidated Appeals).
[99] Ibid., paras. 33–9 (leadership of the Secretary-General, role and responsibilities of the Co-ordinator, establishment of Inter-Agency Standing Committee, and country-level co-ordination). The Co-ordinator is to be supported by a secretariat based on a strengthened UNDRO and the consolidation of existing offices dealing with complex emergencies: ibid., para. 36.
[100] Ibid., para. 20: 'Early-warning information should be made available in an unrestricted and timely manner to all interested Governments and concerned authorities, in particular of affected or disaster-prone countries. The capacity of disaster-prone countries to receive, use and disseminate this information should be strengthened ...' Also, para. 35(g), identifying among the Co-ordinator's responsibilities, 'providing consolidated information, including early warning on emergencies, to all interested Governments and concerned authorities ...'
[101] Ibid., para. 35(d).
[102] UN res. 46/182, Annex, para. 36. See *Report* of the Secretary-General, above n. 95.

International Meeting on Humanitarian Aid for Victims of the Conflict in the Former Yugoslavia in Geneva on 29 July 1992. On the basis of the *Comprehensive Response to the Humanitarian Crisis in former Yugoslavia* (CRHC) presented by the High Commissioner,[103] the international community launched a special effort to protect and bring assistance to those in need. A joint inter-agency mission assessed requirements during August 1992, resulting in a Plan of Action and UN Consolidated Inter-Agency Appeal for the period September 1992—March 1993 and revised from time to time thereafter.

The inter-agency activities included programmes co-ordinated in the field by UNHCR, and designed and implemented together with UNICEF, WFP, WHO, IOM, the ICRC, the European Commission and international and local NGOs. These covered, for example, the distribution by air and land of food and winterization material, the provision of health services, and assistance to survivors of war trauma, including rape and sexual assault. In addition to addressing survival needs, UNHCR aimed to provide protection and assistance to individuals as close as possible to their homes, while promoting the concept and practice of temporary protection for those compelled to flee their country of origin. In many instances, programme delivery depended on the efforts of UNPROFOR, the United Nations Protection Force in former Yugoslavia, while the cessation of hostilities remained very much in the hands of the political decision-makers and the diplomatic efforts of the International Conference on Former Yugoslavia. The experience may provide many lessons for future operations, but is widely considered to have fallen far short of expectations and by some, to have compromised UNHCR's primary responsibility to provide international protection.[104]

1.4 OTHER INTERNATIONAL AND INTERGOVERNMENTAL ORGANIZATIONS AND AGENCIES

1.4.1 *International Organization for Migration (IOM)*

Founded outside the United Nations as the Intergovernmental Committee for European Migration in 1951, the International Organization for Migration now brings together some eighty-three States. It is premised on one human right in particular—freedom of movement, and the preamble of the revised Constitution, adopted in 1989, recognizes that migration assistance at an international level is often required 'to ensure the orderly flow of migration movements throughout the world and to facilitate . . . settlement and . . . integration'.[105]

[103] UN doc. HCR/IMFY/1992/2, 24 July 1992.

[104] See Mooney, E. D., 'Presence, *ergo* Protection? UNPROFOR, UNHCR and the ICRC in Croatia and Bosnia and Herzegovina', 7 *IJRL* 407 (1995); Mendiluce, J. M., 'War and disaster in the former Yugoslavia: The limits of humanitarian action,' in *World Refugee Survey—1994*, 16; and below, Ch. 7, s. 3.5.

[105] Perruchoud, R., 'From the Intergovernmental Committee for European Migration to the International Organization for Migration', 1 *IJRL* 501 (1989). For the revised Constitution, see Annexe 1, No. 9. The Constitution recognizes a number of key organizational and developmental principles: the relationship between migration and economic, social and cultural conditions in developing countries; and close co-operation and co-ordination on migration and refugee matters, among States, international organizations, governmental and non-governmental.

In the organization's first years of operation, it focused on displaced persons and refugees in, and orderly migration from, Europe.[106] Since them, IOM's objectives and functions have become world-wide and include orderly and planned migration for employment purposes; the movement of qualified human resources, including family members; the organized transfer of refugees, displaced persons and other persons compelled to leave their country of origin; technical assistance and advisory services on migration policies, legislation, administration and programmes; and the provision of a forum in which States and organizations concerned can exchange views and experiences, and promote co-operation and co-ordination on migration issues.[107] IOM is also involved in migration information, both in its own right and in co-operation with UNHCR.[108]

IOM's working concept of displaced persons includes refugees within the sense of the OAU Convention or the Cartagena Declaration, as well as those in flight from man-made disasters. It also assists asylum seekers in various countries, who have either been accepted under the immigration programmes of third States, or have elected to return home voluntarily. In 1972, it helped many stateless persons and former citizens of Uganda, then facing expulsion. In September 1990, in a United Nations inter-agency context, IOM assumed responsibility for the repatriation of third country nationals displaced or expelled in the aftermath of the Iraqi invasion of Kuwait.[109] In September 1991, working with UNHCR and within the context of the Comprehensive Plan of Action for Indo-Chinese refugees, IOM signed a memorandum of understanding with the Socialist Republic of Vietnam, with respect to the return of Vietnamese citizens from countries of refuge in South East Asia.[110]

---

[106] See 'Continued Effectiveness of the Organization in view of New Challenges': *Report* of the Director General on the Implementation of Resolution No. 749 (LVII) of 26 May 1988: IOM doc. MC/1631 (13 Oct. 1989).

[107] See Perruchoud, R., 'Persons falling under the Mandate of the International Organization for Migration, to Whom the Organization may Provide Migration Services', 4 *IJRL* 205, 211f (1992). The breadth of IOM's mandate means that it is often well-placed to provide appropriate services to individuals whose status is unclear, or who are not the responsibility of any other organization, such as rejected asylum seekers or internally displaced persons.

[108] IOM's information activities relating to migratory flows in the early 1990s included surveys on socio-economic profiles of potential migrants in Eastern and Central Europe and the CIS: see IOM, *Feasibility Study on the Establishment of a Migration Information System/Activity for Central and Eastern Europe and the Commonwealth of Independent States*, Final Report, Sept. 1992; see also IOM doc. MC/1741. para. 196. IOM has implemented country-specific programmes, including dissemination of information to would-be migrants, in Romania and other countries. Drawing on experience gained under the Comprehensive Plan of Action for Indo-Chinese Refugees and in the aftermath of the mass movement to Italy in 1991, a joint IOM/UNHCR migration information programme was initiated in Albania in 1992. It aimed to provide accurate and credible information to the local population regarding legal emigration procedures, visa criteria and living conditions in various countries of potential destination, as well as information on difficulties facing those who migrate in an irregular fashion.

[109] *Refugee Reports*, 28 Sept. 1990.

[110] IOM also participated in the UNHCR-funded repatriation programme to South Africa; see IOM doc. MC/1741, para. 266.

In Europe, IOM operates programmes of limited assistance to asylum seekers whose claims have been definitively rejected, or who have withdrawn their applications. The focus is on pre-departure assistance, re-installation and, occasionally, also on counselling and re-insertion in the labour market.[111] Although IOM does not have a 'protection' function, strictly so-called, its presence in receiving countries can have distinct advantages for returnees, often amounting to protection in fact, through informal monitoring.[112]

1.4.2 International Committee of the Red Cross

In many respects, the International Committee of the Red Cross (ICRC) has comparable protection responsibilities to UNHCR, but under the system consolidated by the 1949 Geneva Conventions and the 1977 Additional Protocols. Article 8, common to the first three Geneva Conventions, and article 9 of the Fourth Convention, each provide for their respective provisions to 'be applied with the co-operation and under the scrutiny of the Protecting Powers whose duty it is to safeguard the interests of the Parties to the conflict'. Each Convention likewise recognizes the 'humanitarian activities which the International Committee of the Red Cross or any other impartial humanitarian organization may . . . undertake for the protection of . . .' persons within their scope, and for their relief.[113] In addition, the Conventions provide for the appointment of substitutes for the Protecting Powers, such as 'an organization which offers all guarantees of impartiality and efficacy'.[114]

Humanitarian objectives and the role of the ICRC are stressed throughout each of the four Geneva Conventions, in common article 3, and in their

---

[111] These activities are complementary to many other IOM programmes, for example, with respect to migration generally or in the field of return of talent. See further, 'Transmigration and Remigration of Refused Asylum Seekers: Case Studies,' paper submitted by IOM to the International Conference, *Refugees in the World: The European Community's Response*, The Hague, 7–8 Dec. 1989. Doc. RWECR/2.2 (Aug. 1989). In a paper submitted in 1991 to the UNHCR Executive Committee Working Group on Solutions and Protection, IOM explained the relevant special assistance as including pre-departure counselling, pre-departure material assistance, documentation, transport, reception, post-arrival assistance, and safeguards in countries of origin. In the period 1979–91, IOM implemented a programme for the Reintegration or Emigration of Asylum-Seekers from Germany (REAG), under which some 82,618 individuals were assisted, either with return (41,108) or migration to a third country (41,510). A similar programme in Belgium since 1984 (REAB) has benefited some 2,060 persons, and programmes have also been established with Switzerland (1987) and Italy (1988) for the return and labour reinsertion of unsuccessful Chilean asylum applicants. See also IOM doc. MC/INF/222.

[112] See Perruchoud, R., 'Persons falling under the Mandate of the International Organization for Migration, to Whom the Organization may Provide Migration Services,' 4 *IJRL* 205 (1992).

[113] See art. 9 of the First (wounded and sick, medical personnel and chaplains), Second (including shipwrecked persons), and Third (prisoners of war) Conventions; and art. 10 of the Fourth Convention (civilian persons).

[114] Art. 10 of the First, Second and Third Conventions; art. 11 of the Fourth Convention. The Conventions further provide for Protecting Powers to 'lend their good offices' with a view to settling disputes: art. 11 of the First, Second and Third Conventions; art. 12 of the Fourth Convention. Compare generally art. 5, 1977 Protocol I, and see Veuthey, M., *Guérilla et droit humanitaire*, (1983), 329–32.

respective provisions on protected persons and the meaning of protection.[115] In addition to its activities under the Conventions, the ICRC is recognized as retaining its right of initiative,[116] the freedom to engage in 'toute initiative humanitaire, . . . toute action que les conventions n'auraient pas prévues mais qui serait nécessaire pour la protection des victimes'.[117]

1.4.3 Regional organizations

The protection of refugees may also be promoted, directly and indirectly, by regional organizations, including, for example, the Organization of African Unity,[118] the Organization of American States, and the Council of Europe. These have generated, among others, instruments such as the 1969 OAU Convention on the Specific Aspects of Refugee Problems in Africa, the 1969 American Convention on Human Rights, the 1950 European Convention on Human Rights, the 1959 European Agreement on the Abolition of Visas for Refugees, the 1972 European Agreement on Social Security and its Supplementary Agreement, the 1967 European Agreement on Consular Functions, together with the Protocol concerning the Protection of Refugees, and the 1980 European Agreement on Transfer of Responsibility for Refugees.[119]

The necessity for inter-agency and inter-State co-operation in migration and refugee matters has been increasingly recognized in multiple fora, including the Organization (formerly the Conference) on Security and Co-operation in Europe.[120] Although the OSCE process may fall short of the high normative character of an international treaty, co-operation has been a central element in each meeting, the focus of which is increasingly detailed.[121] At the CSCE Vienna Meeting in 1986-7, participating States covered a range of relevant

[115] See, in particular, common article 3, 1949 Geneva Conventions; art. 81, 1977 Additional Protocol I; Veuthey, above n. 114, 332-4. With respect to the ICRC's functions on behalf of interned enemy civilians or other protected persons; see arts. 41, 78, 132-4, Fourth Geneva Convention (1949); art 75, Additional Protocol 1; arts. 4-6, Additional Protocol 2.

[116] Art. 9 of the first three Conventions; art. 10 of the Fourth Convention.

[117] Veuthey, above n. 114, 332-3.

[118] See Bakwesegha, C. J., 'The Role of the Organization of African Unity in Conflict Prevention, Management and Resolution', 7 *IJRL Special Issue—Summer 1995*, 207; Oloka-Onyango, J., 'The Place and Role of the OAU Bureau for Refugees in the African Refugee Crisis', 6 *IJRL* 34 (1994).

[119] Besides promoting legal instruments and monitoring mechanisms, the Council of Europe's activities have also included community relations, training of police and immigration officers, and programmes to combat intolerance and xenophobia. See, among many others, 'Community Relations and Solidarity in European Society,' Interim report on the community relations project by the Committee of Experts on Community Relations (MG-CR): CE doc. MG-CR (89) 3 rev. (1989); 'Intolerance and Human Rights,' Background Document prepared by the Directorate of Human Rights for the Colloquy, 'Human Rights without Frontiers,' Strasbourg, 30 Nov.—1 Dec. 1989: CE doc. DH-ED-COLL (89) 5.

[120] The 1992 appointment of a CSCE High Commissioner for National Minorities is perhaps the most evident illustration of regional concern and intention to act.

[121] Principle IX of the Declaration on Principles guiding Relations between Participating States, Helsinki Final Act, 1 Aug. 1975, declared: 'The participating States will develop their co-operation with one another and with all States in all fields in accordance with the purposes and principles of the United Nations . . .' Text in 1975 *Digest of United States Practice in International Law*, 8, 10.

issues, among them the freedom to leave any country, including one's own, and to return there, and the entitlement of refugees to repatriate.[122]

The final document of the CSCE Copenhagen Conference on the Human Dimension in June 1990 also endorsed basic human rights, including freedom of movement and a comprehensive right to effective remedies.[123] Even as they stressed the desirability of freer movement, participating States also declared that 'they will consult and, where appropriate, co-operate in dealing with problems that might emerge as a result of the increased movement of persons'.[124] In November 1990, CSCE States adopted the Charter of Paris for a New Europe, with guidelines for strengthening democratic institutions, fostering 'the rich contribution of national minorities,' combating all forms of ethnic hatred and discrimination, 'as well as persecution on religious and ideological grounds'.[125]

Notwithstanding the formal, non-obligatory nature of much of the OSCE process, the repeated endorsement of basic principles by participating States is important evidence of a consolidating norm of co-operation, sufficiently broad to include the relations of States between themselves and practical inter-agency co-operation.

1.4.4 Non-governmental organizations (NGOs)

Protection concerns reveal a commonality of interest; *effective* protection demands a purposeful degree of co-operation, by no means limited to States or international organizations. For example, in 1980, the Economic and Social Council recognized the 'essential role played by inter-governmental organizations, the International Committee of the Red Cross and other non-governmental organizations' in meeting humanitarian needs in emergency situations.[126] Many

---

[122] Conference on Security and Co-operation in Europe (CSCE): Concluding Document from the Vienna Meeting (4 Nov. 1986—17 Jan. 1987): 28 *ILM* 527 (1989). The Concluding Document specifically identified (a) general principles, including human rights, freedom of movement and repatriation of refugees; (b) co-operation on, among other areas, migrant workers; (c) co-operation in humanitarian and other fields, including human contacts and the freedom to leave and to return; and (d) the human dimension—human rights, human contacts and other humanitarian issues.

[123] The participating States reaffirmed 'that the protection and promotion of the rights of migrant workers have their human dimension'. They are the concern of all, and as such should be addressed within the CSCE process: CSCE: Document of the Copenhagen Meeting of the Conference on the Human Dimension: 29 June 1990: 29 *ILM* 1305 (1990). See arts. (9.5), (11), (22).

[124] Ibid., art. (20). Significantly, at the Moscow Meeting, it was accepted that a participating State may request a CSCE mission 'to address or contribute to the resolution of questions in its territory relating to the human dimension of the CSCE'. On 28 Sept. 1992, the Republic of Estonia invited a CSCE ODIHR mission of experts to study Estonian citizenship legislation and to compare it and its implementation with CSCE standards and international human rights norms; see Fehervary, A., 'Citizenship, Statelessness and Human Rights: Recent Developments in the Baltic States', 5 *IJRL* 392 (1993).

[125] CSCE: Charter of Paris for a New Europe, 21 Nov. 1990: 30 *ILM* 190 (1991).

[126] ECOSOC res. 1980/43, 23 Jul. 1980. Amnesty International, the Anti-Slavery Society, the Minority Rights Group and the International Commission of Jurists are typical of those NGOs whose activities can be called 'protection'. The international role of NGOs in the human rights field has been confirmed and developed, among others, through the mechanism of consultative status with ECOSOC (under art. 71 of the UN Charter) and thereby also with bodies such as the Commission on Human Rights.

hundreds of national and international NGOs are involved in assisting and protecting refugees and asylum seekers around the world. Among the widely known are *Médecins sans Frontières*, which specializes in bringing medical care and health services to refugees in emergency camps and settlements; the *US Committee for Refugees*, which regularly carries out field visits and publishes situational and issues papers focusing on areas of concern; the *European Council on Refugees and Exiles*, a forum established in 1973 for co-operation between more than sixty western European NGOs concerned with refugees and the right of asylum; the various *Refugee Councils* in the Netherlands, the United Kingdom and other European countries, which provide legal or other counselling, or seek to influence national policy on refugees and asylum seekers; as well as *human rights organizations* whose reporting, monitoring and lobbying activities include refugees and the persecuted as a natural extension to their mandate.[127]

For example, there is a clear complementarity between protection of refugees and *Amnesty International's* statutory concern with 'prisoners of conscience', that is, men and women 'imprisoned, detained or otherwise physically restricted by reason of their political, religious or other conscientiously held beliefs or by reason of their ethnic origin, sex, colour or language, provided that they have not used or advocated violence'.[128]

2. The protection of refugees in international law

Day-to-day protection activities are necessarily dictated by the needs of refugees and asylum seekers, but a summary reading of both the UNHCR Statute and the 1951 Convention gives a general picture. There are, first, both direct and indirect aspects to the protection function, with the latter comprising UNHCR's promotion activities already mentioned. Direct protection activities, including intervention on behalf of individuals or groups, involve protection of the refugee's basic human rights, for example, non-discrimination, liberty, and security of the person.[129] UNHCR is also concerned specifically with the following: (1) the prevention of the return of refugees to a country or territory in

---

[127] For a comprehensive listing of organizations working in the human rights/refugee field, see Human Rights Internet *Reporter*, (1994), vol. 15, supp.

[128] Art. 1(a), Statute of Amnesty International, as amended by the 12th International Council, Louvain, Belgium, 6–9 Sept. 1979: *1980 Report*, appx. 1, 383.

[129] In many ways, UNHCR acts much as does a national consul, although formal recognition of this role was a divisive issue at the 1963 United Nations Conference on Consular Relations and no article thereon was agreed; see UN doc. A/CONF.25/L6, setting out UNHCR's position. The 1967 European Convention on Consular Functions has gone some way, to protect refugees *against* the exercise of consular functions by consuls who are nationals of the refugees' country of origin: *ETS* No. 61, art. 47. Art. 2(2) of the Protocol to the same convention, moreover, expressly recognizes a protection role for the consuls of a refugee's State of habitual residence, 'in consultation, whenever possible, with the Office of the United Nations High Commissioner for Refugees'. For a view of the 'collective vision' of UNHCR lawyers and their role, see Kennedy, D., 'International Refugee Protection', 8 *HRQ* 1 (1986).

which their life or liberty may be endangered;[130] (2) access to a procedure for the determination of refugee status; (3) the grant of asylum; (4) the prevention of expulsion; (5) release from detention; (6) the issue of identity and travel documents; (7) the facilitation of voluntary repatriation; (8) the facilitation of family reunion; (9) the assurance of access to educational institutions; (10) the assurance of the right to work and the benefit of other economic and social rights; (11) treatment generally in accordance with international standards, not excluding access to and by UNHCR, the provision of physical and medical assistance, and personal security; and (12) the facilitation of naturalization. Of these, the first four, together with the general function, are traditionally considered to be of prime importance, with the principle of *non-refoulement* standing as the essential starting-point in the search for permanent solutions. However, the measures to which refugees have been subject, and the conditions under which they must frequently live, have given added weight to claims for personal security, family reunion, assistance, and international efforts to achieve solutions.

As a matter of international law, the precise standard of treatment to be accorded to refugees will vary, depending on whether the State in which they find themselves has ratified the Convention and Protocol or any other relevant treaty. It may further depend on whether the refugee falls within the narrow or broad sense of the term, is lawfully or unlawfully in the territory of the State, or has been formally recognized as a refugee.

2.1 GENERAL INTERNATIONAL LAW

With regard to basic human rights, the lawfulness or otherwise of presence is as irrelevant as the distinction between national and alien.[131] Certain provisions of the 1966 Covenants on human rights are indicative of standards going beyond a purely treaty-based regime. Article 2(2) of the Covenant on Civil and Political Rights, for example, obliges the State to respect and to ensure the rights declared to 'all individuals within its territory and subject to its jurisdiction'. The same article elaborates a principle of non-discrimination in broad terms, including national or social origin, birth or other status, within the list of prohibited grounds of distinction. Article 4(1), it is true, permits derogation in certain circumstances,[132] and contains a narrower statement of the principle of non-discrimination that would allow States to distinguish between nationals and aliens. Nevertheless, any measures in derogation must be consistent with States'

[130] This in turn may cover a wide range of activities. During the height of the conflict in El Salvador, UNHCR 'roving protection officers' patrolled the border on the Honduras side, leading asylum seekers to refugee camps, and often interceding directly with Honduran military to prevent forced return. In other situations, protection may mean maintaining a watching brief at airports and in transit areas, to try to prevent summary removals, or interceding with legal arguments to ensure that claims generally receive substantive determination.
[131] Applicable standards, with particular regard to immigration, are analysed in more detail in Goodwin-Gill, *Movement of Persons*, Chs. iv and v.
[132] Derogation is permitted in 'time of public emergency which threatens the life of the nation and the existence of which is officially proclaimed'.

other obligations under international law,[133] and no derogation is allowed from those provisions which guarantee the right to life, or which forbid torture or inhuman treatment, slavery, servitude, or conviction or punishment under retroactive laws. The right to recognition as a person before the law and the right to freedom of conscience, thought, and religion are also declared in absolute terms.[134]

The Covenant is in force and has been widely ratified,[135] while certain rights and standards also possess a positive foundation in general international law. In one oft quoted dictum, the International Court of Justice observed that 'the principles and rules concerning the basic human rights of the human person, including protection from slavery and racial discrimination',[136] figure within the class of obligations owed by States *erga omnes*, that is to the international community of States as a whole. Although this concept is not without its difficulties, the rights in question frequently appear in conventions among those from which no derogation is permitted, even in exceptional circumstances. Other rights of a similar fundamental character ought likewise to benefit everyone, and they would include the right to life; the right to be protected against torture or cruel or inhuman treatment or punishment; the right not to be subject to retroactive criminal penalties and the right to recognition as a person before the law.[137] Such rights clearly allow for no distinction between national and alien, whether the latter be a migrant, visitor, refugee, or asylum seeker, and whether lawfully or unlawfully in the State.[138] The obligations of respect and protection are incumbent on States, irrespective of ratification of treaties, and refugees ought in principle to benefit, whether admitted on a temporary, indefinite, or a permanent basis. In practice, however, this objective may remain elusive, particularly where the State of refuge is unable or unwilling to take the necessary

[133] Thus, in view of the peremptory character of the rule of non-discrimination on the ground of race, measures taken against a particular class of foreign nationals determinable solely by reference to such characteristics would not be justified.

[134] Art. 4(2). Cf. annexe III, Elles, *International Provisions protecting the Human Rights of Non-Citizens*: UN doc. E/CN.4/Sub.2/392/Rev.1, (1980), 57.

[135] At 31 Dec. 1994, 129 States were parties to the Covenant.

[136] *Barcelona Traction* case, ICJ *Rep.*, 1970, 3, at 32.

[137] See Goodwin-Gill, *Movement of Persons*, 72–3, 85–7; and with respect to persecution, see above Ch. 2, s. 5.

[138] Cf. ILO Migrant Workers (Supplementary Provisions) Convention 1975 (no. 143). Art. 1 affirms that 'Each Member for which this Convention is in force undertakes to respect the basic human rights of all migrant workers'. The ILO Committee of Experts proposed for inclusion within this category of rights, the right to life, to protection against torture, cruel, inhuman or degrading treatment or punishment, liberty and security of the person, protection against arbitrary arrest and detention, and the right to a fair trial: *Migrant Workers*, report of the Committee of Experts, International Labour Conference, 66th Session, 1980, 68–9. Art. 9(1) of this same convention requires further that illegal migrant workers, whose position cannot be regularized, should receive 'equal treatment' for themselves and their families in respect of rights arising out of past employment in matters of pay, social security, etc. See also Goodwin-Gill, G. S., 'International Law and Human Rights: Trends concerning International Migrants and Refugees', 23 *Int.Mig.Rev.* 526 (1989).

measures. Refugees have thus fallen victim to external, armed aggression;[139] to attacks by pirates resulting in murder, rape, abduction, and robbery;[140] to abandonment when in distress at sea;[141] to threats to life and security by paramilitary 'death squads';[142] to forced conscription, even as children;[143] to arbitrary detention and torture;[144] and to rape and other sexual violence.[145] The exercise of protection on such occasions is a difficult and delicate task, whether attempted by UNHCR or by concerned States, and the problem is further exacerbated where the injury takes place in an area formally beyond the jurisdiction of any State. While international solidarity may manifest itself in calls for action, practical results can be far harder to obtain.

Once refugees have secured admission, however, the goal of attaining a lasting solution to their plight would seem to entail certain further standards of treatment geared to that objective. In 1981, a Group of Experts considered the implications of the concept of temporary refuge, and proposed a list of some sixteen 'basic human standards' which, in its view, should govern the treatment of those temporarily admitted; these were duly endorsed by the Executive Committee and the General Assembly later that year.[146] The objective, the initiative for which drew especially on generally negative practices in South East Asia, was rather the promotion of certain practically attainable standards, than

---

[139] Summary reports on the risks and injuries faced by refugees are included in UNHCR's annual 'Notes' on International Protection, submitted each year to the Executive Committee, and in UNHCR's reports to the Economic and Social Council; some examples are provided below and in the following nn. Armed attacks against refugee camps are cited in the various 'Notes' on International Protection, including UN docs. A/AC.96/643 (1984), paras. 2, 19–20; A/AC.96/660 (1985), paras. 3, 20–2; A/AC.96/680 (1986), paras. 34–46; A/AC.96/694 (1987), para. 42; A/AC.96/713 (1988), paras. 26ff; A/AC.96/728 (1989), paras. 40ff; A/AC.96/777 (1991), para. 29.

[140] On piracy and the anti-piracy programme, see UNHCR, 'Notes' on International Protection: UN docs. A/AC.96/579 (1980), para. 11; A/AC.96/623 (1983), para. 19; A/AC.96/643 (1984), paras. 19, 23; A/AC.96/660 (1985), paras. 23ff; A/AC.96/680 (1986), para. 53; A/AC.96/694 (1987), para. 36; A/AC.96/713 (1988), para. 36; A/AC.96/728 (1989), paras. 50–1.

[141] On rescue at sea; see UNHCR, 'Notes' on International Protection: UN docs. A/AC.96/643 (1984), paras. 19, 24; A/AC.96/660 (1985), paras. 24–5; A/AC.96/694 (1987), para. 37; A/AC.96/713 (1988), para. 36.

[142] *Report* of the UNHCR to the Economic and Social Council: UN doc. E/1981/45, para. 31.

[143] On forced recruitment, see UNHCR, 'Notes' on International Protection: UN docs. A/AC.96/694 (1987), para. 41; A/AC.96/713 (1988), para. 24; A/AC.96/728 (1989), paras. 46–8; A/AC.96/777 (1991), para. 29; A/AC.96/815 (1993), para. 31; See Cohn, I. & Goodwin-Gill, G. S., *Child Soldiers*, (1994), 77–8.

[144] On detention, see UNHCR, 'Notes' on International Protection: UN docs. A/AC.96/660 (1985), paras. 26–9; A/AC.96/680 (1986), para. 22; A/AC.96/694 (1987), para. 33; A/AC.96/713 (1988), paras. 16–23; see further below, Ch. 7, s. 1.1. On torture, see UN doc. A/AC.96/815 (1993), para. 38.

[145] On rape and sexual violence apart from piracy, see UNHCR, 'Notes' on International Protection: UN doc. A/AC.96/815 (1993), para. 30; also 'Note on refugee women and international protection': UN doc. EC/SCP/59 (28 Aug. 1990), paras. 19–28; 'Information Note on UNHCR's Guidelines on the Protection of Refugee Women': UN doc. A/AC.96/822; 'Report of the 17–18 May Meeting of the Sub-Committee of the Whole on International Protection': UN doc. EC/SCP/83 930 Sept. 1993), paras. 19–32; 'Report of the Working Group on Refugee Women and Children': UN doc. EC/SCP/85 (29 Jun. 1994), paras. 39ff.

[146] Executive Committee Conclusion No. 22 (1981); also UNGA res. 36/125, 14 Dec. 1981.

the formulation of rules. The Executive Committee thus reiterated the need to observe fundamental rights, including the principle of non-discrimination. It also recommended that asylum seekers be located by reference to their safety and well-being, as well as the security of the State of refuge;[147] that they be provided with the basic necessities of life; that the principle of family unity be respected and that assistance with tracing of relatives be given; that minors and unaccompanied children be adequately protected; that the sending and receiving of mail, and receipt of material assistance from friends be allowed; that, where possible, appropriate arrangements be made for the registration of births, deaths, and marriages; that asylum seekers be permitted to transfer to the country in which a lasting solution is found, any assets brought into the country of temporary refuge; and that all necessary facilities be granted to enable the attainment of a satisfactory durable solution, including voluntary repatriation.

These recommendations are not of a normative character, although a rules base can certainly be found for many of them among basic human rights principles.[148] They were formulated primarily with a view to reaching solutions which, in the case of refugees from Indochina, meant first asylum followed by third country resettlement. UNHCR has sought to maintain such standards of treatment in the 'temporary protection' debate of the 1990s. Here, the first objective has been to obtain a prompt response to the protection needs of those in flight from conflict in former Yugoslavia, on the assumption that voluntary return, rather than resettlement, will eventuate in due course. However, given the particular circumstances, UNHCR has also argued that beneficiaries of temporary protection in Europe should also have early access to the labour market, to education, and to be joined by family members. Where the period of protection is prolonged, measures of social and economic integration should be implemented, that is, temporary protection should be converted into a more permanent and secure status.[149]

2.2 TREATIES AND MUNICIPAL LAW

Basic human rights derive their force from customary international law, and indicate the content of the *general* obligations which control and structure the treatment by States of nationals and aliens. For States which have ratified treaties specifically benefiting refugees, the particular standards required ought to be easier to determine. This, however, raises the problem of the obligation, if any, requiring ratifying States to incorporate or otherwise implement the provisions of the treaties in question in their municipal law. The 1951 Convention contains no provision requiring legislative incorporation or any other formal

---

[147] With respect to military attacks on refugee camps and settlements, see Ch. 7, s. 1.3.1.

[148] The Executive Committee was somewhat more peremptory, however, in its statement on co-operation with UNHCR: Executive Committee Conclusion No. 22 (1981), ch. III.

[149] See UNHCR, 'Temporary Protection: Information Note, Informal Meeting of Government Experts on the Implementation of Temporary Protection,' Geneva, 20 Apr. 1995; see also above, Ch. 5, s. 3.

implementing step; indeed, article 36, which obliges States to provide information on national legislation, refers only to such laws and regulations as States 'may' adopt to ensure application of the Convention. Similarly, nothing is said with regard to the establishment of procedures for the determination of refugee status, or otherwise for ascertaining and identifying those who are to benefit from the substantive provisions of the Convention.

Although it offers little assistance in the solution of specific problems, the *general* duty of a party to a treaty to ensure that its domestic law is in conformity with its international obligations is beyond contradiction.[150] The governing principles, however, do not include an obligation as such to incorporate the provisions of treaties into domestic law.[151] The fundamental distinction is between an obligation of conduct or means, and an obligation of result.[152] This is often easier to declare than to apply, but it remains crucial in any assessment of a State's performance in the light of its participation in international treaties. Obligations of conduct tend on the whole to be less frequent than obligations of result, and are commonly encountered where action is required at the level of direct relations between States. Obligations of result, on the other hand, incorporating acknowledgement of the principle of choice of means, are most usually found where States are required to bring about a certain situation within their system of internal law.[153]

So, for example, article 22(1) of the 1961 Vienna Convention on Diplomatic Relations declares a clear obligation of conduct: '[t]he premises of the mission shall be inviolable. The agents of the receiving State may not enter them, except with the consent of the head of the mission'.[154] In this case, the internationally required conduct is that of omission by the organs of the receiving State; in other cases, positive action may be required. Thus, States parties to the 1965 Convention on the Elimination of All Forms of Racial Discrimination agree, among others, 'to amend, rescind or nullify any laws or regulations which have the effect of creating or perpetuating racial discrimination wherever it exists'.[155] Similarly, the specific *enactment* of legislation may be required, as by article 20 of the 1966 Covenant on Civil and Political Rights: '[a]ny propaganda for war shall be prohibited by law'.[156] In all such cases, the international obligation

---

[150] McNair, *The Law of Treaties*, (1961), 78–9; see also Brownlie, I., *Principles of Public International Law* (4th ed. 1990), 35–7; Brownlie, I., *System of the Law of Nations: State Responsibility (Part I)*, (1983), 241–76; *Treatment of Polish Nationals in Danzig*, PCIJ ser. A/B no. 44 at 24; *Greco-Bulgarian Communities*, PCIJ, ser. B, no. 17, 32; *Free Zones*, PCIJ ser. A, no. 24, 12; ser. A/B, no. 46, 167; art. 27, 1969 Vienna Convention on the Law of Treaties; *Advisory Opinion, Applicability of the Obligation to Arbitrate under Section 21 of the United Nations Headquarters Agreement of 26 June 1947*, ICJ *Rep.*, 1988, 12.

[151] The International Court has stressed that failure to enact legislation necessary to ensure fulfilment of international obligations will not relieve a State of responsibility; see *Exchange of Greek and Turkish Populations*, PCIJ ser. B, no. 10, 20.

[152] See generally *Yearbook of the ILC* (1977), ii, 11–50.   [153] Ibid., 13.

[154] 500 UNTS 95; Brownlie, I., *Basic Documents in International Law*, (4th ed., 1995), 217.

[155] Art. 2(1)(c): 660 *UNTS* 195.

[156] Text annexed to UNGA res. 2200(XXI), 16 Dec. 1966. Some States have made reservations to this article, on the basis of its inconsistency with the freedom of expression recognized in art.

requires a specifically determined course of conduct; ascertaining if the obligation has been fulfilled simply turns on whether the State's act or omission is or is not in fact in conformity with the internationally required conduct, the sufficient injury being the breach of legal duty.[157]

International obligations requiring the achievement of a specified result often concede the State's full freedom in its choice of means for implementation. Article 22(2) of the 1961 Vienna Convention on Diplomatic Relations declares the receiving State's 'special duty to take all appropriate steps to protect the premises of the mission', but defines those steps no further. Article 10 of the ILO Migrant Workers (Supplementary Provisions) Convention 1975 (No. 143) obliges '[e]ach Member for which the Convention is in force . . . to declare and pursue a national policy designed to promote and to guarantee, *by methods appropriate to national conditions and practice*, equality of opportunity and treatment . . .'[158] The obligation of result is especially common in standard-setting treaties (for example, treaties of establishment guaranteeing most-favoured-nation treatment) and in human rights instruments. On occasion, full freedom of choice can be implied from the terms of the treaty itself, while in other cases a preference for the adoption of legislative measures will be indicated. Nevertheless, though legislation may be considered appropriate, even essential, it is evidently only one way in which the internationally required result can be obtained. It is not so much the law which counts, as that compliance with international obligations be assured. As the International Law Commission noted in 1977: '. . . so long as the State has not failed to achieve *in concreto* the result required by an international obligation, the fact that it has not taken a certain measure which would have seemed

19. See *Multilateral Treaties deposited with the Secretary-General: Status as at 31 December 1994:* UN doc. ST/LEG/SER.E/13 (1995), 118–26, recording reservations by Australia, Belgium, Denmark, Finland, Iceland, Ireland, Luxembourg, Malta, Netherlands, New Zealand, Norway, Sweden, Switzerland, UK and the US.

[157] *United States Diplomatic and Consular Staff in Tehran, (USA v. Iran),* ICJ *Rep.,* 1980, 3 at 30–1. The International Law Commission's draft articles on State responsibility include: 'Article 16. There is a breach of an international obligation by a State when an act of the State is not in conformity with what is required of it by that obligation . . . Article 20. There is a breach by a State of an international obligation requiring it to adopt a particular course of conduct when the conduct of that State is not in conformity with that required of it by that obligation': *Yearbook of the ILC* (1977), ii, 10–11. In commenting on the irrelevance whether harmful consequences actually result, the ILC suggests as one example that art. 10(3) of the 1966 Covenant on Economic, Social, and Cultural Rights ('States Parties . . . recognize that [child employment in certain circumstances] should be prohibited and punishable by law') is breached by simple failure to enact legislation. This conclusion seems erroneous; art. 2(1) of the Covenant refers expressly to 'achieving progressively the full realization of the rights recognized', while art. 10 alone in that instrument employs the ambivalent 'should', rather than the peremptory 'shall'. The provision in question is rather an obligation of result, than of conduct. On the terminological issue, cf. 1979 International Convention on Maritime Search and Rescue (IMCO, 1979), annexe I, art. 1.1: ' "Shall" is used . . . to indicate a provision, the uniform application of which by all Parties is required in the interest of safety of life at sea.'

[158] See also art. 24, ILO Constitution, whereby every member State 'binds itself effectively to observe within its jurisdiction any Convention to which it is a party'; 1949 Geneva Conventions, common art. 1: 'The High Contracting Parties undertake to respect and to ensure respect for the present Convention in all circumstances'.

especially suitable for that purpose—in particular, that it has not enacted a law—cannot be held against it as a breach of that obligation'.[159]

In two human rights treaties concluded in the 1960s, States are called upon to enact such 'legislative or other measures as may be necessary'[160] to give effect to rights; and to 'prohibit and bring to an end' certain conduct, 'by all appropriate means, including legislation as required by circumstances'.[161] Words such as 'necessary' and 'appropriate' indicate that the State enjoys discretion in its choice of implementing measures, but the standard of compliance remains an international one. The question is that of effective or efficient implementation of the treaty provisions, *in fact*, and in the light of the principle of effectiveness of obligations.[162] Just as taking the theoretically most appropriate measures of implementation is not conclusive as to the fulfilment of an international obligation, so failing to take such measures is not conclusive as to breach.[163] The same holds good with regard to a State's adoption of a potentially obstructive measure, so long as such measure does not itself create a specific situation incompatible with the required result; what counts is what in fact results, not enactment and promulgation, but application and enforcement.[164]

In theory at least, the test of implementation of an international obligation of result might appear as straightforward as that for an obligation of conduct: [c]ompare the result in fact achieved with that which the State ought to have

---

[159] The ILC invoked particularly clear statements of the principle submitted by Poland and Switzerland to the Preparatory Committee of the 1930 Hague Conference for the Codification of International Law; cited in *Yearbook of the ILC* (1977), ii, 23.

[160] Art. 2(2), 1966 Covenant on Civil and Political Rights. See also, OAS Additional Protocol to the American Convention on Human Rights in the area of Economic, Social and Cultural (Protocol of San Salvador, 14 Nov. 1988), art. 2: 'If the exercise of the rights set forth in this Protocol is not already guaranteed by legislative or other provisions, the States Parties undertake to adopt, in accordance with their constitutional processes and the provisions of this Protocol, such legislative or other measures as may be necessary for making those rights a reality': 28 *ILM* 156 (1989).

[161] Art. 2(1)(d), 1965 International Covenant on the Elimination of All Forms of Racial Discrimination.

[162] See generally Lauterpacht, H., *The Development of International Law by the International Court,* (1958) 257, 282; art. 31(1), 1969 Vienna Convention on the Law of Treaties; McNair, *Treaties,* 540–1.

[163] See *Tolls on the Panama Canal* (1911–12): Hackworth, *Digest,* vi, 59 (views of the US); *German Interests in Polish Upper Silesia* (Merits), PCIJ (1926) ser. A, no. 7, 19. The Permanent Court's reference in the *German Settlers in Poland* case to the necessity for '. . . equality in fact . . . as well as ostensible legal equality in the sense of absence of discrimination in the words of the law': PCIJ (1923) ser. B, no. 6, 24, is founded on an equivalent principle. See further *Yearbook of the ILC* (1977), ii, 23–7.

[164] Judgment of the European Court of Human Rights, *Ireland* v. *United Kingdom* (Appl. 5301/71), ser. A, no. 25, paras. 236ff. Art. 1 of the European Convention provides: 'The High Contracting Parties shall secure to everyone within their jurisdiction the rights and freedoms defined . . .' Cf. *Abdulaziz, Cabales and Balkandali* v. *United Kingdom,* 28 May 1985, Ser. A, no. 94, where the European Court found, among others, a violation of art. 13 (requiring an effective remedy for everyone whose rights and freedoms are violated), in a case in which discrimination on the ground of sex was the result of norms incompatible in this respect with the European Convention. Since the Convention was not incorporated into UK law, there could be no 'effective remedy' (paras. 92, 93). See the reservations expressed by Judge Bernhardt on this point in a concurring opinion, and further below Ch. 8, s. 2.2.1.

achieved.[165] In practice, however, major problems of interpretation and appreciation arise in view of, amongst others, the relative imprecision of the terminology employed in standard-setting conventions; the variety of legal systems and practices of States; the role of discretion, first, in the State's initial choice of means, and secondly, in its privilege on occasion to require resort to such remedial measures as it may provide; and finally the possibility that the State may be entitled to avoid responsibility by providing an 'equivalent alternative'[166] to the required result, such as compensation for arbitrary detention. The question whether a State has fulfilled an obligation of result must be examined in the light of the initial means chosen for implementation, the remedies available in the event that an initially incompatible situation ensues, and the option, if permitted by the obligation, of substituting an equivalent alternative result in the event that the principal required result is rendered unattainable.

In the context of standard setting, local remedies are especially important;[167] their availability and effectiveness will often determine the question of fulfilment or breach of obligation, the 'generation' of international responsibility and the implementation of this responsibility.[168] Nevertheless, it is also clear that a treaty-based standard of treatment may be expressed as an obligation of *conduct*, in which case no requirement of exhaustion of local remedies would arise.[169] In

---

[165] Cf. ILC draft art. 21: '(1) There is a breach by a State of an international obligation requiring it to achieve, by means of its own choice, a specified result if, by the conduct adopted, the State does not achieve the result required of it by that obligation. (2) When the conduct of the State has created a situation not in conformity with the result required of it by an international obligation, but the obligation allows that this or an equivalent result may nevertheless be achieved by subsequent conduct of the State, there is a breach of the obligation only if the State also fails by its subsequent conduct to achieve the result required of it by that obligation.' *Yearbook of the ILC* (1977), ii, 18f.

[166] Ibid., 22, 28.

[167] The local remedies rule is firmly based in general international law, and also figures in human rights instruments; see, for example, art. 26, 1950 European Convention on Human Rights; art. 11(3), 14(7)(a), 1965 International Convention on the Elimination of All Forms of Racial Discrimination; art. 41(1)(c), 1966 Covenant on Civil and Political Rights, art. 5(2)(b), Optional Protocol thereto.

[168] *Yearbook of the ILC*, (1977), ii, 36. Cf. ILC draft art. 22: 'When the conduct of a State has created a situation not in conformity with the result required of it by an international obligation concerning the treatment to be accorded to aliens, whether natural or juridical persons, but the obligation allows that this or an equivalent result may nevertheless be achieved by subsequent conduct of the State, there is a breach of the obligation only if the aliens concerned have exhausted the effective local remedies available to them without obtaining the treatment called for by the obligation or, where that is not possible, an equivalent treatment'. The United States expressed reservations as to the 'possibility that in the further drafting of Article 22 a "substantive" approach to the calculation of damages as of the exhaustion of local remedies might result in the accrual of interest not from time of injury, but at the time of exhaustion'. 1977 *Digest of United States Practice in International Law* 762.

[169] *Yearbook of the ILC* (1977), ii, 30–50 at 48. Schachter, O., 73 *AJIL* 464 f. (1979) doubted whether proposed US reservations designed, according to the State Department, to harmonize the treaties with existing provisions of domestic law, but in fact aiming to avoid any need to modify the said law, can be regarded as compatible with the object and purpose of the Covenant, especially in the light of the obligations of conduct which he found in art. 2. He argued that the object of art. 2 is to require all parties to adopt measures wherever necessary to give effect to the Covenant; reservations intended to deprive art. 2 of all effect themselves challenge the general principle reflected in art. 27 of the Vienna Convention on the Law of Treaties.

the present context, the principle of *non-refoulement* of refugees, including non-rejection at the frontier, falls within this category of obligation.

The difficulties attaching to the general issue of incorporation are illustrated by two occasions on which the United Kingdom's performance in the light of its international obligations was called in question. In 1979, that country was examined by the Human Rights Committee with regard to its report on the implementation of the Covenant on Civil and Political Rights. The United Kingdom's representative disagreed with the view that States were obliged to adopt positive measures;[170] what mattered was the treatment that people received and the way in which the law worked in practice.[171] This position was maintained when incorporation and effective implementation of the 1951 Convention relating to the Status of Refugees were discussed in the House of Commons in May 1979,[172] continuing a debate begun the previous year in the House of Lords.[173] The Minister for State noted that nothing in the Convention required incorporation, and that it imposed no obligation and offered no guidance in the matter of procedures for the determination of refugee status.[174] While accepting that the Executive Committee's 1977 recommendations[175] might comprehend 'the basic requirements for the effective implementation of the Convention', he nevertheless felt that the United Kingdom's existing procedure was sufficient.

The arguments regarding legislative implementation and establishment of a procedure, while formally correct in the light of obligations actually assumed,

[170] One expert noted that the UK had no written constitution and that the Covenant was not part of its internal legal order; if there were no laws, he wondered how the Committee could determine the degree of compliance with the Covenant: Mr Movchan, expert from the Soviet Union: UN doc. CCPR/C/SR.147, paras. 8, 9; a more lively account appears in United Nations press releases HR/1792-4, 25-6 Apr. 1979. At the time, the Soviet Union figured among those States which, despite the apparently express requirement of art. V of the Genocide Convention, had not found it necessary to enact specific legislation: Ruhashyankiko, *Study of the Question of the Prevention and Punishment of the Crime of Genocide* (1978): UN doc. E/CN.4/Sub. 2/416, para. 501. Another expert believed that art. 2(2) required the adoption of specific measures and that it was not sufficient to state that existing laws were consonant with the Covenant: Mr Sadi, expert from Jordan: UN doc. CCPR/C/SR.147, para. 13.
[171] Mr Richard (UK): UN doc. CCPR/C/SR.147, para. 18 and SR.149, para. 18; also Mr Cairncross (UK): ibid., SR.147, para. 32.
[172] 967 HC Deb. cols. 1363-81 (25 May 1979).
[173] 392 HL Deb. cols. 799-819 (22 May 1978). The debate arose out of a UNHCR note to the British government proposing various reforms, in particular, that 'all those provisions of the 1951 Convention and the 1967 Protocol which are not provided for in the existing law', should be specifically incorporated; and that there should be established 'a formal procedure for the determination of refugee status by an independent body' in accordance with UNHCR Executive Committee recommendations: ibid., cols. 815-16 (Lord Wells-Pestell).
[174] 967 HC Deb. col. 1376 (Mr Raison). A similar argument was stated the previous year in the Executive Committee by the UK's representative, Mr Gould, who noted that 'the States Parties to the 1951 Convention and the 1967 Protocol were under a duty to comply with those instruments and it was entirely for them to decide whether the provisions of those texts should for that purpose be incorporated in their national law': UN doc. A/AC.96/SR.302, para. 17, commenting on UN doc. A/AC.96/555, para. 6; also UN doc. A/AC.96/553, paras. 517-18.
[175] Executive Committee Conclusion No. 8 (1977).

fail to go to the heart of the matter, which is effectiveness of implementation. That incompatibilities with the Convention had developed was impliedly admitted in the announcement of certain changes in practice.[176] United Kingdom law, like that of many countries, was of general application, making no special provision for refugees. It therefore needed to be supplemented by a judicious use of administrative discretion, both to avoid the application of the general law and to secure appropriate benefits. Under article 28 of the Convention, for example, refugees lawfully staying in the territory of contracting States are entitled to be issued with travel documents. If 'refugee status' is not recognized at law, and if no procedure exists whereby claims to refugee status can be determined, it may be difficult, if not impossible, for the contracting State effectively to implement its international obligations.[177]

In addition to assuming obligations with regard to the status and treatment of refugees, States ratifying the 1951 Convention and the 1967 Protocol necessarily undertake to implement those instruments in good faith. The choice of means in implementing most of the provisions is left to the States themselves; they may select legislative incorporation, administrative regulation, informal and *ad hoc* procedures, or a combination thereof. In no case will mere formal compliance itself suffice to discharge a State's responsibility; the test is whether, in the light of domestic law and practice, including the exercise of administrative discretion, the State has attained the international standard of reasonable efficacy and efficient implementation of the treaty provisions concerned.[178]

The effective implementation of the 1951 Convention must therefore first take into account the fact that States parties have undertaken particularly important obligations governing (a) the legal definition of the term 'refugee'; (b) the application of the Convention to refugees without discrimination; (c) the issue of travel documents to refugees; (d) the treatment of refugees entering illegally; (e) the expulsion of refugees; and (f) the *non-refoulement* of refugees. These topics all fall, somewhat loosely, within the field of immigration or aliens law; such law itself is most usually of general application, so that if special measures are not taken to single out the refugee, he or she is likely to be denied the rights and benefits

---

[176] 967 HC Deb. cols. 1379–80.

[177] See also art. 24(3), under which States agree to extend to refugees the benefits of treaties covering the maintenance of acquired rights and rights in the process of acquisition in regard to social security. Again, effective implementation would appear to be contingent on effective procedures for the determination of status. Compare Belgian law; 'lorsqu'un conflit existe entre un norme de droit interne et une norme de droit international qui a des effets directs dans l'ordre juridique interne, la règle établie par le traite doit prévaloir': Tribunal civil (Réf.)-Bruxelles. 8 oct. 1993. C/ Etat belge, *RDDE*, No. 75, sept.–oct. 1993, 454, 459.

[178] That the situation of refugees and asylum seekers in the UK continued to be unsatisfactory may be inferred from the enactment finally of the Asylum and Immigration Appeal Act 1993, and from a comparison of its provisions and the relevant immigration rules (HC No. 395, in force 1 Oct. 1994) with those prevailing formerly. See Stevens, D., 'Re-introduction of the United Kingdom Asylum Bill', 5 *IJRL* 91 (1993).

due under the Convention and Protocol.[179] Secondly, the Convention defines a status to which it attaches consequences, but says nothing about procedures for identifying those who are to benefit. While the choice of means may be left to States, some such procedure would seem essential for the effective implementation and fulfilment of Convention obligations. It should be available to deal with claims to refugee status, whether made in the context of applications for asylum either at the border or after admission, for a travel document, for a social security benefit, or in an appeal against expulsion.[180]

Specific *legislative* action in the above matters may well be sufficient to remove the refugee from the ambit of the general law; it might therefore be considered a necessary condition for effective implementation. The establishment of a procedure for the determination of refugee status, given the object and purpose of the instruments in question, may likewise be considered a further necessary condition. Whether in any given case such measures, either together or alone, are sufficient conditions for effective implementation remains to be judged in the light of the actual workings of the municipal system as a whole.

3. A note on nationality issues affecting Palestinians

3.1 THE 'NATIONALITY' OF PALESTINIANS

Palestine was a British mandate during the time of the League of Nations, up until 15 May 1948. Under the mandates system, the local inhabitants were not to be considered as nationals of the administering powers, although they might benefit from the exercise of diplomatic protection.[181] Palestinian citizenship was regulated by United Kingdom statutory instrument,[182] and included acquisition by birth, but a Palestinian citizen was not a British subject.[183] Palestinian citizenship, as a product of the mandatory's authority, terminated with the mandate and with the proclamation of the State of Israel, even though there is some authority in international law for the continuance of certain internal laws upon

---

[179] Similar considerations may apply to other human rights instruments that have an impact on State powers to expel or refuse admission to non-nationals, such as the 1984 Convention against Torture (art. 3), or the 1966 Covenant on Civil and Political Rights (art. 7). States are only now beginning to appreciate the necessity to ensure that such issues are accommodated in appropriate decision-making procedures.

[180] The State again benefits from choice of means, but the standard of effective implementation itself will be affected by the practice of other States and the recommendations of bodies such as the Executive Committee. So far as it elects to apply exclusionary principles premised on other States' responsibilities, the lawfulness of actions will be determined in light of other relevant principles; see above Ch. 2, 5.2. Cf. art. 6, 1954 Caracas Convention on Territorial Asylum (below, Annexe 2, No. 3) which declares that States are under *no* obligation to make any distinction in the laws, regulations, or administrative acts applicable to aliens, solely because they are political asylees or refugees.

[181] See League Council resolution, 22 Apr. 1923: *Official Journal*, 1923, 604. Administering powers did not acquire sovereignty over the territories in question; see per Judge McNair, *South West Africa Case*, ICJ *Rep.*, 1950, 128, 150.

[182] Palestinian Citizenship Order 1925, S.R. & O., 1925, No. 25.

[183] *R* v. *Ketter* [1940] 1 KB 787.

the cession or abandonment of territory.[184] Israel had no nationality legislation until 1952.

Nationality falls, prima facie, within the reserved domain of domestic jurisdiction; that is, international law recognizes that each State determines who are its citizens, and how such citizenship shall be obtained or transmitted.[185] International law is not indifferent to those claimed or disclaimed, but the amount of positive guidance is limited, and much depends upon the context. For international law purposes, States do not enjoy the freedom to denationalize their nationals in order to expel them as 'non-citizens';[186] however, if the effects of such denationalization are internal only, for example, the denial of civic rights, international law traditionally has had little to say on the matter.[187] There is likewise no obligation in international law to naturalize a resident non-citizen, even though such non-citizen may over time and for certain international law purposes acquire the effective nationality of the State of residence.[188]

The existence of a State implies a body of nationals, and a population within a relatively well-defined territory is an accepted criterion of statehood. In early decisions, however, Israeli courts held that with the termination of the Palestine mandate, former Palestine citizens had lost their citizenship without acquiring any other.[189] This view was rejected in one case only, where the fact of residence and the international law governing succession of States were invoked.[190] For the purposes of Israeli municipal law, however, the issue was resolved by the Supreme Court in *Hussein* v. *Governor of Acre Prison*, and by the 1952 Nationality Law.

In *Hussein's* case, the Court agreed that Palestinian citizenship had come to an end, and that former Palestine citizens had not become Israeli citizens.[191] The Nationality Law confirmed the repeal of the Palestine Citizenship Orders

[184] Cf. debates in the UK on the Palestine Act, cited in O'Connell, D. P., *State Succession in Municipal Law and International Law*, vol. 1, (1967), 128–9.

[185] *Nationality Decrees Case*, PCIJ, (1923), Ser. B, No. 4, pp. 23–4; Schwarzenberger, G., *International Law*, (3rd ed., 1957), vol. I, 354; Oppenheim, *International Law*, (8th ed., 1955), vol. I, 642–3; O'Connell, *International Law*, (2nd ed., 1970), 670; Weis, P., *Nationality and Statelessness in International Law*, (2nd ed., 1979), 239.

[186] Cf. O'Connell, *State Succession*, above n. 184, 498–9.

[187] Cf. *Kahane (Successor)* v. *Parisi and Austrian State*, 5 *Ann. Dig.* (1929–30), No. 131, in which the tribunal regarded Romanian Jews as Romanian nationals; even though Romania withheld citizenship, it did not consider them to be stateless persons. With developments in related human rights, international law is unlikely to remain silent today.

[188] Cf. *Nottebohm Case*, ICJ *Rep.*, 1955, 4.

[189] *Oseri* v. *Oseri* (1953) 8 PM 76; 17 ILR 111 (1950); this decision of the Tel Aviv District Court, ostensibly based on the fact of termination of Palestinian citizenship, may also have been inspired by a desire not to recognize Palestinian Arabs as citizens of Israel.

[190] See *A.B.* v. *M.B.* 17 ILR 110 (1950); Zeltner J. said: 'So long as no law has been enacted providing otherwise, my view is that every individual who, on the date of the establishment of the State of Israel, was resident in the territory which today constitutes the State of Israel, is also a national of Israel.'

[191] (1952) 6 PD 897, 901; 17 ILR 111 (1950). See also *Nakara* v. *Minister of the Interior* (1953) 7 PD 955; 20 ILR 49.

1925–42, retroactively to the day of the establishment of the State of Israel. It declared itself the exclusive law on citizenship, which was available by way of return,[192] residence, birth, and naturalization.[193] Former Palestinian citizens of Arab origin might be incorporated in the body of Israeli citizens, provided they met certain conditions: they must have been registered under the Register of Inhabitants Ordinance on 1 March 1952; have been inhabitants of Israel on the day of entry into force of the Nationality Law (14 July 1952); and have been in Israel, or an area which became Israel, from the day of establishment of the State to the day of entry into force of the law, or have entered legally during that period.[194] These strict requirements meant that the majority of those displaced by the conflict in 1948 were effectively denied Israeli citizenship. If international law raised a presumption of entitlement to local citizenship for residents at the moment of establishment of the State,[195] subsequent developments have made any such claims redundant.[196]

Palestinian refugees were admitted to neighbouring countries on what was expected to be a temporary basis; local citizenship, for the most part, was not available. In Lebanon, the majority of Palestinians are unable to obtain citizenship,[197] even though prima facie some appear to qualify under the law. In these circumstances, many Palestinians, not being recognized as a citizen or national of any State, were therefore to be considered stateless persons.

3.2 PALESTINIANS, STATELESSNESS AND PROTECTION

At the same time that Israel has denied citizenship to the majority of Palestinian Arabs, the Arab countries of refuge have, for the most part,[198] consistently rejected local integration and citizenship as a solution to a problem which, in their view, can only be resolved by repatriation and self-determination. With

---

[192] Under the Law of Return, 5710, 1950. [193] Nationality Law, 5712, 1952, s. 1.

[194] Section 3. There were some authorized returns for the purposes of family reunion.

[195] Cf. Goodwin-Gill, G. S., *International Law and the Movement of Persons between States*, (1978), 4–11. Succession of States commonly links citizenship to residence, with frequent recognition of the right of option; see examples cited ibid., 7, n. 4.

[196] Under s. 30(a) of the Prevention of Infiltration (Offences and Jurisdiction) Law 1954, the Minister of Defence is empowered to order the deportation of an infiltrator, defined by s. 1 as a person who has entered Israel knowingly and unlawfully, and who, at any time between 29 Nov. 1947 (the date of the UN decision to partition Palestine) and his entry was a national, resident or visitor in the Arab countries hostile to Israel, or a former Palestine citizen or resident who had left his ordinary place of residence in an area which became part of Israel. By contrast, the Jordanian Nationality Law of 4 Feb. 1954 (following a 1949 amendment of the 1928 Trans-Jordan Nationality Law) conferred citizenship on all inhabitants of the West Bank and on residents who had been Palestinian citizens before 15 May 1948, were ordinarily resident in Jordan, and not Jewish. See generally, *Laws concerning Nationality*, UN Leg. Ser., 1954, 1959; also US Department of State, *Country Reports on Human Rights Practices for 1987*, (1988), 1205, for the view that Jordanian citizens of Palestinian origin enjoy an 'unrestricted right to live, work, and own property.'

[197] US Department of State, *Country Reports on Human Rights Practices for 1987*, (1988), 1229. See also UN doc. A/AC.96/SR.485 (1993), para. 25 (Lebanon)—the responsibility for ensuring the return of Palestinians lay with the international community; Lebanese and Palestinians had categorically refused all forms of settlement in Lebanon.

[198] The exception is Jordan; see above, n. 196.

limited exceptions, Palestinian refugees have not been granted (and for the most part, have not sought) citizenship in the countries of refuge. From the international law perspective, they are therefore stateless persons,[199] notwithstanding the recognition accorded by some States to the entity 'Palestine', and notwithstanding the United Nations' recognition of the Palestine Liberation Organization as the legitimate representative of the Palestinian people.[200] For many Palestinian citizens by birth, such citizenship will have lapsed or terminated with the events of 1948; and likewise for many, no other citizenship will have been acquired in the interim.

Courts in the Federal Republic of Germany have frequently addressed the legal situation of Palestinians and ruled on their claims to asylum. The Constitution (*Grundgesetz* = Basic Law) of the Federal Republic recognizes an individual right of asylum in favour of the 'politically persecuted',[201] and the 1951 Convention is also incorporated into local law. The asylum provision and the Convention definition are not co-terminous, however, as jurisprudence confirms. In a 1974 decision, the Federal Administrative Court[202] ruled that, even without the article 1D exclusion clause, a Palestinian from Lebanon could not successfully found a claim to asylum on his flight from Israel in 1948. The applicant was stateless, and both the Constitution and the 1951 Convention provided protection only with respect to persecution feared in his land of former habitual residence.[203] In a 1980 case, the Administrative Court at Ansbach considered that a stateless Palestinian, who resided lawfully in Lebanon and who held a Lebanese refugee passport, could look in the first instance to the Lebanese authorities for protection against persecution by the Palestinian Liberation Organization. Asylum in the Federal Republic of Germany could only be

[199] A stateless person is defined as 'a person who is not considered as a national by any State under the operation of its law': art. 1, 1954 UN Convention relating to the Status of Stateless Persons: 360 *UNTS* 117. Cf. 1961 UN Convention on the Reduction of Statelessness: UN doc. A/CONF.9/15, Final Act, recommending that 'persons who are stateless de facto should as far as possible be treated as stateless de jure to enable them to acquire an effective nationality'. See also United Nations, *A Study of Statelessness*, (1949), 8–9 and generally.

[200] Pending further consolidation of the peace process, the status of Palestine as a State in the sense of international law (having a permanent population, a defined territory, government and the capacity to enter into relations with other States, including full membership of international organizations), remains undetermined; see art. 1, 1933 Montevideo Convention on Rights and Duties of States: 165 *LNTS* 19; 28 *AJIL* Supp., (1934), 75. For the present, there is thus no Palestinian passport, that entitles the holder to return to the State of Palestine, but only such travel documents as may be issued by, and allow return to, the holder's State of residence. For a long time, many States did not accept such documents; for example, under the *Immigration Regulations 1978*, any document purporting to be a Palestinian passport is not recognized as a valid travel document for the purpose of entering Canada. On the importance of 'returnability', see Goodwin-Gill, *Movement of Persons*, 44–6.

[201] 'Politisch Verfolgte geniessen Asylrecht': *Grundgesetz*, art. 16.2,2; now replaced by art. 16a.

[202] The *Bundesverwaltungsgericht* is the final court of appeal in administrative matters.

[203] BVerwG 8 Okt. 1974; *DOV* 1975, 286; BVerwG 12 Feb. 1985–9 C 45.84: 'Das Land der gewöhnlicher Aufenthalt ist für den Kläger (stl. Palestinenser) der Libanon.' = 'For the appellant, a stateless Palestinian, the State of usual residence is Lebanon.' (Author's translation)

claimed where protection in Lebanon was denied, or where it was impossible for the applicant to enjoy the minimum conditions of life.[204]

A number of German decisions, however, acknowledged the existence of a Palestinian 'quasi-State' in southern Lebanon, at least until the Israeli invasion of 1982,[205] when the factual and legal situation changed. From June 1982, the Lebanese government introduced a number of measures against Palestinian refugees; in particular, those who had participated in the fighting were required to leave Lebanon, and others overseas were refused renewal of their (Lebanese-issued) travel documents. The government stated that its objective was to reduce the number of Palestinians in the country to around 50,000.[206] In a 1985 decision, the German Federal Administrative Court held that these measures were not dictated by 'Convention' reasons (that is, by considerations of race, religion, nationality, membership of a particular social group or political opinion); they were in the nature of preventive or police measures, directed against stateless persons. In the view of the Court, residence in the Lebanon on the basis of various international agreements or undertakings could be terminated wherever the persons concerned violated national security or public order, for example, by participating in a civil war.

Under German law, these rulings entail non-eligibility for asylum under the Constitution; in practice, Palestinian refugees in the Federal Republic of Germany were 'tolerated', that is, their (international) status as 'refugees' was acknowledged, so far as they were allowed to remain, although without formal status.[207] From an international law perspective, however, the lawfulness of the severance of the link between Palestinians and the Lebanon is far from clear. Over time, resident non-nationals acquire vested rights, and for some purposes may even require to be treated like nationals. States of residence retain discretionary powers in the matter of expulsion and termination of residence, but these

[204] VG Ansbach 7 Aug. 1980—AN 13643-X/78(XV). The court also noted that Palestinians had no possibility in practice of living outside PLO-run camps, or of obtaining regular permission to work. Cf. VG Gelsenkirchen 11 Jan. 1983—14 K 10.729/82, in which the court considered, without regard to international law, that there was no duty on Lebanon to protect the stateless within its territory, even where their presence was tolerated, and that its duty of care was limited to nationals.

[205] See for example, BVerwG 2 Jan. 1980—1 B 476.79. The availability of an internal flight alternative has often been relied on as a reason for rejecting asylum applications; see also VG Stuttgart 1 Apr. 1981—A 13 K 491/80.

[206] Minority Rights Group, *The Palestinians*, (1984), 12; US Department of State, *Country Reports*, above n. 196, 1229. In 1989, the number registered with UNRWA was 288,180: United States Committee on Refugees, *World Refugee Survey—1988 in Review*, (1989), 33.

[207] On the other hand, a policy denying naturalization to the children of Palestinians born in the Federal Republic has been implemented by the Federal Minister of the Interior, on the basis that Palestinians are *not* stateless, but persons of uncertain nationality (*Staatsangehörigkeit ungeklärt*). In this manner an attempt is made to avoid the obligation incumbent on the Federal Republic of Germany in virtue of its ratification of the 1961 Convention on the Reduction of Statelessness, incorporated by *Ausführungsgesetz zu dem Abkommen vom 30. August 1961 zur Verminderung der Staatenlösigkeit und zu dem Übereinkommen vom 13. September 1973 zur Verringerung der Fälle von Staatenlösigkeit*, 29 Juni 1977, *BGBl.* I s. 1101.

must be exercised within the limits allowed by international law.[208] The rights of other States are also clearly involved in the cancellation or non-renewal of travel documents; in appropriate circumstances, third States which had admitted Palestinians in reliance on Lebanese-issued documents guaranteeing returnability, and on the strength of established practices of renewal, might have been entitled to claim Lebanon's continuing responsibility.[209] That claim will become less compelling over time, however, and may be extinguished by intervening residence or documentation by another State.

Statelessness is often a mixed question of law and fact. It is a matter of law in a negative sense, in that a stateless person is defined as a person who is not recognized as a citizen by any State under its law. It is also a factual issue, in that statelessness may result from historical events; and it may be perpetuated by reason of failure to acquire a new nationality. Evidence conclusively determinative of statelessness, like all evidence of negative conditions, will often be missing, however, and inferences as to the lack of protection may have to be drawn from all the circumstances, including any available documentation and historical context.

Palestinians who, for any reason, are not included in the peace settlement (that is, they do not or are not able to return to Palestinian territory, and/or to obtain protection from the Palestinian authorities), will likely come within the terms of article 1D of the Convention. If required to leave their countries of habitual residence in the future, then their situation not having been 'definitively settled in accordance with the relevant resolutions adopted by the General Assembly', they will be entitled to international protection as refugees or, in the alternative, as stateless persons.

---

[208] Goodwin-Gill, *Movement of Persons*, Chs. XI–XIII.   [209] Ibid., 44–50.

Chapter 7

PROTECTION, SOLUTIONS, PREVENTION AND CO-OPERATION

While the previous chapter considered the institutions and basic principles of international protection, the focus here is on particular problems and challenges.

1. General protection issues

1.1 DETENTION

That States have the competence to detain non-nationals pending removal or pending decisions on their entry is confirmed in judicial decisions and the practice of States.[1] From the international law perspective, therefore, the issue is not whether the power is recognized, but whether its exercise or duration are limited in the case of refugees and asylum seekers by operation of law or principle.

The 1951 Convention explicitly acknowledges that States retain the power to limit the freedom of movement of refugees, for example, in exceptional circumstances, in the interests of national security, or if necessary after illegal entry.[2] Article 31's non-penalization provision[3] is of limited application, and the 1951 Conference of Plenipotentiaries discussed the possibility of detention 'for a few days' to verify identity.[4] Article 31(2) seems to imply that thereafter States may only impose restrictions on movement which are 'necessary', for example, on security grounds or in the special circumstances of a mass influx, although restrictions are generally to be applied only until status is regularized or admission obtained into another country.

---

[1] See, for example, *Attorney-General for Canada* v. *Cain* [1906] AC 542; *Shaughnessy* v. *US ex rel. Mezei*, 345 US 206 (1953); art. 5, 1950 European Convention on Human Rights; Note, 'The indefinite detention of excluded aliens: statutory and constitutional justifications and limitations', 82 *Mich. L. Rev.* 61 (1983). Cf. the argument that the community's right of self-definition justifies a degree of exclusiveness and lesser responsibility towards the non-belonger: Martin, D., 'Due Process and the treatment of aliens', 44 *Uni. Pittsburgh L.R.* 165, (1983); Aleinikoff, T. A., 'Aliens, due process and "community ties": A response to Martin', ibid., 237.

[2] Art. 9 of the 1951 Convention permits a State to take 'provisional measures' against a particular person, 'pending a determination that that person is in fact a refugee and that the continuance of such measures is necessary in the interests of national security'. The Convention does not limit the period of detention, require review of its legality or its necessity, or otherwise confine the discretion of the State. For reservations to arts. 9 and 26, see below Ch. 8, s. 1.2. For background, see Goodwin-Gill, G. S., 'International Law and the detention of refugees and asylum-seekers', 20 *Int. Mig. Rev.* 193, 205–9 (1986); Goodwin-Gill, G. S., 'The detention of non-nationals, with particular reference to refugees and asylum-seekers', 9 *In Defense of the Alien*, (1986), 138, 141–6.

[3] See above, Ch. 4, s. 3.2.5.

[4] See generally UN docs. A/CONF.2/SR.13, 13–15; SR.14, 4, 10–11; SR.35, 11–13, 15–16, 19.

Apart from the few days for investigation, it may be argued that the drafters of the 1951 Convention intended that further detention would need to be justified as necessary under article 31(2), or exceptional under article 9.[5] This receives some support from article 32 on the expulsion of lawfully resident refugees, which limits the grounds and calls for certain procedural guarantees. In addition, a refugee under order of expulsion is to be allowed a reasonable period within which to seek legal entry into another country, although States do retain discretion to apply 'such internal measures as they may deem necessary'.[6] In short, a number of limitations on the detention of refugees can be inferred from the provisions of the 1951 Convention, and references to 'necessary' measures of detention imply an objective standard, subject to independent review.[7]

If the 1951 Convention and 1967 Protocol offer only limited protection against detention, human rights law goes further. Although State practice recognizes the power to detain in the immigration context, human rights treaties affirm that no one shall be subject to *arbitrary* arrest or detention.[8] The first line of protection thus requires that all detention must be in accordance with and authorized by law; the second, that detention should be reviewed as to its legality and necessity, according to the standard of what is reasonable and necessary in a democratic society.[9] Arbitrary embraces not only what is illegal, but also what is unjust.[10]

[5] On art. 9, see Ch. 8, s. 1.2.   [6] On art. 32, see·Ch. 8, s. 1.2.3.

[7] See Samuels, H., 'The Detention of Vietnamese Asylum Seekers in Hong Kong: *Re Pham Van Hgo and 110 Others*', 41 *ICLQ* 422 (1992), for an interesting summary of the detention of 111 Vietnamese whose ship was damaged, and who wanted repairs and then to sail on the Japan. Instead they were detained, successfully challenged the legality of their detention, were re-arrested, and eventually released, and determined to be refugees and allowed to remain pending resettlement.

[8] See, for example, art. 9, 1966 Covenant on Civil and Political Rights; art. 5, 1950 European Convention; art. 2, Protocol 4, European Convention; art. 7, 1969 American Convention; art. 6, 1981 African Charter on Human and Peoples' Rights; also art. 5, 1985 United Nations Declaration on the Human Rights of Individuals who are not Nationals of the Country in which They Live: UNGA res. 40/144, 13 Dec. 1985, Annex. In *Gisbert* v. *US Attorney General* 988 F.2d 1437 (5th Cir., 1993), however, the court held that customary international law prohibitions against prolonged arbitrary detention cannot supersede US statute, the Attorney General's actions and judicial decisions.

[9] Emergency powers and the inherent limitations to many human rights are nevertheless a problem for refugees and asylum seekers, given the generality and vagueness of the wording of exceptions (public emergency, life of the nation, national security, *ordre public*, necessary in a democratic society), but also by experience with State practice in the face of actual or perceived threats. See generally Higgins, R., 'Derogations under Human Rights Treaties', 48 *BYIL* 281 (1976–7). Judicial decisions like *Fernandez-Roque* v. *Smith* 567 F. Supp. 1115 (1981) are relatively rare. Here, the District Court for the Northern District of Georgia considered that the government's power to detain nonnationals was conditional on there being clear and convincing evidence that those affected were likely to abscond, or posed a risk to national security, or a significant and serious threat to persons or property. Reversing this decision, 734 F.2d 576 (1984), the Court of Appeals (11th Cir.) concluded that the applicants lacked a sufficient constitutional liberty interest, and did not address the international law arguments. Cf. *Barrera-Echavarria* v. *Rison* 21 F.3d 314 (9th Cir., 1994): 8 years imprisonment of an excluded alien who had arrived from Cuba with the Mariel boatlift because US government considered him a danger to society violated his Fifth Amendment rights because such extended detention was 'excessive in relation to its regulatory goal'.

[10] This interpretation was adopted in the work of the Commission on Human Rights on the right of everyone to be free from arbitrary arrest, detention and exile; see UN doc. E/CN.4/826/Rev.1,

The *conditions* of detention may also put in question a State's compliance with generally accepted standards of treatment, including the prohibition on cruel, inhuman or degrading treatment; the special protection due to the family and to children;[11] and the general recognition given to basic procedural rights and guarantees.[12]

The detention of refugees and asylum seekers was considered by the Executive Committee at its 37th session in 1986, where the debate in the Sub-Committee of the Whole on International Protection was long, often heated, and divided between those anxious to ensure that detention remained an exception and those who sought the widest powers in controlling movement and entry.[13] For the purposes of discussion, UNHCR had proposed that 'the word "detention" [be] employed to signify confinement in prison, closed camp or other restricted area, on the assumption that there is a qualitative difference between detention and other restrictions on freedom of movement'.[14]

Several States regretted that the UNHCR 'Note' did not deal with issues of practical concern, such as fraudulent or destroyed documentation, mass influx, detention as a deterrent to 'irregular movements', or during the process of adjudicating claims. Article 31 was considered to be of limited application, benefiting only those 'coming directly' from a country in which their life or freedom was threatened. Other States viewed detention as prima facie a violation of rights; detention for the purpose of deterrence, it was said, went beyond the spirit of the Convention, and entry in search of asylum should not be considered an unlawful act. As the Sub-Committee was unable to reach agreement in

paras 23–30. Also, Hassan, 'The word "arbitrary" as used in the Universal Declaration of Human Rights: "Illegal or Unjust"?' 10 *Harv. Int'l L.J.* 225 (1969); Lillich, R., 'Civil Rights', in Meron, T., ed., *Human Rights in International Law*, (1984) 15, 12lf.

[11] See Tribunal civil (Réf.)-Bruxelles, 25 nov. 1993, No. 56.865, *D.D. & D.N. c/ Etat belge, Min. de l'Interieur et Min. de la santé publique, de l'Environnment et de l'Intégration sociale*, in which the court found the detention of an asylum seeker and her new-born baby to be inhuman and degrading, contrary to arts. 3 and 8 of the European Convention on Human Rights: *RDDE*, No. 76, nov.–dec. 1993, 604. For a particularly strong indictment of detention and its effects on children, see McCallin, M., 'Living in Detention: A review of the psychological well-being of Vietnamese children in the Hong Kong detention centres', International Catholic Child Bureau, Geneva, (1992).

[12] Cf. *United States Diplomatic and Consular Staff in Tehran*, where the International Court of Justice observed that, 'Wrongfully to deprive human beings of their freedom and to subject them to physical constraint in conditions of hardship is in itself manifestly incompatible with the principles of the Charter of the United Nations, as well as with the fundamental principles enunciated in the Universal Declaration of Human Rights': ICJ *Rep.*, 1980, 42, para 91. See also, among a variety of standard-setting documents, the UN Standard Minimum Rules for the Treatment of Prisoners, the Code of Conduct of Law Enforcement Officials, and the Principles of Medical Ethics relevant to the Role of Health Personnel, particularly Physicians, in the Protection of Prisoners and Detainees against Torture and Other Cruel, Inhuman or Degrading Treatment or Punishment: Texts in United Nations, *Human Rights: A Compilation of International Instruments*: UN doc. ST/HR/1/Rev.2 (1983), 75, 83, 86.

[13] The following report is based not on formal records, but on a contemporaneous record by the author who attended all the sessions and conducted the country-by-country survey on which UNHCR's note on detention was partly based. See also Goodwin-Gill, above n. 2.

[14] UNHCR, *Note* on accession to international instruments and the detention of refugees and asylum seekers: UN doc. EC/SCP/44 (19 Aug. 1986), paras. 25–51, at 25.

its alloted time, a working group was established on the High Commissioner's initiative, and continued to meet throughout the remainder of the session.

During the working group meetings, the Netherlands representative, supported by the German delegate, reverted to the question of definition, apparently concerned at the uses which might be made of that proposed by UNHCR. The Austrian representative thought attempting a definition inappropriate, and that the report of Plenary might mention that some representatives thought the definition too wide, others too narrow. The Netherlands representative, indeed, suggested that a paragraph be added to the effect that States were free, in the exercise of their sovereignty, to define detention at will.[15] The United States representative objected, such a proposal being entirely unacceptable from the human rights perspective. The United Kingdom representative, referring to detention for the purpose of establishing the basis of an application, said that this meant determining whether an entertainable claim existed, whether the individual enjoyed protection elsewhere, or was making an abusive or repetitive claim; it was not meant to justify unlimited detention.

The Working Group finally reached consensus, its report and conclusions being presented to the Plenary Session of the Executive Committee and duly adopted.[16] Although not as progressive as some had hoped for,[17] and by no means as committed to detention as exception which had been UNHCR's goal, the Conclusions nevertheless accept the principle that 'detention should normally be avoided'. However, the Executive Committee expressly recognized that,

if necessary, detention may be resorted to only on grounds prescribed by law to verify identity; to determine the elements on which the claim to refugee status or asylum is based; to deal with cases where refugees or asylum seekers have destroyed their travel and/or identity documents or have used fraudulent documents in order to mislead the authorities of the State in which they intend to claim asylum; or to protect national security or public order.[18]

---

[15] The Netherlands representative also argued, though without support, that holding people at an airport or port of entry, both for the purposes of enquiry and pending a decision on an asylum application, did not amount to detention, in that the persons concerned remained free to leave the country. It was pointed out that this begged precisely the questions which remained to be answered, such as refugee status and/or a right to enter another country. Cf. Hoge Raad der Nederlanden. 9 dec. 1988. *Shokuh c/ Pays-Bas*, in which the court held further to art. 5 of the European Convention on Human Rights that an alien who is not allowed to remain but is nevertheless on Dutch territory may only be detained as provided by law, and that holding in the transit zone of an airport constitutes deprivation of liberty within the meaning of that article: *RDDE*, No. 52, jan.–fév. 1989, 16.

[16] *Report* of the 37th Session (1986): UN doc. A/AC.96/688, para. 128. Conscious of the criticism of conditions in reception centres during the 1980s, including by UNHCR in a controversial report, the German representative commented that his government understood the conclusions to be without prejudice to current practice. See Executive Committee Conclusion No. 44 (1986); for text, see Annexe 3 below.

[17] Cf. Takkenberg, L., 'Detention and other restrictions of the freedom of movement of refugees and asylum seekers: The European perspective', in Bhabha, J. & Coll, G., *Asylum Law and Practice in Europe and North America*, (1992), 178, 180–4.

[18] Executive Committee Conclusion No. 44 (1986), para. (b).

It also noted that 'fair and expeditious procedures' for determining refugee status are an important protection against prolonged detention; and that 'detention measures taken in respect of refugees and asylum seekers should be subject to judicial or administrative review'.

1.1.1 Detention and mass influx

In the case of a mass influx, the principles contained in article 31 remain applicable; State practice, however, reflects a general tendency to use closed or restricted camps as an interim solution, pending repatriation or third country resettlement.[19] One commentator in 1951 considered that article 26 on freedom of movement would not be violated in 'special situations where refugees have to be accommodated in special camps or in special areas even if this does not apply to aliens generally'.[20] Such measures are now the usual response in situations of large-scale influx, justified by reference to national security, community welfare, and even 'humane deterrence'. Both case by case determination of refugee status and case by case review of confinement may indeed be unrealistic, and there *may* also exist good reasons—racial, cultural, religious, economic—why alternatives to detention cannot be used in any particular context; but the conditional nature of these statements should not be overlooked.

The Executive Committee's 1981 conclusions on the protection of asylum seekers in situations of mass influx make basic provision for the conditions of detention.[21] Other international standards, as applicable to individuals as to large groups, include the prohibition on forced or compulsory labour. At the 1951 Conference the practice of labour contract and group settlement schemes was defended, under which refugees who were admitted were required to remain in a particular job for a particular time.[22] Today, however, objections would likely be based on a variety of treaty provisions.[23]

1.2 ACCESS

The question of *access* to protection and assistance has acquired critical dimensions over the last years, touching directly on issues of territorial sovereignty, control and the reserved domain of domestic jurisdiction. Denial of access has thus been the objective for many States anxious to avoid the requirement to abide by certain peremptory obligations, such as *non-refoulement*; refugees and asylum seekers are directly 'interdicted' while outside territorial jurisdiction, or their

[19] Just as there are a number of notable exceptions, including the use of settlements with a self-sufficiency component in Africa, Central America and Pakistan, and special temporary legal regimes for refugees from conflict, so also 'interim' settlements may endure for many years.

[20] Robinson, N., *The 1951 Convention relating to the Status of Refugees: A Commentary*, (1953), 133, n. 207.

[21] See above, Ch. 6, s. 2.1.　　　　　　　　　[22] UN doc. E/AC.32/SR.11, p. 6.

[23] See art. 2, 1930 ILO Convention (No. 29) concerning Forced Labour; art. 1, 1957 ILO Convention (No. 105) concerning the Abolition of Forced Labour. In 1984 the ILO Committee of Experts noted that German legislation allowed for asylum seekers to be required to perform 'socially useful work' if they wished to maintain welfare entitlements. It called on the government to bring law and practice into conformity with ILO Convention No. 29 on Forced Labour.

movements are increasingly controlled indirectly, through the application of restrictive visa policies and/or carrier sanctions. Those who arrive on the territory of the State may also be denied access to a procedure for the determination of asylum or refugee status, or to courts and tribunals generally for the protection of their rights, or to the sources of information that ought to be the essential foundation for informed decision-making. Even where refugees secure admission, they may also be denied access to relief or basic services, such as health care and education. Access has another dimension in situations of conflict, when internally displaced populations requiring humanitarian assistance become hostages to fortune, with international efforts to relieve their suffering linked to political or military advantages sought by one or other side.

The question of access to countries and therefore also of procedures for the determination of refugee status and the grant of asylum falls between competing responsibilities, only some of which are clearly regulated by rules of international law. For example, State agents who intercept refugees on the high seas and return them directly to a country in which they are persecuted violate the principle of *non-refoulement*. On the other hand, State agents who, by refusing a visa to individuals having a well-founded fear of persecution thereby prevent or obstruct their flight to safety do not breach the prohibition on *returning* refugees to persecution. The 'right to seek' asylum is certainly restricted, but State practice to date has not recognized directly correlative duties obliging States to adjust visa or immigration policies accordingly. On the contrary, States have repeatedly insisted on their right to apply visa and related controls, including sanctions against transportation companies which bring undocumented or insufficiently documented passengers to their ports and airports.

Visas are frequently used to 'control' movements, not just from countries which are the source of migration-related problems (such as movement in search of employment); but also from countries in conflict, where a substantial number of those leaving or seeking to leave likely have a well-founded fear of persecution or other valid reasons for flight. In some circumstances, such controls may indeed reflect a reasonable, non-abusive policy and programme of restriction, for example, where other protection opportunities exist, such as an 'internal flight alternative' or internationally guaranteed safety zone, where the quality of the protection is such as to warrant their acceptability. In other circumstances, no such alternatives may exist, and the possibility of abuse of rights arises.[24] State practice, however, provides little direct support for this line of argument alone, suggesting that it may best be advanced in conjunction with principles of solidarity and co-operation, and with due regard to causes.[25]

The reverse of denial of access to refuge is the refusal to allow international organizations, relief workers and non-governmental organizations to have access to refugees, asylum seekers, returnees, internally displaced persons, camps and

[24] See below, s. 3.5.4.   [25] See below, s. 4.

settlements. This may happen incidentally to internal conflicts, insecurity and the resultant disintegration of social institutions and law and order; or it may be done deliberately, as part of political or military strategy.[26] Without access to and by refugees, the displaced, and those affected by conflict, and without the monitoring and oversight inherent in the provision even of relief, rights are more likely to be violated and the objectives of protection and solutions less likely to be obtained.

Bringing its own refugee and displacement perspective to the issue, the UNHCR Executive Committee has also focused on the problem of access.[27] The 1994 Conclusion on Internally Displaced Persons, for example, calls on the governments concerned 'to ensure safe and timely humanitarian access to persons in need of protection and assistance, including the internally displaced and victims of armed conflict, as well as refugees within their territories'.[28] In two 1993 conclusions on the personal security of refugees, and on refugee protection and sexual violence, the Executive Committee urged States 'to take all measures necessary to prevent or remove threats to the personal security of refugees and asylum seekers in border areas and elsewhere, including by affording . . . prompt and unhindered access to them, . . . to provide effective physical protection . . . and to ensure safe access for humanitarian assistance and relief workers'.[29]

Not surprisingly, the Security Council has repeatedly stressed the importance it attaches to 'unhindered access by international humanitarian organizations to all those in need of assistance',[30] and to 'unimpeded access for humanitarian assistance to the civilian population in need'.[31] Together with State practice, a right of humanitarian access (to receive relief/to provide relief) is emerging.[32]

1.3 PERSONAL SECURITY AND RELATED MEASURES

Efforts to provide protection or bring humanitarian assistance to threatened populations in conflict-stricken areas have frequently exposed relief workers to

[26] Executive Committee Conclusion on the Refugee Situation in Africa (1992), paras. (a), (f): *Report* of the 43rd Session: UN doc. A/AC.96/804.

[27] In 1992, the Executive Committee also called upon the High Commissioner, among other things, 'to develop, whenever required, modalities to gain access to and deliver protection and assistance to the affected populations in conformity with the mandate of UNHCR': *Report* of the 43rd Session: UN doc. A/AC.96/804. Executive Committee Conclusion No. 22 (1981) also deals with access by UNHCR in peremptory terms; see above, Ch. 5, s. 5.2.

[28] Executive Committee Conclusion No. 75 (1994). Its conclusion the same year on the refugee situation in Africa noted that access to and delivery of protection and humanitarian assistance continued to be impeded: *Report* of the 45th Session: UN doc. A/AC.96/839.

[29] Executive Committee Conclusions No. 72 (1993), para. (b); No. 73 (1993), para. (b).

[30] SC res. 706, 15 Aug. 1991, on Iraq.

[31] SC res. 834, 1 Jun. 1993, on Angola; SC res. 822, 20 Apr. 1993, on the Nagorno-Karabakh conflict; SC res. 820, 17 Apr. 1993, on Bosnia-Herzegovina; SC res. 916, 5 May 1994, on Mozambique; SC res. 931, 29 Jun. 1994, on Aden—urging all concerned to provide 'humanitarian access and facilitate the distribution of relief supplies to those in need wherever they may be located'.

[32] Bettati, M., 'The right of humanitarian intervention or the right of free access to victims?' ICJ *Review*, No. 49, 1 (Dec. 1992); Sandoz, Y., '"Droit" or "devoir" d'ingérence and the right to assistance: the issues involved', ibid., 12; Kouchner, B., *Le malheur des autres*, (1992).

personal danger, and many have been killed or wounded in the course of their duties. Refugees and the internally displaced have also been the object of attacks, used as political pawns by opposing sides, as shields for military operations or as sources of supplies and combatants. Recent practice suggests the emergence of a principle of *humanitarian access*, on the one hand, and a rule protecting relief workers, on the other. International law also prohibits military and armed attacks on refugee camps and settlements, at least so far as they maintain their civilian and humanitarian character.

1.3.1 Refugees and asylum seekers

Neither UNHCR nor any other international agency has any secure place of asylum and no formal way to protect the personal security of refugees and asylum seekers, which in principle remains largely the responsibility of governments. Refugees and asylum seekers are often exposed to danger during flight, however, particularly in areas of military activity, and on occasion, UNHCR protection officers have been there to guide new arrivals to places of safety.[33] UNHCR has also successfully called for the establishment of safe havens, particularly for refugees awaiting enforced departure from their country of asylum.[34] In 1980, the Executive Committee called on UNHCR and others to intensify efforts to protect refugees in danger from pirate attacks at sea;[35] by then many had been killed or assaulted, and many women and girls raped or abducted. Bilateral and multilateral actions involving UNHCR, States and NGOs eventually produced an anti-piracy programme and a decline in the percentage of boats attacked.[36] Programmes for victims of violence (including rape, torture and other forms of persecution) are thus a natural and practical extension of the protection function, oriented also towards re-integration of the individual and thereby towards a durable solution.[37]

In addition, refugee camps, settlements and centres need to be places of safety, located in light of the security of the refugees, while remaining accessible. This means taking account of the possibility of armed attacks, whether from within or without State territory.[38] Internal policing may also be required, as well as external protection against harassment or forced recruitment. The UNHCR

[33] UNHCR's border presence in Thailand and Honduras in the 1980s, in particular, ensured that many found refuge.
[34] With respect to foreign refugees in Chile after the 1973, see UN doc. A/AC.96/508, (1974), 5; *Report* to the General Assembly, 29 GAOR, Supp. 12A, 28: UN doc. A/9612/Add.1 (1974); also UNHCR, *Handbook for Emergencies*, Pt. II, (1983), paras. 13.2, 13.3.8.
[35] Executive Committee Conclusion No. 20 (1981).
[36] 'Note on International Protection': UN doc. A/AC.96/660, 23 Jul. 1985, para. 23; see also above, Ch. 6, s. 2.1.
[37] See UNHCR, 'Note on Refugee Women and International Protection': UN doc. EC/SCP/39, 8 Jul. 1985; *Report* of the Sub-Committee: UN doc. A/AC.96/671, paras. 8–19; *Report* of the Executive Committee, 37th Session: UN doc. A/AC.96/673, para. 115(4), (1985).
[38] See Mtango, E-E., 'Military and Armed Attacks on Refugee Camps', in Loescher, G. and Monahan, L., eds., *Refugees and International Relations*, (1989), 87.

Executive Committee first looked at the question of military attacks in 1982, following a number of raids in southern Africa. The debate turned out to be protracted, and controversial, with varying emphasis placed upon the necessity to maintain the civilian and humanitarian character of such camps; conclusions on the subject were not agreed until five years later.[39]

1.3.2 Women refugees

During refugee movements, women and girls risk further violations of their human rights, and have repeatedly been targeted as victims of rape and abduction.[40] Their passage to safety may have to be bought at the price of sexual favours, and even within the relative security of a refugee camp or settlement and bearing additional responsibilities as heads of households, they face discrimination in food distribution, access to health, welfare and education services—doubly disadvantaged as refugees and as women. These facts were common knowledge for years, but apart from the particular attention given to piracy attacks in the South China Sea, the protection of women refugees did not appear on the agenda of the UNHCR Executive Committee until 1985. At that time, the primary question was not so much the physical security or systemic discrimination which women face in flight and in refuge, but whether women might constitute a particular social group, membership of which could give rise in appropriate circumstances to a well-founded fear of persecution.[41]

From 1988 onwards, however, women have featured regularly, with particular reference to questions of safety, discrimination, and sexual exploitation.[42] In

[39] For background, see UNHCR, 'Military Attacks on Refugee Camps and Settlements in Southern Africa and Elsewhere': UN doc. EC/SCP/23 (Oct. 1982); *Report* of the Sub-Committee: UN doc. A/AC.96/613 (1982), paras. 12–21; *Report* of the 33rd Session (1982): UN doc. A/AC.96/614, paras. 42(i), 63, 70(3); *Report* of the Sub-Committee: UN doc. A/AC.96/629 (1983), paras. 13–16; *Report* of the 34th Session (1983): UN doc. A/AC.96/631, paras. 93–5, 97(4); *Report* by Ambassador Felix Schnyder, 'Military Attacks on Refugee Camps and Settlements in Southern Africa and Elsewhere': UN doc. EC/SCP/26 (Mar. 1983); also UN doc. EC/SCP/31 (Aug. 1983); UN doc. EC/SCP/27 (June 1983); 'Draft Principles on Military Attacks': UN doc. EC/SCP/32 (Sept. 1983); UN doc. EC/SCP/34 and Add.1 (July 1984); *Report* of the Sub-Committee: UN doc. A/AC.96/649 (1984) and Add.1, paras. 6–13; UN doc. EC/SCP/38; *Report* of the Sub-Committee: UN doc. A/AC.96/671 (9 Oct. 1985), paras. 20–6; *Report* of the 37th Session (1986): UN doc. A/AC.96/688 and Corr.1, para. 129; 'Note' on Military and Armed Attacks on Refugee Camps and Settlements: UN doc. EC/SCP/47, 10 Aug. 1987; *Report* of the Sub-Committee: UN doc. A/AC.96/700, 5 Oct. 1987, paras. 21–30; *Report* of the 38th Session: UN doc. A/AC.96/702, 22 Oct. 1987, para. 206: Executive Committee Conclusion No. 48 (1987) on Military and Armed Attacks on Refugee Camps and Settlements; for text, see Annexe 3, below. In its 1988 'Note' on International Protection: UN doc. A/AC.96/713, paras. 24–36, UNHCR noted that the effect of the 1987 Conclusion was yet to be to be felt, provided statistics of attacks in one African country (para. 28), and suggested various remediable measures, such as relocation (31–4).

[40] See above on piracy, Ch. 6, s. 2.1.

[41] See 'Refugee Women and International Protection': UN doc. EC/SCP/39 (1985); *Report* of the Sub-Committee: UN doc. A/AC.96/671 (9 Oct. 1985), paras. 8–19; Executive Committee Conclusion No. 39 (1985). On gender as a basis for persecution and the social group question, see further below, Ch. 9, s. 3.2.4.

[42] See UNHCR, *Note on International Protection:* UN doc. A/AC.96/713, (15 Aug. 1988), para. 36; *Note on International Protection:* UN doc. A/AC.96/728 (2 Aug. 1989), paras. 30–6; Also, Johnsson,

1990, under pressure from a number of governments, UNHCR first raised the possibility of developing a *policy* on refugee women,[43] while also looking at their specific needs in the refugee determination context, and in that of physical safety.[44] With respect to the latter, UNHCR noted that special measures were needed in camps and settlements in order to protect women from abuse, especially women heads of household and single women.[45] Action was also required to ensure the provision of food, water and relief supplies, to meet health and reproductive health needs, to provide education and to promote skills training and economic activities. Women also face problems in making their voices heard on important decisions, such as voluntary repatriation.[46]

Guidelines on the protection of refugee women were drafted in 1991 for the use of UNHCR personnel,[47] but the following year the United States representative remarked in the Executive Committee that protection of women and children was still not of sufficient concern to many UNHCR field offices.[48] The following year produced a comprehensive note on certain aspects of sexual violence against women,[49] which in turn led to an equally wide-ranging conclusion.[50] Also in 1993, the UN General Assembly adopted the Declaration on the Elimination of Violence against Women,[51] recognizing that this is an issue of international concern and that all States have an obligation to work towards its

A. B., 'The International Protection of Women Refugees', 1 *IJRL* 221 (1989); Kelly, N., 'Report on the International Consultation on Refugee Women, held in Geneva, 15–19 November 1988', 1 *IJRL* 233 (1989).

[43] *UNHCR Policy on Refugee Women:* UN doc. A/AC.96/754 (20 Aug. 1990).

[44] 'Note on Refugee Women and International Protection': UN doc. EC/SCP/59 (28 Aug. 1990).

[45] Such measures should include not only counselling and assistance to victims of sexual violence and prosecution and punishment of offenders, but also basic preventive steps, such as adequate lighting in camps, or planting thorn bushes around women's areas.

[46] Ibid., paras. 29–56; *Report* of the Sub-Committee: UN doc. A/AC.96/758 (2 Oct. 1990); Executive Committee Conclusion No. 64 (1990).

[47] See 'Information Note on UNHCR's Guidelines on the Protection of Refugee Women': UN doc. EC/SCP/67 (22 July 1991), Annexe; 'Progress Report on Implementation of the UNHCR Guidelines on the Protection of Refugee Women': UN doc. EC/SCP/74 (22 July 1992); 'Progress Report on Implementation of the UNHCR Policy on Refugee Women': UN doc. EC/SC.2/55 (26 Aug. 1992); *Report* of the Sub-Committee: UN doc. A/AC.96/802 (6 Oct. 1992), paras. 35–46.

[48] UN doc. A/AC.96/SR.472 (1992), para. 71 (USA): 'The number of women who were still victims of rape was the best example of the failure of traditional protection measures.'

[49] 'Note on Certain Aspects of Sexual Violence against Women': UN doc. A/AC.96/822 (12 Oct. 1993). Originally issued as a 'conference room paper', it was re-issued as a session document at the express request of the Executive Committee. *Report* of the 44th Session: UN doc. A/AC.96/821, para. 21(m).

[50] Executive Committee Conclusion No. 73 (1993) on Refugee Protection and Sexual Violence; for text, see below, Annexe 3. Guidelines on preventing and responding to sexual violence have also been drafted: 'Report of the Working Group on Refugee Women and Refugee Children': UN doc. EC/SCP/85 (5 July 1994), para. 42. As part of overall policy, it was also proposed that UNHCR sign 'gender clauses' with implementing partners, such as NGOs, requiring them to provide equal and appropriate benefits to refugee women, and to employ female staff members in relevant functions: ibid., para. 56. Extracts from the guidelines were published in 7 *IJRL* (1995).

[51] UNGA res. 48/104, 20 Dec. 1993; Charlesworth, H., 'The Declaration on the Elimination of All Forms of Violence against Women', *ASIL Insight*, No. 3, (1994).

eradication. It interprets such violence widely in article 1, as 'any act of gender-based violence that results in, or is likely to result in, physical, sexual or psychological harm or suffering to women, including threats of such acts, coercion or arbitrary deprivation of liberty, whether occurring in public or private life'. Moreover, such violence is seen not so much in terms of individual behaviour, as a 'manifestation of historically unequal power relationships between men and women', which may occur in the family, in the general community, or be perpetrated or condoned by the State. It recognizes that some groups, such as refugee women, women belonging to minority groups, indigenous women, and women in situations of armed conflict, are especially vulnerable.

In an environment in which implementation depends so substantially on traditional power structures, male and society attitudes, it remains to be seen how effective this Declaration and UNHCR's Guidelines will be in contributing to the prevention or mitigation of sexual violence and the promotion of equity among refugees.

1.3.3 Child refugees

The need for special care and protection for *all* children was first recognized internationally in the 1924 League of Nations declaration on the rights of the child.[52] Though followed by a series of similar and related declarations,[53] another sixty-five years were to pass before the international community acknowledged both the very special status of children, and the value of States entering into a treaty on their behalf. The 1989 UN Convention on the Rights of the Child, now ratified by more that 180 States, is a critical milestone in legal protection generally. In fact, however, neither the 1951 Convention nor the Convention on the Rights of the Child, *so far as they address the situation of children as refugees*, provide an entirely satisfactory legal basis. The 1951 Convention does little more than recommend measures to ensure family unity and protection, and provide for access at least to primary education. Article 22 of the Convention on the Rights of the Child (CRC) endorses the entitlement of refugee children to 'appropriate protection and humanitarian assistance', but essentially by cross-referencing the body of the Convention and other international instruments, while emphasizing co-operation in tracing and family reunion. On the other hand, and unlike many other human rights treaties, the CRC has no general derogation clause for times of emergency. Consequently, the CRC may ensure that in some circumstances children are better protected than adults.[54] States

---

[52] Generally, see Ressler, E., Boothby, N. and Steinbock, D., *Unaccompanied Children: Care and Protection in Wars, Natural Disasters and Refugee Movements,* (1988).

[53] See for example the 1959 UN Declaration on the Rights of the Child and the 1974 UN Declaration on the Protection of Women and Children in Emergencies and Armed Conflicts.

[54] See Cohn, I., 'The Convention on the Rights of the Child: What it Means for Children in War,' 3 *IJRL* 291 (1991); under the CRC, there is thus no possibility to derogate from arts. 37 or 40 (torture, arbitrary detention, administration of justice guarantees); McCallin, M., 'The Convention on the Rights of the Child: An Instrument to Address the Psychosocial Needs of Refugee

parties to the CRC undertake to 'respect and ensure the rights' proclaimed to 'each child within their jurisdiction'. A child who takes refuge in the territory of a State party benefits as much from its provisions as child nationals of that country.

The idea of the child as someone entitled to *special protection* derives in part from the specific context of the 1949 Geneva Conventions and international humanitarian law—the laws of war. States are obliged, for example, to allow the free passage of assistance intended for children under 15 and expectant mothers, or required to facilitate the good functioning of institutions for the care of children in occupied territory.[55] The 1977 Additional Protocols go further, expressly confirming the special protection due to children. Article 77 of *Additional Protocol I*,[56] declares in its opening paragraph that

Children shall be the object of special respect and shall be protected against any form of indecent assault. The Parties to the conflict shall provide them with the care and aid they require, whether because of their age or for any other reason.

Both the Geneva Conventions and the Additional Protocols repeatedly link the protection of the child to the maintenance of *family life*.[57] Even in cases of internment, families should be kept together, and every effort made to promote the reunion of families separated by reason of armed conflict. The general intent is to preserve family life and, by inference, the natural process of child development. Similar objectives are clear in the human rights context, where States have recognized that the family should receive 'protection by society and the State'; and that 'special measures of protection and assistance should be taken on behalf of all children and young persons.'[58] Together with the principle of the best interests of the child as a primary consideration,[59] these principles put in question any solution for child refugees that might either 'officially' remove the child from the actual or potential family environment, or have the effect of leaving the child without care and support, for example, on return to the country of origin when family have not been found and interim arrangements in the country of refuge are no longer viable.

UNHCR brought the situation of refugee children before the Executive Committee in 1987, stating its intention to include within its protection and Children', 2 *IJRL Special Issue—September 1990* 82; Cohen, C. P., 'The Rights of the Child: Implications for Change in the Care and Protection of Refugee Children' 3 *IJRL* 675 (1991).

[55] A complete account of the provisions intended to benefit children during armed conflict is beyond the scope of the present analysis. Some twenty-five articles in the Geneva Conventions and the Additional Protocols deal with the special protection of children.

[56] See also art. 4, *Additional Protocol II*, confirming the obligation to provide children with the requisite care and aid, and referring expressly to education, family reunion, limitations on recruitment, and temporary evacuation.

[57] See Singer, S., 'The protection of children during armed conflict situations', *International Review of the Red Cross*, May–June 1986, 133.

[58] Art. 23(1), 1966 Covenant on Civil and Political Rights; and art. 10(3), 1966 Covenant on Economic, Social and Cultural Rights, respectively.

[59] CRC art. 3(1); see also art. 4, 1990 African Charter on the Rights and Welfare of the Child.

assistance activities, 'refugees, asylum seekers and displaced persons of concern to UNHCR, up to the age of 18, unless under applicable national law, the age of majority is less'.[60] In a comprehensive conclusion adopted the same year, the Executive Committee condemned the violence often facing refugee children, reiterated the 'widely-recognized principle that children must be among the first to receive protection and assistance', and recognized that the situation of refugee children 'often gives rise to special protection and assistance problems as well as to problems in the area of durable solutions'.[61] In 1988, UNHCR issued the first edition of its *Guidelines on Refugee Children*, confirming its policy not only to intervene with governments to ensure that they defend the safety and liberty of refugee children, but also 'to assume direct responsibility in many situations for protecting the safety and liberty of refugee children.' Revised in 1994, these *Guidelines* recognize the centrality of the CRC as 'a normative frame of reference' for UNHCR's action, laying down legally required standards and legally established goals.[62] The sections on particularly vulnerable children and solutions reflect that content.[63]

The *Guidelines* emphasize that all work with children must be founded on detail and verification, and that action should begin as soon as possible to trace relatives and to promote family reunion.[64] Children can become separated for many reasons, including abduction, where they are sent out of the country of origin by parents who remain behind, or they become separated when parents return home. Military recruitment of minors,[65] detention or internment of parents, and the actions of aid workers have also led to children being separated from their families.[66]

Where tracing is successful, family reunion can still be delayed, for example, because of immigration restrictions. Several States have made reservations to the

[60] UNHCR, 'Note on Refugee Children': UN doc. E/SCP/46, 9 July 1987, para. 8.

[61] Executive Committee Conclusion No. 47; see also Executive Committee Conclusion No. 59. The Executive Committee has adopted conclusions on refugee children every year since 1991, although none as comprehensive as that adopted in 1987. See also 'UNHCR Policy on Refugee Children': UN doc. EC/SCP/82 (6 Aug. 1993); 'Programming for the Benefit of Refugee Children': UN doc. EC/SC.2/CRP.15 (25 Aug. 1993); *Report* of the Working Group on Refugee Women and Refugee Children: UN doc. EC/SCP/85 (5 July 1994).

[62] UNHCR, *Refugee Children: Guidelines on Protection and Care*, Geneva, (1994), 19. Also, 'UNHCR Policy on Refugee Children': UN doc. EC/SCP/82 (6 Aug. 1993)—identifying the primary goals as ensuring the protection and healthy development of refugee children and durable solutions appropriate to immediate and long-term developmental needs (para. 25); 'Report of the Working Group on Refugee Women and Refugee Children': UN doc. EC/SCP/85 (5 July 1994).

[63] UNHCR, *Guidelines*, 121–49.

[64] Ibid., 128–9. Close cross-border co-operation is also essential, but may be difficult to arrange in highly politicized or conflict situations. Computerized tracing systems are beginning to be developed, and other agencies, such as the International Committee of the Red Cross (ICRC), have considerable long-term experience in tracing family members separated as a result of conflict; co-ordination with such agencies is essential in order to enhance the prospects of finding separated family members.

[65] See Cohn, I. and Goodwin-Gill, G. S., *Child Soldiers*, (1994), 77–8, 152–3.

[66] UNHCR, *Guidelines*, 122.

CRC provisions on family reunion, despite the importance otherwise given to the family as the basic unit of society. Restrictions on family reunion possibilities also result from the conditions attached to certain types of status, such as temporary protection which, although they facilitate the grant of refuge, may be so circumscribed as to frustrate fundamental rights relating to the family, and seriously undermine the best interests of the child.[67]

The situation of refugee children differs substantially from that of children still living in their country of birth. They may be orphaned, with relatives in different countries, and they may be living with an unrelated family which would like to adopt them.[68] Reaching the most appropriate solution, however, becomes more difficult when there is no national decision-making body competent to make or confirm arrangements for a child's future. For example, UNHCR recognizes that while family reunion is the primary aim for unaccompanied refugee children, adoption can be considered, where reunion either would not be in the best interests of the child, or is not likely to be realized within a reasonable time, normally at least two years.[69]

Although UNHCR considers that the authorities of the country of asylum have the necessary legal responsibility to take adoption decisions, in practice such States do not always accept that refugee children on their territory are 'habitually resident' within the meaning of the Hague Convention in respect of Intercountry Adoption.[70] The situation is further complicated by the fact that in a 'normal' inter-country adoption, the State of origin also bears a substantial responsibility to decide whether the child should benefit.[71]

These jurisdictional and practical concerns in the area of adoption seems equally valid with respect to international child abduction. The 1980 Hague

[67] Recognizing this basic premise, the UNHCR/UNICEF guidelines on evacuation of children from conflict areas emphasize the first priority is to enable families to meet the needs of children in their care; and the second, if evacuation is considered necessary, 'that children be evacuated as part of a family unit, children being kept with their primary care givers': Ressler, E. M., *Evacuation of Children from Conflict Areas: Considerations and Guidelines*, UNHCR/UNICEF, Geneva, (1992), 23. Where evacuation without parents occurs, records must be kept and the operation closely monitored with a view to bringing about family reunion as soon as possible; see UNHCR/UNICEF Joint Statements on the evacuation of children from former Yugoslavia; reprinted ibid., 25–32.

[68] Ibid., 22.

[69] UNHCR, *Guidelines*, 130–1. Adoption is also not to be carried out if it against the expressed wishes of the child or the parent; or if 'voluntary repatriation in conditions of safety and dignity appears feasible in the near future and options in the child's country of origin would provide better for the psychological and cultural needs of the child than adoption in the country of asylum or a third country': ibid., 131. See also McLeod, M., 'Legal Protection of Refugee Children separated from their Parents: Selected Issues', 27 *Int. Mig.* 295 (1989).

[70] Cf. *Convention on the Civil Aspects of International Child Abduction*, Explanatory Report by Elisa Pérez-Vera, (1980), paras. 66–7.

[71] See, for example, the extensive scope of art. 4, 1993 Convention on Protection of Children and Co-operation in respect of Intercountry Adoption; also, UNGA res. 41/85, 3 Dec. 1986. Declaration on Social and Legal Principles relating to the Protection and Welfare of Children, with Special Reference to Foster Placement and Adoption Nationally and Internationally.

Convention[72] is again premised on the relatively 'normal' situation of interference by one party with another's custody rights. It aims 'to protect children internationally from the harmful effects of their wrongful removal or retention and to establish procedures to ensure their prompt return to the State of their habitual residence.' Children *are* abducted in the course of refugee movements; some are taken forcibly into a country of asylum, others are abducted from refugee camps and settlements, for example, to work or take part in military operations, and still others are targeted for 'illegal' adoption. Although some cases of abduction will involve removal in the sense of the 1980 Hague Convention, the greatest need is for comparable procedures to protect children against other, more common abductions.

The absence of rules, the lack of national and international bodies with jurisdictional competence and authority to act prejudices refugee children at both ends of the spectrum. On the one hand, they commonly fall outside the protective umbrella of the procedures and institutions established by the State under the relevant conventions; on the other hand, they can be denied timely access to the one durable solution that may be appropriate in their case, adoption, solely by reason of the inability or unwillingness of national authorities to act on their behalf.

In October 1994, the Special Commission on the Implementation of the 1993 Convention on adoption co-operation adopted a recommendation which goes some way towards meeting needs and filling gaps. Referring to the situations of refugee children and children who are internationally displaced as a result of disturbances in their countries, the Special Commission proposed a number of principles to be considered in applying the Convention.[73] First, States should not discriminate against refugee and displaced children in determining whether they are habitually resident. Moreover, the 'State of origin' should be considered to be 'the State where the child is residing after being displaced.'[74] The competent authorities in any such State should take particular care in the case of proposed inter-country adoptions, to ensure that 'all reasonable measures' have been taken to trace family and bring about reunion; that repatriation for reunion purposes is not feasible or desirable, either because the child cannot receive appropriate care, or benefit from 'satisfactory protection';[75] to obtain the necessary consents and, 'so far as is possible under the circumstances', to ensure that all relevant information regarding the child has been collected.[76] In this regard, the

---

[72] Convention on the Civil Aspects of International Child Abduction, adopted by the Fourteenth Session, 25 Oct. 1980.

[73] Hague Conference on Private International Law, Special Commission on the Implementation of the Convention of 29 May 1993, 17–21 Oct. 1994, Work. Doc. No. 39 (21 Oct. 1994).

[74] Ibid., para. 1.

[75] With respect to tracing and repatriation, co-operation with other national and international bodies, particularly UNHCR, is recommended. Para. 4 further proposes that 'the States shall facilitate the fulfilment, in respect to children referred to in this Recommendation, of the protection mandate of the United Nations High Commissioner for Refugees'.

[76] Ibid., para. 2.

authorities must also take particular care 'not to harm the well-being of persons still within the child's country'.[77]

If implemented in practice, these recommendations may remedy some of the problems. Nonetheless, the variety of issues and difficulties standing between refugee and internationally displaced children and a solution to their problems strongly suggests that a supplementary legal instrument may be called for, in order to protect against abduction and unlawful adoption. Two related objectives may help delineate the nature of the solution and the agency for its implementation: first, such agency should be able to initiate and facilitate communication and assistance between the refugee child's country of origin and the country of asylum or potential 'receiving State', as appropriate, with a view to achieving a solution that is in the best interests of the child; and secondly, if no such links can be established, for any reason, it should be the international substitute for the Central Authority, if any, 'normally' competent for the child, and assume the role and responsibilities of such Authority as set out in the relevant conventions, adjusted to the particular situation of displacement. Whether that agency should be UNHCR, which already enjoys competence to provide international protection to refugees, and is recognized as entitled to act on their behalf in dealings with governments, is another matter. In the circumstances, an agency having child welfare and child rights experience may be better placed to assume these particular responsibilities.

1.3.4 Relief workers

In recent emergencies, relief workers have been the object of kidnappings, threats, aerial bombardment and fighting between different factions.[78] The Security Council has repeatedly demanded that all parties take the necessary steps to ensure the safety of UN personnel, among others, in former Yugoslavia;[79] Cambodia;[80] Somalia;[81] and Mozambique.[82]

In 1992, the UN General Assembly also expressed its concern, and the following year urged support for initiatives 'concerning the safety of United Nations and associated personnel, in particular the consideration of new measures to enhance (their) safety'.[83] The resolutions in question refer specifically to

---

[77] Ibid., para. 3.

[78] See UN Commission on Human Rights, *Report on the Situation of Human Rights in the Sudan:* UN doc. E/CN.4/1994/48, paras. 34, 116.

[79] On behalf of UNPROFOR and international humanitarian agencies, see SC resolutions 758, 8 June 1992, para. 7; 761, 29 June 1992, para. 8; 770, 13 Aug. 1992, para. 6—'UN and other personnel engaged in the delivery of humanitarian assistance'; 859, 24 Aug. 1993, para. 4.

[80] SC res. 810, 8 Mar. 1993, para. 18.   [81] SC res. 897, 4 Feb. 1994, para. 8.

[82] SC res. 912, 21 Apr. 1994, preamble—expressing concern for the safety and security 'of personnel of non-governmental organizations who are assisting in implementing the peace process and in distributing humanitarian relief'. See also SC res. 966, 8 Dec. 1994, on Angola, para. 10.

[83] UNGA res. 47/105, 16 Dec. 1992, para. 20—UNHCR staff and other relief workers; see also UNGA resolutions 48/116, 20 Dec. 1993, para. 22; 49/169, 23 Dec. 1994, para. 17.

'international *and local staff* undertaking humanitarian work', which has obvious implications for jurisdiction and responsibility. The UNHCR Executive Committee also has endorsed the necessity for safety for relief workers.[84]

In 1993, the General Assembly established an *ad hoc* committee to draw up an international convention on 'the safety and security of United Nations and associated personnel'.[85] A year later the Sixth Committee (Legal) duly submitted a 29-article draft, annexed to a resolution stressing the importance of speedily concluding a comprehensive review of compensation for death, disability, injury or illness attributed to peace-keeping services, in order to develop equitable arrangements and ensure expeditious reimbursement.[86] In December 1994, the General Assembly adopted the Convention and opened it for signature.[87]

The Convention defines United Nations personnel as persons engaged or deployed by the Secretary-General as members of a military, police or civilian component of a United Nations operation, as well as officials and experts on missions of the United Nations and its specialized agencies. It extends to associated personnel, that is, persons assigned by a government or an intergovernmental organization, under agreement to carry out activities directly connected with a United Nations operation. Also included are those engaged by the Secretary-General or a specialized agency, or deployed by a humanitarian non-governmental organization or agency under agreement with the Secretary-General or with a specialized agency. However, the Convention will *not* apply to a UN operation authorized by the Security Council as an enforcement action under Chapter VII of the Charter, in which personnel are engaged as combatants against organized armed forces and to which the law of international armed conflict applies.

The Convention obliges States parties to establish jurisdiction over those who commit crimes against personnel involved in United Nations operations; defines the duties of States to ensure the safety and security of personnel and to release or return personnel captured or detained; and calls on host States and United Nations to conclude agreements on the status of the United Nations operations and personnel.

[84] See UNHCR, Executive Committee Conclusion No. 72 (1993); Executive Committee Conclusion on the Security of UNHCR Staff (1994), *Report* of the 45th Session (1994): UN doc. A/AC.96/839, para. 28; Conclusion on the Situation of Refugees, Returnees and Displaced Persons in Africa (1994): ibid., para. 29(m). On a related issue, see Wiseberg, L. S., 'Protecting Human Rights Activists and NGOs: What More can be Done?' 13 *HRQ* 525 (1991).

[85] UNGA res. 48/37, 9 Dec. 1993, on the question of responsibility for attacks on United Nations and associated personnel and measures to ensure that those responsible for such attacks are brought to justice.

[86] UN doc. A/C.6/49/L.9. The Sixth Committee approved the draft resolution without a vote, although a number of States expressed reservations with respect to the consent of the receiving State, definitions, transit, extradition, and jurisdiction over nationals abroad.

[87] UNGA res. 49/59, 9 Dec. 1994—Convention on the Safety of United Nations and Associated Personnel; text also in 7 *IJRL* 526 (1995).

2. Internally displaced persons (IDPs)

From an international law perspective, primary responsibility for the protection of and assistance to internally displaced persons rests with the territorial State, in virtue of its sovereignty and the principle of non-intervention. In practice, internal displacement often occurs as a result of civil conflict, in situations where the authority of the central government is itself in dispute, and its capacity or willingness to provide protection and assistance are equally in doubt.

Internally displaced persons are by no means a new item on the international agenda. In the late 1940s, for example, Greece suggested that international help also be extended to those displaced internally by civil war. They might not need 'legal protection', but their material needs exceeded the resources of a country such as itself, ravaged by domestic conflict and foreign occupation.[88] Both Pakistan and India emphasized that the United Nations should take a universal approach, not excluding refugees merely by reason of the fact that they possessed the nationality of the country in which they now found themselves. The Pakistani representative noted that statelessness, or lack of legal protection, might be a problem, but it was perhaps the least of misfortunes for those dying of disease and starvation.[89] Eleanor Roosevelt, for the United States, on the other hand, stressed that the United Nations' responsibility should be to provide for a specific category of refugees, namely, those who required *legal* protection. Refugees within their own countries, who still enjoyed the protection of their governments, did not come within the scope of the discussion, though they might be in great need of material assistance.[90]

UNHCR's relief and rehabilitation programmes for refugees and returnees have included those 'displaced within the country' since at least 1972, when ECOSOC and the General Assembly endorsed operations in the Sudan.[91] The same year the General Assembly kept the mandate door open by asking the High Commissioner to continue to participate, at the Secretary-General's request, in 'those humanitarian endeavours of the United Nations for which his Office has particular expertise and experience'.[92] Resolutions in later years con-

---

[88] See GAOR, 4th Sess., Third Committee, Summary Records, 110 (1949).

[89] Ibid., 116 (Pakistan), 123 (India), 128 (Pakistan), 144 (India, stating that it was not convinced of the need for an international organization whose sole responsibility would be to provide legal protection, when its own refugees were dying of starvation), 146 (Pakistan).

[90] Ibid., 132. With what seems irony in retrospect, Mrs Roosevelt also commented on the need to preserve the essentially deliberative character of the United Nations, in face of the increasing tendency to drive the organization into the field of international relief: ibid., 135. See also GAOR, 4th Sess., Plenary, 2 Dec. 1949, 473.

[91] See ECOSOC res. 1705(LIII), 27 Jul. 1972, referring to Sudan and to 'the assistance required for voluntary repatriation, rehabilitation and resettlement of the refugees returning from abroad, as well as of persons displaced within the country'; also UNGA res. 2958(XXVII), 12 Dec. 1972.

[92] UNGA res. 2956(XXVII), 12 Dec. 1972. Para. 9 of the UNHCR Statute requires the High Commissioner to 'follow policy directives' from the General Assembly and ECOSOC and to 'engage in such additional activities . . . as the General Assembly may determine within the limits of the resources placed at his disposal'.

tained frequent references to 'displaced persons', though generally without qua_
ification as internal or external. So far as the context remained assistance activities to refugees, returnees and displaced persons,[93] it is reasonable to infer an
expectation that such programmes might usefully benefit the internally displaced; this is also in line with the then growing recognition of the necessity to
link assistance for refugees and returnees to the general question of development.

In the period 1988–91, the General Assembly, under pressure from major
donors, began to emphasize the necessity for better *co-ordination* of relief programmes for the internally displaced,[94] a task initially entrusted to UNDP
Resident Representatives.[95] In 1990, ECOSOC requested a system-wide review
to assess the experience and capacity of UN organizations involved in assistance
to all refugees, displaced persons and returnees,[96] which was duly followed by
the Commission on Human Rights focusing on the need of internally displaced
persons (IDPs) for relief assistance *and* protection.[97] The Commission requested
the Secretary-General to appoint a representative on IDPs, a role entrusted to
Francis Deng in July 1992. The Representative presented the first of several
reports the following year,[98] and identified his goal as the development of 'a doctrine of protection specifically tailored to the needs of the internally displaced,'[99]
provisionally described as 'persons who have been forced to flee their homes sud-
denly or unexpectedly in large numbers, as a result of armed conflict, internal
strife, systematic violations of human rights or natural or man-made disasters;
and who are within the territory of their own country'.[100]

During the period in question, UNHCR had phased out its operations in
northern Iraq, continued to be deeply involved in former Yugoslavia, and
was becoming increasingly engaged in conflict situations featuring internal and

[93] See, for example, UNGA resolutions 3454(XXX), 9 Dec. 1975; 31/35, 30 Nov. 1976; 34/60,
29 Nov. 1979; 35/41, 25 Nov. 1980; 40/118, 13 Dec. 1985.

[94] UNGA res. 43/116, 8 Dec. 1988. See generally Plender, R., 'The Legal Basis of International
Jurisdiction To Act with Regard to the Internally Displaced', 6 *IJRL* 345 (1994).

[95] UNGA resolutions 44/136, 15 Dec. 1989; 45/137, 14 Dec. 1990.

[96] ECOSOC res. 1990/78, 27 Jul. 1990, para. 1.

[97] CHR res. 1992/73, 5 Mar. 1992; UN doc. E/CN.4/1992/L.11/Add.6; CHR res. 1991/25,
5 Mar. 1991. See also *Analytical Report* of the Secretary-General on Internally Displaced Persons: UN
doc. E/CN.4/1992/23, 14 Feb. 1992.

[98] *Comprehensive Study on the Human Rights Issues relating to Internally Displaced Persons*: UN doc.
E/CN.4/1993/35; Internally Displaced Persons. *Report* of the Representative of the Secretary-
General: UN doc. E/CN.4/1994/44; See the series of addenda, 'Profiles in Displacement': Sri
Lanka: UN doc. E/CN.4/1994/44/Add.1 (25 Jan. 1994); Colombia: UN doc. E/CN.4/
1995/50/Add.1 (3 Oct. 1994); Burundi: UN doc. E/CN.4/1995/50/Add.2 (28 Nov. 1994); also
published in 14 *RSQ*, Nos. 1 and 2, (1995); also, Deng, F. M., 'The International Protection of the
Internally Displaced', 7 *Special Issue—Summer 1995*, 74.

[99] UN doc. E/CN.4/1994/44, para. 28; text in 6 *IJRL* 291 (1994); also UN doc.
E/CN.4/1995/50; text in 14 *RSQ*, Nos. 1 and 2, 192 (1995). For suggestions on the standards issue,
see Petrasek, D., 'New Standards for the Protection of Internally Displaced Persons: A Proposal for
a Comprehensive Approach', 14 *RSQ*, Nos. 1 and 2, 285 (1995).

[100] An alternative wording would delete the words 'in large numbers', which are irrelevant to a
definition premised on displacement and need; and replace 'who are within the territory of their
own country' with 'who have not crossed an internationally recognized State border'.

external displacement. Given its growing involvement with IDPs,[101] UNHCR published internal guidelines in April 1993, setting out a number of legal considerations and criteria.[102] While emphasizing that UNHCR 'does not have a general competence' for IDPs, the guidelines otherwise take their lead from paragraph 14 of UN General Assembly resolution 47/105, identifying the criteria for engagement as a *specific request* from the Secretary-General or other competent authority, and the *consent of the State* concerned.[103] The Executive Committee, in turn, reaffirmed its support for UNHCR's role with IDPs, while stressing that its involvement should focus on situations that 'call for the Office's particular expertise', and pay 'due regard to the complementary mandates and specific expertise of other relevant organizations as well as the availability of sufficient resources'.[104] The UN General Assembly confirmed this approach in resolution 48/116 in December of the same year.[105]

The protection aspects of IDPs, a separate item on the Executive Committee agenda in 1994, were examined on the basis of a paper presented by UNHCR to an inter-sessional meeting in May.[106] Paragraph 11 of the Note offered

[101] IDPs were considered in a desultory way by the UNHCR Executive Committee Working Group on Solutions and Protection: UN doc. EC/SCP/64, 12 Aug. 1991, paras. 43–9, 54(k), 55(l), but no substantive observations or recommendations emerged.

[102] UNHCR, *UNHCR's Role with Internally Displaced Persons*, IOM/33/93–FOM/33/93, 28 Apr. 1993.

[103] Interestingly, the UNHCR guidelines acknowledge the possible role of other relevant entities, presumably authorities in fact, if not in law. UNGA res. 46/182, 19 Dec. 1991, on the Strengthening of the Co-ordination of Humanitarian Emergency Assistance also stressed consent and respect for sovereignty, territorial integrity, and national unity: ibid., Annex, para. 3, but did not exclude the possibility of negotiating the provision of emergency assistance 'by obtaining the consent of *all parties concerned*': ibid., para. 35(d). One commentator has noted with respect to the discussions leading to Additional Protocol II of the 1949 Geneva Conventions that 'States strongly opposed any reference to offers of relief, even emanating from neutral third parties, which might constitute an interference in their internal affairs', and that Additional Protocol II consequently contains minimal provisions on relief (art. 18(2)): Macalister-Smith, P., *International Humanitarian Assistance: Disaster Relief Actions in International Law and Organization*, (1985), 31, cited in Plender, R., 'The Legal Basis of International Jurisdiction To Act with Regard to the Internally Displaced', 6 *IJRL* 345 (1994).

[104] UNHCR Executive Committee, General Conclusion on International Protection: *Report* of the 44th Session (1993): UN doc. A/AC.96/821, para. (s). Cf. the view of the Netherlands, favouring the assignment of 'general competence to UNHCR to provide protection to internally displaced persons and local populations under siege in refugee-like and potential refugee-generating situations': UN doc. A/AC.96/SR.482 (1993), para. 31.

[105] UNGA res. 48/116, 20 Dec. 1993, para. 12. See also UNGA res. 48/135, 20 Dec. 1993, in which the General Assembly welcomed, 'the decision by the Executive Committee . . . to extend, on a case-by-case basis and under specific circumstances, protection and assistance to the internally displaced . . .'

[106] See UNHCR, 'Note on the Protection Aspects of UNHCR Activities on behalf of Internally Displaced Persons': UN doc. EC/1994/SCP/CRP.2, 4 May 1994; text also in 6 *IJRL* 485 (1994). Also, *Report* of the 18–19 May 1994 Meeting of the Sub-Committee of the Whole on International Protection: UN doc. EC/SCP/89 (29 Sept. 1994), paras. 6–36. Cf. Petrasek, D., 'New Standards for the Protection of Internally Displaced Persons: A Proposal for a Comprehensive Approach', 14 *RSQ*, Nos. 1 and 2, 285 (1995); Norwegian Refugee Council & Refugee Policy Group, 'Round table Discussion on United Nations Human Rights Protection for Internally Displaced Persons', Nyon, Switzerland, Feb. 1993; Refugee Policy Group, 'Human Rights Protection for Internally Displaced Persons'. Report of an International Conference, 24–5 June 1991; Cohen, R., 'Human Rights

UNHCR's 'operational definition', framed in terms of the Office's traditional refugee functions, and including 'those in a refugee-like situation, . . . persons fleeing persecution, armed conflict or civil strife, rather than victims of physical disasters'.[107] The Conclusion on IDPs adopted by the Executive Committee at its 45th Session in October 1994, while emphasizing the primary responsibility of the State for the welfare and protection of persons displaced within its territory, also recognized that,

actions by the international community, *in consultation and co-ordination with the concerned State*, on behalf of the internally displaced may contribute to the easing of tensions and the resolution of problems resulting in displacement, and constitute important components of a comprehensive approach to the prevention and solution of refugee problems.[108]

The Executive Committee encouraged the High Commissioner to continue to apply the internal guidelines referred to above, but also emphasized, as it had done earlier with respect to prevention,[109] that 'activities on behalf of internally displaced persons must not undermine the institution of asylum, including the right to seek and enjoy in other countries asylum from persecution'. Finally, it laid great stress on the necessity for inter-agency co-operation.[110]

Besides the UN agencies regularly working with the internally displaced, such as UNICEF, WHO and WFP, other organizations likely to be involved in assistance and related activities include IOM and the ICRC. The IOM Constitution mandates the provision of migration services to the displaced, and internal displacement is approached largely as an aspect of internal migration. The ICRC has a clear legal interest, deriving from the fact that most IDPs move as a consequence of armed conflict, and its mandate is to ensure the application of international humanitarian law. The ICRC's paramount consideration in any operation remains the interest of the victims, rather than attention to categories, or to ulterior objectives, such as the avoidance of transfrontier flight.[111]

Protection for Internally Displaced Persons', RPG, (1991); Refugee Policy Group, 'Internally Displaced Persons in Africa: Assistance Challenges and Opportunities', (1992).

[107] The ICRC representative, Yves Sandoz, commented with respect to this proposal: 'Les critères opérationnels ne devraient pas être trop dogmatiques. Il nous paraît que l'effort fait pour ramener l'activité du HCR dans le mandat originel de l'Institution—si important et louable soit cet effort—relève parfois d'une certaine acrobatie. Peut-on réellement dire que c'était le cas dans le cadre de Bosnie-Herzégovine?' Sandoz, Y., 'Déclaration du Comité international de la Croix-Rouge', Sous-Comité plenier sur la protection internationale du Comité executif du programme du Haut Commissaire, 18 mai 1994.

[108] Executive Committee Conclusion No. 75 (1994), para. (h) (emphasis supplied). A distinction may be drawn between so-called humanitarian intervention and the provision of humanitarian assistance. As the editors of the ninth edition of Oppenheim have observed, 'even in a situation of conflict within a State, humanitarian assistance will not constitute intervention, so long as it is given (or perhaps is at least available) without discrimination between the parties to the conflict': *Oppenheim's International Law*, 9th ed., Jennings R. Y. and Watts, A., Vol. I, 444; cited by Plender, above n. 103, at 356.

[109] See below, s. 3.5.4.

[110] Executive Committee Conclusion No. 75 (1994), paras. (r), (s)—referring to the leadership of the Emergency Relief Co-ordinator; (t).

[111] For a brief but clear statement of ICRC's role with IDPs, see Sandoz, above n. 107.

Increasing international attention to the problems of IDPs, their functional needs and institutional requirements, will likely have an impact on the traditional requirement of consent as a pre-condition to the provision of relief. The classical model of the sovereign State is hardly redundant after Iraq,[112] and although it may repay re-evaluation in light of the implications of membership in the United Nations, a number of States remain concerned at the extension of the UN's sphere of interest.[113] Nevertheless, it is increasingly difficult for States to resist criticism of internal policies and practices that result in displacement.[114] International 'findings' on these issues could conceivably become part of a process leading to the provision of international relief, even including protection, that is *not* contingent on request or consent, and not limited to the relatively rare instances in which State authority has effectively disappeared.

At this point, definitions will have a role to play, either in an operational sense, as triggers to action; or jurisdictionally, by delimiting the competence of different organizations. The criterion of size ('large numbers') may be an appropriate pre-condition to launching international assistance, while not having crossed a frontier may determine which agency should assume overall responsibility, for example, the Department of Humanitarian Affairs or UNHCR.[115]

3. Solutions and prevention

A refugee movement necessarily has an international dimension, but neither general international law nor treaty obliges any State to accord durable solutions. Indeed, some consider such a development undesirable, as tending to relieve the country of origin of its responsibility to establish the conditions permitting return, while also 'institutionalizing' exile at the expense of human rights.[116] The General Assembly initiative on co-operation to avert new flows of

---

[112] In April 1991, three States—Cuba, Yemen, and Zimbabwe—voted against SC res. 688, the sole and somewhat ambiguous 'authority' for humanitarian operations in northern Iraq.

[113] In the Commission on Human Rights in 1992, India, Bangladesh and a number of other Third World countries all expressed deep reservations on the proposal for an independent expert to study human rights issues related to the internally displaced. In Sept. 1992, China, India and Zimbabwe also abstained on SC resolutions 770 and 776 where, amongst other things, the Security Council endorsed military protection of humanitarian assistance and convoys of released detainees in former Yugoslavia.

[114] See, for example, UNGA resolutions 47/142, 18 Dec. 1992, 48/147, 20 Dec. 1993, and 49/198, 23 Dec. 1994, expressing alarm at 'the large number of internally displaced persons and victims of discrimination in the Sudan, including members of minorities who have been forcibly displaced in violation of their human rights and who are in need of relief assistance and of protection'.

[115] See among others, Borgen, J. et al., 'Institutional Arrangements for Internally Displaced Persons: The Ground Level Experience,' Norwegian Refugee Council, 1 *Report* (1995).

[116] See views expressed by Australia in 1981 on the German Federal Republic's initiative regarding international co-operation to avert new flows of refugees: *Report* of Secretary-General: UN doc. A/36/582, 23 Oct. 1981, 5. Similar sentiments were expressed by other countries, including Belgium (at 9), Egypt (at 15), Qatar (at 36), with varying emphasis depending on each State's perception of the initiative. Cf. Executive Committee Conclusions No. 67 (1991), para. (g)—resettlement 'only as a last resort'; and No. 68 (1992), para. (s)—voluntary repatriation as 'the preferred solution'.

refugees both reaffirmed 'the right of refugees to return to their homes in their homelands', but also the right of those not wishing to return to receive adequate compensation.[117] The former continues to hold primary position in the hierarchy of solutions, but the right of refugees to compensation has still a fairly weak normative base in international law and, like the putative duty to provide solutions, possibly little to recommend it. The subject of damages for the expulsion of foreign nationals remains controversial,[118] and there are few precedents concerning refugees.[119] Although the principle of compensating the victims of violations of human rights has much to commend it, introducing a financial substitute for State and community obligations risks lending respectability to ethnic, religious and ideological cleansing.[120]

The fact that, apart from the duty of the State to readmit its nationals, solutions fall generally outside the area of legal obligation, justifies close attention to the policies and positions of States, particularly as revealed in statements in the UNHCR Executive Committee and in their practice. UNHCR's primary responsibility is to provide international protection to refugees and to seek 'permanent solutions for the problem of refugees by assisting Governments and, subject to the approval of the Governments concerned, private organizations to facilitate the voluntary repatriation of ... refugees, or their assimilation within new national communities'.[121] It is to provide for protection by, among others, 'assisting ... efforts to promote voluntary repatriation or assimilation', and by 'promoting the admission of refugees, not excluding those in the most destitute categories'. Finally, the High Commissioner is authorised to 'engage in such additional activities, including repatriation and resettlement' as the General Assembly may determine.[122] The latter reference to 'activities' supposes an operational dimension to UNHCR which, since the 1960s and early 1970s, has also provided assistance and *de facto* protection to repatriating refugees and internally displaced persons, and assistance to local populations affected by a refugee influx.[123]

---

[117] UNGA res. 35/124, 11 Dec. 1980; 36/148, 16 Dec. 1981. On 'return' in the Palestinian context, see above Ch. 3, s. 3.2; Ch. 6, s. 1.2.

[118] Goodwin-Gill, *Movement of Persons*, 278–80.

[119] The indemnification of the victims of Nazi persecution by the Federal Republic of Germany is one of the few relevant precedents, as is the payment by the Government of Uganda, through UNHCR, of compensation to 'Asians of undetermined nationality' expelled in 1972; Goodwin-Gill, *Movement of Persons*, 216, n. 1.

[120] But see Lee, L. T., 'The declaration of principles of international law on compensation to refugees: its significance and implications', 6 *JRS* 65 (1993); also, Lee, L. T., 'The right to compensation: Refugees and countries of asylum', 80 *AJIL* 532 (1986).

[121] Statute, para. 1. UNGA res. 428(V), adopting the Statute, also calls upon governments to assist 'the High Commissioner in his efforts *to promote ... voluntary repatriation*'. See generally, Luca, D., 'La notion de "solution" au problème des réfugiés', *Revue de droit international*, janv.–mars 1987, 1; Fonteyne, J. -P., 'Burden-Sharing: An Analysis of the Nature and Function of International Solidarity in Cases of Mass Influx of Refugee', 8 *Aust. YB Int'l Law* 162 (1983).

[122] Statute, para. 9.

[123] To these specific or implied mandate responsibilities must now also be added the special humanitarian tasks entrusted to UNHCR, for example, in former Yugoslavia, including assistance and, within difficult limits, protection of populations at risk in their own land.

Notwithstanding the weight of rule and principle, UNHCR's capacity to obtain protection and asylum for refugees is often closely linked to, if not contingent on, its success in promoting solutions.[124] Evidently also, the absence or failure to provide solutions will have a destabilizing effect on populations, likely leading to further displacement, or to what some States have characterized as irregular movements.[125] The temporary nature of the refugees' predicament has also frequently been acknowledged, particularly in the case of those fleeing internal disorder resulting from independence struggles.[126]

Asylum and local integration are covered in part by Chapter 8, dealing with treaty standards; the present section therefore focuses on the other durable solutions of voluntary repatriation and resettlement, while looking also at related issues of safe return, and 'preventive protection'.

3.1 VOLUNTARY REPATRIATION

The UNHCR Statute calls upon the High Commissioner to facilitate and to promote voluntary repatriation. In recent years, States have repeatedly and insistently called for more attention to be paid to this solution and for UNHCR to do more to promote it.[127]

One of the unresolved theoretical paradoxes of UNHCR's institutional responsibilities is the extent to which its duty to provide international protection pervades the field of cessation of refugee status and voluntary return. Formal categories frequently provide inadequate descriptions of refugee realities, and in practice it is often difficult to be certain whether circumstances have changed to such a degree as to warrant formal termination of refugee status, even supposing that it was ever formally recognized. The assessment of change involves subjective elements of appreciation, in a continuum where the fact of repatriation

---

[124] Cf. Executive Committee General Conclusions on International Protection (1990), *Report* of the 41st Session: UN doc. A/AC.96/760, para. 20(e); and No. 50 (1988), *Report* of the 39th Session: UN doc. A/AC.96/721, para. 22(e), noting the 'close nexus between international protection and solutions'.

[125] See Executive Committee Conclusion No. 58 (1989), para. (b), noting that irregular movements are largely due to 'the absence of educational and employment possibilities and the non-availability of long-term durable solutions by way of voluntary repatriation, local integration and resettlement'.

[126] See, for example, UNGA res. 1500(XV), 5 Dec. 1960, and 1672(XVI), 18 Dec. 1961, regarding refugees from Algeria in Tunisia and Morocco; 1671(XVI), 18 Dec. 1961, regarding refugees from Angola; 2040(XX), 7 Dec. 1965, regarding African refugees generally; UNGA res. 2790(XXVI), 6 Dec. 1971, refugees from East Pakistan during the war of secession; Executive Committee Conclusion No. 18 (1980), para. (a).

[127] See *Report* of the 34th Session of the Executive Committee (1983): UN doc. A/AC.96/631, paras. 31–2; also the views of Australia: UN doc. A/AC.96/SR.354, paras. 36, 42; the UK: ibid., SR.356, para. 63 (suggesting UNHCR adopt the image of goad, rather than catalyst); *Report* of the 35th Session (1984): UN doc. A/AC.96/651, paras. 35, 79; A/AC.96/INF.173 (12 Oct. 1984), Morocco's appeal for the voluntary repatriation of persons from ex-Spanish Sahara in the Tindouf region; also the views of the Netherlands: UN doc. A/AC.96/SR.369, para. 57; Belgium, ibid., SR.370, para. 39; Algeria, ibid., SR.371, para. 58; Morocco, ibid., SR.372, para. 9. Algeria and Morocco have exchanged claim and counterclaim repeatedly in later sessions of the Executive Committee.

may be the sufficient *and* necessary condition, bringing the situation or status of refugee to an end. Moreover, in the uncertain and fluid dynamics which characterize mass exodus, this fact of return can itself be an element in the change of circumstances, contributing to the re-emergence or consolidation of stability and to national reconciliation.[128]

Voluntary repatriation has institutional and human rights dimensions. Both the facilitation and the promotion of voluntary repatriation fall within the province of UNHCR,[129] while the right to return to one's own country locates such efforts squarely in a human rights context.[130] To ignore this dimension and the legal implications arising from the concept of nationality would be to condone exile at the expense of human rights. Voluntary repatriation also involves a dimension of *responsibility*, namely, the responsibility of the international community to find solutions without 'institutionalizing' exile to such a degree that it disregards the interests of individuals and communities.[131]

A particular legal context for protection in repatriation is offered by article V of 1969 OAU Convention,[132] which stresses its essentially voluntary character, the importance of country of origin and country of refuge collaboration, of amnesties and non-penalization, as well as assistance to those returning. Because repatriation may itself cause serious practical difficulties, the General Assembly has increasingly authorized UNHCR involvement in rehabilitation and reintegration programmes,[133] and a fund for durable solutions was at one time

[128] Goodwin-Gill, G. S. 'Voluntary Repatriation: Legal and Policy Issues', in Loescher, G. and Monahan, L., *Refugees and International Relations*, (1989), 255; Cuny, F. C., Stein, B. N. and Reed, P., eds., *Repatriation during Conflict in Africa and Asia*, (1992); Stein, B. N., Cuny, F. C. and Reed, P. eds., *Refugee Repatriation during Conflict*, (1995); Larkin, M. A., Cuny, F. C., and Stein, B. N., *Repatriation under Conflict in Central America*, (1991); Chimni, B. S., 'The Meaning of Words and the Role of UNHCR in Voluntary Repatriation', 5 *IJRL* 442 (1993); Chimni, B. S., 'Perspectives on Voluntary Repatriation: A Critical Note', 3 *IJRL* 541 (1991); Hofmann, R., "Voluntary Repatriation and UNHCR', 44 *ZaöRV* 327 (1984). Also, para. 21, CIREFCA Plan of Action; below, Annexe 5, No. 2.

[129] Statute, paras. 1, 8(c); UNGA res. 428(V), para. 2(d); Executive Committee Conclusion No. 65 (1991), para. (j).

[130] See arts. 9, 13(2), 1948 Universal Declaration of Human Rights; art. 5, 1965 Convention on the Elimination of All Forms of Racial Discrimination; art. 12, 1966 Covenant on Civil and Political Rights; Executive Committee General Conclusion on International Protection, *Report* of the 45th Session (1994): UN doc. A/AC.96/839; para. 19(v); UNGA res. 49/169, 23 Dec. 1994, para. 9. Source countries are sometimes less than enthusiastic about the return of those who have fled, however. When it sought UNHCR assistance with repatriation in 1975, the Provisional Revolutionary Government of South Vietnam emphasized that authorization for return fell within the government's sovereign rights, and that each case would need to be examined: UN doc. A/AC.96/521, para. 105 (Observer for the Democratic Republic of Vietnam). In 1974, the Chilean government legislated to prohibit the return of Chileans on various grounds, such as national security, and a 1978 amnesty left generally unchanged the legal situation of Chilean exiles wishing to repatriate: UN doc. A/33/331, para. 433; also E/CN.4/1310, paras. 129-38 (Study of Reported Violations of Human Rights in Chile, Feb. 1979).

[131] On 'international co-operation' as a principle of international law, see below s. 4.

[132] For text see below, Annexe 2, No. 1.

[133] See UNGA res. 2956(XXVII), 12 Dec. 1972; 3143(XXVIII), 14 Dec. 1973, 3271(XXIX), 10 Dec. 1974, 3454(XXX), 9 Dec. 1975, 31/35, 30 Nov. 1976, 33/26, 29 Nov. 1978, 34/60, 29 Nov. 1979, and 35/41, 25 Nov. 1980.

proposed, to assist developing countries to meet some of the costs.[134] That proposal did not survive as such, but 'Refugee Aid and Development', an initiative sponsored by the High Commissioner in 1985, is now a regular agenda item in the UNHCR Executive Committee.

A potentially active UNHCR role is anticipated in Executive Committee conclusions adopted in 1980 and 1985, the first of which, closely modelled on the OAU Convention, looks towards *facilitation*, rather than the promotion of return movement.[135] These conclusions recognize that voluntary repatriation is generally the most appropriate solution, while stressing the necessity for arrangements to establish voluntariness, in both individual and large-scale movements. Visits to the country of origin by refugees or refugee representatives for the purpose of informing themselves of the situation are seen as useful,[136] and formal guarantees for the safety of returnees are also called for, together with mechanisms to ensure the dissemination of relevant information.[137] The Executive Committee considered that 'UNHCR could appropriately be called upon—with the agreement of the parties concerned—to monitor the situation of returning refugees . . .'

The Executive Committee looked again at voluntary repatriation in 1985.[138] The right of the individual to return was accepted as a fundamental premise, but linked to the principle of the free, voluntary and individual nature of all repatriation movements. UNHCR's mandate was considered broad enough to enable it to take initiatives, including those which might promote favourable conditions. Some, indeed, considered that UNHCR had a responsibility to begin the dialogue, although others cautioned against its becoming entangled in political issues. UNHCR involvement with returnees was recognised as a legitimate concern, particularly where return takes place under amnesty or similar guar-

---

[134] See UN doc. A/AC.96/569 and summary of debate in the Executive Committee: A/AC.96/SR.312, paras. 48–9; (30th Session, 1979); A/AC.96/SR.322, paras. 66–73; SR.323, paras. 14–36 (31st Session, 1980). Some States feared that UNHCR might, through the fund, become involved in developmental activities better left to other international agencies; see A/AC.96/SR.305, para. 16 and SR.319, para. 25 (statements by the Netherlands representative in 1979 and 1980).

[135] See Executive Committee Conclusion No. 18 (1980); UNHCR, Note on Voluntary Repatriation: UN doc. EC/SCP/13, 27 Aug. 1980; *Report* of the Sub-Committee: UN doc. A/AC.96/586, 8 Oct. 1980, paras. 17–29.

[136] Cf. Executive Committee General Conclusion on International Protection (1994), *Report* of the 45th Session: UN doc. A/AC.96/839, para. 19(v).

[137] *Report* of the Sub-Committee: UN doc. A/AC.96/586, paras. 23–4. The 1979 Arusha Conference on the Situation of Refugees in Africa recommended that appeals for repatriation and related guarantees be made known by every possible means: UN doc. A/AC.96/INF.158, paras. 3, 4. The importance of adequate information was also recognized in the 1946 IRO Constitution: see Annex I: Definitions, Part I, Section C, para. 1.

[138] See Executive Committee Conclusion No. 40 (1985); UNHCR, Voluntary Repatriation: UN doc. EC/SCP/41, 1 Aug. 1985; *Report* of the Sub-Committee: UN doc. A/AC.96/671, 9 Oct. 1985; *Report* of the Executive Committee: UN doc. A/AC.96/673, 22 Oct. 1985, paras. 100–6; and for the summary records of debate: UN docs. A/AC.96/SR.385–400.

antee, although legal difficulties might arise with the government of the country of origin.[139]

3.1.1 *Facilitating and promoting*

The duty to provide international protection justifies a cautious distinction between *facilitation* and *promotion*.[140] The former presupposes an informed and voluntary decision by an individual, while the latter anticipates varying degrees of encouragement by outside bodies. For UNHCR, the principal consideration in a promotion context must be the interest of the refugee, and the protection of his or her rights, security and welfare.[141] The individual's right to return will not always prevail over other acquired rights, in the sense of becoming a duty to leave, and a danger in agency-sponsored repatriation operations is that protection ultimately may be compromised. Some critics have challenged UNHCR's role and activities, so far as they appear to support State-inspired policies of 'containment', or promote 'preventive protection' oriented more to reducing admissions and costs, than to the interests of refugees. The promotion of (voluntary) repatriation by governments is seen as suspect, particularly when presented in the context of 'safe return', rather than on the basis of the voluntary choice of the individual.[142]

UNHCR's protection responsibilities require it to obtain the best available information regarding conditions in the country of origin, and an accurate analysis of the extent to which the causes of flows have modified or ceased. Such information must in turn be shared with refugees and governmental and non-governmental agencies involved, including repatriation commissions and implementing partners. UNHCR's duty to provide international protection clearly obliges the Office to refrain from *promotion* where circumstances have not changed, or where instability and insecurity continue;[143] similarly, UNHCR

[139] In brief, Executive Committee Conclusion No. 40 (1985), also stresses the voluntary and individual character of repatriation and the necessity for it to be carried out in conditions of safety, preferably to the refugee's former place of residence, emphasizes the inseparability of causes and solutions, the primary responsibility of States to create conditions conducive to return, and that the UNHCR mandate is broad enough to allow it to promote dialogue, act as intermediary, facilitate communication, and actively pursue return in appropriate circumstances.

[140] Cf. Executive Committee General Conclusion on International Protection: *Report* of the 45th Session (1994): UN doc. A/AC.96/839, para. 19(y), underscoring UNHCR's role in 'promoting, facilitating and co-ordinating voluntary repatriation . . . , including ensuring that international protection continues to be extended to those in need until such time as they can return in safety and dignity . . .'

[141] Ibid., para. 19(ii), endorsing the High Commissioner's efforts with respect to reducing or eliminating the threat of landmines.

[142] On 'safe return' see further below s. 3.2.

[143] The issue of coercion and pressure to return calls for close monitoring, and was central to the controversy which surrounded the second phase of repatriation from Djibouti to Ethiopia in 1986 and 1987; see Goodwin-Gill, 'Voluntary Repatriation', 255, 277–80. See also with respect to Bangladesh and Myanmar, Médecins sans Frontières/Artsen zonder Grenzen, 'Awareness Survey: Rohingya Refugee Camps, Cox's Bazar District, Bangladesh, 15 March 1995', The Netherlands, 1995; and for States' comments: UN doc. A/AC.96/SR.473 (1992), para. 32 (Australia); SR.476, paras. 45–51 (Bangladesh); SR.477, paras. 12–15 (Myanmar).

ought to oversee the application of guarantees or assurances that are integral to the process of return (by being there, by close contact with returnees and implementing agencies, and by activating regional political and human rights mechanisms); and also to contribute morally and materially to successful re-integration in the national community.[144]

Countries of origin and countries of asylum may themselves co-operate to facilitate the return of refugees, either with or without UNHCR involvement. For example, although largely overtaken by persistent conflict, a 1988 agreement between Afghanistan and Pakistan recognized that all refugees should have the opportunity to return in freedom, free choice of domicile and freedom of movement, the right to work and to participate in civic affairs, and the same rights and privileges as other citizens. Pakistan, in turn, agreed to facilitate 'voluntary, orderly and peaceful repatriation', and mixed commissions were also to be established.[145]

Although it can provoke logistical demands often difficult to meet, recognizing the primacy of the refugee's own decision generally makes good sense, even to the extent of *facilitating* repatriation in circumstances which, objectively considered, may be far from ideal.[146] It often does not matter what UNHCR, NGOs, or even States want; if refugees themselves choose to return, so they will, even to situations that outsiders consider highly insecure and undesirable. The virtue of voluntariness lies in the fact that it is an inherent safeguard against *forced* return, while being one manifestation of the 'right to return', to be exercised within a human rights framework, and whether or not Convention refugees in the strict sense are involved. Put another way, voluntariness (the choice of the individual) is justified because in the absence of formal cessation, the refugee is the best judge of when and whether to go back; because it allows for the particular experiences of the individual, such as severe persecution and trauma, to receive due weight; and finally because there is a value in individual choice. The voluntary character of repatriation is the necessary correlative to the subjective

---

[144] Cf. Executive Committee General Conclusion on International Protection: *Report* of the 42nd Session (1991): UN doc. A/AC.96/783, para. 21(j), urging States, among others, to allow their citizens to return 'in safety and dignity to their homes without harassment, arbitrary detention or physical threats . . .'

[145] See Bilateral Agreement between the Republic of Afghanistan and the Islamic Republic of Pakistan on the Voluntary Return of Refugees 27 *ILM* 585 (1988); also Afghanistan–Pakistan–Union of Soviet Socialist Republics–United States: Accords on the Peaceful Resolution of the Situation in Afghanistan, Geneva, 14 Apr. 1988: ibid., 577. Cf. US Committee for Refugees, 'Left out in the Cold: The perilous homecoming of Afghan refugees', Dec. 1992. For other examples of agreements touching on the repatriation of refugees, see India–Sri Lanka: Agreement to Establish Peace and Normalcy in Sri Lanka, Colombo, 29 July 1987: 26 *ILM* 1175 (1987); South Africa–UNHCR, Memorandum of Understanding on the Voluntary Repatriation and Reintegration of South African Returnees: 31 *ILM* 522 (1992); décret-loi du 31 déc. 1989 relatif au rapatriement des citoyens roumains et des anciens citoyens roumains: *Doc. réf.*, No. 103, 5/14 mars 1990, 13.

[146] See Executive Committee Conclusion No. 40 (1985), para. (h), recognizing the importance of 'spontaneous return'.

fear which gave rise to flight; willingness to return negatives that fear, but it requires equal verification.[147]

Voluntary repatriation will continue as the preferred solution to refugee problems, both as a matter of principle (it reflects the right of the citizen to return), and on the ground of self-interest (most States of refuge prefer to limit their obligations to refugees). The success of voluntary repatriation will depend on political factors, however, including the clearly expressed wish of the country of origin that the refugees should return, and on the personal choice of the refugees themselves. Independence, successful secession, an amnesty, or other change of circumstances may indicate that the basis for a claim to refugee status has been removed, and the State of refuge must decide whether this is a sufficient or necessary reason for requiring the individual to quit national territory. This may be justified, for example, where the period of refuge has been relatively short, or where sheer numbers alone have meant that only temporary protection could be accorded. In other cases, however, the former refugee should benefit from standards generally applicable to resident aliens, including respect for any 'acquired right of residence' deriving from lengthy stay, integration, and local connections, establishment of business, marriage, and so forth.[148]

3.2 SAFE RETURN

From having been a description of the preferred consequence or effect of repatriation, the notion of 'safe return' has come to occupy an interim position between the refugee deciding voluntarily to go back home and any other nonnational who, having no claim to international protection, faces deportation or is otherwise required to leave. In 1994, the Executive Committee linked temporary protection (admission to safety, respect for basic human rights, protection against *refoulement*) to 'safe return when conditions permit'.[149] This reflects States' acceptance of an intermediate category in need of protection, but raises questions as to both the obligation to protect and the modalities governing termination of protection. The former has been considered above,[150] while the latter remains controlled by international law only at its outermost boundary. In particular, although the State remains bound by such provisions as prohibit torture or cruel and inhuman treatment, no rule of international law appears formally to require that a State proposing to implement returns take into account and act on assessments of both 'legal' safety and safety in fact, including basic

---

[147] See Goodwin-Gill, G. S., 'Voluntary Repatriation: Legal and Policy Issues', in Loescher, G. and Monahan, L., *Refugees in International Relations*, (1989), 255, where these ideas are developed more fully, with illustrations from a number of repatriation programmes. From a practical perspective, establishing the views of large numbers of refugees can pose problems of logistics and principle, touching issues of information and representative (or not) decision-making.

[148] See further below, Ch. 9, s. 4.1.

[149] Executive Committee General Conclusion on International Protection (1994): *Report* of the 45th Session: UN doc. A/AC.96/839, paras. 19(r), (u).

[150] See above Ch. 4, s. 6.1; Ch. 5, s. 5.

issues like absence of conflict, de-mining, and a working police and justice system.

Increasingly, 'safe return' has become part of the policy thinking of governments, even if the content of temporary protection overall is still being worked out. When 'safe havens' are declared and the UN is present, the idea of safe return also emerges, notwithstanding the actual situation with respect to human rights at large. The 'internal flight alternative' in certain States' jurisprudence is an aspect of the same development.

A central issue in the distinction between voluntary repatriation and safe return is, who decides? International law provides no clear answers to situations involving large movements of people in flight from complex situations of risk. If the conditions that caused flight have fundamentally changed, the 'refugee' is no longer a 'refugee' and, all things being equal, can be required to return home like any other foreign national. That a 'refugee' may voluntarily repatriate seems to imply a decision to return while the conditions for a well-founded fear of persecution continue to exist. State proponents of 'safe return' effectively substitute 'objective' (change of) circumstances for the refugee's subjective assessment, thereby crossing the refugee/non-refugee line.

So far as safe return *may* have a role to play in the construction of policy, its minimum conditions include a transparent process based on credible information, which involves States, UNHCR as the agent of the interest of the international community,[151] and a representative element from among the refugees or displaced themselves. These or equivalent means seem most likely to ensure that the element of risk is properly appreciated, so reducing the chance of States acting in breach of their protection obligations.

3.3 RESETTLEMENT

Resettlement is about refugees moving from a transit or country of first asylum to another, or third, State. Resettlement policy aims to achieve a variety of objectives, the first and perhaps most fundamental being to provide a durable solution for refugees unable to return home or to remain in their country of immediate refuge.[152] A further goal is to relieve the strain on receiving countries, sometimes in a quantitative way, at others in a political way, by assisting them in relations with countries of origin. Resettlement also provides significant potential for the development of a resource base for the return of professional and skilled personnel at some future time when repatriation may become viable; returns to El Salvador and Chile illustrate this process. Finally, resettlement con-

---

[151] Executive Committee General Conclusion on International Protection (1994), above n. 149, para. 19(u) calls on UNHCR, amongst other matters, to provide guidance on the implementation of temporary protection, 'including advice . . . on safe return once the need for international protection has ceased'.

[152] Executive Committee Conclusions No. 22 (1981), IV, para. (3),(4).

tributes to international solidarity and to maintaining the fundamental principles of protection.[153]

Successive refugee crises in Indo-China, Latin America, and Europe, have underlined the necessity for States on occasion to go beyond financial assistance and to offer resettlement opportunities. This 'least preferred option'[154] may be dictated by a variety of factors, including political, economic, and ethnic pressures on the State of first admission, and concern for the security of the refugees themselves. States, however, have very different perceptions as to the desirability of various solutions. Broadly, these demonstrate (a) an emphasis on regional responsibility and local integration; or (b) an emphasis on global responsibility and a broadening of the resettlement burden; or (c) a resistance to local integration, with a corresponding emphasis on extra-regional resettlement. Certain States have also at times expressly accepted responsibility, as countries of first admission, to accept for local integration a proportion of asylum seekers, provided that other States lighten the burden by offering appropriate resettlement opportunities.[155]

Not surprisingly, the self-same reasons which may be advanced against resettlement by certain States (for example, their physical, demographic, and socio-economic limitations, together with the potential for culture shock and problems of adjustment for resettled refugees), are also relied on by other States unwilling to accept refugees for local integration.[156] Economic and social problems caused by large numbers of refugees, in both developing and developed countries,[157] as well as political and security factors, can likewise militate against local acceptance.[158]

---

[153] For a particularly coherent account of resettlement policy from the perspective of UNHCR, see Troeller, G. G., 'UNHCR Resettlement as an Instrument of International Protection', 3 *IJRL* 564 (1991); also, Bach, R. L., 'Third Country Resettlement', in Loescher, G. and Monahan, L., eds., *Refugees and International Relations*, (1989), 313; Salomon, K., *Refugees in the Cold War: Toward a New International Refugee Regime in the Early Postwar Era*, (1991), Ch. 5, 'Resettlement'.

[154] 'Least preferred' by whom?

[155] This view has been expressed by Australia and adopted in regard to refugees disembarked on its shores after rescue at sea; see above, Ch. 4, s. 4.2.

[156] See, for example, the views expressed by the Netherlands: UN doc. A/AC.96/SR.295, para. 2 and by UNHCR: ibid., SR.299, para. 13 (1978). On problems of adjustment faced by resettled refugees, see Chan, K. B. and Indra, D. M., eds., *Uprooting, Loss and Adaptation: The Resettlement of Indo-Chinese Refugees in Canada*, (1987); Iredale, R. R. 'The Occupational Adjustment of Indochinese refugees in Australia', (1983); Beach, H. and Ragvald, L., *A New Wave on the Northern Shore: The Indochinese Refugees in Sweden*, (1982); Fifth Seminar on Adaptation and Integration of Permanent Immigrants (Geneva, 6–10 April 1981), 19 *Int. Mig.* 1 (1981); Rutledge, P. J., *The Vietnamese Experience in America* (1992).

[157] See statements by Austria: UN doc. A/AC.96/SR.296, para. 1 (1978); SR.300, para. 29 (1979) and SR.325, paras. 46–7 (1980); and by Italy: ibid., SR.307, para. 48 (1979). On occasion, a commitment to resettlement has also been linked to attempts to 'cap' the numbers of spontaneous asylum seekers; see proposals by Denmark: UN doc. A/AC.96/SR.432 (1988), paras. 7–16.

[158] These factors have been stressed repeatedly by first refuge countries; see statements by Djibouti: UN doc. A/AC.96/SR.307, para. 63 (1979) and SR.319, para. 54 (1980); Malaysia: ibid., SR.306, para. 81 (1979) and Indonesia: ibid., SR.308, para. 42 (1979). The settlement problems of refugees may be further exacerbated by the break-up of families; see Executive Committee

At the individual level, however, resettlement can still mean the difference between life and death.[159] Refugees may be denied basic human rights in the country of first refuge; their lives and freedom may be threatened by local elements motivated by racial, religious or political reasons, or by attacks and assassinations directed from outside. The authorities in turn may be unable or unwilling to offer effective protection. In such circumstances, resettlement becomes not the solution of last resort, but the principal objective. Similar considerations apply to other categories such as children, the disabled, or rescue at sea cases, for whom the exercise of protection without prospect of solution is otherwise quite meaningless.[160] UNHCR, States and the Executive Committee have also recognized that the special protection needs of women refugees may call for resettlement opportunities.

In a background paper entitled 'Resettlement as an Instrument of Protection', submitted to the Sub-Committee of the Whole on International Protection in 1991,[161] UNHCR emphasized the 'last resort' character of resettlement, to be pursued when it is the 'only available measure to guarantee protection and/or offer a refugee a future commensurate with fundamental human rights'. Besides security concerns, resettlement could also contribute to 'humanitarian protection', for women at risk,[162] torture victims, the physically or mentally handicapped, and certain medical and family reunion cases.[163] However, while over

Conclusion No. 24 (1981), para. 7 on tracing and family reunion. Family unity and the right to respect for family life and to protection of the family are recognized in most human rights instruments; see art. 16(3), 1948 Universal Declaration of Human Rights; arts. 17 and 23, 1966 Covenant on Civil and Political Rights; art. 8, European Convention on Human Rights; see also Recommendation B, Final Act of the 1951 Convention. The Indo-China refugee problem highlighted the need to take account of traditional extended family relationships; incorporating recognition of such relationships in resettlement programmes can in turn cause problems, however, as where other migrant groups perceive themselves disadvantaged by comparison.

[159] See Executive Committee General Conclusions on International Protection (1989), *Report* of the 40th Session: UN doc. A/AC.96/737, para. 22(m)—resettlement not only a possible solution, but for some refugees also an urgent protection measure; (1990), *Report* of the 41st Session: UN doc. A/AC.96/760, para. 20(f)—link between protection and resettlement; (1992), *Report* of the 43rd Session: UN doc. A/AC.96/804, para. 21(t)—resettlement as an instrument of protection; and (1993), *Report* of the 44th Session: UN doc. A/AC.96/821, para. 19(q)—and 'a durable solution in specific circumstances'.

[160] On the resettlement of disabled refugee children and the 'Twenty or More Plan', see Executive Committee Conclusion No. 47 (1987), para. (l).

[161] 'Resettlement as an Instrument of Protection: Traditional Problems in achieving this Durable Solution and New Directions in the 1990s': UN doc. EC/SCP/65 (9 July 1991); Troeller, above n. 153.

[162] Cf. Executive Committee Conclusion on Refugee Women (1988), *Report* of the 39th Session: UN doc. A/AC.96/721, para. 26, recognizing that refugee women face particular hazards, especially threats to physical safety and sexual exploitation, and calling for support for special resettlement programmes. See also Executive Committee Conclusion on Refugee Women (1989), *Report* of the 40th Session: UN doc. A/AC.96/737, para. 26(c); Executive Committee Conclusion No. 64 (1990), para. (a)(xi).

[163] UN doc. EC/SCP/65 (9 July 1991), paras. 2, 3, 4. The 'vulnerable' categories potentially eligible for 'humanitarian protection' through resettlement were first defined in guidelines issued in 1990, with a sixth category of 'long-stayers'. Some States expressed concern at the narrow scope of

1.2 million had been resettled out of South East Asia, particularly to protect 'first asylum', future resettlement, in UNHCR's view, would be more protection-oriented and involve smaller numbers.[164] Such down-grading of an important if specialized pillar of the solutions structure doubtless satisfied some of UNHCR's constituency, but may have done little for refugees or international protection at large. A number of countries remain committed to providing places, while others continue to see resettlement as an important and effective means of making concrete the rhetoric of solidarity and co-operation.

Canada's experience as a refugee resettlement country is illustrative. Together with Australia and the United States, it is one of only three countries to run major programmes, although some others either have smaller programmes or are committed to admit disabled refugees or urgent protection cases.[165] As an immigration country, Canada has aimed not only to fulfil foreign policy aims, but also to satisfy often competing domestic concerns, including community expectations in the area of private sponsorship, and national goals, such as economic performance. The Canadian Immigration Act, as amended, together with the Immigration Regulations, provide a legal framework for the selection of Convention refugees and others similarly situated for permanent resettlement in Canada. The Act incorporates the Convention definition, and provides that a refugee or member of a 'designated class' may be admitted for permanent residence if able to meet the selection standards and to show that he or she is likely to become successfully established.[166] In the past, Canada has maintained different types of resettlement programmes, focusing on Convention refugees who have not found permanent solutions elsewhere; and on designated classes requiring resettlement and assistance on humanitarian grounds, such as Indochinese, self-exiles, and political prisoners.[167]

Canadian policy and programmes were extensively revised in the 1990s, away

'vulnerable groups', and suggested additional categories, such as the elderly and children traumatized by war: *Report* of the Sub-Committee of the Whole on International Protection: UN doc. A/AC.96/781 (9 Oct. 1991), paras. 19–26, at 22.

[164] UN doc. EC/SCP/65 (9 July 1991), paras. 13,14 (obstacles to resettlement); 15–19 (future resettlement). Basic statistics illustrate changing times: in the late 1970s/early 1980s, some 200,000 resettlement places were available annually, principally for those in camps in South East Asia; by the mid-1990s, places had fallen to around 50,000, notwithstanding a significant global increase in total refugee numbers.

[165] During the crisis in former Yugoslavia, for example, Denmark established an office in Zagreb to deal with asylum and protection issues, and specifically to ensure that 'persons in need of immediate protection obtained it outside the area of conflict as expeditiously as possible': UN doc. A/AC.96/SR.483 (1993), para. 85.

[166] Immigration Act 1976, s. 6(1); also s. 6(3)—'a member of a class designated by the Governor in Council as a class, the admission of members of which would be in accordance with Canada's humanitarian tradition with respect to the displaced and the persecuted'; see s. 114(1)(d) on the making of regulations. The Governor in Council may also grant exemptions or otherwise facilitate the admission of any person, 'for reasons of public policy or due to the existence of compassionate or humanitarian considerations': s. 114(2).

[167] For a general summary see Immigration Canada, *Canada's Resettlement Programs: New Directions*, (Jan. 1993).

from specific classes and towards a more generic humanitarian designated class.[168] A 1994 policy document recognized that resettlement is the 'least feasible option for the vast majority of the global refugee population, both in terms of the limited role played by most countries and the high costs involved'.[169] From a Canadian perspective, however, resettlement continues to play a role in meeting three principal objectives, namely, protection, burden sharing, and private sponsorship, with the last-mentioned intended to encourage refugee resettlement in partnership with community-based sponsoring groups and organizations. 'Settlement potential' will not be disregarded, although policy emphasizes that 'protection concerns will continue to be given priority' in a number of urgent cases, such as the Women at Risk programme.

During 1995, discussion began on the replacement of designated classes and special programmes with a single *Resettlement from Abroad Class* (RAC).[170] Intended to apply to people identified overseas as requiring humanitarian consideration while remaining 'flexible and comprehensive', the RAC will focus on three separate categories: Convention refugee, source country, and country of first asylum. The first needs no explanation; the second applies to those who, being still in their country of origin, itself listed as a source country,[171] are 'seriously and personally affected by civil war, armed conflict or massive violation of human rights', and have no possibility of a durable solution within a reasonable time-frame.[172] A member of the country of first asylum category includes individuals in a similar situation, save that they have left their country of origin, and a Canadian sponsoring organization has undertaken to assist them.

The Indo-China exodus and the almost automatic resettlement response regardless of refugee status were unique, although policy precedents can be seen in earlier, particularly western, reactions to movements from eastern Europe and of certain minority, mainly Christian groups from the Middle East. Although remarkable numbers were moved, the experience was by no means entirely positive, either for the Indochinese or for the States and communities involved. As the years passed, the solution chosen by the developed world for a particularly tragic instance of humanitarian necessity—temporary refuge in countries of first asylum, assistance from the international community, and resettlement beyond the region generally and without regard to refugee status—operated as a signi-

---

[168] See Citizenship and Immigration Canada, *Into the 21st Century: A Strategy for Immigration and Citizenship*, (1994), 43–54; also 'Declaration on Refugee Protection for Women', 1 June 1994: ibid., annex 5.

[169] Citizenship and Immigration, 'Building a Framework', Nov. 1994.

[170] Citizenship and Immigration, International Refugee and Migration Policy Branch, 'Resettlement from Abroad Class', Discussion Paper, Apr. 1995.

[171] The listing of countries (for both source and first asylum country categories) distinguishes these categories from Convention refugees, and also serves to narrow the range of potential applicants (for example, because not every country in conflict will be listed). The list, to be drawn up in consultation with NGOs, is intended to be easily and quickly amended.

[172] This category will replace the Political Prisoners and Oppressed Persons designated class, open at the time of writing to nationals of Guatemala and El Salvador.

ficant pull factor, both for those in fear for their lives and liberty and for others simply dissatisfied with conditions in their country of origin or anxious to join family overseas.

Recognition of the changed character of the flow from Vietnam led in time to the Comprehensive Plan of Action, with a continuing commitment to resettle those determined to be refugees according to international criteria. The experience overall, however, contributed to a shrinking commitment to resettlement as solution among many States, both at the individual level and in the context of international solidarity, co-operation and burden sharing. In these circumstances, a coherent, practical, let alone normative theory of response remains difficult to argue, save in the most general sense.

3.4 ASSISTANCE AND DEVELOPMENT

A distinction has sometimes been drawn between UNHCR's protection and assistance functions, particularly in light of the additional humanitarian activities periodically entrusted to it, for example, in former Yugoslavia. In practice, however, protection and assistance activities have tended to mingle, as programmes were extended beyond local integration, employment and self-sufficiency projects, to cover returnees and the internally displaced. There is no necessary, hard and fast division between the humanitarian role of meeting material needs, and a legal interest in security and welfare, and at times a clear rights element may be present, for example, in the provision of adequate food.[173]

By 1989, *refugee aid and development* had become well established in the relief and assistance vocabulary, as a way of linking refugees and host communities.[174] Integration programmes and large-scale repatriations almost always involve some sort of contribution to development: from roads, water supplies, and schools, to employment, the provision of seeds, farming equipment and livestock. For agencies such as UNHCR, the question is to determine how far its responsibility extends, and to ascertain respective agency competence for promoting conditions conducive to voluntary repatriation, including support for sustainable development, control of arms supplies and de-mining, and actually organizing and accompanying transport.

The inter-connectedness of assistance, protection and solutions is evident in international action with respect to the situations in Indo-China and Central America. The 1979 United Nations Conference on Indo-Chinese Refugees

---

[173] See arts. 2, 11, 1966 Covenant on Economic, Social and Cultural Rights, and the emphasis on international co-operation. See generally Alston, P. and Tomaševski, K., eds., *The Right to Food*, (1984).

[174] See *Review and Appraisal of the World Population Plan of Action*, (1989), 2–3, Rec. 9; *Report of the International Conference on Population, 1984, Mexico City, 6–14 August 1984*, (1984); Rec. 47 declared that 'High priority' should be given to the 'rehabilitation of expelled and homeless people . . . displaced by natural and man-made catastrophes'. For UNHCR's area of interest, see comment and recommendations excerpted in the *Note on the United Nations International Conference on Population*: UN doc. A/AC.96/INF.170, 3 Sept. 1984.

produced a package of undertakings with respect to material support and resettlement in favour of so-called first asylum countries in South East Asia.[175] Ten years later, the second international conference adopted a Declaration and Comprehensive Plan of Action (CPA) and 'noted with satisfaction' that durable solutions had been found for so many Indo-Chinese, 'as a result of combined efforts on the part of Governments and international organizations concerned'.[176] The Conference nevertheless accepted that a complex problem required a 'comprehensive set of mutually re-enforcing humanitarian undertakings'.[177]

A similar level of co-operation was endorsed by States represented at the May 1989 International Conference which adopted the Declaration and Concerted Plan of Action in Favour of Central American Refugees, Returnees and Displaced Persons.[178] This in turn recognized that solutions to the problems of refugees and displaced persons in the region were intimately linked to the peace process, to development and to economic co-operation. CIREFCA grew out of a political commitment to improve regional stability, and sought to incorporate solutions for the uprooted into a more, comprehensive durable plan.

Although a protection component can be identified in the resolution of the problems of displacement in Indo-China and Central America, the contribution of each to the legal situation is far less clear, whether considered from an institutional or an individual perspective. While the principle of international co-operation between States may have been strengthened, the continuing place of protection within the operational mandate of an organization such as UNHCR, which is called on more and more to provide assistance, poses a range of institutional challenges that have yet to be resolved.

3.5 'PREVENTIVE PROTECTION'

In the present context, 'prevention' means mediating or otherwise ameliorating situations which are most usually the proximate causes of flight. The linkage to

---

[175] See *Report* of the Secretary-General on the Meeting on Refugees and Displaced Persons in South East Asia, Geneva, 20–21 July 1979, and subsequent developments: UN doc. A/34/637.

[176] The draft Declaration and Comprehensive Plan of Action, approved by the Preparatory Meeting for the International Conference on 8 March 1989: *Note by the Secretary-General:* UN doc. A/CONF.148/2, 26 Apr. 1989, were adopted without amendment and by consensus at the June 1989 conference. For text, see below, Annexe 5, No. 1.

[177] Generally on the CPA, see Bronée, S. A., 'The History of the Comprehensive Plan of Action', 5 *IJRL* 534 (1993); Bari, S., 'Refugee Status Determination under the Comprehensive Plan of Action (CPA)' 4 *IJRL* 487 (1992); Helton, A. C., 'Refugee Determination under the Comprehensive Plan of Action; Overview and Assessment', 5 *IJRL* 544 (1993); Mushkat, R., 'Implementation of the CPA in Hong Kong: Compatibility with International Standards?', 5 *IJRL* 559 (1993).

[178] The process and plan of action came to be known as CIREFCA, after the Spanish acronym for the international conference; text below, Annexe 5, No. 2. See also UNHCR, 'Consolidating Peace in Central America through an Inter-Agency Approach to Longer-Term Needs of the Uprooted. Report on the Conclusion of the CIREFCA Process': UN doc. A/AC.96/831, 31 Aug. 1994; Espiell, H. G., Picado, S. and Lanza, L. V., 'Principles and Criteria for the Protection of and Assistance to Central American Refugees, Returnees and Displaced Persons in Central America', 2 *IJRL* 83 (1990).

protection implies that, whatever action is undertaken to deal with the underlying reasons for flight, groups and individuals should not be worse off, in the sense of remaining exposed to danger or risk to life and limb, while also losing the possibility of flight to refuge and asylum. There is no *a priori* limit to the range of activities that might be labelled 'preventive', just as there is no fixed number of causes of exodus.

3.5.1 Fact-finding and the resolution of disputes

At first glance, certain traditional methods of dispute settlement might appear of value for application to situations involving refugees, at least so far as facts in dispute may lead to conflict and displacement.[179] Assuming a value in de-politicization, the Commissions of Inquiry set up under the 1899 Hague Convention were specifically required *not* to pronounce verdicts; their role was limited to ascertaining, rather than judging, the facts, from which the parties were free to draw whatever conclusions they desired.[180] Both these commissions and those established under the Bryan treaties,[181] however, have been little used. Conciliation commissions competent to examine the broader aspects of disputes—political, juridical and factual—have suffered a similar fate, which one commentator attributes to their being identified with the legal process, and as a form of arbitration likely to lead to unwanted rulings.[182] Other writers have observed, with evident justification, that dispute settlement at the international level, 'must rest on political rather than legal institutions and devices, on

---

[179] See generally *Report of the Secretary-General on Methods of Fact-Finding:* UN docs. A/5694 (1964); A/6228 (1966).

[180] The 1899 Hague Convention for the Pacific Settlement of International Disputes further excluded Commissions of Inquiry from disputes involving honour or vital interests. Art. 16(4) of the Additional Facility declared: 'The Report shall be limited to findings of fact. The Report shall not contain any recommendations to the parties, nor shall it have the character of an award.' Art. 17 added that the parties shall be entirely free as to the effect to be given to the Report. Compare art. 53 on *arbitrations*: 'The award shall be final and binding on the parties'; and art. 33(1) on *conciliation*, providing that it shall be the duty of the conciliation commission, 'to clarify the issues in dispute and to endeavour to bring about agreement between them on mutually acceptable terms'. Art. 34(1), on the same subject, declares that the parties shall co-operate in good faith with the conciliation commission in order to enable it to carry out its functions, and shall give their most serious consideration to its recommendations. Compare Rolin's view of the essence of conciliation as a thorough examination, which distinguishes it from good offices, followed by a non-binding recommendation, which distinguishes it from arbitration: 49(II) *Annuaire de l'Institut de Droit International* (1961), 226; Bar-Yaacov, N., *The Handling of International Disputes by Means of Inquiry*, (1974), 237.

[181] UN doc. A/5964 (1964), para. 62 and following. Bar-Yaacov, *International Disputes*, 114–17, 134–6. The Bryan commissions were competent as to the factual aspects of all disputes, apart from those capable of arbitration.

[182] Bar-Yaacov, *International Disputes*, 198–246, 245. Note also that in a request for interim measures under art. 41 of its Statute, the ICJ 'cannot make definitive findings of fact or of imputability, and the right of each party to dispute the facts alleged against it, to challenge the attribution to it of responsibility for those facts, and to submit arguments in respect of the merits, must remain unaffected by the Court's decision': *Genocide Convention Case*, ICJ *Rep.*, 1993, 345, para. 44; Merrills, J. G., 'Interim Measures of Protection in the Recent Jurisprudence of the International Court of Justice', 44 *ICLQ* 90, 105 (1995).

balancing conflicting interests, on negotiation, bargaining, and the search for a mutually acceptable solution rather than a trial in a court of law'.[183]

The United Nations itself has not been notably successful in developing methods of fact-finding and inquiry as effective instruments in the resolution of international disputes.[184] Fact-finding apart from formal dispute settlement procedures nevertheless remains of crucial importance, and knowledge of facts is essential to effective decision-making by those charged with finding solutions. In his 1982 *Report on the Work of the Organization,* the Secretary-General, apparently wary of the Security Council's increasing recourse to 'informal consultations', suggested greater use of article 99 of the Charter.[185] He proposed that the UN's preventive role could be made more effective by developing 'a wider and more systematic capacity for fact-finding in potential conflict areas', and that the Council itself could devise swifter, more responsive procedures for sending good offices missions, military or civilian observers, or other UN presence. With reference to refugee movements rather than conflict as such, the Group of Governmental Experts in 1986 urged the main organs of the UN to make fuller use of their respective competencies, 'with a view to considering at the earliest possible stage situations and problems' which could give rise to massive flows of refugees. It further recommended that the Secretary-General make full use of his authority, give continuing attention to the question of averting new massive flows, ensure that timely and fuller information is available, analysed and assessed within the Secretariat, share the information, and strive for prompt and more effective action by UN agencies and Member States.[186] The General Assembly adopted these conclusions and recommendations in December 1986, and the following year the Secretary-General took a first, ultimately short-lived, implementing step and established an Office for Research and the Collection of Information.[187]

For many years, the nature of the General Assembly and the Security Council contributed to a level of politicization, evident in the composition, mandate and pronouncements of those organs which have been established, alien to the attainment of mutually acceptable solutions. Indeed, it may have been unrealistic to expect that such bodies could ever be non-political, or attain the desired

---

[183] Northedge F. S. and Bonelan, M. D., *International Disputes: The Political Aspects,* (1981), 320; summarized with approval in Bar-Yaacov, *International Disputes,* 245.

[184] One exception, perhaps, has been the role from time to time of United Nations forces in observing ceasefires and related activities. See Bar-Yaacov, *International Disputes,* 247–73; cf. *Report of the Secretary-General on the Work of the Organization,* Sept. 1982: UN doc. A/37/1, 7. On the other hand, UN efforts to establish a Panel for Inquiry and Conciliation (see UNGA res. 268 (III), 28 Apr. 1949) and a Register of Experts on Fact-Finding (see UNGA res. 2329 (XXII), 13 Dec. 1967) have had few concrete results.

[185] 'The Secretary General may bring to the attention of the Security Council any matter which in his opinion may threaten the maintenance of international peace and security'.

[186] *Report* of the Group of Governmental Experts: UN doc. A/41/324, 13 May 1986, paras, 68, 70–2; for relevant extracts see below, Annexe 4, No. 2.

[187] On ORCI and related developments, see above, Ch. 6, s. 1.3.

levels of 'impartiality, efficiency and rectitude',[188] although developments in the relations between States during the 1990s have opened up new possibilities. In 1991, the General Assembly adopted a 'Declaration on Fact-finding by the United Nations in the field of the Maintenance of International Peace and Security', recognizing that the UN's ability in this respect 'depends to a large extent on its acquiring detailed knowledge about the factual circumstances of any dispute or situation'.[189] The Declaration in turn accepted that fact-finding missions might be undertaken by the Security Council, the General Assembly and the Secretary-General, in the context of their respective responsibilities.

In a general sense, fact-finding is as important in the formulation of policies of prevention and response as in dispute settlement. Any effective system of protection, intercession and assistance depends on accurate sources of information, including access to systematic and authoritative reporting on conditions in any country which may bear on refugee flows, such as war or inter-communal conflict of an ethnic, religious or political nature, widespread violations of human rights, and even ecological and natural disasters.[190] Such information will allow the formulation of policies for flows and returns, and a more accountable determination of the validity of claims to protection.

3.5.2 *The United Nations and its possibilities*

The initiatives on mass exodus and measures to avert flows of refugees helped to open debate on the potential for United Nations machinery to reach solutions to humanitarian problems. The General Assembly may recommend measures for the peaceful adjustment of any situation, regardless of origin, which it deems likely to impair the general welfare or friendly relations between States.[191] This certainly appears wide enough to allow for action on the occasion of any refugee exodus, but historically General Assembly involvement has been indirect and after the fact. Thus, it has repeatedly stressed the necessity for States to uphold relevant legal and humanitarian principles and to provide solutions to refugee problems. It has also approved action by UNHCR on specific issues,[192] but has refrained from participation in the resolution of situations, other than calling generally for appropriate action to deal with causes.[193] Earlier precedents still

---

[188] UN doc. A/37/1, 5–8; or as para. 3 of the Declaration on Fact-Finding puts it, 'Fact-finding should be comprehensive, objective, impartial and timely.'

[189] UNGA res. 46/59, 9 Dec. 1991.

[190] Rusu, S., 'Refugees, Information and Solutions: The Need for Informed Decision-Making', 13 *RSQ*, No. 1, 4 (1994). Also UNHCR, 'Informed Decision-Making in Protection: The Role of Information': UN doc. EC/SCP/CRP.6 (27 Sept. 1983).

[191] Art. 14, United Nations Charter; this competence is subject to the overall responsibility of the Security Council under art. 12. Art. 14 was invoked in UNGA res. 1542 (XV), 14 Dec. 1960, calling on Portugal to submit information regarding its non-self-governing territories; see Bar-Yaacov, *International Disputes*, 313–4.

[192] See, for example, UNGA res. 2790 (XXVI), 6 Dec. 1971, on assistance to East Pakistan refugees through the UN focal point and UN humanitarian assistance to East Pakistan.

[193] See UNGA res. 49/169, 23 Dec. 1994, preamble; 48/116, 20 Dec. 1993, preamble; also UNGA res. 48/139, 20 Dec. 1993, 'Human rights and mass exoduses', paras. 15, 21.

show the degree of politicization which can affect any 'dispute' between States and which, given voting patterns in the General Assembly, will more likely lead to stalemate than effective solutions.[194]

Latterly, with the 'disappearance' of Cold War restraints, more has been expected of the Security Council in dealing with humanitarian issues. Like the General Assembly, it too may establish the subsidiary organs it deems necessary for the performance of its functions,[195] but under Chapter VII of the Charter, it also has authority to take a variety of measures to deal with humanitarian problems.[196] Resolution 688 on northern Iraq, adopted by the Security Council on 5 April 1991, remains ambiguous, controversial and probably specific to the circumstances of the time. Perhaps more significant from the perspective of an evolving international responsibility to provide protection was the memorandum of understanding agreed by the United Nations and the Government of Iraq some two weeks later, in which the latter expressly welcomed 'United Nations efforts to promote the voluntary return home of Iraqi displaced persons and to take humanitarian measures to avert new flows of refugees and displaced persons from Iraq'.[197] The subsequent implementation of this understanding, although not without problems, nevertheless internationalized humanitarian operations and may serve as significant precedent.

3.5.3 *UNHCR and 'preventive protection'*

UNHCR was slower to associate itself with causes and prevention than might have been supposed, given its function of providing international protection and seeking permanent solutions. Certain statutory provisions long had an inhibiting effect, particularly paragraph 2, prescribing that the work of the Office shall be 'of an entirely non-political character (and) shall be humanitarian and social'. No work on behalf of refugees can ever be truly non-political, particularly where it involves protection, but UNHCR invoked this proviso in 1981 when formally declining to contribute to the initiative on international co-operation to avert new flows of refugees: while it assists in the solution of refugee problems, UNHCR 'cannot concern itself with the circumstances which have brought

[194] In 1946 and 1947, after the Security Council proved unable to reach agreement on principles and modalities for establishing peace in the Balkans, the United States brought the situation before the General Assembly. UNGA res. 109(II), 21 Oct. 1947, called on the States involved to 'co-operate in the settlement of the problems arising out of the presence of refugees . . . through voluntary repatriation wherever possible and (to) take effective measures to prevent the participation of such refugees in political or military activity'. On the various dimensions of the refugee problem and the political and other difficulties in finding solutions, see Goodwin-Gill, G. S., 'Different Types of Forced Migration Movements as an International and National Problem', in Rystad, G., ed., *The Uprooted: Forced Migration as an International Problem in the Post-War Era*, (1991), 15, 31–3.

[195] See United Nations Charter, arts. 24, 29, and 34. Cf. UN Commission of Investigation concerning Greek Frontier Incidents, established by SC res. 15 (1946); UN doc. A/5694 (1964), paras. 249-59.

[196] Gowlland-Debbas, V., 'Security Council Enforcement Action and Issues of State Responsibility', 43 *ICLQ* 55 (1994).

[197] Memorandum of Understanding, para. 2; for text, see 3 *IJRL* 359 (1991).

them into existence'.[198] Although abstention in some cases will be politic, it is not necessarily dictated by the 'non-political' directive; and if this is a jurisdictional restriction on competence, it must be subsidiary to UNHCR's two fundamental objectives, protection and solutions.[199]

The necessity to deal with causes was acknowledged in several earlier Executive Conclusions,[200] but UNHCR's understanding of *preventive measures* was initially limited to what could or should be done, for example, to ensure the personal safety of refugees, reduce armed attacks on camps, or meet the needs of refugee women.[201] Economic and development aid was linked in 1990 to the prevention of *migratory* flows,[202] but in 1991, the General Assembly mentioned the promotion of solutions through preventive measures,[203] and thereafter UNHCR highlighted steps that might be taken in countries of origin with regard to the promotion of human rights, or to removing or reducing the factors that force displacement.[204] Implementing appropriate action successfully, while

---

[198] *Report* of the Secretary-General: UN doc. A/36/582, 43.

[199] Where protection necessitates determining refugee status, it always involves consideration of causes. Similarly, UNHCR would hardly be justified in promoting or facilitating repatriation where it had express knowledge that the conditions which had produced the initial exodus still persisted.

[200] Executive Committee Conclusions No. 22 (1980), para. (6); No. 40 (1985), para. (c). See the following General Conclusions on International Protection: (1982), *Report* of the 33rd Session: UN doc. A/AC.96/614, para. 42(e)—referring to efforts in *other* fora; (1986), *Report* of the 37th Session: UN doc. A/AC.96/688, para. 125(e); (1987), *Report* of the 38th Session: UN doc. A/AC.96/702, para. 204(k)—urging the international community to do its utmost to address causes; (1988), *Report* of the 39th Session: UN doc. A/AC.96/721, para. 22(d); (1991), *Report* of the 42nd Session: UN doc. A/AC.96/783, para. 21(h), (i)—calling on the High Commissioner to explore new options for preventive strategies. Also Conclusions on durable solutions (1989), *Report* of the 40th Session: UN doc. A/AC.96/737, para. 23(b)(ii); and on the Note on International Protection (1990), *Report* of the 41st Session, UN doc. A/AC.96/760, para. 21(1)(i)—with a reference to mediation as an effective method to contain problems; and (vi). In 1983, Australia had called for more emphasis on political solutions in countries of origin: UN doc. A/AC.96/SR.354, para. 36, while in 1985, Turkey stated that action to prevent refugee movements was of a political nature and therefore not within UNHCR's competence: UN doc. A/AC.96/SR.388, para. 48.

[201] See, for example, UNHCR, 'Notes' on International Protection, (1983): UN doc. A/AC.96/623, para. 26; (1986): UN doc. A/AC.96/680, para. 45; (1987): UN doc. A/AC.96/694, para. 39; also UNGA res. 40/118, para. 4; UNGA res. 41/124, para. 5.

[202] As UN High Commissioner for Refugees Stoltenberg put it, 'in order to secure admission and asylum for those in need of protection, there was need to address the larger issue of migratory flows. *Persecution and oppression had to be met by asylum;* migratory flows had to be met by preventive economic and development aid. To blur the distinction might be detrimental to the specific interests of refugees, but to ignore the links . . . would be unrealistic': UN doc. A/AC.96/SR.453, paras. 55–6 (1990) (emphasis added).

[203] UNGA res. 46/106, 16 Dec. 1991, Preamble and para. 9.

[204] See UNHCR, 'Notes' on International Protection, (1992): UN doc. A/AC.96/799, para. 30; (1993): UN doc. A/AC.96/815, para. 36. The 'Notes' for 1993 and 1994 included sections respectively on 'Prevention and Solutions' and 'The Need for Protection in Countries of Origin'. See also Executive Committee General Conclusions on International Protection (1992), *Report* of the 43rd Session : UN doc. A./AC.96/804, para. 21(o); (1993), *Report* of the 44th Session: UN doc. A/AC.96/821 paras. 19(n), (dd), (ee)—calling on the international community to address causes in a concerted, comprehensive manner; (1994), *Report* of the 45th Session: UN doc. A/AC.96/839, para. 19(s); and Executive Conclusion No. 75 (1994) on Internally Displaced Persons, para. (b).

maintaining basic principles and mandate responsibilities, is another matter, however.

In 1992, the Special Rapporteur on former Yugoslavia concluded that many displaced persons would not have to seek refuge abroad, 'if their security could be guaranteed and if they could be provided with both sufficient food supplies and adequate medical care'.[205] UNHCR's strategy of 'preventive protection' consequently anticipated monitoring the treatment of ethnic minority groups, mediation, exposing the practice of forced relocation, and other measures to improve respect for human rights. The presence of international relief organizations and NGOs, it was thought, would 'build confidence in fragile security situations',[206] but the resulting reality was rather different.[207]

3.5.4 *Prevention and the refugee dimension*

In 1993, the Executive Committee emphasized that 'UNHCR's activities in the field of prevention must be complementary to its international protection responsibilities and consistent with the principles of international human rights and humanitarian law and that the institution of asylum must not in any way be undermined'.[208] The failure of regional and international efforts to provide an adequate degree of internal protection calls into question State actions otherwise intended to contain, restrict or prevent movement out of former Yugoslavia, for whatever good or bad reason. The prevention of movements in search of asylum by stopping flight rather than removing causes, is no solution and may indeed amount to an abuse of rights. State practices and objectives,

[205] *Report* on human rights in former Yugoslavia: UN doc. E/CN.4/1992/S–1/10, (1992), para. 25(b). The United Nations High Commissioner for Refugees also spoke of the 'basic right of the individual not to be forced into exile': Sadako Ogata, Statement to the Commission on Human Rights, Geneva, 3 Mar. 1993.

[206] UNHCR, 'A Comprehensive Response to the Humanitarian Crisis in the former Yugoslavia': UN doc. HCR/IMFY/1992/2, 24 July 1992, paras. 7–9.

[207] For detailed accounts of the human rights situation, see the periodic reports submitted by Tadeusz Mazowiecki, Special Rapporteur of the Commission on Human Rights, further to Commission resolutions 1994/72 (9 Mar. 1994), (1993/7 (23 Feb. 1993) and 1992/S–1/1 (14 Aug. 1992): UN docs. E/CN.4/1995/10 (4 Aug. 1994); E/CN.4/1995/4 (10 June 1994); E/CN.4/1994/110 (21 Feb. 1994); E/CN.4/1994/47 (17 Nov. 1993); E/CN.4/1994/8 (6 Sept. 1993); E/CN.4/1994/6 (26 Aug. 1993); E/CN.4/1994/4 (19 May 1993); E/CN.4/1994/3 (5 May 1993); E/CN.4/1993/50 (10 Feb. 1993); E/CN.4/1992/S–1/10 (27 Oct. 1992); also, E/CN.4/1994/26/Add.1 (15 Dec. 1993)—question of enforced or involuntary disappearances; E/CN.4/1993/62 (6 Jan. 1993)—implementation of the declaration on the elimination of all forms of intolerance and of discrimination based on religion or belief. For comment on the efficacy of international protection measures see, for example, Mooney, E. D., 'Presence, *ergo* protection? UNPROFOR, UNHCR and the ICRC in Croatia and Bosnia and Herzegovina', 7 *IJRL* 407 (1995); Thorburn, J., 'Transcending Boundaries: Temporary Protection and Burden-Sharing in Europe', ibid., 459; Landgren, K., 'Safety Zones and International Protection: A Dark Grey Area', ibid., 436; Higgins, R., 'The United Nations and Former Yugoslavia', 69 *International Affairs* 3 (1993); Grant, S., 'Protection Mechanisms and the Yugoslav Crisis', *Interights Bulletin*, 8:1 (1994).

[208] Executive Committee General Conclusion on International Protection (1993), *Report* of the 44th Session: UN doc. A/AC.96/821, para. 19(u). Also, 'Note on International Protection': UN doc. A/AC.96/777 (1991), paras. 43–4, 47; UN doc. A/AC.96/SR.463 (1991), paras. 30–49 (Mrs Ogata).

which limit directly the human right to leave and seek asylum, will therefore only be valid[209] if *effective protection* of human rights is provided to those who would otherwise flee.[210]

UNHCR's involvement in supplying humanitarian relief in the guise of 'preventive protection' is open to precisely equivalent criticism. Without otherwise intending to deal with the question of mandate responsibility, the High Commissioner's Special Representative for former Yugoslavia remarked in 1994 that UNHCR had been used as 'a palliative, an alibi, an excuse to cover the lack of political will to confront the reality of the war . . . with the necessary political and, perhaps, military means'.[211] Novel international exercises to provide protection on site and somehow or other to deal with causes for flight have diminished the perception in some quarters that the right to leave in search of asylum is fundamental. Turkey's decision to close its border to Kurdish refugees and the support or non-objection of a substantial part of the international community, challenged the principle of non-rejection at the frontier,[212] although arguably they also removed the factual/legal basis for departure in search of asylum. In other cases, however, international measures have been inadequate to the purpose, and the rights of those obliged to remain have not been sufficiently protected as to avoid the necessity for flight in search of asylum.

Given the protection orientation and objectives of refugee and human rights law, the limited notion of the right to leave to seek asylum from persecution may be the only aspect of the right to leave one's country in international law to impose any duty on other States. In this sense, the nearest correlative duty may be not to frustrate the exercise of that right in such a way as to leave individuals exposed to persecution or other violation of their human rights; and that correspondingly intentional policies and practices of containment *without protection* constitute an abuse of rights.[213]

---

[209] Which is *not* the same as 'legal'.

[210] See Frelick, B., ' "Preventive Protection" and the Right to Seek Asylum: A Preliminary Look at Bosnia and Croatia', 4 *IJRL* 439 (1992); cf. Goodwin-Gill, G. S., 'The Right to Leave, the Right to Return and the Question of a Right to Remain', in Gowlland-Debbas, V., *The Problem of Refugees in the Light of Contemporary International Law Issues*, (1995), 95.

[211] Mendiluce, J. -M., 'War and Disaster in the Former Yugoslavia: The Limits of Humanitarian Action', *World Refugee Survey—1994*, 10, 14. Cf. UN High Commissioner Ogata's contrasting optimistic references in 1992 to 'increasingly effective initiatives to provide protection . . . to displaced populations' in countries such as former Yugoslavia: UN doc. A/AC.96/SR.472, para. 49. For Turkey, the main lesson from Bosnia was that peace-keeping could not be carried out in tandem with an ongoing war: UN doc. A/AC.96/SR.485, paras. 65–76 (1993), while the High Commissioner significantly qualified the success of any UNHCR activities as contingent on larger international efforts to resolve underlying causes: UN doc. A/AC.96/SR.481, para. 42 (1993).

[212] See above, Ch. 4, s. 3.2.

[213] To paraphrase a former ILC Rapporteur on State Responsibility, a 'primary' rule of international law forbids the 'abusive' exercise of rights of control over the movement of persons, which rights will be violated if certain limits are exceeded in the course of their exercise, or if they are exercised with the (sole) intention of harming others. Cf. Ago, R., *Second Report on State Responsibility*, UN doc. A/CN.4/233: Yearbook of the ILC, 1970–II, 191, 193.

3.5.5 *Prevention: some preliminary conclusions*

A comprehensive and *effective* mechanism to prevent or mitigate refugee movements will need to draw on disparate elements and experience, while also being
linked to a clear set of *protection* objectives.[214] Traditional dispute settlement
methods, such as inquiry, arbitration, mediation and conciliation, should not be
dismissed out of hand, particularly in their regional forms.[215] Although largely
premised on the type of *inter-State* dispute that does not necessarily exist in the
context of coerced displacement,[216] certain internal disputes regarding minority
and autonomy claims may be sufficiently analogous to lend themselves to resolution by these means.

Less formal approaches, including good offices missions, contacts groups and
regional intercessions, also have some potential for moderating situations likely
to lead to flight.[217] Finally, and notwithstanding such egregious failures as former Yugoslavia, local protection may be necessary and practical. Interventions
in Somalia and northern Iraq have illustrated possibilities and limits, but also
the urgent necessity for institutional reforms capable of producing coherent and
informed policies.[218] Whatever final form international protection efforts take,
their success will depend on interrelated factors and objectives, including mechanisms to provide early notice of events, such as political and armed conflicts; a
capacity to act towards the objective of resolution or mediation; preparedness;
co-operative structures allowing for appropriate sharing of responsibilities; and
a continuing capacity to monitor peace arrangements, human rights, and population movements and returns.

In attempting to face up to the problems in former Yugoslavia, the Security

---

[214] Cf. Executive Committee General Conclusion on International Protection (1993), *Report* of the
44th Session: UN doc. A/AC.96/821, para. 19(u), above note 201; also, 'Note on International
Protection': UN doc. A/AC.96/815, paras. 34–8 (1993).

[215] Bakwesegha, C. J., 'The Role of the Organization of African Unity in Conflict Prevention,
Management and Resolution', 7 *IJRL Special Issue—Summer 1995*—207; Dieng, A., 'Addressing the
Root Causes of Forced Population Displacements in Africa: A Theoretical Model', 7 *IJRL Special
Issue—Summer 1995*—119.

[216] Irredentist or secessionist movements and disputed territorial claims may give rise to such
issues, of course.

[217] Hindsight raises the question whether it might not have been possible to avoid the massive
movement out of Vietnam by appropriate intercessions and economic assistance in the late 1970s;
or whether the political conflict in Sri Lanka could have been diverted into mutually acceptable
forms of shared political responsibility by similar interventions in the early 1980s. In many cases,
however, politicization and polarization may have reached such a level as to make outside involvement quite redundant.

[218] This is obviously a larger question than that of the refugee in international law; for discussion, see Childers, E. and Urquhart, B., *Strengthening International Response to Humanitarian Emergencies*,
New York, Oct. 1991. Note however, the dictum of the International Court of Justice in the
Nicaragua case: 'there can be no doubt that the provision of strictly humanitarian aid to persons or
forces in another country, whatever the political obligations or objectives cannot be regarded as
unlawful intervention, or in any way contrary to international law' (para. 242); and for general comments, Chandrahasan, N., 'Use of Force to ensure Humanitarian Relief—A South Asian Precedent
examined', 42 *ICLQ* 664 (1993).

Council reached consensus on the existence of a threat to international peace and security, and agreement on certain basic principles, namely, international monitoring; access to camps, prisons and detention centres; the prohibition of forcible expulsions or attempts to change the ethnic composition of the population; the delivery of aid; the protection of international humanitarian relief programmes and the safety of personnel; co-operation in the evacuation of special humanitarian cases; assistance to the displaced in returning voluntarily to their homes; international investigation of grave breaches of international humanitarian law, and individual responsibility for such breaches.[219]

A basis for United Nations involvement in protection operations might begin with a finding by an international mechanism, on the basis of accurate and trustworthy information, of an imminent or actual threat to peace and security in the form of internal or external displacement, conflict or generalized violence. Experience nevertheless argues strongly for a clear separation between enforcement and humanitarian operations.[220] United Nations 'protection' operations would have humanitarian (and therefore limited) objectives to provide relief, to establish corridors of peace and even safety zones, or to monitor events, pending mediation or other forms of conflict resolution through political process. Provided the methods of operation were internationally implemented and openly supervised, accountable and subject to review, the UN's involvement, undertaken in fulfilment of the international community's responsibility to provide protection, could hardly constitute a threat to the territorial integrity or political independence of any State. Any such formal objection might anyway be considered irrelevant in situations involving the disintegration of formerly existing States, or the total absence of governmental authority.

4. International co-operation

The general principle of co-operation with respect to persons moving across borders flows from the obligations assumed by Member States under the Charter of the United Nations, and as members of the international community.[221] Commenting on the typhus epidemic in Poland after the First World War and the resulting need for collective measures, Schwarzenberger observed that, 'No compulsion exists for a State to join in any such co-operative effort. It is its own self-interest which prompts it to do so.'[222] Although today the institutions of international co-operation are more comprehensive, more universal, and more

---

[219] See for example, Security Council resolutions 743, 21 Feb. 1992; 752, 15 May 1992; 764, 13 July 1992; 770, 13 Aug. 1992; 771, 13 Aug. 1992; 776, 14 Sept. 1992; and 780, 6 Oct. 1992; text also in 4 *IJRL* 376 (1992). Cf. Goodwin-Gill, G. S., 'UNHCR and International Protection: Old Problems—New Directions', 5 *IJRL* 1 (1993).

[220] Cf. Mooney, 'Presence, *ergo* protection?', above n. 207; Gowlland-Debbas, 'Security Council Enforcement Action', above n. 196.

[221] UN Charter, arts. 1, 13.1(b), 55, 56.

[222] Schwarzenberger, G., *Power Politics*, (2nd rev. ed., 1954), 228.

firmly established, the underlying truth remains, emphasizing the degree to which co-operation in practice still depends upon the formal consent of States.

The *Declaration on Principles of International Law concerning Friendly Relations and Co-operation among States in accordance with the Charter of the United Nations* outlines the basic approach:

States have the duty to co-operate with one another, irrespective of the differences in their political, economic and social systems, in the various spheres of international relations, in order to maintain international peace and security and to promote international economic stability and progress, the general welfare of nations and international co-operation free from discrimination based on such differences.[223]

The principle of co-operation in the present context reflects recognition of the inherently *international* dimension to the movements of persons across borders.

Increasing numbers of refugees notwithstanding, the 1984 United Nations International Conference on Population Conference found 'broad agreement' that through international co-operation within the framework of the United Nations an attempt should be made to avert the causes of new flows of refugees, with due regard to the principle of non-intervention in the internal affairs of sovereign States. There was nevertheless a 'need for *continuing international co-operation in finding durable solutions* . . . and for the provision of *support and assistance to first countries of asylum*'.[224]

The Comprehensive Plan of Action on the problems in South East Asia contemplated measures to deter clandestine departures from the country of origin, including mass media activities and regular consultation between the countries concerned; encouragement of regular departure (emigration/immigration) programmes; provisions for reception and temporary refuge for new arrivals; region-wide refugee status determination procedures; resettlement undertakings for long-stayers and for new arrivals found to be refugees; and repatriation of non-refugees. To ensure continued co-ordination and adaptation, a Steering Committee was established, consisting of 'representatives of all Governments making specific commitments' under the CPA.[225]

The undertakings given on such occasions, considered together with the actions thereafter introduced at national and regional level, are thus necessarily elements in the evolution of rules with respect to international co-operation in the relief and resolution of the problems of refugees and the displaced.

Perhaps the most striking instance of a formal obligation to assist is found in

[223] See UNGA res. 2625(XXV), 24 Oct. 1970, Annex, Principle (d): The duty of States to co-operate with one another in accordance with the Charter. The resolution, which 'approves the Declaration', was adopted without vote.

[224] 1984 United Nations International Conference on Population, Recommendation 47: UNHCR, *Note* on the United Nations International Conference on Population: UN doc. A/AC.96/INF.170, 3 Sept. 1984.

[225] Cf. Statement of the Fourth Steering Committee: Reaffirmation of the Comprehensive Plan of Action: 3 *IJRL* 367 (1991). A similar level of co-operation was endorsed by States party to the CIREFCA process; see above n. 178.

the 1989 Lomé IV Convention, concluded between the European Community and African, Caribbean and Pacific (ACP) countries.[226] In a strikingly direct fashion, article 254 provides,

1. Emergency assistance *shall be accorded* to ACP States faced with serious economic and social difficulties of an exceptional nature resulting from natural disasters or extraordinary circumstances having comparable effects . . .
2. The Community *shall take adequate steps* to facilitate speedy action which is required to meet immediate needs for which emergency assistance is intended . . . (emphasis supplied)

Examples such as this show States' recognition of the need to co-operate, in particular, to ensure that movements across borders do not place an undue or disproportionate burden on receiving States. To a significant degree, and so far as it focuses on the situation of refugees and externally displaced persons, this emerging principle reflects the practice of some States at least, within a policy framework established, in part, in the Preamble to the 1951 Convention relating to the Status of Refugees:

Considering that the grant of asylum may place unduly heavy burdens on certain countries, and that a satisfactory solution of a problem of which the United Nations has recognized the international scope and nature cannot therefore be achieved without international co-operation,
Expressing the wish that all States, recognizing the social and humanitarian nature of the problem of refugees, will do everything within their power to prevent this problem from becoming a cause of tension between States . . .

That framework is being filled out in successive responses to refugee crises which, given the voluntarist structure of refugee institutions, have to be met without benefit of assessed contributions. A significant level of practical co-operation nevertheless exists, even if material contributions and political or moral support for the displaced waver and formal obligations are elusive.[227] Certainly, the principles of co-operation and international solidarity have been consistently endorsed within the Executive Committee of the UNHCR Programme. In 1988, for example, it reaffirmed that 'refugee problems are the concern of the international community and their resolution is dependent on the will and capacity of States to respond in concert and wholeheartedly, in a spirit of true humanitarianism and international solidarity'.[228] And in 1990, it emphasized,

the close nexus between international protection, international solidarity, material assistance and the provision of solutions through voluntary repatriation, integration in countries of asylum, or resettlement, and calls upon the High Commissioner to continue his

---

[226] For text, see 28 *ILM* 1382 (1989).

[227] Cf. Morris, N., 'Refugees: Facing Crisis in the 1990s—A Personal View from within UNHCR', 2 *IJRL Special Issue—September 1990*, 38; also, Guest, I., 'The United Nations, the UNHCR, and Refugee Protection—A Non-Specialist Analysis', 3 *IJRL* 585 (1991).

[228] Executive Committee Conclusion No. 52 (1988) on International Solidarity and Refugee Protection.

efforts to ensure that protection measures are fully integrated into assistance and durable solutions programmes.[229]

Comprehensive responses to the problems of persons moving across borders clearly depend upon significant measures of international co-operation for their success.[230]

National self-interest may prevail when States are confronted with population displacements on their borders, but national goals will often be best achieved through co-operation with others. An emerging principle requires States to co-operate, in accordance with the principles of international solidarity and burden sharing, in promoting solutions through voluntary repatriation, by dealing with causes; and through local integration or resettlement for people in distress who, owing to a well-founded fear of being persecuted for reasons of race, religion, national or ethnic origin, social group or political opinion, are unable or unwilling to return to their own country. By contrast with article 254 on *emergency* assistance, article 255 of the Lomé IV Convention proposes a less categoric obligation with respect to refugee-related matters, in terms resonating more closely with the continuing dominance of discretion:

1. Assistance *may* be granted to ACP States taking in refugees or returnees to meet acute needs not covered by emergency assistance, to implement in the longer term projects and action programmes aimed at self-sufficiency and the integration or reintegration of such people.
2. Similar assistance . . . *may* be envisaged to help with the voluntary integration or re-integration of persons who have had to leave their homes as a result of conflicts or natural disasters. In implementing this provision account shall be taken of all the factors leading to the displacement in question including the wishes of the population concerned and the responsibilities of the government in meeting the needs of its own people. (Emphasis supplied)

While these first two paragraphs are oriented towards assistance, with the objective of solutions, paragraph 3 emphasizes the developmental nature of the assistance granted, and paragraph 4 stresses the necessity for flexibility and rapid

---

[229] Executive Committee General Conclusions on International Protection, (1990): *Report* of the 41st Session: UN doc. A/AC.96/760, para. 20; (1992): *Report* of the 43rd Session: UN doc. A/AC.96/804 para. 21(a); (1993): *Report* of the 44th Session: UN doc. A/AC.96/821, para. 19(h); (1994): *Report* of the 45th Session: UN doc. A/AC.96/839 para. 19(h).

[230] On proposals for a 'New International Humanitarian Order', see letter of 28 Oct. 1981 from the Permanent Representative of Jordan to the United Nations: UN doc. A/36/245; UNGA res. 36/136, 14 Dec. 1981; 37/201, 18 Dec. 1982; 38/125, 16 Dec. 1983; 42/120 and 42/121, 7 Dec. 1987, 43/129, 8 Dec. 1988; *Report* of the Third Committee, Draft resolution II: UN doc. A/45/751 (21 Nov. 1990); *Report* of the Secretary-General, Development and International Economic Co-operation, New international humanitarian order: moral aspects of development: UN doc. A/40/591 (11 Sept. 1985); *Report* of the Secretary-General submitted pursuant to General Assembly res. 38/125: UN doc. A/40/348 (9 Oct. 1985); GAOR, 3rd Ctte., 6 Dec. 1985: UN doc. A/C.3/40/SR.69; *Report* of the Third Committee, Draft res. III, Promotion of international co-operation in the humanitarian field; also Draft Res. I, Humanitarian assistance to victims of natural disasters and similar emergency situations: UN doc. A/45/751 (21 Nov. 1990).

action in implementation.[231] Although the formal statement of obligation may
be less striking than that in article 254, a clear intention to provide assistance is
revealed in a Joint Declaration annexed to the Convention. Specifically, the parties agree to give particular attention to projects that assist the voluntary repatriation and reintegration of refugees; the needs of women, children, the aged or
the handicapped among refugees or displaced persons; and closer co-ordination
between States and agencies.[232] Exactly how effective these provisions have been
in mobilising European Union assistance is another matter, however, and
requires further evaluation.

[231] Para. 4 further provides: 'The assistance may be implemented, if the ACP State so agrees, in
conjunction with specialized organizations, including those of the United Nations, or by the
Commission direct.'
[232] Annex LII: Joint Declaration on art. 255.

Chapter 8

TREATY STANDARDS

The main treaties governing the status and treatment of refugees have attracted wide, if not universal acceptance, although they do not in fact either comprehend every refugee known to the world, or, in many cases, offer any but the most basic guarantees. Nevertheless, both the 1951 Convention and the 1967 Protocol are increasingly and widely accepted; for those found to qualify, the benefits for which they call are often improved upon in actual practice, and supplemented substantially by the provisions of regional and related instruments. The Convention and the Protocol represent a point of departure in considering the appropriate standard of treatment of refugees, often exceeded, but still at base proclaiming the fundamental principles of protection, without which no refugee can hope to attain a satisfactory and lasting solution to his or her plight. The present chapter briefly examines the provisions of these and related agreements, with a view to determining the appropriate convention standards of treatment applicable to refugees and asylum seekers, whether lawfully or unlawfully in the territory of contracting States.[1]

1. The 1951 Convention and the 1967 Protocol relating to the Status of Refugees

The importance of the 1951 Convention as a statement of the minimum rights of refugees has been stressed repeatedly in the preceding chapters. Time has shown its provisions to be inadequate to deal with certain aspects of today's refugee problems,[2] but its principal objective was always the regulation of issues of legal status and treatment, rather than the grand design of universally acceptable solutions. It should not be forgotten that the Convention has its origin in the cold war climate of the late 1940s and early 1950s, when concern centred on refugees in Europe. Similarly, the very European flavour of many of the provisions can be readily understood when it is realized that of the twenty-six States which participated in drafting and adopting the Convention, seventeen were from Europe and four more of a Western European/North American disposi-

---

[1] As of 1 Jun. 1997, 134 States had ratified the 1951 Convention and/or the 1967 Protocol. For full texts, see Annexe 1, Nos. 4 and 5; and for States parties, Annexe 6, No. 1.

[2] This assessment, made in the first edition of this work, is regrettably even more justified today. See, however, Jackson, I. C., 'The 1951 Convention relating to Status of Refugees: A Universal Basis for Protection', 3 *IJRL* 403 (1991).

tion.[3] What is remarkable is that the 1951 Convention still attracts both ratifications and support among States from all regions.

By resolution 429(V) of 14 December 1950, the United Nations General
Assembly decided to convene a Conference of Plenipotentiaries to draft and sign
a convention on refugees and stateless persons; it duly met in July 1951, but was
able only to complete its work with regard to the former.[4] The Conference took
as its basis for discussion a draft prepared by the *Ad hoc* Committee on Refugees
and Stateless Persons, adopted at its second session in Geneva in August 1950,[5]
save that the Preamble was that adopted by the Economic and Social Council,[6]
while article 1 was as recommended by the General Assembly and annexed to
resolution 429(V). The Conference also unanimously adopted five recommendations covering travel documents, family unity, non-governmental organizations,
asylum, and application of the Convention beyond its contractual scope.

As noted in Chapter 1, article 1 limited the definition of refugees by reference
not only to a well-founded fear of persecution, but also to a dateline (those resulting from 'events occurring before 1 January 1951'), and offered States the option
of further restricting their obligations to refugees resulting from events occurring
in Europe before the critical date. It was the object of the 1967 Protocol to remove
that stipulative date, but the geographical option remains.[7] For convenience's
sake, the 1967 Protocol has been referred to as 'amending' the 1951 Convention; in fact, it does no such thing. The Protocol is an independent instrument,
not a revision within the meaning of article 45 of the Convention.[8] States parties to the Protocol, which can be ratified or acceded to by a State without
becoming a party to the Convention,[9] simply agree to apply articles 2 to 34 of

[3] Superficial criticism of the western/European focus of the 1951 Convention generally fails to
note that the invitation to participate in the Conference of Plenipotentiaries was extended to *all*
United Nations member States. As one participant noted at the time, the non-appearance of so many
non-European States contributed in no small degree to the initial orientation of art. 1; see UN doc.
A/CONF.2/SR.3, p. 12 (M. Rochefort).

[4] The proposed Protocol formed the basis of the 1954 Convention relating to the Status of
Stateless Persons: 360 *UNTS* 117, finalized after a further conference. For background and review,
see Batchelor, C. A., 'Stateless Persons: Some Gaps in International Protection', 7 *IJRL* 232 (1995).

[5] UN doc. E/1850. This draft, that adopted by the *Ad Hoc* Committee at its first session (UN doc.
E/1618), and the draft prepared by the UN Secretariat (UN doc. E/AC.32/2) are reproduced in
Takkenberg, A. and Tahbaz, C. C., *The Collected travaux préparatoires of the 1951 Convention relating to the
Status of Refugees*, 3 vols., (1988). See also Robinson, N., *Convention relating to the Status of Refugees: A
Commentary*, (1953), 181–9, 190–214.

[6] ECOSOC res. 319 B II (XI), 11 Aug. 1950.

[7] At 1 Jun. 1997, six States maintained the geographical limitation: Congo, Hungary,
Madagascar, Malta, Monaco, and Turkey: *Multilateral Treaties deposited with the Secretary-General: Status
as at 31 December 1994*, (1995): UN doc. ST/LEG/SER.E/13, 208, 209; updated through
CDR/UNHCR, *RefWorld* CD-ROM, 4th ed., Jul. 1997.

[8] See generally Weis, P., 'The 1967 Protocol relating to the Status of Refugees and some
Questions of the Law of Treaties', 42 *BYIL* 39 (1967).

[9] Cape Verde, Swaziland, the United States and Venezuela have acceded only to the Protocol,
while Madagascar, Monaco, Namibia and St. Vincent and the Grenadines are party only to the
Convention. There are some advantages in ratifying only the Protocol, for example, with respect to
dispute settlement; see n. 12 below. Swaziland's accession to the Protocol alone in Jan. 1969

the Convention to refugees defined in article 1 thereof, as if the dateline were omitted.[10] While reservations are generally permitted under both instruments,[11] the integrity of certain articles is absolutely protected, including articles 1 (definition); 3 (non-discrimination), 4 (religion), 16(1) (access to courts), and 33 (*non-refoulement*).[12] A number of existing reservations are also of doubtful validity. Guatemala, for example, has purported to accede to the Convention and Protocol, 'with the reservation that it will not apply provisions of those instruments in respect of which the Convention allows reservations if those provisions contravene constitutional precepts in Guatemala or norms of public order under domestic law'. Belgium, France, Germany, Italy, Luxembourg, and the Netherlands have objected to the lack of clarity, considering it impossible for other States parties to determine the scope of a reservation expressed in such broad terms and which refers for the most part to domestic law.[13]

1.1 REQUIRED STANDARDS OF TREATMENT

As was the case with some of the inter-war arrangements,[14] the objective of the 1951 Convention and the 1967 Protocol is both to establish certain fundamental rights, such as *non-refoulement*, and to prescribe certain standards of treatment. The refugee may be stateless and therefore, as a matter of law, unable to secure the benefits accorded to nationals of his or her country of origin. Alternatively, even if nationality is retained, the refugee's unprotected status can make obtaining such benefits a practical impossibility. The Convention consequently pro-

appears to have been inspired in part by a desire to 'accede' as a Member of the UN, rather than to become a party to the Convention by way of 'succession': *Multilateral Treaties*, 232. The UK had extended the territorial application of the 1951 Convention to Swaziland in 1960, but not the 1967 Protocol, which the UK ratified in 1968.

[10] Art. I of the Protocol. Note also art. I(3), on the geographical limitation.

[11] See generally Blay, S. K. N. and Tsamenyi, B. M., 'Reservations and Declarations under the 1951 Convention and the 1967 Protocol relating to the Status of Refugees', 2 *IJRL* 527 (1990).

[12] Under the Convention, reservations are further prohibited with respect to arts. 36–46, which include a provision entitling any party to a dispute to refer the matter to the International Court of Justice (art. 38). The corresponding provision of the Protocol (art. IV) may be the subject of reservation, and such has been made by Botswana, China, Congo, El Salvador, Ghana, Jamaica, Rwanda, Tanzania and Venezuela. It is also not clear from art. VII of the Protocol whether reservations may be made to art. II (co-operation with the United Nations); they are clearly permissible under the corresponding Convention provision (art. 35), although none has been made; cf. Peru's declaration on ratification of the Protocol.

[13] *Multilateral Treaties*, 217. See also Malta's reservations, excluding entirely application of arts. 7(2), 14, 23, 27 and 28, and qualifying arts. 7(3),(4)(5), 8, 9, 11, 17, 18, 31, 32, and 34 as applicable 'to Malta compatibly with its own special problems, its peculiar position and characteristics': ibid., 213. Cf. objections by Finland, Germany, Ireland, Norway, Portugal and Sweden to reservations lodged by Bangladesh, Djibouti, Indonesia, Jordan, Kuwait, Qatar and Tunisia, with respect to the 1989 Convention on the Rights of the Child: ibid., 200–1.

[14] Art. 37 lists the agreements replaced, as between the parties, by the Convention.

[15] Art. 7(1). The Republic of Korea does not accept the provision on exemption from legislative reciprocity; Honduras understands art. 7 to mean 'that it shall accord to refugees such facilities and treatment as it shall deem appropriate at its discretion, taking into account the economic, social, democratic and security needs of the country'. Note also arts. 5, 6, 13, 18, 19, 21, 22(2); see further below on art. 26.

poses, as a minimum standard, that refugees should receive at least that treatment which is accorded to aliens generally.[15] Most-favoured-nation treatment[16]
is called for in respect of the right of association (article 15),[17] and the right to
engage in wage-earning employment (article 17(1)). The latter is of major importance to the refugee in search of an effective solution, but it is also the provision
which has attracted most reservations.[18] Many States have thus emphasized that
the reference to most-favoured-nation shall not be interpreted as entitling
refugees to the benefit of special or regional customs, or economic or political
agreements.[19] Other States have expressly rejected most-favoured-nation treatment, limiting their obligation to accord only that standard applicable to aliens
generally,[20] while some view article 17 merely as a recommendation,[21] or agree
to apply it 'so far as the law allows'.[22]

National treatment, finally, is to be granted in respect of a wide variety of matters, including the freedom to practice religion and as regards the religious education of children (article 4); the protection of artistic rights and industrial
property (article 14); access to courts, legal assistance, and exemption from the
requirement to give security for costs in court proceedings *(cautio judicatum solvi)*
(article 16);[23] rationing (article 20); elementary education (article 22(1)),[24] public
relief (article 23);[25] labour legislation and social security (article 24(1));[26] and fiscal charges (article 29).

1.2 STANDARDS APPLICABLE TO REFUGEES AS REFUGEES

Although the stipulative provisions of article 1 are excluded from reservation,
three States have made declarations which may affect claims to refugee status.

[16] Goodwin-Gill, G. S., *International Law and the Movement of Persons between States*, (1978), 186 and
note, and sources cited.

[17] Cf. reservation by Ecuador, limiting acceptance of art. 15, 'so far as those provisions are in
conflict with the constitutional and statutory provisions ... prohibiting aliens, and consequently
refugees, from being members of political bodies'.

[18] For reservations, see *Multilateral Treaties*, 208 (Convention); 230 (Protocol).

[19] See reservations by Angola, Belgium, Brazil, Burundi, Cape Verde, Denmark, Finland,
Guatemala, Iran, Luxembourg, Madagascar, Netherlands, Norway, Peru, Portugal, Spain, Sweden,
Uganda and Venezuela. Also Kiss, A., 'La convention européenne et la clause de la nation la plus
favorisée', *Ann. Fr.* 478–89 (1957).

[20] Bahamas, Honduras, Ireland, Liechtenstein, Malawi, Mozambique, Switzerland, Zambia and
Zimbabwe.

[21] Austria, Burundi, Ethiopia and Sierra Leone; Papua New Guinea does not accept any obligation with respect to art. 17(1).

[22] Jamaica; see also reservations by Malta, Sweden, the UK, and Zambia.

[23] China has excluded application of this entire article.

[24] Ethiopia, Malawi, Monaco, Mozambique and Zambia consider this provision a recommendation only; Swaziland and Papua New Guinea accept no obligation.

[25] Iran, Monaco and Zimbabwe consider this a recommendation only, while it is not accepted
by Malta; for Canada's interpretation of the phrase 'lawfully staying' in both arts. 23 and 24, see
further below, n. 76.

[26] Reservations have been made to this article by Canada, Finland, Honduras, Iran, Jamaica,
Liechtenstein, Malawi, Monaco, New Zealand, Sweden, Switzerland, the UK, and the US. Turkey
has declared that refugees shall not enjoy greater rights than Turkish citizens in Turkey. Poland does
not accept art. 24(2).

The Netherlands, for example, declared on ratification that Ambionese transported to that country after 17 December 1949 (the date of Indonesia's accession to independence) were not considered eligible for refugee status. Turkey, on the other hand, stated on signature that it considered the Convention should apply also to 'Bulgarian refugees of Turkish extraction . . . who, being unable to enter Turkey, might seek refuge on the territory of another Contracting State'.[27] Somalia, somewhat portentously, declared that its accession to the Convention was not to be construed so as to prejudice or adversely affect 'the national status or political aspiration of displaced people from Somali territories under alien domination'.[28] Such evidently political statements, not amounting to reservations, appear to have had little if any substantive effect on the application of the Convention generally or on the interpretation of the refugee definition.

Of greater importance is the varying degree to which States have been prepared to accept and to apply benefits and standards of treatment established by the Convention on behalf of refugees as refugees. Article 8, for example, makes a half-hearted attempt to exempt refugees from the application of exceptional measures which might otherwise affect them by reason only of their nationality. Several States have made reservations, of which some exclude entirely any obligation, some regard the article as a recommendation only, while others expressly retain the right to take measures based on nationality in the interests of national security.[29] Article 9, indeed, expressly preserves the right of States to take 'provisional measures' on the grounds of national security against a particular person, 'pending a determination by the Contracting State that that person is in fact a refugee and that the continuance of such measures is necessary . . . in the interests of national security'. Nevertheless, this has not prevented certain States from seeking further to entrench their powers by way of reservation.[30] Similar concern is evident in States' responses to article 26, which prescribes such freedom of movement for refugees as is accorded to aliens generally in the same circumstances. Eleven States have made reservations, eight of which expressly retain the right to designate places of residence, either generally, or on grounds of national security, public order (*ordre public*) or the public interest.[31]

---

[27] In 1989, 320,000 Bulgarians of Turkish ethnic origin did indeed cross into Turkey; see above, Ch. 4, s. 2.5.1. On ratification, Turkey also expressed its understanding that the terms 'reavailment' and 'reacquisition' in art. 1C implied not only a request by the individual concerned, but also the consent of the State in question.

[28] Ethiopia in 1979 objected to this declaration, stating 'that it does not recognize it as valid on the ground that there are no Somali territories under alien domination'. In Oct. 1983, Argentina submitted to the Secretary-General a 'formal objection' to the UK's extension, in 1956, of the 1951 Convention to the Falkland/Malvinas Islands: *Multilateral Treaties*, 220, n. 1. The UK declared that the objection was without effect: ibid., 115, n. 16.

[29] Reservations by Ethiopia, Fiji, Finland, Israel, Jamaica, Madagascar, Malta, Spain, Sweden, Uganda, and the UK.

[30] Reservations by Angola, Ethiopia, Fiji, Finland, Jamaica, Madagascar, Malta, Uganda, and the UK.

[31] Reservations by Angola, Burundi, Greece, Honduras, Malawi, Mozambique, Netherlands, Rwanda, Spain, Sudan, Zambia, and Zimbabwe. Botswana has made an 'open' reservation, Iran

Burundi, reflecting concerns shared by many African countries and reiterated in the 1969 OAU Convention,[32] declares that it accepts article 26 provided refugees (a) do not choose their place of residence in a region bordering on their country of origin; and (b) refrain in any event, when exercising their right to move freely, from any activity or incursion of a subversive nature with respect to the country of which they are nationals.[33]

The principal articles still to be considered fall loosely into two groups: first, those under which States parties agree to provide certain facilities to refugees; and secondly, those by which States have undertaken to recognize and protect certain 'rights' on behalf of refugees. The first group includes the provision of administrative assistance (article 25);[34] the issue of identity papers (article 27);[35] the issue of travel documents (article 28);[36] the grant of permission to transfer assets (article 30); and the facilitation of naturalization (article 34).[37] Within the second group are included the following specific 'rights':[38] recognition of the law of personal status (article 12);[39] exemption from penalties in respect of illegal entry or presence (article 31);[40] limitations on the liability to expulsion (article 32);[41] and the benefit of *non-refoulement* (article 33).

considers art. 26 to be a recommendation only, while Papua New Guinea accepts no obligation. At the 1951 Conference, it was said that art. 26 was not infringed where, under a labour contract or group-settlement scheme, refugees who were admitted were required to remain in a particular job for a particular time: UN doc. E/AC.32/SR.11, 6. Robinson further considered that art. 26 would not be breached in the case of 'special situations where refugees have to be accommodated in special camps or in special areas even if this does not apply to aliens generally': *Commentary*, 133, n. 207. See further below, s. 1.2.2.

[32] Arts. II(6) and III.

[33] Corliss, S., 'Asylum State Responsibility for the Hostile Acts of Foreign Exiles', 2 *IJRL* 181 (1990).

[34] Some common law countries, where affidavits and statutory declarations may take the place of official documents, have made reservations; see, for example, those of Fiji, Ireland, Jamaica, Uganda, and the UK. Finland and Sweden have also limited their obligations.

[35] See Executive Committee Conclusion No. 35 (1984), recommending that States provide such documents and also issue provisional documentation to asylum seekers; see also UNHCR, 'Identity Documents for Refugees': UN doc. EC/SCP/33 (July 1984); *Report* of the Sub-Committee of the Whole on International Protection: UN doc. A/AC.96/649 and Add. 1, paras. 22–30—incidentally observing that registration and documentation in situations of large scale influx should be without prejudice to subsequent case-by-case determination: paras. 29–30.

[36] Finland does not accept an obligation to issue travel documents, but agrees to recognize those issued by other contracting States. Israel agrees to issue CTDs subject to the limitations provided for in its passport law, while Zambia does not consider itself bound to issue a travel document with a return clause, where another State has accepted a refugee from Zambia.

[37] Honduras, Malawi, Mozambique and Swaziland accept no obligation to accord more favourable facilities than those ordinarily available to aliens; Papua New Guinea accepts no obligation.

[38] Art. 10, which protects certain types of residence otherwise affected by the events of the Second World War, is not considered further. For art. 11, in respect of refugee seamen, see above, Ch. 4, s. 4.2.

[39] The general rule is that personal status shall be governed by the law of a refugee's country of domicile or residence. Finland and Sweden maintain that status is governed by the law of nationality; Botswana and Israel do not accept art. 12, while Spain reserves its position with regard to para. 1.

[40] Honduras has reserved the right, equally with respect to arts. 26 and 31, to designate, change or limit the place of residence or restrict the freedom of movement of refugees. Papua New Guinea accepts no obligation under art. 31.

[41] Not accepted by Papua New Guinea.

1.2.1 The Convention Travel Document: article 28

Article 28 of the 1951 Convention maintains the practice of issuing travel documents to refugees, initiated under the League of Nations, and provides in paragraph 2 for documents issued under earlier arrangements to continue to be
recognized.[42] The operative part of article 28 is succinct: '[t]he Contracting
States shall issue to refugees lawfully staying in their territory travel documents
for the purpose of travel outside their territory unless compelling reasons of
national security or public order otherwise require . . .' The criterion of entitlement, 'lawfully staying', is examined more fully below, but the words of this provision may well place the refugee in a better position with regard to the issue of
travel documentation than the citizen of the State in which he or she resides.[43]
A Schedule to the Convention prescribes the form of the travel document and
makes provision, among other matters, for renewal, recognition, and return to
the State of issue. Article 28(1) also empowers States, in their discretion, to issue
travel documents to refugees not linked to them by the nexus of lawful stay, who
may be present temporarily or even illegally.[44]

Where the applicant for a travel document is indeed a refugee within the
Convention and/or the Protocol, and meets the requirement of lawful stay, article 28 permits few exceptions to the obligation to issue. The reference to 'compelling' reasons of national security and public order as justifying an exception
clearly indicates that restrictive interpretation is called for. It was thus emphasized at the 1951 Conference that the refugee is not required to justify his or her
proposed travel;[45] on the other hand, paragraph 14 of the Schedule to the
Convention (which declares that the Schedule's provisions in no way affect laws
and regulations governing admission, transit, residence, establishment, and
departure), might be interpreted as permitting a somewhat broader range of

[42] See also Recommendation A of the Final Act.
[43] Generally on passports and the right to travel, see Goodwin-Gill, *Movement of Persons*, Ch. II.
Robinson notes that at the 1951 Conference, the representative of Venezuela, despite the wording
of art. 28(1), held to the view that the issue of travel documents to refugees would not be considered
mandatory in the absence of a similar obligation benefitting nationals: *Commentary*, 135, n. 212. Cf.
Turkey's 'general' declaration that 'no provisions of [the] Convention may be interpreted as granting to refugees greater rights than those accorded to Turkish citizens in Turkey'.
[44] Amended regulations governing the issue of CTDs in the US provide for the issue of a refugee
travel document to a refugee whose presence is lawful, 'unless compelling reasons of national security or public order otherwise require'. However, lawful presence 'does not include brief presence as
a transit or crewman, or any other presence so brief as not to signify residence even of a temporary
nature'. Travel documents may be issued in discretion to any other refugee, and 'sympathetic consideration shall be given to such an application' unless it is intended to expel or exclude the individual in question: 8 *CFR* §223a.3. A 1986 amendment provided that for 'reasons of national
security, a refugee travel document shall not be issued to a lawful permanent resident alien who
intends to travel to, in, or through Libya, unless such travel is for journalistic activity by a person
who is regularly employed in such capacity by a newsgathering organization, or the applicant establishes that his or her trip is justified by urgent and compelling humanitarian considerations': 51 *Fed.
Reg.* 12596, 14 Apr. 1986.
[45] UN docs. E/AC.32/SR.16, 13–15; SR.42, 5–7; A/CONF.2/SR.12, 4–13; SR.17, 4–11; see
previous n.

restrictions. In this context, 'public order' (*ordre public*) still remains a relatively fluid concept, and certain States have not excluded the possibility of applying to the issue of Convention travel documents the same restrictions as they would apply with regard to national passports.[46]

A more serious obstacle in practice to the issue of Convention travel documents can result from the absence within a State's administration of any procedure for consideration and determination of applications for refugee status. Even where such procedures do exist, they may be limited to consideration of refugee status in the context of asylum, that is, at the point at which questions of admission, residence, and expulsion arise. The refugee admitted under a resettlement programme, or allowed to remain otherwise than by reference to his or her refugee status (for example, as a student or business person, or by reason of marriage to a local citizen) may be unable, quite simply, to invoke such status and thereby to secure treatment in accordance with the Convention. The standard of reasonably efficient and efficacious implementation suggests that some sort of procedure is required, if States are to meet their obligations under provisions such as article 28.

The Schedule prescribes the format of the Convention travel document,[47] and further regulates its issue and renewal, extension, recognition by other States, and guarantee of the holder's returnability to the issuing country.[48] Geographical validity for the largest possible number of countries is called for, and the document is to be valid for one or two years, at the discretion of the issuing State.[49] Renewal shall be by the State of issue, so long as the holder has not established lawful residence in another country,[50] and diplomatic and consular offices abroad are to be empowered to effect limited extensions of validity.[51] Contracting States undertake to recognize Convention travel documents issued by other parties (even, it may be supposed, if they do not accept that the holder is a refugee) and to accept them for visa purposes.[52] Paragraph 13(1) of the Schedule makes clear the obligation of the issuing State to readmit the holder of one of its travel documents, 'at any time during the period of its validity'.[53] Paragraph 13(3) nevertheless empowers States 'in exceptional cases, or in

[46] See the reservation by Israel; also the comment by an unidentified State representative in the Executive Committee's Sub-Committee of the Whole on International Protection in 1978: UN doc. A/AC.96/558, para. 34, who noted that issue would be precluded, among others, to a refugee who was not fulfilling family maintenance obligations.

[47] See generally UNHCR, 'Note on Travel Documents for Refugees': UN doc. EC/SCP/10 (1978).

[48] On 'returnability' as an essential incident to travel documentation, see Goodwin-Gill, *Movement of Persons*, 44–6.

[49] Schedule, paras. 4, 5.   [50] Ibid., paras. 6(1), 11, 12.

[51] Schedule, para. 6(2); see also para. 6(3).

[52] Schedule, paras. 7, 8, 9. The obligation to recognize CTDs, of course, does not oblige States to admit their holders.

[53] The return clause only gradually became an integral part of the refugee travel document; see Goodwin-Gill, *Movement of Persons*, 42–4. Some States, on a bilateral basis, have agreed to re-admission even after expiration of validity; see, for example, arts. 2 and 4, 1974 Austria–France

cases where the refugee's stay is authorized for a specific period . . .' to limit the return clause to not less than three months. Article 28 already acknowledges States' discretionary competence to issue travel documents to refugees not otherwise 'lawfully staying' in their territory. The Schedule confirms that discretion, by allowing States to avoid any long-term responsibility towards refugees whom they wish simply to assist with resettlement in a third State.[54] In practice, however, it is clear that excessive limitation of the return clause can result in serious problems for refugees, who may find themselves unable to return to the country of issue of their travel document and yet without any entitlement to residence elsewhere.[55]

With the aim of resolving some at least of those issues, a number of States have concluded agreements regulating 'transfer of responsibility' for refugees who change their lawful residence from one country to another. Paragraph 6 of the Schedule predicates responsibility for renewal and extension of CTDs on the fact that 'the holder has not established lawful residence in another territory and resides lawfully in the territory' of the renewing authority. Paragraph 11, in turn, predicates transfer of responsibility for the issue of a CTD on the fact that the refugee 'has lawfully taken up residence in the territory of another Contracting State'. Given the divergence in national immigration laws and concepts, these terms are clearly capable of many different interpretations. Inter-State agreements have therefore attempted to provide objective criteria for ascertaining the moment of transfer. Article 2(1) of the 1980 European Agreement, for example, declares:

Responsibility shall be considered to be transferred on the expiry of a period of two years of actual and continuous stay in the second State with the agreement of its authorities or earlier if the second State has permitted the refugee to remain in its territory either on a permanent basis or for a period exceeding the validity of the travel document.

The same article provides a method of calculation of the relevant period, and permits disregard of stay allowed solely for study, training, or medical care, and of periods of imprisonment.[56]

Finally, paragraph 15 of the Schedule to the Convention declares that neither

Agreement on the Residence of Refugees (collected with other related instruments in Council of Europe doc. EXP/AT.Re(77) 3, 21–3.). A similar provision is included in art. 4, 1980 European Agreement on Transfer of Responsibility for Refugees: *ETS* no. 107.

[54] Robinson, *Commentary*, 145; see also the general discussion in *Report* of the Executive Committee, 29th Session, (1978): UN doc. A/AC.96/558, paras. 35–7.

[55] See UNHCR, 'Note on Asylum': UN doc. EC/SCP/12, paras. 19–23 (1979); *Report* of the Executive Committee, 30th Session, (1979): UN doc. A/AC.96/572, paras. 60, 72(2)(m), (n). In 1978, the Observer for Botswana, in urging other countries to offer resettlement opportunities, noted that it was unfair that Botswana should be asked to readmit those who had gone abroad for education, solely because it had been the country of first refuge: UN doc. A/AC.96/SR.302, para. 14. Zambia has reserved the right not to issue a travel document with a return clause, 'where a country of second asylum has accepted or indicated its willingness to accept a refugee from Zambia'.

[56] Art. 2(2). Temporary absences not exceeding three months on any one occasion or six months in all are not deemed to interrupt stay.

the issue of a CTD nor entries on it shall affect the status of the holder, particularly as to nationality, and paragraph 16 affirms that the CTD holder is not entitled to diplomatic protection by the issuing State, and that that State acquires no right to exercise such protection.[57] In practice, however, diplomatic assistance falling short of full protection is often accorded by issuing States, while the fact of possession of a CTD would constitute prima facie evidence at least of the holder's entitlement to protection by UNHCR.[58]

1.1.2 Treatment of refugees entering illegally: article 31

Article 31 has already been analysed in its relation to the principle of *non-refoulement* and asylum, and separately with respect to detention.[59] Although not comprehensive, this provision serves as a point of departure in determining the minimum standard of treatment to be accorded to those whose situation remains unregularized in the country of first refuge. It applies first to refugees who, 'coming directly from a territory where their life or freedom was threatened in the sense of article 1, enter or are present . . . without authorization, provided they present themselves without delay to the authorities and show good cause for their illegal entry or presence'. Such refugees are not to be subjected to 'penalties', which appears to comprehend prosecution, fine, and imprisonment, but not administrative detention.[60] Article 31(2) makes it clear that States may impose 'necessary' restrictions on movement, which would include those prompted by security considerations or special circumstances like a large influx.[61] Such measures also come within article 9, and are an exception to the freedom of movement called for by article 26. Article 31(2) nevertheless calls for restrictions to be applied only until status in the country of refuge is regularized,[62] or admission obtained into another country; moreover, contracting States are to allow refugees a reasonable period and all necessary facilities to obtain such admission. Those facilities clearly include access to the representatives of other States and of UNHCR. The United Kingdom considered that provisional detention was not ruled out if necessary to investigate the circumstances of entry.

---

[57] Cf. Grahl-Madsen, A., 'Protection of Refugees by their Country of Origin', 11 *Yale J.I.L.* 362 (1986), arguing for a rule under which the State of origin of refugees, 'by breaking its ties with a refugee', loses any right to exercise protection until such time as the refugee willingly returns.

[58] See Reiterer, M., *The Protection of Refugees by their State of Asylum*, (1984).

[59] See above, Ch. 4, s. 3.2.5; Ch. 7, s. 1.1.

[60] See discussion at the 1951 Conference: UN docs. A/CONF.2/SR.13, pp. 13–15; SR.14, pp. 4, 10–11; SR.35, pp. 10–20; also art. 5, 1954 Caracas Convention on Territorial Asylum; below, Annexe 2, No. 3. Cf. Campiche, M. -P., 'Entrée illégale et séjour irrégulier des réfugiés et requérants d'asile: La pratique des cantons', *Asyl*, 1994/3, 51–7, showing different sanctions practice and different interpretations prevailing among the 'frontier' cantons with respect to both Swiss law and art. 31.

[61] Robinson, *Commentary*, 154.

[62] Cf. art. 9: 'pending a determination . . . that [the] person is in fact a refugee . . .' Vietnamese detained after arriving in Hong Kong after 2 July 1982 were to be given 'all reasonable facilities' to obtain authorization to enter another State, or to leave Hong Kong, with or without such authorization: Immigration Amendment Ordinance 1982 (no. 42/82) s. 7 (adding new s. 13D).

The Conference President likewise distinguished between detention to investigate and penalties for illegal entry, the latter being prohibited where entry was justified.[63]

1.2.3 Expulsion of refugees: article 32

Article 32, which limits the circumstances in which refugees 'lawfully in their territory' may be expelled by contracting States, has also been analysed above in the context of *non-refoulement*.[64] The meaning of 'lawfully' in article 32 is examined further below, and for the present it suffices to recall that this provision limits expulsion to grounds of national security or public order;[65] that it requires a decision to be reached in accordance with due process of law; that some form of appeal should be generally permitted; and that the refugee should be allowed a reasonable period in which to seek admission into another country. As with most Convention provisions, and subject always to conformity with its other obligations under international law, the State clearly enjoys choice of means with regard to its implementation of article 32. Thus, it may be sufficient to adopt internal, *ad hoc* administrative procedures regulating the exercise of the discretion to set removal machinery in motion, so that formal incorporation of the limitations on expulsion is not necessary. Moreover, some uncertainty surrounds the precise implications of the reference to decisions in accordance with due process of law. The French version of the text (*'une décision rendue conformément à la procédure prévue par la loi'*) suggests that formal compliance with the law is all that is required.[66] Alternatively, the concept of due process today can be considered to

---

[63] UN doc. A/CONF.2/SR.35, pp. 10–20. In the *Ad hoc* Committee in 1950, the Swiss delegate proposed that immunity from penalty also be accorded to those who assisted refugees to enter illegally; States were more concerned about smuggling organizations, however, and the problem of identifying those acting in good faith. Turning down the idea, the US representative suggested that its spirit be reflected in the summary records: UN doc. E/AC.32/SR.40, pp. 4–9. Cf. *Doc. réf.*, 208: 16 jan./1 fév. 1993, 2, reporting the conviction of M. and Mme Colak for 'aide à l'entrée, à la circulation ou au séjour irrégulier d'étrangers en France'. They travelled to the border between Hungary and Croatia and helped twelve relatives to get out and then into France. The family members were caught, reconducted to the border with Germany, but later allowed to return to France with visas and to apply for asylum. The couple were sentenced to 15 months suspended and fined 2000 francs.

[64] See above, Ch. 4, s. 3.2.4.

[65] In 1991, France expelled a recognized Moroccan refugee, Abdelmoumen Diouri, resident since 1974, to Gabon, under the 'urgence absolue' procedure, on the grounds of his 'contacts' with groups and foreign powers prejudicial to public security and national interests. He returned to France after the *tribunal administratif de Paris*, following the advice of the *commissaire du gouvernement* found that 'les conditions de l'urgence absolue n'étaient pas réunies, pas plus que la nécéssité impérieuse pour la sûreté de l'Etat et la sécurité publique'. The Conseil d'Etat rejected the Minister's appeal in Oct. 1991, the *commissaire du gouvernement* accepting that while M. Diouri could present a public security threat, those conditions did not exist at the time of his expulsion. See *Doc. réf.*, 150: 17/26 juin. 1991, 1; 151: 27 juin/6 juill. 1991, 1; 152: 7/16 juill. 1991; 161: 5/14 oct. 1991, 1. Also, Tiberghien, F., 'L'expulsion des réfugiés: Problèmes legislatifs et jurisprudentiels', *Doc. réf.*, no. 73, 5/14 mars 1989, Suppl., CJ, 1–8.

[66] This appears to be Ireland's interpretation, as stated on ratification: above, n. 5. Cf. Uganda's reservation to art. 32: 'Without recourse to legal process the Government . . . shall, in the public interest, have the unfettered right to expel any refugee . . . and may at any time apply such internal

include, as minimum requirements, (a) knowledge of the case against one, (b) an opportunity to submit evidence to rebut that case, (c) reasoned negative decisions, and (d) the right to appeal against an adverse decision before an impartial tribunal independent of the initial decision-making body. It is a moot point to what extent these higher standards of procedural due process are now required by general international law.[67]

1.2.4 *Non-refoulement: article 33*

The scope of the principle of *non-refoulement*, both as a treaty rule and as a rule of general international law, has been fully analysed in Chapter 4.

1.3 THE CRITERIA OF ENTITLEMENT TO TREATMENT IN ACCORDANCE WITH THE CONVENTION

Some provisions of the Convention are limited to refugees 'lawfully staying' in contracting States, some apply to those 'lawfully in' such States, while others apply to refugees *tout court*, whether lawfully or unlawfully present. Regrettably, there is little consistency in the language of the Convention, be it English or French, but three general categories may be distinguished: simple presence, lawful presence, and lawful residence; for some purposes also reference may be required to the concept of habitual residence.

1.3.1 *Simple presence*

Some benefits extend to refugees, by virtue of their status alone as refugees, without in any way being dependent upon their legal situation. Article 33, for example, refers simply to refugees, as does article 3.[68] Articles 2, 4, and 27 are predicated on the fact of presence ('the country in which he finds himself'; 'refugees within their territories'; 'any refugee in their territory'/ *'du pays où il se trouve'; 'réfugiés sur leur territoire'; 'tout réfugié se trouvant sur leur territoire'*), while article 31 is specifically applicable to cases of illegal entry or presence ('in their territory without authorization'/ *'se trouve sur leur territoire sans autorisation'*).

1.3.2 *Lawful presence*

Lawful presence is to be distinguished from lawful residence; it implies admission in accordance with the applicable immigration law, for a temporary purpose, for example, as a student, visitor, or recipient of medical attention. Owing to the different approaches adopted within national systems, the distinction is often difficult to maintain in practice. For the purposes of the Convention, articles 18, 26, and 32 apply to refugees whose presence is lawful ('lawfully in'/ *'qui se trouvent régulièrement'*).[69]

measures as the Government may deem necessary in the circumstances; so however that any action taken by the Government . . . in this regard shall not operate to the prejudice of the provisions of art. 33 . . .'

[67] Cf. Goodwin-Gill, *Movement of Persons*, 227–8, 238–40, 308–9.   [68] See also art. 16(1).

[69] Cf. art. 11, which refers to refugees 'regularly serving as crew members/ *régulièrement employés comme membres de l'équipage*'.

The extension of article 32 benefits to refugees who are merely lawfully present in contracting States, even if only on a temporary basis, may be disputed in the light of State practice. Thus, article 43 of the 1979 Swiss law on asylum affords the benefit of restricted grounds of expulsion to the refugee '*auquel la Suisse a accordé l'asile*'.[70] A similar approach is found in other jurisdictions,[71] and in principle there appears to be no reason why the temporarily present refugee should not be subject to the same regime of deportation as applies to aliens generally. It may be assumed that he or she will still enjoy the right of return to the State which issued a travel document and the benefit of article 33 will apply in any event. It may be argued that the grounds of public order/*ordre public* include breach of any aspect of a country's immigration or aliens law,[72] in which case little substantive protection is offered to distinguish the refugee lawfully present from the refugee lawfully resident. On balance, article 32 should be interpreted as a substantial limitation upon the State's power of expulsion, but with its benefits confined to lawfully resident refugees, that is, those in the State on a more or less indefinite basis.

1.3.3 *Lawful residence*

Finally, many articles apply only to refugees lawfully resident in the contracting State, that is, those who are, as it were, enjoying asylum in the sense of residence and lasting protection. Again the terminology varies. Article 25 refers to States 'in whose territory (the refugee) is residing'/'*sur le territoire duquel il réside*'. Articles 14 and 16(2) invoke the country of the refugee's 'habitual residence'/'*résidence habituelle*', while articles 15, 17(1), 19, 21, 23, 24, and 28 employ, in English, the somewhat imprecise term 'lawfully staying'.[73] The corresponding phrase in the French text is '*résident régulièrement*' (or some variation thereof); it is evident from the *travaux préparatoires* concerning article 28, for example, that the English phrase was selected for its approximation to the French term, particularly as the concept of residence in common law systems is often replete with contradiction. The terminology adopted in the Convention, however, is not free from difficulty. It was noted at the second session of the *Ad hoc* Committee in 1950 that a resident in France may be a privileged, ordinary, or temporary resident.[74] The cases of

---

[70] FF 1979 II 977.

[71] See, for example, *Kan Kim Lin* v. *Rinaldi* 361 F.Supp. 177, 186 (1973); aff'd., 493 F.2d (1974), the Court, referring to the *travaux préparatoires* on art. 32, observed that the term 'lawfully in their territory' would 'exclude a refugee who, while lawfully admitted, has overstayed the period for which he was admitted or was authorized to stay or who had violated any other condition attached to his admission or stay'. In *Chim Ming* v. *Marks* 505 F.2d 1170 (1974), the Court of Appeals considered that the 'only rational interpretation' of the phrase was 'one consistent with the definition of unlawfulness in article 31 as involving the status of being in a nation "without authorization". Since a nation's immigration laws provide authorization, one unlawfully in the country is in violation of those laws.'

[72] See cases cited in Goodwin-Gill, *Movement of Persons*, 298, n. 1, and generally, 295-9.

[73] See also the terminology of residence used in paras. 6 and 11 of the Schedule.

[74] UN doc. E/AC.32/SR.42, 11-20.

those present only for a short period of time might cause problems, but in the view of the French representative, '. . . an examination of the various articles in which the words "résident régulièrement" appeared would show that they all implied a settling down and consequently a certain length of residence'.[75] In order to obtain the benefit of the articles cited above, the refugee must show something more than mere lawful presence.[76] Generalizations are difficult in the face of different systems of immigration control, but evidence of permanent, indefinite, unrestricted or other residence status, recognition as a refugee, issue of a travel document, grant of a re-entry visa, will raise a strong presumption that the refugee should be considered as lawfully staying in the territory of a contracting State. It would then fall to that State to rebut the presumption by showing, for example, that the refugee was admitted for a limited time and purpose, or that he or she is in fact the responsibility of another State.[77]

1.3.4 Habitual residence

The phrase 'former habitual residence' appears in article 1A(2) of the 1951 Convention to identify the country with respect to which a stateless person might establish his or her status as a refugee, on the basis of a well-founded fear of persecution. In this context, the drafters gave little attention to the precise meaning of the phrase, the *Ad hoc* Committee observing simply that the expression did not refer to a locality, but to 'the country in which (the refugee) had resided and where he had suffered or fears he would suffer persecution if he returned'.[78] Habitual residence for a stateless person would necessarily seem to imply some degree of security, of status, of entitlement to remain and to return, which were in part the objectives of inter-government arrangements of the inter-war period.[79] Where the term 'habitual residence' is used in other articles of the 1951

---

[75] Ibid., 12.

[76] In its reservation to arts. 23 and 24, Canada states that it interprets 'lawfully staying' as referring only to refugees admitted for permanent residence; refugees admitted for temporary residence are to be accorded the same treatment with respect to those articles as is accorded to visitors generally.

[77] Cf. the approach adopted in the bilateral agreements cited above, n. 53. The Protocol to the 1962 Switzerland-Federal Republic of Germany agreement on transfer of responsibility, for example, while discounting periods of stay for educational, medical, or convalescence purposes, deems authorization of establishment to arise, *'lorsque le réfugié a obtenu une autorisation de séjour illimitée ou lorsqu'il peut justifier d'une résidence régulière de trois ans . . .'* The agreements in question deal with transfer of responsibility *between States*, and no such period of elapsed residence is required for the refugee seeking to invoke the benefit of Convention articles *vis-à-vis* his or her country of asylum.

[78] UN doc. E/1618, p. 39. UNHCR, *Handbook on Procedures and Criteria for the Determination of Refugee Status*, (1979), paras. 101, 104–5. See also CRR, 13 sept. 1991, *Joude Faycal*, 142.572: *Doc. réf.* no. 178, 22/31 mars 1992, Suppl., CJ, 2—a stateless claimant having no 'habitual residence' was found not therefore to be a Convention refugee. Commenting on the jurisprudence of the *Commission de recours*, Tiberghien concludes that habitual residence implies the possession of a travel document or, at least, the possibility of entering and leaving the country of residence: ibid., 3.

[79] See United Nations, *A Study of Statelessness*, (1949), Introduction and Part I.

Convention, it signifies more than a stay of short duration, but was apparently not intended necessarily to imply permanent residence or domicile.[80]

'Domicile', indeed, is a term of art fraught with problems in common law and other jurisdictions, and is distinguished from residence in article 12 of the Convention:

1. The personal status of a refugee shall be governed by the law of the country of his domicile or, if he has no domicile, by the law of the country of his residence.

States practice differs on the law that should govern issues of personal status (legal capacity, capacity to marry, family rights, succession, and so forth); some have opted for the law of the individual's domicile, and others for the law of the individual's State of nationality. Article 12 is intended to address the problems that may arise for refugees, but it is not always easy to determine when one domicile has been abandoned, and another acquired;[81] hence, the use of the residuary concept of residence.[82]

'Habitual residence' and even 'residence' alone involve elements of fact and intention. For example, whether those admitted for permanent residence to Canada do in fact establish such residence in Canada does not necessarily follow, as citizenship courts have confirmed. On the one hand, residency is now conceded to have an 'extended meaning', (that is, it is flexible enough to accommodate periods of absence).[83] On the other hand, the grant of the special status of citizenship requires more than a place of abode and an intent to return;[84] it requires that the individual 'centralize his or her mode of living' in Canada, and this in turn may depend upon additional factors, such as family ties, only temporary links overseas, and continuing connections with Canada (bank accounts, investments, and the like).[85]

---

[80] Art. 14 provides that the same protection of artistic rights and industrial property is to be accorded to refugees in their country of habitual residence, as is accorded to nationals. See debate in the Conference of Plenipotentiaries: UN doc. A/CONF.2/SR.7, p. 20; SR.8, p. 6; SR.23, p. 26.

[81] Domicile involves both subjective and objective factors. See *Trottier* v. *Dame Lionel Rajotte* [1940] SCR 203, in which the Supreme Court of Canada stated that the principles governing change of domicile of origin or birth are that a domicile of origin cannot be lost until a new domicile has been acquired. This involves two factors: the acquisition of residence in fact in a new place, and the intention of permanently settling there. Leaving a country with the intention of never returning is not enough, in the absence of a permanent residence established in another country, 'general and indefinite in its future contemplation'.

[82] See *Ad hoc* Committee on Statelessness and Related Problems: UN doc. E/AC.7/SR.8, paras. 14, 19; SR.9, para. 2.

[83] *Re Citizenship Act and in re Antonios E. Papadogiorgakis* [1978] 2 FC 208. This case, it has been said, 'imposed on the courts an enquiry covering both intention and fact, neither of these elements being considered determinative by itself': per Joyal J. in *Canada (Secretary of State)* v. *Nakhjavani* [1987] FCJ No. 721.

[84] In *Canada (Secretary of State)* v. *Nakhjavani* [1987] FCJ No. 721, the court found that the respondents, stateless persons holding Canadian certificates of identity, maintained a pied-à-terre in Canada, but resided principally in Haifa, Israel, by reason of the husband's religious and administrative duties on behalf of the Baha'i Faith. Their brief visits to Canada did not qualify them for citizenship.

[85] See *Re Chan* [1988] FCJ No. 323, a successful appeal against refusal of citizenship. The

In determining the country of former habitual residence, the exact purpose for which the determination is required must first be identified. Both the 1951 Convention and municipal law rely on different conceptions of residence for different purposes, as the above sections show. Similarly, in municipal law, certain benefits, such as social security or relief from deportation,[86] may require a qualifying period of residence, while entitlements such as citizenship generally require evidence of greater commitment to the community.

The identification of the country of former habitual residence can serve either of two purposes: (1) to clarify which State, if any, is properly to be considered as the putative State of persecution in a claim to refugee status by a stateless person; or (2) to establish which State is 'responsible' for the individual concerned, in the sense of having an obligation to readmit him or her, and/or to deal with any claim to refugee status or to treatment under the 1951 Convention.

2. Refugees as the beneficiaries of other instruments, including regional agreements

Refugees may also benefit, directly and indirectly, from a wide variety of other international agreements, many of which have been cited in the preceding chapters. The following summary account is intended merely to flag some of the apparent advantages and disadvantages of parallel systems of protection. In some cases, they have been little used on behalf of refugees and asylum seekers; in other cases, States are only now becoming aware that their human rights obligations also may require specific measures of incorporation; and in still others, provisions with a particular human rights focus have proven inadequate to protect those in search of refuge or asylum.

Particularly important are those instruments of universal or potentially universal application which incorporate a supervisory or treaty monitoring mechanism, such as the 1966 Covenants on Civil and Political Rights, and on Economic, Social and Cultural Rights; the 1984 Convention against Torture; the 1989 Convention on the Rights of the Child; the 1949 Geneva Convention

---

applicant had completed undergraduate and graduate training in Canada, and had left for Hong Kong only after experiencing difficulties in finding a job in Canada commensurate with his qualifications. He kept rooms in his parents' house, made frequent return trips, maintained strong family ties and other social relations, took only temporary, furnished accommodation overseas, kept bank accounts and filed income tax returns. He was held to meet the residency requirements of the Citizenship Act.

[86] For example, under the UK Commonwealth Immigrants Act 1962, no recommendation for deportation was to be made against a Commonwealth citizen who satisfied the court that he or she was 'ordinarily resident' in the UK, and had been continuously so resident for at least five years prior to the date of conviction of a relevant criminal offence. The Immigration Act 1971 maintained the like immunity. In France, under the former system, 'privileged residents' enjoyed similar benefits, as does the class of *Aufenthaltsberechtigter* in the German Federal Republic—those resident for five years who have adapted themselves economically and socially to local life.

relative to the Protection of Civilian Persons in time of War[87] and Protocol 1 thereto;[88] conventions dealing with the safety of life at sea;[89] International Labour Organization conventions, including Convention No. 118 concerning Equality of Treatment of Nationals and Non-Nationals in Social Security, 1962,[90] and Convention No. 97 concerning Migration for Employment, 1949.[91]

Specific aspects of the refugee problem have been the subject of instruments such as the 1957 refugee seamen agreement and the 1973 protocol thereto,[92] or of protocols annexed to agreements such as the 1971 revision of the Universal Copyright Convention;[93] such protocols derive from article 14, common to both the 1951 Convention relating to the Status of Refugees and the 1954 Convention relating to the Status of Stateless Persons, and a like protocol has also been proposed for consideration by the Diplomatic Conference on the Revision of the 1883 Paris Convention for the Protection of Industrial Property.

Clearly also, refugee and related population displacements will need to be dealt with in the context of any inter-State arrangement relating, for example, to free trade and free movement of labour. The 1992 Maastricht Treaty, for example, anticipates the harmonization of refugee and asylum policy in the European Union.[94] The 1990 Dublin Convention and the 1990 Convention on the Application of the Schengen Agreement in turn aim for common rules and practices in handling asylum cases, particularly with respect to determination and the removal of rejected cases.[95]

In Africa, the 1969 OAU Convention has been widely ratified;[96] Latin

---

[87] 75 *UNTS* 287, arts. 26, 44, 70.

[88] Adopted in 1977 (arts. 73, 74, and 85); text in *Official Records of the Diplomatic Conference on the Reaffirmation and Development of International Humanitarian Law applicable in Armed Conflicts*, Geneva, 1974–77, vol. 3.

[89] See art. 11, 1910 Brussels Convention for the Unification of Certain Rules of Law relating to Assistance and Salvage at Sea; art. 12, 1958 Geneva Convention on the High Seas; Regulations 10 and 15, 1960 International Convention on the Safety of Life at Sea; 1979 International Convention on Maritime Search and Rescue, art. I and annexe, paras. 2.1.1, 2.1.10, and 5.3.3.8; art. 98, 1982 United Nations Convention on the Law of the Sea.

[90] Arts. 1 and 10(1).   [91] Annexe II, art. 11.

[92] Text in UNHCR, *Collection of International Instruments concerning Refugees*, (1979), 48, 54.

[93] Ibid., 179.

[94] 1992 Treaty of Maastricht = Treaty on the European Union, 7 Feb. 1992: EC *Official Journal* C.191, 29 Jun. 1992; Joly, D., 'The Porous Dam: European Harmonization on Asylum in the Nineties', 6 *IJRL* 159 (1994).

[95] 1990 Dublin Convention Determining the State Responsible for Examining Applications for Asylum lodged in one of the Member States of the European Communities; 1990 Convention on the Application of the Schengen Agreement of 14 June 1985 relating to the Gradual Suppression of Controls at Common Frontiers, between the Governments of States Members of the Benelux Economic Union, the Federal Republic of Germany and the French Republic. For text, see Annexe 2, Nos. 13 and 14.

[96] For States parties, see below Annexe 6, No. 1. See also Oloka-Onyango, J., 'Human Rights, the OAU Convention and the Refugee Crisis in Africa', 3 *IJRL* 453 (1991); id., 'The Place and Role of the OAU Bureau for Refugees in the African Refugee Crisis', 6 *IJRL* 34 (1994); generally see OAU/UNHCR Commemorative Symposium on Refugees and the Problems of Forced Population Displacements in Africa, Addis Ababa, 8–10 September 1994, 7 *IJRL, Special Issue—Summer 1995*.

America is covered by a complex network of treaties and asylum practices,[97] while a large number of arrangements have been concluded under the auspices of the Council of Europe, dealing with such varied topics as visa-free travel for refugees;[98] national treatment in social security matters;[99] consular protection;[100] and transfer of responsibility.[101]

The variety of instruments affecting refugees does not permit very many useful generalizations. How refugees are defined will often differ from agreement to agreement, while in other contexts refugees and asylum seekers will need to attach their claims to one or other right protected by the convention in question. The criteria of entitlement will necessarily vary, depending on the nature of the right claimed.

2.1 UNIVERSAL TREATY MONITORING BODIES

The *Human Rights Committee* was established in 1976 to monitor the application of the 1966 Covenant on Civil and Political Rights and its Optional Protocol. It comprises eighteen experts, elected for a four-year term by the one hundred and twenty-nine States which had ratified that treaty by 31 December 1994, and meets twice a year. It considers reports from States Parties and hears complaints by other States or individuals against those States which have ratified the Optional Protocol (80 States at 31 December 1994). The inter-State complaints procedure is unused, and the individual procedure under the Optional Protocol has become the Committee's second principal activity. The Committee has already had occasion to deal with issues arising in the immigration and refugee areas.[102]

The *Committee on Economic, Social and Cultural Rights* held its first session in 1987, in succession to a series of working groups set up by ECOSOC. Like its civil

---

[97] See 1889 Montevideo Treaty on International Penal Law; 1928 Havana Convention on Asylum; 1933 Montevideo Convention on Political Asylum; 1940 Montevideo Treaty on International Penal Law (revising that of 1889); 1954 Caracas Convention on Territorial Asylum (Annexe 2, No. 3); 1954 Caracas Convention on Diplomatic Asylum (Annexe 2, No. 4). See also Cuellar, R., García-Sayán, D., Montaño, J., Diegues, M. and Valladares Lanza, L., 'Refugee and Related Developments in Latin America: The Challenges Ahead', 3 *IJRL* 482 (1991); D'Alotto, A. & Garretón, R., 'Developments in Latin America: Some Further Thoughts', ibid., 499; Gros Espiell, H., Picado, S. & Valladares Lanza, L., 'Principles and Criteria for the Protection of and Assistance to Central American Refugees, Returnees and Displaced Persons in Central America', 2 *IJRL* 83 (1990).

[98] The 1959 European agreement on the abolition of visas for refugees (*ETS* no. 31) aims for visa-free travel between contracting States for refugees holding CTDs issued by, and residing in, any contracting State; it is limited to visits not exceeding three months, undertaken otherwise than for employment.

[99] See, for example, arts. 1(o), (p), 2, 4, 1972 European Convention on Social Security: *ETS* no. 78; also EEC Regulation 1408/71, art. 1, 2.

[100] See above, s. 1.1.1.   [101] Ibid.

[102] See further Opsahl, T., 'The Human Rights Committee', in Alston, P., *The United Nations and Human Rights*, (1992), 369; McGoldrick, D., *The Human Rights Committee: Its Role in the Development of the International Covenant on Civil and Political Rights*, (1991); Human Rights Committee, 'General Comments', No. 15 (The position of aliens under the Covenant): UN doc. CCPR/C/21/Rev.1 (19 May 1989).

and political rights counterpart, the Committee comprises eighteen members, but elected under the authority of ECOSOC, and not under the Covenant on Economic, Social and Cultural Rights. Its mandate is to assist ECOSOC to do its job, rather than to exercise direct supervisory responsibilities, and it has not so far had to deal with refugee-related questions.[103]

The *Committee against Torture*, set up under article 17 of the 1984 United Nations Convention against Torture and other Cruel, Inhuman or Degrading Treatment or Punishment to monitor implementation, is composed of ten experts elected by States parties to serve in their personal capacity. Eighty-six States were party to the convention at 31 December 1994, and all *must* accept a reporting obligation. Uniquely, the Committee against Torture also has the power to investigate cases on its own initiative, where it receives 'reliable information which appears to it to contain well-founded indications that torture is being systematically practised *in the territory* of a State party'.[104] Not surprisingly, given the Convention's express reference to the principle of *non-refoulement* in article 3, the Committee against Torture is increasingly receiving refugee-related cases, a number of which have been referred to above.[105]

The most recently established body is the *Committee on the Rights of the Child*. Composed of ten independent members, the committee's mandate is similar to those described above, including the examination of country reports on measures taken to implement the provisions of the 1989 Convention on the Rights of the Child, ratified by one hundred and seventy-seven States by 31 November 1995. This Convention specifically mentions refugee children in article 22,[106] and the Committee may expect to deal with problems of protection in the future.

2.2 REGIONAL TREATY MONITORING BODIES

The European and the American conventions on human rights provide for supervisory and petitions procedures at both individual and State level.

The *European Commission on Human Rights* and the *European Court of Human Rights* are the principal investigatory and adjudicatory organs in Europe, with certain responsibilities also shared by the Committee of Ministers. The European Convention allows claims to be brought by States, individuals or groups. With the entry into force of the Eleventh Protocol, a single full-time court will replace the existing Commission and Court of Human Rights, and the right of individual petition will no longer be optional.

---

[103] One hundred and thirty-eight States were parties at 1 Jun. 1997. See generally Alston, P., 'The Committee on Economic, Social and Cultural Rights', in Alston, P., *The United Nations and Human Rights*, 473.

[104] Art. 20(1). Although this is an optional procedure, States have to *opt out* of the art. 20 process under art. 28. See further Byrnes, A., 'The Committee against Torture', in Alston, P., ed., *The United Nations and Human Rights*, 509.

[105] See above, Ch. 4, s. 3.2.6; Gorlick, B., 'Refugee Protection and the Committee against Torture', 7 *IJRL* 504 (1995).

[106] See further below, Ch. 9, s. 3.1.

The 1969 American Convention on Human Rights provides for the *Inter-American Court of Human Rights* and continues the role of the *Inter-American Commission on Human Rights*, which had already exercised certain responsibilities under the earlier American Declaration of the Rights of Man.[107] The general approach of these institutions is similar to that of their European counterparts.

The *African Commission on Human and People's Rights*, meeting in private sessions, also examines communications concerning gross violations of human rights.

2.2.1 Refugees, asylum seekers and the European Convention: an assessment

The European Convention on Human Rights, at first glance, appears to offer substantial protection possibilities to refugees and asylum seekers.[108] Article 3, for example, prohibits torture and cruel or inhuman treatment, article 13 requires a remedy for every victim of a violation of protected rights, while even article 8 may be of indirect value, through the protection accorded to the family and the manner in which it has been applied to 'second generation migrants'.[109] The jurisprudence of the European Court and the European Commission of Human Rights also seem to hold considerable precedential value,[110] with a series of consistent rulings in immigration and removal cases that seem to impose significant limitations on sovereign powers.

[107] See, for example, Inter-American Human Rights Commission, *Haitian refugee Cases*, Case No. 10.675, Inter-Am. C.H.R. 334, OEA/Ser.L/V/II.85, doc. 9 rev. (1994)—ruling on the issue of admissibility that interdiction and return policies appeared to violate the American Declaration of Human Rights, the American Convention on Human Rights as supplemented by art. 18, Vienna Convention on the Law of Treaties, arts. 55, 56, UN Charter, the Universal Declaration of Human Rights, the 1951 Convention and 1967 Protocol relating to the Status of Refugees, and customary international law.

[108] On the uses of the European Convention, see Steenbergen, Hanneke D. M., 'The Relevance of the European Convention on Human Rights for Asylum Seekers', in Baehr, Peter R. and Tessenyi, Geza, eds., *The New Refugee Hosting Countries: Call for Experience-Space for Innovation.* (Dec. 1991), 45. See also Einarsen, T., 'The European Convention on Human Rights and the Notion of an Implied Right to *de facto* Asylum', 2 *IJRL* 361 (1990).

[109] On the extent of the family relationship, see for example, *Berrehab* (3/1987/126/177), 21 June 1988; *Keegan* v. *Ireland* (16/1993/411/490), 26 May 1994; on expulsion of second generation migrants, see *Djeroud Case* (34/1990/225/289), 23 Jan. 1991; *Lamguindaz* v. *United Kingdom*, (48/1992/393/471), 28 June 1993; *Beldjoudi* v. *France* (55/1990/246/317), 26 Mar. 1992.

[110] What a State may do in times of public emergency is limited and potentially subject to regional control. However, the margin of appreciation is wide and where control will be exercised is not easy to determine; *Brannigan and McBride* v. *United Kingdom* (5/1992/350/423–4), 26 May 1993—in determining whether the life of the nation is threatened by a public emergency and how far it is necessary to go in attempting to overcome the emergency, a wide margin of appreciation should be left to the national authorities, accompanied by a 'European supervision'. This permissible discretion may be reflected in acceptance of lower thresholds for lawful arrest; see, for example, *Fox, Campbell and Hartley* (18/1989/178/234–6), 30 Aug. 1990; also *Murray* v. *United Kingdom* (13/1993/408/487), 28 Oct. 1994. On the requirements that restrictive measures must be in accordance with law, adopted in pursuit of a legitimate aim, and necessary in a democratic society, that is, 'justified by a pressing social need and ... proportionate to the legitimate aim pursued', see *Moustaquim* v. *Belgium* (31/1989/191/291), 18 Feb. 1991, para. 43; *Beldjoudi* v. *France* (55/1990/246/317), 26 Mar. 1992; *Kokkinakis* v. *Greece* (3/1992/348/421), 25 May 1993; *Otto-Preminger-Institut* v. *Austria* (11/1993/406/485), 20 Sept. 1994; *Berrehab* (3/1987/126/177), 21 June 1988.

The reality, however, is somewhat different, at least so far as the Court, rather than the Commission is concerned.[111] The distance between the international protection of refugees and article 3 of the European Convention has been repeatedly confirmed, even as the European Court has purported to lay down general principles of apparently wider application. In *Cruz Varas*, for example, the Court held that expulsion of an asylum seeker may engage the responsibility of the expelling State under article 3, 'where substantial grounds have been shown for believing that the person concerned faced a real risk of being subjected to torture or to inhuman or degrading treatment or punishment in the country to which he was returned . . .' However, the Court also stressed that the ill-treatment must attain a minimum level of severity, and in applying article 3, it has consistently maintained a high standard of proof ('substantial grounds', 'real risk'), while simultaneously conceding considerable substantive and procedural room to national authorities.[112]

In *Vilvarajah and Others* v. *UK*, for example, the Court found, on the facts, that the applicants' situation was no worse than that of other members of the Tamil community, who might well be detained and ill-treated: '[a] mere possibility of ill-treatment . . . in such circumstances, is not in itself sufficient to give rise to a breach of Article 3'.[113]

Article 13 has also proven something of a non-starter. It requires that '[e]veryone whose rights and freedoms . . . are violated shall have an effective remedy before a national authority . . .' On the one hand, this has been construed to mean that an actual breach of the Convention is not an essential pre-condition to the availability of a remedy, but that neither must a remedy be made available for 'any supposed grievance', only for that which is 'an arguable one in terms of the Convention'.[114] On the other hand, the Court has also repeatedly stated that there is no obligation to incorporate the Convention into domestic law, and that article 13 'does not go so far as to guarantee a remedy allowing a Contracting State's laws as such to be challenged before a national authority on

---

[111] On the positive side in the context of entry and removal of non-nationals, see *Bozano* Case, (5/1985/91/138), 18 Dec. 1976; *Abdulaziz, Cabales and Balkandali* (15/1983/71/ 107–9), 28 May 1985.

[112] *Cruz-Varas* v. *Sweden*, (46/1990/237/307), 20 Mar 1991, Ser. A, vol. 201. The Court indicated that in assessing the degree of risk, it will look at all the material placed before it, including any obtained on its own initiative; that in judging State actions, it will look at facts known at time of alleged exposure to risk, but will also take into account information later available to confirm or refute the appreciation made at the time of the applicant's fears.

[113] *Vilvarajah* v. *United Kingdom*, (45/1990/236/302–306), 20 Oct. 1991, Ser. A, vol. 215, paras. 103, 107, 111. Cf. Hailbronner, K., '*Non-Refoulement* and "Humanitarian" Refugees: Customary International Law or Wishful Legal Thinking?' 26 *Virg. JIL* 857 (1986), whose argument from the European case law supports the proposition that art. 3 does not establish a (European Convention) right of refuge for those in flight from civil war, but does not answer the claim for a right of refuge in general or customary international law.

[114] *Case of Boyle and Rice* (19/1986/117/165–6), 27 Apr. 1988, para. 52; *Plattform 'Ärzte für das Leben'* (5/1987/128/179), 21 June 1988; *Powell and Rayner* v. *UK* (3/1989/163/219), 21 Feb. 1990; see also Pettiti and Walsh, diss., in *Brannigan and McBride* v. *UK* (5/1992/350/423–4), 26 May 1993.

the ground of being contrary to the Convention'.[115] This effectively debars claimants in States that have not specifically incorporated the Convention, or where it is not otherwise a part of domestic law, from seeking a local remedy for its breach.

Article 13 has been construed especially narrowly in proceedings involving non-nationals, refugees and asylum seekers. In *Vilvarajah* it was argued that judicial review is not an effective remedy when what is at issue is the merits of a decision, in this case, the reasonableness of claimants' fear of persecution.[116] The Court maintained its acceptance of judicial review as explained in the *Soering* case, on the ground that the reviewing court was nonetheless able to review 'reasonableness' and strike down decisions 'tainted with illegality, irrationality or procedural impropriety'.[117] It was left to the Irish judge, Judge Walsh, to point out that the comparison with *Soering* was inappropriate, for there the facts were not in dispute; a remedy that excludes the competence to make a decision on the merits, he said, cannot meet the requirements of article 13.[118] The Court, however, attached particular importance to the knowledge and experience of the United Kingdom authorities in dealing with asylum claims such as those before it, concluding that 'substantial grounds' had not been established to show a breach of article 3.[119]

The protection that might otherwise be expected for the refugee and the

---

[115] *The Sunday Times* v. *UK (No. 2)* (50/1990/241/312), 26 Nov. 1991, para. 61; *Observer and Guardian* v. *UK* (51/1990/242/313), 26 Nov. 1991, para. 76; *James and Others*, 21 Feb. 1986, p. 47, paras. 84–5; *Case of the Holy Monasteries* v. *Greece* (10/1993/405/483–4), 9 Dec. 1994, para. 90.

[116] *Vilvarajah and Others* v. *UK* (45/1990/236/302–6), 30 Oct. 1991.

[117] Ibid., para. 123. The Court was impressed by the fact that applicants had actually succeeded with judicial review in a number of cases; ibid., paras. 89–93. *Soering* case, Ser. A., No. 161 (1/1989/161/217), 7 July 1989; Lillich, Richard B. 'Notes and Comments: The *Soering* Case', 85 *AJIL* 128 (1991); Van den Wyngaert, C., 'Applying the European Convention on Human Rights to Extradition: Opening Pandora's Box?' 39 *ICLQ* 757 (1990).

[118] See also Walsh diss. in *Brannigan and McBride* v. *UK* (5/1992/350/423–4), 26 May 1993: 'The application of Article 13 does not depend upon a violation being proved … (Habeas corpus) depends upon showing a breach of national laws. It is not available for a claim that the detention is illegal by reason only of a breach of the Convention.' For an instance of judicial review in positive terms, see Ward, I., 'The Story of M: A Cautionary Tale from the United Kingdom', 6 *IJRL* 194 (1994).

[119] Cf. Hampson, F. J., 'The Concept of an "Arguable Claim" under Article 13 of the European Convention on Human Rights', 39 *ICLQ* 891 (1990). Note also that in the context of art. 6(1) (determination of civil rights and obligations or any criminal charge), the Court has ruled that decisions of administrative authorities that do not themselves satisfy the requirements of that article should be subject to subsequent control by a 'judicial body that has full jurisdiction': *Albert and Le Compte* v. *Belgium*, 10 Feb. 1983, p.16, para. 29; also *Ortenberg* v. *Austria* (33/1993/428/507), 25 Nov. 1994, paras. 29–34; *Beaumartin* v. *France*, (35/1993/430/509), 24 Nov. 1994, in which the Court held, again with respect to art. 6(1), that 'Only an institution that has full jurisdiction and satisfies a number of requirements, such as independence of the executive and also of the parties, merits the designation "tribunal",' within the meaning of article 6(1). The Conseil d'Etat, which referred questions of treaty interpretation to the executive for (binding) decision, did not meet these requirements. *Hadjianastassiou* v. *Greece*, (69/1991/321/393), 16 Dec. 1992—national courts must indicate with sufficient clarity the grounds on which they base their decision, which makes it possible for the accused to exercise usefully available rights of appeal.

asylum seeker has been further undermined by the Court's interpretation of the term 'victim of a violation' in article 25(1).[120] *Vijayanathan and Pusparajah* v. *France* involved a direction to two Sri Lankans to leave French territory, after rejection of their request to be granted refugee status.[121] The government objected that the applicants were not 'victims', and the Court agreed. No *expulsion* order had been made against them, and the direction to leave French territory was not enforceable in itself,[122] even though the 'directions' amounted to an order to leave France within one month or be liable to the penalty of imprisonment and a fine.[123] The Court gave particular credence, however, to evidence of the practice of the French authorities with respect to asylum claims by Sri Lankans, including their use of information sources, case by case assessments, and the low incidence of actual expulsions.[124] As in *Vilvarajah*, what counted for the Court was the authorities' knowledge and experience, and little weight was accorded to the applicants' request for a review of the merits.

The interpretation of 'victim' in *Vijayanathan and Pusparajah* appears to be manifestly inconsistent with the view expressed by the Court in *Open Door and Dublin Well Woman* v. *Ireland*, to the effect that article 25 entitles individuals to contend that a law violates their rights by itself, in the absence of an individual measure of implementation, if they run the risk of being directly affected by it.[125]

---

[120] 'The Commission may receive petitions . . . from any person . . . claiming to be a victim of a violation by one of the High Contracting Parties of the rights set forth in this Convention . . .' See now also Protocol No. 11, replacing the existing European Commission and Court, but maintaining the same terminology in new art. 34.

[121] *Vijayanathan and Pusparajah* v. *France*, (75/1991/327/399–400), Ser. A., vol. 241–B, 27 Aug. 1992.

[122] If an expulsion order were made, it could be appealed with suspensive effect: art. 22, ordonnance du 2 nov. 1945 as amended.

[123] Minimum one month, maximum one year; minimum 2,000 francs, maximum 20,000 francs, possibly followed by prohibition on residence and expulsion per art. 19, ordonnance du 2 nov. 1945; Judgment of the Court, paras. 10, 15. The court did not consider whether the deliberate perpetuation of such a situation of insecurity and illegality by the State might itself be a violation of art. 3.

[124] Judgment of the Court, paras. 34–8, 44. See also *X* v. *Switzerland*, Appl. No. 14912/89, 1 Oct. 1990; Achermann, A., 'Neuansetzung einer Ausreisefrist für "Tolerierte"—Bemerkungen zum Entscheid der Europäischen Menschenrechtskommission i.S. X. c. Schweiz vom 1.10.1990, Beschwerde Nr. 14912/89', *Asyl*, 1991/2, 19–20. In the decision reviewed, the European Commission found the application manifestly ill-founded, given that government had given assurances of non-removal and/or if removal was contemplated, that the claimant would be 'granted sufficient opportunity to challenge the expulsion, if possible before the Swiss authorities, and in any event before the European Commission'. In the circumstances, there was no serious reason to believe a violation of arts. 2 or 3 was likely, and the applicant could not claim to be a victim of an alleged violation.

[125] *Case of Open Door and Dublin Well Woman* v. *Ireland* (64/1991/316/387–8), 29 Oct. 1992, paras. 43–4. This case involved an injunction issued to prevent the corporate applicants and their employees from providing certain information to pregnant women; two of the four individual applicants were counsellors employed by the agency concerned, and two were 'women of child-bearing age': 'Although it has not been asserted that (the two women concerned) are pregnant, it is not disputed that they belong to a class of women of child-bearing age which may be adversely affected by the restrictions imposed by the injunction. They are not seeking to challenge *in abstracto* the compatibility of Irish law with the Convention since they run the risk of being directly prejudiced by the measure complained of. They can thus claim to be "victims" within the meaning of Article 25 (1).'

The reasons why the European Convention fails to provide any or any adequate protection to refugees and asylum seekers in Europe are fairly straightforward. First, asylum, as the Court has pointed out on several occasions, is not, 'as such', protected by the Convention.[126] The asylum seeker, therefore, must try to bring his or her claim within one or other Convention right, such as article 3 or article 8, but here the European Court has adopted a restrictive approach, at least with respect to asylum seekers. Why this is so is less clear, but it may well reflect the Court's view, on the whole, that asylum touches still too closely the sovereign sensibilities of States, and that for now it is best left alone. This certainly explains why the Court thought it appropriate, in *Vilvarajah*, to mention if not to comment on the United Kingdom government's stated fear that,

The consequences of finding a breach of Article 3 in the present case would be that all other persons in similar situations facing random risks on account of civil turmoil in the State in which they lived, would be entitled not to be removed, thereby permitting the entry of a potentially very class of people with the attendant serious social and economic consequences.[127]

It also explains why the Court is especially keen to stress the 'wide' margin of appreciation enjoyed by States in this field, and to accord particular weight to governmental 'knowledge and experience' in dealing with asylum claims as a further reason for not intervening.

The few inroads so far made on sovereign discretion also have a policy explanation. Thus, the court's interference with the deportation of second generation migrants is explicable as the defence of a relatively known and manageable population, whose acquired residence claims anyway already have some basis in general international law through the doctrine of effective nationality. Similarly, family reunion claims, while they do breach the wall in a few places, are also closely circumscribed in terms of the necessary family relationship, and subject to other questions of appreciation, such as the ability or lack of ability to establish family life elsewhere.

Even the so-called 'landmark' case of *Soering*, which many have upheld as so potentially useful a precedent in asylum cases,[128] proves on closer examination to be worth considerably less. National extradition proceedings tend, after all, to ignore the 'humanitarian' aspects of the case, except so far as these are covered by the shrinking concept of political offence, or reflect a regional concern for 'prejudice' or discrimination on the traditional grounds. In *Soering*, the essential facts were not in dispute, and the core issue was whether as a matter of law the fate awaiting the claimant amounted to torture or inhumane or degrading treatment within the meaning of article 3. No answer having been given by the

---

[126] See, among many others, *Vilvarajah*, para. 102.   [127] *Vilvarajah*, para. 105.
[128] If so much can be demanded for the actual or suspected criminal, how can it be denied to the innocent refugee?

domestic tribunal, before which the question could not have been raised,[129] the European Court filled a gap, in effect putting European States on notice of the need also to factor such considerations into the extradition process.

With respect to asylum, on the other hand, most if not all European States already have some sort of procedure for dealing with the 'humanitarian' claim, at least so far as it is based on a well-founded fear of persecution. National procedures, in theory, bring experienced decision-makers to the task of establishing the facts, assessing credibility, and appreciating the existence or non-existence of risk. Indeed, national asylum and refugee status procedures constitute precisely the area or margin of appreciation that the European institutions want to avoid.

It is ironic that the European Court has read into article 3 evidential tests which, for asylum seekers, are unlikely ever to be satisfied; and that in doing so, the Court has reproduced its own version of the *Wednesbury* rules, a principle of United Kingdom judicial review limiting the circumstances in which a court may substitute its own discretionary decision or appreciation of the facts for that of the administrative agency or tribunal having responsibility in the area under review. In a much quoted dictum, Lord Greene, MR, said:

If a decision . . . is so unreasonable that no reasonable authority would ever have come to, then the courts can interfere . . . but to prove a case of that kind would require something overwhelming.[130]

Critics of such justified non-intervention have sometimes characterized it as the 'lunacy rules': [o]nly in cases of proven insanity on the part of the decision-maker will the court intervene. More moderate commentators nevertheless see the principle as an extreme and inadequate basis for supervision.[131] The European Court now appears to have adopted the *Wednesbury* standard as its own; for example, claimants must produce 'concrete evidence' of a 'real risk' of torture, and so forth. Concrete evidence has not been defined, but a 'real risk' is clearly more than a 'reasonable risk' or a 'serious possibility', such as is accepted by many national tribunals,[132] and appears to require that the likelihood of relevant prejudicial treatment be established as more likely than not, that is, on a balance of probabilities or more.

Even where the evidence of risk was too strong to ignore, asylum seekers have failed, for example, by narrow rulings of article 25. In addition, in *Cruz Varas* the Court accepted the non-binding nature of a request for postponement of removal.

The record of the European Court can be contrasted with that of the European Commission on Human Rights, where proceedings, even if not carried through to a final report or decision, do appear frequently to have bene-

[129] At least not in the UK, where the European Convention has not been incorporated and does not have the force of law.

[130] *Associated Provincial Picture Houses Ltd.* v. *Wednesbury Corporation* [1948] 1 KB 223, 230.

[131] See Judge Walsh's dissent in *Vilvarajah* for a short, cogent critique of the deficiencies of judicial review in UK law.

[132] See above, Ch. 2, s. 3.

fited refugees and asylum seekers.[133] Indeed, in *The Chahal Family* v. *United Kingdom*, the European Commission found unanimously that the principal applicant would be at risk of a violation of article 3 if returned to his country of origin, India.[134] The Commission noted that the guarantees in article 3 of the Convention 'are of an absolute character, permitting no exception', and that they provide correspondingly wider guarantees than articles 32 and 33 of the 1951 Convention. With respect to the evidence, the Commission paid particular attention to the government's recognition of violence and widespread human rights violations by the policy and security forces in the Punjab at the relevant time, that the applicant's evidence of political activity and his own experiences were uncontested, and that while there had been an improvement in the situation, there was no 'solid evidence that the police are now under democratic control or that the judiciary has been able fully to reassert its own independent authority'.[135] With respect to the claim under article 13, the Commission distinguished the decision of the European Court of Human Rights in *Vilvarajah*, finding that removals in national security cases were a matter of 'unchallengeable executive discretion'. The courts were unlikely to have all the facts before them, and in most cases would be powerless to intervene, however strong the risk of treatment contrary to article 3. The power of review was therefore 'too restrictive to satisfy the requirements of article 13'.[136]

Whether the Court will follow the same line of reasoning remains to be seen. In previous decisions, its reluctance to intervene appears to have been implicitly supported by evidence that the claimant has had an opportunity to present his or her claim. The Court has never ruled, however, on minimum procedural requirements, although the fact that 'asylum' is not considered a 'civil right' within the meaning of article 6 again leaves States with considerable room for manoeuvre. Even if many of the most egregious instances of denial of asylum have been 'reversed' as a result of the initiation and later withdrawal of proceedings before the European institutions, this is hardly satisfactory from a standard-setting perspective. A reasonable inference from decisions on article 13, article 6, and article 3, is that judges of the European Court of Human Rights are no more willing than government officials to extend the protection of the European Convention on Human Rights to the non-citizen of Europe, having merely a 'humanitarian' claim and no family, residential or other tie.[137]

---

[133] For example, the following applications were struck off, following a friendly settlement: 23580/94 v. France (applicant threatened with expulsion; refugee status granted); 14985/89 v. United Kingdom (refusal of asylum; exceptional leave to remain granted); 18434/91 v. France (expulsion of recognized refugee; order annulled); 21406 v. Sweden (expulsion cancelled).

[134] Appl. 22414/93, 27 June 1995.

[135] Ibid., paras. 108–12. The Commission was impressed by the Indian Government's good faith assurance as to the applicant's safety, but was 'not satisfied that the assurance provides an effective guarantee': para. 113.   [136] Ibid., paras. 144, 149–52.

[137] For a proposal for an additional protocol to the European Convention, developed by the author in the course of discussions with participants in the European Council on Refugees and Exiles, see below Annexe 4, No. 10.

2.3 REFUGEES AND THE RESPONSIBILITIES OF ASYLUM STATES

States remain under no obligation to grant asylum, while protection within a State 'implies only the normal exercise of territorial sovereignty'.[138] Save in so far as it does not trespass upon a State's other obligations under international law, the sovereign act comprising the beneficial exercise of territorial jurisdiction is entitled to respect by all other States, including the country of origin of the refugees. General Assembly resolutions and those of regional organizations have repeatedly stressed that the grant of asylum 'is a peaceful and humanitarian act and that, as such, it cannot be regarded as unfriendly by any other State'.[139] This principle has also been reiterated in regional treaty arrangements.[140] At the same time, it has been recognized that the grant of asylum imports the continuing responsibility of the State 'not to allow knowingly its territory to be used for acts contrary to the rights of other States'.[141] The State granting asylum becomes, as it were, under a duty to take reasonable care to ensure that its hospitality is not abused to the detriment of other States. Again, this general issue has been the subject of recommendation and specific undertakings.

Article 4 of the 1967 Declaration on Territorial Asylum, for example, requires States not to permit those granted asylum 'to engage in activities contrary to the purposes and principles of the United Nations'. The Preamble to the 1969 OAU Convention announces a distinction between the refugee in search of a peaceful and normal life and one who flees solely for the purpose of 'fomenting subversion'. The latter's activities are to be discouraged. Article II(6) calls for the settlement of refugees at a reasonable distance from the frontier of their country of origin. Article III expressly calls upon refugees to refrain from subversive activities, and requires States to prohibit refugees from attacking member States, 'by any activity likely to cause tension . . . and in particular by use of arms, through the press, or by radio'. The 1954 Caracas Convention on Territorial Asylum recognizes that the exercise of 'freedom of expression of thought' by refugees shall not ground a complaint by a third State, save in the case of 'systematic propaganda through which they incite to the use of force or violence against the government of the complaining State'.[142] Similarly, no State has the right to request restriction of refugees' freedom of assembly and association, unless that freedom is being exercised for the purpose of 'fomenting the use of force or violence against the government of the soliciting State'.[143]

---

[138] *Asylum* case, ICJ *Rep.*, 1950, 266, at 274.

[139] Preamble, 1967 Declaration on Territorial Asylum; see also para. 3, Council of Europe, 1977 Declaration on Territorial Asylum.

[140] See, for example, art. II(2), 1969 OAU Convention; art. 1, 1954 Caracas Convention on Territorial Asylum.

[141] *Corfu Channel* case, ICJ *Rep.*, 1949, 4, 22; *Alabama* Arbitration (1872): Moore, *Arbitrations*, 653; Corliss, S., 'Asylum State Responsibility for the Hostile Acts of Foreign Exiles', 2 *IJRL* 181 (1990); Johnsson, A. B., 'The Duties of Refugees', 3 *IJRL* 579 (1991).

[142] Art. 7.

[143] Art. 8. See also art. 9, providing that, on request, an asylum State shall watch over or intern

The provisions of these treaties may lend some colour to the general principles of international law which lie at the basis of State responsibility for the activities of those granted asylum in its territory, namely, that States shall refrain in their international relations from the threat or use of force; and shall not intervene in matters within the domestic jurisdiction of any State.[144]

at a reasonable distance from the frontier, 'notorious leaders' of subversive movements and those inclined to join them. Cf. art. 18, 1954 Caracas Convention on Diplomatic Asylum; arts. 3, 4, 1984 South Africa–Mozambique Agreement on Non-Aggeression and Good Neighbourliness: 23 *ILM* 282 (1984).

[144] See the Declaration on Principles of International Law concerning Friendly Relations and Co-operation among States in accordance with the Charter of the United Nations, annexe to UNGA res. 2625(XXV), 24 Oct. 1970. That there remain major differences between States on certain core issues relating to protection is evident from the protracted and often confrontational debate in the Executive Committee on the subject of military attacks on refugee camps and settlements in Southern Africa and elsewhere. See above Ch. 7, s. 1.3.1.

Chapter 9

PROTECTION IN MUNICIPAL LAW

Whether a State takes steps to protect refugees within its jurisdiction and if so, which steps, are matters very much in the realm of sovereign discretion. For States parties to the Convention and Protocol, however, the outer limits of that discretion are confined by the principle of effectiveness of obligations, and the measures it adopts will be judged by the international standard of reasonable efficacy and efficient implementation. Legislative incorporation may not itself be expressly called for, but effective implementation requires, at least some form of procedure whereby refugees can be identified, and some measure of protection against laws of general application governing admission, residence, and removal. State practice understandably reveals widely divergent methods of implementation, from which it is difficult to extract any easy formula for determining adequacy and sufficiency. The effectiveness of formal measures depends not only upon the overall efficacy of a State's internal administrative and judicial system, but also upon the particular problems with which that system is faced. Procedures designed for the individual asylum seeker may fail to absorb, let alone survive, a mass influx; the needs of the latter, moreover, will often differ radically, requiring less sophisticated, often purely material solutions, at least in the short term.

A potentially useful distinction is that between refugee status, on the one hand, and the legal consequences which flow from that status, on the other hand; the latter may include an entitlement to residence formally recognized by municipal law or simply eligibility for consideration under a discretionary power only distantly confined by international law. In practice, that distinction is often difficult to maintain, particularly where status is itself the criterion for residence and where normal residence requirements—relating, for example, to character or potential for assimilation—may filter back to influence the decision whether someone is a refugee. Similarly, the mere fact that a State treats refugees separately from others will not be conclusive evidence of effective protection. A refugee enjoys fundamental human rights common to citizens and foreign nationals; where these are generally assured, where due process of law is acknowledged, and where measures of appeal and judicial review permit examination of the merits and the legality of administrative decisions, then the refugee also may be sufficiently protected.

The present chapter recalls the more or less common criteria applied by States in deciding who should be recognized as a refugee; considers the 'minimum requirements' for effective procedures for determination of status; examines a number of practical problems and special issues involved in the decision-making process; and concludes with some assessments of the status of refugee in municipal law.

1. Definitions and procedures

States' differing approaches to the problem of definition have already been mentioned.[1] The criteria of the 1951 Convention are commonly adopted, with additional provision often made for others who, while not refugees in the strict sense, may yet be considered as having valid reasons for equivalent treatment. The practice in extradition laws of recognizing the 'political offender' as someone worthy of exceptional treatment has also been noted. Similar jurisdictions may employ similar concepts of political offence, but the act of characterization is dominated by municipal law considerations. Although it is not concerned with political offences as such,[2] international law is directly concerned with the treatment anticipated for the returned offender. Increasingly, States are incorporating the criterion of liability to persecution or prejudice as the underlying rationale, the international standard precluding return.

1.1 REFUGEE STATUS AND ASYLUM PROCEDURES: GENERAL STANDARDS

The basic refugee definition, both in international law and in the form adopted by municipal systems, is highly individualistic. It supposes a dispassionate case-by-case examination of subjective and objective elements, which may well prove impractical in the face of large numbers, although they too require the benefit of certain minimum standards.[3] For asylum seekers generally, the very existence of procedures for the determination of status can guarantee both *non-refoulement* and treatment in accordance with the relevant international instruments. At its session on protection in 1977, the Executive Committee expressed the hope that all States parties to the Convention and Protocol would establish such procedures and also give favourable consideration to UNHCR participation.[4] The Committee further recommended basic procedural requirements, designed at such a level of generality as to be capable of adoption by most States.[5]

[1] See above, Ch. 1, s. 6.   [2] See above, Ch. 3, s. 4.2.
[3] See Report of the 1979 Arusha Conference, recommendations on the term 'refugee' and determination of refugee status: UN doc. A/AC.96/INF/158, at 9 (1979).
[4] The UN General Assembly also consistently calls for 'fair and efficient procedures'.
[5] See Avery, C., 'Refugee Status Decision-making: The Systems of Ten Countries', 19 *Stan. J.I.L.*, 235 (1983). The accounts of national procedures in the first edition of this book have not been continued, given frequent changes in the law, and the availability of more in-depth analysis. See, among others, Bovard, A., 'La procédure d'asile suisse', *Doc. réf.*, no. 213, supp., 30 mars/12 avr. 1993; Anker, D. E., 'Determining Asylum Claims in the United States: Report of the Findings and Recommendations of an Empirical Study of Adjudication before the Immigration Court', 2 *IJRL* 252 (1990); Barcroft, P., 'Immigration and Asylum Law in the Republic of Ireland: Recent Developments and proposed Statutory Reform', 7 *IJRL* 84 (1995); Beyer, G. A., 'Establishing the United States Asylum Officers Corps: A First Report', 4 *IJRL* 455 (1992); Crawford, J., 'Australian

Formal procedures for the determination of refugee status clearly go far towards securing the effective internal implementation and application of the 1951 Convention and the 1967 Protocol. In adopting the UNHCR Statute in 1950, the General Assembly urged governments to co-operate with the High Commissioner not only by becoming parties to international conventions, but also by taking the necessary steps of implementation. In succeeding years the General Assembly has repeated this call, inviting States in particular to improve the legal status of refugees residing in their territory. One of UNHCR's principal objectives has long been the establishment of fair and expeditious procedures for the determination of refugee status,[6] preferably guaranteeing 'full access' by those in search of asylum,[7] and with the opportunity for independent review of negative decisions.[8]

Although neither the Convention nor the Protocol formally require procedures as a necessary condition for full implementation, their object and purpose of protection and assurance of fundamental rights and freedoms for refugees without discrimination, argue strongly for the adoption of such effective internal measures. At its 1977 session, the Executive Committee elaborated this approach, not only urging governments to establish formal procedures,[9] but also recommending the following basic procedural requirements:[10]

Immigration Law and Refugees: The 1989 Amendments', 2 *IJRL* 626 (1990); Fonteyne, J., 'Overview of Refugee Determination Procedures in Australia', 6 *IJRL* 253 (1994); European Consultation on Refugees and Exiles, 'Fair and Efficient Procedures for Determining Refugee Status: A Proposal', 2 *IJRL Special Issue—September 1990* 112; Federal Ministry of the Interior, 'Recent Developments in the German Law on Asylum', 6 *IJRL* 265 (1994); Marx, R., 'The Criteria for the Determination of Refugee Status in the Federal Republic of Germany', 4 *IJRL* 151 (1992); Hernandez, C.E., 'Asylum and Refugee Status in Spain', 4 *IJRL* 57 (1992); Gortázar C. F., 'The Implementation Rules of the new Spanish Asylum Law', 7 *IJRL* 506 (1995); Iza, A. O., 'The Asylum and Refugee Procedure in the Argentine Legal System', 6 *IJRL* 643 (1994); Kussbach, E., 'The 1991 Austrian Asylum Law', 6 *IJRL* 227 (1994); Maluwa, T., 'The Domestic Implementation of International Refugee Law: A Brief Note on Malawi's Refugee Act of 1989', 3 *IJRL* 503 (1991); Stevens, D., 'Re-introduction of the United Kingdom Asylum Bill', 5 *IJRL* 91 (1993); Stravropoulou, M., 'Refugee Law in Greece', 6 *IJRL* 53 (1994); Yamagami, S., 'Determination of Refugee Status in Japan', 7 *IJRL* 60 (1995); ECRE, *Asylum in Europe*, vol. 2, (1994)—descriptions of procedures in Denmark, Finland, Germany, Hungary, and Switzerland.

[6] UNHCR, 'Note on International Protection': UN doc. A/AC.96/694, (3 Aug. 1987), paras. 13, 25–8.

[7] UN High Commissioner Jean-Pierre Hocké: UN doc. A/AC.96/SR.425 (1988), para. 66. See also various UNHCR 'Notes' on International Protection: UN doc. A/AC.96/750 (27 Aug. 1990), para. 15; UN doc. A/AC.96/777 (9 Sept. 1991), paras. 25–6.

[8] UNHCR, 'Note on International Protection': UN doc. A/AC.96/815 (31 Aug. 1993), para. 19.

[9] *Report* of the 28th Session (1977): UN doc. A/AC.96/549, para. 36. Compare Council of Europe Recommendation no. R(81) 16 on the harmonization of national procedures relating to asylum, adopted by the Committee of Ministers on 5 Nov. 1981.

[10] Executive Committee Conclusion No. 8 (1977). Although these conclusions were followed up in 1982, States were not generally prepared to accept stricter procedural requirements. Instead, they expressed concern about the need to safeguard procedures in the face of manifestly unfounded and abusive applications; there were also different perceptions of UNHCR's role in the determination of refugee status, and something less than wholehearted endorsement; see *Report* of the Sub-Committee of the Whole on International Protection: UN doc. A/AC.96/613, paras. 37–8; also *Report* of the 33rd Session (1982): UN doc. A/AC.96/614, paras. 65–6, 70(4). See further below, s. 2.1.2.

1. The competent official (for example, immigration officer or border police officer) to whom applicants address themselves at the border or in the territory of a contracting State, should have clear instructions for dealing with cases which might come within the purview of the relevant international instruments. The official should be required to act in accordance with the principle of *non-refoulement* and to refer such cases to a higher authority.

2. Applicants should receive the necessary guidance as to the procedure to be followed.

3. There should be a clearly identified authority—wherever possible a single central authority—with responsibility for examining requests for refugee status and taking a decision in the first instance.

4. Applicants should be given the necessary facilities, including the services of competent interpreters for submitting their case to the authorities concerned. Applicants should also be given the opportunity, of which they should be duly informed, to contact a representative of UNHCR.

5. Applicants recognized as refugees should be informed accordingly and issued with documentation certifying refugee status.

6. Applicants not recognized should be given a reasonable time to appeal for a formal reconsideration of the decision, either to the same or a different authority, whether administrative or judicial, according to the prevailing system.

7. Applicants should be permitted to remain in the country pending decisions on the initial request by the competent authority referred to in paragraph (3) above, unless it has been established by that authority that the request is clearly abusive. They should also be permitted to remain in the country while an appeal to a higher administrative authority or to the courts is pending.

1.2 THE ROLE OF UNHCR IN NATIONAL PROCEDURES

Participation by UNHCR in the determination of refugee status derives sensibly from its supervisory role and from the obligations of States parties to co-operate with the Office, and it allows UNHCR to monitor closely matters of status and of the entry and removal of asylum seekers. The procedures themselves will differ, necessarily, in the light of States' own administrative and judicial framework; so too will the nature and degree of involvement of UNHCR. The fundamental issue, however, remains the same—identifying those who should benefit from recognition of their refugee status, and ensuring, so far as is practical, consistent and generous interpretations of essentially international criteria.

In a few countries, UNHCR participates in the decision-making process; in others, the local office may attend hearings in an observer capacity, while in yet others the exact role may be determined *ad hoc*, for example, by intervening at appellate level, or by submitting *amicus curiae* briefs. The summary information provided to UNHCR by governments in 1989 revealed some five levels of participation, from no formal role, through observer on an advisory committee or similar, voting member of an appeals body, joint decision-maker, to being informed of cases and being asked for views from time to time.[11]

[11] See UNHCR, 'Note on Procedures for the Determination of Refugee Status under International Instruments': UN doc. A/AC.96/INF.152/Rev.8 (12 Sept. 1989).

Generally, UNHCR's procedural responsibilities may be summarized as contributing to the effective identification of refugees in need of protection. This may entail: (1) offering an assessment of the applicant's credibility in the light of the claim and of conditions known to exist in his or her country of origin;[12] (2) providing information on the treatment of similar cases or similar legal points in other jurisdictions;[13] (3) representing the international community's interest by providing authoritative interpretations of fundamental concepts, such as 'well-founded fear', and persecution; and (4) promoting an application of the Convention and Protocol that best agrees with their humanitarian objectives.

1.3 DUE PROCESS IN THE DETERMINATION OF REFUGEE STATUS

International law has little to say with respect to the procedural aspects of due process, particularly as the responsibility of the State for the fulfilment of its obligations turns essentially on what results in fact. The UNHCR Executive Committee recommendations offer a very basic agenda, comprising guidance to applicants, the provision of competent interpreters, a reasonable time to 'appeal for formal reconsideration' of a negative decision, 'either to the same or a different authority, whether administrative or judicial, according to the prevailing system'. They are not binding, but indicate a practically necessary minimum if refugees are to be identified and accorded protection in accordance with international obligations. Reviewing the United States asylum process in 1990, Martin identified the tension, common to all States involved in refugee determination, between the 'asylum tradition' and the 'need for control'. He singled out a number of critical issues in the overall process, including lack of clarity in the applicable legal standards; the problem of the coast of Bohemia, that is, the 'images' or preconceptions that each participant brings to the refugee/asylum issue; the limited availability of essential facts on which to base an informed decision; cross-cultural communication problems; and the practical necessity for speedy decisions.[14]

Reaching decisions quickly and removing those who are found not to require international protection are perceived by many States as essential to reduce

---

[12] UNHCR's duty to provide international protection to refugees also requires that it provide information known to it regarding conditions in an asylum seeker's country of origin, at least if such information is critical for the determination of refugee status. Because of the political sensitivities involved, and also because UNHCR is not always equipped to collect, assess and analyse relevant information, increasing reliance is placed on information in the public domain, to which appropriate standards of verification and corroboration can be applied in an objective manner; see further below, s. 2.2.2.

[13] Developed and expanded in UNHCR's Centre for Documentation on Refugees, REFCAS (a case law database) contains abstracts of refugee and refugee-related decisions from numerous jurisdictions. Selected abstracts are also published regularly in the *International Journal of Refugee Law*. During 1995, REFCAS became accessible on the Internet, first via a Gopher site and on the World Wide Web during 1996.

[14] Martin, D. A., 'Reforming Asylum Adjudication: On Navigating the Coast of Bohemia', 138 *Uni. Penn. L.R.* 1247 (1990).

instances of abuse and to render the asylum process more manageable.[15] In practice, few have succeeded in marrying an efficient and expeditious national process (and national legal traditions) to the fulfilment of international obligations.

Procedural rights nevertheless remain very much within the area of 'choice of means' among States parties to the Convention and Protocol; national procedures vary considerably, drawing mostly on local legal culture and due process traditions. Those in the United States, for example, have a constitutional right to a full and fair hearing,[16] while applicants for admission are entitled to such due process as may be accorded by statute. Notice of the 'right to apply for asylum' is often limited, however, for example, to those in custody or otherwise subject to immigration processing.[17] In Canada, oral hearings are accorded at each level,[18] and the claimant is entitled to be assisted by an interpreter.[19] In the United States, there is no right to the interpretation of the entire proceedings, but only of questions directed to the claimant and responses thereto.[20] In other

---

[15] For suggested reforms of the US system, including specialized adjudicators and a non-adversarial proceeding, see Martin, 'On Navigating the Coast of Bohemia', 1338; for implementation, development and assessments of the new system, see Beyer, G. A., 'Affirmative Asylum Adjudication in the United States', 6 *Geo. Imm. L.J.* 253 (1992); Beyer, G. A., 'Establishing the United States Asylum Officers Corps: A First Report', 4 *IJRL* 455 (1992).

[16] *Wong Yang Sung* v. *McGrath* 339 US 33 (1950).

[17] See, for example, *Orantes-Hernandez* v. *Meese* 685 F. Supp. 1488, (DC CD Calif.), aff'd 919 F.2d 549 (9th Cir. 1990), where the Court, among others, ordered the INS to advise class members (citizens of El Salvador in INS custody) of their rights to be represented by an attorney, to request a deportation hearing, and to apply for asylum; a copy of a list of free legal services was also to be supplied; see now 8 §208.5(a), requiring the INS to provide the appropriate application forms and, if available, a list of persons or private agencies able to assist in the preparation of the application, but only when such alien 'expresses fear of persecution or harm upon return to his country of origin or to agents thereof'. In Canadian law, before any substantive evidence is given at an inquiry in immigration-related matters such as admissibility, the adjudicator is required to give the person concerned an opportunity to claim Convention refugee status: Immigration Act, s. 43.

[18] See *Singh* case [1985] SCR 177; confirmed in the *Immigration Act*, s. 69.1(4). Swiss law lays down a right to an asylum procedure as well as a right to be granted asylum, provided the relevant legal conditions are fulfilled: Kälin, W., 'The Legal Condition of Refugees in Switzerland', 24 *Swiss Reports presented at the XIVth International Congress of Comparative Law*, 57, 57–8 (1994).

[19] The right to an interpreter has been upheld by the Federal Court of Appeal. In *Owusu* v. *Minister of Employment and Immigration* [1989] FCJ No. 33, the Court noted that the right only comes into play when the need for an interpreter is demonstrated in the circumstances of a particular case. In *Ming* v. *Minister of Employment and Immigration* [1990] FCJ No. 173, the Court observed that the applicant was entitled to a *competent* interpreter, citing Wilson J. in *Sociétés Acadiens du Nouveau-Brunswick Inc.* v. *Association of Parents for Fairness in Education* [1986] 1 SCR 549, 622: 'the ability to understand and be understood is a minimal requirement of due process.' See also Conseil d'Etat, 29 juin 1990, No. 35.346 (IIIe ch), *Nwokolo c/ Etat belge*—if an interpreter has not been or appears not to have been used, this is a violation of European Convention and 1951 Convention rights, so far as the claimant has not had the chance properly to defend his or her rights: *RDDE*, No. 60, sept.–oct. 1990, 245; Conseil d'Etat, 19 fev. 1992, No. 38.798 (IIIe ch.), *Manou c/ Etat belge*—where another refugee claimant was used as interpreter, but had little knowledge of the applicant's language, the court quashed the decision to refuse suspension of removal: *RDDE*, No. 69, mai–juin–juillet–août, 1992, 191.

[20] But see *El Rescate Legal Services* v. *Executive Office for Immigration Review* 727 F. Supp. 557 (CD Calif., 1989). For concerns as to the adequacy of interpretation, see Anker, D., 'Determining Asylum Claims in the United States—Summary Report of an Empirical Study of the Adjudication of Asylum Claims before the Immigration Court', 2 *IJRL* 252, 257 (1990).

jurisdictions, the availability of interpretation may depend upon the 'nature' of the proceedings, being limited sometimes to criminal cases, or of the 'civil' character of the right in question.[21]

Jurisdictional differences also govern the right to counsel, with the United States recognizing the right but at no expense to the government,[22] while the Canadian system provides that every claimant has, and shall be informed of, the right to counsel, in certain circumstances at government expense.[23]

An important related issue, both for claimants and for States, is that of confidentiality of proceedings. Again, the interest of the asylum seeker, including the necessity to protect friends and family in the country of origin, will often run counter to legal traditions of public hearings and open courts.[24] Many jurisdictions provide for confidentiality in matrimonial cases, however, and in proceedings involving juveniles or sexual assault. Where the principle of open court has constitutional status, a balance between the advantages of confidentiality and the public interest may yet be achieved. This might be done, for example, by legislating a presumption in favour of *in camera* proceedings, save that where a member of the public seeks to attend, the claimant would have the onus of showing that the life, liberty or security of any person might be endangered if the hearing were held in open court.[25]

Most jurisdictions require decision-makers to base their determinations on evi-

---

[21] See Julien-Laferrière, F., 'Le contentieux en matière de réfugiés en France: deux arrêts récents': *Doc. réf.*, no. 139, 27 fevr./8 mars 1991, Suppl., 7–9, citing Conseil d'Etat, 7 nov. 1990, 93.993, *Serwaah*, at 8, to the effect that the right to an interpreter laid down in art. 6(3) of the European Convention on Human Rights applies only in penal proceedings. As Julien-Laferrière notes, '. . . le Conseil d'Etat, comme la Cour et la Commission de Strasbourg, a opéré la distinction entre la cause –la qualité de réfugié–et les effets–le statut du réfugié–qui seraient de nature différente: droit de caractère administratif pour la première, droits de caractère civil pour les seconds. On peut s'interroger sur le bien-fondé de ce raisonnement . . .' In his view, since status is subordinate to recognition, it is more logical to treat the whole of the matter as relating to civil rights.

[22] Immigration and Nationality Act, §242(b). There is no *Sixth Amendment* right to counsel, as at a criminal trial, and the right is essentially a *statutory* right, strengthened by *Fifth Amendment* due process requirements. Counsel have a very limited role at the first instance proceeding before an Asylum Officer: 8 CFR §208.9(b). See also *Ukrainian–American Bar Association* v. *Shultz* 695 F.Supp. 33 (D.D.C. 1988), in which plaintiffs obtained order, based the First Amendment right to communicate effectively, requiring INS to furnish each person seeking asylum from a Soviet or East Bloc country with written information describing the Association's offer to provide free legal services and how to contact.

[23] The right to counsel is protected by the Canadian *Charter of Rights and Freedoms*, and costs are generally met through legal aid schemes. See Immigration Act, ss. 30(2)(3), 69(1). The right does not extend to investigations at ports of entry, however; see *Dehghani* v, *MEI* [1993] 1 SCR 1053.

[24] In Canada, for example, hearings before the Convention Refugee Determination Division (CRDD) of the Immigration and Refugee Board are held *in camera*, and randomly selected initials are used in and identifying information removed from decisions selected for publication in QuickLaw's CRDD database. Once claimants seek review in the Federal Court, however, they are identified by name.

[25] See McAllister, D. M., 'Refugees and Public Access to Immigration Hearings in Canada: A Clash of Constitutional Values', 2 *IJRL* 562 (1990); *Pacific Press* v. *Minister of Employment and Immigration* [1991] FCJ No. 331 (Federal Court of Appeal); also Wilson J. in *Edmonton Journal* v. *Alberta* [1989] SCJ No. 124 (Supreme Court of Canada).

dence adduced at the hearing which is found to be credible and trustworthy in the circumstances, and to take account of all the evidence.[26] The claimant in turn is generally entitled to present evidence, to challenge that submitted against his or her case,[27] and sometimes also to cross-examine witnesses.[28] Finally, the claimant should be advised of the decision which, if negative, should be accompanied by written reasons.

Reasons for decisions are an essential pre-requisite for fundamental justice, allowing the applicant for refugee status to know why his or her claim has been refused and to make a meaningful appeal or application for review. The reasons alone will be practically meaningless, however, unless accompanied by a statement of the relevant facts.[29] The reasons requirement provides justification for the decision, showing that the decision-maker has identified the material facts in the applicant's claim; identified relevant country of origin evidence and assessed its weight; assessed the credibility of the applicant; identified and interpreted the relevant rule or rules of law; applied the law to the facts in a reasoned way (to show, for example, whether what the claimant fears is persecution, or whether the group to which he or she belongs is a 'social group', or whether he or she has what amounts to a well-founded fear); and determined whether the claimant is a refugee.[30]

1.3.1 Appeal or review

The Executive Committee employed somewhat ambiguous language with respect to appeal or review from initial decisions on asylum or refugee status,

---

[26] Cf. *Hamilton* v. *Minister of Employment and Immigration* [1990] FCJ No. 720—decision-making bodies must consider all relevant evidence placed before them, must base their findings on the evidence and not arbitrarily reject evidence which is uncontradicted and not obviously implausible.

[27] Conseil d'Etat, 18 nov. 1987, 78.981, *Bokwa Kimbolo*, *Doc. réf.*, no. 35, 11/20 mars 1988, Suppl., CJ., 5: the CRR rapporteur having failed to share relevant documents with the claimant, 'le caractère contradictoire de la procédure n'a pas été respecté . . .'

[28] The availability of 'cross-examination' depends very much on the nature of the procedure, whether adversarial (as generally in the US and the UK), or investigatory (as in Canada). Martin also doubts whether rebuttal evidence, cross-examination and confrontation provide 'the best way to resolve controversies involving disputes over adjudicative facts', (citing Davis, K. C., *Administrative Law Treatise*, (2nd. ed., 1980), ss.15.3 at 144): Martin, D. A., 'Reforming Asylum Adjudication: On Navigating the Coast of Bohemia', 138 *Uni. Penn. L.R.* 1247, 1346 (1990). See further below, s. 2.2.3.

[29] See per Estey, J., in *Northwestern Utilities Ltd.* v. *City of Edmonton* [1979] 1 SCR 684, 705; *MEI* v. *Miah* [1995] FCJ No. 381—no need to give reasons for positive decisions, but if given, must be adequate.

[30] Among the many reviews of refugee and administrative decision-making in Canada, for example, see *Report* of the Task Force on *The Refugee Status Determination Process*, (1981), 52–3, noting that reasons given are rarely substantial, seldom relating the facts on which they are based, containing little in the way of reasoning, and amounting to little more than conclusions. Other reviewers have stressed the need for *adequacy*; see Ratushny, E., *A new refugee status determination process for Canada*, (1984), at 35 (reasons which are 'proper, adequate and intelligent'); Plaut, W. G., *Refugee Determination in Canada*, (1985), at 127 ('Cogent, proper reasons . . .'). On administrative tribunal practice generally, see Law Reform Commission of Canada, *Independent Administrative Agencies*, Report No. 26, (1985), 64; *Obtaining Reasons before applying for Judicial Scrutiny—Immigration Appeal Board*, Report No. 18, 7–8; *Independent Administrative Agencies*, Report No. 26, (1985), 63–4: reasons should be given wherever the decision amounts to a total or partial denial of a requested action, or is otherwise adverse to the interests of a participant, and ideally should be developed as part of the decision-making exercise.

merely recommending that claimants have 'a reasonable time to *appeal for a for-mal reconsideration* of the decision', and leaving open both the identity and com-position of the re-examining body,[31] and the administrative or judicial nature of the process.

Many States have responded to the 'crisis of numbers' in refugee procedures by abolishing appeals, or levels of appeal, or by confining review to legal issues. It is difficult and perhaps unwise to generalize across systems, but experience nev-ertheless suggests that while the initial decision-maker may be best placed to judge certain issues, such as the personal credibility of the claimant,[32] restricting later review to a narrow category of legal issues may not be the most effective way to address the problem and ensure that international obligations are satisfied.[33]

The limits of article 13 of the European Convention on Human Rights and of review processes limited to the lawfulness of decisions have been considered above.[34] International law generally favours a second look at asylum claims, if only from the perspective of the effectiveness of obligations.[35] At both national and international levels, some sort of appeal, going both to facts and to legality, offers the best chance of correcting error and ensuring consistency. Such an appeal is even more important where the national application of international criteria is subordinated to regional mechanisms of 'harmonization', for example, within the Dublin and Schengen schemes.[36]

2. The determination process

2.1 ADMISSIBILITY AND PRELIMINARY QUESTIONS

The principle of access to a fair and efficient procedure for the determination of claims to asylum and refugee status has long been a cardinal principle in

[31] Cf. Conseil d'Etat, 7 nov. 1990, 93.993, *Serwaah*, cited in Julien-Laferrière, above n. 21, in which the court ruled that as the *Commission des recours de réfugiés* does not determine questions of civil obligation, its composition (including a member of the council of OFPRA, the initial decision-maker), does not violate art. 6 of the European Convention.

[32] Courts generally are reluctant to overturn first instance credibility findings, where supported by evidence in the record. See Legomsky, S. H., 'Political Asylum and the Theory of Judicial Review', 73 *Minnesota L.R.* 1205 (1989); Blum, C. P., 'The Ninth Circuit and the Protection of Asylum Seekers since the Passage of the Refugee Act of 1980', 23 *San Diego L.R.* 327, 364f (1986).

[33] Tiberghien, F., 'L'étendue du contrôle du Conseil d'Etat sur les decisions de la Commission des Recours', *Doc. réf.*, no. 55, Suppl., CJ, 1–4: although in principle control may be exercised on the basis of error of fact, as well as law, in practice initial decision-makers rarely rely on an imma-terial fact or completely misinterpret the facts presented. Part of the problem is also due to contin-uing attachment to individual case-by-case determination, even for manifestly well-founded claims. See also Greene, I. and Schaffer, P., 'Leave to Appeal and Leave to commence Judicial Review in Canada's Refugee Determination System: Is the Process Fair?' 4 *IJRL* 71 (1992).

[34] See Ch. 8, s. 3.

[35] See Tribunal civil (Réf.)-Bruxelles, 8 oct. 1993, *X c/ Etat belge*, to the effect that the right to an effective remedy in the case of breach of fundamental rights constitutes an essential element of the rule of law: *RDDE*, No. 75, sept.–oct. 1993, 454.

[36] See Groenendijk, C. A., 'The Competence of the EC Court of Justice with respect to inter-governmental Treaties on Immigration and Asylum', 4 *IJRL* 531 (1992).

UNHCR's protection policy, and has been endorsed with equal consistency by the UN General Assembly.[37] In practice, however, various devices may be employed to keep asylum seekers from the procedural door, ranging from visa policies, through carrier sanctions, to admissibility requirements of varying severity.

2.1.1 *Jurisdictional issues: Identifying the State responsible for determining a claim*

Debate over the right of access to procedures and the related question of responsibility to determine claims has continued in various fora. The UNHCR Executive Committee in 1985, for example, examined the question of so-called irregular movements of refugees and asylum seekers, defined to include those who move, without first obtaining authorization, from countries in which they have already found protection in order to seek asylum or permanent resettlement elsewhere.[38] Executive Committee Conclusion No. 58, finally adopted in 1989, recognized that there might be compelling reasons for such onward movement, and emphasized that return should only be contemplated where the refugee was protected against *refoulement*, allowed to remain in the country in question, and treated in accordance with basic human rights standards pending a durable solution.

Since then, both the Executive Committee and the United Nations General Assembly have repeatedly endorsed the general principle of access to refugee procedures,[39] and the specific need for agreement on responsibility.[40] Some States have been careful to emphasize that *non-refoulement* does not stand in the

---

[37] See for example, the 1988 statement by UN High Commissioner for Refugees Jean-Pierre Hocké: 'UNHCR's concern was that fair and efficient asylum procedures guaranteeing full access by those in search of asylum should be the undisputed basis for all future developments': UN doc. A/AC.96/SR.425, para. 66; full text annexed to *Report* of the 39th Session: UN doc. A/AC.96/721 (1988). Also, UNGA res. 48/116, 20 Dec. 1993, para. 4; 49/169, 23 Dec. 1994—the latter calling for access to procedures, 'or, as appropriate, to other mechanisms to ensure that persons in need of international protection are identified and granted . . . protection,'while not diminishing the protection afforded to refugees under the terms of the 1951 Convention, the 1967 Protocol and relevant regional instruments' (para. 5).

[38] UNHCR, 'Irregular Movements of Asylum Seekers and Refugees': UN doc. EC/SCP/40/Rev.1; *Report* of the Sub-Committee of the Whole on International Protection: UN doc. A/AC.96/671 (Oct. 1985); *Report* of the 36th Session of the Executive Committee: UN doc. A/AC.96/673, (Oct. 1985), paras. 77–82. Adoption of the Conclusions was delayed until 1989, owing to German reservations.

[39] See, for example, UNGA res. 49/169, 23 Dec. 1995, para. 5, reiterating 'the importance of ensuring access, for all persons seeking international protection, to fair and efficient procedures for the determination of refugee status . . .'

[40] See for example Executive Committee General Conclusion on International Protection No. 71 (1993), *Report* of the 44th Session: UN doc. A/AC.96/821, para. 19(k), (l), recognizing 'the advisability of concluding agreements among States directly concerned . . . to provide for the protection of refugees through the adoption of common criteria and related arrangements to determine which State shall be responsible for considering an application for asylum . . . and for granting the protection required...,' and emphasizing 'that such procedures, measures and agreements must include safeguards adequate to ensure . . . that persons in need of international protection are identified and that refugees are not subject to *refoulement*'.

way of returns to 'safe third countries',[41] while others have stressed the dangers inherent in refusing admission at the border 'for purely administrative reasons'.[42] Generally, however, States have accepted that 'the fundamental criterion when considering resort to the notion (of safe third country), was protection against *refoulement*'.[43]

The resolution on 'host third countries', for example, adopted in December 1992 by European Community Ministers responsible for immigration, proposes a number of 'fundamental requirements' as a precondition to the identification of a State as one to which asylum seekers and refugees may be returned. Specifically, the applicant's life or freedom must not be threatened in the country in question, within the meaning of article 33 of the 1951 Convention; he or she must not be exposed to torture or inhuman or degrading treatment; either the applicant must already have been granted protection, or have had a previous opportunity to contact the country's authorities to seek protection;[44] and finally, the applicant 'must be afforded effective protection in the host third country against *refoulement*, within the meaning of the Geneva Convention'.[45] This formulation is by no means free of ambiguity, however, and there is also no *necessary* connection between having had 'a previous opportunity' to apply for asylum/refugee status and thereafter being able to access the full range of refugee protection. Nevertheless, this approach has been largely followed in practice, particularly among European States.

[41] Mr Wrench (UK): UN doc. A/AC.96/SR.430, para. 53, (1988). This interpretation was reiterated the following year; see UN doc. A/AC.96/SR.442, para. 51 (1989).

[42] Mr Strassera (Argentina): UN doc. A/AC.96/SR. 442, para. 46 (1989).

[43] *Report* of the Sub-Committee of the Whole on International Protection: UN doc. A/AC.96/781 (9 Oct. 1991), para. 34. The notion of 'internal flight alternative' raises similar questions relating to the availability of protection, though in a quite different context. See decision of the Bundesverfassungsgericht = Federal Constitutional Court, 10 July 1989, *BverfGe* 2 BvR 502/86, 2 BvR 1000/86, 2 BvR 961/86, noting that an internal flight alternative presupposes that the territory in question offers the asylum seeker reasonable protection against persecution: Case Abstract No. *IJRL/0084*: 3 *IJRL* 343 (1991); also *Rasaratnam* v. *Canada (Minister of Employment and Immigration)*, [1991] FCJ No. 1256; [1992] FC 706, in which the Canadian Federal Court of Appeal held that for an internal flight alternative to exist, the decision-maker should be satisfied, 'on a balance of probabilities that there was no serious possibility of the applicant being persecuted in Colombo, and that, in all the circumstances, including circumstances particular to him, conditions in Colombo were such that it would not be unreasonable for the Appellant to seek refuge there': Case Abstract No. *IJRL/0099*: 3 *IJRL* 95 (1992). Cf. *Amanullah and Wahidullah* v. *Cobb* 862 F.2d 362 (1st Cir. 1988), in which detained Afghan asylum seekers withdrew their asylum appeal after receiving assurances that they would not be returned to Afghanistan from India. The Indian government thereupon refused to indicate that it would accept the returnees and not send them back to their country of origin, and also stated that it did not accept any obligation as 'country of first refuge'. The claimants were allowed to reinstate their appeal.

[44] Alternatively, there must be clear evidence of admissibility to a third country.

[45] Ministers of the Member States of the European Communities responsible for Immigration, Resolution on a harmonized approach to questions concerning host third countries, London, 30 Nov.–1 Dec. 1992; text in ECRE, 'Safe Third Countries: Myths and Realities', (1995), appx. C. See Julien-Laferrière, F., 'Commentaire des résolutions et conclusions adoptées par le Conseil européen d'Edimbourg sur le pays où il n'existe pas de risques sérieux de persécution, les pays tiers d'accueil et les demandes manifestement infondées', *Doc. réf.* no. 205–6, supp., 17 déc. 1992.

Thus, the July 1993 constitutional amendments in the Federal Republic of Germany provide that the right of asylum may not be invoked by those entering from a Member State of the European Communities or from a third country where application of the 1951 Convention and the European Convention on Human Rights is guaranteed.[46] In the United Kingdom, the Asylum and Immigration Appeals Act 1993 established a 'fast-track' appeal procedures for asylum seekers refused on the basis of safe third country. The immigration rules closely follow the resolution cited above, and provide that asylum claims will not normally be considered on their merits if the applicant can be sent to a country, 'in which the life or freedom of the asylum applicant would not be threatened (within the meaning of Article 33 of the Convention) and the government of which would not send the applicant elsewhere in a manner contrary to the principles of the Convention and the Protocol'.[47] The rules further provide that an applicant will only be removed if, not having arrived directly from the country in which persecution is claimed to be feared, he or she 'had an opportunity at the border or within the territory of a third country to make contact with that country's authorities in order to seek their protection'.[48]

The rationale for this policy was explained in a paper prepared by the United Kingdom delegation in Geneva, as a contribution to discussion within the UNHCR Executive Committee.[49] 'Protection needs', it is said, distinguish refugees from other migrants, and 'once refugees have reached a country from which they could safely seek protection it is that country's obligations under the 1951 Convention which are engaged, and any subsequent migratory movements do not normally result in the transfer of those obligations'.[50] The United Kingdom nevertheless noted that full account must be taken of a State's obligations with respect to *non-refoulement*, including indirect *refoulement*.[51] Safe third

---

[46] Art. 16a(2), *Grundgesetz* (Basic Law); see *AsylVfG* 1993, art. 26a, prescribing that asylum may not be claimed where the applicant comes from a safe third State; besides the Members of the European Union, the following States had been listed as safe at 31 Jan. 1995: Czech Republic, Norway, Poland, Switzerland. See also art. 27, excluding the applicant who has already found protection against persecution; residence for three months or more raises a presumption that protection has been found, which can be rebutted by credible evidence of a risk of expulsion to a State in which the claimant fears persecution. Marx, R., *Asylverfahrensgesetz: Kommentar* (1995); also Blay, S. and Zimmermann, A., 'Recent Changes in German Refugee Law: A Critical Assessment', 88 *AJIL* 361 (1994); Ablard, T. and Novak, A., 'L'évolution du droit d'asile en Allemagne jusqu'à la réforme de 1993', 7 *IJRL* 260, 276–87 (1995); Hailbronner, K., 'The Concept of "Safe Country" and Expeditious Asylum Procedures: A Western European Perspective', 5 *IJRL* 31, 46ff (1994).

[47] Immigration Rules (HC 395, in force 1 Oct. 1994), para. 345.

[48] Ibid. An applicant may also be removed if there is clear evidence of admissibility to a third country.

[49] UK Delegation, Geneva, 'Sending Asylum Seekers to Safe Third Countries', 7 *IJRL* 119 (1995); the notion of safe third country is considered to be somewhat wider than other terms, such as 'host third country' or 'first country of asylum', and includes countries to which the claimant has not in fact been, if there is a country to which he or she can nevertheless be safely sent. See also UNHCR's reply, 'The Concept of "Protection Elsewhere"', ibid., 123.

[50] Ibid., 121. See also Hailbronner, K., 'The Right to Asylum and the Future of Asylum Procedures in the European Community', 2 *IJRL* 341, 348 (1990).

[51] Cf. *R.* v. *Secretary of State for the Home Department, ex parte Bugdaycay; in re Musisi* [1987] AC 514.

country removals must therefore take account of receiving country practice, as well as their formal legal obligations, and no return should take place if there are 'substantial grounds for thinking that the third country would send the applicant on to a country of claimed persecution without properly considering the case'.[52] Finally, although consultations are desirable, and agreements for the allocation of responsibility are best, they are not a precondition to removal.

Canada's 1976 Immigration Act, as amended, conditions eligibility to have an asylum claim determined on the applicant not having been recognized as a Convention refugee in a country to which he or she may still be returned; and on not having come, 'directly or indirectly', from a 'prescribed' country (that is, one which complies with article 33 of the 1951 Convention), other than his or her country of origin.[53] Finally, the Minister is empowered to conclude agreements 'with other countries for the purpose of facilitating the co-ordination and implementation of immigration policies and programs including . . . agreements for sharing the responsibility for examining refugee claims and for sharing information concerning persons who travel between countries that are parties to such agreements'.[54] Although available in various forms since 1988, Canada's 'safe country' provisions were not implemented for a variety of practical and political reasons.[55] Towards the end of 1995, however, agreement appeared likely on a memorandum of understanding with the United States, dealing with responsibilities for refugee and asylum applicants transiting the territory of one, en route to the other.[56]

As part of the process of regional harmonization or co-ordination of immigration, asylum and visa policies, European States concluded two agreements in

[52] Note the careful use of language relating to the degree of risk, essentially reproducing the language of art. 3, 1984 Convention against Torture. For assessments of returns to unsafe conditions, see Amnesty International British Section. 'United Kingdom: Deficient Policy and Practice for the Protection of Asylum Seekers', London, Nov. 1990; Amnesty International, *Turkey—Selective Protection: Discriminatory treatment of non-European refugees and asylum-seekers*, (Mar. 1994: AI Index EUR 44/16/94)—recommending no return of any non-European asylum seeker to Turkey.

[53] *Immigration Act, 1976*, as amended, s. 46.01(1); coming from a country in which the applicant was present solely for the purpose of joining a flight to Canada is disregarded. The Act further provides that a claim is inadmissible where the country that the person claims to have left or outside of which he or she claims to have remained by reason of fear of persecution is 'prescribed' as one that respects human rights: ibid., s. 69.1(10.1); for the power to make regulations prescribing such countries, see s. 114(1)(s), (s1).

[54] Ibid., s. 108.1.

[55] Plaut, whose report contributed significantly to the process of Canadian legislative reform, recommended against 'prior protection' as a ground of inadmissibility, arguing that though it 'appears accessible to objective judgment . . . the actual determination of whether a claimant in fact enjoys the protection of another country is frequently highly complex': Plaut, W. G., *Refugee Determination in Canada*, (1985), 103–4. As Achermann and Gattiker note, under the revised German law, the substantive aspects of 'protection elsewhere' are no longer taken into account. In 'safe third country', but not 'safe country of origin' cases, a simple administrative decision is now involved, based on the legislated fact of entry from a country considered safe: Achermann and Gattiker, 'Safe Third Countries', 28–9.

[56] See also Melander, G., 'The Principle of "Country of First Asylum" from a European Perspective', in Bhabha, J. and Coll, G., eds., *Asylum Law and Practice in Europe and North America*, (1992), 122.

1990, namely, the Dublin and Schengen Conventions.[57] These agreements have simple, limited objectives: to determine which participating State is responsible for deciding the asylum claim of an individual within the area of application; to provide in appropriate cases for the readmission of such individual, and for the exchange of information; and to confirm the responsibility of the State for the removal of unsuccessful applicants from European Union or Schengen territory, as the case may be. Responsibility is based on formal elements, including the presence of family members (defined strictly) having refugee status, the issue of visas, residence permits, or authorization to enter the territory by one or other State.[58] Additional declared purposes include the identification of a *single* responsible State, thereby reducing the likelihood of multiple, successive applications; and the elimination of the 'orbiting' of asylum seekers, by *requiring* claims to be determined by the State so identified.

Both Dublin and Schengen are premised on the assumption that member States will implement a common standard, namely, the protection of refugees as defined in the 1951 Convention/1967 Protocol, in particular, by the determination of claims. Relevant procedural and substantive questions, such as due process, rights to counsel or interpreters, appeal and review, as well as interpretations of definitional elements in the international standard, are not dealt with, however. Arrangements such as these could certainly improve the situation of refugees and reduce the number requiring protection,[59] especially as participating States under-

[57] The Convention determining the State Responsible for Examining Applications for Asylum Lodged in one of the Member States of the European Communities (Dublin Convention) was signed by eleven Member States on 15 June 1990, and was signed and ratified by the twelfth State, Denmark, on 12 June 1991. By 31 Dec. 1995, France, Germany, Greece, Italy, Luxembourg, Portugal and the UK had also ratified the Convention, which will enter into force only when all Member States are parties. The Schengen Supplementary Convention, also concluded in June 1990, entered into force between Belgium, France, Germany, Luxembourg, the Netherlands, Portugal and Spain on 26 March 1995: Italy and Greece have signed, but entry into force has been delayed in each case. As and when the Dublin Convention enters into force, the Schengen scheme will likely be abolished; see art. 142. On 29 March 1991, the Schengen States concluded an agreement with Poland, under which the latter agreed to readmit persons found in Schengen territory in an irregular situation; it came into force on 1 May 1991 for Germany, France, Italy, Luxembourg and Poland; see Achermann, A. and Gattiker, M., 'Safe Third Countries: European Developments', 7 *IJRL* 19, 24, 36–7 (1995). See generally Joly, D., 'The Porous Dam: European Harmonization on Asylum in the Nineties', 6 *IJRL* 159 (1994); also Achermann, A., 'Schengen und Asyl: Das Schengener Übereinkommen als Ausgangspunkt der Harmonisierung europäischer Asylpolitik', in Achermann, A., Bieber, R., Epiney, A., Wehner, R., *Schengen und die Folgen*, (1995), 79; Meijers, H., et al., *Schengen: Internationalisation of Central Chapters of the Law on Aliens, Refugees, Security and the Police*, (1991); Mahmoud, S., 'The Schengen Information System: An Inequitable Data Protection Regime', 7 *IJRL* 179 (1995).

[58] See arts. 3, 4–8, 10, Dublin Convention; also art. 2, in which States reaffirm their obligations under the 1951 Convention/1967 Protocol without geographic restriction, and 'their commitment' to co-operate with UNHCR.

[59] Cf. UNHCR Statute, para. 8(a),(b). See Hailbronner, K., 'Perspectives of a Harmonization of the Law of Asylum after the Maastricht Summit', 29 *CMLR* 917 (1992), for the view that Dublin and Schengen cannot be characterized as in breach of the 1951 Convention or the European Convention on Human Rights, there being no obligation in the former either to determine a refugee claim or not to return applicants to third States (at 925–6). He notes, however, that safe third

take to determine the asylum claims for which they are responsible. The reality, however, is less engaging; far from effectively providing for a substantive decision on every asylum claim lodged in the European Union, article 3(5) of the Dublin Convention expressly reserves to each member State, 'the right . . . to send an applicant for asylum to a third State'. Indeed, the Dublin scheme for attributing responsibility *only* comes into operation if there is no other non-European Union State to which the claimant may be sent by a member State, 'pursuant to its national laws'.

This intent was confirmed by the Ministers responsible for immigration, in their 1992 resolution on a harmonized approach to so-called host third countries. This provides that formal identification of a host third country shall *precede* the substantive examination of an asylum application; and in language that is far from clear and unambiguous, that the application 'may not' be examined if there is a host third country; and that the Dublin Convention shall apply only if the asylum applicant 'cannot in practice be sent to a host third country'. If no such country exists, a member State will consider whether another member State is responsible, and if so, hand over the applicant.[60] Although the notion of a single responsible State obliged to determine an asylum claim was hailed, among others, as bringing an end to refugees in orbit and making the right to seek asylum effective, this prospect is limited to those refugees and asylum seekers who cannot be sent out of Europe. As Achermann and Gattiker have observed, '[t]he principle of the responsible State has thus been turned upside down; expulsion to a third State is no longer the exception but the rule'.[61]

Having a 'safe third country' rule in national legislation is one thing; being able effectively to implement it, quite another; in places, a marked chasm separates rhetoric and reality, whether it relates to other States' compliance with obligations towards refugees and asylum seekers, or to the effectiveness of removals policies. The United Kingdom considers that although consultations are desirable and agreements for the allocation of responsibility are best, they are not a precondition to removal.[62] Several European States have backed up their domestic provisions with a network of readmission agreements, principally with States in Central and Eastern Europe. Traditionally, such agreements provide for and facilitate the readmission by States of their own citizens. In addition, they now generally also apply to third country nationals who have crossed a common border, and can thus be used to return asylum seekers to a 'safe third

country policies can work only on the basis of international agreements which establish States' willingness to assume jurisdiction (at 936). Also, Hailbronner, K., 'The Concept of "Safe Country" and Expeditious Asylum Procedures: A Western European Perspective', 5 *IJRL* 31 (1993).

[60] Paras. 1, 3. The second Member State, in turn, may re-examine the possibility of removal to a host third country.

[61] Achermann and Gattiker, 'Safe Third Countries', 23.

[62] UK Delegation, Geneva, 'Sending Asylum Seekers to Safe Third Countries', 7 *IJRL* 119, 122 (1995); Immigration Rules, para. 345.

country',[63] even though they contain no provision obliging the receiving State to consider any such claims on their merits, let alone to provide protection.[64]

Both practice and principle suggest that inter-State agreements on responsibility, return, and procedural and substantive guarantees, including *non-refoulement*, are essential if the protection of refugees is to be effective.[65]

In a note presented to the Executive Committee in 1991, UNHCR called attention to many difficulties of application with the safe third country concept, both at the threshold of identification and thereafter, on implementation. Relevant issues of concern include uncertainty with respect to the length of stay, standards of application, treatment, and monitoring.[66] The discussion in the Sub-Committee revealed various positions; one representative suggested that the only relevant criterion in deciding on return was the risk of *refoulement*;[67] others that the notion of safe third country should be taken into account before resort to determination of status under the 1951 Convention, and that there should be 'no forum shopping'.[68] No conclusions were adopted, save that it was agreed to give the subject further attention. Different views have in fact surfaced over the years, with some States emphasizing that the right to seek asylum did not imply the right to travel to a particular country in order to apply;[69] some, that the individual's choice should be respected, while still others noted the overall negative impact of such measures, or specifically, that they were coming under pressure to take more refugees and asylum seekers in order to protect western Europe.[70]

In 1993, UNHCR stated that the return of those who have obtained effective protection in another country is permissible, subject to the conditions laid down in Executive Committee Conclusion No. 58 (1989) on irregular movements. Practical problems, however, included determining whether another country in which an asylum seeker can reasonably be expected to request asylum will in fact accept responsibility for examining the request and granting protection.

[63] Achermann and Gattiker, 'Safe Third Countries', 23–5; UNHCR, 'Overview of Readmission Agreements', Sept. 1993. For an early multilateral agreement, limited to nationals, see 1957 European Agreement on the Movement of Persons between Member States of the Council of Europe: *ETS* No. 25; and for the 1989 agreement between France and Spain, see décret no. 89–275 du 28 avr. 1989: *J.O.*, 4 mai 1989, No. 5710.

[64] Achermann and Gattiker, 'Safe Third Countries', 36–7.

[65] See Amnesty International British Section, *Playing Human Pinball: Home Office Practice in 'Safe Third Country' Asylum Cases*, June 1995. This comprehensive and compelling report by Richard Dunstan tracks sixty cases over a nine month period, to show that the policy on safe third country denials had achieved nothing, with the Home Office rescinding its original decision in the majority of cases and agreeing to consider the claims on their merits.

[66] *Background Note on the Safe Country Concept and Refugee Status:* UN doc. EC/SCP/68 (26 July 1991), paras. 11–17.

[67] A point also made by Norway in 1993: UN doc. A/AC.96/SR.483 (1993), para. 21.

[68] *Report* of the Sub-Committee of the Whole on International Protection: UN doc. A/AC.96/781 (9 Oct. 1991), paras. 34–7.

[69] UN doc. A/AC.96/SR.472 (1992), para. 78 (UK, on behalf of the European Community and Member States).

[70] See UN doc. A/AC.96/SR.485 (1993), para. 2 (Brazil); UN doc. A/AC.96/SR.475 (1992), para. 37 (Poland).

Examples of summary removals onwards in turn confirmed that exclusion from asylum procedures is a substantive issue requiring appropriate procedural safeguards, including an opportunity to rebut any presumption that a State is 'safe' with respect to the individual concerned, together with prior consent and co-operation of the country of return. UNHCR also called attention to the problem of return from countries with developed procedures to those with none or with few resources, which was likely to result in the serious risk of denial of protection.[71]

The Conclusions on irregular movements of refugees and asylum seekers are commonly invoked as a source of common standards for returns to so-called safe third countries. Although considered by many States to be well-balanced, at the time of their adoption they produced a substantial batch of 'interpretative declarations'. Among them, Turkey considered that the conclusions did not apply to those 'who are merely in transit in other country';[72] Italy considered them limited to *recognized* Convention refugees and to asylum seekers who have *already found protection* on the basis of the principles of the Convention and Protocol; Thailand opposed any hierarchy among durable solutions that gave priority to local settlement before third country resettlement; Germany, with Austria concurring, asserted that a 'formal residence permit' was not a necessary precondition to return; while Greece thought that first asylum countries should bear the burden of refugees on an equitable basis, that 'the will of a refugee to choose freely the country of . . . destination should not be overlooked . . .', and that with respect to returns, the 'sovereignty of the State and its rules and regulations under which entry is allowed cannot be ignored'.[73]

State practice and the views of States reveal a clear division between those who would argue that the international responsibility (of other States) to determine status and provide protection is engaged by the fact of passage through or earlier presence in their territory; and those who look for more substantial evidence of connection or attach greater weight to the wishes or intentions of the asylum seeker, either as a matter of principle or because this leads in fact to a more equitable spread of refugees and asylum seekers.[74] Among the persistent

---

[71] *Note on International Protection:* UN doc. A/AC.96/815 (31 Aug. 1993), paras. 20–2; *Report* of the Sub-Committee of the Whole on International Protection: UN doc. A/AC.96/819 (5 Oct. 1993), para. 13—one delegate queried whether it was right to hold a sending State indirectly responsible for *refoulement* effected by a third country.

[72] See *Report* of the Sub-Committee: UN doc. A/AC.96/671 (9 Oct. 1985), para. 68.

[73] Executive Committee Conclusion No. 58 (1989), para. 25; p. 23, N, Interpretative declarations; below, Annexe 3. For a review of Danish law and practice, see Kjaerum, M., 'The Concept of Country of First Asylum', 4 *IJRL* 514 (1992); the concept can be used either as an admissibility question, or as a 'kind of national exclusion clause' (515f). However, the decision-maker must first decide whether the asylum seeker is in need of protection, *before* looking at whether another country is more appropriate; this has the advantage of providing a fall-back if removal to the other State does not come through (517). Note also that the burden of proof is on the Danish authorities; it is not for the applicant to prove that protection is not available (522).

[74] Cf. Parliamentary Assembly of the Council of Europe. CE Doc. 6633, 16 June 1992. 'Report on migratory flows in Czechoslovakia, Hungary and Poland.' Rapporteurs, Miss Guirado, Miss

objectors, Turkey has consistently voiced its opposition to safe third country returns, also arguing that resettlement should not continue as the solution of last resort, lest first asylum or transit countries be required to shoulder most of the burden.[75] In 1990, Turkey declared that it was wrong to perceive transit countries as permanent havens where the movement farther west or north could be contained. In the absence of voluntary repatriation, equitable burden-sharing should be the guiding principle, with the choice of solution based on the desire of the refugees and asylum seekers themselves and conditions in the host country. The principle of first asylum should not be used to impose the necessity of hosting increasingly large numbers of refugees for an indefinite period of time.[76]

The fact of an asylum seeker's presence in or transit through a State does raise certain issues of jurisdiction. However, at first glance and from the perspective of customary international law, these appear more permissive than mandatory, in the sense that such State *may* determine whether an asylum seeker is a refugee, but is not *obliged* so to determine unless minded to return the individual to a country in which his or her life or freedom may be threatened. Possible exceptions, such as arise in the case of obligations to extradite or to prosecute, are almost exclusively based on formal agreements.

State practice, apart from the responsibility-determining context of the Dublin and Schengen Conventions, has been mostly unilateral, in the sense that one or other State has declined to consider an asylum application or extend protection, after determining, generally without consultation, that another State was responsible. Alternatively, asylum seekers have been dealt with under general bilateral agreements on the readmission of nationals and non-nationals, but without the issue of responsibility for asylum determination being considered.

There is certainly no consistent practice among 'sending' and 'receiving' States as would permit the conclusion that any rule exists with respect to the return of refugees and asylum seekers to safe third countries, simply on the basis of a brief or transitory contact. Equally, it cannot be said that, in relation to the 1951 Convention, there is 'any subsequent practice in the application of the treaty which establishes the agreement of the parties regarding its

---

Szelényi—proposing that Member States should share the burden 'with the new immigration countries through practical co-operation and the provision of financial assistance as well as the acceptance of asylum seekers and migrants from the countries of first asylum'; also Parliamentary Assembly of the Council of Europe. CE Doc. 7052, 23 Mar. 1994. 'Report on the right of asylum.' Rapporteur: Mr Franck—proposing common action, among other things, to reduce friction over sharing asylum responsibilities; Parliamentary Assembly of the Council of Europe. CE Doc. 6413, 12 Apr. 1991. 'Report on Europe of 1992 and refugee policies.' Rapporteur: Sir John Hunt.

[75] UN doc. A/AC.96/SR.388 (1985), para. 52; SR.407 (1986), paras. 45–8; SR.426 (1988), paras. 19–20; also SR.427 (1988), para. 69 (Sudan); paras. 10 (China); SR.430 (1988), para. 66 (Turkey).

[76] UN doc. A/AC.96/SR.456 (1990), paras. 6–7; see also SR.468 (1991), paras. 15, 20—the fundamental right of asylum seekers to be free to choose the country they wished to go to had to be accepted.

interpretation'.[77] In the absence of any applicable agreement, such returns therefore run the risk of violating article 33 of the 1951 Convention, for example, where the receiving State fails to provide protection.[78] Writing in 1989, Crawford and Hyndman included the practice of sending asylum seekers on to other States as one of 'three heresies' in the application of the 1951 Convention.

It is . . . clear that more than one State may share joint responsibility for decisions which result in the *refoulement* of a refugee . . . It follows that a State may not rely on the obligation of another State party to the Convention, even where there are good grounds for saying that the latter State is indeed under a particular obligation with respect to the refugee, if that reliance is likely to result in a violation of Article 33.[79]

Returns may also breach other applicable human rights provisions, where the process of refusal and return amounts to cruel, inhuman or degrading treatment.[80] The standards of the International Civil Aviation Authority on the return of inadmissible travellers govern an essentially administrative situation,[81] and are not intended by themselves to activate the substantial treaty-based protection responsibilities involved in refugee determination.

So far as States have accepted returned asylum seekers, either unilaterally or on the strength of readmission agreements, this process is flawed from the refugee protection perspective, because it is not indissolubly linked to the obligation of the receiving State to proceed to a substantive evaluation of the asylum claim, if any, and to provide protection in appropriate cases.

While the UNHCR Executive Committee has recognized 'connection or close links' with another State as a discretionary basis for refusal to consider an asylum claim, it has approved returns only to countries in which refugees or asylum seekers 'have already found protection', if they are protected there against *refoulement*, are permitted to remain and are treated in accordance with recognized basic human standards. The European resolution on so-called host third countries also confirms that returns are conditional upon the availability of a certain minimum standard of protection.

[77] Art. 31(3)(b), 1969 Vienna Convention on the Law of Treaties. Hailbronner, K., 'The Concept of "Safe Country" and Expeditious Asylum Procedures: A Western European Perspective', 5 *IJRL* 31 (1993), finds as yet no agreement within Europe on key terms, such as how long an asylum seeker needs to have stayed in a country, or what is considered safe.

[78] This could easily arise, for example, where the receiving State denies admission to its asylum procedure because of lapse of time since first contact; or where it sends the asylum seeker to another country deemed to be responsible, which then *refoules* the individual; or where it sends the claimant to a State that only considers those who come directly from their country of origin, which then passes him or her back to a transit State that in turn applies exclusion on the basis of a geographical limitation on its obligations.

[79] Crawford, J. and Hyndman, P., 'Three Heresies in the Application of the Refugee Convention', 1 *IJRL* 155, 171 (1989). See also the authors' review of a number of Australian cases, including *Azemoudeh* (at 168), returned by Australia to Hong Kong, thereafter to India and probably then to his country of origin.

[80] On the earlier practice of 'shuttlecocking' migrants, see Goodwin-Gill, G. S., *International Law and the Movement of Persons between States*, (1978), 287–8.

[81] See generally Feller, E., 'Carrier Sanctions and International Law', 1 *IJRL* 48, 53–5, 65 (1989).

The most that can be said at present is that international law permits the return of refugees and asylum seekers to another State if there is substantial evidence of admissibility, such as possession of a Convention travel document or other proof of entitlement to enter. A supplementary rule or practice may be emerging at the European regional level, which will allow return if there is evidence of a *sufficient* 'territorial connection' with another State, such as is laid down in the Dublin and Schengen Conventions.[82] Compliance with article 33 of the 1951 Convention is a further key factor in the criteria for safe third country status. *Non-refoulement* is most likely to be observed if there is access to an fair and effective procedure for the determination of claims to refugee status, in accordance with prevailing international standards. However, formal effectiveness may be prejudiced by restrictions on access, for example, because of time limits, geographical limitations on the extent of obligations, policy reasons affecting particular groups, or legal reasons affecting certain classes, such as illegal entrants. In either case, actual return is likely to satisfy a best practice standard only if the receiving State is able to provide certain effective guarantees, including (1) willingness to readmit asylum seekers; (2) acceptance of responsibility to determine claims to refugee status, notwithstanding departure from the country in question or the circumstances of initial entry; (3) the treatment of applicants during the determination process in accordance with generally accepted standards;[83] and (4) some provision with respect to subsistence and human dignity issues, such as social assistance or access to the labour market in the interim, family unity, education of children, and so forth. Besides the question of fulfilment of obligations deriving from the 1951 Convention/1967 Protocol, a country's human rights record will also be relevant. This may include both procedural and substantive standards, including questions of remedies, non-discriminatory or equivalent treatment with local nationals, and protection of fundamental human rights.

Ironically, the essential error in the safe third country debate has been to approach the question as a substantive one of protection and (assumed) obligations. Rather, it should be seen as procedural, but premised on the participation of States in a formal regime of responsibility and protection, regulated by treaty. The debate and the legislation must be recast away from the notion of 'safe third country', with all its substantive implications, and in favour of formal agreements with other States on the precise issues of responsibility to determine claims and common standards of treatment that are in accord with the 1951 Convention and applicable human rights instruments.[84] Merely attributing responsibility,

---

[82] In a recent article, Marx suggests that removals without consent amount to abuse of rights, and also criticizes the adequacy of existing re-admission agreements: Marx, R., '*Non-refoulement*, Access to Procedures and Responsibility to Determine Claims', 7 *IJRL* 383, 396–7 (1995).

[83] Ideally, such standards will deal with detention or other restrictions on liberty, the length of proceedings, the availability of interpreters, legal advice, access to UNHCR, and so forth.

[84] In 1991, the Council of the Presidency of the European Community committed itself to harmonization of asylum procedures by 31 Dec. 1993. It also agreed that readmission agreements with

however, is likely to fall short of securing effective protection or the fullest implementation of international obligations.

Although the standards of protection endorsed in the British statement above have much to recommend them, United Kingdom practice fully confirms the practical difficulties of making safe third country policy work in the absence of agreement.[85] Only within the area of application of the Dublin and Schengen Conventions is there an obligation to determine a claim for asylum; but even there, inadequate protection is possible (considered from an international law perspective), because of variations in procedural entitlements and aberrant interpretations of refugee criteria.[86]

2.1.2 *Substantive issues: manifestly unfounded claims and the 'safe country of origin' exception*

Since the 1980s, many States have complained of abuse of their asylum procedures by those who did not need or deserve international protection, and of the resulting costs, delays and injury to 'genuine' refugees. Delays in determination have certainly been due in part to the numbers of claimants (although refugee procedures have never been renowned for their expedition), and to the fact that systems oriented to case by case determination operate within legal regimes governed by the rule of law and subject to appeal and review. Countries in conflict and other proven locations of human rights violations nevertheless also continued to produce outflows of asylum seekers, although the process of individual assessment did not always meet the needs, either of claimants or of the receiving community.

In such circumstances, pre-screening, admissibility thresholds and accelerated procedures appear to offer advantages, permitting the speedy rejection (and removal) of those not requiring protection; and the prompt recognition of refugees and others who do. The means chosen to achieve these ends, however, are not always best suited to ensure the fulfilment of international obligations.

third States should be examined, and recognized the desirability of elaborating common positions on immigration at international meetings: Council of the Presidency, Luxembourg, 28–9 June 1991: Doc. ROV SN/151/3/91; see also Communication from the Commission on Immigration and Asylum Policies, 23 Feb. 1994, to the Council and the European Parliament. With the entry into force of the Treaty on European Union (the Maastricht Treaty), asylum policy is a matter of 'common interest': Art. K.1. A standard bilateral readmission agreement with third States was adopted by the Council for Justice and Home Affairs in 1994; see ECRE, 'Safe Third Countries: Myths and Realities', (1995), app. E; Inter-governmental Consultations, 'Working Paper on Readmission Agreements', (Aug. 1994). A June 1995 res. on minimum guarantees for asylum procedures set a very low level. Cf. Amnesty International, 'Europe: Harmonization of asylum policy. Accelerated procedures for "manifestly unfounded" asylum claims and the "safe country" concept', AI EC Project, Brussels, Nov. 1992; European Council on Refugees and Exiles (ECRE), 'A European policy in the light of established principles,' Apr. 1994.

[85] Amnesty International British Section, *Playing Human Pinball: Home Office Practice in 'Safe Third Country' Asylum Cases*, (1995).

[86] The critical areas of difference include the relevance of agents of persecution, persecution in the context of civil war, among others.

'Accelerated procedures' may be either positive or negative. Except with respect to temporary protection policies for readily identifiable groups, *positive* procedures are relatively rare, even though, by taking account of success rates and being based in accurate and up-to-date country information, they can significantly reduce the burden on national decision-making systems.[87] The case for *negative* accelerated procedures is harder to make. Few countries can be prescribed with confidence as entirely non-refugee producing, although obviously experience over time and accumulated information and analysis tend to raise evidential presumptions that may be practically insurmountable. International obligations with respect to the protection of refugees and human rights are nevertheless persuasive authority for individual examination, although again the key may lie in the information used to determine whether a particular country is presumptively safe. Provided it is available, verified and public, a coherent body of country of origin information will raise exclusionary *presumptions* of which the asylum seeker will be aware, but which may be rebutted by the particular facts of the claim. The threshold is raised, permitting easier identification of unfounded cases, offering a visible deterrent to those who would use asylum procedures for immigration purposes, but nevertheless remaining open to the exceptional instance.

In 1982 and 1983 the Executive Committee considered the problem of manifestly unfounded or abusive applications, considered as those which,

are clearly fraudulent or not related to the criteria for the granting of refugee status laid down in the 1951 ... Convention nor to any other criteria justifying the grant of asylum.[88]

The Executive Committee nevertheless acknowledged that determinations in such cases have a substantive character, and require appropriate procedural guarantees. In all cases, applicants should receive a complete personal interview by a fully qualified official and, whenever possible, by an official of the authority competent to determine refugee status; that authority alone should determine the unfounded or abusive character of such applications, and review, simplified if necessary, should be available before rejection at the frontier or removal.[89]

---

[87] Shortly after the new procedure came into operation in Canada in 1989, an 'expedited' procedure was also introduced. Refined over time, it allowed claims generally conforming with the profile of previously successful cases from particular source countries to be batched for (positive) decision without the necessity for personal appearance by the applicant.

[88] Executive Committee Conclusions Nos. 28 (1982) and 30 (1983); for full text, see below Annexe 3. Also UNHCR, 'Follow-up on earlier Conclusions of the Sub-Committee of the Whole—The Determination of Refugee Status with regard to the Problem of Manifestly Unfounded or Abusive Applications': UN doc. EC/SCP/29 (Aug. 1993); *Report* of the Sub-Committee: UN doc. A/AC.96/629 (1983), paras. 4–12.

[89] The very idea of manifestly unfounded claims (MUC) has been disputed. For example, Plaut noted that 'Language itself stands in the way of a workable MUC concept. *Webster's International Dictionary* defines "manifest" as "capable of being easily understood or recognized at once by the mind" ... But taking the vast differences of sense perception and reasoning into consideration, frequently what is manifest to some is often not so to others. Refugee claims are generally of that

This limited sense of the 'manifestly unfounded' has not been maintained in practice, particularly among some European States. For example, a resolution adopted by the EU Ministers responsible for immigration in 1992 equates manifestly unfounded applications with claims by applicants who 'are not in genuine need of protection . . . within the terms of the Geneva Convention'.[90] This includes not only those where there is 'clearly no substance', or where the claim is based 'on deliberate deception or is an abuse of asylum procedures',[91] but also applications which fall within the provisions on host third countries.[92] Claims with 'no substance' are described as those in which the grounds of the application are outside the scope of the 1951 Convention, in which there is no reference to fear of persecution on Convention grounds, but instead to the search for employment or better living conditions; in which the applicant provides no indication that he or she 'would be exposed to fear of persecution' (sic), the story contains no circumstantial or personal details, 'is manifestly lacking in any credibility', or 'inconsistent, contradictory or fundamentally improbable'.

Clearly, this ill-drafted formulation trespasses on the realm of substantive determination. It is also open to further misapplication, so far as States may be inspired to read back into its terms their preferred or legislated interpretations of the refugee definition, for example, that there can be no (Convention-based) fear of persecution in situations of civil conflict;[93] or that an 'internal flight alternative' exists; or that certain policies or practices should be discounted in the evaluation of claims.[94]

Several countries have amended their law to make 'manifestly unfounded' the

kind. They address themselves to experiences and conditions in other countries well removed from direct observation'. He concluded that the concept was 'logically so narrow as to be practically unworkable', and that as an enforcement tool it was 'open to administrative misapplication': Plaut, G., 'Refugee determination in Canada', (1985), 96, 99.

[90] Preamble, Ministers of the Member States of the European Communities responsible for Immigration, Resolution on manifestly unfounded applications for asylum, London, 30 Nov.–1 Dec. 1992; text in ECRE, 'Safe Third Countries: Myths and Realities', (1995), appx. C). This elision is manifestly inappropriate, begging precisely the question which refugee procedures exist to answer. In this, it contradicts even Executive Committee Conclusion No. 30 (1983), which is claimed as the inspiration. Cf. Conseil d'Etat, 8 fevrier 1994, No. 46.086, extr. urgence (VIè ch.réf.), *Mayita Mbamu Didier c/ Etat belge*, finding in a case involving no serious contradictions, that it cannot be said that the claim is 'manifestly unfounded' because the applicant has not presented any element capable of establishing, in his or her case, serious indications of a well-founded fear: *RDDE*, No. 78, mai–avril–juin 1994, 148.

[91] Defined further in paras. 6–10. The resolution is also a regrettable example of manifestly incompetent drafting as in para. 7: 'Member States may consider under the provisions of paragraph 2 above an application for asylum from claimed persecution which is clearly limited to a specific geographical area where effective protection is readily available for that individual in another part of his own country to which it would be reasonable to expect him to go, in accordance with article 33.1 of the Geneva Convention'.

[92] See above, s. 2.1.1.

[93] As is implied by certain French and German rulings; see above, Ch. 2, s. 5.2.3.

[94] For example, during 1995 the Australian government was reported to be drafting legislation which would not allow a foreign government's fertility policies and legislation to be taken into account in the determination of the existence of a particular social group.

basis for inadmissibility to the full asylum procedure, or for liability to summary removal.[95] In addition to 'lack of substance', credibility and documentary grounds, some States have also introduced the notion of 'safe country of origin' as a legislated presumption against admissibility. In a paper submitted to the Executive Committee in 1991, UNHCR had argued that, so far as it might exclude whole groups from the asylum process, 'safe country of origin' could amount to a reservation in fact to article 1A(2) of the Convention, contrary to article 42, or to a new geographical limitation incompatible with the intent of the 1967 Protocol. A procedural role might be acceptable, however, which either channelled claims into an expedited hearing, or raised rebuttable evidentiary presumptions.[96]

The European Ministers' resolution on manifestly unfounded applications refers to parallel conclusions adopted on countries in which there is generally no serious risk of persecution, but also emphasize that Member States will 'consider the individual claims of all applicants from such countries and any specific indications presented by the applicant which might outweigh a general presumption'. The factors to be taken into account include previous recognition rates, human rights in law and practice, democratic institutions and stability. A country will be considered 'safe', where it,

can be clearly shown, in an objective and verifiable way, normally not to generate refugees or where it can be clearly shown, in an objective and verifiable way, that circumstances which might in the past have justified recourse to the 1951 Geneva Convention have ceased to exist.[97]

---

[95] See, for example, section 15c, *Vremdelingenwet* (amendment to Netherlands aliens law, in force 1 Jan. 1994); art. 17, *Asylgesetz 1991* (Austrian asylum law); art. 30(3), *Asylverfahrensgesetz 1992/1993* (German asylum procedure law); art. 16, *loi sur l'asile* (Swiss asylum law). In one or another form, the laws also include the use of false or forged documents and failure to co-operate as additional grounds. See also Julien-Laferrière, F., 'Droit d'asile et politique d'asile en France', *Asyl* 1993/4, 75, noting that while 'manifestly unfounded' is not defined by the law, administrative practice and the jurisprudence of the *tribunaux de grande instance*, (especially from Bobigny, which has jurisdiction over Roissy-Charles de Gaulle airport), suggests that it includes, among others, persecution claims which do not appear serious because of lack of precision, incoherence or stereotypical account.

[96] 'Background Note on the Safe Country Concept and Refugee Status': UN doc. EC/SCP/68 (26 July 1991), paras. 5 7. See also *Report* of the Sub-Committee: UN doc. A/AC.96/781 (9 Oct. 1991), paras. 32–3; UN doc. A/AC.96/SR.463 (1991), paras. 71–2 (Netherlands). Amnesty International has recommended that special procedures in such cases should only allow for expedited appeal; see 'Europe—Harmonization of asylum policy: Accelerated procedures for "manifestly unfounded" asylum claims and the "safe country" concept', AI EC Project, Brussels, Nov. 1992; also European Council on Refugees and Exiles, 'A European Policy in the light of established principles', Apr. 1994, recommending that safe country assessments be based on reliable and impartial information, subject to open and parliamentary control, and available to applicants.

[97] Joly, D., 'The Porous Dam: European Harmonization on Asylum in the Nineties', 6 *IJRL* 159, 170–1 (1994), citing various published and unpublished European Union documents; Hailbronner, K., 'The Concept of "Safe Country" and Expeditious Asylum Procedures: A Western European Perspective', 5 *IJRL* 31, 56–8 (1993). The reference to what is 'objective and verifiable' would seem to imply reliance on publicly available information sources, subject to review.

In this sense also, the 1993 constitutional changes in Germany provide that nationals from countries designated as safe by the legislature shall be presumed not to be politically persecuted.[98] The legal criterion for designation as 'safe' is that on the basis of the legal situation, the application of the law and general political circumstances, it can be assumed that neither political persecution nor inhuman or degrading treatment or punishment are practised.[99] Claimants from such designated countries are channelled into a shortened procedure, where the claimant may seek to rebut the presumption.[100] It is not yet clear what types of evidence must be produced to rebut the presumption, or what standard of proof must be satisfied.[101]

The problem with the general assessments implied by the safe country of origin device is precisely that they are general, and consequently operate at a quite different level from the realm of the particular which is central to the refugee definition laid down in the 1951 Convention. Their role can only be evidential, and while good information is the surest basis for good refugee decisions, there will always be a danger of *refoulement* wherever the general is preferred to the particular circumstances of the individual case.[102]

---

[98] *Grundgesetz* (Basic Law), art. 16a, para. 3; *Asylverfahrensgesetz*, art. 29a; Blay, S. and Zimmermann, A., 'Recent Changes in German Refugee Law: A Critical Assessment', 88 *AJIL* 361 (1994); Hailbronner, K., 'The Concept of "Safe Country" and Expeditious Asylum Procedures: A Western European Perspective', 5 *IJRL* 31 (1993). Also, section 15f, *Vreemdelingenwet* (amendment to Netherlands aliens law, in force 1 Jan. 1995, adding arrival from a country in which there is no serious risk of persecution to the manifestly unfounded category); art. 17, *Asylgesetz 1991* (Austrian asylum law); art. 16(2), *loi sur l'asile* (Swiss asylum law); Julien-Laferrière, 'Droit d'asile et politique d'asile en France', above n. 95.

[99] The original list included Bulgaria, Czech Republic, Gambia, Ghana, Hungary, Poland, Romania, Senegal and the Slovak Republic; Gambia was removed during 1995.

[100] *Grundgesetz* (Basic Law), art. 16a, para. 3; *Asylverfahrensgesetz*, art. 18a (airport arrivals). A claimant denied access under s. 15c, *Vreemdelingenwet* (Netherlands aliens law) may appeal to the *Vreemdelingenkamer* (special aliens court), but this has no suspensive effect; the claimant may apply for suspension of removal in summary proceedings which must be begun within twenty-four hours. See also the Swiss procedure for decisions of 'non-entrée en matière' = no inquiry into the merits: art. 16(2), *loi sur l'asile*—'Si le requérant vient (d'un pays sur), il n'est pas entré en matière sur sa demande ou son recours, *à moins que des indices de persécution n'apparaissent en cours d'audition*' (emphasis added); Bois, P., 'La non-entrée en matière selon l'art. 16 I litt. a LAS et le recours contre le retrait de l'effet suspensif', *Asyl*, 1990/4, 11.

[101] With respect to arrivals in Germany from 'safe third countries', a chamber of the federal constitutional court ruled in preliminary injunction proceedings that the (continuing) constitutional status of the right to asylum implies an individual right to present evidence of personal risk, for examination by the administrative courts: *BVerfG* 2 BvR 1507/93, 22 July 1993; *NZW*, Beilage 1/93. This interpretation, which significantly undercuts the otherwise *automatic* exclusion from the procedure, was under review by the full court at the end of 1995.

[102] Hailbronner therefore misstates the issues when he argues that art. 33 imposes no limit on the ways in which the objective elements in the refugee definition may be decided, and more particularly, when stating that safe country determinations 'involving elements of discretion must remain within the area of the government's political responsibility': 'Concept of "Safe Country" and Expeditious Asylum Procedures', 53, 56. This line of argument begs the question, whether an individual is at risk of persecution, which is precisely *not* a question of discretion, but of determination and therefore in itself subject to review.

2.2 GETTING TO 'YES'; GETTING TO 'NO'

The 1951 Convention/1967 Protocol do not require a refugee to have fled by reason of persecution, or that persecution should actually have occurred. The focus is more on the future, but there are inherent weaknesses in a system of protection founded, as international law would seem to require, upon essays in prediction. Although subjective fear is a relevant factor, the key issues are nevertheless factual, and the key question is whether there are sufficient facts to permit the finding that, if returned to his or her country of origin, the claimant would face a serious risk of harm. The credibility of the applicant and the weight of the evidence are thus of critical importance.

The UNHCR *Handbook on Procedures and Criteria for Determining Refugee Status,* prepared at the request of States members of the UNHCR Executive Committee, deals in large measure with some of the practical problems of determining refugee status, from the standard of proof to guidelines for the conduct of hearings. It acknowledges the general legal principle that the burden of proof lies on the person submitting a claim, but recalls that an applicant for refugee status is normally in a particularly vulnerable situation which may occasion serious difficulties in presenting the case.[103] Although an applicant must generally prove the *facts* on which he or she relies on a balance of probabilities, the legal test for the *risk* of persecution is not set so high.[104] In practice also, many of the facts relating to conditions in the country of origin will be common knowledge, or will be capable of proof on the basis of authoritative documentary information. In such circumstances, what counts is the personal situation of the applicant, who will often be unable to support his or her statements with 'hard evidence'. Ideally, these factors will influence both the procedure and evidentiary requirements, leading to a hearing in which the claimant is best able to present his or her story, and to decision-making premised on appropriate standards of proof.[105]

The minimum outline for refugee status procedures is relatively straightforward, as are the guidelines for examiners and decision-makers. The basic issues involve establishing the narrative of flight, including the reasons, clarifying country of origin conditions, and reaching an assessment of the whole in light of the essentially future orientation of the refugee definition. Asylum applicants have a responsibility to tell the truth and present their case fully, but counsel and examiners too have a duty and a role to play in the process of presentation. This is not a rule of law, but a general notion flowing from the nature of the

---

[103] *Handbook,* paras. 190, 196. Particular care will be needed in cases involving torture; see Dignam, Q., 'The Burden of Proof: Torture and Testimony in the Determination of Refugee Status in Australia', 4 *IJRL* 343 (1992).

[104] On evidence and the standard of proof, see *Handbook,* paras. 37–43; and for more detailed analysis, see above Ch. 2, s. 3.

[105] On evidentiary requirements and the benefit of the doubt, see *Handbook,* paras. 197–9; 203–5.

proceedings, where the ultimate objective, recognizing and protecting refugees, may otherwise get lost in the process.

Experience shows that the refugee status determination process is often unstructured. Decision-makers commonly rely on instinct and a feel for credibility, but with inadequate attention to the problems of assessment, identification of material facts, the weight of the evidence, and standards of proof. Even where decisions are felt to be correct, lack of confidence can result from systematically basing oneself on subjective assessments and failing to articulate clearly the various steps which lead to particular conclusions and the reasons which justify each stage. Such lack of confidence can increasingly undermine the capacity to deal effectively with the caseload, whatever the strengths or weaknesses of individual applications, and no matter how many unstructured decisions are in fact right.

Considered in its simplest form, the process of determining refugee status involves no more than the application of a legal formula to a particular set of facts. In practice, there are many inherent problems. Decision-makers, for example, must be able to elicit relevant information from the narrative which is the applicant's story; to assess the credibility of applicants, witnesses and experts, and to justify decisions on credibility; to weigh the evidence rationally; to determine and state what are the material facts; to apply the law to the facts; to take decisions and to justify those decisions by reference to reasons and principle. This in turn requires a degree of competence, even skill in the arts of questioning, interviewing, and examination, and the capacity to bring out the relevant elements from an individual narrative; the use of interpreters; the use of country of origin and jurisprudential information, and discrimination in the selection of such information; and evaluation and assessment.

In addition, a sound knowledge of the legal and procedural framework is called for, including its national and international aspects, and a sensitivity to other influential factors in the process, for example, the subjective element of fear, both as a dimension of the refugee definition and of the proceedings themselves; cultural factors which influence the narration of events, practices of truth and concealment, and the attribution of family and other relationships of greater and lesser dependence; and the relationship of group fear to individual cases.

2.2.1 *The interview, examination or hearing*

The object of the interview, examination or hearing is to encourage and obtain a narrative, and an understanding of the applicant's reasons for leaving, or refusing to return to, his or her country of origin. The process itself, whether conducted directly or through counsel, is one of communication, in which all behaviour, even silence or inactivity, may convey its own message. Moreover, communication operates on many levels, including the content or the information transmitted; and the context, which explains what the message is about. Context includes not only the words used and the manner of their presentation, but also the reactive aspects which flow from environment, questioning and expectations. For the message sent is not necessarily the message received, either because examiner and applicant move in different contexts and are misreading each other's responses; or because of an absence of shared symbols, such as language and culture; or because of the emotion attendant on the process (the intimidating aspect of proceedings, the trauma of recalling torture, sexual abuse, ill-treatment or other suffering).

In a process of case-by-case determination, the hearing must nevertheless be used to elucidate the applicant's reasons for flight and unwillingness to return, in the light of what is known about conditions in the country of origin, as gathered from what the applicant says, from other information provided, and from the decision-maker's own knowledge. The facts given must in turn be interpreted in light of the applicable legal criteria—the *well-foundedness* of the fear, whether what is feared is *persecution* and whether the persecution feared is *attributable* to any of the *reasons* specified in the 1951 Convention.

Often what is important in a person's narrative are *events*, and in particular, their *impact* on the claimant as an individual. Events may be *proximate and personal*, in the sense that the applicant has actually experienced, for example, torture, brutality, discrimination or imprisonment; or they may be more *distant*, though no less relevant, such as the related experience of others which the applicant (and the observer) perceives to bear upon his or her own case.[106] If there are patterns of persecution of those who share similar characteristics, that may suffice to raise a strong presumption of a reasonable possibility or serious risk of persecution. A credible information base, in turn, will help to show whether such patterns do in fact exist.

Having identified the events which are central to the applicant's story, the decision-maker must evaluate the *apprehensions*, the *fears* founded upon them. Are they *reasonable* in the circumstances; are they *well-founded*, in the sense of revealing a serious risk of persecution?

In articulating decisions on individual cases, a framework of rights and interests, reasons, restrictions and likelihood can be helpful. First, what are the *rights or interests* of the applicant that are claimed to be at risk? Where do they stand in the hierarchy of importance? Secondly, upon what *grounds*, for what *reasons*, are those rights or interests the object of attention? Next, what is the nature of the *restriction or measure* which it is feared may affect, repress, deny, or injure the

---

[106] The US Asylum Regulations, 8 CFR §208.13(b)(2), provide: '(i) In evaluating whether the applicant has sustained his burden of proving that he has a well-founded fear of persecution, the Asylum Officer or Immigration Judge shall not require the applicant to provide evidence that he would be singled out individually for persecution if: (A) He establishes that there is a pattern or practice in his country of nationality or last habitual residence of persecution of groups of persons similarly situated to the applicant on account of race, religion, nationality, membership in a particular social group, or political opinion; and (B) He establishes his own inclusion in and identification with such group of persons such that his fear of persecution upon return is reasonable.'

rights and interests in issue? Are questions of proportionality involved? Are there any competing State or community interests?

Finally, although this fact is integral to the whole process, how *likely* is it that the applicant may be the victim of measures which otherwise must be considered as persecution within the meaning of the Convention? Is there a reasonable, or serious possibility of such measures eventuating? Is the risk one which, on balance, can be discounted? Or is the nature of the interest such that even an otherwise remote possibility cannot be disregarded, particularly in light of the overall objective of the process, which is to provide protection, to ensure that dignity and integrity and fundamental human rights are assured.

The question of the likelihood of persecution is in practice inseparable from the personal circumstances of the individual considered in light of the general situation prevailing in the country of origin. Likelihood may vary over time and space, depending for example, on fluctuations in conflicts, or on the physical proximity of individuals to localities in which law and order do not prevail.

2.2.2 *Uses and abuses of country and other information*

The hearing rarely provides enough information, and although nowadays there are few limits to the sources that might be consulted, extensive searches often raise rather than answer questions. Credible and trustworthy information is nevertheless increasingly recognized as the essential foundation for good decisions. States and decision-makers have long maintained document collections of newspaper items, foreign broadcast reports, governmental and non-governmental human rights assessments, analyses from embassies in source countries of origin, and so forth.

The inherent difficulties of coherently assessing the authority of such disparate sources and the necessity to inform decision-makers spread across five regions led the Canadian Immigration and Refugee Board to establish, from the beginning, a Documentation Centre with the objective of becoming 'the principal resource in Canada for the provision of credible and trustworthy evidence relevant to the process of refugee determination, including country of origin information and information on jurisprudential questions'.[107] The Centre undertook

---

[107] Immigration and Refugee Board Documentation Centre (IRBDC), Mandate, Ottawa, 1989; the terminology of 'credible and trustworthy information' was taken from the *Immigration Act*, as amended. See generally, Rusu, S., 'The Development of Canada's Immigration and Refugee Board Documentation Centre', 1 *IJRL* 319 (1989); Houle, F., 'The Credibility and Authoritativeness of Documentary Information in Determining Refugee Status: The Canadian Experience', 6 *IJRL* 6 (1994). For examples of information and country papers from the IRBDC, see 'Haiti: The Impact of the September 1991 Coup (June 1992)', 4 *IJRL* 217 (1992); 'CIS, Baltic States and Georgia: Nationality Legislation' (April 1992), 4 *IJRL* 230 (1992); 'Bulgaria: Political Parties and Groups' (April 1991), 3 *IJRL* 273 (1991); 'Bulgaria: The Impact of Reform' (May 1991), 3 *IJRL* 288 (1991); 'Lebanon—Country Profile', 1 *IJRL* 331 (1989). On standards for human rights reporting and assessment, see Barsh, R. L., 'Measuring Human Rights: Problems of Methodology and Purpose', 15 *HRQ* 87 (1993); Donnelly, J. and Howard, R. E., 'Assessing Nations Human Rights Performance: A Theoretical Framework', 10 *HRQ* 214 (1988); also Symposium: Statistical Issues in the Field of Human Rights, 8 *HRQ* 592 (1986), including Stohl, M., Carleton, D., Lopez, G., and Samuels, S.,

to disseminate such information to the major actors in the refugee determination process, to provide 'objective, reliable and cogent analysis and evaluations', to acquire, disseminate and exchange information, and to establish legal and country of origin databases. The legal database, selected decisions from the Convention Refugee Determination Division, was later in turn opened on-line to the public by QuickLaw, the principal Canadian legal database provider.

As part of its commitment to producing and disseminating authoritative information, the IRB Documentation Centre (now the Documentation, Information and Research Branch—DIRB) based itself exclusively on material in the public domain, and guidelines published in 1990 stressed that every factual statement or report, in principle, should be corroborated by three different sources. The important principles of public domain information and corroboration have also been incorporated in the collection and dissemination practices of other centres, including UNHCR's Centre for Documentation on Refugees (CDR) which in turn has become an international focal point for collection, analysis and dissemination of bibliographic, legal, country, UN, UNHCR, and other relevant material.[108]

There can be no doubting the value of accurate, in-depth, up-to-date and trustworthy information in the refugee determination context. For example, refugees may have fled a country as a result of counter-insurgency operations. The fuller picture will show the historical origins of the conflict, such as resistance to dispossession of historical land rights; the protagonists (such as the military, representing a dominant non-indigenous elite); the policies (such as institutionalized or systemic discrimination against particular ethnic, linguistic, religious, or economic groups or classes); and the tactics (such as the abduction, torture and arbitrary killing of group representatives). A complete picture will never be available, but a comprehensive approach will contribute significantly to identifying refugee-related reasons for flight. Knowing past patterns and

'States Violation of Human Rights: Issues and Problems of Measurement', ibid., 592; Goldstein, R. J., 'The Limitations of Using Quantitative Data in Studying Human Rights Abuses', ibid., 607; Reiter, R. B., Zunzunequi, M. V. and Quiroga, J., 'Guidelines for Field Reporting of Basic Human Rights Violations', ibid., 628; Banks, D. L., 'The Analysis of Human Rights Data over Time', ibid., 654.

[108] CDR/UNHCR's resources include a variety of databases which can be consulted on-line, and through the Internet. In Jan. 1996, CDR published the bulk of its (externally accessible) information on CD-ROM, *RefWorld/RefMonde*. Databases of relevance to refugee determination include RefLeg (national refugee legislation); RefInt (refugee and human rights instruments, with States parties and reservations); RefCas (abstracts of refugee and refugee-related cases; a selection from the database is published in each issue of the *International Journal of Refugee Law*). Complementary databases include UNHCR Executive Committee documents; United Nations documents (General Assembly and Security Council resolutions; Commission of Human Rights documents; as well as a wide range of reports from governmental and non-governmental sources, such as the US Department of State, the Refugee Information Center of the US Immigration and Naturalization Service, the Canadian IRB, the UK Refugee Legal Centre, Amnesty International, Human Rights Watch, and the Minority Rights Group). See further below, Select Bibliography—Country Information Sources.

present conditions enables one to make reasonably accurate predictions about the future; about the way certain elements are likely to react and interact; and therefore about the degree of security awaiting those returned or returning to their country of origin.

Documentary evidence, particularly electronically accessible country reports, have a seductive air, often seeming sufficient to decide the case. But like any other material, documentary evidence must still be assessed and put in context, whether it relates personally to the claimant, or to conditions in the country of origin. Information of the latter kind often gives only a general impression, more or less detailed, of what is going on. Like the refugee determination process itself, it has the artificial quality of freezing time, in a way which can lead to single events acquiring greater significance than is their due.[109] Situations remain fluid, however. Recognizing that and drawing the right sorts of inference from evidence acknowledged as credible and trustworthy, are nevertheless the hallmarks of sound decisions.

2.2.3 *Assessing credibility and drawing inferences from the evidence*

Refugee claims made by people from different backgrounds raise a variety of issues. The cross-cultural dimension is obvious on some levels, but the decision-maker's understanding of credibility is almost always affected by the fact that he or she is dealing with 'filtered' knowledge. Simply considered, there are just two issues: first, could the applicant's story have happened, or could his or her apprehensions come to pass, on their own terms, given what we know from available country of origin information? Secondly, is the applicant personally believable? If the story is consistent with what is what is known about the country of origin, then the basis for the right inferences has been laid.

Inconsistencies must be assessed as material or immaterial. *Material* inconsistencies go to the heart of the claim, and concern, for example, the key experiences that are the cause of flight and fear. Being crucial to acceptance of the story, applicants ought in principle to be invited to explain contradictions and clarify confusions.

Inconsistency may be *immaterial* if it relates to incidentals, such as travel details, or distant dates of lesser significance. A statement from which different inferences can be drawn, however, is not an inconsistency, and generally a negative inference as to credibility ought only to be based on inconsistencies that are material or substantial; a series of minor inconsistencies and contradictions may nevertheless combine together to cast doubt on the truthfulness of the claimant. In practice, negative inferences will often be drawn from the claimant's destruction of documents, withholding of information, failure to provide evidence of

---

[109] See, for example, Norway's view in *1987*, namely, that since the conclusion of the peace agreement with India, 'there was no further basis for receiving asylum seekers from Sri Lanka'. UN doc. A/AC.96/SR.415 (1987) para. 52.

identity,[110] and persistent vagueness in response, particularly where the claimant is also unable or unwilling to provide a reasonable explanation.

Holes or inconsistencies that appear in the fabric of the narrative can be dealt with through question and answer, provided some care is used in the choice of questions. Research shows that errors in testimony increase dramatically in response to specific questions (25 per cent–33 per cent more errors), by comparison with spontaneous testimony given in the form of a free report.[111] Such free reports also tend to be sketchy and incomplete, however, and can be most effectively filled out by using 'open', rather than 'closed' questions. The open question solicits views, opinions, thoughts and feelings, founded on personal experience; the closed question invites the monosyllabic answer, yes or no; a simple statement of fact; a closed answer.[112]

The process of narration is also a process of communication, and all behaviour, even silence or inactivity, may convey its own message. But the message sent is not necessarily the message received. Participants misread each other's responses; they lack a vocabulary of shared symbols; they may be affected by the emotion of the moment or of past suffering.

Although witness behaviour, such as the manner of expression, politeness, firmness of speech, nervousness or openness, is sometimes considered a good guide to credibility, cultural differences will often invalidate this approach. Similarly, to work successfully, cross-examination requires a fairly sophisticated understanding of a language common to all the parties, but is quite unsuited to the questioning of one not fluent, or where question and answer must pass through the medium of an interpreter.[113]

Indeed, the use of interpreters in a manner which will best elicit the narrative of the claimant is something of an art.[114] Translation is *not* a mechanical process, but a two-way, sometimes three-way street, that places particular responsibilities on every participant in the refugee determination process. The interpreter is both link and obstacle; *link*, because he or she facilitates an oral dialogue; and *obstacle*, because the questioner's intentions may be misunderstood, either because of a failure to communicate clearly and coherently, or because both parties do not possess a common basis of understanding and values. What the

---

[110] CRR, 14 sept. 1987, 28.685, Opoku Agyemang. *Doc. réf.*, no. 35, 11/20 mars 1988, Suppl., CJ., 1: 'en l'absence de documents permettant d'établir l'identité réelle de l'intéressé . . . son recours n'est pas recevable . . .'

[111] 'Free reports', however, can be far more time-consuming.

[112] For example, ask not, 'When did you leave your country?' but, 'Why did you leave, . . . and when was this?' Not, 'Were you ever mistreated?' but, 'Please describe any difficulties you had . . .' Not, 'Do you like your government?' but, 'How do you feel about your government?' Not, 'Are you willing to return?' but, 'How do you feel about returning, and what do you think might happen?'

[113] On the limits of cross-examination, see Eggleston, Sir Richard, 'What is Wrong with the Adversary System?' 49 *Australian Law Journal* 428 (1975); also, 'Is Your Cross-Examination Really Necessary?' *Proceedings of the Medico-Legal Society of Victoria*, vol. IX, 84 (1961).

[114] See Kälin, W., 'Troubled Communication: Cross–Cultural Misunderstandings in the Asylum Hearing', 20 *Int. Mig. Rev.* 230 (1986); also, in another not unrelated context, Mirdal, G. M., 'The Interpreter in Cross-Cultural Therapy', 26 *Int. Mig.* 327 (1988)

applicant say's comes across *filtered* and then has to pass by the decision-maker's own baggage of preconceptions. Accepted universals, like time, family, common sense, are upset by other peoples' world views.[115]

Refugee claims are not like other cases; they rarely present hard facts, let alone positive proof or corroboration. More often than not, the decision-maker must settle for inferences instead, that is, conclusions drawn from the generally inadequate material available. In the absence of hard evidence, the possibility of persecution must be inferred from the personal circumstances of the applicant, and from the general situation prevailing in the country of origin. The credibility of testimony is thus both an essential pre-condition to the drawing of inferences relating to refugee status; and a matter of inference in itself. Inference in this context does not mean the strict logical consequences of known premises, or the process of reaching results by deduction or induction from something known or assumed. Rather, it is the practical business of arriving at a conclusion which, although not logically derivable from the assumed or known, *nonetheless possesses some degree of probability relative to those premises.*

Conjecture must be distinguished from inference, though the line is often difficult to draw:

A conjecture may be plausible but it is of no legal value, for its essence is that of a mere guess. An inference in the legal sense, on the other hand, is a deduction from the evidence, and if it is a reasonable deduction it may have the validity of legal proof. The attribution of an occurrence to a cause is ... always a matter of inference.[116]

Thus, an inference as to the facts (what happened), or as to the credibility of the claimant (is he or she to be believed) must be based on the evidence and be reasonably open to the decision-maker.[117]

3. Selected issues

3.1 CHILDREN AS ASYLUM SEEKERS

A preliminary issue in all cases involving children and young persons, is whether they are accompanied. In principle, this has no bearing on whether they are

[115] Alvarez, L. and Loucky, J., 'Inquiry and Advocacy: Attorney-Expert Collaboration in the Political Asylum Process', 11 *NAPA Bulletin* 43 (1992) (American Anthropological Association); with reference to claims involving Maya from Huehuetenango, Guatemala, the authors examine practical problems in using expert testimony in asylum proceedings, including the role of the anthropologist in countering political interference, cultural insensitivity, lack of impartiality, and lack of information.

[116] *Minister for Employment and Immigration* v. *Satiacum* [1989] FCJ NO. 505; (1989) 99 NR 171, Federal Court of Appeal of Canada, citing Lord MacMillan in *Jones* v. *Great Western Railway Co.* (1930) 47 TLR 39 at 45.

[117] For examples of the application of this rule from Canadian case law see *Ye* v. *Minister of Employment and Immigration* [1992] FCJ No. 584; *Anthonypillai* v. *MEI* [1992] FCJ No. 944; *Lai* v. *MEI* [1989] FCJ No. 826, (1989) 8 ImmLR (2d) 245; *Owusu-Ansah* v. *MEI* [1989] FCJ No. 442, (1989) ImmLR (2d) 106; *Frimpong* v. *MEI* [1989] FCJ No. 441.

refugees, but may affect how their claims are dealt with, as well as the solutions which may be proposed. Unaccompanied children, in particular, need special attention, and a guardian or other person competent to protect their interests.[118]

The UNHCR *Handbook* locates the refugee status of accompanied dependants, including children, in the context of family unity. If the head of the family is recognized as a refugee then, all things being equal,[119] the 'dependants are normally granted refugee status according to the principle of family unity'.[120] Practical reasons and procedural convenience subordinate individual claims to an alternative principle, and the child's status is relegated to that of dependency.[121] Whereas this may be sufficient and reflect social realities in the case of accompanied children, a more comprehensive approach is required for the unaccompanied in search of protection. Here the UNHCR *Handbook*, drafted some ten years before the Convention on the Rights of the Child, still focuses on refugee status as a primary consideration. With this underlying premise, the *Handbook* somewhat misleadingly invokes 'mental development and maturity' as the criterion for determining the existence of a well-founded fear of persecution.[122]

The approach to refugee status in terms of maturity is misguided for several reasons. First, there is no necessary connection between any particular level of maturity and the existence of a well-founded fear of persecution. Secondly, children are as capable as adults of feeling fear; their maturity may affect merely their capacity to understand the events or conditions which are the basis of that fear. Thirdly, a child's maturity is irrelevant to the question whether he or she may be persecuted. Fourthly, and above all, the principle of the *best interests of the child* requires that decisions on behalf of the child be taken on the basis of all the circumstances, including his or her personal situation and the conditions

[118] Cf. art. 22(1), Convention on the Rights of the Child: 'States Parties shall take appropriate measures to ensure that a child who is seeking refugee status . . . shall, whether unaccompanied or accompanied by his or her parents or by any other person, receive appropriate protection and humanitarian assistance in the enjoyment of applicable rights set forth in the present Convention and in other international human rights or humanitarian instruments to which the said States are Parties.'

[119] Provided, for example, that the dependant is not excludable, or a citizen having the protection of another country.

[120] UNHCR, *Handbook on Procedures and Criteria for Determining Refugee Status*, (1979), paras. 181–8, 184.

[121] The *Handbook* nevertheless leaves open the possibility of individual entitlement: 'the principle of family unity operates in favour of dependants, and *not against them*': ibid., para. 185 (emphasis added).

[122] Ibid., para. 214. Cf. para. 215: 'It can be assumed that—in the absence of indications to the contrary—a person of 16 or over may be regarded as sufficiently mature to have a well-founded fear of persecution. Minors under 16 years of age may normally be assumed not to be sufficiently mature.' See Commission permanente de recours des refugies, (Belgium), 12 mai 1993, No. 93/021/R1115(Iè ch.franc.), holding that a 16 year old was sufficiently mature to claim refugee status in his own right: *RDDE*, No. 77, jan.-fev. 1994, 41. See also 'Note on Refugee Children': UN doc. EC/SCP/46 (31 Aug. 1987), paras. 14–16. Ch. 8, UNHCR, *Refugee Children: Guidelines on Protection and Care*, (1994), updates the *Handbook*, but maintains an emphasis on status determination.

prevailing in the child's country of origin. The welfare of the child, and the special protection and assistance which are due in accordance with international standards, prevail over the narrow concerns of refugee status. What is required is a decision for and on behalf of the unaccompanied child, which takes account of the best interests of the child and effectively contributes to his or her full development, preferably in the environment of the family. To channel children in flight into refugee status procedures will often merely interpose another obstacle between the child and a solution.

That being said, however, in some jurisdictions a successful refugee claim may be the only way by which to access child welfare services. The United Kingdom immigration rules, for example, appear to be premised on the assumption that a child arriving alone is in need of protection and assistance. So far as such child may apply for asylum, the rules require priority treatment, close attention to welfare needs, and care in interviewing.[123] Nevertheless, the child's best interests are a primary concern. The likelihood of risk of harm in his or her country of origin must be factored in, but in many cases the most appropriate solution may still be reunion with family members who have remained behind.[124] Equally, prolonged detention in a closed camp has a serious negative effect on any child's development, and needs to be avoided through prompt and appropriate decision-making.[125]

3.2 EMERGENT SOCIAL GROUPS[126]

In the United States case of *Sanchez-Trujillo* v. *INS*, asylum applicants from El Salvador based their claim on membership of a class that included young, urban, working class males, who were further identified as unwilling to serve in the armed forces of their country.[127] Anticipating the need to 'identify a cognizable group', the claimants adduced fairly cogent statistical evidence showing the numbers of such young, urban non-combatant males who figured among the disappeared and the dead, to which they added personal testimony and experience. The court found little guidance in the UNHCR *Handbook* reference to 'persons of similar background, habits or social status', considering instead that a social group implied 'a collection of people closely affiliated with each other who are actuated by some common impulse or interest'. Moreover, 'a voluntary associational relationship' was also required, 'which imparts some common

---

[123] For a particularly clear guide to UK law and procedure, see Guedalla, V., 'Representing unaccompanied refugee children in the asylum process', *Childright*, Dec. 1994, No. 112. Also, Carlier, J. -Y., 'La demande d'asile introduite par un mineur non accompagné', *RDDE*, 19–20 mai 1994, 94–102.

[124] Some two thirds of the 'best interests' decisions by the Special Committees established under the CPA were for reunion with family members still in Vietnam; see 'Programming for the Benefit of Refugee Children': UN doc. EC/SC.2/CRP.15 (25 Aug. 1993), para. 15; cf. O'Donnell, D., 'Resettlement or Repatriation: Screened-out Vietnamese Child Asylum Seekers and the Convention on the Rights of the Child', 6 *IJRL* 382 (1994).

[125] See McCallin, 'Living in Detention'.

[126] On 'social group' generally, see Ch. 2, s. 4.2.4.   [127] 801 F.2d 1571 (9th Cir. 1986).

characteristic that is fundamental to their identity'. In the court's view, 'family members' were a prototypical example, conveniently meeting its criteria of affiliation, common interest, or association. The family also has the advantage of being finite; it is usually small, readily identifiable, and terminable with difficulty. Potentially larger categories, including so-called statistical groups, such as the red-headed, the blue-eyed, or the over six-feet tall,[128] were dismissed, even though such arbitrary classifications have been the basis for persecutory practices in the past. Like others before and since, this court was evidently anxious to guard against 'sweeping demographic divisions' that encompass a plethora of different lifestyles, varying interests, diverse cultures and contrary political leanings.

3.2.1 The possible categories of social group

The social group category has given rise to several, not always easily reconcilable, judgments in Canada. Many claims have been based on the consequences of China's 'one-child policy', so far as parents of one or more children might run the risk of forcible sterilization; others have been lodged by women who feared 'domestic' violence in their own country and were unable to obtain protection locally; while one leading case concerned a former terrorist group member, who feared retribution at the hands of the group.[129]

In *Cheung*, the Federal Court of Appeal held that 'women in China who have (more than) one child and are faced with forced sterilization satisfy enough of the ... criteria to be considered a particular social group'.[130] The conjunction of group criteria and the risk of consequences, however, is unsatisfactory from a theoretical and analytical perspective.[131] In *Chan*, another case based on fear of forced sterilization (this time by a father), a majority of the Supreme Court dismissed the appeal on the ground that the appellant had not discharged the burden of proof, with respect either to the subjective or objective elements.[132]

[128] Cf. Helton, A. C., 'Persecution on Account of Membership in a Social Group as a Basis for Refugee Status', 15 *Col. Hum. Rts. L.R.* 39 (1983).
[129] See, among others, *Cheung* v. *MEI* [1993] 2 FC 314 (Federal Court of Appeal; hereafter *Cheung*); *Ward* v. *Attorney-General of Canada* [1993] 2 SCR 689 (Supreme Court of Canada; hereafter *Ward*); and *Chan* v. *MEI* [1993] 3 FC 675 (Federal Court of Appeal), [1995] SCJ No. 78 (Supreme Court of Canada; hereafter *Chan*).
[130] [1993] 2 FC 314, 320; the court in *Chan* considered that the words 'more than' had been omitted accidentally. The court in *Cheung* relied on the social group test propounded in *MEI* v. *Mayers* [1993] 1 FC 154 (Federal Court-Trial Division): '(1) a natural or non-natural group of persons with (2) similar shared background, habits, social status, political outlook, education, values, aspirations, history, economic activity or interests, often interests contrary to those of the prevailing government, and (3) sharing basic, innate, unalterable characteristics, consciousness, and solidarity or (4) sharing a temporary but voluntary status, with the purpose of their association being so fundamental to their human dignity that they should not be required to alter it'.
[131] Cf. Macklin, A., '*Canada (Attorney-General)* v. *Ward*: A Review Essay', 6 *IJRL* 362 (1994).
[132] A majority of the Federal Court of Appeal, [1993] 3 FC 675, dismissed the claim, Heald, JA holding that the facts did not support a finding of sufficient risk of sterilization, and Desjardins, JA, that the group of which the claimant asserted membership was not a particular social group within the meaning of the Convention. See also Board of Immigration Appeals, *Chang*, A27 202–715, 12

Ward concerned a resident of Northern Ireland who had voluntarily joined
the Irish National Liberation Army (INLA), a terrorist group dedicated to the
political union of Ulster and the Irish Republic. Detailed to guard innocent
hostages, he facilitated their escape on learning that they were to be executed.
The INLA in turn 'court-martialled' and tortured him and decided that he
should be killed. Amongst other grounds, he claimed to fear persecution by
reason of membership in the particular social group constituted by the INLA.
The Supreme Court of Canada held that the group of INLA members were not
a 'particular social group'; its membership was not characterized by an innate
characteristic or an unchangeable historical fact, while its objectives also could
not be said to be so fundamental to the human dignity of its members.[133]

The Supreme Court in *Ward* approved the approach adopted in *Mayers,
Cheung* and *Acosta*,[134] and recognized also that the process of interpreting particular social group should reflect certain themes, namely, human rights and anti-
discrimination. It considered that there were three possible categories of social
group: (1) those defined by an innate or unchangeable characteristic, for example, individuals fearing persecution by reason of gender, linguistic background
and sexual orientation; (2) those whose members voluntarily associate for
reasons so fundamental to their human dignity that they should not be forced
to forsake the association, for example, human rights activists;[135] and (3) those
associated by a former voluntary status, unalterable due to its historical permanence. Given that 'one's past is an immutable part of the person',[136] the third
category belongs essentially to the first.

3.2.2 *The categories of association*

The *Ward* judgment is of major importance on a variety of issues, but the analysis of the social group question raises a number of concerns. What is meant by
'groups associated by a former voluntary status', is far from clear. The Court
said that this sub-category was included 'because of historical intentions'.
However, there is no evidence to suggest that those apparently intended to benefit from the social group provision, the former capitalists of eastern Europe, were

May 1989 (Int. Dec. 3107), not finding the birth control policy persecutory on its face, but a matter of case by case evaluation. The ruling in practice was significantly modified by policy instructions.

[133] Why the refugee claim was based on social group was never clear. The claimant's fear was
not based on membership, but on his actions in a political context, motivated by conscience; political opinion was first raised by UNHCR in its intervenor brief; see *Ward*, [1993] 2 SCR 689, 740.
Also, Bagambiire, D., 'Terrorism and Convention Refugee Status in Canadian Immigration Law:
The Social Group Category according to *Ward v. Canada*', 5 *IJRL* 183 (1993), which considers the
earlier Federal Court of Appeal decision.

[134] See above, Ch. 2, s. 4.2.4.

[135] In *Cheung*, particular weight was attached to a woman's reproductive liberty as a basic right
fundamental to human dignity. Women in China who have more than one child were 'united or
identified by a purpose which is so fundamental to their human dignity that they should not be
required to alter it': [1993] 2 FC 314, 322.

[136] *Ward*, [1993] 2 SCR 689, 739.

ever formally associated one with another. They may have been, but equally they may not. What counted at the time was the fact that they were not only *internally* linked by having engaged in a particular type of (past) economic activity, but also *externally* defined, partly if not exclusively, by the perceptions of the new ruling class.[137]

As the Supreme Court in fact recognized, capitalists were persecuted historically, 'not because of their contemporaneous activities but because of their past status *as ascribed to them by the Communist leaders.*'[138] In this sense, they were persecuted not because they were *former* capitalists, but because they *were* former capitalists; not because of what they had done in the past, but because of what they were considered to be today; not because of any actual or imagined voluntary association, but because of the perceived threat of the class (defined *incidentally* by what they had once done) to the new society. The approach of the new ruling class to the capitalist class reveals a clear overlap between *past* activity and/or status and the perception of a *present* threat to the new society.[139]

Having proposed a 'limiting' approach to social group,[140] it is hardly surprising that the Supreme Court at first seems conservative in its list of innate or unchangeable characteristics: 'such bases as gender, linguistic background and sexual orientation'.[141] In fact, this approach is not as restrictive as might appear; the list is clearly illustrative, and in principle other innate or unchangeable factors relevant to non-discrimination in the enjoyment of fundamental rights may also be included, such as ethnic or cultural factors, education, family background, property, birth or other status, national or social origin; in short, the very sorts of *social* factors that are or ought to be irrelevant to the enjoyment of fundamental human rights.

Economic activity, shared values, outlook and aspirations should not be excluded, because either they are part of the unchangeable past,[142] or they describe, if only generally, the idea of individuals associated for reasons

---

[137] New ruling *social group*? Thus, in the sense of the text, the government of the Socialist Republic of Vietnam announced its intention to 'restructure' society and abolish the 'bourgeoisie': Foreign Language Press, *The Hoa in Vietnam*, Hanoi, 1978.

[138] *Ward*, [1993] 2 SCR 689, 731, emphasis supplied.

[139] In one sense, the 'grouping' will often be independent of will, so that the requirement of voluntary associational relationship, if adopted in all cases, not only introduces an unjustified, additional evidential burden on the claimant (under the guise of interpretation), but also departs from the jurisprudence of earlier years, admittedly sparse, which nonetheless recognized the existence of a social group among individuals, who displayed little if any *voluntary* association relationship with others similarly situated. See, however, La Forest J, diss., in *Chan* [1993] SCJ No. 78, para. 87, also quoting Macklin, 'Review Essay', at 375.

[140] 'Foreign governments should be accorded leeway in their definition of what constitutes antisocial behaviour of their nationals. Canada should not overstep its role in the international sphere by having its responsibility engaged whenever any group is targeted': *Ward*, [1993] 2 SCR 689, 738–9. See also *Chan* [1995] SCJ No. 78, La Forest J, diss., para. 65.

[141] *Ward*, [1993] 2 SCR 689, 739.

[142] In which case it is irrelevant that economic activity is not a matter of fundamental human rights; what counts is that the activity 'links' people who then, on the basis of perceptions among the ruling class or society at large, are subject to treatment amounting to persecution.

fundamental to their human dignity, and the sort of 'value' association which voluntary participants ought not to be required to forsake.

3.2.3 Common victimization

In *Ward*, the Supreme Court was clearly of the view that an association of people should not be characterized as a particular social group, 'merely by reason of their common victimization as the objects of persecution'.[143] The essential question, however, is whether the persecution feared is the *sole* distinguishing factor that results in the identification of the particular social group. Taken out of context, this question is too simple, for wherever persecution under the law is the issue, legislative provisions will be but one facet of broader policies and perspectives, *all* of which contribute to the identification of the group, adding to its pre-existing characteristics.

For example, parents with one or more children can be considered as an identifiable social group because of (1) their factual circumstances and (2) the way in which they are treated in law and by society. Arbitrary laws might subject red-headed people, mothers of one or more children, and thieves to a variety of penalties, reflecting no more than the whims of the legislator. Where such laws have a social and political context and purpose, and touch on fundamental human rights, such as personal integrity or reproductive control, then a rational basis exists for identifying red-headed people and mothers of one or more children as a particular social group, *in their particular circumstances*, while excluding thieves.[144] For the purposes of the Convention definition, internal linking factors cannot be considered in isolation, but only in conjunction with external defining factors, such as perceptions, policies, practices and laws.

Treatment amounting to persecution thus remains relevant in identifying a particular social group, where it reflects State policy towards a particular class. As the penal law embodies State policy on criminals, so other laws and practices may illustrate policy towards individuals or groups who assert fundamental rights, for example, with respect to family life or conscience.[145] In both cases, the penalties help to identify the group at risk; so far as they also exceed the limits of reasonableness and proportionality, they may also cross the line from permissible 'sanction' for contravention of a particular social policy into impermissible persecution.

3.2.4 Women, social group and refugee status

From the perspective of the 1951 Convention, the problem with much of the violence against women is precisely that it is perceived, either as 'domestic' or as individual and non-attributable to the State or other political structure. The term 'domestic violence' is commonly used to describe spousal violence applied

---

[143] *Ward*, [1993] 2 SCR 689, 729; also *Chan* [1993] 3 FC 675 (FCA).
[144] See Macklin, 'A Review Essay', at 371–8.
[145] See above Ch. 2, s. 4.3.2.2, on conscientious objection to military service.

in a domestic setting, out of the public eye, and for reasons personal to the aggressor. It is 'private', unlike the 'public' dimension to so much political, ethnic or religious persecution, and it tends to serve individual, usually male, ends, such as aggression, sadism, oppression or subjection.[146] Violence is non-attributable when perpetrated by random individuals for personal reasons, including soldiers, policemen, or other holders of public authority, such as civil officials or State religious leaders, when acting outside or beyond authority.

Executive Committee Conclusion No. 39 (1985) merely recognizes that States, 'in the exercise of their sovereignty', may interpret 'social group' to include women who face harsh or inhuman treatment for having transgressed the social mores of their community.[147] Many societies have long turned a blind eye to domestic violence, on the ground that unless it was 'excessive', it was not a proper matter for State involvement or State penalties. The *policy* implicit in such a laissez-faire approach, not surprisingly, has found its reaction in the proposition that *all* violence against women is political, or in its slightly less radical variant, that all violence against women should be presumed to be political unless and until the State is shown to provide effective protection. Thus, it is argued, being a woman is a sufficiently political statement in itself, so far as violence against women, domestic, sexual or public, is part of the process of oppression.

Within the scheme of international protection offered by the 1951 Convention relating to the Status of Refugees and its national counterparts, such an approach has found no support. Women claimants may yet come within the refugee definition, drawing by analogy on rights-based approaches in other circumstances, on increasing sensitivity to the frequently systemic character of denials of rights to women, and on underlying obligations incumbent on all States to protect the human rights of everyone within their territory and subject to their jurisdiction. The 1993 UN Declaration on the Elimination of Violence against Women,[148] for example, acknowledges that all States have an obligation to work towards its eradication.

What might at first glance appear 'domestic' may enter the public arena and therefore the traditional refugee domain when it passes into the ambit of State-sanctioned or State-tolerated oppression. This raises evidential considerations of some magnitude, however, and at a certain point cases call rather for a value judgment, than a purely factual assessment of conditions in this or that country.

---

[146] See generally, Castel, J. R., 'Rape, Sexual Assault and the Meaning of Persecution', 4 *IJRL* 39 (1992); Thomas, D. Q. and Beasley, M. E., 'Domestic Violence as a Human Rights Issue', 15 *HRQ* 36 (1993).

[147] For full text, see below Annexe 3; also UNHCR, 'Note on Refugee Women and International Protection': UN doc. EC/SCP/39 (July 1985), para. 7, citing a similar resolution adopted by the European Parliament in 1984. The first edition of this work suggested that it *may* be the case that the discrimination suffered by women in many countries on account of their sex alone, though severe, is not yet sufficient to justify the conclusion that they, as a group, have a fear of persecution within the meaning of the Convention. Times have changed.

[148] UNGA res. 48/104, 20 Dec. 1993. See also 1994 Inter-American Convention on the Prevention, Punishment and Eradication of Violence against Women: 33 *ILM* 1534 (1994).

There are nevertheless precedents recognizing the essentially 'political' purposes of other gender-related persecution, including the enforcement of conformity to a particular religious, cultural or social view of society; such persecution has included torture or oppression by State agents at the individual level, as well as more generalized harassment by sections of the public.[149] Rape by a soldier, policeman or person in authority, for example, may be characterized as the unauthorized private act of an individual, and therefore not persecution. An examination of the context in which the act takes place, however, may disclose a manifestation of public State authority; the conditions and the occasion may as much be the responsibility of the State, as the failure to provide an effective remedy. For women suffer particular forms of persecution *as women*, and not just or specifically because of political opinion or ethnicity. Even though men too may be sexually abused, their gender is not a consideration. Women may be raped because of their politics, but they are also raped because they are women and because rape inflicts a particular indignity and promotes a particular structure of male power.[150]

Even if 'domestic' violence is given a public, political face, there is still some distance between the act and the *reasons* in the Convention definition.[151] The State is unwilling or unable to prevent or punish such violence as might otherwise amount to persecution, but *why* is the claimant so affected? The language of political opinion does not readily fit, and the question is whether membership of a particular social group will establish the sufficient link.

If it is assumed that gender, in principle, is a sufficient identifying factor held in common, so that all women may comprise a social group,[152] is this sufficient for Convention purposes to show that the woman who faces domestic or even public violence is persecuted *for reasons of* membership in that group? The answer may lie in further sub-categorization. Taking account of conditions in a particu-

---

[149] Art. 1 of the 1993 UN Declaration interprets violence against women widely: 'any act of gender-based violence that results in, or is likely to result in, physical, sexual or psychological harm or suffering to women, including threats of such acts, coercion or arbitrary deprivation of liberty, whether occurring in public or private life'. Such violence is seen not so much in terms of individual behaviour, but as a 'manifestation of historically unequal power relationships between men and women', which may occur in the family, in the general community, or be perpetrated or condoned by the State.

[150] Spijkerboer, citing examples from former Yugoslavia, argues that gender is rarely the reason for persecution, but a factor that dictates the form of persecution; that is, the fact of risk is not related to gender, because had they been men they would still have been persecuted, though in different ways: *Women and Refugee Status: Beyond the public/private distinction*. Emancipation Council. (1994), 26–7.

[151] See Kelly, N., 'Guidelines for Women's Asylum Claims', 6 *IJRL* 517 (1994); Mawani, N., 'Introduction to the Immigration and Refugee Board of Canada Guidelines on Gender-Related Persecution', 5 *IJRL* 240 (1993); 'IRB: Guidelines on Gender-Related Persecution', 5 *IJRL* 278 (1993); Hausammann, C., 'Die Beurteilung frauenspezifischer Verfolgung in Asylverfahren', Erster Teil, *Asyl*, 1991/4 7; Zweiter Teil, 1992/1, 3.

[152] Spijkerboer, however, would characterize forcible sterilization as persecution for political opinion, concluding that social group premised on gender 'depoliticises' women's position, and denies the quintessential role their convictions play in their claim to refugee status: *Women and Refugee Status*, 41, 46.

lar country, it may become clear that the group within the group is identifiable by reference to the fact of their liability, exposure, or vulnerability to violence in an environment that denies them protection. Such a social group of women may be additionally identifiable by reference to other descriptors, such as race or class, which leads to their being denied protection in circumstances in which other women in the same society are not (so) affected or deprived. They face violence amounting to persecution, and other denials of rights, because of their gender, their race and their class and *because they are unprotected*.[153] Clearly, gender *is* used by societies to organize or distribute rights and benefits; where it is also used to deny rights or inflict harm, the identification of a gender-defined social group has the advantage of external confirmation.[154]

3.2.5 A social view of 'social group'

Although courts and tribunals in different jurisdictions have wrestled with the concept of particular social groups, none has so far produced a coherent, cogent approach valid for all times and places. Clearly, there are social groups other than those that share immutable characteristics, or which combine for reasons fundamental to their human dignity. Drawing the contours of such groups by reference to the likelihood of persecution confuses the issues of identity and risk, despite the fact that each is relevant to the other. The individualized approach of the Convention refugee definition requires attention to personal circumstances, time and place, all of which may combine to distinguish those at risk from others who may share similar characteristics and yet not be in danger. Although there will be policy pressures to limit refugee categories in periods of increased population displacement, there is no rational basis for denying protection to individuals who, even if divided in lifestyle, culture, interests and politics, may yet be linked across another dimension of affinity.

If such groups are not excluded as a matter of policy, then decision-makers may need to accept that, with respect to a particular social group, there is

---

[153] Laws of general application can operate similarly. The refugee sub-group, that is, the group within the larger group of those conforming or reluctantly conforming, is identified by the fact of prosecution and/or liability to sanction, considered together with the assertion by the sub-group of certain fundamental rights, such as those relating to conscience or belief.

[154] This approach has certain inherent disadvantages, however. Macklin, for example, identifies the 'risk factor' in both *Mayers* (a domestic violence case; above n. 130) and *Cheung* (a forcible sterilization case; above n. 130) as one's identity as a woman: 'A Review Essay', at 377. While helpfully inclusive at one level, such a gender base also *excludes*, leaving other similarly situated claimants potentially unprotected; for example, a male claimant threatened with forcible sterilization; or the battered partner in a same-sex relationship whose gender evidently is *not* a factor in his or her victimization. See Vivian Smith, 'Opening doors on gay partner abuse', *Globe and Mail*, 29 July 1993; Renzetti, C. M., 'Building a second closet: third party responses to victims of Lesbian partner abuse', 38 *Family Relations* 157 (1989); Island, D. and Letellier, P., *Men who beat the men who love them*, (1991). The fact that proportionately more women are beaten by men in heterosexual relationships provides no rational justification for denying protection in other relationships, and these questions put in issue the value or appropriateness of trying to force the refugee protection system alone to provide answers to problems for which it is singularly ill-equipped.

probably no single coherent definition, but rather a set of variables, a 'range of permissible descriptors'. These would include, for example, (1) the fact of voluntary association, where such association is equivalent to a certain *value* and not merely the result of accident or incident, unless that in turn is affected by (3); (2) involuntary linkages, such as family, shared past experience, or innate, unalterable characteristics; and (3) the perception of others.

In the cases considered above, the courts inclined towards relatively simple bases of categorization, relying on innate or unchangeable characteristics and notions of association for reasons fundamental to human dignity. There are many 'natural' meanings of 'social', however, which have received little or no attention, but which may also prove a sufficient and appropriate basis for defining or describing social groups for the purposes of the Convention. Beyond the ideas of individuals associated, allied or combined, characterized by mutual intercourse, united by some common tie, stand those who, in simple sociological terms, are *groups in society*, in the ordinary, everyday sense which describes the constitution or make-up of the community at large. This is most evident in the use of language to describe, for example, the landlord class, the working class, the ruling class, the bourgeoisie, the middle class, even the criminal class. The principle of non-discrimination, linked to fundamental rights, serves to distinguish between those deserving protection, because their social origins or situation now put them at risk; and those who do not, such as those who are liable to penalties for breach of the law, considered in its ordinary, common law sense.

If a sociological approach is adopted to the notion of groups in society, then apparently unconnected and unallied individuals may indeed satisfy the criteria: mothers; mothers and families with two children; women at risk of domestic violence; capitalists; former capitalists; homosexuals;[155] and so forth. Whether they then qualify as refugees having a well-founded fear of persecution by reason of their membership in a particular social group will depend on answers to related questions, including the perceptions of the group shared by other groups or State authorities, policies and practices vis-à-vis the group, and the risk, if any, of treatment amounting to persecution.

3.3 INTERPRETATION OF INTERNATIONAL INSTRUMENTS: THE USES AND LIMITS OF TRAVAUX PRÉPARATOIRES

No treaty is self-applying and the meaning of words, such as 'well-founded', 'persecution', 'expel', 'return' or '*refouler*,' is by no means self-evident. The Vienna Convention on the Law of Treaties confirms that a treaty 'shall be interpreted in good faith in accordance with the ordinary meaning to be given to the terms of the treaty in the context and in the light of its object and purpose'.[156] For the

---

[155] See *Navaez v. Canada (Minister of Citizenship and Immigration)* [1995] FCJ No. 219.

[156] Art. 31(1), 1969 Vienna Convention on the Law of Treaties: UN doc. A/CONF.39/27; Brownlie, I., *Basic Documents in International Law*, (4th ed., 1995), 388. Art. 31(2) defines 'context' as follows: 'The context for the purpose of the interpretation of a treaty shall comprise, in addition to the text, including its preamble and annexes: (a) any agreement relating to the treaty which was

1951 Convention relating to the Status of Refugees, this means interpretation by reference to the object and purpose of extending the protection of the international community to refugees, and assuring to 'refugees the widest possible exercise of . . . fundamental rights and freedoms'.[157]

Article 31(3) provides further that account shall also be taken of any subsequent agreement between the parties, or any subsequent practice bearing on the interpretation of the treaty, as well as 'any relevant rules of international law applicable in the relations between the parties'. This subsequent agreement and practice can be derived or inferred, amongst others, from the actions of the States parties at diplomatic level, including the adoption or promulgation of unilateral interpretative declarations; and at the national level, in the promulgation of laws and the implementation of policies and practices. The rules of treaty interpretation permit recourse to 'supplementary means of interpretation' (including the preparatory work, or *travaux préparatoires*) only where the meaning of the treaty language is 'ambiguous or obscure; or leads to a result which is manifestly absurd or unreasonable'.[158] If the meaning of the treaty is clear from its text when viewed in light of its context, object and purpose, supplementary sources are unnecessary and inapplicable, and recourse to such sources is discouraged.[159]

During the Conference leading up to the Vienna Convention on the Law of Treaties, the United States and the United Kingdom adopted opposing positions on resort to preparatory works, the former favouring their use and the latter, together with France, arguing against the practice. The United Kingdom objected that,

preparation work was almost invariably confusing, unequal and partial: confusing because it commonly consisted of the summary records of statements made during the process of negotiations, and early statements on the positions of delegations might express the intention of the delegation at that stage, but bear no relation to the ultimate text of the treaty; unequal, because not all delegations spoke on any particular issue; and partial because it excluded the informal meetings between heads of delegations at which final compromises were reached and which were often the most significant feature of any negotiation.[160]

made between all the parties in connection with the conclusion of the treaty; (b) any instrument which was made by one or more parties in connection with the conclusion of the treaty and accepted by the other parties as an instrument related to the treaty.'

[157] 1951 Convention, Preamble.

[158] Art. 32: 'Recourse may be had to supplementary means of interpretation, including the preparatory work of the treaty and the circumstances of its conclusion, in order to confirm the meaning resulting from the application of art. 31, or to determine the meaning when the interpretation according to art. 31: (a) leaves the meaning ambiguous or obscure; or (b) leads to a result which is manifestly absurd or unreasonable.'

[159] This principle has long been established in international law; see, for example, *Interpretation of Article 3(2) of the Treaty of Lausanne*, 1925 PCIJ (Ser. B) No. 12, at 22; *The Lotus Case*, 1927 PCIJ (Ser. A) No. 10, at 16; *Admission to the United Nations Case*, 1950 ICJ *Rep.* 8. See generally, American Law Institute, *Restatement of the Law, Third, Foreign Relations Law of the United States*, (1987), vol. 1, §325; McNair, *The Law of Treaties*, (1961), Ch. XXIII.

[160] Vienna Conference Records: UN doc. A/CONF. 39/11, (1968), 178.

Or as the French put it, '[i]t was much less hazardous and much more equitable when ascertaining the intention of the parties to rely on what they had agreed in writing, rather than to seek outside the text elements of intent which were far more unreliable, scattered as they were through incomplete or unilateral documents'.[161]

International courts occasionally resort to the preparatory works, but within fairly well defined limits. In *Interpretation of Article 3(2) of the Treaty of Lausanne*, for example, the Permanent Court of International Justice noted,

> Since the Court is of opinion that Article 3 is in itself sufficiently clear to enable the nature of the decision to be reached by the Council under the terms of that article to be determined, the question does not arise whether consideration of the work done in the preparation of the Treaty of Lausanne (*les travaux préparatoires*) would also lead to the conclusions set out above.[162]

The International Court of Justice has adopted the same reasoning:

> When the Court can give effect to a provision of a treaty by giving to the words used in it their natural and ordinary meaning, it may not interpret the words by seeking to given them some other meaning.[163]

For better or worse, refugee status decision-makers (and commentators . . .) make frequent use of the *travaux préparatoires* to the 1951 Convention. Many key terms are vague, undefined and open to interpretation, but the results of inquiry into the background, as the present analysis shows, can be rather mixed. On the one hand, clear statements of drafting intentions are rare; yet on the other hand, the debates in the General Assembly, the Third Committee, the Economic and Social Council and, to a lesser extent, at the 1951 Conference itself, provide a fascinating insight into the politics of a highly sensitive and emotive issue. If some sentiments and statements seem frozen in time, others show the continuity of concern and, perhaps too rarely, confirmation of a pervasive humanitarianism.

4. The status of refugees and the termination of refugee status in municipal law

A fully comprehensive survey of the status and rights of refugees in municipal law is beyond the scope of this work, which is primarily concerned with international law. The following is therefore intended merely to sketch out some of

---

[161] Ibid., 176.

[162] *Interpretation of Article 3(2) of the Treaty of Lausanne*, PCIJ, Ser. B, No. 12, (1925), 22. See also the *Lotus* Case, PCIJ, Ser. A, No. 10, (1927), 16: '. . . there is no occasion to have regard to preparatory work if the text of a convention is sufficiently clear in itself.'

[163] *Admission to the United Nations* Case, ICJ Rep., 1950, 8. See also *State of Arizona* v. *State of California* (1934) 292 US 341, at 359, 360, in which the US Supreme Court said that the rule permitting resort to preparatory work 'has no application to oral statements made by those engaged in negotiating the treat which were not embodied in any writing and were not communicated to the government of the negotiator or to its ratifying body'.

the areas requiring attention if an effective national and international system of protection is to be maintained.

A first distinction exists between those States which have and those which have not ratified the relevant international instruments. For certain States parties, the very act of ratification may cause the treaty to have internal effect, so that it can be relied upon at law by the refugee who seeks to establish status or to secure a particular advantage or standard of treatment.[164] Even in such countries, however, specific measures of incorporation may be appropriate, particularly in procedural matters. In other States, including many with a common law tradition, specific legislation is essential if the concept of refugee status is to have any legal content, and if standards of treatment are to be legally enforceable, rather than dependent upon executive discretion.

The divorce between refugee status, on the one hand, and asylum in the sense of a lasting solution, on the other hand, has been analysed above; States are bound by one consequence of refugee status, *non-refoulement*, but retain discretion in the grant of asylum. Between the obligation and the liberty, refugees may yet find themselves in a limbo of varying degrees of legal and administrative security. Many States in practice allow or tolerate the presence of asylum seekers pending the conclusion of procedures for the determination of status.[165] Other countries permit residence pending decision, although departure to a third country can be required.[166] Temporary residence, again under varying conditions, is also granted to asylum seekers pending resettlement elsewhere. Legislation introduced in Hong Kong in 1981 went so far as to *define* a Vietnamese refugee as a person who '(a) was previously resident in Vietnam; and (b) is permitted to remain in Hong Kong as a refugee pending his resettlement elsewhere'.[167] The law provided for sanctions to encourage onward movement by making it a condition of stay that an offer of resettlement elsewhere should not be refused 'without reasonable excuse'.[168]

In many countries, formal recognition of refugee status is the practical precursor to the grant of asylum in the sense of lawful residence. On occasion, asylum follows as a matter of legal right or of administrative practice. In other cases, however, it is clear that even recognized refugees are, openly or tacitly, expected

---

[164] See, for example, art. 65 of the Constitution of the Netherlands, under which self-executing treaties have the force of law as from their publication, taking precedence over existing statutes and those which follow. See also arts. 25 and 59, Constitution of the Federal Republic of Germany; arts. 53 and 55, 1958 Constitution of France.

[165] See, for example, Conseil d'etat, *Préfet de l'Hérault c./ M. Dakoury*, 13 déc. 1991, confirming the asylum seeker's right to temporary residence.

[166] See above, s. 2.1.1.

[167] Immigration Amendment Ordinance 1981 (no. 35/81) s. 2; Mushkat, R., 'Hong Kong as a country of temporary refuge: an interim analysis', 12 *Hong Kong LJ* 157 (1982).

[168] Ibid. s. 3 (adding new s. 13A(3) to the principal ordinance). Further amendments in 1982, intended to discourage further arrivals, prescribed wide powers of detention and removal of Vietnamese arriving after 2 July of that year: Immigration Amendment Ordinance 1982 (no. 42/82), s. 7.

to move on to other countries. Where asylum in the sense of residence does follow, then the precise standards of treatment to be accorded will again depend
upon the standing of the relevant international treaties in the local law and upon
the provisions of any incorporating legislation. Finally, protection against extradition, expulsion and *refoulement* may be secured by law indirectly (for example,
where deportation appeals tribunals are empowered to take all relevant factors
into account); or directly, by express restrictions upon the permissible grounds
of expulsion and choice of destination.

4.1 REFUGEE STATUS AND THE 'OPPOSABILITY' OF DECISIONS

The existence of an international legal definition of refugees raises the question
of the opposability of determinations of refugee status by UNHCR and individual States parties to the 1951 Convention. UNHCR is charged with protection
of refugees and is alone competent to decide who comes within its jurisdiction
under the Statute or any relevant General Assembly resolution. Given States'
acquiescence in UNHCR's protection function, its determinations of status are in
principle binding on States, at least so far as meeting its mandate responsibilities
is concerned. The very definition of refugees, however, incorporates areas of
appreciation, so that in practice UNHCR's position on individuals and groups
may be challenged. Nevertheless, as noted in another context,[169] UNHCR's
opinions must be considered by objecting States in good faith and a refusal to
accept its determinations requires substantial justification.[170]

The 'international character' of refugee status was expressly recognized in
Executive Committee Conclusion No. 12 (1978) on the extraterritorial effect of
determinations.[171] The Committee noted that States parties to the Convention
and Protocol undertake to recognize and accept for visa purposes CTDs issued
by other States,[172] and that in certain circumstances refugees resident in one
contracting State may exercise rights in another.[173] It considered that the purpose of the Convention and Protocol implied that refugee status determined by
one contracting State would be recognized also by other contracting States.
Determinations, moreover, should only be questioned in exceptional cases, such
as fraud or cessation.[174]

Neither the Convention nor the Protocol in fact makes any express provision
for extraterritorial effect. The undertaking to 'recognize the validity' of travel
documents issued under article 28 is arguably limited to their validity for visa,

---

[169] See above, Ch. 6, s. 1.1.1.

[170] UNHCR's decisions on refugee status, although possessing an international character, do not
have the same binding character as, say, the 'housekeeping' or technical resolutions of international
organizations, which may directly create obligations for member States.

[171] See UN doc. EC/SCP/9.   [172] 1951 Convention, Schedule, para. 7.

[173] See, for example, arts. 14 and 16(3).

[174] For full text, see Annexe 3, below. It was also accepted that a decision by one State *not* to recognize refugee status does not preclude another State from examining a new request by the person concerned.

identity, and returnability purposes. However, just as a passport is generally accepted as prima facie proof of nationality,[175] so as a matter of comity if not obligation, ought the CTD to be accepted as evidence that the holder possesses the international legal status of refugee. State practice either for or against the Executive Committee's recommendations is sparse, and the occasions on which one State will challenge another's determinations are likely to be rare. A refugee who has offended the law can generally be deported to the State which issued the travel document. A more acute problem arises, however, where the extradition is sought of a refugee recognized in one State but physically present in another. Where the requesting State is the country of origin, the protecting or asylum State may justifiably object to the potential *refoulement* of 'its' refugee. In such a case the refusal to accept the latter's determination of status, followed by extradition of the refugee, constitutes a putative wrong to the protecting State.

4.2 THE PRINCIPLE OF ACQUIRED RIGHTS

The justification for refugee status may come to an end in a variety of circumstances, without the individual at the same time constituting a threat to the security of the State of asylum. The question then arises whether that State, in the exercise of its discretion generally over the conditions of residence of foreign nationals, is entitled to require the former refugee to leave its territory. As a matter of law, and at first glance, this aspect of sovereign competence cannot be doubted. In practice, however, it is common to find that, once asylum is granted, the issue of refugee status is reviewed only if, by their own actions, refugees render themselves liable to deportation (for example, by engaging in criminal activity). Where refugee status ceases in other cases, then the individual becomes subject to the ordinary law governing the residence of foreign nationals. The corollary is that he or she is entitled to the same standards of treatment, including the right not to be arbitrarily expelled. This right, it has been argued elsewhere, entails not only that decisions on expulsion be in accordance with law, but that the foreign national's 'legitimate expectations' be taken into account, including such 'acquired rights' as may derive from long residence and establishment, business, marriage, and local integration.[176]

---

[175] Goodwin-Gill, *Movement of Persons*, 45–9.
[176] Ibid., 178–9, 230, 255–61, 294.

ANNEXES

TABLE OF CONTENTS

Annexe 1
Basic Instruments

Annexe 2
Selected Regional Instruments

Annexe 3
UNHCR Executive Committee
Selected Conclusions on International Protection

Annexe 4
Miscellaneous Texts

Annexe 5
Comprehensive Arrangements for Refugees

Annexe 6
States Parties to the 1951 Convention, the 1967 Protocol, and the 1969 OAU Convention; Delegations participating in the 1984 Cartagena Declaration; and Members of the Executive Committee of the High Commissioner's Programme
(at 1 June 1997)

ANNEXE 1
BASIC INSTRUMENTS
1. 1946 Constitution of the International Refugee Organization—Extracts

Entry into force: 20 August 1948

Text: 18 *UNTS* 3

Preamble

The Governments accepting this Constitution, recognizing:

that genuine refugees and displaced persons constitute an urgent problem which is international in scope and character;

that as regards displaced persons, the main task to be performed is to encourage and assist in every way possible their early return to their country of origin;

that genuine refugees and displaced persons should be assisted by international action, either to return to their countries of nationality or former habitual residence, or to find new homes elsewhere, under the conditions provided for in this Constitution; or in the case of Spanish Republicans, to establish themselves temporarily in order to enable them to return to Spain when the present Falangist regime is succeeded by a democratic regime;

that resettlement and reestablishment of refugees and displaced persons be contemplated only in cases indicated clearly in the Constitution;

that genuine refugees and displaced persons, until such time as their repatriation or resettlement and reestablishment is effectively completed, should be protected in their rights and legitimate interests, should receive care and assistance and, as far as possible, should be put to useful employment in order to avoid the evil and anti-social consequences of continued idleness; and that the expenses of repatriation to the extent practicable should be charged to Germany and Japan for persons displaced by those Powers from countries occupied by them:

Have agreed, for the accomplishment of the foregoing purposes in the shortest possible time, to establish and do hereby establish, a non-permanent organization to be called the International Refugee Organization, a specialized agency to be brought into relationship with the United Nations . . .

ANNEX 1: DEFINITIONS

General Principles

1. The following general principles constitute an integral part of the definitions as laid down in Parts I and II of this Annex.

(a) The main object of the Organization will be to bring about a rapid and positive solution of the problem of bona fide refugees and displaced persons, which shall be just and equitable to all concerned.

(b) The main task concerning displaced persons is to encourage and assist in every way possible their early return to the countries of origin, having regard to the principles laid down in paragraph (c) (ii) of the resolution adopted by the General Assembly of the United Nations on 12 February 1946 regarding the problem of refugees (Annex III).

(c) As laid down in the resolution adopted by the Economic and Social Council on 16 February 1946, no international assistance should be given to traitors, quislings and war criminals, and nothing should be done to prevent in any way their surrender and punishment.

(d) It should be the concern of the Organization to ensure that its assistance is not exploited in order to encourage subversive or hostile activities directed against the Government of any of the United Nations.

(e) It should be the concern of the Organization to ensure that its assistance is not exploited by persons in the case of whom it is clear that they are unwilling to return to their countries of origin because they prefer idleness to facing the hardships of helping in the reconstruction of their countries, or by persons who intend to settle in other countries for purely economic reasons, thus qualifying as emigrants.

(f) On the other hand it should equally be the concern of the Organization to ensure that no bona fide and deserving refugee or displaced person is deprived of such assistance as it may be in a position to offer.

(g) The Organization should endeavour to carry out its functions in such a way as to avoid disturbing friendly relations between nations. In the pursuit of this objective, the Organization should exercise special care in cases in which the re-establishment or resettlement of refugees or displaced persons might be contemplated, either in countries contiguous to their respective countries of origin or in non-self-governing countries. The Organization should give due weight, among other factors, to any evidence of genuine apprehension and concern felt in regard to such plans, in the former case, by the country of origin of the persons involved, or, in the latter case, by the indigenous population of the non-self-governing country in question.

2. To ensure the impartial and equitable application of the above principles and of the terms of the definition which follows, some special system of semi-judicial machinery should be created, with appropriate constitution, procedure and terms of reference.

Part I: Refugees and Displaced Persons within the Meaning of the
Resolution adopted by the Economic and Social Council of the United Nations on 16
February 1946

Section A—Definition of Refugees

1. Subject to the provisions of sections C and D and of Part II of this Annex, the term 'refugee' applies to a person who has left, or who is outside of, his country of nationality or of former habitual residence, and who, whether or not he had retained his nationality, belongs to one of the following categories:

(a) victims of the Nazi or fascist regimes or of regimes which took part on their side in the Second World War, or of the quisling or similar regimes which assisted them against the United Nations, whether enjoying international status as refugees or not;

(b) Spanish Republicans and other victims of the Falangist regime in Spain, whether enjoying international status as refugees or not;

(c) persons who were considered refugees before the outbreak of the Second World War, for reasons of race, religion, nationality or political opinion.

2. Subject to the provisions of sections C and D and of Part II of this Annex regarding the exclusion of certain categories of persons, including war criminals, quislings and traitors, from the benefits of the Organization, the term 'refugee' also applies to a person, other than a displaced person as defined in section B of this Annex, who is outside of his country of nationality or former habitual residence, and who, as a result of events subsequent to the outbreak of the Second World War, is unable or unwilling to avail himself of the protection of the Government of his country of nationality or former nationality.

3. Subject to the provisions of Section D and of Part II of this Annex, the term 'refugee' also applies to persons who, having resided in Germany or Austria, and being of Jewish origin or foreigners or stateless persons, were victims of Nazi persecution and were detained in, or were obliged to flee from, and were subsequently returned to, one of those countries as a result of enemy action, or of war circumstances, and have not yet been firmly resettled therein.

4. The term 'refugee' also applies to unaccompanied children who are war orphans or whose parents have disappeared, and who are outside their countries of origin. Such children, sixteen years of age or under, shall be given all possible priority assistance, including, normally, assistance in repatriation in the case of those whose nationality can be determined.

Section B—Definition of Displaced Persons

The term 'displaced person' applies to a person who, as a result of the actions of the authorities of the regimes mentioned in Part I, section A, paragraph 1(a) of this Annex has been deported from, or has been obliged to leave his country of nationality or of former habitual residence, such as persons who were compelled to undertake forced labour or who were deported for racial, religious or political reasons. Displaced persons will only fall within the mandate of the Organization subject to the provisions of sections C and D of Part I and to the provisions of Part II of this Annex. If the reasons for their displacement have ceased to exist, they should be repatriated as soon as possible in accordance with article 2, paragraph 1(a) of this Constitution, and subject to the provision of paragraph (c), sub-paragraphs (ii) and (iii) of the General Assembly resolution of 12 February 1946 regarding the problem of refugees . . . [1]

[1] In the resolution referred to, UNGA res. 8(1) on the question of refugees, the General Assembly decided to refer the problem to the Economic and Social Council for thorough examination, recommending that it establish a special committee to this end, and that it take the following principles into consideration (para. (c)): '(i) this problem is international in scope and nature; (ii) no refugees or displaced persons who have finally and definitely, in complete freedom, and after receiving full knowledge of the facts, including adequate information from the governments of their countries of origin, expressed valid objection to returning to their country of origin . . . shall be compelled to return to their country of origin. The future of such refugees or displaced persons shall become the concern of whatever international body may be recognized or established . . . (iii) the main task concerning displaced persons is to encourage and assist in every way possible their early return to their countries of origin. Such assistance may take the form of promoting the conclusion of bilateral

Section C—Conditions under which 'Refugees' and 'Displaced Persons' will become the Concern of the Organization

1. In the case of all the above categories except those mentioned in section A, paragraphs 1(b) and 3 of this Annex, persons will become the concern of the Organization in the sense of the resolution adopted by the Economic and Social Council on 16 February 1946 if they can be repatriated, and the help of the Organization is required in order to provide for their repatriation, or if they have definitely, in complete freedom and after receiving full knowledge of the facts, including adequate information from the Governments of their countries of nationality or former habitual residence, expressed valid objections to returning to those countries.

(a) The following shall be considered as valid objections:

(i) persecution, or fear, based on reasonable grounds of persecution because of race, religion, nationality or political opinions, provided these opinions are not in conflict with the principles of the United Nations, as laid down in the Preamble of the Charter of the United Nations;

(ii) objections of a political nature judged by the Organization to be 'valid', as contemplated in paragraph 8(a)[2] of the report of the Third Committee of the General Assembly as adopted by the Assembly on 12 February 1946;

(iii) in the case of persons falling within the category mentioned in section A, paragraphs 1(a) and 1(c) compelling family reasons arising out of previous persecution, or, compelling reasons of infirmity or illness.

(b) The following shall normally be considered 'adequate information': information regarding conditions in the countries of nationality of the refugees and displaced persons concerned, communicated to them directly by representatives of the Governments of these countries, who shall be given every facility for visiting camps and assembly centres of refugees and displaced persons in order to place such information before them.

2. In the case of all refugees falling within the terms of Section A paragraph 1(b) of this Annex, persons will become the concern of the Organization in the sense of the resolution adopted by the Economic and Social Council of the United Nations on 16 February 1946, so long as the Falangist regime in Spain continues. Should that regime be replaced by a democratic regime they will have to produce valid objections against returning to Spain corresponding to those indicated in paragraph 1(a) of this section.

Section D—Circumstances in which Refugees and Displaced Persons will cease to be the Concern of the Organization

Refugees or displaced persons will cease to be the concern of the Organization:

---

arrangements for mutual assistance in the repatriation of such persons having regard to the principles laid down in paragraph (c)(ii) . . .' Paragraph (d) provided that 'no action taken as a result of this resolution shall be of such a character as to interfere with the surrender and punishment of war criminals, quislings and traitors . . .'

[2] Paragraph 8 (a). 'In answering the representative of Belgium, the Chairman stated that it was implied that the international body would judge what were, or what were not, "valid objections"; and that such objections clearly might be of a "political nature".'

(a) when they have returned to the countries of their nationality in United Nations territory, unless their former habitual residence to which they wish to return is outside their country of nationality; or

(b) when they have acquired a new nationality; or

(c) when they have, in the determination of the Organization become otherwise firmly established; or

(d) when they have unreasonably refused to accept the proposals of the Organization for their resettlement or repatriation; or

(e) when they are making no substantial effort towards earning their living when it is possible for them to do so, or when they are exploiting the assistance of the Organization.

Part II: Persons who will not be the Concern of the Organization

1. War criminals, quislings and traitors.

2. Any other persons who can be shown:

(a) to have assisted the enemy in persecuting civil populations of countries, Members of the United Nations; or

(b) to have voluntarily assisted the enemy forces since the outbreak of the Second World War in their operations against the United Nations.[3]

3. Ordinary criminals who are extraditable by treaty.

4. Persons of German ethnic origin, whether German nationals or members of German minorities in other countries, who:

(a) have been or may be transferred to Germany from other countries;

(b) have been, during the Second World War, evacuated from Germany to other countries;

(c) have fled from, or into, Germany, or from their places of residence into countries other than Germany in order to avoid falling into the hands of Allied armies.

5. Persons who are in receipt of financial support and protection from their country of nationality, unless their country of nationality requests international assistance for them.

6. Persons who, since the end of hostilities in the Second World War:

(a) have participated in any organization having as one of its purposes the overthrow by armed force of the Government of their country of origin, being a Member of the United Nations; or the overthrow by armed force of the Government of any other Member of the United Nations, or have participated in any terrorist organization;

(b) have become leaders of movements hostile to the Government of their country of origin being a Member of the United Nations or sponsors of movements encouraging refugees not to return to their country of origin;

---

[3] Mere continuance of normal and peaceful duties, not performed with the specific purpose of aiding the enemy against the Allies or against the civil population of territory in enemy occupation, shall not be considered to constitute 'voluntary assistance'. Nor shall acts of general humanity, such as care of wounded or dying, be so considered except in cases where help of this nature given to enemy nationals could equally well have been given to Allied nationals and was purposely withheld from them.

(c) at the time of application for assistance, are in the military or civil service of a foreign State.

2. 1948 Universal Declaration of Human Rights—Extracts

Adopted by the United Nations General Assembly on 10 December 1948

Text: UNGA resolution 217 A(III)

Article 13

1. Everyone has the right to freedom of movement and residence within the borders of each State.

2. Everyone has the right to leave any country, including his own, and to return to his country.

Article 14

1. Everyone has the right to seek and to enjoy in other countries asylum from persecution.

2. This right may not be invoked in the case of prosecutions genuinely arising from non-political crimes or from acts contrary to the purposes and principles of the United Nations.

Article 15

1. Everyone has the right to a nationality.

2. No one shall be arbitrarily deprived of his nationality nor denied the right to change his nationality.

3. 1950 Statute of the Office of the United Nations High Commissioner for Refugees

GENERAL ASSEMBLY RESOLUTION 428(V) OF 14 DECEMBER 1950

The General Assembly,
In view of its resolution 319 A (IV) of 3 December 1949,

1. Adopts the Annex to the present resolution, being the Statute of the Office of the United Nations High Commissioner for Refugees;

2. Calls upon Governments to co-operate with the United Nations High Commissioner for Refugees in the performance of his functions concerning refugees falling under the competence of his office, especially by:

(a) Becoming parties to international conventions providing for the protection of refugees, and taking the necessary steps of implementation under such conventions;

(b) Entering into special agreements with the High Commissioner for the execution of measures calculated to improve the situation of refugees and to reduce the number requiring protection;

(c) Admitting refugees to their territories, not excluding those in the most destitute categories;

(d) Assisting the High Commissioner in his efforts to promote the voluntary repatriation of refugees;

(e) Promoting the assimilation of refugees, especially by facilitating their naturalization;

(f) Providing refugees with travel and other documents such as would normally be provided to other aliens by their national authorities, especially documents which would facilitate their resettlement;

(g) Permitting refugees to transfer their assets and especially those necessary for their resettlement;

(h) Providing the High Commissioner with information concerning the number and condition of refugees, and laws and regulations concerning them;

3. Requests the Secretary-General to transmit the present resolution, together with the Annex attached thereto, also to States non-members of the United Nations, with a view to obtaining their co-operation in its implementation.

ANNEX: STATUTE OF THE OFFICE OF THE UNITED NATIONS HIGH COMMISSIONER FOR REFUGEES

Chapter I—General Provisions

1. The United Nations High Commissioner for Refugees, acting under the authority of the General Assembly, shall assume the function of providing international protection, under the auspices of the United Nations, to refugees who fall within the scope of the present Statute and of seeking permanent solutions for the problem of refugees by assisting Governments and, subject to the approval of the Governments concerned, private organizations to facilitate the voluntary repatriation of such refugees, or their assimilation within new national communities.

In the exercise of his functions, more particularly when difficulties arise, and for instance with regard to any controversy concerning the international status of these persons, the High Commissioner shall request the opinion of the advisory committee on refugees if it is created.

2. The work of the High Commissioner shall be of an entirely non-political character; it shall be humanitarian and social and shall relate, as a rule, to groups and categories of refugees.

3. The High Commissioner shall follow policy directives given him by the General Assembly or the Economic and Social Council.

4. The Economic and Social Council may decide, after hearing the views of the High Commissioner on the subject, to establish an advisory committee on refugees, which shall consist of representatives of States Members and States non-members of the United

Nations, to be selected by the Council on the basis of their demonstrated interest in and devotion to the solution of the refugee problem.

5. The General Assembly shall review, not later than at its eighth regular session, the arrangements for the Office of the High Commissioner with a view to determining whether the Office should be continued beyond 31 December 1953.

Chapter II—Functions of the High Commissioner

6. The competence of the High Commissioner shall extend to:

A. (i) Any person who has been considered a refugee under the Arrangements of 12 May 1926 and of 30 June 1928 or under the Conventions of 28 October 1933 and 10 February 1938, the Protocol of 14 September 1939 or the Constitution of the International Refugee Organization.

(ii) Any person who, as a result of events occurring before 1 January 1951 and owing to well-founded fear of being persecuted for reasons of race, religion, nationality or political opinion, is outside the country of his nationality and is unable or, owing to such fear or for reasons other than personal convenience, is unwilling to avail himself of the protection of that country; or who, not having a nationality and being outside the country of his former habitual residence, is unable or, owing to such fear or for reasons other than personal convenience, is unwilling to return to it.

Decisions as to eligibility taken by the International Refugee Organization during the period of its activities shall not prevent the status of refugee being accorded to persons who fulfil the conditions of the present paragraph;

The competence of the High Commissioner shall cease to apply to any person defined in section A above if:

(a) He has voluntarily re-availed himself of the protection of the country of his nationality; or

(b) Having lost his nationality, he has voluntarily re-acquired it; or

(c) He has acquired a new nationality, and enjoys the protection of the country of his new nationality; or

(d) He has voluntarily re-established himself in the country which he left or outside which he remained owing to fear of persecution; or

(e) He can no longer, because the circumstances in connection with which he has been recognized as a refugee have ceased to exist, claim grounds other than those of personal convenience for continuing to refuse to avail himself of the protection of the country of his nationality. Reasons of a purely economic character may not be invoked; or

(f) Being a person who has no nationality, he can no longer, because the circumstances in connection with which he has been recognized as a refugee have ceased to exist and he is able to return to the country of his former habitual residence, claim grounds other than those of personal convenience for continuing to refuse to return to that country;

B. Any other person who is outside the country of his nationality, or if he has no nationality, the country of his former habitual residence, because he has or had well-founded fear of persecution by reason of his race, religion, nationality or political opinion and is unable or, because of such fear, is unwilling to avail himself of the protection of the government of the country of his nationality, or, if he has no nationality, to return to the country of his former habitual residence.

7. Provided that the competence of the High Commissioner as defined in paragraph 6 above shall not extend to a person:

(a) Who is a national of more than one country unless he satisfies the provisions of the preceding paragraph in relation to each of the countries of which he is a national; or

(b) Who is recognized by the competent authorities of the country in which he has taken residence as having the rights and obligations which are attached to the possession of the nationality of that country; or

(c) Who continues to receive from other organs or agencies of the United Nations protection or assistance; or

(d) In respect of whom there are serious reasons for considering that he has committed a crime covered by the provisions of treaties of extradition or a crime mentioned in article VI of the London Charter of the International Military Tribunal or by the provisions of article 14, paragraph 2, of the Universal Declaration of Human Rights.

8. The High Commissioner shall provide for the protection of refugees falling under the competence of his Office by:

(a) Promoting the conclusion and ratification of international conventions for the protection of refugees, supervising their application and proposing amendments thereto;

(b) Promoting through special agreements with Governments the execution of any measures calculated to improve the situation of refugees and to reduce the number requiring protection;

(c) Assisting governmental and private efforts to promote voluntary repatriation or assimilation within new national communities;

(d) Promoting the admission of refugees, not excluding those in the most destitute categories, to the territories of States;

(e) Endeavouring to obtain permission for refugees to transfer their assets and especially those necessary for their resettlement;

(f) Obtaining from Governments information concerning the number and conditions of refugees in their territories and the laws and regulations concerning them;

(g) Keeping in close touch with the Governments and inter-governmental organizations concerned;

(h) Establishing contact in such manner as he may think best with private organizations dealing with refugee questions;

(i) Facilitating the co-ordination of the efforts of private organizations concerned with the welfare of refugees.

9. The High Commissioner shall engage in such additional activities, including repatriation and resettlement, as the General Assembly may determine, within the limits of the resources placed at his disposal.

10. The High Commissioner shall administer any funds, public or private, which he receives for assistance to refugees, and shall distribute them among the private and, as appropriate, public agencies which he deems best qualified to administer such assistance.

The High Commissioner may reject any offers which he does not consider appropriate or which cannot be utilized. The High Commissioner shall not appeal to Governments for funds or make a general appeal, without the prior approval of the General Assembly. The High Commissioner shall include in his annual report a statement of his activities in this field.

11. The High Commissioner shall be entitled to present his views before the General Assembly, the Economic and Social Council and their subsidiary bodies.

The High Commissioner shall report annually to the General Assembly through the Economic and Social Council; his report shall be considered as a separate item on the agenda of the General Assembly.

12. The High Commissioner may invite the co-operation of the various specialized agencies.

Chapter III — Organization and Finances

13. The High Commissioner shall be elected by the General Assembly on the nomination of the Secretary-General. The terms of appointment of the High Commissioner shall be proposed by the Secretary-General and approved by the General Assembly. The High Commissioner shall be elected for a term of three years, from 1 January 1951.

14. The High Commissioner shall appoint, for the same term, a Deputy High Commissioner of a nationality other than his own.

15. (a) Within the limits of the budgetary appropriations provided, the staff of the Office of the High Commissioner shall be appointed by the High Commissioner and shall be responsible to him in the exercise of their functions.

(b) Such staff shall be chosen from persons devoted to the purposes of the Office of the High Commissioner.

(c) Their conditions of employment shall be those provided under the staff regulations adopted by the General Assembly and the rules promulgated thereunder by the Secretary-General.

(d) Provision may also be made to permit the employment of personnel without compensation.

16. The High Commissioner shall consult the Government of the countries of residence of refugees as to the need for appointing representatives therein. In any country recognizing such need, there may be appointed a representative approved by the Government of that country. Subject to the foregoing, the same representative may serve in more than one country.

17. The High Commissioner and the Secretary-General shall make appropriate arrangements for liaison and consultation on matters of mutual interest.

18. The Secretary-General shall provide the High Commissioner with all necessary facilities within budgetary limitations.

19. The Office of the High Commissioner shall be located in Geneva, Switzerland.

20. The Office of the High Commissioner shall be financed under the budget of the United Nations. Unless the General Assembly subsequently decides otherwise, no expen-

diture other than administrative expenditures relating to the functioning of the Office of the High Commissioner shall be borne on the budget of the United Nations and all other expenditures relating to the activities of the High Commissioner shall be financed by voluntary contributions.

21. The administration of the Office of the High Commissioner shall be subject to the Financial Regulations of the United Nations and to the financial rules promulgated thereunder by the Secretary-General.

22. Transactions relating to the High Commissioner's funds shall be subject to audit by the United Nations Board of Auditors, provided that the Board may accept audited accounts from the agencies to which funds have been allocated. Administrative arrangements for the custody of such funds and their allocation shall be agreed between the High Commissioner and the Secretary-General in accordance with the Financial Regulations of the United Nations and rules promulgated thereunder by the Secretary-General.

4. 1951 Convention relating to the Status of Refugees

Text: 189 *UNTS* 150

Entry into force: 22 April 1954

FINAL ACT OF THE UNITED NATIONS CONFERENCE OF PLENIPOTENTIARIES ON THE STATUS OF REFUGEES AND STATELESS PERSONS

I

The General Assembly of the United Nations, by Resolution 429(V) of 14 December 1950, decided to convene in Geneva a Conference of Plenipotentiaries to complete the drafting of, and to sign, a Convention relating to the Status of Refugees and a Protocol relating to the Status of Stateless Persons.

The Conference met at the European Office of the United Nations in Geneva from 2 to 25 July 1951.

The Governments of the following twenty-six States were represented by delegates who all submitted satisfactory credentials or other communications of appointment authorizing them to participate in the Conference:

Australia	Italy
Austria	Luxembourg
Belgium	Monaco
Brazil	Netherlands
Canada	Norway
Colombia	Sweden
Denmark	Switzerland (the Swiss delegation
Egypt	also represented Liechtenstein)
France	Turkey

Federal Republic of Germany	United Kingdom of Great Britain
Greece	and Northern Ireland
Holy See	United States of America
Iraq	Venezuela
Israel	Yugoslavia

The Governments of the following two States were represented by observers:

Cuba

Iran

Pursuant to the request of the General Assembly, the United Nations High Commissioner for Refugees participated, without the right to vote, in the deliberations of the Conference.

The International Labour Organization and the International Refugee Organization were represented at the Conference without the right to vote.

The Conference invited a representative of the Council of Europe to be represented at the Conference without the right to vote.

Representatives of . . . Non-Governmental Organizations in Consultative relationship with the Economic and Social Council were also present as observers . . .

[List of Non-Governmental Organizations omitted].

Representatives of Non-Governmental Organizations which have been granted consultative status by the Economic and Social Council as well as those entered by the Secretary-General on the Register referred to in Resolution 288 B(X) of the Economic and Social Council, paragraph 17, had under the rules of procedure adopted by the Conference the right to submit written or oral statements to the Conference.

The Conference elected Mr Knud Larsen, of Denmark, as President, and Mr A. Herment, of Belgium, and Mr Talat Miras, of Turkey, as Vice-Presidents.

At its second meeting, the Conference, acting on a proposal of the representative of Egypt, unanimously decided to address an invitation to the Holy See to designate a plenipotentiary representative to participate in its work. A representative of the Holy See took his place at the Conference on 10 July 1951.

The Conference adopted as its agenda the Provisional Agenda drawn up by the Secretary-General (A/CONF.2/2/Rev.l). It also adopted the Provisional Rules of Procedure drawn up by the Secretary-General, with the addition of a provision which authorized a representative of the Council of Europe to be present at the Conference without the right to vote and to submit proposals (A/CONF.2/3/Rev.l).

In accordance with the Rules of Procedure of the Conference, the President and Vice-Presidents examined the credentials of representatives and on 17 July 1951 reported to the Conference the results of such examination, the Conference adopting the report.

The Conference used as the basis of its discussions the draft Convention relating to the Status of Refugees and the draft Protocol relating to the Status of Stateless Persons prepared by the *Ad hoc* Committee on Refugees and Stateless Persons at its second session held in Geneva from 14 to 25 August 1950, with the exception of the preamble and article 1 (Definition of the term 'refugee') of the draft Convention. The text of the preamble before the Conference was that which was adopted by the Economic and Social Council on 11 August 1950 in Resolution 319 B II (XI). The text of article 1 before the Conference was that recommended by the General Assembly on 14 December 1950 and contained in the Annex to Resolution 429(V). The latter was a modification of the text as it had been adopted by the Economic and Social Council in Resolution 319 B II(XI).[4]

The Conference adopted the Convention relating to the Status of Refugees in two readings. Prior to its second reading it established a Style Committee composed of the President and the representatives of Belgium, France, Israel, Italy, the United Kingdom of Great Britain and Northern Ireland and the United States of America, together with the High Commissioner for Refugees, which elected as its Chairman Mr G. Warren, of the United States of America. The Style Committee re-drafted the text which had been adopted by the Conference on first reading, particularly from the point of view of language and of concordance between the English and French texts.

The Convention was adopted on 25 July by 24 votes to none with no abstentions and opened for signature at the European Office of the United Nations from 28 July to 31 August 1951. It will be re-opened for signature at the permanent headquarters of the United Nations in New York from 17 September 1951 to 31 December 1952.

The English and French texts of the Convention, which are equally authentic, are appended to this Final Act.

II

The Conference decided, by 17 votes to 3 with 3 abstentions, that the titles of the chapters and of the articles of the Convention are included for practical purposes and do not constitute an element of interpretation.

III

With respect to the draft Protocol relating to the Status of Stateless Persons, the Conference adopted the following resolution:

'*The Conference,*

'*Having considered* the draft Protocol relating to the Status of Stateless Persons,

'*Considering* that the subject still requires more detailed study,

'*Decides* not to take a decision on the subject at the present Conference and refers the draft Protocol back to the appropriate organs of the United Nations for further study.'

IV

The Conference adopted unanimously the following recommendations:

A

'*The Conference,*

'*Considering* that the issue and recognition of travel documents is necessary to facilitate the movement of refugees, and in particular their resettlement,

'*Urges* Governments which are parties to the Inter-Governmental Agreement on Refugee Travel Documents signed in London on 15 October 1946, or which recognize travel documents issued in accordance with the Agreement, to continue to issue or to recognize such travel documents, and to extend the issue of such documents to refugees as defined in article 1 of the Convention relating to the Status of Refugees or to recognize

---

[4] The texts referred to in the paragraph above are contained in document A/CONF.2/1.

the travel documents so issued to such persons, until they shall have undertaken obligations under article 28 of the said Convention.'

B

'*The Conference,*

'*Considering* that the unity of the family, the natural and fundamental group unit of society, is an essential right of the refugee, and that such unity is constantly threatened, and

'*Noting* with satisfaction that, according to the official commentary of the *Ad hoc* Committee on Statelessness and Related Problems (E/1618, p. 40), the rights granted to a refugee are extended to members of his family,

'*Recommends* Governments to take the necessary measures for the protection of the refugee's family especially with a view to:

'(1) Ensuring that the unity of the refugee's family is maintained particularly in cases where the head of the family has fulfilled the necessary conditions for admission to a particular country,

'(2) The protection of refugees who are minors, in particular unaccompanied children and girls, with special reference to guardianship and adoption.'

C

'*The Conference,*

'*Considering* that, in the moral, legal and material spheres, refugees need the help of suitable welfare services, especially that of appropriate non-governmental organizations,

'*Recommends* Governments and inter-governmental bodies to facilitate, encourage and sustain the efforts of properly qualified organizations.'

D

'*The Conference,*

'*Considering* that many persons still leave their country of origin for reasons of persecution and are entitled to special protection on account of their position,

'*Recommends* that Governments continue to receive refugees in their territories and that they act in concert in a true spirit of international co-operation in order that these refugees may find asylum and the possibility of resettlement.'

E

'*The Conference,*

'*Expresses* the hope that the Convention relating to the Status of Refugees will have value as an example exceeding its contractual scope and that all nations will be guided by it in granting so far as possible to persons in their territory as refugees and who would not be covered by the terms of the Convention, the treatment for which it provides.'

In Witness Whereof the President, Vice Presidents and the Executive Secretary of the Conference have signed this Final Act.

Done at Geneva this twenty-eighth day of July one thousand nine hundred and fifty-one in a single copy in the English and French languages, each text being equally authentic. Translations of this Final Act into Chinese, Russian and Spanish will be prepared by the Secretary-General of the United Nations, who will, on request, send copies thereof to each of the Governments invited to attend the Conference.

The President of the Conference:	Knud Larsen
The Vice Presidents of the Conference:	A. Herment. Talat Miras
The Executive Secretary of the Conference:	John P. Humphrey

CONVENTION RELATING TO THE STATUS OF REFUGEES

Preamble

The High Contracting Parties,

Considering that the Charter of the United Nations and the Universal Declaration of Human Rights approved on 10 December 1948 by the General Assembly have affirmed the principle that human beings shall enjoy fundamental rights and freedoms without discrimination,

Considering that the United Nations has, on various occasions, manifested its profound concern for refugees and endeavoured to assure refugees the widest possible exercise of these fundamental rights and freedoms,

Considering that it is desirable to revise and consolidate previous international agreements relating to the status of refugees and to extend the scope of and protection accorded by such instruments by means of a new agreement,

Considering that the grant of asylum may place unduly heavy burdens on certain countries, and that a satisfactory solution of a problem of which the United Nations has recognized the international scope and nature cannot therefore be achieved without international co-operation,

Expressing the wish that all States, recognizing the social and humanitarian nature of the problem of refugees will do everything within their power to prevent this problem from becoming a cause of tension between States,

Noting that the United Nations High Commissioner for Refugees is charged with the task of supervising international conventions providing for the protection of refugees, and recognizing that the effective co-ordination of measures taken to deal with this problem will depend upon the co-operation of States with the High Commissioner,

Have agreed as follows:

Chapter I—General Provisions

Article 1
Definition of the term 'Refugee'

A. For the purposes of the present Convention, the term 'refugee' shall apply to any person who:

(1) Has been considered a refugee under the Arrangements of 12 May 1926 and 30 June 1928 or under the Conventions of 28 October 1933 and 10 February 1938, the Protocol of 14 September 1939 or the Constitution of the International Refugee Organization;

Decisions of non-eligibility taken by the International Refugee Organization during the period of its activities shall not prevent the status of refugee being accorded to persons who fulfil the conditions of paragraph 2 of this section;

(2) As a result of events occurring before 1 January 1951 and owing to a well-founded fear of being persecuted for reasons of race, religion, nationality, membership of a particular social group or political opinion, is outside the country of his nationality and is unable or, owing to such fear, is unwilling to avail himself of the protection of that country; or who, not having a nationality and being outside the country of his former habitual residence as a result of such events, is unable or, owing to such fear, is unwilling to return to it.

In the case of a person who has more than one nationality, the term 'the country of his nationality' shall mean each of the countries of which he is a national, and a person shall not be deemed to be lacking the protection of the country of his nationality if, without any valid reason based on well-founded fear, he has not availed himself of the protection of one of the countries of which he is a national.

B. (1) For the purposes of this Convention, the words 'events occurring before 1 January 1951' in Article 1, Section A, shall be understood to mean either

(a) 'events occurring in Europe before 1 January 1951'; or

(b) 'events occurring in Europe or elsewhere before 1 January 1951', and each Contracting State shall make a declaration at the time of signature, ratification or accession, specifying which of these meanings it applies for the purpose of its obligations under this Convention.

(2) Any Contracting State which has adopted alternative (a) may at any time extend its obligations by adopting alternative (b) by means of a notification addressed to the Secretary-General of the United Nations.

C. This Convention shall cease to apply to any person falling under the terms of Section A if:

(1) He has voluntarily re-availed himself of the protection of the country of his nationality; or

(2) Having lost his nationality, he has voluntarily re-acquired it, or

(3) He has acquired a new nationality, and enjoys the protection of the country of his new nationality; or

(4) He has voluntarily re-established himself in the country which he left or outside which he remained owing to fear of persecution; or

(5) He can no longer, because the circumstances in connection with which he has been recognized as a refugee have ceased to exist, continue to refuse to avail himself of the protection of the country of his nationality;

Provided that this paragraph shall not apply to a refugee falling under Section A(1) of this Article who is able to invoke compelling reasons arising out of previous persecution for refusing to avail himself of the protection of the country of nationality;

(6) Being a person who has no nationality he is, because of the circumstances in connection with which he has been recognized as a refugee have ceased to exist, able to return to the country of his former habitual residence;

Provided that this paragraph shall not apply to a refugee falling under section A(1) of this Article who is able to invoke compelling reasons arising out of previous persecution for refusing to return to the country of his former habitual residence.

D. This Convention shall not apply to persons who are at present receiving from organs or agencies of the United Nations other than the United Nations High Commissioner for Refugees protection or assistance.

When such protection or assistance has ceased for any reason, without the position of such persons being definitively settled in accordance with the relevant resolutions adopted by the General Assembly of the United Nations, these persons shall *ipso facto* be entitled to the benefits of this Convention.

E. This Convention shall not apply to a person who is recognized by the competent authorities of the country in which he has taken residence as having the rights and obligations which are attached to the possession of the nationality of that country.

F. The provisions of this Convention shall not apply to any person with respect to whom there are serious reasons for considering that:

(a) he has committed a crime against peace, a war crime, or a crime against humanity, as defined in the international instruments drawn up to make provision in respect of such crimes;

(b) he has committed a serious non-political crime outside the country of refuge prior to his admission to that country as a refugee;

(c) he has been guilty of acts contrary to the purposes and principles of the United Nations.

Article 2
General obligations

Every refugee has duties to the country in which he finds himself, which require in particular that he conform to its laws and regulations as well as to measures taken for the maintenance of public order.

Article 3
Non-discrimination

The Contracting States shall apply the provisions of this Convention to refugees without discrimination as to race, religion or country of origin.

Article 4
Religion

The Contracting States shall accord to refugees within their territories treatment at least as favourable as that accorded to their nationals with respect to freedom to practise their religion and freedom as regards the religious education of their children.

Article 5
Rights granted apart from this Convention

Nothing in this Convention shall be deemed to impair any rights and benefits granted by a Contracting State to refugees apart from this Convention.

Article 6
The term 'in the same circumstances'

For the purposes of this Convention, the term 'in the same circumstances' implies that any requirements (including requirements as to length and conditions of sojourn or residence) which the particular individual would have to fulfil for the enjoyment of the right in question, if he were not a refugee, must be fulfilled by him, with the exception of requirements which by their nature a refugee is incapable of fulfilling.

Article 7
Exemption from reciprocity

1. Except where this Convention contains more favourable provisions, a Contracting State shall accord to refugees the same treatment as is accorded to aliens generally.

2. After a period of three years' residence, all refugees shall enjoy exemption from legislative reciprocity in the territory of the Contracting States.

3. Each Contracting State shall continue to accord to refugees the rights and benefits to which they were already entitled, in the absence of reciprocity, at the date of entry into force of this Convention for that State.

4. The Contracting States shall consider favourably the possibility of according to refugees, in the absence of reciprocity, rights and benefits beyond those to which they are entitled according to paragraphs 2 and 3, and to extending exemption from reciprocity to refugees who do not fulfil the conditions provided for in paragraphs 2 and 3.

5. The provisions of paragraphs 2 and 3 apply both to the rights and benefits referred to in Articles 13, 18, 19, 21 and 22 of this Convention and to rights and benefits for which this Convention does not provide.

Article 8
Exemption from exceptional measures

With regard to exceptional measures which may be taken against the person, property or interests of nationals of a foreign State, the Contracting States shall not apply such measures to a refugee who is formally a national of the said State solely on account of such nationality. Contracting States which, under their legislation, are prevented from applying the general principle expressed in this Article, shall, in appropriate cases, grant exemptions in favour of such refugees.

Article 9
Provisional measures

Nothing in this Convention shall prevent a Contracting State, in time of war or other grave and exceptional circumstances, from taking provisionally measures which it considers to be essential to the national security in the case of a particular person, pending a determination by the Contracting State that that person is in fact a refugee and that the continuance of such measures is necessary in his case in the interests of national security.

Article 10
Continuity of residence

1. Where a refugee has been forcibly displaced during the Second World War and removed to the territory of a Contracting State, and is resident there, the period of such enforced sojourn shall be considered to have been lawful residence within that territory.

2. Where a refugee has been forcibly displaced during the Second World War from the territory of a Contracting State and has, prior to the date of entry into force of this Convention, returned there for the purpose of taking up residence, the period of residence before and after such enforced displacement shall be regarded as one uninterrupted period for any purposes for which uninterrupted residence is required.

Article 11
Refugee seamen

In the case of refugees regularly serving as crew members on board a ship flying the flag of a Contracting State, that State shall give sympathetic consideration to their establishment on its territory and the issue of travel documents to them or their temporary admission to its territory particularly with a view to facilitating their establishment in another country.

Chapter II—Juridical Status
Article 12
Personal status

1. The personal status of a refugee shall be governed by the law of the country of his domicile or, if he has no domicile, by the law of the country of his residence.

2. Rights previously acquired by a refugee and dependent on personal status, more particularly rights attaching to marriage, shall be respected by a Contracting State, subject to compliance, if this be necessary, with the formalities required by the law of that State, provided that the right in question is one which would have been recognized by the law of that State had he not become a refugee.

Article 13
Movable and immovable property

The Contracting States shall accord to a refugee treatment as favourable as possible and, in any event, not less favourable than that accorded to aliens generally in the same circumstances, as regards the acquisition of movable and immovable property and other rights pertaining thereto, and to leases and other contracts relating to movable and immovable property.

Article 14
Artistic rights and industrial property

In respect of the protection of industrial property, such as inventions, designs or models, trade marks, trade names, and of rights in literary, artistic, and scientific works, a refugee shall be accorded in the country in which he has his habitual residence the same protection as is accorded to nationals of that country. In the territory of any other Contracting State, he shall be accorded the same protection as is accorded in that territory to nationals of the country in which he has his habitual residence.

Article 15
Right of association

As regards non-political and non-profit making associations and trade unions the Contracting States shall accord to refugees lawfully staying in their territory the most favourable treatment accorded to nationals of a foreign country, in the same circumstances.

Article 16
Access to courts

1. A refugee shall have free access to the courts of law on the territory of all Contracting States.

2. A refugee shall enjoy in the Contracting State in which he has his habitual residence the same treatment as a national in matters pertaining to access to the Courts, including legal assistance and exemption from *cautio judicatum solvi*.

3. A refugee shall be accorded in the matters referred to in paragraph 2 in countries other than that in which he has his habitual residence the treatment granted to a national of the country of his habitual residence.

Chapter III—Gainful Employment

Article 17
Wage-earning employment

1. The Contracting State shall accord to refugees lawfully staying in their territory the most favourable treatment accorded to nationals of a foreign country in the same circumstances, as regards the right to engage in wage-earning employment.

2. In any case, restrictive measures imposed on aliens or the employment of aliens for the protection of the national labour market shall not be applied to a refugee who was already exempt from them at the date of entry into force of this Convention for the Contracting State concerned, or who fulfils one of the following conditions:

(a) He has completed three years' residence in the country;

(b) He has a spouse possessing the nationality of the country of residence. A refugee may not invoke the benefits of this provision if he has abandoned his spouse;

(c) He has one or more children possessing the nationality of the country of residence.

3. The Contracting States shall give sympathetic consideration to assimilating the rights of all refugees with regard to wage-earning employment to those of nationals, and in particular of those refugees who have entered their territory pursuant to programmes of labour recruitment or under immigration schemes.

Article 18
Self-employment

The Contracting States shall accord to a refugee lawfully in their territory treatment as favourable as possible and, in any event, not less favourable than that accorded to aliens generally in the same circumstances, as regards the right to engage on his own account in agriculture, industry, handicrafts and commerce and to establish commercial and industrial companies.

Article 19
Liberal professions

1. Each Contracting State shall accord to refugees lawfully staying in their territory who hold diplomas recognized by the competent authorities of that State, and who are desirous of practising a liberal profession, treatment as favourable as possible and, in any event, not less favourable than that accorded to aliens generally in the same circumstances.

2. The Contracting States shall use their best endeavours consistently with their laws and constitutions to secure the settlement of such refugees in the territories, other than the metropolitan territory, for whose international relations they are responsible.

Chapter IV—Welfare

Article 20
Rationing

Where a rationing system exists, which applies to the population at large and regulates the general distribution of products in short supply, refugees shall be accorded the same treatment as nationals.

Article 21
Housing

As regards housing, the Contracting States, in so far as the matter is regulated by laws or regulations or is subject to the control of public authorities, shall accord to refugees lawfully staying in their territory treatment as favourable as possible and, in any event, not less favourable than that accorded to aliens generally in the same circumstances.

Article 22
Public education

1. The Contracting States shall accord to refugees the same treatment as is accorded to nationals with respect to elementary education.

2. The Contracting States shall accord to refugees treatment as favourable as possible, and, in any event, not less favourable than that accorded to aliens generally in the same circumstances, with respect to education other than elementary education and, in particular, as regards access to studies, the recognition of foreign school certificates, diplomas and degrees, the remission of fees and charges and the award of scholarships.

Article 23
Public relief

The Contracting States shall accord to refugees lawfully staying in their territory the same treatment with respect to public relief and assistance as is accorded to their nationals.

Article 24
Labour legislation and social security

1. The Contracting States shall accord to refugees lawfully staying in their territory the same treatment as is accorded to nationals in respect of the following matters:

(a) In so far as such matters are governed by laws or regulations or are subject to the control of administrative authorities: remuneration, including family allowances where these form part of remuneration, hours of work, overtime arrangements, holidays with pay, restrictions on home work, minimum age of employment, apprenticeship and training, women's work and the work of young persons, and the enjoyment of the benefits of collective bargaining;

(b) Social security (legal provisions in respect of employment injury, occupational diseases, maternity, sickness, disability, old age, death, unemployment, family responsibilities and any other contingency which, according to national laws or regulations, is covered by a social security scheme), subject to the following limitations:

(i) There may be appropriate arrangements for the maintenance of acquired rights and rights in course of acquisition;

(ii) National laws or regulations of the country of residence may prescribe special arrangements concerning benefits or portions of benefits which are payable wholly out of public funds, and concerning allowances paid to persons who do not fulfil the contribution conditions prescribed for the award of a normal pension.

2. The right to compensation for the death of a refugee resulting from employment injury or from occupational disease shall not be affected by the fact that the residence of the beneficiary is outside the territory of the Contracting State.

3. The Contracting States shall extend to refugees the benefits of agreements concluded between them, or which may be concluded between them in the future, concerning the maintenance of acquired rights and rights in the process of acquisition in regard to social security, subject only to the conditions which apply to nationals of the States signatory to the agreements in question.

4. The Contracting States will give sympathetic consideration to extending to refugees so far as possible the benefits of similar agreements which may at any time be in force between such Contracting States and non-contracting States.

Chapter V—Administrative measures

Article 25
Administrative assistance

1. When the exercise of a right by a refugee would normally require the assistance of authorities of a foreign country to whom he cannot have recourse, the Contracting States

in whose territory he is residing shall arrange that such assistance be afforded to him by their own authorities or by an international authority.

2. The authority or authorities mentioned in paragraph 1 shall deliver or cause to be delivered under their supervision to refugees such documents or certifications as would normally be delivered to aliens by or through their national authorities.

3. Documents or certifications so delivered shall stand in the stead of the official instruments delivered to aliens by or through their national authorities, and shall be given credence in the absence of proof to the contrary.

4. Subject to such exceptional treatment as may be granted to indigent persons, fees may be charged for the services mentioned herein, but such fees shall be moderate and commensurate with those charged to nationals for similar services.

5. The provisions of this Article shall be without prejudice to Articles 27 and 28.

Article 26
Freedom of movement

Each Contracting State shall accord to refugees lawfully in its territory the right to choose their place of residence and to move freely within its territory, subject to any regulations applicable to aliens generally in the same circumstances.

Article 27
Identity papers

The Contracting States shall issue identity papers to any refugee in their territory who does not possess a valid travel document.

Article 28
Travel documents

1. The Contracting States shall issue to refugees lawfully staying in their territory travel documents for the purpose of travel outside their territory unless compelling reasons of national security or public order otherwise require, and the provisions of the Schedule to this Convention shall apply with respect to such documents. The Contracting States may issue such a travel document to any other refugee in their territory; they shall in particular give sympathetic consideration to the issue of such a travel document to refugees in their territory who are unable to obtain a travel document from the country of their lawful residence.

2. Travel documents issued to refugees under previous international agreements by parties thereto shall be recognized and treated by the Contracting States in the same way as if they had been issued pursuant to this article.

Article 29
Fiscal charges

1. The Contracting States shall not impose upon refugee duties, charges or taxes, of any description whatsoever, other or higher than those which are or may be levied on their nationals in similar situations.

2. Nothing in the above paragraph shall prevent the application to refugees of the laws and regulations concerning charges in respect of the issue to aliens of administrative documents including identity papers.

Article 30
Transfer of assets

1. A Contracting State shall, in conformity with its laws and regulations, permit refugees to transfer assets which they have brought into its territory, to another country where they have been admitted for the purposes of resettlement.

2. A Contracting State shall give sympathetic consideration to the application of refugees for permission to transfer assets wherever they may be and which are necessary for their resettlement in another country to which they have been admitted.

Article 31
Refugees unlawfully in the country of refuge

1. The Contracting States shall not impose penalties, on account of their illegal entry or presence, on refugees who, coming directly from a territory where their life or freedom was threatened in the sense of Article 1, enter or are present in their territory without authorization, provided they present themselves without delay to the authorities and show good cause for their illegal entry or presence.

2. The Contracting States shall not apply to the movements of such refugees restrictions other than those which are necessary and such restrictions shall only be applied until their status in the country is regularized or they obtain admission into another country. The Contracting States shall allow such refugees a reasonable period and all the necessary facilities to obtain admission into another country.

Article 32
Expulsion

1. The Contracting States shall not expel a refugee lawfully in their territory save on grounds of national security or public order.

2. The expulsion of such a refugee shall be only in pursuance of a decision reached in accordance with due process of law. Except where compelling reasons of national security otherwise require, the refugee shall be allowed to submit evidence to clear himself, and to appeal to and be represented for the purpose before competent authority or a person or persons specially designated by the competent authority.

3. The Contracting States shall allow such a refugee a reasonable period within which to seek legal admission into another country. The Contracting States reserve the right to apply during that period such internal measures as they may deem necessary.

Article 33
Prohibition of expulsion or return ('refoulement')

1. No Contracting State shall expel or return ('refouler') a refugee in any manner whatsoever to the frontiers of territories where his life or freedom would be threatened on

account of his race, religion, nationality, membership of a particular social group or political opinion.

2. The benefit of the present provision may not, however, be claimed by a refugee whom there are reasonable grounds for regarding as a danger to the security of the country in which he is, or who, having been convicted by a final judgment of a particularly serious crime, constitutes a danger to the community of that country.

Article 34
Naturalization

The Contracting States shall as far as possible facilitate the assimilation and naturalization of refugees. They shall in particular make every effort to expedite naturalization proceedings and to reduce as far as possible the charges and costs of such proceedings.

Chapter VI—Executory and transitory provisions

Article 35
Co-operation of the national authorities with the United Nations

1. The Contracting States undertake to co-operate with the Office of the United Nations High Commissioner for Refugees, or any other agency of the United Nations which may succeed it, in the exercise of its functions, and shall in particular facilitate its duty of supervising the application of the provisions of this Convention.

2. In order to enable the Office of the High Commissioner or any other agency of the United Nations which may succeed it, to make reports to the competent organs of the United Nations, the Contracting States undertake to provide them in the appropriate form with information and statistical data requested concerning:

(a) the condition of refugees,

(b) the implementation of this Convention, and

(c) laws, regulations and decrees which are, or may hereafter be, in force relating to refugees.

Article 36
Information on national legislation

The Contracting States shall communicate to the Secretary-General of the United Nations the laws and regulations which they may adopt to ensure the application of this Convention.

Article 37
Relation to previous Conventions

Without prejudice to Article 28, paragraph 2, of this Convention, this Convention replaces, as between parties to it, the Arrangements of 5 July 1922, 31 May 1924, 12 May 1926, 30 June 1928 and 30 July 1935, the Conventions of 28 October 1933 and 10 February 1938, the Protocol of 14 September 1939 and the Agreement of 15 October 1946.

Chapter VII—Final clauses

Article 38
Settlement of disputes

Any dispute between parties to this Convention relating to its interpretation or application, which cannot be settled by other means, shall be referred to the International Court of Justice at the request of any one of the parties to the dispute.

Article 39
Signature, ratification and accession

1. This Convention shall be opened for signature at Geneva on 28 July 1951 and shall hereafter be deposited with the Secretary-General of the United Nations. It shall be open for signature at the European Office of the United Nations from 28 July to 31 August 1951 and shall be re-opened for signature at the Headquarters of the United Nations from 17 September 1951 to 31 December 1952.

2. This Convention shall be open for signature on behalf of all States Members of the United Nations, and also on behalf of any other State invited to attend the Conference of Plenipotentiaries on the Status of Refugees and Stateless Persons or to which an invitation to sign will have been addressed by the General Assembly. It shall be ratified and the instruments of ratification shall be deposited with the Secretary-General of the United Nations.

3. This Convention shall be open from 28 July 1951 for accession by the States referred to in paragraph 2 of this Article. Accession shall be effected by the deposit of an instrument of accession with the Secretary-General of the United Nations.

Article 40
Territorial application clause

1. Any State may, at the time of signature, ratification or accession, declare that this Convention shall extend to all or any of the territories for the international relations of which it is responsible. Such a declaration shall take effect when the Convention enters into force for the State concerned.

2. At any time thereafter any such extension shall be made by notification addressed to the Secretary-General of the United Nations and shall take effect as from the ninetieth day after the day of receipt by the Secretary-General of the United Nations of this notification, or as from the date of entry into force of the Convention for the State concerned, whichever is the later.

3. With respect to those territories to which this Convention is not extended at the time of signature, ratification or accession, each State concerned shall consider the possibility of taking the necessary steps in order to extend the application of this Convention to such territories, subject, where necessary for constitutional reasons, to the consent of the governments of such territories.

Article 41
Federal clause

In the case of a Federal or non-unitary State, the following provisions shall apply:

(a) With respect to those Articles of this Convention that come within the legislative jurisdiction of the federal legislative authority, the obligations of the Federal Government shall to this extent be the same as those of Parties which are not Federal States,

(b) With respect to those Articles of this Convention that come within the legislative jurisdiction of constituent States, provinces or cantons which are not, under the constitutional system of the federation, bound to take legislative action, the Federal Government shall bring such Articles with a favourable recommendation to the notice of the appropriate authorities of States, provinces or cantons at the earliest possible moment.

(c) A Federal State Party to this Convention shall, at the request of any other Contracting State transmitted through the Secretary-General of the United Nations, supply a statement of the law and practice of the Federation and its constituent units in regard to any particular provision of the Convention showing the extent to which effect has been given to that provision by legislative or other action.

Article 42
Reservations

1. At the time of signature, ratification or accession, any State may make reservations to articles of the Convention other than to Articles 1, 3, 4, 16(1), 33, 36–46 inclusive.

2. Any State making a reservation in accordance with paragraph 1 of this article may at any time withdraw the reservation by a communication to that effect addressed to the Secretary-General of the United Nations.

Article 43
Entry into force

1. This Convention shall come into force on the ninetieth day following the day of deposit of the sixth instrument of ratification or accession.

2. For each State ratifying or acceding to the Convention after the deposit of the sixth instrument of ratification or accession, the Convention shall enter into force on the ninetieth day following the date of deposit by such State of its instrument of ratification or accession.

Article 44
Denunciation

1. Any Contracting State may denounce this Convention at any time by a notification addressed to the Secretary-General of the United Nations.

2. Such denunciation shall take effect for the Contracting State concerned one year from the date upon which it is received by the Secretary-General of the United Nations.

3. Any State which has made a declaration or notification under Article 40 may, at any time thereafter, by a notification to the Secretary-General of the United Nations, declare

that the Convention shall cease to extend to such territory one year after the date of receipt of the notification by the Secretary-General.

Article 45
Revision

1. Any Contracting State may request revision of this Convention at any time by a notification addressed to the Secretary-General of the United Nations.

2. The General Assembly of the United Nations shall recommend the steps, if any, to be taken in respect of such request.

Article 46
Notifications by the Secretary-General of the United Nations

The Secretary-General of the United Nations shall inform all Members of the United Nations and non-member States referred to in Article 39:

(a) of declarations and notifications in accordance with Section B of Article 1;

(b) of signatures, ratifications and accessions in accordance with Article 39;

(c) of declarations and notifications in accordance with Article 40;

(d) of reservations and withdrawals in accordance with Article 42;

(e) of the date on which this Convention will come into force in accordance with Article 43;

(f) of denunciations and notifications in accordance with Article 44;

(g) of requests for revision in accordance with Article 45.

IN FAITH WHEREOF the undersigned, duly authorized, have signed this Convention on behalf of their respective Governments,

DONE at GENEVA, this twenty-eighth day of July, one thousand nine hundred and fifty-one, in a single copy, of which the English and French texts are equally authentic and which shall remain deposited in the archives of the United Nations, and certified true copies of which shall be delivered to all Members of the United Nations and to the non-member States referred to in Article 39.

Schedule[5]

Paragraph 1

1. The travel document referred to in Article 28 of this Convention shall be similar to the specimen annexed hereto.

2. The document shall be made out in at least two languages, one of which shall be English or French.

Paragraph 2

Subject to the regulations obtaining in the country of issue, children may be included in the travel document of a parent or, in exceptional circumstances, of another adult refugee.

[5] The Annex with details of the Specimen Travel Document is omitted.

Paragraph 3

The fees charged for issue of the document shall not exceed the lowest scale of charges for national passports.

Paragraph 4

Save in special or exceptional cases, the document shall be made valid for the largest possible number of countries.

Paragraph 5

The document shall have a validity of either one or two years, at the discretion of the issuing authority.

Paragraph 6

1. The renewal or extension of the validity of the document is a matter for the authority which issued it, so long as the holder has not established lawful residence in another territory and resides lawfully in the territory of the said authority. The issue of a new document is, under the same conditions, a matter for the authority which issued the former document.

2. Diplomatic or consular authorities, specially authorized for the purpose, shall be empowered to extend, for a period not exceeding six months, the validity of travel documents issued by their Governments.

3. The Contracting States shall give sympathetic consideration to renewing or extending the validity of travel documents or issuing new documents to refugees no longer lawfully resident in their territory who are unable to obtain a travel document from the country of their lawful residence.

Paragraph 7

The Contracting States shall recognize the validity of the documents issued in accordance with the provisions of Article 28 of this Convention.

Paragraph 8

The competent authorities of the country to which the refugee desires to proceed shall, if they are prepared to admit him and if a visa is required, affix a visa on the document of which he is the holder.

Paragraph 9

1. The Contracting States undertake to issue transit visas to refugees who have obtained visas for a territory of final destination.

2. The issue of such visas may be refused on grounds which would justify refusal of a visa to any alien.

Paragraph 10

The fees for the issue of exit, entry or transit visas shall not exceed the lowest scale of charges for visas on foreign passports.

Paragraph 11

When a refugee has lawfully taken up residence in the territory of another Contracting State, the responsibility for the issue of a new document, under the terms and conditions of Article 28, shall be that of the competent authority of that territory, to which the refugee shall be entitled to apply.

Paragraph 12

The authority issuing a new document shall withdraw the old document and shall return it to the country of issue, if it is stated in the document that it should be so returned; otherwise it shall withdraw and cancel the document.

Paragraph 13

1. Each Contracting State undertakes that the holder of a travel document issued by it in accordance with Article 28 of this Convention shall be re-admitted to its territory at any time during the period of its validity.

2. Subject to the provisions of the preceding sub-paragraph, a Contracting State may require the holder of the document to comply with such formalities as may be prescribed in regard to exit from or return to its territory.

3. The Contracting States reserve the right, in exceptional cases, or in cases where the refugee's stay is authorized for a specific period, when issuing the document, to limit the period during which the refugee may return to a period of not less than three months.

Paragraph 14

Subject only to the terms of paragraph 13, the provisions of this Schedule in no way affect the laws and regulations governing the conditions of admission to, transit through, residence and establishment in, and departure from, the territories of the Contracting States.

Paragraph 15

Neither the issue of the document nor the entries made thereon determine or affect the status of the holder, particularly as regards nationality.

Paragraph 16

The issue of the document does not in any way entitle the holder to the protection of the diplomatic or consular authorities of the country of issue, and does not confer on these authorities a right of protection.

5. 1967 Protocol relating to the Status of Refugees

Entry into force: 4 October 1967

Text: 606 *UNTS* 267

Preamble

The States Parties to the present Protocol,

Considering that the Convention relating to the Status of Refugees done at Geneva on 28 July 1951 (hereinafter referred to as the Convention) covers only those persons who have become refugees as a result of events occurring before 1 January 1951,

Considering that new refugee situations have arisen since the Convention was adopted and that the refugees concerned may therefore not fall within the scope of the Convention,

Considering that it is desirable that equal status should be enjoyed by all refugees covered by the definition in the Convention irrespective of the dateline 1 January 1951, *Have agreed as follows:*

Article I
General provision

1. The States Parties to the present Protocol undertake to apply Articles 2 to 34 inclusive of the Convention to refugees as hereinafter defined.

2. For the purpose of the present Protocol, the term 'refugee' shall, except as regards the application of paragraph 3 of this Article, mean any person within the definition of Article 1 of the Convention as if the words 'As a result of events occurring before 1 January 1951 and . . .' and the words '. . . a result of such events', in Article 1 A(2) were omitted.

3. The present Protocol shall be applied by the States Parties hereto without any geographic limitation, save that existing declarations made by States already Parties to the Convention in accordance with Article 1 B(1)(a) of the Convention, shall, unless extended under Article 1 B(2) thereof, apply also under the present Protocol.

Article II
Co-operation of the national authorities with the United Nations

1. The States Parties to the present Protocol undertake to co-operate with the Office of the United Nations High Commissioner for Refugees, or any other agency of the United Nations which may succeed it, in the exercise of its functions, and shall in particular facilitate its duty of supervising the application of the provisions of the present Protocol.

2. In order to enable the Office of the High Commissioner, or any other agency of the United Nations which may succeed it, to make reports to the competent organs of the United Nations, the States Parties to the present Protocol undertake to provide them with the information and statistical data requested, in the appropriate form, concerning:
(a) The condition of refugees;

(b) The implementation of the present Protocol;

(c) Laws, regulations and decrees which are, or may hereafter be, in force relating to refugees.

Article III
Information on national legislation

The States Parties to the present Protocol shall communicate to the Secretary-General of the United Nations the laws and regulations which they may adopt to ensure the application of the present Protocol.

Article IV
Settlement of disputes

Any dispute between States Parties to the present Protocol which relates to its interpretation or application and which cannot be settled by other means shall be referred to the International Court of Justice at the request of any one of the parties to the dispute.

Article V
Accession

The present Protocol shall be open for accession on behalf of all States Parties to the Convention and of any other State Member of the United Nations or member of any of the specialized agencies or to which an invitation to accede may have been addressed by the General Assembly of the United Nations. Accession shall be effected by the deposit of an instrument of accession with the Secretary-General of the United Nations.

Article VI
Federal clause

In the case of a Federal or non-unitary State, the following provisions shall apply:

(a) With respect to those articles of the Convention to be applied in accordance with Article I, paragraph 1, of the present Protocol that come within the legislative jurisdiction of the federal legislative authority, the obligations of the Federal Government shall to this extent be the same as those of States Parties which are not Federal States.

(b) With respect to those articles of the Convention to be applied in accordance with Article I, paragraph 1, of the present Protocol that come within the legislative jurisdiction of constituent States, provinces or cantons which are not, under the constitutional system of the federation, bound to take legislative action, the Federal Government shall bring such articles with a favourable recommendation to the notice of the appropriate authorities of States, provinces or cantons at the earliest possible moment;

(c) A Federal State Party to the present Protocol shall, at the request of any other State Party hereto transmitted through the Secretary-General of the United Nations, supply a statement of the law and practice of the Federation and its constituent units in regard to any particular provision of the Convention to be applied in accordance with Article I, paragraph 1, of the present Protocol, showing the extent to which effect has been given to that provision by legislative or other action.

Article VII
Reservations and declarations

1. At the time of accession, any State may make reservations in respect of Article IV of the present Protocol and in respect of the application in accordance with Article I of the present Protocol of any provisions of the Convention other than those contained in Articles 1, 3, 4, 16 (1) and 33 thereof, provided that in the case of a State Party to the Convention reservations made under this Article shall not extend to refugees in respect of whom the Convention applies.

2. Reservations made by States Parties to the Convention in accordance with Article 42 thereof shall, unless withdrawn, be applicable in relation to their obligations under the present Protocol.

3. Any State making a reservation in accordance with paragraph 1 of this Article may at any time withdraw such reservation by a communication to that effect addressed to the Secretary-General of the United Nations.

4. Declarations made under Article 40, paragraphs 1 and 2, of the Convention by a State Party thereto which accedes to the present Protocol shall be deemed to apply in respect of the present Protocol, unless upon accession a notification to the contrary is addressed by the State Party concerned to the Secretary-General of the United Nations. The provisions of Article 40, paragraphs 2 and 3, and of Article 44, paragraph 3, of the Convention shall be deemed to apply *mutatis mutandis* to the present Protocol.

Article VIII
Entry into force

1. The present Protocol shall come into force on the day of deposit of the sixth instrument of accession.

2. For each State acceding to the Protocol after the deposit of the sixth instrument of accession, the Protocol shall come into force on the date of deposit by such State of its instrument of accession.

Article IX
Denunciation

1. Any State Party hereto may denounce this Protocol at any time by a notification addressed to the Secretary-General of the United Nations.

2. Such denunciation shall take effect for the State Party concerned one year from the date on which it is received by the Secretary-General of the United Nations.

Article X
Notifications by the Secretary-General of the United Nations

The Secretary-General of the United Nations shall inform the States referred to in Article V above of the date of entry into force, accessions, reservations and withdrawals of reservations to and denunciations of the present Protocol, and of declarations and notifications relating hereto.

Article XI

Deposit in the archives of the Secretariat of the United Nations

A copy of the present Protocol, of which the Chinese, English, French, Russian and Spanish texts are equally authentic, signed by the President of the General Assembly and by the Secretary-General of the United Nations, shall be deposited in the archives of the Secretariat of the United Nations. The Secretary-General will transmit certified copies thereof to all States Members of the United Nations and to the other States referred to in Article V above.

GENERAL ASSEMBLY RESOLUTION 2198 (XXI) OF
16 DECEMBER 1966

Protocol relating to the Status of Refugees

The General Assembly,

Considering that the Convention relating to the Status of Refugees, signed at Geneva on 28 July 1951, covers only those persons who have become refugees as a result of events occurring before 1 January 1951,

Considering that new refugee situations have arisen since the Convention was adopted and that the refugees concerned may therefore not fall within the scope of the Convention,

Considering that it is desirable that equal status should be enjoyed by all refugees covered by the definition in the Convention, irrespective of the date line of 1 January 1951,

Taking note of the recommendation of the Executive Committee of the Programme of the United Nations High Commissioner for Refugees that the draft Protocol relating to the Status of Refugees should be submitted to the General Assembly after consideration by the Economic and Social Council, in order that the Secretary-General might be authorized to open the Protocol for accession by Governments within the shortest possible time,

Considering that the Economic and Social Council, in its resolution 1186 (XLI) of 18 November 1966, took note with approval of the draft Protocol contained in the addendum to the report of the United Nations High Commissioner for Refugees and concerning measures to extend the personal scope of the Convention and transmitted the addendum to the General Assembly,

1. *Takes note* of the Protocol relating to the Status of Refugees, the text of which is contained in the addendum to the report of the United Nations High Commissioner for Refugees;

2. *Requests* the Secretary-General to transmit the text of the Protocol to the States mentioned in article V thereof, with a view to enabling them to accede to the Protocol.[6]

---

[6] The Protocol was signed by the President of the General Assembly and by the Secretary-General on 31 January 1967.

6. 1967 UN Declaration on Territorial Asylum

Adopted by the General Assembly of the United Nations on 14 December 1967

Text: UNGA resolution 2312 (XXII)

The General Assembly,

Recalling its resolutions 1839 (XVII) of 19 December 1962, 2100 (XX) of 20 December 1965 and 2203 (XXI) of 16 December 1966 concerning a declaration on the right of asylum,

Considering the work of codification to be undertaken by the International Law Commission in accordance with General Assembly resolution 1400 (XIV) of 21 November 1959,

Adopts the following Declaration:

DECLARATION ON TERRITORIAL ASYLUM

The General Assembly,

Noting that the purposes proclaimed in the Charter of the United Nations are to maintain international peace and security, to develop friendly relations among all nations and to achieve international co-operation in solving international problems of an economic, social, cultural or humanitarian character and in promoting and encouraging respect for human rights and for fundamental freedoms for all without distinction as to race, sex, language or religion,

Mindful of the Universal Declaration of Human Rights, which declares in article 14 that:

'1. Everyone has the right to seek and to enjoy in other countries asylum from persecution.'

'2. This right may not be invoked in the case of prosecutions genuinely arising from non-political crimes or from acts contrary to the purposes and principles of the United Nations.'

Recalling also article 13, paragraph 2, of the Universal Declaration of Human Rights, which states: 'Everyone has the right to leave any country, including his own, and to return to his country',

Recognizing that the grant of asylum by a State to persons entitled to invoke article 14 of the Universal Declaration of Human Rights is a peaceful and humanitarian act and that, as such, it cannot be regarded as unfriendly by any other State,

Recommends that, without prejudice to existing instruments dealing with asylum and the status of refugees and stateless persons, States should base themselves in their practices relating to territorial asylum on the following principles:

Article 1

1. Asylum granted by a State, in the exercise of its sovereignty, to persons entitled to invoke article 14 of the Universal Declaration of Human Rights, including persons struggling against colonialism, shall be respected by all other States.

2. The right to seek and to enjoy asylum may not be invoked by any person with respect to whom there are serious reasons for considering that he has committed a crime against

peace, a war crime or a crime against humanity, as defined in the international instruments drawn up to make provision in respect of such crimes.

3. It shall rest with the State granting asylum to evaluate the grounds for the grant of asylum.

Article 2

1. The situation of persons referred to in article 1, paragraph 1, is, without prejudice to the sovereignty of States and the purposes and principles of the United Nations, of concern to the international community.

2. Where a State finds difficulty in granting or continuing to grant asylum, States individually or jointly or through the United Nations shall consider, in a spirit of international solidarity, appropriate measures to lighten the burden on that State.

Article 3

1. No person referred to in article 1, paragraph 1, shall be subjected to measures such as rejection at the frontier or, if he has already entered the territory in which he seeks asylum, expulsion or compulsory return to any State where he may be subjected to persecution.

2. Exception may be made to the foregoing principle only for overriding reasons of national security or in order to safeguard the population, as in the case of a mass influx of persons.

3. Should a State decide in any case that exception to the principle stated in paragraph 1 of this article would be justified, it shall consider the possibility of granting to the person concerned, under such conditions as it may deem appropriate, an opportunity, whether by way of provisional asylum or otherwise, of going to another State.

Article 4

States granting asylum shall not permit persons who have received asylum to engage in activities contrary to the purposes and principles of the United Nations.

7. 1984 United Nations Convention Against Torture and Other Cruel, Inhuman or Degrading Treatment or Punishment—Extracts

Entry into force: 26 June 1987

Text: UNGA resolution 39/46, 10 December 1984

Article 1

1. For the purposes of this Convention, the term 'torture' means any act by which severe pain or suffering, whether physical or mental, is intentionally inflicted on a person for

such purposes as obtaining from him or a third person information or a confession, pu̇ ishing him for an act he or a third person has committed or is suspected of having com mitted, or intimidating or coercing him or a third person, or for any reason based on discrimination of any kind, when such pain or suffering is inflicted by or at the instigation of or with the consent or acquiescence of a public official or other person acting in an official capacity. It does not include pain or suffering arising only from, inherent in or incidental to lawful sanctions.

2. This article is without prejudice to any international instrument or national legislation which does or may contain provisions of wider application.

Article 2

1. Each State Party shall take effective legislative, administrative, judicial or other measures to prevent acts of torture in any territory under its jurisdiction.

2. No exceptional circumstances whatsoever, whether a state of war or a threat of war, internal political instability or any other public emergency, may be invoked as a justification of torture.

3. An order from a superior officer or a public authority may not be invoked as a justification of torture.

Article 3

1. No State Party shall expel, return ('refouler') or extradite a person to another State where there are substantial grounds for believing that he would be in danger of being subjected to torture.

2. For the purpose of determining whether there are such grounds, the competent authorities shall take into account all relevant considerations including, where applicable, the existence in the State concerned of a consistent pattern of gross, flagrant or mass violations of human rights.

. . .

Article 11

Each State Party shall keep under systematic review interrogation rules, instructions, methods and practices as well as arrangements for the custody and treatment of persons subjected to any form of arrest, detention or imprisonment in any territory under its jurisdiction, with a view to preventing any cases of torture.

Article 12

Each State Party shall ensure that its competent authorities proceed to a prompt and impartial investigation, wherever there is reasonable ground to believe that an act of torture has been committed in any territory under its jurisdiction.

Article 13

Each State Party shall ensure that any individual who alleges he has been subjected to torture in any territory under its jurisdiction has the right to complain to, and to have his case promptly and impartially examined by, its competent authorities. Steps shall be taken to ensure that the complainant and witnesses are protected against all ill-treatment or intimidation as a consequence of his complaint or any evidence given.

Article 14

1. Each State Party shall ensure in its legal system that the victim of an act of torture obtains redress and has an enforceable right to fair and adequate compensation, including the means for as full rehabilitation as possible. In the event of the death of the victim as a result of an act of torture, his dependants shall be entitled to compensation.

2. Nothing in this article shall affect any right of the victim or other persons to compensation which may exist under national law.

Article 15

Each State Party shall ensure that any statement which is established to have been made as a result of torture shall not be invoked as evidence in any proceedings, except against a person accused of torture as evidence that the statement was made.

Article 16

1. Each State Party shall undertake to prevent in any territory under its jurisdiction other acts of cruel, inhuman or degrading treatment or punishment which do not amount to torture as defined in article 1, when such acts are committed by or at the instigation of or with the consent or acquiescence of a public official or other person acting in an official capacity. In particular, the obligations contained in articles 10, 11, 12 and 13 shall apply with the substitution for references to torture of references to other forms of cruel, inhuman or degrading treatment or punishment.

2. The provisions of this Convention are without prejudice to the provisions of any other international instrument or national law which prohibits cruel, inhuman or degrading treatment or punishment or which relates to extradition or expulsion.

. . .

8. 1989 United Nations Convention on the Rights of the Child—Extracts

Entry into force: 20 September 1990

Text: UNGA resolution 44/25, 20 November 1989

Article 1

For the purposes of the present Convention, a child means every human being below the age of eighteen years unless, under the law applicable to the child, majority is attained earlier.

Article 2

1. States Parties shall respect and ensure the rights set forth in the present Convention to each child within their jurisdiction without discrimination of any kind, irrespective of the child's or his or her parent's or legal guardian's race, colour, sex, language, religion, political or other opinion, national, ethnic or social origin, property, disability, birth or other status.

2. States Parties shall take all appropriate measures to ensure that the child is protected against all forms of discrimination or punishment on the basis of the status, activities, expressed opinions, or beliefs of the child's parents, legal guardians, or family members.

Article 3

1. In all actions concerning children, whether undertaken by public or private social welfare institutions, courts of law, administrative authorities or legislative bodies, the best interests of the child shall be a primary consideration.

2. States Parties undertake to ensure the child such protection and care as is necessary for his or her well-being, taking into account the rights and duties of his or her parents, legal guardians, or other individuals legally responsible for him or her, and, to this end, shall take all appropriate legislative and administrative measures.

3. States Parties shall ensure that the institutions, services and facilities responsible for the care or protection of children shall conform with the standards established by competent authorities, particularly in the areas of safety, health, in the number and suitability of their staff, as well as competent supervision.

Article 4

States Parties shall undertake all appropriate legislative, administrative, and other measures for the implementation of the rights recognized in the present Convention. With regard to economic, social and cultural rights, States Parties shall undertake such measures to the maximum extent of their available resources and, where needed, within the framework of international co-operation.

. . .

Article 12

1. States Parties shall assure to the child who is capable of forming his or her own views the right to express those views freely in all matters affecting the child, the views of the child being given due weight in accordance with the age and maturity of the child.

2. For this purpose, the child shall in particular be provided the opportunity to be heard in any judicial and administrative proceedings affecting the child, either directly, or through a representative or an appropriate body, in a manner consistent with the procedural rules of national law.

. . .

Article 19

1. States Parties shall take all appropriate legislative, administrative, social and educational measures to protect the child from all forms of physical or mental violence, injury or abuse, neglect or negligent treatment, maltreatment or exploitation, including sexual abuse, while in the care of parent(s), legal guardian(s), or any other person who has the care of the child.

2. Such protective measures should, as appropriate, include effective procedures for the establishment of social programmes to provide necessary support for the child and for those who have the care of the child, as well as for other forms of prevention and for identification, reporting, referral, investigation, treatment and follow-up of instances of child maltreatment described heretofore, and, as appropriate, for judicial involvement.

Article 20

1. A child temporarily or permanently deprived of his or her family environment, or in whose own best interests cannot be allowed to remain in that environment, shall be entitled to special protection and assistance provided by the State.

2. States Parties shall in accordance with their national laws ensure alternative care for such a child.

3. Such care could include, *inter alia*, foster placement, *kafalah* of Islamic law, adoption or if necessary placement in suitable institutions for the care of children. When considering solutions, due regard shall be paid to the desirability of continuity in a child's upbringing and to the child's ethnic, religious, cultural and linguistic background.

Article 21

States Parties that recognize and/or permit the system of adoption shall ensure that the best interests of the child shall be the paramount consideration and they shall:

(a) Ensure that the adoption of a child is authorized only by competent authorities who determine, in accordance with applicable law and procedures and on the basis of all pertinent and reliable information, that the adoption is permissible in view of the child's status concerning parents, relatives and legal guardians and that, if required, the persons concerned have given their informal consent to the adoption on the basis of such counselling as may be necessary;

(b) Recognize that inter-country adoption may be considered as an alternative means of child's care, if the child cannot be placed in a foster or an adoptive family or cannot in any suitable manner be cared for in the child's country of origin;

(c) Ensure that the child concerned by inter-country adoption enjoys safeguards and standards equivalent to those existing in the case of national adoption;

(d) Take all appropriate measures to ensure that, in inter-country adoption, the placement does not result in improper financial gain for those involved in it;

(e) Promote, where appropriate, the objectives of the present article by concluding bilateral or multilateral arrangements or agreements, and endeavour, within this framework, to ensure that the placement of the child in another country is carried out by competent authorities or organs.

1. States Parties shall take appropriate measures to ensure
refugee status or who is considered a refugee in accordance with ap~~r~~
or domestic law and procedures shall, whether unaccompanied or accom~~,is seeking~~
or her parents or by any other person, receive appropriate protection and huma~~n...~~ ~~is~~ ~~tional~~
assistance in the enjoyment of applicable rights set forth in the present Convention and
in other international human rights or humanitarian instruments to which the said States
are Parties.

2. For this purpose, States Parties shall provide, as they consider appropriate, co-
operation in any efforts by the United Nations and other competent intergovernmental
organizations or non-governmental organizations co-operating with the United Nations
to protect and assist such a child and to trace the parents or other members of the family of any refugee child in order to obtain information necessary for reunification with his
or her family. In cases where no parents or other members of the family can be found,
the child shall be accorded the same protection as any other child permanently or temporarily deprived of his or her family environment for any reason, as set forth in the present Convention.

9. 1987 Constitution of the International Organization for Migration

The present text incorporates into the Constitution of the Intergovernmental Committee
for European Migration (former designation of the Organization; original Constitution of
19 October 1953 in force 30 November 1954) the amendments adopted on 20 May 1987,
which in turn entered into force on 14 November 1989.

Preamble

The High Contracting Parties,

Recalling the Resolution adopted on 5 December 1951 by the Migration Conference in
Brussels,
Recognizing that the provision of migration services at an international level is often
required to ensure the orderly flow of migration movements throughout the world and
to facilitate, under the most favourable conditions, the settlement and integration of the
migrants into the economic and social structure of the country of reception,

that similar migration services may also be required for temporary migration, return
migration and intra-regional migration,

that international migration also includes that of refugees, displaced persons and other
individuals compelled to leave their homelands, and who are in need of international
migration services,

that there is a need to promote the co-operation of States and international organizations with a view to facilitating the emigration of persons who desire to migrate to countries where they may achieve self-dependence through their employment and live with
their families in dignity and self-respect,

...iate the creation of new economic opportunities in receiving
...iationship exists between migration and the economic, social and
that mi... ..is in developing countries,
countrie co-operation and other international activities for migration the needs of
cul... ...ping countries should be taken into account,

that there is a need to promote the co-operation of States and international organizations, governmental and non-governmental, for research and consultation on migration issues, not only in regard to the migration process but also the specific situation and needs of the migrant as an individual human being,

that the movement of migrants should, to the extent possible, be carried out with normal transport services but that, on occasion, there is a need for additional or other facilities,

that there should be close co-operation and co-ordination among States, international organizations, governmental and non-governmental, on migration and refugee matters,

that there is a need for the international financing of activities related to international migration,

Do hereby establish the International Organization for Migration, hereinafter called the Organization, and

Accept this Constitution.

Chapter I—Purposes and Functions

Article 1

1. The purposes and functions of the Organization shall be:

(a) to make arrangements for the organized transfer of migrants, for whom existing facilities are inadequate or who would not otherwise be able to move without special assistance, to countries offering opportunities for orderly migration;

(b) to concern itself with the organized transfer of refugees, displaced persons and other individuals in need of international migration services for whom arrangements may be made between the Organization and the States concerned, including those States undertaking to receive them;

(c) to provide, at the request of and in agreement with the States concerned, migration services such as recruitment, selection, processing, language training, orientation activities, medical examination, placement, activities facilitating reception and integration, advisory services on migration questions, and other assistance as is in accord with the aims of the Organization;

(d) to provide similar services as requested by States, or in co-operation with other interested international organizations, for voluntary return migration, including voluntary repatriation;

(e) to provide a forum to States as well as international and other organizations for the exchange of views and experiences, and the promotion of co-operation and co-ordination of efforts on international migration issues, including studies on such issues in order to develop practical solutions.

2. In carrying out its functions, the Organization shall co-operate closely with international organizations, governmental and non-governmental, concerned with migration,

refugees and human resources in order, *inter alia*, to facilitate the national activities in these fields. Such co-operation shall be carried ~~n of inter-~~ respect of the competences of the organizations concerned. ~~mutual~~

3. The Organization shall recognize the fact that control of standards of admis. the number of immigrants to be admitted are matters within the domestic jurisdiction States, and, in carrying out its functions, shall conform to the laws, regulations and policies of the States concerned.

Chapter II—Membership

Article 2

The Members of the Organization shall be:

(a) the States being Members of the Organization which have accepted this Constitution according to Article 34, or to which the terms of Article 35 apply;

(b) other States with a demonstrated interest in the principle of free movement of persons which undertake to make a financial contribution at least to the administrative requirements of the Organization, the rate of which will be agreed to by the Council and by the State concerned, subject to a two-thirds majority vote of the Council and upon acceptance by the State of this Constitution.

Article 3

Any Member State may give notice of withdrawal from the Organization effective at the end of a financial year. Such notice must be in writing and must reach the Director General of the Organization at least four months before the end of the financial year. The financial obligations to the Organization of a Member State which has given notice of withdrawal shall include the entire financial year in which notice is given.

Article 4

1. If a Member State fails to meet its financial obligations to the Organization for two consecutive financial years, the Council may by a two-thirds majority vote suspend the voting rights and all or part of the services to which this Member State is entitled. The Council shall have the authority to restore such voting rights and services by a simple majority vote.

2. Any Member State may be suspended from membership by a two-thirds majority vote of the Council if it persistently violates the principles of this Constitution. The Council shall have the authority to restore such membership by a simple majority vote.

Chapter III—Organs

Article 5

There are established as the organs of the Organization:

(a) the Council;

(b) the Executive Committee;

Chapter IV—Council

Article 6

The functions of the Council, in addition to those mentioned in other provisions of this Constitution, shall be:

(a) to determine the policies of the Organization;

(b) to review the reports and to approve and direct the activities of the Executive Committee;

(c) to review the reports and to approve and direct the activities of the Director General;

(d) to review and approve the programme, the Budget, the expenditure and the accounts of the Organization;

(e) to take any other appropriate action to further the purposes of the Organization.

Article 7

1. The Council shall be composed of representatives of the Member States.

2. Each Member State shall have one representative and such alternates and advisers as it may deem necessary.

3. Each Member State shall have one vote in the Council.

Article 8

The Council may admit, upon their application, non-member States and international organizations, governmental or non-governmental, concerned with migration, refugees or human resources as observers at its meetings under conditions which may be prescribed in its rules of procedure. No such observers shall have the right to vote.

Article 9

1. The Council shall meet in regular session once a year.

2. The Council shall meet in special session at the request of:

(a) one third of its members;

(b) the Executive Committee;

(c) the Director General or the Chairman of the Council in urgent circumstances.

3. The Council shall elect, at the beginning of each regular session, a Chairman and other officers for a one-year term.

Article 10

The Council may set up such sub-committees as may be required for the proper discharge of its functions.

The Council shall adopt its own rules of procedure.

Chapter V—Executive Committee

Article 12

The functions of the Executive Committee shall be:

(a) to examine and review the policies, programmes and activities of the Organization, the annual reports of the Director General and any special reports;

(b) to examine any financial or budgetary questions falling within the competence of the Council;

(c) to consider any matter specifically referred to it by the Council, including the revision of the Budget, and to take such action as may be deemed necessary thereon;

(d) to advise the Director General on any matters which he may refer to it;

(e) to make, between sessions of the Council, any urgent decisions on matters falling within the competence of the Council, which shall be submitted for approval by that body at its next session;

(f) to present advice or proposals to the Council or the Director General on its own initiative;

(g) to transmit reports and/or recommendations to the Council on the matters dealt with.

Article 13

1. The Executive Committee shall be composed of the representatives of nine Member States. This number may be increased by a two-thirds majority vote of the Council, provided it shall not exceed one third of the total membership of the Organization.

2. These Member States shall be elected by the Council for two years and shall be eligible for re-election.

3. Each member of the Executive Committee shall have one representative and such alternates and advisers as it may deem necessary.

4. Each member of the Executive Committee shall have one vote.

Article 14

1. The Executive Committee shall meet at least once a year. It shall meet, as necessary, in order to perform its functions, at the request of:

(a) its Chairman;

(b) the Council;

(c) the Director General after consultation with the Chairman of the Council;

(d) a majority of its members.

2. The Executive Committee shall elect a Chairman and a Vice-Chairman from among its members for a one-year term.

424

Article 15

...utive Committee may, subject to review by the Council, set up such sub-com-
...es as may be required for the proper discharge of its functions.

Article 16

The Executive Committee shall adopt its own rules of procedure.

Chapter VI—Administration

Article 17

The Administration shall comprise a Director General, a Deputy Director General and such staff as the Council may determine.

Article 18

1. The Director General and the Deputy Director General shall be elected by a two-thirds majority vote of the Council and may be re-elected. Their term of office shall normally be five years but may, in exceptional cases, be less if a two-thirds majority of the Council so decides. They shall serve under contracts approved by the Council, which shall be signed on behalf of the Organization by the Chairman of the Council.

2. The Director General shall be responsible to the Council and the Executive Committee. The Director General shall discharge the administrative and executive functions of the Organization in accordance with this Constitution and the policies and decisions of the Council and the Executive Committee and the rules and regulations established by them. The Director General shall formulate proposals for appropriate action by the Council.

Article 19

The Director General shall appoint the staff of the Administration in accordance with the staff regulations adopted by the Council.

Article 20

1. In the performance of their duties, the Director General, the Deputy Director General and the staff shall neither seek nor receive instructions from any State or from any authority external to the Organization. They shall refrain from any action which might reflect adversely on their position as international officials.

2. Each Member State undertakes to respect the exclusively international character of the responsibilities of the Director General, the Deputy Director General and the staff and not to seek to influence them in the discharge of their responsibilities.

3. Efficiency, competence and integrity shall be the necessary considerations in the recruitment and employment of the staff which, except in special circumstances, shall be recruited among the nationals of the Member States of the Organization, taking into account the principle of equitable geographical distribution.

Article 30

1. Texts of proposed amendments to this Constitution shall be communicated by the Director General to Governments of Member States at least three months in advance of their consideration by the Council.

2. Amendments shall come into force when adopted by two-thirds of the members of the Council and accepted by two-thirds of the Member States in accordance with their respective constitutional processes, provided, however, that amendments involving new obligations for Members shall come into force in respect of a particular Member only when that Member accepts such amendments.

Article 31

Any dispute concerning the interpretation or application of this Constitution which is not settled by negotiation or by a two-thirds majority vote of the Council shall be referred to the International Court of Justice in conformity with the Statute of the Court, unless the Member States concerned agree on another mode of settlement within a reasonable period of time.

Article 32

Subject to approval by two-thirds of the members of the Council, the Organization may take over from any other international organization or agency the purposes and activities of which lie within the purposes of the Organization such activities, resources and obligations as may be determined by international agreement or by mutually acceptable arrangements entered into between the competent authorities of the respective organizations.

Article 33

The Council may, by a three-quarters majority vote of its members, decide to dissolve the Organization.

Article 34[7]

This Constitution shall come into force, for those Governments Members of the Intergovernmental Committee for European Migration which have accepted it in accordance with their respective constitutional processes, on the day of the first meeting of that Committee after:

(a) at least two-thirds of the Members of the Committee, and

(b) a number of Members whose contributions represent at least 75 per cent of the Administrative part of the Budget, shall have communicated to the Director their acceptance of this Constitution.

---

[7] Arts. 34 and 35 were implemented at the time of the entry into force of the Constitution on 30 Nov. 1954.

Article 35

Those Governments Members of the Intergovernmental Committee for European Migration which have not by the date of coming into force of this Constitution communicated to the Director their acceptance of this Constitution may remain Members of the Committee for a period of one year from that date if they contribute to the administrative requirements of the Committee in accordance with paragraph 2 of Article 25, and they shall retain during that period the right to accept the Constitution.

Article 36

The English, French and Spanish texts of this Constitution shall be regarded as equally authentic.

1. Organization of African Unity: 1969 Convention on the Specific Aspects of Refugee Problems in Africa

Entry into force: 20 June 1974

Text: 1000 *UNTS* 46

Preamble

We, the Heads of State and Government assembled in the city of Addis Ababa, from 6–10 September 1969,

1. *Noting with concern* the constantly increasing numbers of refugees in Africa and desirous of finding ways and means of alleviating their misery and suffering as well as providing them with a better life and future,

2. *Recognizing* the need for an essentially humanitarian approach towards solving the problems of refugees,

3. *Aware*, however, that refugee problems are a source of friction among many Member States, and desirous of eliminating the source of such discord,

4. *Anxious* to make a distinction between a refugee who seeks a peaceful and normal life and a person fleeing his country for the sole purpose of fomenting subversion from outside,

5. *Determined* that the activities of such subversive elements should be discouraged, in accordance with the Declaration on the Problem of Subversion and Resolution on the Problem of Refugees adopted at Accra in 1965,

6. *Bearing in mind* that the Charter of the United Nations and the Universal Declaration of Human Rights have affirmed the principle that human beings shall enjoy fundamental rights and freedoms without discrimination,

7. *Recalling* Resolution 2312 (XXII) of 14 December 1967 of the United Nations General Assembly, relating to the Declaration on Territorial Asylum,

8. *Convinced* that all the problems of our continent must be solved in the spirit of the Charter of the Organization of African Unity and in the African context,

9. *Recognizing* that the United Nations Convention of 28 July 1951, as modified by the Protocol of 31 January 1967, constitutes the basic and universal instrument relating to the status of refugees and reflects the deep concern of States for refugees and their desire to establish common standards for their treatment,

10. *Recalling* Resolutions 26 and 104 of the OAU Assemblies of Heads of State and Government, calling upon Member States of the Organization who had not already done

so to accede to the United Nations Convention of 1951 and to the Protocol of 1967 relating to the Status of Refugees, and meanwhile to apply their provisions to refugees in Africa,

11. *Convinced* that the efficiency of the measures recommended by the present Convention to solve the problem of refugees in Africa necessitates close and continuous collaboration between the Organization of African Unity and the Office of the United Nations High Commissioner for Refugees,

Have agreed as follows:

Article I
Definition of the term 'Refugee'

1. For the purposes of this Convention, the term 'refugee' shall mean every person who, owing to well-founded fear of being persecuted for reasons of race, religion, nationality, membership of a particular social group or political opinion, is outside the country of his nationality and is unable or, owing to such fear, is unwilling to avail himself of the protection of that country, or who, not having a nationality and being outside the country of his former habitual residence as a result of such events is unable or, owing to such fear, is unwilling to return to it.

2. The term 'refugee' shall also apply to every person who, owing to external aggression, occupation, foreign domination or events seriously disturbing public order in either part or the whole of his country of origin or nationality, is compelled to leave his place of habitual residence in order to seek refuge in another place outside his country of origin or nationality.

3. In the case of a person who has several nationalities, the term 'a country of which he is a national' shall mean each of the countries of which he is a national, and a person shall not be deemed to be lacking the protection of the country of which he is a national if, without any valid reason based on well-founded fear, he has not availed himself of the protection of one of the countries of which he is a national.

4. This Convention shall cease to apply to any refugee if:

(a) he has voluntarily re-availed himself of the protection of the country of his nationality, or,

(b) having lost his nationality, he has voluntarily reacquired it, or,

(c) he has acquired a new nationality, and enjoys the protection of the country of his new nationality, or,

(d) he has voluntarily re-established himself in the country which he left or outside which he remained owing to fear of persecution, or,

(e) he can no longer, because the circumstances in connection with which he was recognized as a refugee have ceased to exist, continue to refuse to avail himself of the protection of the country of his nationality, or,

(f) he has committed a serious non-political crime outside his country of refuge after his admission to that country as a refugee, or,

(g) he has seriously infringed the purposes and objectives of this Convention.

5. The provisions of this Convention shall not apply to any person with respect to whom the country of asylum has serious reasons for considering that:

(a) he has committed a crime against peace, a war crime, or a crime against humanity, as defined in the international instruments drawn up to make provision in respect of such crimes;

(b) he committed a serious non-political crime outside the country of refuge prior to his admission to that country as a refugee;

(c) he has been guilty of acts contrary to the purposes and principles of the Organization of African Unity;

(d) he has been guilty of acts contrary to the purposes and principles of the United Nations.

6. For the purposes of this Convention, the Contracting State of asylum shall determine whether an applicant is a refugee.

Article II
Asylum

1. Member States of the OAU shall use their best endeavours consistent with their respective legislations to receive refugees and to secure the settlement of those refugees who, for well-founded reasons, are unable or unwilling to return to their country of origin or nationality.

2. The grant of asylum to refugees is a peaceful and humanitarian act and shall not be regarded as an unfriendly act by any Member State.

3. No person shall be subjected by a Member State to measures such as rejection at the frontier, return or expulsion, which would compel him to return to or remain in a territory where his life, physical integrity or liberty would be threatened for the reasons set out in Article I, paragraphs 1 and 2.

4. Where a Member State finds difficulty in continuing to grant asylum to refugees, such Member State may appeal directly to other Member States and through the OAU, and such other Member States shall in the spirit of African solidarity and international cooperation take appropriate measures to lighten the burden of the Member State granting asylum.

5. Where a refugee has not received the right to reside in any country of asylum, he may be granted temporary residence in any country of asylum in which he first presented himself as a refugee pending arrangement for his resettlement in accordance with the preceding paragraph.

6. For reasons of security, countries of asylum shall, as far as possible, settle refugees at a reasonable distance from the frontier of their country of origin.

Article III
Prohibition of Subversive Activities

1. Every refugee has duties to the country in which he finds himself, which require in particular that he conforms with its laws and regulations as well as with measures taken

for the maintenance of public order. He shall also abstain from any subversive activities against any Member State of the OAU.

2. Signatory States undertake to prohibit refugees residing in their respective territories from attacking any State Member of the OAU, by any activity likely to cause tension between Member States, and in particular by use of arms, through the press, or by radio.

Article IV
Non-Discrimination

Member States undertake to apply the provisions of this Convention to all refugees without discrimination as to race, religion, nationality, membership of a particular social group or political opinions.

Article V
Voluntary Repatriation

1. The essentially voluntary character of repatriation shall be respected in all cases and no refugee shall be repatriated against his will.

2. The country of asylum, in collaboration with the country of origin, shall make adequate arrangements for the safe return of refugees who request repatriation.

3. The country of origin, on receiving back refugees, shall facilitate their resettlement and grant them the full rights and privileges of nationals of the country, and subject them to the same obligations.

4. Refugees who voluntarily return to their country shall in no way be penalized for having left it for any of the reasons giving rise to refugee situations. Whenever necessary, an appeal shall be made through national information media and through the Administrative Secretary-General of the OAU, inviting refugees to return home and giving assurance that the new circumstances prevailing in their country of origin will enable them to return without risk and to take up a normal and peaceful life without fear of being disturbed or punished, and that the text of such appeal should be given to refugees and clearly explained to them by their country of asylum.

5. Refugees who freely decide to return to their homeland, as a result of such assurances or on their own initiative, shall be given every possible assistance by the country of asylum, the country of origin, voluntary agencies and international and intergovernmental organizations, to facilitate their return.

Article IV
Travel Documents

1. Subject to Article III, Member States shall issue to refugees lawfully staying in their territories travel documents in accordance with the United Nations Convention relating to the Status of Refugees and the Schedule and Annex thereto, for the purpose of travel outside their territory, unless compelling reasons of national security or public order otherwise require. Member States may issue such a travel document to any other refugee in their territory.

2. Where an African country of second asylum accepts a refugee from a country of first asylum, the country of first asylum may be dispensed from issuing a document with a return clause.

3. Travel documents issued to refugees under previous international agreements by States Parties thereto shall be recognized and treated by Member States in the same way as if they had been issued to refugees pursuant to this Article.

Article VII
Co-operation of the National Authorities with the Organization of African Unity

In order to enable the Administrative Secretary-General of the Organization of African Unity to make reports to the competent organs of the Organization of African Unity, Member States undertake to provide the Secretariat in the appropriate form with information and statistical data requested concerning:

(a) the condition of refugees;

(b) the implementation of this Convention, and

(c) laws, regulations and decrees which are, or may hereafter be, in force relating to refugees.

Article VIII
Co-operation with the Office of the United Nations High Commissioner for Refugees

1. Member States shall co-operate with the Office of the United Nations High Commissioner for Refugees.

2. The present Convention shall be the effective regional complement in Africa of the 1951 United Nations Convention on the Status of Refugees.

Article IX
Settlement of Disputes

Any dispute between States signatories to this Convention relating to its interpretation or application, which cannot be settled by other means, shall be referred to the Commission for Mediation, Conciliation and Arbitration of the Organization of African Unity, at the request of any one of the Parties to the dispute.

Article X
Signature and Ratification

1. This Convention is open for signature and accession by all Member States of the Organization of African Unity and shall be ratified by signatory States in accordance with their respective constitutional processes. The instruments of ratification shall be deposited with the Administrative Secretary-General of the Organization of African Unity.

2. The original instrument, done if possible in African languages, and in English and French, all texts being equally authentic, shall be deposited with the Administrative Secretary-General of the Organization of African Unity.

3. Any independent African State, Member of the Organization of African Unity, may at any time notify the Administrative Secretary-General of the Organization of African Unity of its accession to this Convention.

Article XI
Entry into force

This Convention shall come into force upon deposit of instruments of ratification by one-third of the Member States of the Organization of African Unity.

Article XII
Amendment

This Convention may be amended or revised if any Member State makes a written request to the Administrative Secretary-General to that effect, provided however that the proposed amendment shall not be submitted to the Assembly of Heads of State and Government for consideration until all Member States have been duly notified of it and a period of one year has elapsed. Such an amendment shall not be effective unless approved by at least two-thirds of the Member States Parties to the present Convention.

Article XIII
Denunciation

1. Any Member State Party to this Convention may denounce its provisions by a written notification to the Administrative Secretary-General.

2. At the end of one year from the date of such notification, if not withdrawn, the Convention shall cease to apply with respect to the denouncing State.

Article XIV

Upon entry into force of this Convention, the Administrative Secretary-General of the OAU shall register it with the Secretary-General of the United Nations, in accordance with Article 102 of the Charter of the United Nations.

Article XV
Notifications by the Administrative Secretary-General of the Organization of African Unity

The Administrative Secretary-General of the Organization of African Unity shall inform all Members of the Organization:

   (a) of signatures, ratifications and accessions in accordance with Article X;

   (b) of entry into force, in accordance with Article XI;

   (c) of requests for amendments submitted under the terms of Article XII;

   (d) of denunciations, in accordance with Article XIII.

. . .

2. 1981 African Charter on Human and Peoples' Rights—Extracts

Entry into Force: 1 October 1986

Text: 21 *ILM* 58 (1982)

Article 12

1. Every individual shall have the right to freedom of movement and residence within the borders of a State provided he abides by the law.

2. Every individual shall have the right to leave any country including his own, and to return to his country. This right may only be subject to restrictions, provided for by law for the protection of national security, law and order, public health or morality.

3. Every individual shall have the right, when persecuted, to seek and obtain asylum in other countries in accordance with the law of those countries and international conventions.

4. A non-national legally admitted in a territory of a State Party to the present Charter, may only be expelled from it by virtue of a decision taken in accordance with the law.

5. The mass expulsion of non-nationals shall be prohibited. Mass expulsion shall be that which is aimed at national, racial, ethnic or religious groups.

. . .

Article 23

1. All peoples shall have the right to national and international peace and security. The principles of solidarity and friendly relations implicitly affirmed by the Charter of the United Nations and reaffirmed by that of the Organization of African Unity shall govern relations between States.

2. For the purpose of strengthening peace, solidarity and friendly relations, States parties to the present Charter shall ensure that:

(a) any individual enjoying the right of asylum under Article 12 of the present Charter shall not engage in subversive activities against his country of origin or any other State party to the present Charter;

(b) their territories shall not be used as bases for subversive or terrorist activities against the people of any other State party to the present Charter.

. . .

3. 1954 Caracas Convention on Territorial Asylum

Entry into force: 29 December 1954

Text: OAS Official Records, OEA/Ser.X/1. Treaty Series 34

The Governments of the Member States of the Organization of American States, desirous of concluding a Convention regarding Territorial Asylum, have agreed to the following articles:

Article 1

Every State has the right, in the exercise of its sovereignty, to admit into its territory such persons as it deems advisable, without, through the exercise of this right, giving rise to complaint by any other State.

Article 2

The respect which, according to international law, is due to the jurisdictional right of each State over the inhabitants in its territory, is equally due, without any restriction whatsoever, to that which it has over persons who enter it proceeding from a State in which they are persecuted for their beliefs, opinions, or political affiliations, or for acts which may be considered as political offenses.

Any violation of sovereignty that consists of acts committed by a government or its agents in another State against the life or security of an individual, carried out on the territory of another State, may not be considered attenuated because the persecution began outside its boundaries or is due to political considerations or reasons of state.

Article 3

No State is under the obligation to surrender to another State, or to expel from its own territory, persons persecuted for political reasons or offenses.

Article 4

The right of extradition is not applicable in connection with persons who, in accordance with the qualifications of the solicited State, are sought for political offenses, or for common offenses committed for political ends, or when extradition is solicited for predominantly political motives.

Article 5

The fact that a person has entered into the territorial jurisdiction of a State surreptitiously or irregularly does not affect the provisions of this Convention.

Article 6

Without prejudice to the provisions of the following articles, no State is under the obligation to establish any distinction in its legislation, or in its regulations or administrative acts applicable to aliens, solely because of the fact that they are political asylees or refugees.

Article 7

Freedom of expression of thought, recognized by domestic law for all inhabitants of a State, may not be ground of complaint by a third State on the basis of opinions expressed publicly against it or its government by asylees or refugees, except when these concepts constitute systematic propaganda through which they incite to the use of force or violence against the government of the complaining State.

Article 8

No State has the right to request that another State restrict for the political asylees or refugees the freedom of assembly or association which the latter States's internal legislation grants to all aliens within its territory, unless such assembly or association has as its purpose fomenting the use of force or violence against the government of the soliciting State.

Article 9

At the request of the interested State, the State that has granted refuge or asylum shall take steps to keep watch over, or to intern at a reasonable distance from its border, those political refugees or asylees who are notorious leaders of a subversive movement, as well as those against whom there is evidence that they are disposed to join it.

Determination of the reasonable distance from the border, for the purpose of internment, shall depend upon the judgment of the authorities of the State of refuge.

All expenses incurred as a result of the internment of political asylees and refugees shall be chargeable to the State that makes the request.

Article 10

The political internees referred to in the preceding article shall advise the government of the host State whenever they wish to leave its territory. Departure therefrom will be granted, under the condition that they are not to go to the country from which they came and the interested government is to be notified.

Article 11

In all cases in which a complaint or request is permissible in accordance with this Convention, the admissibility of evidence presented by the demanding State shall depend on the judgment of the solicited State.

Article 12

This Convention remains open to the signature of the Member States of the Organization of American States, and shall be ratified by the signatory States in accordance with their respective constitutional procedures.

Article 13

The original instrument, whose texts in the English, French, Portuguese, and Spanish languages are equally authentic, shall be deposited in the Pan American Union, which shall send certified copies to the governments for the purpose of ratification. The instruments of ratification shall be deposited in the Pan American Union; this organization shall notify the signatory governments of said deposit.

Article 14

This Convention shall take effect among the States that ratify it in the order in which their respective ratifications are deposited.

Article 15

This Convention shall remain effective indefinitely, but may be denounced by any of the signatory States by giving advance notice of one year, at the end of which period it shall cease to have effect for the denouncing State, remaining, however, in force among the remaining signatory States. The denunciation shall be forwarded to the Pan American Union which shall notify the other signatory States thereof.

4. 1954 Caracas Convention on Diplomatic Asylum

Entry into force: 29 December 1954

Text: OAS Official Records, OEA/Ser.X/1. Treaty Series 34

The Governments of the Member States of the Organization of American States, desirous of concluding a Convention on Diplomatic Asylum, have agreed to the following articles:

Article 1

Asylum granted in legations, war vessels, and military camps or aircraft, to persons being sought for political reasons or for political offenses shall be respected by the territorial State in accordance with the provisions of this Convention. For the purposes of this Convention, a legation is any seat of a regular diplomatic mission, the residence of chiefs of mission, and the premises provided by them for the dwelling places of asylees when the number of the latter exceeds the normal capacity of the buildings. War vessels or military aircraft that may be temporarily in shipyards, arsenals, or shops for repair may not constitute a place of asylum.

Article 2

Every State has the right to grant asylum; but it is not obligated to do so or to state its reasons for refusing it.

Article 3

It is not lawful to grant asylum to persons who, at the time of requesting it, are under indictment or on trial for common offenses or have been convicted by competent regular courts and have not served their respective sentence, nor to deserters from land, sea, and air forces, save when the acts giving rise to the request for asylum, whatever the case may be, are clearly of a political nature.

Persons included in the foregoing paragraph who de facto enter a place that is suitable as an asylum shall be invited to leave or, as the case may be, shall be surrendered to the local authorities, who may not try them for political offenses committed prior to the time of the surrender.

Article 4

It shall rest with the State granting asylum to determine the nature of the offense or the motives for the persecution.

Article 5

Asylum may not be granted except in urgent cases and for the period of time strictly necessary for the asylee to depart from the country with the guarantees granted by the Government of the territorial State, to the end that his life, liberty, or personal integrity may not be endangered, or that the asylee's safety is ensured in some other way.

Article 6

Urgent cases are understood to be those, among others, in which the individual is being sought by persons or mobs over whom the authorities have lost control, or by the authorities themselves, and is in danger of being deprived of his life or liberty because of political persecution and cannot, without risk, ensure his safety in any other way.

Article 7

If a case of urgency is involved, it shall rest with the State granting asylum to determine the degree of urgency of the case.

Article 8

The diplomatic representative, commander of a warship, military camp, or military airship, shall, as soon as possible after asylum has been granted, report the fact to the Minister of Foreign Affairs of the territorial State, or to the local administrative authority if the case arose outside the capital.

Article 9

The official furnishing asylum shall take into account the information furnished to him by the territorial Government in forming his judgment as to the nature of the offense or the existence of related common crimes; but this decision to continue the asylum or to demand a safe-conduct for the asylee shall be respected.

Article 10

The fact that the Government of the territorial State is not recognized by the State granting asylum shall not prejudice the application of the present Convention, and no act carried out by virtue of this Convention shall imply recognition.

Article 11

The Government of the territorial State, may, at any time, demand that the asylee be withdrawn from the country, for which purpose the said State shall grant a safe-conduct and the guarantees stipulated in Article 5.

Article 12

Once asylum has been granted, the State granting asylum may request that the asylee be allowed to depart for foreign territory, and the territorial State is under obligation to grant immediately, except in case of force majeure, the necessary guarantees, referred to in Article 5, as well as the corresponding safe-conduct.

Article 13

In the cases referred to in the preceding articles the State granting asylum may require that the guarantees be given in writing, and may take into account, in determining the rapidity of the journey, the actual conditions of danger involved in the departure of the asylee.

The State granting asylum has the right to transfer the asylee out of the country. The territorial State may point out the preferable route for the departure of the asylee, but this does not imply determining the country of destination.

If the asylum is granted on board a warship or military airship, departure may be made therein, but complying with the previous requisite of obtaining the appropriate safe-conduct.

Article 14

The State granting asylum cannot be held responsible for the prolongation of asylum caused by the need for obtaining the information required to determine whether or not the said asylum is proper, or whether there are circumstances that might endanger the safety of the asylee during the journey to a foreign country.

Article 15

When, in order to transfer an asylee to another country it may be necessary to traverse the territory of a State that is a party to this Convention, transit shall be authorized by the latter, the only requisite being the presentation, through diplomatic channels, of a safe-conduct, duly countersigned and bearing a notation of his status as asylee by the diplomatic mission that granted asylum. En route, the asylee shall be considered under the protection of the State granting asylum.

Article 16

Asylees may not be landed at any point in the territorial State or at any place near thereto, except for exigencies of transportation.

Article 17

Once the departure of the asylee has been carried out, the State granting asylum is not bound to settle him in its territory; but it may not return him to his country of origin, unless this is the express wish of the asylee.

If the territorial State informs the official granting asylum of its intention to request the subsequent extradition of the asylee, this shall not prejudice the application of any provision of the present Convention. In that event, the asylee shall remain in the territory of the State granting asylum until such time as the formal request for extradition is received, in accordance with the juridical principles governing that institution in the State granting asylum. Preventive surveillance over the asylee may not exceed thirty days.

Payment of the expenses incurred by such transfer and of preventive control shall devolve upon the requesting State.

Article 18

The official furnishing asylum may not allow the asylee to perform acts contrary to the public peace or to interfere in the internal politics of the territorial State.

Article 19

If as a consequence of a rupture of diplomatic relations the diplomatic representative who granted asylum must leave the territorial State, he shall abandon it with the asylees.

If this is not possible for reasons independent of the wish of the asylee or the diplomatic representative, he must surrender them to the diplomatic mission of a third State, which is a party to this Convention, under the guarantees established in the Convention.

If this is also not possible, he shall surrender them to a State that is not a party to this Convention and that agrees to maintain the asylum. The territorial State is to respect the said asylum.

Article 20

Diplomatic asylum shall not be subject to reciprocity.
Every person is under its protection, whatever his nationality.

Article 21

The present Convention shall be open for signature by the Member States of the Organization of American States and shall be ratified by the signatory States in accordance with their respective constitutional procedures.

Article 22

The original instrument, whose texts in the English, French, Spanish, and Portuguese languages are equally authentic, shall be deposited in the Pan American Union, which shall send certified copies to the governments for the purpose of ratification. The instruments of ratification shall be deposited in the Pan American Union, and the said organization shall notify the signatory governments of the said deposit.

Article 23

The present Convention shall enter into force among the States that ratify it in the order in which their respective ratifications are deposited.

Article 24

The present Convention shall remain in force indefinitely, but may be denounced by any of the signatory States by giving advance notice of one year, at the end of which period it shall cease to have effect for the denouncing State, remaining in force, however, among the remaining signatory States. The denunciation shall be transmitted to the Pan American Union, which shall inform the other signatory States thereof.

5. 1969 American Convention on Human Rights—Extracts

Entry into force: 18 July 1978

Text in 9 *ILM* 99, reproducing OAS, Official Records: OEA/Ser.K/XVI/1.1. doc. 65, Rev. 1, Corr. 1 of 7 January 1970

Article 20

1. Every person has the right to a nationality.

2. Every person has the right to the nationality of the State in whose territory he was born if he does not have the right to any other nationality.

3. No one shall be arbitrarily deprived of his nationality or of the right to change it.

. . .

Article 22
Freedom of Movement and Residence

1. Every person lawfully in the territory of a State Party has the right to move about in it and to reside in it subject to the provisions of the law.

2. Every person has the right to leave any country freely, including his own.

3. The exercise of the foregoing rights may be restricted only pursuant to a law to the extent necessary in a democratic society to prevent crime or to protect national security, public safety, public order, public morals, public health, or the rights or freedoms of others.

4. The exercise of the rights recognized in paragraph 1 may also be restricted by law in designated zones for reasons of public interest.

5. No one can be expelled from the territory of the State of which he is a national or be deprived of the right to enter it.

6. An alien lawfully in the territory of a State Party to this Convention may be expelled from it only pursuant to a decision reached in accordance with law.

7. Every person has the right to seek and be granted asylum in a foreign territory, in accordance with the legislation of the State and international conventions, in the event he is being pursued for political offenses or related common crimes.

8. In no case may an alien be deported or returned to a country, regardless of whether or not it is his country of origin, if in that country his right to life or personal freedom is in danger of being violated because of his race, nationality, religion, social status, or political opinions.

9. The collective expulsion of aliens is prohibited.

6. 1981 Inter-American Convention on Extradition— Extracts

Entry into force: 28 March 1982

Text: *Treaty Series No. 60*: OEA/Ser.A/36

Article 4
Grounds for denying extradition

Extradition shall not be granted:

1. When the person sought has completed his punishment or has been granted amnesty, pardon or grace for the offense for which extradition is sought, or when he has been acquitted or the case against him for the same offense has been dismissed with prejudice.

2. When the prosecution or punishment is barred by the statute of limitations according to the laws of the requesting State or the requested State prior to the presentation of the request for extradition.

3. When the person sought has been tried or is to be tried before an extraordinary or ad hoc tribunal of the requesting State.

4. When, as determined by the requested State, the offense for which the person is sought is a political offense, an offense related thereto, or an ordinary criminal offense prosecuted for political reasons. The requested State may decide that the fact that the victim of the punishable act in question performed political functions does not in itself justify the designation of the offense as political.

5. When, from the circumstances of the case, it can be inferred that persecution for reasons of race, religion or nationality is involved, or that the position of the person sought may be prejudiced for any of these reasons.

6. With respect to offenses that in the requested State cannot be prosecuted unless a complaint or charge has been made by a party having a legitimate interest.

. . .

Article 6
Right of asylum

No provision of this Convention may be interpreted as a limitation on the right of asylum when its exercise is appropriate.

7. 1984 Cartagena Declaration on Refugees

Adopted at a Colloquium entitled 'Coloquio Sobre la Protección Internacional de los Refugiados en América Central, México y Panamá: Problemas Jurídicos y Humanitarios' held at Cartagena, Colombia from 19–22 November 1984

Text: OAS/Ser.L/V/II.66, doc. 10, rev. 1, pp. 190–3

Conclusions and Recommendations

I

Recalling the conclusions and recommendations adopted by the Colloquium held in Mexico in 1981 on Asylum and International Protection of Refugees in Latin America, which established important landmarks for the analysis and consideration of this matter;

Recognizing that the refugee situation in Central America has evolved in recent years to the point at which it deserves special attention;

Appreciating the generous efforts which have been made by countries receiving Central American refugees, notwithstanding the great difficulties they have had to face, particularly in the current economic crisis;

Emphasizing the admirable humanitarian and non-political task which UNHCR has been called upon to carry out in the Central American countries, Mexico and Panama in accordance with the provisions of the 1951 United Nations Convention and the 1967 Protocol, as well as those of resolution 428 (V) of the United Nations General Assembly, by which the mandate of the United Nations High Commissioner for Refugees is applicable to all States whether or not parties to the said Convention and/or Protocol;

Bearing in mind also the function performed by the Inter-American Commission on Human Rights with regard to the protection of the rights of refugees in the continent;

Strongly supporting the efforts of the Contadora Group to find an effective and lasting solution to the problem of Central American refugees, which constitute a significant step in the negotiation of effective agreements in favour of peace in the region;

Expressing its conviction that many of the legal and humanitarian problems relating to refugees which have arisen in the Central American region, Mexico and Panama can only be tackled in the light of the necessary co-ordination and harmonization of universal and regional systems and national efforts;

II

Having acknowledged with appreciation the commitments with regard to refugees included in the Contadora Act on Peace and Co-operation in Central America, the bases of which the Colloquium fully shares and which are reproduced below:

(a) 'To carry out, if they have not yet done so, the constitutional procedures for accession to the 1951 Convention and the 1967 Protocol relating to the Status of Refugees.'

(b) 'To adopt the terminology established in the Convention and Protocol referred to in the foregoing paragraph with a view to distinguishing refugees from other categories of migrants.'

(c) 'To establish the internal machinery necessary for the implementation, upon accession, of the provisions of the Convention and Protocol referred to above.'

(d) 'To ensure the establishment of machinery for consultation between the Central American countries and representatives of the Government offices responsible for dealing with the problem of refugees in each State.'

(e) 'To support the work performed by the United Nations High Commissioner for Refugees (UNHCR) in Central America and to establish direct co-ordination machinery to facilitate the fulfilment of his mandate.'

(f) 'To ensure that any repatriation of refugees is voluntary, and is declared to be so on an individual basis, and is carried out with the co-operation of UNHCR.'

(g) 'To ensure the establishment of tripartite commissions, composed of representatives of the State of origin, of the receiving State and of UNHCR with a view to facilitating the repatriation of refugees.'

(h) 'To reinforce programmes for protection of and assistance to refugees, particularly in the areas of health, education, labour and safety.'

(i) 'To ensure that programmes and projects are set up with a view to ensuring the self-sufficiency of refugees.'

(j) 'To train the officials responsible in each State for protection of and assistance to refugees, with the co-operation of UNHCR and other international agencies.'

(k) 'To request immediate assistance from the international community for Central American refugees, to be provided either directly, through bilateral or multilateral agreements, or through UNHCR and other organizations and agencies.'

(l) 'To identify, with the co-operation of UNHCR, other countries which might receive Central American refugees. In no case shall a refugee be transferred to a third country against his will.'

(m) 'To ensure that the Governments of the area make the necessary efforts to eradicate the causes of the refugee problem.'

(n) 'To ensure that, once agreement has been reached on the bases for voluntary and individual repatriation, with full guarantees for the refugees, the receiving countries permit official delegations of the country of origin, accompanied by representatives of UNHCR and the receiving country, to visit the refugee camps.'

(o) 'To ensure that the receiving countries facilitate, in co-ordination with UNHCR, the departure procedure for refugees in instances of voluntary and individual repatriation.'

(p) 'To institute appropriate measures in the receiving countries to prevent the participation of refugees in activities directed against the country of origin, while at all times respecting the human rights of the refugees.'

III

The Colloquium adopted the following conclusions:

1. To promote within the countries of the region the adoption of national laws and regulations facilitating the application of the Convention and the Protocol and, if necessary, establishing internal procedures and mechanisms for the protection of refugees. In addition, to ensure that the national laws and regulations adopted reflect the principles and criteria of the Convention and the Protocol, thus fostering the necessary process of systematic harmonization of national legislation on refugees.

2. To ensure that ratification of or accession to the 1951 Convention and the 1967 Protocol by States which have not yet taken these steps is unaccompanied by reservations limiting the scope of those instruments, and to invite countries having formulated such reservations to consider withdrawing them as soon as possible.

3. To reiterate that, in view of the experience gained from the massive flows of refugees in the Central American area, it is necessary to consider enlarging the concept of a refugee, bearing in mind, as far as appropriate and in the light of the situation prevailing in the region, the precedent of the OAU Convention (article I, paragraph 2) and the doctrine employed in the reports of the Inter-American Commission on Human Rights. Hence the definition or concept of a refugee to be recommended for use in the region is one which, in addition to containing the elements of the 1951 Convention and the 1967 Protocol, includes among refugees persons who have fled their country because their lives, safety or freedom have been threatened by generalized violence, foreign aggression, internal conflicts, massive violation of human rights or other circumstances which have seriously disturbed public order.

4. To confirm the peaceful, non-political and exclusively humanitarian nature of grant of asylum or recognition of the status of refugee and to underline the importance of the internationally accepted principle that nothing in either shall be interpreted as an unfriendly act towards the country of origin of refugees.

5. To reiterate the importance and meaning of the principle of *non-refoulement* (including the prohibition of rejection at the frontier) as a corner-stone of the international protection of refugees. This principle is imperative in regard to refugees and in the present state of international law should be acknowledged and observed as a rule of *jus cogens*.

6. To reiterate to countries of asylum that refugee camps and settlements located in frontier areas should be set up inland at a reasonable distance from the frontier with a view to improving the protection afforded to refugees, safeguarding their human rights and implementing projects aimed at their self-sufficiency and integration into the host society.

7. To express its concern at the problem raised by military attacks on refugee camps and settlements which have occurred in different parts of the world and to propose to the Governments of the Central American countries, Mexico and Panama that they lend

their support to the measures on this matter which have been proposed by the High Commissioner to the UNHCR Executive Committee.

8. To ensure that the countries of the region establish a minimum standard of treatment for refugees, on the basis of the provisions of the 1951 Convention and 1967 Protocol and of the American Convention on Human Rights, taking into consideration the conclusions of the UNHCR Executive Committee, particularly No. 22 on the Protection of Asylum Seekers in Situations of Large-Scale Influx.

9. To express its concern at the situation of displaced persons within their own countries. In this connection, the Colloquium calls on national authorities and the competent international organizations to offer protection and assistance to those persons and to help relieve the hardship which many of them face.

10. To call on States parties to the 1969 American Convention on Human Rights to apply this instrument in dealing with asilados and refugees who are in their territories.

11. To make a study, in countries in the area which have a large number of refugees, of the possibilities of integrating them into the productive life of the country by allocating to the creation or generation of employment the resources made available by the international community through UNHCR, thus making it possible for refugees to enjoy their economic, social and cultural rights.

12. To reiterate the voluntary and individual character of repatriation of refugees and the need for it to be carried out under conditions of absolute safety, preferably to the place of residence of the refugee in his country of origin.

13. To acknowledge that reunification of families constitutes a fundamental principle in regard to refugees and one which should be the basis for the regime of humanitarian treatment in the country of asylum, as well as for facilities granted in cases of voluntary repatriation.

14. To urge non-governmental, international and national organizations to continue their worthy task, co-ordinating their activities with UNHCR and the national authorities of the country of asylum, in accordance with the guidelines laid down by the authorities in question.

15. To promote greater use of the competent organizations of the inter-American system, in particular the Inter-American Commission on Human Rights, with a view to enhancing the international protection of asilados and refugees. Accordingly, for the performance of this task, the Colloquium considers that the close co-ordination and co-operation existing between the Commission and UNHCR should be strengthened.

16. To acknowledge the importance of the OAS/UNHCR Programme of Co-operation and the activities so far carried out and to propose that the next stage should focus on the problem raised by massive refugee flows in Central America, Mexico and Panama.

17. To ensure that in the countries of Central America and the Contadora Group the international norms and national legislation relating to the protection of refugees, and of human rights in general, are disseminated at all possible levels. In particular, the Colloquium believes it especially important that such dissemination should be undertaken

with the valuable co-operation of the appropriate universities and centres of higher education.

IV

The Cartagena Colloquium therefore

Recommends:

— That the commitments with regard to refugees included in the Contadora Act should constitute norms for the 10 States participating in the Colloquium and be unfailingly and scrupulously observed in determining the conduct to be adopted in regard to refugees in the Central American area.

— That the conclusions reached by the Colloquium (III) should receive adequate attention in the search for solutions to the grave problems raised by the present massive flows of refugees in Central America, Mexico and Panama.

— That a volume should be published containing the working document and the proposals and reports, as well as the conclusions and recommendations of the Colloquium and other pertinent documents, and that the Colombian Government, UNHCR and the competent bodies of OAS should be requested to take the necessary steps to secure the widest possible circulation of the volume in question.

— That the present document should be proclaimed the 'Cartagena Declaration on Refugees'.

— That the United Nations High Commissioner for Refugees should be requested to transmit the contents of the present declaration officially to the heads of State of the Central American countries, of Belize and of the countries forming the Contadora Group.

Finally, the Colloquium expressed its deep appreciation to the Colombian authorities, and in particular to the President of the Republic, Mr Belisario Betancur, the Minister for Foreign Affairs, Mr Augusto Ramírez Ocampo, and the United Nations High Commissioner for Refugees, Mr Poul Hartling, who honoured the Colloquium with their presence, as well as to the University of Cartagena de Indias and the Regional Centre for Third World Studies for their initiative and for the realization of this important event. The Colloquium expressed its special recognition of the support and hospitality offered by the authorities of the Department of Bolivar and the City of Cartagena. It also thanked the people of Cartagena, rightly known as the 'Heroic City', for their warm welcome.

In conclusion, the Colloquium recorded its acknowledgement of the generous tradition of asylum and refuge practised by the Colombian people and authorities.

Cartagena de Indias, 22 November 1984

8. 1950 European Convention on Human Rights and Fundamental Freedoms—Extracts

Entry into force: 3 September 1953

Text: *ETS*, No. 5

Article 1

The High Contracting Parties shall secure to everyone within their jurisdiction the rights and freedoms defined in Section 1 of this Convention.

. . .

Article 3

No one shall be subjected to torture or to inhumane or degrading treatment or punishment.

. . .

Article 13

Everyone whose rights and freedoms as set forth in this Convention are violated shall have an effective remedy before a national authority notwithstanding that the violation has been committed by persons acting in an official capacity.

Article 14

The enjoyment of the rights and freedoms set forth in this Convention shall be secured without discrimination on any ground such as sex, race, colour, language, religion, political or other opinion, national or social origin, association with a national minority, property, birth or other status.

Article 15

1. In time of war or other public emergency threatening the life of the nation any High Contracting Party may take measures derogating from its obligations under this Convention to the extent strictly required by the exigencies of the situation, provided that such measures are not inconsistent with its other obligations under international law.

2. No derogation from Article 2, except in respect of deaths resulting from lawful acts of war, or from Article 3, 4 (paragraph 1) and 7 shall be made under this provision.

3. Any High Contracting Party availing itself of this right of derogation shall keep the Secretary-General of the Council of Europe fully informed of the measures which it has taken and the reasons therefor. It shall also inform the Secretary-General of the Council of Europe when such measures have ceased to operate and the provisions of the Convention are again being fully executed.

9. 1963 Protocol No. 4 to the European Convention on the Protection of Human Rights and Fundamental Freedoms— Extracts

Entry into force: 2 May 1968

Text: *ETS* No. 46

Article 2

1. Everyone lawfully within the territory of a State shall, within that territory, have the right to liberty of movement and freedom to choose his residence.

2. Everyone shall be free to leave any country, including his own.

3. No restrictions shall be placed on the exercise of these rights other than such as are in accordance with law and are necessary in a democratic society in the interests of national security or public safety, for the maintenance of 'ordre public', for the prevention of crime, for the protection of health or morals, or for the protection of the rights and freedoms of others.

4. The rights set forth in paragraph 1 may also be subject, in particular areas, to restrictions imposed in accordance with law and justified by the public interests in a democratic society.

Article 3

1. No one shall be expelled, by means either of an individual or of a collective measure, from the territory of the State of which he is a national.

2. No one shall be deprived of the right to enter the territory of the State of which he is a national.

Article 4

Collective expulsion of aliens is prohibited.

10. 1957 European Convention on Extradition—Extracts

Entry into force: 18 April 1960

Text: *ETS*, No. 24

Article 3
Political offences

1. Extradition shall not be granted if the offence in respect of which it is requested is regarded by the requested Party as a political offence or as an offence connected with a political offence.

2. The same rule shall apply if the requested Party has substantial grounds for believing that a request for extradition for an ordinary criminal offence has been made for the purpose of prosecuting or punishing a person on account of his race, religion, nationality or political opinion, or that that person's position may be prejudiced for any of these reasons.

3. The taking or attempted taking of the life of a Head of State or a member of his family shall not be deemed to be a political offence for the purposes of this Convention.

4. This Article shall not affect any obligations which the Contracting Parties may have undertaken or may undertake under any other international convention of a multilateral character.

. . .

Article 21

1. Transit through the territory of one of the Contracting Parties shall be granted on submission of a request . . . provided that the offence concerned is not considered by the Party requested to grant transit as an offence of a political or purely military character having regard to Articles 3 and 4 of the Convention.

11. 1975 Additional Protocol to the European Convention on Extradition—Extracts

Entry into force: 20 August 1979

Text: *ETS* No. 86

Article 1

For the application of Article 3 of the Convention, political offences shall not be considered to include the following:

(a) the crimes against humanity specified in the Convention on the Prevention and Punishment of the Crime of Genocide adopted on 9 December 1948 by the General Assembly of the United Nations;

(b) the violations specified in Article 50 of the 1949 Geneva Convention for the Amelioration of the Condition of the Wounded and Sick in Armed Forces in the Field, Article 51 of the 1949 Geneva Convention for the Amelioration of the Condition of Wounded, Sick and Shipwrecked Members of Armed Forces at Sea, Article 130 of the 1949 Geneva Convention relative to the Treatment of Prisoners of War and Article 147 of the 1949 Geneva Convention relative to the Protection of Civilian Persons in Time of War;

(c) any comparable violations of the laws of war having effect at the time when this Protocol enters into force and of customs of war existing at that time, which are not already provided for in the above-mentioned provisions of the Geneva Conventions.

12. 1977 European Convention on the Suppression of Terrorism—Extracts

Entry into force: 4 August 1970

Text: *ETS* No. 90

Article 1

For the purposes of extradition between Contracting States, none of the following offences shall be regarded as a political offence or as an offence connected with a political offence or as an offence inspired by political motives:

(a) an offence within the scope of the Convention for the Suppression of Unlawful Seizure of Aircraft, signed at The Hague on 16 December 1970;

(b) an offence within the scope of the Convention for the Suppression of Unlawful Acts against the Safety of Civil Aviation, signed at Montreal on 23 September 1971;

(c) a serious offence involving an attack against the life, physical integrity or liberty of internationally protected persons, including diplomatic agents;

(d) an offence involving kidnapping, the taking of a hostage or serious unlawful detention;

(e) an offence involving the use of a bomb, grenade, rocket, automatic firearm or letter or parcel bomb if this use endangers persons;

(f) an attempt to commit any of the foregoing offences or participation as an accomplice of a person who commits or attempts to commit such an offence.

Article 2

1. For the purposes of extradition between Contracting States, a Contracting State may decide not to regard as a political offence or as an offence connected with a political offence or as an offence inspired by political motives a serious offence involving an act of violence, other than one covered by Article 1, against the life, physical integrity or liberty of a person.

2. The same shall apply to a serious offence involving an act against property, other than one covered by Article 1, if the act created a collective danger for persons.

3. The same shall apply to an attempt to commit any of the foregoing offences or participation as an accomplice of a person who commits or attempts to commit such an offence.

Article 3

The provisions of all extradition treaties and arrangements applicable between Contracting States, including the European Convention on Extradition, are modified as between Contracting States to the extent that they are incompatible with this Convention.

. . .

Article 5

Nothing in this Convention shall be interpreted as imposing an obligation to extradite if the requested State has substantial grounds for believing that the request for extradition for an offence mentioned in Article 1 or 2 has been made for the purpose of prosecuting or punishing a person on account of his race, religion, nationality or political opinion, or that that person's position may be prejudiced for any of these reasons.

Article 6

1. Each Contracting State shall take such measures as may be necessary to establish its jurisdiction over an offence mentioned in Article 1 in the case where the suspected offender is present in its territory and it does not extradite him after receiving a request for extradition from a Contracting State whose jurisdiction is based on a rule of jurisdiction existing equally in the law of the requested State.

2. This Convention does not exclude any criminal jurisdiction exercised in accordance with national law.

Article 7

A Contracting State in whose territory a person suspected to have committed an offence mentioned in Article 1 is found and which has received a request for extradition under the conditions mentioned in Article 6, paragraph 1, shall, if it does not extradite that person, submit the case, without exception whatsoever and without undue delay, to its competent authorities for the purpose of prosecution. Those authorities shall take their decision in the same manner as in the case of any offence of a serious nature under the law of that State.

Article 8

1. Contracting States shall afford one another the widest measure of mutual assistance in criminal matters in connection with proceedings brought in respect of the offences mentioned in Article 1 or 2. The law of the requested State concerning mutual assistance in criminal matters shall apply in all cases. Nevertheless this assistance may not be refused on the sole ground that it concerns a political offence or an offence connected with a political offence or an offence inspired by political motives.

2. Nothing in this Convention shall be interpreted as imposing an obligation to afford mutual assistance if the requested State has substantial grounds for believing that the request for mutual assistance in respect of an offence mentioned in Article 1 or 2 has been made for the purpose of prosecuting or punishing a person on account of his race, religion, nationality or political opinion or that that person's position may be prejudiced for any of these reasons.

3. The provisions of all treaties and arrangements concerning mutual assistance in criminal matters applicable between Contracting States, including the European Convention on Mutual Assistance in Criminal Matters, are modified as between Contracting States to the extent that they are incompatible with this Convention.

13. 1990 Dublin Convention Determining the State Responsible for Examining Applications for Asylum lodged in one of the Member States of the European Communities

Entry into force: Following signature of all EU Member States

[The EC Member States]

Having regard to the objective, fixed at the European Council meeting in Strasbourg on 8 and 9 December 1989, of the harmonization of their asylum policies;

Determined, in keeping with their common humanitarian tradition, to guarantee adequate protection to refugees in accordance with the terms of the Geneva Convention of 28 July 1951 and the New York Protocol of 31 January 1967 relating to the Status of Refugees, hereinafter referred to as the 'Geneva Convention' and the 'New York Protocol' respectively;

Considering the joint objective of an area without internal frontiers in which the free movement of persons shall, in particular, be ensured, in accordance with the provisions of the Treaty establishing the European Economic Community, as amended by the Single European Act;

Aware of the need, in pursuit of this objective, to take measures to avoid any situations arising, with the result that applicants for asylum are left in doubt for too long as regards the likely outcome of their applications and concerned to provide all applicants for asylum with a guarantee that their applications will be examined by one of the Member States and to ensure that applicants for asylum are not referred successively from one Member State to another without any of these States acknowledging itself to be competent to examine the application for asylum;

Desiring to continue the dialogue with the United Nations High Commissioner for Refugees in order to achieve the above objectives;

Determined to co-operate closely in the application of this Convention through various means, including exchanges of information,

Have Decided to Conclude this Convention . . . .

Article 1

1. For the purposes of this Convention:

(a) *Alien means:* any person other than a national of a Member State;

(b) *Application for asylum means:* a request whereby an alien seeks from a Member State protection under the Geneva Convention by claiming refugee status within the meaning of Article 1 of the Geneva Convention, as amended by the New York Protocol;

(c) *Applicant for asylum means:* an alien who has made an application for asylum in respect of which a final decision has not yet been taken;

(d) *Examination of an application for asylum means:* all the measures for examination, decisions or rulings given by the competent authorities on an application for asylum, except for procedures to determine the State responsible for examining the application for asylum pursuant to this Convention;

(e) *Residence permit means*: any authorization issued by the authorities of a Member State authorizing an alien to stay in its territory, with the exception of visas and 'stay permits' issued during examination of an application for a residence permit or for asylum;

(f) *Entry visa means*: authorization or decision by a Member State to enable an alien to enter its territory, subject to other entry conditions being fulfilled;

(g) *Transit visa means*: authorization or decision by a Member State to enable an alien to transit through its territory or pass through the transit zone of a port or airport, subject to other transit conditions being fulfilled;

2. The nature of the visa shall be assessed in the light of the definitions set out in paragraph 1, points (f) and (g).

Article 2

The Member States reaffirm their obligations under the Geneva Convention, as amended by the New York Protocol, with no geographic restriction of the scope of these instruments, and their commitment to co-operating with the services of the United Nations High Commissioner for Refugees in applying these instruments.

Article 3

1. Member States undertake to examine the application of any alien who applies at the border or in their territory to any one of them for asylum.

2. That application shall be examined by a single Member State, which shall be determined in accordance with the criteria defined in this Convention. The criteria set out in Articles 4 to 8 shall apply in the order in which they appear.

3. That application shall be examined by that State in accordance with its national laws and its international obligations.

4. Each Member State shall have the right to examine an application for asylum submitted to it by an alien, even if such examination is not its responsibility under the criteria defined in this Convention, provided that the applicant for asylum agrees thereto.

The Member State responsible under the above criteria is then relieved of its obligations, which are transferred to the Member State which expressed the wish to examine the application. The latter State shall inform the Member State responsible under the said criteria if the application has been referred to it.

5. Any Member State shall retain the right, pursuant to its national laws, to send an applicant for asylum to a third State, in compliance with the provisions of the Geneva Convention, as amended by the New York Protocol.

6. The process of determining the Member State responsible for examining the application for asylum under this Convention shall start as soon as an application for asylum is first lodged with a Member State.

7. An applicant for asylum who is present in another Member State and there lodges an application for asylum after withdrawing his or her application during the process of determining the State responsible shall be taken back, under the conditions laid down in Article 13, by the Member State with which that application for asylum was lodged, with

a view to completing the process of determining the State responsible for examining the application for asylum.

This obligation shall cease to apply if the applicant for asylum has since left the territory of the Member States for a period of at least three months or has obtained from a Member State a residence permit valid for more than three months.

Article 4

Where the applicant for asylum has a member of his family who has been recognized as having refugee status within the meaning of the Geneva Convention, as amended by the New York Protocol, in a Member State and is legally resident there, that State shall be responsible for examining the application, provided that the persons concerned so desire.

The family member in question may not be other than the spouse of the applicant for asylum or his or her unmarried child who is a minor of under eighteen years, or his or her father or mother where the applicant for asylum is himself or herself an unmarried child who is a minor of under eighteen years.

Article 5

1. Where the applicant for asylum is in possession of a valid residence permit, the Member State which issued the permit shall be responsible for examining the application for asylum.

2. Where the applicant for asylum is in possession of a valid visa, the Member State which issued the visa shall be responsible for examining the application for asylum, except in the following situations:

(a) if the visa was issued on the written authorization of another Member State, that State shall be responsible for examining the application for asylum. Where a Member State first consults the central authority of another Member State, inter alia for security reasons, the agreement of the latter shall not constitute written authorization within the meaning of this provision.

(b) where the applicant for asylum is in possession of a transit visa and lodges his application in another Member State in which he is not subject to a visa requirement, that State shall be responsible for examining the application for asylum.

(c) where the applicant for asylum is in possession of a transit visa and lodges his application in the State which issued him or her with the visa and which has received written confirmation from the diplomatic or consular authorities of the Member State of destination that the alien for whom the visa requirement was waived fulfilled the conditions for entry into that State, the latter shall be responsible for examining the application for asylum.

3. Where the applicant for asylum is in possession of more than one valid residence permit or visa issued by different Member States, the responsibility for examining the application for asylum shall be assumed by the Member States in the following order:

(a) the State which issued the residence permit conferring the right to the longest period of residency or, where the periods of validity of all the permits are identical, the State which issued the residence permit having the latest expiry date;

(b) the State which issued the visa having the latest expiry date where the various visas are of the same type;

(c) where visas are of different kinds, the State which issued the visa having the longest period of validity, or where the periods of validity are identical, the State which issued the visa having the latest expiry date. This provision shall not apply where the applicant is in possession of one or more transit visas, issued on presentation of an entry visa for another Member State. In that case, that Member State shall be responsible.

4. Where the applicant for asylum is in possession only of one or more residence permits which have expired less than two years previously or one or more visas which have expired less than six months previously and enabled him or her actually to enter the territory of a Member State, the provisions of paragraphs 1, 2 and 3 of this Article shall apply for such time as the alien has not left the territory of the Member States.

Where the applicant is in possession of one or more residence permits which have expired more than two years previously or one or more visas which have expired more than six months previously and enabled him or her to enter the territory of a Member State and where an alien has not left Community territory, the Member State in which the application is lodged shall be responsible.

Article 6

When it can be proved that an applicant for asylum has irregularly crossed the border into a Member State by land, sea or air, having come from a non-member State of the European Communities, the Member State thus entered shall be responsible for examining the application for asylum.

That State shall cease to be responsible, however, if it is proved that the applicant has been living in the Member State where the application for asylum was made at least six months before making his application for asylum. In that case it is the latter Member State which is responsible for examining the application for asylum.

Article 7

1. The responsibility for examining an application for asylum shall be incumbent upon the Member State responsible for controlling the entry of the alien into the territory of the Member States, except where, after legally entering a Member State in which the need for him or her to have a visa is waived, the alien lodges his or her application for asylum in another Member State in which the need for him or her to have a visa for entry into its territory is also waived. In this case, the latter State shall be responsible for examining the application for asylum.

2. Pending the entry into force of an agreement between Member States on arrangements for crossing external borders, the Member State which authorizes transit without a visa through the transit zone of its airports shall not be regarded as responsible for control on entry, in respect of travellers who do not leave the transit zone.

3. Where the application for asylum is made in transit in an airport of a Member State, that State shall be responsible.

Article 8

Where no Member State responsible for examining the application for asylum can be designated on the basis of the other criteria listed in this Convention, the first Member

State with which the application for asylum is lodged shall be responsible for examining it.

Article 9

Any Member State, even when it is not responsible under the criteria laid out in this Convention, may, for humanitarian reasons, based in particular on family or cultural grounds, examine an application for asylum at the request of another Member State, provided that the applicant so desires.

If the Member State thus approached accedes the request, responsibility for examining the application shall be transferred to it.

Article 10

1. The Member State responsible for examining an application for asylum according to the criteria set out in this Convention shall be obliged to:

(a) Take charge under the conditions laid down in Article 11 of an applicant who has lodged an application for asylum in a different Member State.

(b) Complete the examination of the application for asylum.

(c) Readmit or take back under the conditions laid down in Article 13 an applicant whose application is under examination and who is irregularly in another Member State.

(d) Take back, under the conditions laid down in Article 13, an applicant who has withdrawn the application under examination and lodged an application in another Member State.

(e) Take back, under the conditions laid down in Article 13, an alien whose application it has rejected and who is illegally in another Member State.

2. If a Member State issues to the applicant a residence permit valid for more than three months, the obligations specified in paragraph 1, points (a) to (e) shall be transferred to that Member State.

3. The obligations specified in paragraph 1, points (a) to (d) shall cease to apply if the alien concerned has left the territory of the Member States for a period of at least three months.

4. The obligations specified in paragraph 1, points (d) and (e) shall cease to apply if the State responsible for examining the application for asylum, following the withdrawal or rejection of the application, takes and enforces the necessary measures for the alien to return to his country of origin or to another country which he may lawfully enter.

Article 11

1. If a Member State with which an application for asylum has been lodged considers that another Member State is responsible for examining the application, it may, as quickly as possible and in any case within the six months following the date on which the application was lodged, call upon the other Member State to take charge of the applicant.

If the request that charge be taken is not made within the six-month time limit, responsibility for examining the application for asylum shall rest with the State in which the application was lodged.

2. The request that charge be taken shall contain indications enabling the authorities of that other State to ascertain whether it is responsible on the basis of the criteria laid down in this Convention.

3. The State responsible in accordance with those criteria shall be determined on the basis of the situation obtaining when the applicant for asylum first lodged his application with a Member State.

4. The Member State shall pronounce judgment on the request within three months of receipt of the claim. Failure to act within that period shall be tantamount to accepting the claim.

5. Transfer of the applicant for asylum from the Member State where the application was lodged to the Member State responsible must take place not later than one month after acceptance of the request to take charge or one month after the conclusion of any proceedings initiated by the alien challenging the transfer decision if the proceedings are suspensory.

6. Measures taken under Article 18 may subsequently determine the details of the process by which applicants shall be taken in charge.

Article 12

Where an application for asylum is lodged with the competent authorities of a Member State by an applicant who is on the territory of another Member State, the determination of the Member State responsible for examining the application for asylum shall be made by the Member State on whose territory the applicant is. The latter Member State shall be informed without delay by the Member State which received the application and shall then, for the purpose of applying this Convention, be regarded as the Member State with which the application for asylum was lodged.

Article 13

1. An applicant for asylum shall be taken back in the cases provided for in Article 3(7) and in Article 10 as follows:

(a) The claim for the applicant to be taken back must provide indications enabling the State with which the claim is lodged to ascertain that it is indeed responsible in accordance with Article 3(7) and with Article 10;

(b) the State called upon to take back the applicant shall give an answer to the request within eight days of the matter being referred to it. Should it acknowledge responsibility, it shall then take back the applicant for asylum as quickly as possible and at the latest one month after it agrees to do so.

2. Measures taken under Article 18 may at a later date set out the details of the procedure for taking the applicant back.

Article 14

1. Member States shall conduct mutual exchanges with regard to:
— national legislative or regulatory measures or practices applicable in the field of asylum:

— statistical data on monthly arrivals of applicants for asylum, and their breakdown by nationality. Such information shall be forwarded quarterly through the General Secretariat of the Council of the European Communities, which shall see that it is circulated to the Member States and the Commission of the European Communities and to the United Nations High Commissioner for Refugees.

2. The Member States may conduct mutual exchanges with regard to:
— general information on new trends in applications for asylum;
— general information on the situation in the countries of origin or of provenance of applicants for asylum.

3. If the Member State providing the information referred to in paragraph 2 wants it to be kept confidential, the other Member States shall comply with this wish.

Article 15

1. Each Member State shall communicate to any Member State that so requests such information on individual cases as is necessary for:
— determining the Member State which is responsible for examining the application for asylum;
— examining the application for asylum;
— implementing any obligation arising under this Convention.

2. This information may only cover:
— personal details of the applicant, and, where appropriate, the members of his family (full name; where appropriate, former name; nicknames or pseudonyms; nationality, present and former; date and place of birth);
— identity and travel papers (references, validity, date of issue, issuing authority, place of issue, etc.);
— other information necessary for establishing the identity of the applicant;
— places of residence and routes travelled;
— residence permits or visas issued by a Member State;
— the place where the application was lodged;
— the date any previous application for asylum was lodged, the date the present application was lodged, the stage reached in the proceedings and the decision taken, if any.

3. Furthermore, one Member State may request another Member State to let it know on what grounds the applicant for asylum bases his or her application and, where applicable, the grounds for any decisions taken concerning the applicant. It is for the Member State from which the information is requested to decide whether or not to impart it. In any event, communication of the information requested shall be subject to the approval of the applicant for asylum.

4. This exchange of information shall be effected at the request of a Member State and may only take place between authorities the designation of which has been communicated to the Committee provided for under Article 18.

5. The information exchanged may only be used for the purposes set out in paragraph 1. In each Member State such information may only be communicated to the authorities and courts and tribunals entrusted with:

— determining the Member State which is responsible for examining the application for asylum;

— examining the application for asylum;

— implementing any obligation arising under this Convention.

6. The Member State that forwards the information shall ensure that it is accurate and up-to-date.

If it appears that this Member State has supplied information which is inaccurate or which should not have been forwarded, the recipient Member State shall be immediately informed thereof. They shall be obliged to correct such information or to have it erased.

7. An applicant for asylum shall have the right to receive, on request, the information exchanged concerning him or her, for such time as it remains available.

If he or she establishes that such information is inaccurate or should not have been forwarded, he or she shall have the right to have it corrected or erased. This right shall be exercised in accordance with the conditions laid down in paragraph 6.

8. In each Member State concerned, the forwarding and receipt of exchanged information shall be recorded.

9. Such information shall be kept for a period not exceeding that necessary for the ends for which it was exchanged. The need to keep it shall be examined at the appropriate moment by the Member States concerned.

10. In any event, the information thus communicated shall enjoy at least the same protection as is given to similar information in the Member State which receives it.

11. If data are not processed automatically but are handled in some other form, every Member State shall take the appropriate measures to ensure compliance with this Article by means of effective controls. If a Member State has a monitoring body of the type mentioned in paragraph 12, it may assign the control task to it.

12. If one or more Member States wish to computerize all or part of the information mentioned in paragraphs 2 and 3, such computerization is only possible if the countries concerned have adopted laws applicable to such processing which implement the principles of the Strasbourg Convention of 28 February 1981 for the Protection of Individuals, with regard to Automatic Processing of Personal Data and if they have entrusted an appropriate national body with the independent monitoring of the processing and use of data forwarded pursuant to this Convention.

Article 16

1. Any Member State may submit to the Committee referred to in Article 18 proposals for revision of this Convention in order to eliminate difficulties in the application thereof.

2. If it proves necessary to revise or amend this Convention pursuant to the achievement of the objectives set out in Article 8a of the Treaty establishing the European Economic Community, such achievement being linked in particular to the establishment of a harmonized asylum and a common visa policy, the Member State holding the Presidency of the Council of the European Communities shall organize a meeting of the Committee referred to in Article 18.

3. Any revision of this Convention or amendment hereto shall be adopted by the Committee referred to in Article 18. They shall enter into force in accordance with the provisions of Article 22.

Article 17

1. If a Member State experiences major difficulties as a result of a substantial change in the circumstances obtaining on conclusion of this Convention, the State in question may bring the matter before the Committee referred to in Article 18 so that the latter may put to the Member States measures to deal with the situation or adopt such revisions or amendments to this Convention as appear necessary, which shall enter into force as provided for in Article 16(3).

2. If, after six months, the situation mentioned in paragraph 1 still obtains, the Committee, acting in accordance with Article 18(2), may authorize the Member State affected by the change to suspend temporarily the provisions of this Convention, without such suspension being allowed to impede the achievement of the objectives mentioned in Article 8a of the Treaty establishing the European Economic Community or contravene other international obligations of the Member States.

3. During the period of suspension, the Committee shall continue its discussions with a view to revising the provisions of this Convention, unless it has already reached an agreement.

Article 18

1. A Committee shall be set up comprising one representative of the Government of each Member State.

The Committee shall be chaired by the Member State holding the Presidency of the Council of the European Communities.

The Commission of the European Communities may participate in the discussions of the Committee and the working parties referred to in paragraph 4.

2. The Committee shall examine, at the request of one or more Member States, any question of a general nature concerning the application or interpretation of this Convention.

The Committee shall determine the measures referred to in Article 11(6) and Article 13(2) and shall give the authorization referred to in Article 17(2).

The Committee shall adopt decisions revising or amending the Convention pursuant to Articles 16 and 17.

3. The Committee shall take its decisions unanimously, except where it is acting pursuant to Article 17(2), in which case it shall take its decisions by a majority of two-thirds of the votes of its members.

4. The Committee shall determine its rules of procedure and may set up working parties.

The Secretariat of the Committee and of the working parties shall be provided by the General Secretariat of the Council of the European Communities.

Article 19

As regards the Kingdom of Denmark, the provisions of this Convention shall not apply to the Faroe Islands nor to Greenland unless a declaration to the contrary is made by the Kingdom of Denmark. Such a declaration may be made at any time by a communication to the Government of Ireland which shall inform the Governments of the other Member States thereof.

As regards the French Republic, the provisions of this Convention shall apply only to the European territory of the French Republic.

As regards the Kingdom of the Netherlands, the provisions of this Convention shall apply only to the territory of the Kingdom of the Netherlands in Europe.

As regards the United Kingdom, the provisions of this Convention shall apply only to the United Kingdom of Great Britain and Northern Ireland. They shall not apply to the European territories for whose external relations the United Kingdom is responsible unless a declaration to the contrary is made by the United Kingdom. Such a declaration may be made at any time by a communication to the Government of Ireland, which shall inform the Governments of the other Member States thereof.

Article 20

This Convention shall not be the subject of any reservations.

Article 21

1. This Convention shall be open for the accession of any State which becomes a member of the European Communities. The instruments of accession will be deposited with the Government of Ireland.

2. It shall enter into force in respect of any State which accedes thereto on the first day of the third month following the deposit of its instrument of accession.

Article 22

1. This Convention shall be subject to ratification, acceptance or approval. The instruments of ratification, acceptance or approval shall be deposited with the Government of Ireland.

2. The Government of Ireland shall inform the Governments of the other Member States of the deposit of the instruments of ratification, acceptance or approval.

3. This Convention shall enter into force on the first day of the third month following the deposit of the instrument of ratification, acceptance or approval by the last signatory State to take this step.

The State with which the instruments of ratification, acceptance or approval are deposited shall inform the Member States of the date of entry into force of this Convention.

Dublin
15 June 1990

14. 1990 Convention on the Application of the Schengen Agreement of 14 June 1985 relating to the Gradual Suppression of Controls at Common Frontiers, between the Governments of States Members of the Benelux Economic Union, the Federal Republic of Germany and the French Republic (Unofficial translation)—Extracts

Entry into force: 25 March 1995

TITLE I

Definitions

Article 1

For the purposes of this Convention:

Internal borders:	shall mean the common land borders of the Contracting Parties, together with airports used for domestic flights and sea ports used for regular shipments exclusively arriving from or destined for other ports in the territory of the Contracting Parties, without calling at ports outside these territories;
External borders:	shall mean the land and sea borders and the airports and sea ports of the Contracting Parties, provided they are not internal frontiers;
Domestic flight:	shall mean any flight exclusively from or to the territory of the Contracting Parties, without landing on the territory of a third State;
Third State:	shall mean any State other than the Contracting Parties;
Alien:	shall mean any person other than a national of a Member State of the European Communities;
Alien reported as a person not to be permitted entry:	shall mean any alien reported as a person not to be permitted entry under the Schengen Information System in accordance with article 96;
Border crossing point:	shall mean any crossing point authorised by the competent authorities for the crossing of external borders
Border control:	shall mean a check made at a border with respect to the intention to cross the border, regardless of any other reason;

Carrier:	shall mean any natural or legal person professionally engaged in the transport of passengers by air, sea or land;
Residence permit:	shall mean any form of authorization issued by a Contracting Party and conferring the right of residence on its territory. This definition does not include temporary admission to the territory of a Contracting State for the purpose of processing an application for asylum or an application for a residence permit;
Application for asylum:	shall mean any application submitted in writing, orally or otherwise by an alien at the external frontier or within the territory of a Contracting Party for the purpose of obtaining refugee status under the Geneva Convention of 28 July 1951 relating to the Status of Refugees, as amended by the New York Protocol of 31 January 1967, and thereby obtaining a right of residence;
Applicant for asylum:	shall mean any alien who has submitted an application for asylum within the meaning of this Convention, on which no final decision has yet been made;
Processing an asylum application:	shall mean all the investigative and decision-making procedures and steps taken to implement final decisions relating to an application for asylum, except the determination of the Contracting Party responsible for processing the application for asylum according to the provisions of this Convention.

. . .

Chapter 7
Responsibility for processing applications for asylum

Article 28

The Contracting Parties reaffirm their obligations under the Geneva Convention of 28 July 1951 relating to the Status of Refugees, as amended by the New York Protocol of 31 January 1967, with no geographic restriction of the scope of these texts, and their undertaking to co-operate with the officials of the United Nations High Commissioner for Refugees in applying these instruments.

Article 29

1. The Contracting Parties undertake to process any application for asylum lodged by an alien within the territory of one of them.

2. This obligation does not require a Contracting Party to authorize any applicant for asylum to enter or remain in its territory.

Every Contracting Party retains the right to refuse entry to an applicant for asylum or to remove him to a third State, on the basis of its own laws and in conformity with its international obligations.

3. Irrespective of the Contracting Party to which the alien addresses an application for asylum, only one Contracting Party shall be responsible for processing it. Such Contracting Party shall be determined according to the criteria defined in article 30.

4. Notwithstanding paragraph 3, every Contracting Party retains the right, in particular for reasons relating to domestic law, to process an application for asylum even if responsibility for doing so lies with another Contracting Party under this Convention.

Article 30

1. The Contracting Party responsible for processing an application for asylum shall be determined as follows:

(a) If a Contracting Party has issued a visa of any kind or a residence permit to the applicant for asylum, it shall be responsible for processing the application. If the visa was issued on the authority of another Contracting Party, the Contracting Party which gave the authorization shall be responsible.

(b) If two or more Contracting Parties have issued a visa of any kind or a residence permit, to the applicant for asylum, the responsible Contracting Party shall be that which issued the visa or residence permit having the latest date of expiry.

(c) As long as the applicant for asylum has not left the territory of the Contracting Parties, the responsibility defined in subparagraphs (a) and (b) shall continue even if the period of validity of the visa, whatever its nature, or of the residence permit, has expired. If the applicant for asylum has left the territory of the Contracting Parties after the issue of the visa or the residence permit, these documents shall be the basis of responsibility under subparagraphs (a) and (b) unless they have since expired according to national law.

(d) If the applicant for asylum is exempted by the Contracting Parties from the visa requirement, the Contracting Party through whose external borders the applicant for asylum entered the territory of the Contracting Parties shall be responsible.

Until the harmonization of visa policies has been completed, and if the applicant for asylum is exempted by certain Contracting Parties only from the visa requirement the Contracting Party through whose external borders the applicant for asylum entered the territories of the Contracting Parties by virtue of a visa exemption shall be responsible, subject to the provisions of subparagraphs (a), (b) and (c).

If the application for asylum is submitted to a Contracting Party which has issued a transit visa to the applicant, whether or not the applicant has passed through passport control, and if the transit visa was issued after the country of transit had ascertained from the consular or diplomatic authorities of the Contracting Party of destination that the applicant for asylum satisfied the conditions for entry to the Contracting Party of destination, the Contracting Party of destination shall be responsible for processing the application.

(e) If the applicant for asylum entered the territory of the Contracting Parties without being in possession of one or more documents, as determined by the Executive Committee, permitting the crossing of the border, the Contracting Party through whose external border the applicant for asylum entered the territory of the Contracting Parties shall be responsible.

(f) If an alien whose application for asylum is being processed by one of the Contracting Parties submits a new application, the responsible Contracting Party shall be the one processing the first application.

(g) If an alien, having previously made an application for asylum which has been the subject of a final decision by one of the Contracting Parties, submits a further application, the responsible Contracting Party shall be the one which processed the previous application, unless the applicant has left the territory of the Contracting Parties.

2. If a Contracting Party has undertaken to process an application for asylum under article 29, paragraph 4, the Contracting Party responsible under paragraph 1 of this Article shall be relieved of its obligations.

3. If the Contracting Party responsible cannot be designated on the basis of the criteria defined in paragraphs 1 and 2, the Contracting Party to which the application for asylum has been submitted shall be responsible.

Article 31

1. The Contracting Parties shall seek to determine as quickly as possible which of them is responsible for processing an application for asylum.

2. If an application for asylum is addressed to a Contracting Party which is not responsible under article 30 by an alien within its territory, that Contracting Party may request the responsible Contracting Party to take charge of the applicant for asylum with a view to processing his application.

3. The responsible Contracting Party shall take charge of the applicant for asylum referred to in paragraph 2, if requested to do so within six months of the filing of the application for asylum. If no request is made within this time limit, the Contracting Party with which the application for asylum was lodged shall be responsible for processing it.

Article 32

The Contracting Party responsible for processing an application for asylum shall ensure that this is done in accordance with its national law.

Article 33

1. If an applicant for asylum is illegally present in the territory of another Contracting Party during the asylum procedure, the responsible Contracting Party shall be bound to take him back.

2. Paragraph 1 shall not apply where the other Contracting Party has issued the applicant for asylum a residence permit valid for one year or more. In this case, the responsibility for processing the application is transferred to the other Contracting Party.

Article 34

1. The responsible Contracting Party shall take back an alien whose application for asylum has been finally rejected and who has entered the territory of another Contracting Party without being authorized to reside there.

2. Paragraph 1 shall not apply, however, where the responsible Contracting Party has ensured the removal of the alien from the territories of the Contracting Parties.

Article 35

1. A Contracting Party which has recognized an alien as a refugee and which has granted him the right of residence shall take responsibility for processing an application for asylum from a member of his family, if the persons concerned so agree.

2. For the purposes of paragraph 1, a family member shall be the spouse or unmarried child under eighteen years of the refugee or, if the refugee is an unmarried child under eighteen years, his father or mother.

Article 36

Any Contracting Party responsible for processing an application for asylum may, for humanitarian reasons based in particular on family or cultural reasons, request another Contracting Party to assume responsibility, where the person concerned so desires. The Contracting Party to which the request is made shall decide whether it can grant it.

Article 37

1. The competent authorities of the Contracting Parties shall, as soon as possible, exchange information with respect to:

(a) new regulations or measures adopted in regard to the law on asylum or the processing of applicants for asylum, not later than the date of their entry into force;

(b) statistical data concerning monthly arrivals of applicants for asylum, indicating the principal countries of origin, and decisions on applications for asylum, to the extent that they are available;

(c) the emergence of or significant increases in certain groups of applicants for asylum, and any information available in this regard;

(d) key decisions pertaining to the law on asylum.

2. The Contracting Parties also undertake to co-operate closely in gathering information on the situation in the countries of origin of applicants for asylum, in order to reach a common assessment.

3. Any instruction given by a Contracting Party concerning the confidential treatment of the information communicated by it shall be respected by the other Contracting Parties.

Article 38

1. Each Contracting Party shall transmit to any other Contracting Party that requests it such information in its possession concerning an applicant for asylum which is necessary to:

— determine the Contracting Party responsible for processing an application for asylum;

— process an application for asylum;

— implement the obligations arising under this Chapter.

2. Such information shall deal only with the following matters:

(a) identity (family name and first name, any previous names or pseudonyms, date and place of birth, present and previous nationality of the applicant for asylum and, where appropriate, the members of his family);

(b) identity and travel documents (references, validity, date of issue, issuing authority, place of issue, etc.);

(c) any other information necessary for establishing the identity of the applicant;

(d) places of residence and routes travelled;

(e) residence permits or visas issued by a Contracting Party;

(f) the place where the application for asylum was lodged;

(g) where appropriate, the date of any previous application, the date of the present application, the stage reached in the procedure, and the decision taken.

3. In addition, one Contracting Party may request another Contracting Party to notify it of the grounds invoked by an applicant for asylum in support of his application and, where applicable, the grounds for any decision taken concerning him. The Contracting Party so requested shall decide whether to accede to the request. In every case, the communication of such information shall be subject to the consent of the applicant for asylum.

4. Exchanges of information shall be effected at the request of a Contracting Party, and may only take place between authorities whose designation has been communicated to the Executive Committee by each Contracting Party.

5. The information exchanged may be used only for the purposes set out in paragraph 1. Such information may be communicated only to the authorities and courts competent to

— determine the Contracting Party responsible for processing an application for asylum;

— process an application for asylum;

— implement the obligations arising under this Chapter.

6. The Contracting Party that forwards the information shall ensure that it is accurate and up to date.

If it appears that this Contracting Party has supplied information which is inaccurate or which should not have been forwarded, the recipient Contracting Parties shall be informed without delay. They shall be obliged to correct such information or to delete it.

7. An applicant for asylum has the right to receive, on request, any information exchanged concerning him, for so long as it remains available.

If the applicant for asylum establishes that such information is inaccurate or should not have been forwarded, he has the right to require that it be corrected or deleted. Corrections shall be made in accordance with paragraph 6.

8. In each Contracting Party concerned, the transmission and receipt of information exchanged shall be recorded.

9. The information transmitted shall be kept for a period not exceeding that necessary for the purpose for which it was exchanged. The need to keep such information shall be examined at the appropriate moment by the Contracting Party concerned.

10. In every case, the information transmitted shall enjoy at least the same protection as is given to similar information under the law of the Contracting Party which receives it.

11. If data are not processed automatically but are handled in some other form, every Contracting Party shall take the appropriate measures to ensure compliance with this Article by means of effective controls. If a Contracting Party has a monitoring body of the type mentioned in paragraph 12, it may assign the control task to it.

12. If one or more Contracting Parties wish to computerize all or part of the information mentioned in paragraphs 2 and 3, such computerization is only possible if the Contracting Parties concerned have adopted laws applicable to such processing which implement the provisions of the Convention of the Council of Europe of 28 January 1981 for the Protection of Individuals with regard to Automatic Processing of Personal Data and if they have entrusted an appropriate national body with the independent monitoring of the processing and use of data forwarded pursuant to this Convention.

UNHCR EXECUTIVE COMMITTEE
SELECTED CONCLUSIONS ON INTERNATIONAL PROTECTION[1]

No. 5 (XXVIII)—1977 Asylum[2]

The Executive Committee,

(a) *Noted* with satisfaction the report of the High Commissioner that States have generally continued to follow liberal asylum practices;

(b) *Concerned*, however, that according to the report of the High Commissioner cases continue to occur in which asylum seekers have encountered serious difficulties in finding a country willing to grant them even temporary refuge and that refusal of permanent or temporary asylum has led in a number of cases to serious consequences for the persons concerned;

(c) *Requested* the High Commissioner to draw the attention of Governments to the various international instruments existing in the field of asylum and reiterated the fundamental importance of these instruments from a humanitarian standpoint;

(d) *Appealed* to Governments to follow, or continue to follow, liberal practices in granting permanent or at least temporary asylum to refugees who have come directly to their territory;

(e) *Called* on Governments to co-operate, in a spirit of international solidarity, with the High Commissioner in the performance of his functions—especially with respect to asylum—in accordance with General Assembly Resolution 428(V) of 14 December 1950.

No. 6 (XXVIII)—1977 *Non-refoulement*[3]

The Executive Committee,

(a) *Recalling* that the fundamental humanitarian principle of *non-refoulement* has found expression in various international instruments adopted at the universal and regional levels and is generally accepted by States;

---

[1] The selected Conclusions in this Annexe are drawn from those adopted each year by the UNHCR Executive Committee, and published in its annual *Report* in the UN document series A/AC.96/***; a citation for each of the Conclusions in the present Annexe is provided in the nn. The scheme of numbering is that determined by UNHCR, after each session, and applies to those conclusions considered relevant to international protection. The full set of Conclusions is also available in an annually updated loose-leaf publication from UNHCR, *Conclusions on the International Protection of Refugees adopted by the Executive Committee of the UNHCR Programme*, Geneva, 1979 to date. Since 1989, the previous October's conclusions have appeared regularly in the first issue each year of the *International Journal of Refugee Law*; and since 1995, all Executive Committee Conclusions have been available on-line through CDR/UNHCR's Internet gopher, and in *RefWorld/RefMonde*, CDR/UNHCR's CD-ROM collection of databases.

[2] *Report* of the 28th Session: UN doc. A/AC.96/549, para. 53.3.

[3] *Report* of the 28th Session: UN doc. A/AC.96/549, para. 53.4.

(b) *Expressed* deep concern at the information given by the High Commissioner that, while the principle of *non-refoulement* is in practice widely observed, this principle has in certain cases been disregarded;

(c) *Reaffirms* the fundamental importance of the observance of the principle of *non-refoulement*—both at the border and within the territory of a State of persons who may be subjected to persecution if returned to their country of origin irrespective of whether or not they have been formally recognized as refugees.

No. 7 (XXVIII)—1977   Expulsion[4]

The Executive Committee,

(a) *Recognized* that, according to the 1951 Convention, refugees lawfully in the territory of a Contracting State are generally protected against expulsion and that in accordance with Article 32 of the Convention expulsion of a refugee is only permitted in exceptional circumstances;

(b) *Recognized* that a measure of expulsion may have very serious consequences for a refugee and his immediate family members residing with him;

(c) *Recommended* that, in line with Article 32 of the 1951 Convention, expulsion measures against a refugee should only be taken in very exceptional cases and after due consideration of all the circumstances, including the possibility for the refugee to be admitted to a country other than his country of origin;

(d) *Recommended* that, in cases where the implementation of an expulsion measure is impracticable, States should consider giving refugee delinquents the same treatment as national delinquents and that States examine the possibility of elaborating an international instrument giving effect to this principle;

(e) *Recommended* that an expulsion order should only be combined with custody or detention if absolutely necessary for reasons of national security or public order and that such custody or detention should not be unduly prolonged.

No. 8 (XXVIII)—1977   Determination of Refugee Status[5]

The Executive Committee,

(a) *Noted* the report of the High Commissioner concerning the importance of procedures for determining refugee status;

(b) *Noted* that only a limited number of States parties to the 1951 Convention and the 1967 Protocol had established procedures for the formal determination of refugee status under these instruments;

(c) *Noted,* however, with satisfaction that the establishment of such procedures was under active consideration by a number of Governments;

---

4 *Report* of the 28th Session: UN doc. A/AC.96/549, para. 53.5.
5 *Report* of the 28th Session: UN doc. A/AC.96/549, para. 53.6.

(d) *Expressed* the hope that all Governments parties to the 1951 Convention and the 1967 Protocol which had not yet done so would take steps to establish such procedures in the near future and give favourable consideration to UNHCR participation in such procedures in appropriate form;

(e) *Recommended* that procedures for the determination of refugee status should satisfy the following basic requirements:

(i) The competent official (e.g. immigration officer or border police officer) to whom the applicant addresses himself at the border or in the territory of a Contracting State, should have clear instructions for dealing with cases which might come within the purview of the relevant international instruments. He should be required to act in accordance with the principle of *non-refoulement* and to refer such cases to a higher authority.

(ii) The applicant should receive the necessary guidance as to the procedure to be followed.

(iii) There should be a clearly identified authority—wherever possible a single central authority—with responsibility for examining requests for refugee status and taking a decision in the first instance.

(iv) The applicant should be given the necessary facilities, including the services of a competent interpreter, for submitting his case to the authorities concerned. Applicants should also be given the opportunity, of which they should be duly informed, to contact a representative of UNHCR.

(v) If the applicant is recognized as a refugee, he should be informed accordingly and issued with documentation certifying his refugee status.

(vi) If the applicant is not recognized, he should be given a reasonable time to appeal for a formal reconsideration of the decision, either to the same or to a different authority, whether administrative or judicial, according to the prevailing system.

(vii) The applicant should be permitted to remain in the country pending a decision on his initial request by the competent authority referred to in paragraph (iii) above, unless it has been established by that authority that his request is clearly abusive. He should also be permitted to remain in the country while an appeal to a higher administrative authority or to the courts is pending.

(f) *Requested* UNHCR to prepare, after due consideration of the opinions of States parties to the 1951 Convention and the 1967 Protocol, a detailed study on the question of the extra-territorial effect of determination of refugee status in order to enable the Committee to take a considered view on the matter at a subsequent session taking into account the opinion expressed by representatives that the acceptance by a Contracting State of refugee status as determined by other States parties to these instruments would be generally desirable;

(g) *Requested* the Office to consider the possibility of issuing—for the guidance of Governments—a handbook relating to procedures and criteria for determining refugee status and circulating—with due regard to the confidential nature of individual requests and the particular situations involved—significant decisions on the determination of refugee status.

No. 12 (XXIX)—1978   Extraterritorial Effect of the Determination of Refugee Status[6]

The Executive Committee,

(a) *Considered* that one of the essential aspects of refugee status, as defined by the 1951 Convention and the 1967 Protocol, is its international character;

(b) *Recognized* the desirability for maintenance and continuity of refugee status once it has been determined by a Contracting State;

(c) *Noted* that several provisions of the 1951 Convention enable a refugee residing in one Contracting State to exercise certain rights—as a refugee—in another Contracting State and that the exercise of such rights is not subject to a new determination of his refugee status;

(d) *Noted* that persons considered as refugees under Article 1 A(1) of the Convention maintain their refugee status unless they fall under a cessation or exclusion clause;

(e) *Noted* that refugees, holders of a Convention Travel Document issued by one Contracting State, are enabled to travel as refugees to other Contracting States;

(f) *Considered* that the very purpose of the 1951 Convention and the 1967 Protocol implies that refugee status determined by one Contracting State will be recognized also by the other Contracting States;

(g) *Recognized,* therefore, that refugee status as determined in one Contracting State should only be called into question by another Contracting State in exceptional cases when it appears that the person manifestly does not fulfil the requirements of the Convention, e.g. if facts become known indicating that the statements initially made were fraudulent or showing that the person concerned falls within the terms of a cessation or exclusion provision of the 1951 Convention;

(h) *Further* recognized that a decision by a Contracting State not to recognize refugee status does not preclude another Contracting State from examining a new request for refugee status made by the person concerned.

No. 13 (XXIX)—1978   Travel Documents for Refugees[7]

The Executive Committee,

(a) *Reaffirmed* the importance of the issue of travel documents to refugees for temporary travel outside their country of residence and for resettlement in other countries;

(b) *Urged* all States parties to the 1951 Convention and/or the 1967 Protocol to issue to all refugees, lawfully staying in their territory and who wish to travel, travel documents as provided for in the 1951 Convention (article 28, schedule and annex);

(c) *Recommended* that such Convention Travel Documents should have a wide validity, both geographically and in time, and should contain—as provided for in paragraph 13 of the schedule—a return clause with the same period of validity, in the absence of very special circumstances, as that of the travel document itself;

[6] *Report* of the 29th Session: UN doc. A/AC.96/559, para. 68.2.
[7] *Report* of the 29th Session: UN doc. A/AC.96/559, para. 68.3.

(d) *Recommended* that in order to avoid unnecessary hardship a refugee requesting an extension of validity or renewal of his Convention Travel Document should not be required to return to the issuing country for that purpose and should be enabled to secure such extension of validity or renewal of the Convention Travel Document, also for periods beyond six months, by or through the diplomatic or consular representatives of the issuing State;

(e) *Recommended* that, with a view to avoiding divergent interpretations of paragraphs 6 and 11 of the schedule and the resulting hardships to refugees, Contracting States make appropriate arrangements, including the adoption of bilateral or multilateral agreements, concerning the transfer of responsibility for the issue of Convention Travel Documents;

(f) *Expressed* the hope that bilateral and multilateral arrangements, concluded with a view to facilitating travel by their nationals, e.g. as regards the simplification of visa formalities or the abolition of visa fees, be extended by Contracting States also to refugees lawfully residing in their respective territory;

(g) *Expressed* the hope that States which are not parties to the 1951 Convention or the 1967 Protocol will issue to refugees lawfully residing in their territory appropriate travel documents under conditions as similar as possible to those attaching to the issue of 1951 Convention Travel Documents;

(h) *Expressed* appreciation for the Note on Travel Documents for Refugees (EC/SCP/10) submitted by the High Commissioner, was in general agreement with its contents and recommended that, in an appropriate form and together with the above conclusions, it be communicated to Governments by the High Commissioner in support of his efforts to promote the issue of travel documents to refugees in accordance with internationally accepted standards.

No. 15 (XXX)—1979   Refugees without an Asylum Country[8]

The Executive Committee,

Considered that States should be guided by the following considerations:

General principles

(a) States should use their best endeavours to grant asylum to bona fide asylum seekers;

(b) Action whereby a refugee is obliged to return or is sent to a country where he has reason to fear persecution constitutes a grave violation of the recognized principle of *non-refoulement*;

(c) It is the humanitarian obligation of all coastal States to allow vessels in distress to seek haven in their waters and to grant asylum, or at least temporary refuge, to persons on board wishing to seek asylum;

(d) Decisions by States with regard to the granting of asylum shall be made without discrimination as to race, religion, political opinion, nationality or country of origin;

(e) In the interest of family reunification and for humanitarian reasons, States should facilitate the admission to their territory of at least the spouse and minor or dependent

[8] *Report* of the 30th Session: UN doc. A/AC.96/572, para. 72(2).

children of any person to whom temporary refuge or durable asylum has been granted;

Situations involving a large-scale influx of asylum seekers

(f) In cases of large-scale influx, persons seeking asylum should always receive at least temporary refuge. States which because of their geographical situation, or otherwise, are faced with a large-scale influx should as necessary and at the request of the State concerned receive immediate assistance from other States in accordance with the principle of equitable burden-sharing. Such States should consult with the Office of the United Nations High Commissioner for Refugees as soon as possible to ensure that the persons involved are fully protected, are given emergency assistance, and that durable solutions are sought;

(g) Other States should take appropriate measures individually, jointly or through the Office of the United Nations High Commissioner for Refugees or other international bodies to ensure that the burden of the first asylum country is equitably shared;

Situations involving individual asylum seekers

(h) An effort should be made to resolve the problem of identifying the country responsible for examining an asylum request by the adoption of common criteria. In elaborating such criteria the following principles should be observed:

(i) The criteria should make it possible to identify in a positive manner the country which is responsible for examining an asylum request and to whose authorities the asylum seeker should have the possibility of addressing himself;

(ii) The criteria should be of such a character as to avoid possible disagreement between States as to which of them should be responsible for examining an asylum request and should take into account the duration and nature of any sojourn of the asylum seeker in other countries;

(iii) The intentions of the asylum seeker as regards the country in which he wishes to request asylum should as far as possible be taken into account;

(iv) Regard should be had to the concept that asylum should not be refused solely on the ground that it could be sought from another State. Where, however, it appears that a person, before requesting asylum, already has a connection or close links with another State, he may if it appears fair and reasonable be called upon first to request asylum from that State;

(v) The establishment of criteria should be accompanied by arrangements for regular consultation between concerned Governments for dealing with cases for which no solution has been found and for consultation with the Office of the United Nations High Commissioner for Refugees as appropriate;

(vi) Agreements providing for the return by States of persons who have entered their territory from another contracting State in an unlawful manner should be applied in respect of asylum seekers with due regard to their special situation.

(i) While asylum seekers may be required to submit their asylum request within a certain time limit, failure to do so, or the non-fulfilment of other formal requirements, should not lead to an asylum request being excluded from consideration;

(j) In line with the recommendation adopted by the Executive Committee at its twenty-eighth session (document A/AC.96/549, paragraph 53(6), (E)(i)), where an asylum seeker addresses himself in the first instance to a frontier authority the latter should not reject his application without reference to a central authority;

(k) Where a refugee who has already been granted asylum in one country requests asylum in another country on the ground that he has compelling reasons for leaving his present asylum country due to fear of persecution or because his physical safety or freedom are endangered, the authorities of the second country should give favourable consideration to his asylum request;

(l) States should give favourable consideration to accepting, at the request of the Office of the United Nations High Commissioner for Refugees, a limited number of refugees who cannot find asylum in any country;

(m) States should pay particular attention to the need for avoiding situations in which a refugee loses his right to reside in or to return to his country of asylum without having acquired the possibility of taking up residence in a country other than one where he may have reasons to fear persecution;

(n) In line with the purpose of paragraphs 6 and 11 of the Schedule to the 1951 Convention, States should continue to extend the validity of or to renew refugee travel documents until the refugee has taken up lawful residence in the territory of another State. A similar practice should as far as possible also be applied in respect of refugees holding a travel document other than that provided for in the 1951 Convention.

No. 17 (XXXI)—1980   Problems of Extradition affecting Refugees[9]

The Executive Committee,

(a) *Considered* that cases in which the extradition of a refugee or of a person who may qualify as a refugee is requested may give rise to special problems;

(b) *Reaffirmed* the fundamental character of the generally recognized principle of *non-refoulement*;

(c) *Recognized* that refugees should be protected in regard to extradition to a country where they have well-founded reasons to fear persecution on the grounds enumerated in Article 1(A)(2) of the 1951 United Nations Convention relating to the Status of Refugees;

(d) *Called* upon States to ensure that the principle of *non-refoulement* is duly taken into account in treaties relating to extradition and as appropriate in national legislation on the subject;

(e) *Expressed* the hope that due regard be had to the principle of *non-refoulement* in the application of existing treaties relating to extradition;

(f) *Stressed* that nothing in the present conclusions should be considered as affecting the necessity for States to ensure, on the basis of national legislation and international instruments, punishment for serious offences, such as the unlawful seizure of aircraft, the taking of hostages and murder;

(g) *Stressed* that protection in regard to extradition applies to persons who fulfil the criteria of the refugee definition and who are not excluded from refugee status by virtue

[9] *Report* of the 31st Session: UN doc. A/AC.96/588, para. 48(2).

of Article 1(F)(b) of the 1951 United Nations Convention relating to the Status of Refugees.

No. 18 (XXXI)—1980   Voluntary Repatriation[10]

The Executive Committee,

(a) *Recognized* that voluntary repatriation constitutes generally, and in particular when a country accedes to independence, the most appropriate solution for refugee problems;

(b) *Stressed* that the essentially voluntary character of repatriation should always be respected;

(c) *Recognized* the desirability of appropriate arrangements to establish the voluntary character of repatriation, both as regards the repatriation of individual refugees and in the case of large-scale repatriation movements, and for UNHCR, whenever necessary, to be associated with such arrangements;

(d) *Considered* that when refugees express the wish to repatriate, both the government of their country of origin and the government of their country of asylum should, within the framework of their national legislation and, whenever necessary, in co-operation with UNHCR take all requisite steps to assist them to do so;

(e) *Recognized* the importance of refugees being provided with the necessary information regarding conditions in their country of origin in order to facilitate their decision to repatriate; recognized further that visits by individual refugees or refugee representatives to their country of origin to inform themselves of the situation there—without such visits automatically involving loss of refugee status—could also be of assistance in this regard;

(f) *Called* upon governments of countries of origin to provide formal guarantees for the safety of returning refugees and stressed the importance of such guarantees being fully respected and of returning refugees not being penalized for having left their country of origin for reasons giving rise to refugee situations;

(g) *Recommended* that arrangements be adopted in countries of asylum for ensuring that the terms of guarantees provided by countries of origin and relevant information regarding conditions prevailing there are duly communicated to refugees, that such arrangements could be facilitated by the authorities of countries of asylum and that UNHCR should as appropriate be associated with such arrangements;

(h) *Considered* that UNHCR could appropriately be called upon—with the agreement of the parties concerned—to monitor the situation of returning refugees with particular regard to any guarantees provided by the governments of countries of origin;

(i) *Called* upon the governments concerned to provide repatriating refugees with the necessary travel documents, visas, entry permits and transportation facilities and, if refugees have lost their nationality, to arrange for such nationality to be restored in accordance with national legislation;

(j) *Recognized* that it may be necessary in certain situations to make appropriate arrangements in co-operation with UNHCR for the reception of returning refugees and/or to establish projects for their reintegration in their country of origin.

[10] *Report* of the 31st Session: UN doc. A/AC.96/588, para. 48(3).

No. 19 (XXXI)—1980   Temporary Refuge[11]

The Executive Committee,

(a) *Reaffirmed* the essential need for the humanitarian legal principle of *non-refoulement* to be scrupulously observed in all situations of large-scale influx;

(b) *Recalled* the conclusions on the question of temporary refuge adopted by the Executive Committee at its thirtieth session and, in particular:

(i) that in the case of large-scale influx, persons seeking asylum should always receive at least temporary refuge; and

(ii) that States which, because of their geographical situation or otherwise, are faced with a large-scale influx, should as necessary and at the request of the State concerned receive immediate assistance from other States in accordance with the principle of equitable burden-sharing;

(c) *Took note* of the extensive practice of granting temporary refuge in situations involving a large-scale influx of refugees;

(d) *Stressed* the fundamental importance of the provisions of the 1951 United Nations Convention relating to the Status of Refugees and the 1967 Protocol, and of the 1967 United Nations Declaration on Territorial Asylum and the need for constant advice by UNHCR on the practical application of these provisions by countries exposed to a large-scale influx of refugees;

(e) *Stressed* the exceptional character of temporary refuge and the essential need for persons to whom temporary refuge has been granted to enjoy basic humanitarian standards of treatment;

(f) *Recognized* the need to define the nature, function and implications of the grant of temporary refuge;

(g) *Considered* that the practice of temporary refuge had not been sufficiently examined and should be further studied, particularly in regard to (i) procedures for the admission of refugees, (ii) their status pending a durable solution, (iii) the implications of temporary refuge for international solidarity, including burden sharing;

(h) *Decided* to request the High Commissioner to convene as soon as possible a representative group of experts to examine temporary refuge in all its aspects within the framework of the problems raised by large-scale influx and to provide the group with all possible assistance.

No. 20 (XXXI)—1980   Protection of Asylum Seekers at Sea[12]

The Executive Committee,

(a) *Noted* with grave concern the continuing incidence of criminal attacks on refugees and asylum seekers in different areas of the world, including military attacks on refugee camps and on asylum seekers at sea;

---

[11] *Report* of the 31st Session: UN doc. A/AC.96/588, para. 48(4).
[12] *Report* of the 31st Session: UN doc. A/AC.96/588, para. 48(5).

(b) *Expressed* particular concern regarding criminal attacks on asylum seekers at sea in the South China Sea involving extreme violence and indescribable acts of physical and moral degradation, including rape, abduction and murder;

(c) *Addressed* an urgent call to all interested Governments to take appropriate action to prevent such criminal attacks whether occurring on the high seas or in their territorial waters;

(d) *Stressed* the desirability for the following measures to be taken by Governments with a view to preventing the recurrence of such criminal attacks:

(i) increased governmental action in the region to prevent attacks on boats carrying asylum seekers, including increased sea and air patrols over areas where such attacks occur;

(ii) adoption of all necessary measures to ensure that those responsible for such criminal attacks are severely punished;

(iii) increased efforts to detect land bases from which such attacks on asylum seekers originate and to identify persons known to have taken part in such attacks and to ensure that they are prosecuted;

(iv) establishment of procedures for the routine exchange of information concerning attacks on asylum seekers at sea and for the apprehension of those responsible, and co-operation between Governments for the regular exchange of general information on the matter;

(e) *Called* upon Governments to give full effect to the rules of general international law—as expressed in the Geneva Convention on the High Seas of 1958—relating to the suppression of piracy;

(f) *Urged* Governments to co-operate with each other and with UNHCR to ensure that all necessary assistance is provided to the victims of such criminal attacks;

(g) *Called* upon the United Nations High Commissioner for Refugees in co-operation with the International Committee of the Red Cross and other interested organizations actively to seek the co-operation of the international community to intensify efforts aimed at protecting refugees who are victims of acts of violence, particularly those at sea.

No. 22 (XXXII)—1981　Protection of Asylum Seekers in Situations of Large-scale Influx[13]

The Executive Committee,

Noting with appreciation the report of the Group of Experts on temporary refuge in situations of large-scale influx, which met in Geneva from 21–24 April 1981, adopted the following conclusions in regard to the protection of asylum seekers in situations of large-scale influx.

I. General

1. The refugee problem has become particularly acute due to the increasing number of large-scale influx situations in different areas of the world and especially in developing

[13] *Report* of the 32nd Session: UN doc. A/AC.96/601, para. 57(2).

countries. The asylum seekers forming part of these large-scale influxes include persons who are refugees within the meaning of the 1951 United Nations Convention and the 1967 Protocol relating to the Status of Refugees or who, owing to external aggression, occupation, foreign domination or events seriously disturbing public order in either part of, or the whole of their country of origin or nationality are compelled to seek refuge outside that country.

2. Asylum seekers forming part of such large-scale influx situations are often confronted with difficulties in finding durable solutions by way of voluntary repatriation, local settlement or resettlement in a third country. Large-scale influxes frequently create serious problems for States, with the result that certain States, although committed to obtaining durable solutions, have only found it possible to admit asylum seekers without undertaking at the time of admission to provide permanent settlement of such persons within their borders.

3. It is therefore imperative to ensure that asylum seekers are fully protected in large-scale influx situations, to reaffirm the basic minimum standards for their treatment pending arrangements for a durable solution, and to establish effective arrangements in the context of international solidarity and burden-sharing for assisting countries which receive large numbers of asylum seekers.

II. Measures of protection

A. *Admission and non-refoulement*

1. In situations of large-scale influx, asylum seekers should be admitted to the State in which they first seek refuge and if that State is unable to admit them on a durable basis, it should always admit them at least on a temporary basis and provide them with protection according to the principles set out below. They should be admitted without any discrimination as to race, religion, political opinion, nationality, country of origin or physical incapacity.

2. In all cases the fundamental principle of *non-refoulement*—including non-rejection at the frontier—must be scrupulously observed.

B. *Treatment of asylum seekers who have been temporarily admitted to a country pending arrangements for a durable solution*

1. Article 31 of the 1951 United Nations Convention relating to the Status of Refugees contains provisions regarding the treatment of refugees who have entered a country without authorization and whose situation in that country has not yet been regularized. The standards defined in this Article do not, however, cover all aspects of the treatment of asylum seekers in large-scale influx situations.

2. It is therefore essential that asylum seekers who have been temporarily admitted pending arrangements for a durable solution should be treated in accordance with the following minimum basic human standards:

(a) they should not be penalized or exposed to any unfavourable treatment solely on the ground that their presence in the country is considered unlawful; they should not be subjected to restrictions on their movements other than those which are necessary in the interest of public health and public order;

(b) they should enjoy the fundamental civil rights internationally recognized, in particular those set out in the Universal Declaration of Human Rights;

(c) they should receive all necessary assistance and be provided with the basic necessities of life including food, shelter and basic sanitary and health facilities; in this respect the international community should conform with the principles of international solidarity and burden-sharing;

(d) they should be treated as persons whose tragic plight requires special understanding and sympathy. They should not be subjected to cruel, inhuman or degrading treatment;

(e) there should be no discrimination on the grounds of race, religion, political opinion, nationality, country of origin or physical incapacity;

(f) they are to be considered as persons before the law, enjoying free access to courts of law and other competent administrative authorities;

(g) the location of asylum seekers should be determined by their safety and well-being as well as by the security needs of the receiving State. Asylum seekers should, as far as possible, be located at a reasonable distance from the frontier of their country of origin. They should not become involved in subversive activities against their country of origin or any other State;

(h) family unity should be respected;

(i) all possible assistance should be given for the tracing of relatives;

(j) adequate provision should be made for the protection of minors and unaccompanied children;

(k) the sending and receiving of mail should be allowed;

(l) material assistance from friends or relatives should be permitted;

(m) appropriate arrangements should be made, where possible, for the registration of births, deaths and marriages;

(n) they should be granted all the necessary facilities to enable them to obtain a satisfactory durable solution;

(o) they should be permitted to transfer assets which they have brought into a territory to the country where the durable solution is obtained; and

(p) all steps should be taken to facilitate voluntary repatriation.

III. Co-operation with the Office of the United Nations High Commissioner for Refugees

Asylum seekers shall be entitled to contact the Office of UNHCR. UNHCR shall be given access to asylum seekers. UNHCR shall also be given the responsibility of exercising its function of international protection and shall be allowed to supervise the well-being of persons entering reception or other refugee centres.

IV. International solidarity, burden-sharing and duties of States

(1) A mass influx may place unduly heavy burdens on certain countries; a satisfactory solution of a problem, international in scope and nature, cannot be achieved without international co-operation. States shall, within the framework of international solidarity

and burden-sharing, take all necessary measures to assist, at their request, States which have admitted asylum seekers in large-scale influx situations.

(2) Such action should be taken bilaterally or multilaterally at the regional or at the universal levels and in co-operation with UNHCR, as appropriate. Primary consideration should be given to the possibility of finding suitable solutions within the regional context.

(3) Action with a view to burden-sharing should be directed towards facilitating voluntary repatriation, promoting local settlement in the receiving country, providing resettlement possibilities in third countries, as appropriate.

(4) The measures to be taken within the context of such burden-sharing arrangements should be adapted to the particular situation. They should include, as necessary, emergency, financial and technical assistance, assistance in kind and advance pledging of further financial or other assistance beyond the emergency phase until durable solutions are found, and where voluntary repatriation or local settlement cannot be envisaged, the provision for asylum seekers of resettlement possibilities in a cultural environment appropriate for their well-being.

(5) Consideration should be given to the strengthening of existing mechanisms and, if appropriate, the setting up of new arrangements, if possible on a permanent basis, to ensure that the necessary funds and other material and technical assistance are immediately made available.

(6) In a spirit of international solidarity, Governments should also seek to ensure that the causes leading to large-scale influxes of asylum seekers are as far as possible removed and, where such influxes have occurred, that conditions favourable to voluntary repatriation are established.

No. 23 (XXXII)—1981   Problems related to the Rescue of Asylum Seekers in Distress at Sea[14]

The Executive Committee,

Adopted the following conclusions on problems related to the rescue of asylum seekers in distress at sea.

1. It is recalled that there is a fundamental obligation under international law for ships' masters to rescue any persons in distress at sea, including asylum seekers, and to render them all necessary assistance. Seafaring States should take all appropriate measures to ensure that masters of vessels observe this obligation strictly.

2. Rescue of asylum seekers in distress at sea has been facilitated by the willingness of the flag States of rescuing ships to provide guarantees of resettlement required by certain coastal States as a condition for disembarkation. It has also been facilitated by the agreement of these and other States to contribute to a pool of resettlement guarantees under the DISERO scheme which should be further encouraged. All countries should continue to provide durable solutions for asylum seekers rescued at sea.

[14] *Report* of the 32nd Session: UN doc. A/AC.96/601, para. 57(3).

3. In accordance with established international practice, supported by the relevant international instruments, persons rescued at sea should normally be disembarked at the next port of call. This practice should also be applied in the case of asylum seekers rescued at sea. In cases of large-scale influx, asylum seekers rescued at sea should always be admitted, at least on a temporary basis. States should assist in facilitating their disembarkation by acting in accordance with the principles of international solidarity and burden-sharing in granting resettlement opportunities.

4. As a result of concerted efforts by many countries, large numbers of resettlement opportunities have been, and continue to be, provided for boat people. In view of this development, the question arises as to whether the first port of call countries might wish to examine their present policy of requiring resettlement guarantees as a precondition for disembarkation. Pending a review of practice by coastal States, it is of course desirable that present arrangements for facilitating disembarkation be continued.

5. In view of the complexity of the problems arising from the rescue, disembarkation and resettlement of asylum seekers at sea, the High Commissioner is requested to convene at an early opportunity a working group comprising representatives of the maritime States and the coastal States most concerned, potential countries of resettlement, and representatives of international bodies competent in this field. The working group should study the various problems mentioned and elaborate principles and measures which would provide a solution and should submit a report on the matter to the Executive Committee at its thirty-third session.

No. 24 (XXXII)—1981   Family Reunification[15]

The Executive Committee,

Adopted the following conclusions on the reunification of separated refugee families.

1. In application of the principle of the unity of the family and for obvious humanitarian reasons, every effort should be made to ensure the reunification of separated refugee families.

2. For this purpose it is desirable that countries of asylum and countries of origin support the efforts of the High Commissioner to ensure that the reunification of separated refugee families takes place with the least possible delay.

3. The generally positive trends in regard to the reunification of separated refugee families are greatly to be welcomed but a number of outstanding problems still need to be resolved.

4. Given the recognized right of everyone to leave any country including his own, countries of origin should facilitate family reunification by granting exit permission to family members of refugees to enable them to join the refugee abroad.

5. It is hoped that countries of asylum will apply liberal criteria in identifying those family members who can be admitted with a view to promoting a comprehensive reunification of the family.

[15] *Report* of the 32nd Session: UN doc. A/AC.96/601, para. 57(4).

6. When deciding on family reunification, the absence of documentary proof of the formal validity of a marriage or of the filiation of children should not *per se* be considered as an impediment.

7. The separation of refugee families has, in certain regions of the world, given rise to a number of particularly delicate problems relating to unaccompanied minors. Every effort should be made to trace the parents or other close relatives of unaccompanied minors before their resettlement. Efforts to clarify their family situation with sufficient certainty should also be continued after resettlement. Such efforts are of particular importance before an adoption—involving a severance of links with the natural family—is decided upon.

8. In order to promote the rapid integration of refugee families in the country of settlement, joining close family members should in principle be granted the same legal status and facilities as the head of the family who has been formally recognized as a refugee.

9. In appropriate cases family reunification should be facilitated by special measures of assistance to the head of family so that economic and housing difficulties in the country of asylum do not unduly delay the granting of permission for the entry of the family members.

No. 28 (XXXIII)—1982   Follow-up on Earlier Conclusions of the Sub-Committee of the Whole on International Protection on the Determination of Refugee Status, *inter alia*, with Reference to the Role of UNHCR in National Refugee Status Determination Procedures[16]

The Executive Committee,

(a) *Considered* the report of the High Commissioner on the progress made in regard to the determination of refugee status (EC/SCP/22/Rev.1);

(b) *Noted* with satisfaction that since the twenty-eighth session of the Executive Committee procedures for the determination of refugee status have been established by a further significant number of States Parties to the 1951 Convention and the 1967 Protocol and that these procedures conform to the basic requirements recommended by the Executive Committee at its twenty-eighth session;

(c) *Reiterated* the importance of the establishment of procedures for determining refugee status and urged those States Parties to the 1951 Convention and the 1967 Protocol which had not yet done so to establish such procedures in the near future;

(d) *Recognized* the need for measures to meet the problem of manifestly unfounded or abusive applications for refugee status. A decision that an application is manifestly unfounded or abusive should only be taken by or after reference to the authority competent to determine refugee status. Consideration should be given to the establishment of procedural safeguards to ensure that such decisions are taken only if the application is fraudulent or not related to the criteria for the granting of refugee status laid down in the 1951 United Nations Convention relating to the Status of Refugees. In view of its importance, the question of manifestly unfounded or abusive applications for refugee status should be

[16] *Report* of the 33rd Session: UN doc. A/AC.96/614, para. 70(4).

further examined by the Sub-Committee at its next meeting, as a separate item on its agenda and on the basis of a study to be prepared by UNHCR;

(e) *Noted* with satisfaction the participation in various forms of UNHCR in procedures for determining refugee status in a large number of countries and recognized the value of UNHCR thus being given a meaningful role in such procedures.

No. 30 (XXXIV)—1983   The Problem of Manifestly Unfounded or Abusive Applications for Refugee Status or Asylum[17]

The Executive Committee,

(a) *Recalled* Conclusion No. 8 (XXVIII) adopted at its twenty-eighth session on the Determination of Refugee Status and Conclusion No. 15 (XXX) adopted at its thirtieth session concerning Refugees without an Asylum Country;

(b) *Recalled* Conclusion No. 28 (XXXIII) adopted at its thirty-third session in which the need for measures to meet the problem of manifestly unfounded or abusive applications for refugee status was recognized;

(c) *Noted* that applications for refugee status by persons who clearly have no valid claim to be considered refugees under the relevant criteria constitute a serious problem in a number of States parties to the 1951 Convention and the 1967 Protocol. Such applications are burdensome to the affected countries and detrimental to the interests of those applicants who have good grounds for requesting recognition as refugees;

(d) *Considered* that national procedures for the determination of refugee status may usefully include special provision for dealing in an expeditious manner with applications which are considered to be so obviously without foundation as not to merit full examination at every level of the procedure. Such applications have been termed either 'clearly abusive' or 'manifestly unfounded' and are to be defined as those which are clearly fraudulent or not related to the criteria for the granting of refugee status laid down in the 1951 United Nations Convention relating to the Status of Refugees nor to any other criteria justifying the granting of asylum;

(e) *Recognized* the substantive character of a decision that an application for refugee status is manifestly unfounded or abusive, the grave consequences of an erroneous determination for the applicant and the resulting need for such a decision to be accompanied by appropriate procedural guarantees and therefore recommended that:

(i) as in the case of all requests for the determination of refugee status or the grant of asylum, the applicant should be given a complete personal interview by a fully qualified official and, whenever possible, by an official of the authority competent to determine refugee status;

(ii) the manifestly unfounded or abusive character of an application should be established by the authority normally competent to determine refugee status;

(iii) an unsuccessful applicant should be enabled to have a negative decision reviewed before rejection at the frontier or forcible removal from the territory. Where arrangements for such a review do not exist, governments should give favourable considera-

---

[17] *Report* of the 34th Session: UN doc. A/AC.96/631, para. 97(2).

tion to their establishment. This review possibility can be more simplified than that available in the case of rejected applications which are not considered manifestly unfounded or abusive.

(f) *Recognized* that while measures to deal with manifestly unfounded or abusive applications may not resolve the wider problem of large numbers of applications for refugee status, both problems can be mitigated by overall arrangements for speeding up refugee status determination procedures, for example by:

(i) allocating sufficient personnel and resources to refugee status determination bodies so as to enable them to accomplish their task expeditiously, and

(ii) the introduction of measures that would reduce the time required for the completion of the appeals process.

No. 35 (XXXV)—1984   Identity Documents for Refugees[18]

The Executive Committee,

(a) *Recognized* the need for refugees to have documentation enabling them to establish their identity and noted that Article 27 of the 1951 United Nations Refugee Convention requires Contracting States to issue identity papers to any refugee in their territory who does not have a valid travel document;

(b) *Recalled* that in a conclusion adopted at its twenty-eighth session (A/32/12/Add.1, para. 53 (6)(e)) the Executive Committee recommended that recognized refugees should be issued documentation certifying their refugee status;

(c) *Noted* with approval the general practice of States to provide refugees with documents, in the form prescribed by their national legislation, enabling them to establish their identity and their refugee status, and recommended that States which have not yet done so should ensure that refugees are provided with such documentation;

(d) *Recommended* that asylum applicants whose applications cannot be decided without delay be provided with provisional documentation sufficient to ensure that they are protected against expulsion or *refoulement* until a decision has been taken by the competent authorities with regard to their application;

(e) *Noted* that in countries where there is no provision for the formal recognition of refugee status, it may be necessary for UNHCR, with the consent of the authorities of the asylum country, to certify that a person is considered a refugee within the UNHCR mandate; and

(f) *Recognized* the value of registering and issuing appropriate documentation to refugees in large-scale influx situations, and recommended that States which have not yet done so should undertake such registration and documentation programmes, where appropriate in co-operation with UNHCR.

---

[18] *Report* of the 35th Session: UN doc. A/AC.96/651, para. 87(3).

No. 39 (XXXVI)—1985 Refugee Women and International Protection[19]

The Executive Committee,

(a) *Welcomed* the initiative of the Office in organizing the Round Table on Refugee Women in Geneva in April 1985;

(b) *Welcomed* further the recommendations regarding the situation of refugee and displaced women adopted by the World Conference to Review and Appraise the Achievements of the United Nations Decade for Women held in Nairobi (Kenya) in July 1985;

(c) *Noted* that refugee women and girls constitute the majority of the world refugee population and that many of them are exposed to special problems in the international protection field;

(d) *Recognized* that these problems result from their vulnerable situation which frequently exposes them to physical violence, sexual abuse, and discrimination;

(e) *Stressed* the need for such problems to receive the urgent attention of Governments and of UNHCR and for all appropriate measures to be taken to guarantee that refugee women and girls are protected from violence or threats to their physical safety or exposure to sexual abuse or harassment;

(f) *Noted* with satisfaction the measures already undertaken by UNHCR to address the protection problems of refugee women and to ensure that they are adequately protected;

(g) *Called* upon States to continue to support UNHCR programmes established with a view to securing protection for refugee women, and UNHCR assistance programmes for refugee women, especially those aimed at helping refugee women become self-sufficient through educational and income-generating projects;

(h) *Recommended* that States, individually, jointly and in co-operation with UNHCR, redefine and reorient existing programmes and, where necessary, establish new programmes to meet the specific problems of refugee women, in particular to ensure the safeguard of their physical integrity and safety, and their equality of treatment. Women refugees should participate in the formulation and implementation of such programmes;

(i) *Stressed* the importance of a more detailed knowledge and understanding of the special needs and problems of refugee women in the international protection field and of gathering statistical, sociological and other data concerning refugee women and girls in order to identify and implement appropriate mechanisms to ensure their effective protection;

(j) *Requested* the High Commissioner to report regularly to members of the Executive Committee on the needs of refugee women, and on existing and proposed programmes for their benefit;

(k) *Recognized* that States, in the exercise of their sovereignty, are free to adopt the interpretation that women asylum seekers who face harsh or inhuman treatment due to their having transgressed the social mores of the society in which they live may be considered as a 'particular social group' within the meaning of Article 1 A(2) of the 1951 United Nations Refugee Convention.

[19] *Report* of the 36th Session: UN doc. A/AC.96/673, para. 115(4).

No. 40 (XXXVI)—1985   Voluntary Repatriation[20]

The Executive Committee,

Reaffirming the significance of its 1980 conclusion on voluntary repatriation as reflecting basic principles of international law and practice, adopted the following further conclusions on this matter:

(a) The basic rights of persons to return voluntarily to the country of origin is reaffirmed and it is urged that international co-operation be aimed at achieving this solution and should be further developed;

(b) The repatriation of refugees should only take place at their freely expressed wish; the voluntary and individual character of repatriation of refugees and the need for it to be carried out under conditions of absolute safety, preferably to the place of residence of the refugee in his country of origin, should always be respected;

(c) The aspect of causes is critical to the issue of solution and international efforts should also be directed to the removal of the causes of refugee movements. Further attention should be given to the causes and prevention of such movements, including the co-ordination of efforts currently being pursued by the international community and in particular within the United Nations. An essential condition for the prevention of refugee flows is sufficient political will by the States directly concerned to address the causes which are at the origin of refugee movements;

(d) The responsibilities of States towards their nationals and the obligations of other States to promote voluntary repatriation must be upheld by the international community. International action in favour of voluntary repatriation, whether at the universal or regional level, should receive the full support and co-operation of all States directly concerned. Promotion of voluntary repatriation as a solution to refugee problems similarly requires the political will of States directly concerned to create conditions conducive to this solution. This is the primary responsibility of States;

(e) The existing mandate of the High Commissioner is sufficient to allow him to promote voluntary repatriation by taking initiatives to this end, promoting dialogue between all the main parties, facilitating communication between them, and by acting as an intermediary or channel of communication. It is important that he establishes, whenever possible, contact with all the main parties and acquaints himself with their points of view. From the outset of a refugee situation, the High Commissioner should at all times keep the possibility of voluntary repatriation for all or for part of a group under active review and the High Commissioner, whenever he deems that the prevailing circumstances are appropriate, should actively pursue the promotion of this solution;

(f) The humanitarian concerns of the High Commissioner should be recognized and respected by all parties and he should receive full support in his efforts to carry out his humanitarian mandate in providing international protection to refugees and in seeking a solution to refugee problems;

(g) On all occasions the High Commissioner should be fully involved from the outset in assessing the feasibility and, thereafter, in both the planning and implementation stages of repatriation;

[20] *Report* of the 36th Session: UN doc. A/AC.96/673, para. 115(5).

(h) The importance of spontaneous return to the country of origin is recognized and it is considered that action to promote organized voluntary repatriation should not create obstacles to the spontaneous return of refugees. Interested States should make all efforts, including the provision of assistance in the country of origin, to encourage this movement whenever it is deemed to be in the interests of the refugees concerned;

(i) When, in the opinion of the High Commissioner, a serious problem exists in the promotion of voluntary repatriation of a particular refugee group, he may consider for that particular problem the establishment of an informal *ad hoc* consultative group which would be appointed by him in consultation with the Chairman and the other members of the Bureau of his Executive Committee. Such a group may, if necessary, include States which are not members of the Executive Committee and should in principle include the countries directly concerned. The High Commissioner may also consider invoking the assistance of other competent United Nations organs;

(j) The practice of establishing tripartite commissions is well adapted to facilitate voluntary repatriation. The tripartite commission, which should consist of the countries of origin and of asylum and UNHCR, could concern itself with both the joint planning and the implementation of a repatriation programme. It is also an effective means of securing consultations between the main parties concerned on any problems that might subsequently arise;

(k) International action to promote voluntary repatriation requires consideration of the situation within the country of origin as well as within the receiving country. Assistance for the reintegration of returnees provided by the international community in the country of origin is recognized as an important factor in promoting repatriation. To this end, UNHCR and other United Nations agencies as appropriate, should have funds readily available to assist returnees in the various stages of their integration and rehabilitation in their country of origin;

(l) The High Commissioner should be recognized as having a legitimate concern for the consequences of return, particularly where such return has been brought about as a result of an amnesty or other form of guarantee. The High Commissioner must be regarded as entitled to insist on his legitimate concern over the outcome of any return that he has assisted. Within the framework of close consultations with the State concerned, he should be given direct and unhindered access to returnees so that he is in a position to monitor fulfilment of the amnesties, guarantees or assurances on the basis of which the refugees have returned. This should be considered as inherent in his mandate;

(m) Consideration should be given to the further elaboration of an instrument reflecting all existing principles and guidelines relating to voluntary repatriation for acceptance by the international community as a whole.

No. 44 (XXXVII)—1986   Detention of Refugees and Asylum Seekers[21]

The Executive Committee,

Recalling Article 31 of the 1951 Convention relating to the Status of Refugees,

Recalling further its Conclusion No. 22 (XXXII) on the treatment of asylum seekers in situations of large-scale influx, as well as Conclusion No. 7 (XXVIII), paragraph (e), on the question of custody or detention in relation to the expulsion of refugees lawfully in a country, and Conclusion No. 8 (XXVIII), paragraph (e), on the determination of refugee status,

Noting that the term 'refugee' in the present Conclusions has the same meaning as that in the 1951 Convention and the 1967 Protocol relating to the Status of Refugees, and is without prejudice to wider definitions applicable in different regions,

(a) *Noted* with deep concern that large numbers of refugees and asylum seekers in different areas of the world are currently the subject of detention or similar restrictive measures by reason of their illegal entry or presence in search of asylum, pending resolution of their situation;

(b) *Expressed* the opinion that in view of the hardship which it involves, detention should normally be avoided. If necessary, detention may be resorted to only on grounds prescribed by law to verify identity; to determine the elements on which the claim to refugee status or asylum is based; to deal with cases where refugees or asylum seekers have destroyed their travel and/or identity documents or have used fraudulent documents in order to mislead the authorities of the State in which they intend to claim asylum; or to protect national security or public order;

(c) *Recognized* the importance of fair and expeditious procedures for determining refugee status or granting asylum in protecting refugees and asylum seekers from unjustified or unduly prolonged detention;

(d) *Stressed* the importance for national legislation and/or administrative practice to make the necessary distinction between the situation of refugees and asylum seekers, and that of other aliens;

(e) *Recommended* that detention measures taken in respect of refugees and asylum seekers should be subject to judicial or administrative review;

(f) *Stressed* that conditions of detention of refugees and asylum seekers must be humane. In particular, refugees and asylum seekers shall, whenever possible, not be accommodated with persons detained as common criminals, and shall not be located in areas where their physical safety is endangered;

(g) *Recommended* that refugees and asylum seekers who are detained be provided with the opportunity to contact the Office of the United Nations High Commissioner for Refugees or, in the absence of such office, available national refugee assistance agencies;

(h) *Reaffirmed* that refugees and asylum seekers have duties to the country in which they find themselves, which require in particular that they conform to its laws and regulations as well as to measures taken for the maintenance of public order;

---

[21] *Report* of the 37th Session: UN doc. A/AC.96/688, para. 128.

(i) *Reaffirmed* the fundamental importance of the observance of the principle of *non-refoulement* and in this context recalled the relevance of Conclusion No. 6 (XXVIII).

No. 47 (XXXVIII)—1987   Refugee Children[22]

The Executive Committee,

(a) *Expressed* appreciation to the High Commissioner for his Report on Refugee Children (EC/SCP/46) and noted with serious concern the violations of their human rights in different areas of the world and their special needs and vulnerability within the broader refugee population;

(b) *Recognized* that refugee children constitute approximately one half of the world's refugee population and that the situation in which they live often gives rise to special protection and assistance problems as well as to problems in the area of durable solutions;

(c) *Reiterated* the widely-recognized principle that children must be among the first to receive protection and assistance;

(d) *Stressed* that all action taken on behalf of refugee children must be guided by the principle of the best interests of the child as well as by the principle of family unity;

(e) *Condemned* the exposure of refugee children to physical violence and other violations of their basic rights, including through sexual abuse, trade in children, acts of piracy, military or armed attacks, forced recruitment, political exploitation or arbitrary detention, and called for national and international action to prevent such violations and assist the victims;

(f) *Urged* States to take appropriate measures to register the births of refugee children born in countries of asylum;

(g) *Expressed* its concern over the increasing number of cases of statelessness among refugee children;

(h) *Recommended* that children who are accompanied by their parents should be treated as refugees if either of the parents is determined to be a refugee;

(i) *Underlined* the special situation of unaccompanied children and children separated from their parents, who are in the care of other families, including their needs as regards determination of their status, provision for their physical and emotional support and efforts to trace parents or relatives; and in this connection, recalled the relevant paragraphs of Conclusion No. 24 (XXXII) on Family Reunification;

(j) *Called* upon the High Commissioner to ensure that individual assessments are conducted and adequate social histories prepared for unaccompanied children and children separated from their parents, who are in the care of other families, to facilitate provision for their immediate needs, the analysis of the long term as well as immediate viability of existing foster arrangements, and the planning and implementation of appropriate durable solutions;

(k) *Noted* that while the best durable solution for an unaccompanied refugee child will depend on the particular circumstances of the case, the possibility of voluntary repatriation should at all times be kept under review, keeping in mind the best interests of the child and the possible difficulties of determining the voluntary character of repatriation;

---

[22] *Report* of the 38th Session: UN doc. A/AC.96/702, para. 205.

(l) *Stressed* the need for internationally and nationally supported programmes geared to preventive action, special assistance and rehabilitation for disabled refugee children and encouraged States to participate in the "Twenty or More" Plan providing for the resettlement of disabled refugee children;

(m) *Noted* with serious concern the detrimental effects that extended stays in camps have on the development of refugee children and called for international action to mitigate such effects and provide durable solutions as soon as possible;

(n) *Recognized* the importance of meeting the special psychological, religious, cultural and recreational needs of refugee children in order to ensure their emotional stability and development;

(o) *Reaffirmed* the fundamental right of refugee children to education and called upon all States, individually and collectively, to intensify their efforts, in co-operation with the High Commissioner, to ensure that all refugee children benefit from primary education of a satisfactory quality, that respects their cultural identity and is oriented towards an understanding of the country of asylum;

(p) *Recognized* the need of refugee children to pursue further levels of education and recommended that the High Commissioner consider the provision of post-primary education within the general programme of assistance;

(q) *Called* upon all States, in co-operation with UNHCR and concerned agencies, to develop and/or support programmes to address nutritional and health risks faced by refugee children, including programmes to ensure an adequate, well-balanced and safe diet, general immunization and primary health care;

(r) *Recommended* regular and timely assessment and review of the needs of refugee children, either on an individual basis or through sample surveys, prepared in co-operation with the country of asylum, taking into account all relevant factors such as age, sex, personality, family, religion, social and cultural background and the situation of the local population, and benefiting from the active involvement of the refugee community itself;

(s) *Reaffirmed* the need to promote continuing and expanded co-operation between UNHCR and other concerned agencies and bodies active in the fields of assistance to refugee children and protection, including through the development of legal and social standards;

(t) *Noted* the importance of further study of the needs of refugee children by UNHCR, other intergovernmental and non-governmental agencies and national authorities, with a view to identification of additional support programmes and reorientation as necessary of existing ones;

(u) *Called* upon the High Commissioner to develop further, in consultation with concerned organizations, guidelines to promote co-operation between UNHCR and these organizations to improve the international protection, physical security, well-being and normal psychosocial development of refugee children;

(v) *Called* upon the High Commissioner to maintain the UNHCR Working Group on Refugee Children at Risk as his focal point on refugee children, to strengthen the Working Group and to inform the members of the Executive Committee, on a regular basis, of its work.

No. 48 (XXXVIII)—1987   Military or Armed Attacks on Refugee Camps and Settlements[23]

The Executive Committee,

Remained gravely preoccupied with the continuing incidence of unlawful attacks on refugees and asylum seekers in different areas of the world, including military or armed attacks on refugee camps and settlements and, in view of the tragic and indiscriminate consequences of these attacks, resulting in untold human misery for the refugees and asylum seekers, believed it was necessary and timely at this session to express its humanitarian concern and condemnation in the strongest terms;

Noted with appreciation those Resolutions of the General Assembly of the United Nations, adopted by consensus, in particular General Assembly Resolution 39/140 (1984), which condemned all violations of the rights and safety of refugees and asylum seekers, in particular those perpetrated by military or armed attacks against refugee camps and settlements;

Predicating this Conclusion on the assumption, *inter alia*, that refugee camps and settlements have an exclusively civilian and humanitarian character and on the principle that the grant of asylum or refuge is a peaceful and humanitarian act that is not to be regarded as unfriendly by another State; hoping to assist in guaranteeing the safety of refugees and asylum seekers, as well as to reinforce their rights, obligations and responsibilities and those of States and international organizations pursuant to relevant rules and principles of international law; and underlining that the rights and responsibilities of States pursuant to the Charter of the United Nations and relevant rules and principles of international law, including international humanitarian law, remained unaltered;

1. *Condemns* all violations of the rights and safety of refugees and asylum seekers and in particular military or armed attacks on refugee camps and settlements.

2. *Strongly* urges States to abstain from these violations, which are against the principles of international law and, therefore, cannot be justified.

3. *Calls* upon States and competent international organizations, in accordance with the principle of international solidarity and in order to alleviate the burden of the country of refuge, to provide, according to their means, all necessary assistance to relieve the plight of the victims of such military and armed attacks on refugee camps and settlements if ever they occur.

4. *Urges* States and other parties to be guided by the following considerations in promoting measures to enhance the protection of refugee camps and settlements;

(a) Refugees in camps and settlements have, together with the basic rights they enjoy, duties deriving from the refuge and protection granted or afforded to them by the country of refuge. In particular, they have duties to conform to the laws and regulations of the State of refuge including lawful measures taken for the maintenance of public order and to abstain from any activity likely to detract from the exclusively civilian and humanitarian character of the camps and settlements.

[23] *Report* of the 38th Session: UN doc. A/AC.96/702, para. 206.

(b) It is essential that States of refuge do all within their capacity to ensure that the civilian and humanitarian character of such camps and settlements is maintained. All other States are called upon to assist them in this regard. To this end relevant organs of the United Nations, within their respective terms of reference, are also called upon to co-operate with all States in providing assistance whenever necessary.

(c) UNHCR and other concerned organs of the United Nations should make every effort, within their respective terms of reference and in keeping with the principles of the United Nations Charter, to promote conditions which ensure the safety of refugees in camps and settlements. For UNHCR this may include maintaining close contact with the Secretary-General of the United Nations and providing liaison, as appropriate, with all the parties concerned. It may also involve making appropriate arrangements with States of refuge on methods of protecting such refugee camps and settlements including, whenever possible, their location at a reasonable distance from the frontier of the country of origin.

(d) States have a duty to co-operate with the High Commissioner in the performance of his humanitarian protection and assistance functions, which can only be effectively accomplished if he has access to camps and settlements of his concern.

No. 52 (XXXIX)—1988   International Solidarity and Refugee Protection[24]

The Executive Committee,

Remaining deeply concerned about the gravity and complexity of refugee problems throughout the world, the serious violations of human rights which accompany them and the dislocation and distress they cause for the millions of individuals involved;

Reaffirming that refugee problems are the concern of the international community and their resolution is dependent on the will and capacity of States to respond in concert and wholeheartedly, in a spirit of true humanitarianism and international solidarity;

Noting that States have obligations or responsibilities to accord protection and a basic standard of treatment to refugees and that these must be performed in good faith;

Noting also that the Office of the United Nations High Commissioner for Refugees was created in the context of an urgent need to provide protection to refugees and that it is this protection function which uniquely characterizes the Office;

1. *Underlined* that States, which have defined the protection role of the Office, have a responsibility to co-operate with it in the fulfilment of its mandate on the basis of the fundamental humanitarian principles which motivate its work;

2. *Noted* that States and UNHCR are joined in the common pursuit of solutions for refugee problems and the international protection of the fundamental rights of refugees;

3. *Stressed* that the principle of international solidarity has a fundamental role to play in encouraging a humanitarian approach to the grant of asylum and in the effective implementation of international protection in general;

---

[24] *Report* of the 39th Session: UN doc. A/AC.96/721, para. 24.

4. *Recalled* that, in all circumstances, the respect for fundamental humanitarian principles is an obligation for all members of the international community, it being understood that the principle of international solidarity is of utmost importance to the satisfactory implementation of these principles;

5. *Invited* all States to continue actively to support the protection functions of the High Commissioner through all appropriate means, both bilateral and multilateral, as well as to abide by their own humanitarian responsibilities towards refugees, including, particularly, to safeguard the right to seek and enjoy asylum from persecution and to ensure full respect for the principle of *non-refoulement*.

No. 53 (XXXIX)—1988   Stowaway Asylum-seekers[25]

The Executive Committee,

Recognizing that stowaway asylum-seekers often find themselves in a particularly vulnerable situation in need of international protection and durable solutions;

Recalling its Conclusion No. 15 (XXX) on Refugees without an Asylum Country adopted at the thirtieth session of the Executive Committee;

Reaffirming the necessity of giving proper attention to the needs of stowaway asylum seekers including arranging for their disembarkation, determining their refugee status and, whenever required, providing them with a durable solution;

Noting that there are at present no general and internationally recognized rules dealing specifically with stowaway asylum seekers and at the same time recognizing that asylum seekers should be given the special consideration that their situation demands;

Recommended that States and UNHCR take into account the following guidelines when dealing with actual cases of stowaway asylum seekers:

1. Like other asylum seekers, stowaway asylum seekers must be protected against forcible return to their country of origin.

2. Without prejudice to any responsibilities of the flag State, stowaway asylum seekers should, whenever possible, be allowed to disembark at the first port of call and given the opportunity of having their refugee status determined by the authorities, provided that this does not necessarily imply durable solution in the country of the port of disembarkation.

3. Normally UNHCR would be requested to assist in finding a durable solution for those found to be refugees, based on all relevant aspects of the case.

---

[25] *Report* of the 39th Session: UN doc. A/AC.96/721, para. 25.

No. 58 (XL)—1989   The Problem of Refugees and Asylum Seekers
who Move in an Irregular Manner from a Country in which they had
already found Protection[26]

(a) The phenomenon of refugees, whether they have been formally identified as such or
not (asylum seekers), who move in an irregular manner from countries in which they have
already found protection, in order to seek asylum or permanent resettlement elsewhere,
is a matter of growing concern. This concern results from the destabilizing effect which
irregular movements of this kind have on structured international efforts to provide

---

[26] The following 'interpretative declarations or reservations' were made with respect to
Conclusion No. 58 (XL), 1989. See *Report* of the 40th Session of the Executive Committee: UN doc.
A/AC.96/737, part N, p. 23: The delegation of Australia wishes it to be pointed out that its endorsement of the draft conclusions is subject to it being clearly understood that refugees and asylum seekers should not necessarily be afforded the same treatment. The delegation of China is of the view
that paragraph (b) of the draft conclusions is not exhaustive in its listing of the reasons why persons
feel impelled to leave when they have already found protection. The delegation of Turkey has
requested that it be made clear that in the light of the discussions and the wording of the draft conclusions, and as the then Director of Protection made clear in 1985, these conclusions do not apply
to refugees and asylum seekers who are merely in transit in another country. This interpretation is
recorded in para. 68 of the Report of the Sub-Committee for 1985. The delegation of Italy wishes
the following declaration recorded: 'Without prejudicing in any way the application, in the context
of bilateral agreements or multilateral ones within the European Community, of criteria other than
those put forth hereunder, the Italian authorities consider that the present Conclusion is only applicable to refugees recognized as such according to the Geneva Convention of 1951 and its 1967
Protocol and in the sphere of application of said Geneva Convention and Protocol, as well as to asylum seekers who have already found protection in the first country of asylum on the basis of the
principles of said Convention and Protocol'. The delegation of Tanzania has stated the following:
'Regarding the issue of irregular movements, Tanzania's responsibility to protect a refugee ceases
the moment he voluntarily leaves Tanzania and Tanzania accepts no obligation to readmit such
refugee either from his country of origin or from a third country.'
    Thailand wishes it placed on record that in its view paragraph (d) cannot be understood as estab-
lishing any hierarchy amongst the durable solutions listed therein, in particular to give priority to
local settlement before third country resettlement. As a country of temporary asylum Thailand, with
areas of severe poverty, could not be expected to grant local settlement. Local integration may be
allowed only where and when local situations permit, after other solutions have been exhausted. The
delegation of the Federal Republic of Germany has the following interpretative declaration to make:
'The Federal Republic of Germany understands that the wording "they are permitted to remain
there" (see section (f)) does not prevent repatriation to the country of first asylum even if a formal
residence permit is lacking. It interprets the term "recognized basic human standards" (see section
(f)) in such a way that this notion does not extend beyond the scope of Art. 42 of the Geneva
Convention relating to the Status of Refugees. Finally, it interprets the term "physical safety" (see
section (g)) in such a way that its scope does not extend beyond the definition of the term "refugee"
contained in Article 1 A(2) of the Geneva Convention relating to the Status of Refugees.' The delegation of Austria has stated that it shares the interpretative statement made by the Federal Republic
of Germany.
    The delegation of Greece has stated with respect to para. (b) that: 'First asylum countries should
bear the burden of refugees on an equitable basis, according to their economic or other potential';
with respect to paragraph (e) it has stated that: 'The will of a refugee to choose freely the country
of his destination should not be overlooked, within the spirit of the Geneva Convention of 1951';
and with respect to paragraph (f) it has stated that: 'In all instances, sovereignty of the State and its
rules and regulations under which entry is allowed cannot be ignored. Other considerations not to
be overlooked are the status of the individual, whether he has applied for asylum or not, length of
stay in a country when having moved from the first asylum country, etc.'

appropriate solutions for refugees. Such irregular movements involve entry into the territory of another country, without the prior consent of the national authorities or without an entry visa, or with no or insufficient documentation normally required for travel purposes, or with false or fraudulent documentation. Of similar concern is the growing phenomenon of refugees and asylum seekers who wilfully destroy or dispose of their documentation in order to mislead the authorities of the country of arrival;

(b) Irregular movements of refugees and asylum seekers who have already found protection in a country are, to a large extent, composed of persons who feel impelled to leave, due to the absence of educational and employment possibilities and the non-availability of long-term durable solutions by way of voluntary repatriation, local integration and resettlement;

(c) The phenomenon of such irregular movements can only be effectively met through concerted action by governments, in consultation with UNHCR, aimed at

(i) identifying the causes and scope of irregular movements in any given refugee situation,

(ii) removing or mitigating the causes of such irregular movements through the granting and maintenance of asylum and the provision of necessary durable solutions or other appropriate assistance measures,

(iii) encouraging the establishment of appropriate arrangements for the identification of refugees in the countries concerned and,

(iv) ensuring humane treatment for refugees and asylum seekers who, because of the uncertain situation in which they find themselves, feel impelled to move from one country to another in an irregular manner;

(d) Within this framework, governments, in close co-operation with UNHCR, should

(i) seek to promote the establishment of appropriate measures for the care and support of refugees and asylum seekers in countries where they have found protection pending the identification of a durable solution and

(ii) promote appropriate durable solutions with particular emphasis firstly on voluntary repatriation and, when this is not possible, local integration and the provision of adequate resettlement opportunities;

(e) Refugees and asylum seekers, who have found protection in a particular country, should normally not move from that country in an irregular manner in order to find durable solutions elsewhere but should take advantage of durable solutions available in that country through action taken by governments and UNHCR as recommended in paragraphs (c) and (d) above;

(f) Where refugees and asylum seekers nevertheless move in an irregular manner from a country where they have already found protection, they may be returned to that country if (i) they are protected there against *refoulement* and (ii) they are permitted to remain there and to be treated in accordance with recognized basic human standards until a durable solution is found for them. Where such return is envisaged, UNHCR may be requested to assist in arrangements for the re-admission and reception of the persons concerned;

(g) It is recognized that there may be exceptional cases in which a refugee or asylum seeker may justifiably claim that he has reason to fear persecution or that his physical safety or freedom are endangered in a country where he previously found protection. Such cases should be given favourable consideration by the authorities of the State where he requests asylum;

(h) The problem of irregular movements is compounded by the use, by a growing number of refugees and asylum seekers, of fraudulent documentation and their practice of wilfully destroying or disposing of travel and/or other documents in order to mislead the authorities of their country of arrival. These practices complicate the personal identification of the person concerned and the determination of the country where he stayed prior to arrival, and the nature and duration of his stay in such a country. Practices of this kind are fraudulent and may weaken the case of the person concerned;

(i) It is recognized that circumstances may compel a refugee or asylum seeker to have recourse to fraudulent documentation when leaving a country in which his physical safety or freedom are endangered. Where no such compelling circumstances exist, the use of fraudulent documentation is unjustified;

(j) The wilful destruction or disposal of travel or other documents by refugees and asylum seekers upon arrival in their country of destination, in order to mislead the national authorities as to their previous stay in another country where they have protection, is unacceptable. Appropriate arrangements should be made by States, either individually or in co-operation with other States, to deal with this growing phenomenon.

No. 59 (XL)—1989   Refugee Children[27]

The Executive Committee,

(a) *Expressed* appreciation for the Report on Refugee Children (A/AC.96/731), noted with concern the serious risks to their safety, immediate welfare and future development faced by many refugee children and recognized the efforts made by the Office of the High Commissioner to improve its effectiveness in responding to their special needs;

(b) *Reaffirmed* its Conclusion [No.47 (XXXVIII)] concerning refugee children and stressed the continuing nature of the guidance provided;

(c) *Commended* the High Commissioner and his Working Group on Refugee Children for the development and dissemination of the *Guidelines on Refugee Children* and for the implementation of a work plan concerning refugee children and called upon UNHCR to seek the active co-operation and collaboration of governments, other United Nations bodies, among them UNICEF, non-governmental organizations and refugees themselves, in the implementation of the guidelines;

(d) *Requested* the High Commissioner to ensure that the needs of refugee children are given particular attention through regularly assessing resources and requirements in each refugee situation; collecting and using in programme planning relevant demographic, socio-economic and cultural information; and monitoring and evaluating the impact of his programmes on refugee children;

(e) *Noted* with serious concern the increasing incidence of nutritional deficiency diseases and malnutrition amongst refugee children dependent upon food aid and called upon

---

[27] *Report* of the 40th Session: UN doc. A/AC.96/737, para. 26.

UNHCR to initiate as a matter of urgency formal discussions with relevant United Nations bodies, donors and other humanitarian organizations to develop collaborative strategies for alleviating the nutritional problems of refugee children and to seek the incorporation into their programmes of appropriate provisions for such needs;

(f) *Recognized* the link between education and durable solutions and encouraged UNHCR to strengthen its efforts in assisting host country governments to ensure the access of refugee children to education, *inter alia*, through the involvement of new organizations and governmental and non-governmental donors, and where necessary through the incorporation of appropriate arrangements in its programmes of assistance;

(g) *Requested* the High Commissioner to continue to give special attention to the needs of unaccompanied minors and inform the Executive Committee at its next session of the details of existing programmes and any difficulties encountered in their implementation;

(h) *Called* upon UNHCR to promote the best possible legal protection of unaccompanied minors, particularly with regard to forced recruitment into armed forces and to the risks associated with irregular adoption;

(i) *Urged* UNHCR to intensify efforts to increase public awareness of the situation and needs of refugee children and of the impact of armed conflict and persecution on them;

(j) *Encouraged* UNHCR to develop training materials to improve the capacity and effectiveness of field personnel in identifying and addressing the protection and assistance needs of refugee children;

(k) *Recalled* its request in its Thirty-seventh Session in 1986 [No.41 (XXXVII)] for the High Commissioner to report regularly to the Executive Committee on the needs of refugee children, and on existing and proposed programmes for their benefit.

No. 64 (XLI)—1990   Refugee Women and International Protection[28]

The Executive Committee,

Noting with serious concern the widespread violations of the rights of refugee women and their specific needs;

Underlining the potential of refugee women and the need to ensure their full participation in analysing their needs and in designing and implementing programmes which make appropriate use of their resources;

Reaffirming its Conclusion No.39 (XXXVI) on Refugee Women and International Protection;

Stressing that all action taken on behalf of women who are refugees must be guided by the relevant international instruments relating to the status of refugees as well as other applicable human rights instruments, in particular, for States parties thereto, the United Nations Convention on the Elimination of All Forms of Discrimination Against Women;

Recognizing that ensuring equal treatment of refugee women and men may require specific action in favour of the former;

Recalling the special relevance of the Nairobi Forward-Looking Strategies on the Advancement of Women and the obligation of the United Nations System as a whole to give effect to its provisions;

---

[28] *Report* of the 41st Session: UN doc. A/AC.96/760, para. 23.

Reiterating the importance of collecting data which allows for the monitoring of progress achieved in meeting the needs of refugee women,

(a) *Urges* States, relevant United Nations organizations, as well as non-governmental organizations, as appropriate, to ensure that the needs and resources of refugee women are fully understood and integrated, to the extent possible, into their activities and programmes and, to this end, to pursue, among others, the following aims in promoting measures for improving the international protection of refugee women:

(i) Promote energetically the full and active participation of refugee women in the planning, implementation and evaluation/monitoring of all sectors of refugee programmes;

(ii) Increase the representation of appropriately trained female staff across all levels of all organizations and entities which work in refugee programmes and ensure direct access of refugee women to such staff;

(iii) Provide, wherever necessary, skilled female interviewers in procedures for the determination of refugee status and ensure appropriate access by women asylum seekers to such procedures, even when accompanied by male family members;

(iv) Ensure that all refugees and the staff of relevant organizations and authorities are fully aware of, and support, the rights, needs and resources of refugee women and take appropriate specific actions;

(v) Integrate considerations specific to the protection of refugee women into assistance activities from their inception, including when planning refugee camps and settlements, in order to be able to deter, detect and redress instances of physical and sexual abuse as well as other protection concerns at the earliest possible moment;

(vi) Extend professional and culturally appropriate gender-based counselling as well as other related services to refugee women who are victims of abuse;

(vii) Identify and prosecute persons who have committed crimes against refugee women and protect the victims of such crimes from reprisals;

(viii) Issue individual identification and/or registration documents to all refugee women;

(ix) Provide all refugee women and girls with effective and equitable access to basic services, including food, water and relief supplies, health and sanitation, education and skills training, and make wage-earning opportunities available to them;

(x) Provide for informed and active consent and participation of refugee women in individual decisions about durable solutions for them;

(xi) Ensure that resettlement programmes make special provisions for refugee women at risk.

(b) *Invites* UNHCR to develop comprehensive guidelines on the protection of refugee women as a matter of urgency in order to give effect to its policy on refugee women as contained in document A/AC.96/754.

No. 67 (XLII)—1991   Resettlement as an Instrument of Protection[29]

The Executive Committee,

Reaffirming the link between international protection and resettlement as an instrument of protection and its important role as durable solution in specific circumstances,

(a) *Calls* upon governments in a position to assist, to establish refugee admission ceilings, in the context of international burden-sharing;

(b) *Requests* States when setting refugee admission ceilings to include an adequate contingency provision which could be available depending on need to address rapidly evolving situations;

(c) *Recognizes* that rapidly evolving situations can result in fluctuating resettlement requirements from one year to another and that admission ceilings should be adaptable to such developments;

(d) *Recognizes* the need for rapid and flexible response to UNHCR resettlement requirements in particular for vulnerable groups and emergency protection cases subject to refugee admission requirements of receiving States;

(e) *Acknowledges* the utility of close consultation with UNHCR in the resettlement activities of the Office;

(f) *Recognizes* that in reviewing UNHCR resettlement requests the protection element inherent in such requests should be taken into account;

(g) *Emphasizes* that UNHCR pursues resettlement only as a last resort, when neither voluntary repatriation nor local integration is possible, when it is in the best interests of the refugees and where appropriate.

No. 69 (XLIII)—1992   Cessation of Status[30]

The Executive Committee,

Recalling Conclusion No. 65 (XLII) which, *inter alia*, underlined the possibility of use of the cessation clauses in Article IC(5) and (6) of the 1951 Convention in situations where a change of circumstances in a country is of such a profound and enduring nature that refugees from that country no longer require international protection, and can no longer continue to refuse to avail themselves of the protection of their country, provided that it is recognized that compelling reasons may, for certain individuals, support the continuation of refugee status,

Taking into account that the application of the cessation clause(s) in the 1951 Convention rests exclusively with the Contracting States, but that the High Commissioner should be appropriately involved, in keeping with the role of the High Commissioner in supervising the application of the provisions of the 1951 Convention as provided for in Article 35 of that Convention,

Noting that any declaration by the High Commissioner that the competence accorded to her by the Statute of her Office with regard to certain refugees shall cease to apply,

---

[29] *Report* of the 42nd Session: UN doc. A/AC.96/783, para. 23.
[30] *Report* of the 43rd Session: UN doc. A/AC.96/804, para. 22.

may be useful to States in connection with the application of the cessation clauses as well as the 1951 Convention,

Believing that a careful approach to the application of the cessation clauses using clearly established procedures is necessary so as to provide refugees with the assurance that their status will not be subject to unnecessary review in the light of temporary changes, not of a fundamental character, in the situation prevailing in the country of origin,

(a) *Stresses* that, in taking any decision on application of the cessation clauses based on 'ceased circumstances' (sic), States must carefully assess the fundamental character of the changes in the country of nationality or origin, including the general human rights situation, as well as the particular cause of fear of persecution, in order to make sure in an objective and verifiable way that the situation which justified the granting of refugee status has ceased to exist;

(b) *Underlines* that an essential element in such assessment by States is the fundamental, stable and durable character of the changes, making use of appropriate information available in this respect, *inter alia*, from relevant specialized bodies, including particularly UNHCR;

(c) *Emphasizes* that the 'ceased circumstances' (sic) cessation clauses shall not apply to refugees who continue to have a well-founded fear of persecution;

(d) *Recognizes* therefore that all refugees affected by a group or class decision to apply these cessation clauses must have the possibility, upon request, to have such application in their cases reconsidered on grounds relevant to their individual case;

(e) *Recommends,* so as to avoid hardship cases, that States seriously consider an appropriate status, preserving previously acquired rights, for persons who have compelling reasons arising out of previous persecution for refusing to re-avail themselves of the protection of their country and recommends also that appropriate arrangements, which would not put into jeopardy their established situation, be similarly considered by relevant authorities for those persons who cannot be expected to leave the country of asylum, due to a long stay in that country resulting in strong family, social and economic links there;

(f) *Recommends* that States, in giving effect to a decision to invoke the cessation clauses, should in all situations deal humanely with the consequences for the affected individuals or groups, and that countries of asylum and countries of origin should together facilitate the return, to assure that it takes place in a fair and dignified manner. Where appropriate, return and reintegration assistance should be made available to the returnees by the international community, including through relevant international agencies.

No. 72 (XLIV)—1993   Personal Security of Refugees[31]

The Executive Committee,

Expressing its deep concern over reports on the alarming frequency of incidents in which refugees and asylum seekers, including women and children, are subjected to violence and mistreatment including killing, torture, military or armed attacks, rape, beatings, intimidation, forced recruitment and arbitrary or inhumane conditions of detention,

---

[31] *Report* of the 44th Session: UN doc. A/AC.96/821, para. 20.

Reaffirming the responsibility of States to respect and ensure the fundamental human rights of refugees and asylum seekers to life, liberty and security of person as well as to freedom from torture or other cruel, inhumane or degrading treatment or punishment,

Recalling previous conclusions dealing with the personal security of refugees, in particular, Conclusions No. 22 (XXXII) on the Protection of Asylum Seekers in Situations of Large-Scale Influx and No. 48 (XXXVIII) on Military or Armed Attacks on Refugee Camps and Settlements,

Stressing the duty of refugees and asylum seekers to conform to the laws and regulations of the country of asylum and abstain from any activity likely to detract from the exclusively civilian and humanitarian character of refugee camps and settlements,

Reaffirming the fundamental importance of the scrupulous observance of the principle of *non-refoulement* for the personal security of refugees,

(a) *Deplores* all violations of the right to personal security of refugees and asylum seekers, in particular organized attacks or the incitement to violence directed against them;

(b) *Urges* States to take all measures necessary to prevent or remove threats to the personal security of refugees and asylum seekers in border areas and elsewhere, including by affording UNHCR and, as appropriate, other organizations approved by the Governments concerned prompt and unhindered access to them, by situating refugee camps and settlements in secure locations, by ensuring the safety of vulnerable groups, by facilitating the issuance of personal documentation, and by involving the refugee community, both women and men, in the organization and administration of their camps and settlements;

(c) *Calls* upon States vigorously to investigate violations of the personal security of refugees and asylum seekers, and where possible to institute criminal prosecution, and where applicable strict disciplinary measures, against all perpetrators of such violations;

(d) *Calls* upon States, in collaboration with UNHCR and, as appropriate, other organizations approved by the Governments concerned, to provide effective physical protection to asylum seekers and refugees and to ensure safe access for humanitarian assistance and relief workers, where necessary through the recruitment and training of personnel specifically assigned the task of protecting refugees and securing supply routes for humanitarian assistance;

(e) *Supports* the High Commissioner's activities to monitor the personal security of refugees and asylum seekers and to take appropriate action to prevent or redress violations thereof, including the expansion of training programmes aimed at enhancing the understanding of refugee protection among law enforcement officials, other concerned Government personnel, and non-governmental organizations;

(f) *Encourages* the High Commissioner to develop, share with the Executive Committee and disseminate widely guidelines containing practical measures that States, UNHCR as well as other international and non-governmental organizations can take to further strengthen the physical protection of refugees and asylum seekers.

No. 73 (XLIV)—1993   Refugee Protection and Sexual Violence[32]

The Executive Committee,

Noting with grave concern the widespread occurrence of sexual violence in violation of the fundamental right to personal security as recognized in international human rights and humanitarian law, which inflicts serious harm and injury to the victims, their families and communities, and which has been a cause of coerced displacement including refugee movements in some areas of the world,

Noting also distressing reports that refugees and asylum seekers, including children, in many instances have been subjected to rape or other forms of sexual violence during their flight or following their arrival in countries where they sought asylum, including sexual extortion in connection with the granting of basic necessities, personal documentation or refugee status,

Recognizing the need for concrete action to detect, deter and redress instances of sexual violence to effectively protect asylum seekers and refugees,

Recognizing further that the prevention of sexual violence can contribute to averting coerced displacement including refugee situations and to facilitating solutions,

Stressing the importance of international instruments relating to refugees, human rights and humanitarian law for the protection of asylum seekers, refugees and returnees against sexual violence,

Bearing in mind the draft Declaration on the Elimination of Violence against Women adopted by the Commission on the Status of Women as well as other measures being taken by the Commission on the Status of Women, the Committee on the Elimination of Discrimination against Women, the Commission on Human Rights, the Security Council and other bodies of the United Nations to prevent, investigate and, as appropriate, according to their mandates, punish sexual violence,

Reaffirming its Conclusions No. 39 (XXXVI), No. 54 (XXXIX), No. 60 (XL) and No. 64 (XLI) concerning refugee women,

(a) *Strongly condemns* persecution through sexual violence, which not only constitutes a gross violation of human rights, as well as, when committed in the context of armed conflict, a grave breach of humanitarian law, but is also a particularly serious offence to human dignity;

(b) *Urges* States to respect and ensure the fundamental right of all individuals within their territory to personal security, *inter alia* by enforcing relevant national laws in compliance with international legal standards and by adopting concrete measures to prevent and combat sexual violence, including:

(i) the development and implementation of training programmes aimed at promoting respect by law enforcement officers and members of military forces of the right of every individual, at all times and under all circumstances, to security of person, including protection from sexual violence,

(ii) implementation of effective, non-discriminatory legal remedies including the facilitation of the filing and investigation of complaints against sexual abuse, the prosecution of offenders, and timely and proportional disciplinary action in cases of abuse of power resulting in sexual violence,

[32] *Report* of the 44th Session: UN doc. A/AC.96/821, para. 21.

(iii) arrangements facilitating prompt and unhindered access to all asylum seekers, refugees and returnees for UNHCR and, as appropriate, other organizations approved by the Governments concerned, and

(iv) activities aimed at promoting the rights of refugee women, including through the dissemination of the *Guidelines on the Protection of Refugee Women* and their implementation, in close co-operation with refugee women, in all sectors of refugee programmes;

(c) *Calls* upon States and UNHCR to ensure the equal access of women and men to refugee status determination procedures and to all forms of personal documentation relevant to refugees' freedom of movement, welfare and civil status, and to encourage the participation of refugee women as well as men in decisions relating to their voluntary repatriation or other durable solutions;

(d) *Supports* the recognition as refugees of persons whose claim to refugee status is based upon a well-founded fear of persecution, through sexual violence, for reasons of race, religion, nationality, membership of a particular social group or political opinion;

(e) *Recommends* the development by States of appropriate guidelines on women asylum seekers, in recognition of the fact that women refugees often experience persecution differently from refugee men;

(f) *Recommends* that refugee victims of sexual violence and their families be provided with adequate medical and psycho-social care, including culturally appropriate counselling facilities, and generally be considered as persons of special concern to States and to UNHCR with respect to assistance and the search for durable solutions;

(g) *Recommends* that in procedures for the determination of refugee status, asylum seekers who may have suffered sexual violence be treated with particular sensitivity;

(h) *Reiterates* the importance of ensuring the presence of female field staff in refugee programmes, including emergency operations, and the direct access of refugee women to them;

(i) *Supports* the High Commissioner's efforts, in co-ordination with other intergovernmental and non-governmental organizations competent in this area, to develop and organize training courses for authorities, including camp officials, eligibility officers, and others dealing with refugees on practical protection measures for preventing and responding to sexual violence;

(j) *Recommends* the establishment by States of training programmes designed to ensure that those involved in the refugee status determination process are adequately sensitized to issues of gender and culture;

(k) *Encourages* the High Commissioner to pursue actively her efforts, in co-operation with bodies and organizations dealing with human rights, to increase awareness of the rights of refugees and the specific needs and abilities of refugee women and girls and to promote the full and effective implementation of the *Guidelines on the Protection of Refugee Women*;

(l) *Calls* upon the High Commissioner to include the issue of sexual violence in future progress reports on the implementation of the *Guidelines on the Protection of Refugee Women*;

(m) *Requests* the High Commissioner to issue as an Executive Committee document and disseminate widely the Note on Certain Aspects of Sexual Violence against Refugee Women.

No. 75 (XLV)—1994   Internally Displaced Persons[33]

The Executive Committee,

(a) *Recognizes* that the involuntary displacement of persons within their own countries is a problem of global dimensions, and that the plight of such internally displaced persons, whose numbers may exceed those of refugees, is a matter of grave humanitarian concern;

(b) *Notes* that the many and varied underlying causes of involuntary internal displacement and of refugee movements are often similar, and that the problems of both refugees and the internally displaced often call for similar measures with respect to prevention, protection, humanitarian assistance, and solutions;

(c) *Reiterates* the need for the international community to seek ways and means to avert involuntary displacements;

(d) *Emphasizes* that since internally displaced persons remain within the territorial jurisdiction of their own countries, the primary responsibility for their welfare and protection lies with the State concerned;

(e) *Urges* the Governments of States where there are internally displaced persons to fulfil their responsibility for their welfare and protection;

(f) *Calls* upon the international community, in appropriate circumstances, to provide timely and speedy humanitarian assistance and support to countries affected by internal displacement to help them fulfil their responsibility towards the displaced;

(g) *Notes* that, in many instances, the internally displaced are present alongside refugees, returnees, or a vulnerable local population, in situations where it is neither reasonable nor feasible to treat the categories differently in responding to their needs for assistance and protection;

(h) *Recognizes* that actions by the international community, in consultation and co-ordination with the concerned State, on behalf of the internally displaced may contribute to the easing of tensions and the resolution of problems resulting in displacement, and constitute important components of a comprehensive approach to the prevention and solution of refugee problems;

(i) *Calls* on the Governments concerned to ensure safe and timely humanitarian access to persons in need of protection and assistance, including the internally displaced and victims of armed conflict, as well as refugees within their territories;

(j) *Recognizes* that resolution 48/116, adopted by the United Nations General Assembly on 20 December 1993, which reaffirmed support for the High Commissioner's efforts, 'on the basis of specific requests from the Secretary-General or the competent principal organs of the United Nations and with the consent of the concerned State, and taking into account the complementarities of mandates and expertise of other relevant organizations, in providing humanitarian assistance and protection to persons displaced within their own country in situations calling for the Office's particular expertise, especially where such efforts could contribute to the prevention or solution of refugee problems', continues to provide an appropriate framework for the involvement of the High Commissioner in situations of internal displacement;

---

[33] *Report* of the 45th Session: UN doc. A/AC.96/839, para. 20.

(k) *Encourages* the High Commissioner to continue the efforts of her Office to put into action its internal criteria and guidelines for UNHCR involvement in situations of internal displacement, as an important contribution towards a more concerted response by the international community to the needs of the internally displaced;

(l) *Emphasizes* that activities on behalf of internally displaced persons must not undermine the institution of asylum, including the right to seek and enjoy in other countries asylum from persecution;

(m) *Recognizes* that international human rights law, international humanitarian law, and, in many cases, national laws include norms providing for the security and protection of the internally displaced as well as those at risk of displacement, and expressed serious concern at the failure of parties involved to respect these norms;

(n) *Acknowledges* the importance of the work of the Representative of the Secretary-General for Internally Displaced Persons and, in particular, his efforts to compile existing international standards in respect of the treatment of the internally displaced, and to develop a code of conduct comprising guiding principles in this regard;

(o) *Calls* on UNHCR to continue its close co-operation with the Representative of the Secretary-General in the fulfilment of his mandate;

(p) *Further* acknowledges the essential role of the International Committee of the Red Cross in disseminating international humanitarian law and in providing protection and humanitarian assistance to those displaced by armed conflict;

(q) *Calls* for the strengthening of efforts in the training and dissemination of international human rights law and international humanitarian law and for the joint promotion, by organizations and agencies concerned, of the implementation of these international standards;

(r) *Considers* that, in addressing the problem of internal displacement, the international community should seek to collaborate to the maximum possible extent with existing humanitarian organizations, including non-governmental organizations, with relevant expertise;

(s) *Encourages* UNHCR to continue its efforts, under the leadership of the Emergency Relief Co-ordinator, and in co-operation with other agencies concerned, to reinforce and structure co-ordination through existing interagency mechanisms, notably the Interagency Standing Committee, in order to improve the response by the international community to the plight of the internally displaced, and stresses the importance in this connection of strengthening mechanisms for the sharing of information;

(t) *Urges* that discussions on interagency aspects of internal displacement be pursued actively in other appropriate fora so as to ensure a comprehensive and coherent approach by the international community to the problem of internally displaced persons.

No. 78 (XLVI)—1995   The Prevention and Reduction of Statelessness and the Protection of Stateless Persons[34]

The Executive Committee,

Recognizing the right of everyone to a nationality and the right not to be arbitrarily deprived of one's nationality,

Concerned that statelessness, including the inability to establish one's nationality, may result in displacement,

Stressing that the prevention and reduction of statelessness and the protection of stateless persons are important in the prevention of potential refugee situations,

(a) Acknowledges the responsibilities already entrusted to the High Commissioner for stateless refugees and with respect to the reduction of statelessness, and encourages UNHCR to continue its activities on behalf of stateless persons, as part of its statutory function of providing international protection and of seeking preventive action, as well as its responsibility entrusted by the General Assembly to undertake the functions foreseen under Article 11 of the 1961 Convention on the Reduction of Statelessness;

(b) Calls upon States to adopt nationality legislation with a view to reducing statelessness, consistent with fundamental principles of international law, in particular by preventing arbitrary deprivation of nationality, and by eliminating provisions which permit the renunciation of a nationality without the prior possession or acquisition of another nationality;

(c) Requests UNHCR actively to promote accession to the 1954 Convention relating to the Status of Stateless Persons and the 1961 Convention on the Reduction of Statelessness, in view of the limited number of States parties to these instruments, as well as to provide relevant technical and advisory services pertaining to the preparation and implementation of nationality legislation to interested States;

(d) Further requests UNHCR actively to promote the prevention and reduction of statelessness through the dissemination of information, and the training of staff and government officials; and to enhance co-operation with other interested organizations;

(e) Invites UNHCR to provide it biennially, beginning at the forty-seventh session of the Executive Committee, with information on activities undertaken on behalf of stateless persons, particularly with regard to the implementation of international instruments and international principles relating to statelessness, and including the magnitude of the problem of statelessness.

[34] *Report* of the 46th Session: UN doc. A/AC.96/860, para. 20.

ANNEXE 4

MISCELLANEOUS TEXTS

1. 1977 Draft UN Convention on Territorial Asylum

Articles considered at the United Nations Conference on Territorial Asylum, Geneva,
10 January–4 February 1977[1]

Text: Report of the United Nations Conference on Territorial Asylum: UN doc.
A/CONF.78/12 (21 April 1977).

Article 1
Grant of Asylum

Each Contracting State, acting in the exercise of its sovereignty, shall endeavour in a
humanitarian spirit to grant asylum in its territory to any person eligible for the benefits
of this Convention.

Additional paragraph

Asylum should not be refused by a Contracting State solely on the ground that it could
be sought from another State. However, where it appears that a person requesting asylum from a Contracting State already has a connection or close links with another State,
the Contracting State may, if it appears fair and reasonable, require him first to request
asylum from that State.

Article 2

1. Each Contracting State may grant the benefits of this Convention to a person seeking asylum, if he, being faced with a definite possibility of:

(a) Persecution for reasons of race, colour, national or ethnic origin, religion, nationality,
kinship, membership of a particular social group or political opinion, including the struggle against colonialism and *apartheid*, foreign occupation, alien domination and all forms
of racism; or

(b) Prosecution or punishment for reasons directly related to the persecution set forth in
(a);

is unable or unwilling to return to the country of his nationality, or, if he has no nationality, the country of his former domicile or habitual residence.

2. The provisions of paragraph 1 of this article shall not apply to any person with respect
to whom there are serious reasons for considering that he is still liable to prosecution or
punishment for:

---

[1] The Committee of the Whole approved and referred to the Drafting Committee, Art. 1, Art.
2, Art. 3, a new Art. on the Question of Family Reunion and a new Art. on the Question of Activities
of Asylees. The Drafting Committee only completed its examination of draft Art.1. None of the draft
Arts. was referred back to the Committee of the Whole for reconsideration. They were not approved
by the Conference in Plenary Session.

(a) A crime against peace, a war crime, or crime against humanity as defined in the international instruments drawn up to make provision in respect of such crimes; or

(a *bis*) Other grave crimes as defined in multilateral conventions to which a Contracting State in which he is seeking asylum is a party; or

(b) An offence which would be a serious criminal offence if committed in the Contracting State from which asylum is requested;

(c) Acts contrary to the Purposes and Principles of the United Nations.

3. The provisions of paragraph 1 of this article shall also not apply to any person requesting territorial asylum for purely economic reasons.

3 *bis*. The provisions of paragraph 1 of this article shall not apply to any person whom there are serious reasons for regarding as a threat or danger to the security of the country in which he is seeking asylum.

Article 3

1. No person eligible for the benefits of this Convention in accordance with article 2, paragraph 1, subparagraphs (a) and (b), who is at the frontier seeking asylum or in the territory of a Contracting State shall be subjected by such Contracting State to measures such as rejection at the frontier, return or expulsion, which would compel him to remain in or return to a territory with respect to which he has a well-founded fear of persecution, prosecution or punishment for any of the reasons stated in Article 2.

2. The benefit of the present provision, however, may not be claimed by a person whom there are reasons for regarding as a danger to the security of the country in which he is, or who, being still liable to prosecution or punishment for, or having been convicted by a final judgment of a particularly serious crime, constitutes a danger to the community in that country or in exceptional cases, by a great number of persons whose massive influx may constitute a serious problem to the security of a Contracting State.

3. Where a Contracting State decides that an exception should be made on the basis of the preceding paragraph, it shall consider the possibility of granting to the person concerned, under such conditions as it may deem appropriate, an opportunity of going to another State.

New Article on the Question of Activities of Asylees

1. A person enjoying the benefits of this Convention shall comply with the laws and regulations of the country granting asylum.

2. To the extent to which it is possible under their law, Contracting States granting asylum shall not permit persons enjoying the benefits of this Convention to engage in activities contrary to the Purposes and Principles of the United Nations as set forth in the Charter.

New Article on the Question of Family Reunion

1. Each Contracting State shall, in the interest of family reunification and for humanitarian reasons, facilitate the admission to its territory of the spouse and minor or dependent children of any person to whom it has granted the benefits of this Convention.

2. These members of the family should, save in exceptional circumstances, be given the same benefits under this Convention as that person.

2. International Co-operation to Avert new Flows of Refugees

GENERAL ASSEMBLY RESOLUTION 41/70, 3 DECEMBER 1986

The General Assembly,

Recalling its resolutions 35/124 of 11 December 1980, 36/148 of 16 December 1981, 37/121 of 16 December 1982, 38/84 of 15 December 1983, 39/100 of 14 December 1984 and 40/166 of 16 December 1985 on international co-operation to avert new flows of refugees,

Having considered the report of the Group of Governmental Experts on International Co-operation to Avert New Flows of Refugees,

1. Commends the Group of Governmental Experts on International Co-operation to Avert New Flows of Refugees for the work it has accomplished by consensus, as reflected in its report;

2. Endorses the conclusions and recommendations contained in the report;

3. Calls upon Member States to respect, for the purpose of improving international co-operation to avert new massive flows of refugees, the recommendations and, in particular, to comply with those contained in paragraphs 66, 67 and 69 of the report;

4. Urges the main organs of the United Nations to make fuller use of their respective competences under the Charter of the United Nations for the prevention of new massive flows of refugees, as envisaged in paragraph 68 of the report;

5. Requests the Secretary-General to take the necessary steps to discharge the functions and responsibilities described in paragraphs 70 and 71 of the report;

6. Further requests the Secretary-General to bring the report to the attention of Member States and, in view of paragraph 72 of the report, of all the relevant organizations, organs and programmes of the United Nations system.

3. Report of the Group of Governmental Experts on International Co-operation to Avert New Flows of Refugees, 1986—Extracts

Text: Note by the Secretary-General. UN doc. A/41/324, 13 May 1986

A. Conclusions

63. The analysis of causes and factors showed that the emergence of massive flows of refugees is the result of a number of complex and often interrelated political, economic and social problems related to, and influenced by, the overall international situation. It may affect the political and social stability, as well as the economic development, of the receiving States, and also carry adverse consequences for the economies of the countries of origin and entire regions, thus endangering international peace and security. Moreover, in view of its complex nature and magnitude, as well as its potentially destabilizing effects, averting massive flows of refugees is a matter of serious concern to the international community as a whole. In the first instance, dealing with this problem is the responsibility of the States directly concerned. Given the character of the problem, the task of averting massive flows of refugees requires improved international co-operation at all levels, in particular in the framework of the United Nations, in full observance of the principle of non-intervention in the internal affairs of sovereign States.

64. The Group felt that measures aimed at the strengthening of international security, the development of good-neighbourly relations and the creation of an atmosphere of confidence would contribute to improving international co-operation to avert massive flows of refugees. In order to be appropriate and effective, this co-operation must address all the complex political, economic and social causes and factors of massive flows of refugees with a view to eliminating them, and it must, while this is being undertaken, contribute to the solution of those problems which are the direct cause of such flows . . .

65. For these purposes, the Group presents the following recommendations.

B. Recommendations

66. The General Assembly should call upon Member States, for the purposes of averting new massive flows of refugees, to respect in particular the following obligations:

(a) States should respect the principles contained in the Charter of the United Nations and, in particular, refrain from the threat or use of force against the territorial integrity or political independence of any State, or in any other matter inconsistent with the purposes of the United Nations, and from intervention in matters within the domestic jurisdiction of any State, in accordance with the Charter, since the violation of the aforementioned principles is particularly prone to cause new massive flows of refugees;

(b) States should use peaceful means to resolve international disputes in such a manner that international peace and security as well as justice are not jeopardized and thus improve situations that suggest a danger of future flows of refugees, in accordance with the provisions of the Charter of the United Nations and the Declaration on Principles of

International Law concerning Friendly Relations and Co-operation among States in accordance with the Charter of the United Nations;

(c) In view of their responsibilities under the Charter of the United Nations and consistent with their obligations under the existing international instruments in the field of human rights, States, in the exercise of their sovereignty, should do all within their means to prevent new massive flows of refugees. Accordingly, States should refrain from creating or contributing by their policies to causes and factors which generally lead to massive flows of refugees;

(d) States should promote civil, political, economic, social and cultural rights and accordingly refrain from denying them to, and discriminating against, groups of their population because of their nationality, ethnicity, race, religion or language, thus directly or indirectly forcing them to leave their country;

(e) States should co-operate with one another in order to prevent future massive flows of refugees. They should promote international co-operation in all its aspects, in particular at the regional and subregional levels, as an appropriate and important means to avert such flows;

(f) States should, wherever new massive flows of refugees occur, respect the existing generally recognized norms and principles of international law governing the rights and obligations of States and refugees directly concerned, including those pertaining to the rights of refugees to be facilitated in returning voluntarily and safely to their homes in their homelands and to receive adequate compensation therefrom, where so established, in cases of those who do not wish to return;

(g) States, individually and collectively, should make provisions and take appropriate measures to avert new flows of refugees which may be caused by natural disasters, as appropriate with the support of the relevant international organizations. In the event these natural disasters or other similar situations occur, States should assist the States concerned to the best of their abilities in order to alleviate the situation, as well as to avert new massive flows of refugees.

67. Taking into account the foregoing, the General Assembly should call upon Member States to co-operate with one another and with the Security Council, the Secretariat and other relevant organs of the United Nations in a fuller and more timely manner for the prevention of new massive flows of refugees and to turn to these organs at the earliest possible stage of the development of such situations.

68. The main organs of the United Nations are urged to make fuller use of their respective competences under the Charter for the prevention of new massive flows of refugees, with a view to considering at the earliest possible stage situations and problems which could give rise to massive flows of refugees.

69. Furthermore, the General Assembly should consider calling upon Member States to comply vigorously with the decisions of the Security Council and to respect the decisions and recommendations of the General Assembly, the Economic and Social Council and other organs pertaining to the prevention of massive flows of refugees.

70. With a view to improving international co-operation for the prevention of new massive flows of refugees, the General Assembly should encourage the Secretary-General to make full use of his competences. To this effect, he should, in particular, in accordance

with the Charter of the United Nations, as well as the relevant mandates of the competent United Nations organs:

(a) Give continuing attention to the question of averting new massive flows of refugees;

(b) Ensure that timely and fuller information relevant to the matter is available within the Secretariat;

(c) Improve co-ordination within the Secretariat for analysing the information, so as to obtain an early assessment on the situations which might give rise to new massive flows of refugees, and to make the necessary information available to the competent United Nations organs in consultation with the States directly concerned;

(d) Help improve the co-ordination, within the Secretariat, of the efforts of United Nations organs and specialized agencies and of Member States concerned for timely and more effective action;

(e) Consider taking such measures as are necessary for the purposes enumerated in this paragraph.

71. In the fulfilment of his mandate in the area of international co-operation to avert new massive flows of refugees, the Secretary-General should act within the limits of financial and personnel resources available to the Secretariat. In doing so, he should bear in mind the ongoing efforts to improve the efficiency of the administrative and financial functioning of the United Nations and, without prejudice to his administration competences and functions, should refrain from creating new divisions or posts for this purpose.

72. In the selection of projects, the relevant economic assistance agencies and other bodies of the United Nations should consider, in consultation with the States directly concerned, giving greater support to those projects that directly or indirectly could help avert new massive refugee flows resulting from the impact of social and economic factors or natural causes in a given region.

4. 1989 UN Principles on the Effective Prevention and Investigation of Extra-Legal, Arbitrary and Summary Executions—Extracts

ECONOMIC AND SOCIAL COUNCIL RESOLUTION 1989/65, 24 MAY 1989, ANNEX

(endorsed by General Assembly resolution 44/162, paragraph 2, 15 December 1989)

1. Governments shall prohibit by law all extra-legal, arbitrary and summary executions and shall ensure that any such executions are recognized as offences under their criminal laws, and are punishable by appropriate penalties which take into account the seriousness of such offences. Exceptional circumstances including a state of war or threat of war, internal political instability or any other public emergency may not be invoked as a justification of such executions. Such executions shall not be carried out under any circumstances including, but not limited to, situations of internal armed conflict, excessive or illegal use of force by a public official or other person acting in an official capacity or

a person acting at the instigation, or with the consent or acquiescence of such person, and situations in which deaths occur in custody. This prohibition shall prevail over decrees issued by governmental authority.

2. In order to prevent extra-legal, arbitrary and summary executions, Governments shall ensure strict control, including a clear chain of command over all officials responsible for the apprehension, arrest, detention, custody and imprisonment as well as those officials authorized by law to use force and firearms.

. . .

4. Effective protection through judicial or other means shall be guaranteed to individuals and groups who are in danger of extra-legal, arbitrary or summary executions, including those who receive death threats.

5. No one shall be involuntarily returned or extradited to a country where there are substantial grounds for believing that he or she may become a victim of extra-legal, arbitrary or summary execution in that country.

5. 1992 UN Declaration on the Protection of All Persons from Enforced Disappearance—Extracts

GENERAL ASSEMBLY RESOLUTION 47/133, 18 DECEMBER 1992

Article 1

1. Any act of enforced disappearance is an offence to human dignity. It is condemned as a denial of the purposes of the Charter of the United Nations and as a grave and flagrant violation of the human rights and fundamental freedoms proclaimed in the Universal Declaration of Human Rights and reaffirmed and developed in international instruments in this field.

2. Any act of enforced disappearance places the persons subjected thereto outside the protection of the law and inflicts severe suffering on them and their families. It constitutes a violation of the rules of international law guaranteeing, *inter alia*, the right to recognition as a person before the law, the right to liberty and security of the person and the right not to be subjected to torture and other cruel, inhuman or degrading treatment or punishment. It also violates or constitutes a grave threat to the right to life.

. . .

Article 7

No circumstances whatsoever, whether a threat of war, a state of war, internal political instability or any other public emergency, may be invoked to justify enforced disappearances.

Article 8

1. No State shall expel, return (*refouler*) or extradite a person to another State where there are substantial grounds to believe that he would be in danger of enforced disappearance.

2. For the purpose of determining whether there are such grounds, the competent authorities shall take into account all relevant considerations including, where applicable, the existence in the State concerned of a consistent pattern of gross, flagrant or mass violations of human rights.

6. Council of Europe—Committee of Ministers Resolution on Asylum to Persons in Danger of Persecution (1967)

Resolution (67) 14 adopted by the Committee of Ministers on 29 June 1967

The Committee of Ministers,

Considering Recommendation 293 (1961) of the Assembly on the right of asylum and Recommendation 434 (1965) of the Assembly on the granting of the right of asylum to European refugees;

Aware of the liberal practice based on humanitarian considerations already followed in regard to asylum by the Governments of member States;

Considering, moreover, that Article 3 of the Convention for the Protection of Human Rights and Fundamental Freedoms provides that no one shall be subjected to inhuman treatment;

Desirous that member Governments should, in a humanitarian spirit, do all that is possible, individually and collectively, to assure to persons in danger of persecution the security and protection of which they stand in need;

Recognizing the need for member Governments to take account both of their obligations under existing international treaties and of the necessity of safeguarding national security and of protecting the community from serious danger,

Recommends that member Governments should be guided by the following principles:

Article 1

They should act in a particularly liberal and humanitarian spirit in relation to persons who seek asylum on their territory;

Article 2

They should, in the same spirit, ensure that no one shall be subjected to refusal of admission at the frontier, rejection, expulsion or any other measure which would have the result of compelling him to return to, or remain in, a territory where he would be in danger of persecution for reasons of race, religion, nationality, membership of a particular social group or political opinion;

Article 3

If, in order to safeguard national security or protect the community from serious danger, a member Government contemplates taking measures which might entail such consequences, it should, as far as possible and under such conditions as it may consider appropriate, accord to the individual concerned the opportunity of going to a country other than that where he would be in danger of persecution;

Article 4

Where difficulties arise for a member State in consequence of its action in accordance with the above recommendations, Governments of other member States should, in a spirit of European solidarity and of common responsibility in this field, consider individually, or in co-operation, particularly in the framework of the Council of Europe, appropriate measures in order to overcome such difficulties.

7. Council of Europe—Committee of Ministers Declaration on Territorial Asylum (1977)

Adopted by the Committee of Ministers on 18 November 1977, at the 278th Meeting of the Ministers' Deputies: CE Doc. B(77)81 (1977)

The Committee of Ministers of the Council of Europe,

Having examined the present situation in the field of territorial asylum;

Taking into account the principles contained in particular in the United Nations Charter, in the Universal Declaration of Human Rights and in the United Nations Declaration on Territorial Asylum of 1967;

Acting in pursuance of the objectives contained in the Statute of the Council of Europe;

Bearing in mind the European Convention on Human Rights,

Having regard to Resolution (67) 14 of 29 June 1967;

Wishing to underline the practice which is common to the member States of the Council of Europe in the field of territorial asylum,

Declares:

Article 1

In fulfilling their humanitarian duties, the member States of the Council of Europe reaffirm their intention to maintain, in particular on the basis of the principles set out in Resolution (67) 14, their liberal attitude with regard to persons seeking asylum on their territory;

Article 2

The member States of the Council of Europe, parties to the 1951 Convention relating to the Status of Refugees, reaffirm their right to grant asylum to any person who, having a well-founded fear of being persecuted for reasons of race, religion, nationality, membership of a particular social group or political opinion, also fulfils the other conditions of eligibility for the benefits of that convention, as well as to any other person they consider worthy of receiving asylum for humanitarian reasons;

Article 3

The member States of the Council of Europe reaffirm that the grant of territorial asylum is a peaceful and humanitarian act and shall not be regarded as an act unfriendly to any other state and shall be respected by all States.

8. Council of Europe—Committee of Ministers Recommendation on Guidelines regarding the Arrival of Asylum Seekers at European Airports (1994)

Recommendation No. R(94)5, adopted by the Committee of Ministers on 21 June 1994 at the 515th Meeting of the Ministers' Deputies:

The Committee of Ministers, under the terms of Article 15.b of the Statute of the Council of Europe,

Considering that the aim of the Council of Europe is to achieve a greater unity between its members;

Recalling the liberal and humanitarian attitude of member States of the Council of Europe with regard to asylum seekers;

Having regard to Recommendation 1163 (1991) of the Parliamentary Assembly on the arrival of asylum seekers at European airports;

Considering that the member States of the Council of Europe since the mid-1980s, as a whole, have been unceasingly confronted by a very large number of asylum requests;

Taking into account that the particular position of asylum seekers at the airports may entail specific difficulties, linked to the reception itself as well as the handling of their requests;

Considering that, without prejudice to other principles applicable in this field, guidelines based on the fundamental principles in the field of human rights should inspire the practices of member States with regard to the protection of asylum seekers at airports, and contribute to the development of legislation and the establishment of an administrative infra-structure concerning the reception of asylum seekers in new host countries,

Recommends that the governments of member States apply the following guidelines:

I
Fundamental principles

1. Member States reaffirm their obligations under the Geneva Convention of 28 July 1951 and the New York Protocol of 31 January 1967 relating to the Status of Refugees,

and also the Convention for the Protection of Human Rights and Fundamental Freedoms of 4 November 1850.

II
Asylum requests

2. The examination of all asylum requests presented at the airport shall be assured, in compliance with the rule of law, on the basis of domestic law and the international obligations of each State.

3. Moreover, each State preserves the possibility of sending an asylum seekers to a third country, subject to respect to (sic) the provisions of the Geneva Convention relating to the Status of Refugees, in particular its Article 33, and with respect to the European Convention on Human Rights, in particular its Article 3.

4. States should also further develop their co-operation with regard to the treatment of asylum requests.

5. The request shall be examined with all diligence required in order not to prolong the stay of the applicant at the airport beyond a period strictly necessary for the handling of such a request.

6. The authorities entrusted with the receipt of applications at the border shall receive training adapted to the specific situation of people seeking asylum. Such authorities should, moreover, have precise instructions on the procedures to be followed.

7. The examination of such requests, including the interview with the applicant, shall be reserved to authorities competent in matters of asylum and appointed for the task.

8. The whole procedure shall be under the supervision of the competent authorities with a view to ensuring compliance with the principles mentioned above.

III
Asylum seekers

9. When the asylum seekers has to stay at the border pending a decision, he or she shall be received and accommodated in an appropriate place, whenever possible provided to that effect.

10. The asylum seeker can be held in such a place only under the conditions and for the maximum duration provided for by law.

11. When the request is received, the asylum seeker shall be informed about the procedure to be followed, and about his or her rights and obligations. This information shall be provided orally or in the form of a written document and, if necessary, with the assistance of an interpreter.

12. The asylum seeker has a right to the assistance of a qualified and impartial interpreter during the interview with the competent authority.

13. The competent authority shall draw the attention of the asylum seeker to the confidential nature of the interview and of the information contained in his or her file.

14. A representative of the United Nations High Commissioner for Refugees shall be allowed to contact the asylum seeker in the airports, according to the procedures of each member State.

15. After the first interview with the competent authorities, the asylum seeker shall be allowed to contact a legal counsellor or lawyer.

16. The reception of the asylum seeker at the border shall be under the best possible conditions.

17. The responsible authority shall provide sufficient accommodation and food and, to the extent possible in case of a prolonged stay, recreational facilities.

18. Medical and social assistance shall be provided.

19. According to the procedures fixed by each member State, the asylum seeker can ask to meet with, among others, a representative of a religion, a lawyer and a representative of the United Nations High Commissioner for Refugees. To that effect, they shall all be allowed access to the place of accommodation.

20. The persons in charge of the reception of asylum seekers shall receive appropriate training to fulfil this task.

9. Asian–African Legal Consultative Committee—Principles Concerning Treatment of Refugees (1966)

Adopted by the Asian-African Legal Consultative Committee (AALCC) at its Eighth Session, Bangkok 1966

Text: AALCC, *The Rights of Refugees: Report of the Committee and Background Materials*, New Delhi, 1966, 207–19

Article 1
Definition of the term 'Refugee'

A refugee is a person who, owing to persecution or well-founded fear of persecution for reasons of race, colour, religion, political belief or membership of a particular social group:

(a) leaves the State of which he is a national, or the Country of his nationality, or, if he has no nationality, the State or Country of which he is a habitual resident; or,

(b) being outside such State or Country, is unable or unwilling to return to it or to avail himself of its protection.

Exceptions

(1) A person having more than one nationality shall not be a refugee if he is in a position to avail himself of the protection of any State or Country of which he is a national.

(2) A person who prior to his admission into the Country of refuge, has committed a crime against peace, a war crime, or a crime against humanity or a serious non-political crime or has committed acts contrary to the purposes and principles of the United Nations shall not be a refugee.

Explanation

The dependants of a refugee shall be deemed to be refugees.

Explanation

The expression 'leaves' includes voluntary as well as involuntary leaving.

Notes

(i) The Delegation of Ghana reserved its position on this Article.

(ii) The Delegations of Iraq, Pakistan and the United Arab Republic expressed the view that, in their opinion, the definition of the term 'Refugee' includes a person who is obliged to leave the State of which he is a national under the pressure of an illegal act or as a result of invasion of such State, wholly or partially, by an alien with a view to occupying the State.

(iii) The Delegations of Ceylon and Japan expressed the view that in their opinion the expression 'persecution' means something more than discrimination or unfair treatment but includes such conduct as shocks the conscience of civilized nations.

(iv) The Delegations of Japan and Thailand expressed the view that the word 'and' should be substituted for the word 'or' in the last line of paragraph (a).

(v) In Exception (2) the words 'prior to his admission into the Country of refuge' were inserted by way of amendment to the original text of the Draft Articles on the proposal of the Delegation of Ceylon and accepted by the Delegations of India, Indonesia, Japan and Pakistan. The Delegations of Iraq and Thailand did not accept the amendment.

(vi) The Delegation of Japan proposed insertion of the following additional paragraph in the Article in relation to proposal under note (iv):

'A person who was outside of the State of which he is a national or the Country of his nationality, or if he has no nationality, the State or the Country of which he is a habitual resident, at the time of the events which caused him to have a well-founded fear of above-mentioned persecution and is unable or unwilling to return to it or to avail himself of its protection shall be considered a refugee.'

The Delegations of Ceylon, India, Indonesia, Iraq and Pakistan were of the view that this additional paragraph was unnecessary. The Delegation of Thailand reserved its position on this paragraph.

Article 2
Loss of Status as Refugee

1. A refugee shall lose his status as refugee if:

(i) he voluntarily returns permanently to the State of which he was a national or the Country of his nationality, to the State or the Country of which he was a habitual resident; or

(ii) he has voluntarily re-availed himself of the protection of the State or Country of his nationality; or

(iii) he voluntarily acquires the nationality of another State or Country and is entitled to the protection of that State or Country.

2. A refugee shall lose his status as a refugee if he does not return to the State of which he is a national, or to the Country of his nationality, or, if he has no nationality, to the State or Country of which he was a habitual resident, or if he fails to avail himself of the protection of such State or Country after the circumstances in which he became a refugee have ceased to exist.

Explanation

It would be for the State of asylum of the refugee to decide whether the circumstances in which he became a refugee have ceased to exist.

Notes

(i) The Delegations of Iraq and the United Arab Republic reserved their position on paragraph I(iii).

(ii) The Delegation of Thailand wished it to be recorded that the loss of status as a refugee under paragraph 1(ii) will take place only when the refugee has successfully re-availed himself of the protection of the State of his nationality because the right of protection was that of his country and not that of the individual.

Article 3
Asylum to a Refugee

1. A State has the sovereign right to grant or refuse asylum in its territory to a refugee.

2. The exercise of the right to grant such asylum to a refugee shall be respected by all other States and shall not be regarded as an unfriendly act.

3. No one seeking asylum in accordance with these Principles should, except for over-riding reasons of national security or safeguarding the populations, be subjected to measures such as rejection at the frontier, return or expulsion which would result in compelling him to return to or remain in a territory if there is a well-founded fear of persecution endangering his life, physical integrity or liberty in that territory.

4. In cases where a State decides to apply any of the above-mentioned measures to a person seeking asylum, it should grant provisional asylum under such conditions as it may deem appropriate, to enable the person thus endangered to seek asylum in another country.

Article 4
Right of Return

A refugee shall have the right to return if he so chooses to the State of which he is a national or to the Country of his nationality and in this event it shall be the duty of such State or Country to receive him.

Article 5
Right to compensation

1. A refugee shall have the right to receive compensation from the State or the Country which he left or to which he was unable to return.

2. The compensation referred to in paragraph 1 shall be for such loss as bodily injury, deprivation of personal liberty in denial of human rights, death of dependants of the refugee or of the person whose dependant the refugee was, and destruction of or damage to property and assets, caused by the authorities of the State or Country, public officials or mob violence.

Notes

(i) The Delegations of Pakistan and the United Arab Republic were of the view that the word 'also' should be inserted before the words 'such loss' in paragraph 2.

(ii) The Delegations of India and Japan expressed the view that the words 'deprivation of personal liberty in denial of human rights', should be omitted.

(iii) The Delegations of Ceylon, Japan and Thailand suggested that the words 'in the circumstances in which the State would incur State responsibility for such treatment to aliens under international law' should be added at the end of paragraph 2.

(iv) The Delegations of Ceylon, Japan, Pakistan and Thailand expressed the view that compensation should be payable also in respect of the denial of the refugee's right to return to the State of which he is a national.

(v) The Delegation of Ceylon was opposed to the inclusion of the words 'or country' in this Article.

(vi) The Delegations of Ceylon, Ghana, India and Indonesia were of the view that in order to clarify the position, the words 'arising out of events which gave rise to the refugee leaving such State or Country' should be added to paragraph 2 of this Article after the words 'mob violence'.

Article 6
Minimum Standard of Treatment

1. A State shall accord to refugees treatment in no way less favourable than that generally accorded to aliens in similar circumstances.

2. The standard of treatment referred to in the preceding clause shall include the rights relating to aliens contained in the Final Report of the Committee on the status of aliens, annexed to these principles, to the extent that they are applicable to refugees.

3. A refugee shall not be denied any rights on the ground that he does not fulfil requirements which by their nature a refugee is incapable of fulfilling.

4. A refugee shall not be denied any rights on the ground that there is no reciprocity in regard to the grant of such rights between the receiving State and the State or Country of nationality of the refugee or, if he is stateless, the State or Country of his former habitual residence.

Notes

(i) The Delegations of Iraq and Pakistan were of the view that a refugee should generally be granted the standard of treatment applicable to the nationals of the country of asylum.

(ii) The Delegation of Indonesia reserved its position on paragraph 3 of the Article.

(iii) The Delegations of Indonesia and Thailand reserved their position on paragraph 4 of the Article.

Article 7
Obligations

A refugee shall not engage in subversive activities endangering the national security of the country of refuge, or in activities inconsistent with or against the principles and purposes of the United Nations.

Notes

(i) The Delegations of India, Japan and Thailand were of the view that the words 'or any other country' should be added after the words 'the country of refuge' in this Article. The other Delegations were of the view that such addition was not necessary.

(ii) The Delegation of Iraq was of the view that the inclusion of the words 'or in activities inconsistent with or against the principles and purposes of the United Nations' was inappropriate as in this Article what was being dealt with was the right and obligation of the refugee and not that of the State.

Article 8
Expulsion and Deportation

1. Save in the national or public interest or on the ground of violation of the conditions of asylum, the State shall not expel a refugee.

2. Before expelling a refugee, the State shall allow him a reasonable period within which to seek admission into another State. The State shall, however, have the right to apply during the period such internal measures as it may deem necessary.

3. A refugee shall not be deported or returned to a State or Country where his life or liberty would be threatened for reasons of race, colour, religion, political belief or membership of a particular social group.

Notes

(i) The Delegations of Ceylon, Ghana and Japan did not accept the text of paragraph 1. In the view of these Delegations the text of this paragraph should read as follows: 'A State shall not expel or deport a refugee save on ground of national security or public order, or a violation of any of the vital or fundamental conditions of asylum.'

(ii) The Delegations of Ceylon and Ghana were of the view that in paragraph 2 the words 'as generally applicable to aliens under such circumstances' should be added at the end of the paragraph after the word 'necessary'.

Article 9

Nothing in these Articles shall be deemed to impair any higher rights and benefits granted or which may hereafter be granted by a State to refugees.

10. Asian–African Legal Consultative Committee—Addendum to Principles Concerning Treatment of Refugees (1970)

Adopted by the Asian-African Legal Consultative Committee at its Eleventh Session, Accra, 1970

Text: AALCC, *Report of the Eleventh Session, Accra (Ghnaa), 1970,* New Delhi, 1970, 171–86

Whereas it appears to the Committee on further consideration that the principles adopted at its Session held in Bangkok in 1966 mainly contemplate the status of what may be called political refugees who have been deprived of the protection of their own Government and do not provide adequately for the case of other refugees or displaced persons;

And whereas the Committee considers that such other refugees or displaced persons should enjoy the benefit of protection of the nature afforded by Articles IV and V of those principles;

Now therefore, the Committee at its Eleventh Session held in Accra between 19th and 20th January, 1970 resolves as follows:

1. Any person who because of foreign domination, external aggression or occupation has left his habitual place of residence, or being outside such place, desires to return thereto by is prevented from so doing by the Government or authorities in control of such place of his habitual residence shall be entitled to return to the place of his habitual residence from which he was displaced.

2. It shall accordingly be the duty of the Government or authorities in control of such place of habitual residence to facilitate by all means at their disposal, the return of all such persons as are referred to in the foregoing paragraph, and the restitution of their property to them.

3. This natural right of return shall also be enjoyed and facilitated to the same extent as stated above in respect of the dependants of all such persons as are referred to in paragraph 1 above.

4. Where such person does not desire to return, he shall be entitled to prompt and full compensation by the Government or the authorities in control of such place of habitual residence as determined, in the absence of agreement by the parties concerned, by an international body designated or constituted for the purpose by the Secretary-General of the United Nations at the request of either party.

5. If the status of such a person is disputed by the Government or authorities in control of such place of habitual residence, or if any other dispute arises, such matter shall also be determined, in the absence of agreement by the parties concerned, by an international body designated or constituted as specified in paragraph 4 above.

11. Proposal for an Additional Protocol to the European Convention on Human Rights

The present proposal, first drafted by the author in February 1990, was revised on the basis of comments received and subsequent developments and presented to an ECRE Seminar on Asylum in Europe in April 1992. Explanatory notes follow the draft articles.

The Governments signatory hereto, being Members of the Council of Europe,

Being resolved to take further steps to ensure the collective enforcement of certain rights and freedoms other than those already included in Section I of the Convention for the Protection of Human Rights and Fundamental Freedoms signed at Rome on 4 November, 1950 (hereinafter referred to as 'the Convention'), or in Articles 1 to 3 of the First Protocol to the Convention, signed at Paris on 20 March 1952, Articles 1 to 4 of the Fourth Protocol to the Convention, signed at Strasbourg on 16 September 1963, Articles 1–2 of the Sixth Protocol to the Convention, signed at Strasbourg on 28 April 1983, or Articles 1 to 5 of the Seventh Protocol, signed at Strasbourg on 22 November 1984,

Have agreed as follows:

Article 1

1. Everyone has the right to seek asylum within the territory of a State.

2. The High Contracting Parties undertake to use their best endeavours, individually and in co-operation with Members of the Council of Europe, to provide permanent or temporary asylum to refugees who satisfy the criteria of article 1 of the 1951 Convention/ 1967 Protocol relating to the Status of Refugees, and to other refugees who have valid reasons for not being required to return to their country of origin.

Article 2

1. No one who seeks asylum at the border or in the territory of a State shall be rejected at the frontier, or expelled or returned in any manner whatsoever to any country in which he or she may be tortured or subjected to inhuman, cruel or degrading treatment or punishment, or in which his or her life or freedom may be endangered for reasons of race, ethnic origin, religion, nationality, membership of a particular social group, association with a national minority, sex, language, political or other opinion, birth or other status.

2. The provisions of paragraph 1 shall not prevent the removal or return of an individual who seeks asylum to the territory of a High Contracting Party, other than the State of such person's nationality, which has undertaken to determine the claim in accordance with applicable international agreements.

3. The provisions of paragraph 1 shall not prevent the removal or expulsion of an individual whose claim to asylum has been denied following appeal or review, or whose expulsion is necessary in the interests of public order or is based on reasons of national security.

Article 3

1. Everyone who seeks asylum shall have access to a fair and expeditious procedure before an independent and impartial authority, shall be allowed to submit reasons in support of the application, and shall have the right to be represented for that purpose before the competent authority, and to be assisted by an interpreter where necessary.

2. Decisions on claims to asylum shall be rendered promptly and negative decisions shall be accompanied by reasons. Everyone whose claim to asylum is rejected shall have the possibility to appeal or to have his or her case reviewed, and shall be permitted to remain in the territory of the State pending final determination of the case.

3. A State may by law limit the right of appeal or review in cases that have been determined by the authority described in paragraph 1 to be manifestly unsupported by objective evidence or an abuse of the right of asylum.

4. An applicant whose case is being appealed or is under review pursuant to paragraph 2 may be expelled before a final determination is made when such expulsion is necessary in the interests of public order or is based on reasons of national security.

5. Asylum proceedings shall be held *in camera* and the personal details of applicants shall not be published unless the applicant consents thereto, or if such publication is in accordance with law, is unlikely to endanger the applicant or members of his or her family, and is reasonably necessary in a democratic society.

6. Nothing in the present Article shall prevent a State from granting asylum in accordance with Article 4 on a group or category basis.

Article 4

1. Everyone whose claim to asylum is accepted shall be permitted to remain in the State temporarily or permanently according to law, until such time as he or she is able to return without serious risk to their country of origin, or until a regional solution is found pursuant to Article 1(2).

2. Everyone who is allowed to remain in a State pursuant to paragraph 1 shall enjoy the rights set forth in Articles 2 and 4 of the Fourth Protocol to the Convention.

Article 5

1. Everyone lawfully in the territory of a State has the right to be united with family members who are not nationals of the State and who are seeking to join him or her. For

the purposes of the present article, family members shall include the spouse, dependent children under eighteen and dependent parents. States shall also give favourable consideration to admitting members of extended families, taking account of relations of affinity and dependence recognized in the culture of minority communities within their territory.

2. This right may be limited or restricted in the case of persons who are admitted to State territory for short periods not exceeding three months, or who are awaiting determination of their status pursuant to Article 3 of the present Protocol, or who are under final order of expulsion, removal or extradition.

Article 6

1. Everyone who seeks to be united with family members pursuant to Article 5 has the right to have his or her application determined fairly and expeditiously. A person whose application is refused shall be informed of the reasons for the decision and shall have the right to have the decision reviewed by higher authority. The exercise of this right, including the grounds on which it may be exercised, shall be governed by law.

2. The right to be united with family members shall not be denied on any ground such as sex, age, race, colour, language, religion, political or other opinion, national or social origin, association with a national minority, property, birth or other status.

Article 7

The High Contracting Parties undertake to adopt the necessary measures to ensure:

a. that the rights and freedoms guaranteed in the present Convention are not exercised by any individual or group for the purpose of promoting or encouraging intolerance, hatred or violence towards any other individual or group;

b. that all members of society enjoy effective protection against discrimination on grounds such as sex, age, race, colour, language, religion, political or other opinion, national or social origin, association with a national minority, property, birth or other status.

c. the creation and maintenance of the conditions within which individuals and groups, in reciprocity and mutual respect, may develop and support their integrity and dignity.

Explanatory Notes

Article 1

1. The principle of asylum has been consistently endorsed by Member States of the Council of Europe, in recommendations of the Committee of Ministers, in their practice, and in their ratification and implementation of international instruments, such as the 1951 Convention and 1967 Protocol relating to the Status of Refugees. Article 1 recalls the provisions of Article 14 of the 1948 Universal Declaration of Human Rights: 'Everyone has the right to seek and to enjoy in other countries asylum from persecution.'

2. *Asylum* is not defined in Article 1, in view of the different perceptions prevailing among States. The general notion is therefore left to be developed by States in their municipal

law, while the core content—the protection against the exercise of jurisdiction by another State that may be accorded to an individual—is given a specific meaning in Article 2. At the same time, the emphasis on the right to *seek* asylum is called for not only by recent State practice, but also by the necessity and the desirability of promoting and ensuring access to determination procedures consonant with the general scheme of values entrenched in the European Convention.

3. Article 1(2) recognizes that States, including Member States of the Council of Europe, continue to hesitate to accord due recognition to the right *to be granted asylum*. Among the many reasons for this hesitancy may be included apprehensions about numbers, particularly for countries of first refuge. This paragraph therefore places the responsibility for solidarity, co-operation and solutions, clearly within the regional context offered by the Council of Europe.

4. Article 1(2) also consolidates European practice into formal recognition of the protection needs, not only of refugees falling within Article 1 of the 1951 Convention/1967 Protocol relating to the Status of Refugees, but also of those who are recognized in European State practice as having other *valid reasons* for not being required to return to their country of origin. Such reasons in the past have included reasonable fear of prejudice or discrimination in the exercise of fundamental rights, war and resistance to war, and serious disturbances of public order.

Article 2

5. Member States of the Council of Europe acknowledge the normative effect of the principle of *non-refoulement*, that is, the prohibition prescribed by article 33 of the 1951 Convention relating to the Status of Refugees, on the return in any manner whatsoever of a refugee to a country in which his or her life or freedom may be threatened for reasons of race, religion, nationality, membership of a particular social group, or political opinion. The European Commission and the European Court of Human Rights have extended analogous protection, sometimes indirectly, in accordance with the terms of Article 3 of the European Convention.

6. Article 2(1) confirms and clarifies the obligations of States party to the European Convention and to the 1951 Convention, and further invokes the standard of non-discrimination endorsed in article 14 of the European Convention. In requiring a first degree of protection for all asylum seekers, 'at the border or within the territory of a State', it recalls the fundamental obligation in Article 1 of the European Convention, under which States, 'shall secure to everyone within their jurisdiction the rights and freedoms defined . . .'

7. Article 2(2) is intended to take account of agreements between States on the responsibility to determine claims to asylum, while emphasizing the controlling context of international obligations, including the present Protocol.

8. Article 2(3) recognizes that States' sovereign powers over the residence and removal of foreign nationals apply with respect to those whose claims to asylum are determined to be without foundation.

Article 3

9. The right to seek asylum, and indeed, the right to benefit from the principle of *non-refoulement*, is largely meaningless unless an applicant is able to present his or her case for determination by an independent, impartial authority. Minimum standards for asylum procedures have been recommended by the Executive Committee of the Programme of the United Nations High Commissioner for Refugees in 1977, and by the Committee of Ministers in 1981 (Recommendation No. R (81) 16).

10. Article 3(1) therefore reiterates the *minimum* procedural requirements, which may be expected to be developed by States in their implementation, in the light of standards laid down for other decision-making processes by the European Commission and the European Court. In particular, it may be anticipated that fair and expeditious procedures will be staffed by trained decision-makers, and that the asylum process will be configured around the best available information sources.

11. Article 3(2) briefly develops the principle of due process, drawing upon Committee of Ministers Recommendation No. R (80) 2 concerning the exercise of discretionary powers by administrative authorities, the general practice of States with respect to review of administrative decisions, and the developing jurisprudence of the European Court of Human Rights with respect to effective remedies, as required by Article 13 of the Convention.

12. Article 3(3) acknowledges that, provided minimum standards of procedural due process and impartiality are satisfied, the integrity of the asylum procedure may require the expeditious disposal of abusive applications or claims that are manifestly unsupported by objective evidence. Although the phrase 'manifestly ill-founded' is used in Article 27(2) of the Convention, the present wording is preferred in order to stress again the importance of accurate information, especially country of origin information, in the assessment of claims.

13. Article 3(4) restates the common exception in favour of the State, where the interests of public order (*ordre public*) or national security prevail.

14. Article 3(5) proposes a basic principle of confidentiality of asylum proceedings, as an exception to the general rule which favours public process. It is considered that *in camera* proceedings are better able to protect both the interests of the State, for example, by reducing the risk of creating claims *sur place*; and those of the applicant, for example, by minimizing the risks to family members or friends remaining in the home country.

15. Finally, Article 3(6) recognizes that the general principle of individual petition and hearing may require to yield in favour of a groups and categories approach to the grant of refuge and protection, particularly where significant numbers of asylum seekers arrive from countries manifestly in turmoil. The cross-reference to Article 4 is intended to establish the basic parameters of refuge, while implicitly acknowledging that the content of refuge can be tailored to specific needs.

Article 4

16. The present text takes account of the fact that many individual States remain reluctant to accept a formal, legal obligation to accord asylum (in the sense of a durable or

lasting solution on their territory), even to those who are recognized as refugees. Article 4(1) recognizes nonetheless that certain legal implications follow from the principle of *refuge through time*, and that a temporary solution at least is due to those with a well-founded claim to asylum, until they are able to return without serious risk to their country of origin; or until a regional solution is found, further to Article 1(2). Such regional solution might entail local settlement, that is, permanent residence, in the country of first refuge, or resettlement in another State.

17. Article 4(2) reiterates the applicability of the general principles of freedom of movement, choice of residence, and freedom to leave any country found in the Fourth Protocol to the European Convention, as well as the prohibition of the collective expulsion of aliens.

Article 5

18. Article 5 builds on the jurisprudence of the European Commission and the European Court of Human Rights, which has recognized that the right in Article 8 of the Convention to respect for family life may entail certain limitations of States' traditional powers to control entry into their territory. It implicitly acknowledges that most Member States of the Council of Europe are in effect multi-cultural, multi-racial communities. Some minorities present on their territory have ancient roots; others are the result of more recent migrations. Many of the latter retain close ties with family members outside the community of Europe, but the due recognition of such ties is often subordinated to rigid immigration criteria, including 'traditional' conceptions of the family itself, or national economic interests.

19. Article 5 therefore accords positive recognition to the principle that the family is the fundamental group unit of society and thereby entitled to protection by the society and the State (Article 23(1), 1966 International Covenant on Civil and Political Rights; Article 10, 1966 International Covenant on Economic and Social Rights; Article 16, 1961 European Social Charter; Articles 9 and 10, 1989 United Nations Convention on the Rights of the Child). At the same time, it recognizes that certain limitations on the principle of family unity may be permissible with respect to persons admitted only temporarily to State territory.

Article 6

20. Article 6 maintains the general principle described briefly above in paragraph 10, namely, that individuals seeking to exercise a right are entitled to prompt and reasoned decisions, and that every exercise of discretionary power by administrative authority should be subject to review. (See also Article 10, 1989 United Nations Convention on the Rights of the Child). Article 6(2) ensures the application of the general principle of non-discrimination in this sensitive field, and adds the additional ground of age to the list of impermissible bases for denial of the right to family unity.

Article 7

21. European institutions and European nations are founded on certain shared values, including principles of tolerance and mutual respect. For many in society, however, the

reality is often very different. Article 7 therefore aims to go beyond mere passive endorsement of the principle of non-discrimination and to accentuate the active dimensions of tolerance, which include *creating* the conditions within which the individuals and groups within Europe's disparate communities may be enabled, on a basis of reciprocity and mutual respect to pursue and fulfil their needs and plans. To this end, it also echoes Article 17, which provides that 'Nothing in this Convention may be interpreted as implying for any State, group or person any right to engage in any activity or perform any act aimed at the destruction of any of the rights and freedoms set forth herein . . .' The essentially programmatic, though no less urgent, objectives of this Article may make it appropriate for regular overview by the Secretary General of the Council of Europe, acting under Article 57 of the Convention.

ANNEXE 5

COMPREHENSIVE ARRANGEMENTS FOR REFUGEES

1. International Conference on Indo-Chinese Refugees, Geneva, 13–14 June 1989: Declaration and Comprehensive Plan of Action

Adopted without amendment and by consensus at the International Conference, Geneva, 13–14 June 1989

Text: Note by the Secretary-General, UN doc. A/CONF.148/2, 26 April 1989[1]

I. DECLARATION

The *Governments of the States* represented in the International Conference on Indo-Chinese Refugees, held at Geneva from 13 to 14 June 1989,

Having reviewed the problems of Indo-Chinese asylum seekers in the South-East Asian region,

Noting that, since 1975, over 2 million persons have left their countries of origin in Indo-China and that the flow of asylum seekers still continues,

Aware that the movement of asylum seekers across frontiers in the South-East Asian region remains a subject of intense humanitarian concern to the international community,

Recalling United Nations General Assembly resolution 3455 (XXX) and the first Meeting on Refugees and Displaced Persons in South-East Asia convened at Geneva in July 1979 under the auspices of the United Nations to address the problem,

Recalling further the 1951 Convention relating to the Status of Refugees and its 1967 Protocol, and related instruments,

Noting with satisfaction that, as a result of combined efforts on the part of Governments and international organizations concerned, a durable solution has been found for over 1.6 million Indo-Chinese,

Preoccupied however by the burden imposed, particularly on the neighbouring countries and territories, as a result of the continuation of the outflow and the presence of large numbers of asylum seekers still in camps,

Alarmed by indications that the current arrangements designed to find solutions for asylum seekers and resolve problems stemming from the outflow may no longer be responsive to the size, tenacity and complexity of the problems in the region,

Recognizing that the resolution of the problem of asylum seekers in the region could contribute positively to a climate of peace, harmony and good neighbourliness,

[1] The following text is reproduced, with minor deletions, from the Draft Declaration and Comprehensive Plan of Action, approved by the Preparatory Meeting for the International Conference on Indo-Chinese Refugees on 8 March 1989 and duly endorsed at the June Conference.

Satisfied that the international community, and in particular the countries directly involved, have responded positively to the call for a new international conference made by the States members of the Association of South-East Asian Nations and endorsed by the Executive Committee of the Programme of the United Nations High Commissioner for Refugees at its thirty-ninth session and by the General Assembly of the United Nations at its forty-third session,

Noting the progress achieved towards a solution of this issue by the various bilateral and multilateral meetings held between the parties concerned prior to the International Conference on Indo-Chinese Refugees,

Noting that the issues arising from the presence of Khmer refugees and displaced persons are being discussed, among the parties directly involved, within a different framework and as such have not been included in the deliberations of the Conference,

Noting with satisfaction the positive results of the Preparatory Meeting for the Conference, held in Kuala Lumpur from 7 to 9 March 1989,

Realizing that the complex problem at hand necessitates the co-operation and understanding of all concerned and that a comprehensive set of mutually re-enforcing humanitarian undertakings, which must be carried out in its totality rather than selectively, is the only realistic approach towards achieving a durable solution to the problem,

Acknowledging that such a solution must be developed in the context of national laws and regulations as well as of international standards,

Have solemnly resolved to adopt the attached Comprehensive Plan of Action.

II. COMPREHENSIVE PLAN OF ACTION

A. *Clandestine departures*

1. Extreme human suffering and hardship, often resulting in loss of lives, have accompanied organized clandestine departures. It is therefore imperative that humane measures be implemented to deter such departures, which should include the following:

(a) Continuation of official measures directed against those organizing clandestine departures, including clear guidelines on these measures from the central government to the provincial and local authorities.

(b) Mass media activities at both local and international level, focusing on:

(i) The dangers and hardship involved in clandestine departures;

(ii) The institution of a status-determination mechanism under which those determined not to be refugees shall have no opportunity for resettlement;

(iii) Absence of any advantage, real or perceived, particularly in relation to third-country resettlement, of clandestine and unsafe departures;

(iv) Encouragement of the use of the regular departure and other migration programmes;

(v) Discouragement of activities leading to clandestine departures.

(c) In the spirit of mutual co-operation, the countries concerned shall consult regularly to ensure effective implementation and co-ordination of the above measures.

B. *Regular departure programmes*

2. In order to offer a preferable alternative to clandestine departures, emigration from Viet-Nam through regular departure procedures and migration programmes, such as the current Orderly Departure Programme, should be fully encouraged and promoted.

3. Emigration through regular departure procedures and migration programmes should be accelerated and expanded with a view to making such programmes the primary and eventually the sole modes of departure.

4. In order to achieve this goal, the following measures will be undertaken:

(a) There will be a continuous and widely publicized media campaign to increase awareness of regular departure procedures and migration programmes for departure from Viet-Nam.

(b) All persons eligible under regular third-country migration programmes, Amerasians and former re-education centre detainees will have full access to regular departure procedures and migration programmes. The problem of former re-education centre detainees will be further discussed separately by the parties concerned.

(c) Exit permits and other resettlement requirements will be facilitated for all persons eligible under regular departure procedures and migration programmes.

(d) Viet-Nam will fully co-operate with the United Nations High Commissioner for Refugees (UNHCR) and the Intergovernmental Committee for Migration (ICM) in expediting and improving processing, including medical processing, for departures under regular departure procedures and migration programmes and will ensure that medical records of those departing comply with standards acceptable to receiving countries.

(e) Viet-Nam, UNHCR, ICM and resettlement countries will co-operate to ensure that air transportation and logistics are sufficient to move expeditiously all those accepted under regular departure procedures and migration programmes.

(f) If necessary, countries in South-East Asia through which people emigrating under regular departure procedures and migration programmes must transit will, with external financial support as appropriate, expand transit facilities and expedite exit and entry procedures in order to help facilitate increased departures under such programmes.

C. *Reception of new arrivals*

5. All those seeking asylum will be given the opportunity to do so through the implementation of the following measures:

(a) Temporary refuge will be given to all asylum seekers, who will be treated identically regardless of their mode of arrival until the status-determination process is completed.

(b) UNHCR will be given full and early access to new arrivals and will retain access, following the determination of their status.

(c) New arrivals will be transferred, as soon as possible, to a temporary asylum centre where they would be provided assistance and full access to the refugee status-determination process.

D. *Refugee status*

6. The early establishment of a consistent region-wide refugee status-determination process is required and will take place in accordance with national legislation and internationally accepted practice. It will make specific provision, *inter alia*, for the following:

(a) Within a prescribed period, the status of the asylum seeker will be determined by a qualified and competent national authority or body, in accordance with established refugee criteria and procedures. UNHCR will participate in the process in an observer and advisory capacity. In the course of that period, UNHCR shall advise in writing each individual of the nature of the procedure, of the implications for rejected cases and of the right to appeal the first-level determination.

(b) The criteria will be those recognized in the 1951 Convention relating to the Status of Refugees and its 1967 Protocol, bearing in mind, to the extent appropriate, the 1948 Universal Declaration of Human Rights and other relevant international instruments concerning refugees, and will be applied in a humanitarian spirit taking into account the special situation of the asylum seekers concerned and the need to respect the family unit. A uniform questionnaire developed in consultation with UNHCR will be the basis for interviews and shall reflect the elements of such criteria.

(c) The *Handbook on Procedures and Criteria for Determining Refugee Status* issued by UNHCR will serve as an authoritative and interpretative guide in developing and applying the criteria.

(d) The procedures to be followed will be in accordance with those endorsed by the Executive Committee of the Programme of the United Nations High Commissioner for Refugees in this area. Such procedures will include, *inter alia*:

(i) The provision of information to the asylum seekers about the procedures, the criteria and the presentation of their cases;

(ii) Prompt advice of the decision in writing within a prescribed period;

(iii) A right of appeal against negative decisions and proper appeals procedures for this purpose, based upon the existing laws and procedures of the individual place of asylum, with the asylum seeker entitled to advice, if required, to be provided under UNHCR auspices.

7. UNHCR will institute, in co-operation with the Governments concerned, a comprehensive regional training programme for officials involved in the determination process with a view to ensuring the proper and consistent functioning of the procedures and application of the criteria, taking full advantage of the experience gained in Hong Kong.

E. *Resettlement*

8. Continued resettlement of Vietnamese refugees benefiting from temporary refuge in South-East Asia is a vital component of the Comprehensive Plan of Action.

1. *Long-Stayers Resettlement Programme*

9. The Long-Stayers Resettlement Programme includes all individuals who arrived in temporary asylum camps prior to the appropriate cut-off date and would contain the following elements:

(a) A call to the international community to respond to the need for resettlement, in particular through the participation by an expanded number of countries, beyond those few currently active in refugee resettlement. The expanded number of countries could include, among others, the following: Australia, Austria, Belgium, Canada, Denmark, Federal Republic of Germany, Finland, France, Ireland, Italy, Japan, Luxembourg, Netherlands, New Zealand, Norway, Spain, Sweden, Switzerland, United Kingdom and United States of America.

(b) A multi-year commitment to resettle all the Vietnamese who have arrived in temporary asylum camps prior to an agreed date, except those persons already found not to be refugees under established status-determination procedure and those who express the wish to return to Viet-Nam. Refugees will be advised that they do not have the option of refusing offers of resettlement, as this would exclude them from further resettlement consideration.

2. *Resettlement Programme for Newly-Determined Refugees*

10. The Resettlement Programme for Newly-Determined Refugees will accommodate all those who arrive after the introduction of status determination procedures and are determined to be refugees. Within a designated period after their transfer to the resettlement area, those determined to be refugees shall receive an orientation briefing from a UNHCR representative that explains the third-country resettlement programme, the length of time current arrivals may be expected to spend in camp awaiting resettlement, and the necessity of adhering to the rules and regulations of the camp.

11. Wherever possible, a pledge shall be sought from the resettlement countries to place all those determined to be refugees, except those expressing the wish to return to Viet-Nam, within a prescribed period. It shall be the responsibility of UNHCR, with the full support of all the resettlement countries and countries of asylum, to co-ordinate efforts to ensure that departures are effected within that time.

F. *Repatriation/Plan of Repatriation*

12. Persons determined not to be refugees should return to their country of origin in accordance with international practices reflecting the responsibilities of States towards their own citizens. In the first instance, every effort will be made to encourage the voluntary return of such persons.

13. In order to allow this process to develop momentum, the following measures will be implemented:

(a) Widely publicized assurances by the country of origin that returnees will be allowed to return in conditions of safety and dignity and will not be subject to persecution.

(b) The procedure for readmission will be such that the applicants would be readmitted within the shortest possible time.

(c) Returns will be administered in accordance with the above principles by UNHCR and ICM, and internationally funded reintegration assistance will be channelled through UNHCR, according to the terms of the Memorandum of Understanding signed with Viet-Nam on 13 December 1988.

14. If, after the passage of reasonable time, it becomes clear that voluntary repatriation is not making sufficient progress towards the desired objective, alternatives recognized as being acceptable under international practices would be examined. A regional holding centre under the auspices of UNHCR may be considered as an interim measure for housing persons determined not to be refugees pending their eventual return to the country of origin.

15. Persons determined not to be refugees shall be provided humane care and assistance by UNHCR and international agencies pending their return to the country of origin. Such assistance would include educational and orientation programmes designed to encourage return and reduce re-integration problems.

G. *Laotian asylum seekers*

16. In dealing with Laotian asylum seekers, future measures are to be worked out through intensified trilateral negotiation between UNHCR, the Lao People's Democratic Republic and Thailand, with the active support and co-operation of all parties concerned. These measures should be aimed at:

(a) Maintaining safe arrival and access to the Lao screening process;

(b) Accelerating and simplifying the process for both the return of the screened out and voluntary repatriation to the Lao People's Democratic Republic under safe, humane and UNHCR-monitored conditions.

17. Together with other durable solutions, third-country resettlement continues to play an important role with regard to the present camp populations of the Laotians.

H. *Implementation and review procedures*

18. Implementation of the Comprehensive Plan of Action is a dynamic process that will require continued co-ordination and possible adaptation to respond to changing situations. In order to ensure effective implementation of the Plan, the following mechanisms shall be established:

(a) UNHCR, with the financial support of the donor community, will be in charge of continuing liaison and co-ordination with concerned Governments and intergovernmental as well as non-governmental organizations to implement the Comprehensive Plan of Action.

(b) A Steering Committee based in South-East Asia will be established. It will consist of representatives of all Governments making specific commitments under the Comprehensive Plan of Action. The Steering Committee will meet periodically under the chairmanship of UNHCR to discuss implementation of the Comprehensive Plan of Action. The Steering Committee may establish sub-committees as necessary to deal with specific aspects of the implementation of the Plan, particularly with regard to status determination, return and resettlement.

(c) A regular review arrangement will be devised by UNHCR, preferably in conjunction with the annual Executive Committee session, to assess progress in implementation of the Comprehensive Plan of Action and consider additional measures to improve the Plan's effectiveness in meeting its objectives.

2. International Conference on Central American Refugees (CIREFCA), Guatemala City, 29–31 May 1989: Declaration and Concerted Plan of Action in Favour of Central American Refugees, Returnees and Displaced Persons— Extracts

Adopted by the International Conference on Central American Refugees (CIREFCA), Guatemala City, 29–31 May 1989

Text: UN doc. CIREFCA/89/14, 31 May 1989 (originally published in Spanish; footnotes omitted)

I
DECLARATION

The Governments of the States represented in the International Conference on Central American Refugees, held at Guatemala City from 29 to 31 May 1989,

Bearing in mind the significance of the Procedure for the Establishment of a Firm and Lasting Peace in Central America, signed by the Presidents of the five countries of Central America at Guatemala City on 7 August 1987, and especially the contents of its point 8,

Recalling the San Salvador Communiqué on Central American Refugees of 9 September 1988, resolution 43/118 of the General Assembly of the United Nations of 8 December 1988, entitled 'International Conference on Central American Refugees', and the resolution of the General Assembly of the Organization of American States of 19 November 1988 entitled 'Central American Refugees and Regional Efforts to solve their Problems',

Taking fully into account the Joint Declaration of the Central American Presidents signed in the Department of La Paz, El Salvador, on 14 February 1989, in which they offer their full support for the Conference,

Noting other expressions of support received, in particular from the Ministers for Foreign Affairs of the Central American States, the Contadora Group and the European Economic Community in the Political Declaration and the Joint Economic Communiqué of the San José Meeting, held at San Pedro Sula, Honduras, on 27 and 28 February 1989,

Recognizing the importance, within the overall United Nations effort for the region, of the Special Plan of Economic Co-operation for Central America, approved by the General Assembly of the United Nations in its resolution 42/231 of 12 May 1988, whose chapter on refugees and displaced persons will have to be complementary to the implementation of the Plan of Action of the Conference,

Bearing in mind that the common effort in favour of refugees, returnees and displaced persons requires the support, co-operation and co-ordination of the various affected and interested Governments, and of the various international organizations involved, particularly the Office of the United Nations High Commissioner for Refugees and the United Nations Development Programme,

Noting that, since the beginning of the conflicts in the region, more than a quarter of a million Central Americans have fled their countries of origin and have received protection and assistance as refugees in neighbouring countries, especially through the meritorious work of the United Nations High Commissioner for Refugees,

Noting furthermore that the crisis in Central America not only has brought about the exodus of refugees which have been identified, recognized and assisted as such, but also has resulted in both internal and external displacements of a considerably higher number of persons than that of refugees and which equally need attention,

Concerned by the intense human suffering caused by this massive uprooting of population groups, which in addition has had a negative impact on the populations that receive them and on the public services and natural resources, among others, available in the countries where they transit,

. . .

22. *Recognize* that solutions to the problems of refugees, returnees and displaced persons form an integral part of the efforts for peace, democracy and development taking place in the region;

And, therefore:

23. *Approve*, in accordance with the principle of international solidarity, the guidelines of the Concerted Plan of Action in Favour of Central American Refugees, Returnees and Displaced Persons, set forth below, support its principles and objectives, and consider it a promising initial framework for future activities and thus re-affirm their commitment to contribute to the establishment of a firm and lasting peace in Central America;

. . .

II
CONCERTED PLAN OF ACTION IN FAVOUR OF CENTRAL AMERICAN REFUGEES, RETURNEES AND DISPLACED PERSONS

Introduction

1. The San Salvador Communiqué of 9 September 1988, which called for the International Conference on Central American Refugees, established the need for national plans and programmes of action in favour of Central American refugees, returnees and displaced persons, identifying concrete solutions to their serious problems to be formulated on a purely humanitarian and non-political basis.

2. In this context, the Governments of the affected countries have formulated, at the national level, detailed diagnostic studies of the massive population movements that have taken place in the region, on the basis of which the present Plan of Action has been prepared. In Part One, which contains the strategy, the basic objectives, fundamentals and project proposals to identify solutions to the problems of Central American refugees, returnees and displaced persons are described. In Part Two, the mechanisms for follow-up and promotion of the Plan of Action are outlined.

Part One
Strategy

A. The present situation

3. In the course of the last ten years, almost two million Central Americans have been displaced in the region as a result of the current crisis. During the same time, numerous assistance programmes have been implemented which have considerably improved the situation of the affected people. In several cases, durable solutions have been found; nevertheless, for the majority of the uprooted population groups, viable and definitive alternatives remain to be identified.

4. In the first instance, a particularly vulnerable group of almost 150,000 persons, recognized and assisted as refugees form part of the uprooted population groups. The great majority have found asylum in Costa Rica (41,000), Honduras (37,000) and Mexico (43,000), with smaller but nevertheless significant numbers in Belize, El Salvador, Guatemala and Nicaragua. In any event, these numbers do not include those persons who fall within the established criteria but have not requested recognition and assistance as refugees and are dispersed throughout almost all the countries of the region.

5. In the second instance, there is another group of persons, returnees, who equally need assistance in order to achieve durable solutions. This involves persons who, at one time, had been refugees and decided to return to their countries of origin. According to figures provided by the respective Governments, there are in the region of 13,500 Guatemalans, 35,000 Nicaraguans and 13,000 Salvadorians.

6. The conflict and crisis have at the same time resulted in the displacement of an important third group of persons who remain homeless within the boundaries of their own countries and without means of subsistence. They are called internally displaced persons and need special assistance, even though they remain subject to the jurisdiction and protection of their authorities of their own countries.

7. In addition, among those affected by the crisis, another group is located outside of their own countries and needs attention owing to their uprooted situation and the additional burden which they may signify to the communities where they live. This group is made up of people who, as a result of the crisis, have been unable to provide for their subsistence or lead a normal life, whether or not their lives, security or liberty have been threatened by the conflict. When, as a result, these persons have been obliged to leave their homes and move to a neighbouring country, they are called, for the purpose of this Plan of Action, externally displaced persons and their situation undoubtedly deserves a more detailed legal and social analysis.

8. Although the magnitude of this problem is difficult to measure, it is thought that, in addition to the number of assisted refugees, some 1.8 million persons are affected in all countries of the region, whether they are obliged to cross an international frontier—among whom there are refugees who have not been recognized as such—or to leave their homes while remaining in their own countries.

B. Basic objectives

9. Since the beginning of the refugee exodus in Central America, the affected countries have responded with emergency and other forms of basic assistance with a view to meeting immediate needs and, in some cases facilitating durable solutions. Even if the magnitude of human suffering has been lightened and emergency situations have been overcome, many refugees still live in precarious conditions. One of the objectives of the present Plan of Action is to identify durable solutions to overcome this problem within the possibilities of the affected countries.

10. From this fundamental objective follows the obligation to respect, in the first place, the right of refugees to return voluntarily to their countries of origin in order to resume a normal life. Consequently, voluntary repatriation, which is the best solution, will be facilitated above all. In those instances where conditions do not yet exist to make this possible, the Plan of Action proposes measures to help refugees play a larger and more positive role in the countries of asylum while awaiting voluntary repatriation, by opening camps—when conditions so permit—and promoting interaction with the local community. It also proposes that alternative solutions be identified for those refugees who are dispersed outside the camps. In exceptional cases, when some refugees cannot remain in the country of asylum, for protection reasons, the possibility of third country resettlement is considered.

11. Even though refugees can make a positive contribution to local communities during their stay—and this has in some instances been the case—it is clear that their presence in massive numbers has produced, or can produce, negative effects in the employment, social services, economic and ecological sectors in the country of asylum which must be given special consideration. It is therefore necessary to assure that programmes are appropriate to the characteristics of the area and are formulated while taking into consideration the standard of living in the asylum country. In view of the possible negative effects mentioned, the Plan of Action has been formulated as well to remedy this situation and, if possible, to contribute to improving conditions in the affected communities. Recent experience has shown that international programmes of co-operation in favour of refugees in rural areas should, for reasons of equality, also benefit the surrounding local population.

12. Concerning the group of displaced persons, the Plan of Action attempts to improve their situation so that they may return and have a normal productive life in their communities of origin whenever possible.

C. Fundamentals of the Plan of Action

13. The Plan of Action is based on the following fundamental principles:

(a) The affected countries consider that both the commitment to re-establish peace in the region and the formulation of proposals for solutions in favour of the affected population groups form an integral part of the efforts towards regional peace and development.

(b) The steps taken towards peace constitute the basis of proposals for solutions in favour of refugees, returnees and displaced persons made in the framework of the

Procedure for the Establishment of a Firm and Lasting Peace in Central America (Esquipulas II), signed by the Presidents of the countries of Central America on 7 August 1987 and reaffirmed in the Joint Declaration of the Central American Presidents, signed in the Department of La Paz, El Salvador, on 14 February 1989.

(c) The problems of refugees, returnees and displaced persons and the proposals for solutions should continue to be treated on a strictly humanitarian and non-political basis; in this context, States are guided above all by considerations of solidarity with the individuals in need and the imperative of identifying humane solutions to their problems, giving priority to the preservation of life and personal safety above any other consideration.

14. The affected States reiterate their commitment to the fundamental principle of human rights and protection of refugees, especially those of *non-refoulement* and abstention from discrimination, expulsion or detention of refugees for having entered illegally the territory of the country. In addition, they reaffirm the continued upholding of the institution of asylum in the region.

15. In the same manner, the affected countries reiterate the importance of the principle according to which refugees are obliged, as any other person, to respect and observe the laws and regulations of the country of asylum, including lawful measures taken for the maintenance of public order. Refugees, for their part, are also under the obligation to avoid any activity which might affect the strictly civilian and humanitarian nature of camps and settlements, and to abstain from any activity incompatible with the regional peace process.

16. In order to ensure the success of the Plan of Action, the affected countries propose to link solution programmes for refugees, returnees and displaced persons with economic and social development in the region.

D. Three-year regional programme

17. In order to reach the stated objectives, the affected countries have reoriented or consolidated their polices with regard to refugees, returnees and displaced persons with a view to proposing programmes and projects for the next three years. Taken together, the policies on which the proposals are based constitute the global strategy adopted by the States described below.

18. This strategy has a dynamic character in so far as the proposals presented by the affected countries are based on an analysis of the current regional situation. The implementation of the Plan of Action will be evaluated in the light of the actual situation in the region through the mechanisms outlined in Part Two of the Plan of Action.

1. Programmes in favour of returnees

19. The voluntary repatriation programmes contain multisectoral projects aimed at facilitating the reintegration of returnees in their communities. These programmes address:

(a) The needs of returnees who receive basic assistance and, in some cases, rehabilitation assistance. The Plan of Action attempts to achieve their economic and social integration, benefiting the community where they return as well;

(b) The needs of future returnees and the receiving communities, in an integrated approach, which begins with the process of return and ends with re-integration. The Plan of Action foresees support to communities in the country of origin in order to create minimum conditions for return, even before such movement starts. The rate of implementation of these programmes will depend on the actual return of returnees.

. . .

21. These programmes reflect the commitment to continue respect for:

(a) The right of refugees to return to their countries of origin as well as to receive information on the prevailing situation to allow them to reach a free decision concerning their return;

(b) The voluntary and individually-manifested character of repatriation;

(c) The necessity that repatriation take place in conditions of security and dignity;

(d) The ability of the refugees to choose their destination in their countries, as well as freedom of movement and free choice of place of residence under the same conditions as other nationals of their countries;

(e) Non-discrimination for having sought asylum;

(f) Access to means of subsistence and to land under the same conditions as other nationals of their countries;

(g) The respective cultural and ethnic values;

(h) The work of the United Nations High Commissioner for Refugees in favour of returnees and his access to them.

The rights referred to in this paragraph are to be implemented in the context of the prevailing legislation in each country.

22. The programmes also aim at regularizing the situation of returnees with regard to the delivery of identity documents and the registry of births, marriages and deaths, and other events occurring in the country of asylum and relating to the civil status of the individual. They also provide for access to citizenship for children of returnees born abroad as well as for foreign spouses, when they so desire, and facilitate the recognition of studies undertaken in the country of asylum.

23. The humanitarian and non-political character of international assistance in favour of voluntary repatriation must be respected by all parties involved throughout the repatriation process.

2. Programmes in favour of refugees

24. The Plan of Action will in course allow refugees to play a larger and more positive role in the countries of asylum and—in those situations where the authorities so decide—to begin an integration process. This will mutually benefit refugees and the receiving communities. The Plan of Action includes integrated projects, often on a community-wide basis, with a view to overcoming the isolation of refugee and assistance projects.

. . .

26. These projects are based on the desire expressed by the Governments to undertake activities in favour of refugees which, in so far as possible, will be adapted to the standard of living of the relevant local communities and will benefit the local population.

Among other activities should be noted the development of employment opportunities, the strengthening of public services, the conservation of natural resources and the enrichment of national cultural heritage, with full respect for the ethnic values of the relevant population groups. Bearing in mind the option of voluntary repatriation, possibilities to contribute to an interchange with the refugees' communities of origin will be considered in the context of the tripartite activities which have been established for such purposes.

27. In accordance with existing laws, the Governments of asylum countries propose to regularize the migratory situation of refugees. To this effect, funds have been foreseen under several projects to reinforce government institutions responsible for supervising the co-ordination and implementation of governmental policies concerning refugees . . .

3. Projects in favour of internally and externally displaced persons

28. The number of internally displaced Central Americans is much greater than that of refugees and their needs can be as important. In the context of seeking solutions to problems caused by the massive displacement of population groups in the region, the affected countries have also included these persons as beneficiaries of multisectoral development projects. Once again, as in the case of other groups of beneficiaries, the programme aiming at facilitating the integration of displaced persons uses an integrated approach in order to achieve its goals and also to benefit the communities where the internally displaced persons are living.

. . .

30. These projects reflect the necessity to provide a humanitarian treatment to internally displaced persons, which presumes, in principle, facilitating the return to their homes and the reconstruction of their communities, or their location in other areas of the national territory or in places where they are actually living. In any of these possibilities, the common objective is the integration of internally displaced persons and their participation in the development process in the same conditions as other nationals of the country.

31. The Plan of Action also foresees assistance to externally displaced persons. The relevant projects include improving infrastructure and providing support to the sectors most affected by the massive presence of externally displaced persons . . .

. . .

32. These projects in favour of externally displaced persons reflect the necessity to provide them with a humanitarian treatment and with integral and multisectoral assistance, taking into consideration as well fostering conditions so that the individuals concerned can lead a normal life. In so far as externally displaced persons voluntarily return to their country, the Plan of Action proposes to facilitate their access to programmes in favour of returnees.

Part Two
Follow-up and promotion mechanisms

A. The Conference and the Special Programme of Economic Co-operation for Central America

33. Bearing in mind that the preparation of the Plan of Action has made it possible to update and complement the chapter on refugees and displaced persons contained in the Special Programme of Economic Co-operation for Central America, it is considered that the combination of humanitarian and development objectives requires a follow-up mechanism able to focus duly on the needs of the beneficiary groups and solve them in an expeditious and flexible manner.

34. The aforementioned requires a flexible mechanism for follow-up and promotion, capable of reaching decisions at the national level while promoting international support, and using instruments already defined in the Special Programme of Economic Co-operation for Central America for sectoral programmes and specific projects. As a result, the affected countries adopt the follow-up and promotion mechanisms described below, in order to enable the specific objectives and proposals contained in the Plan of Action and the mobilization of international co-operation to be implemented, with the collaboration of the Office of the Secretary-General of the United Nations, the United Nations High Commissioner for Refugees and the United Nations Development Programme.

[Paragraphs 35–43 are omitted; they provide details of the follow-up mechanisms, including national co-ordinating committees, support for tripartite bodies, and international reporting structures.]

STATES PARTIES TO THE 1951 CONVENTION, THE 1967
PROTOCOL, AND THE 1969 OAU CONVENTION: DELEGATIONS
PARTICIPATING IN THE 1984 CARTAGENA DECLARATION,
MEMBERS OF THE EXECUTIVE COMMITTEE OF THE HIGH
COMMISSIONER'S PROGRAMME (AT 1 JUNE 1997)

1. The 1951 Convention Relating to the Status of Refugees and the 1967 Protocol

Date of entry into force: 22 April 1954 (Convention); 4 October 1967 (Protocol).

Total Number of States Parties to the 1951 Convention:	130
Total Number of States Parties to the 1967 Protocol:	130
States Parties to both the Convention and Protocol:	126
States Parties to one or both of these instruments:	134

States Parties to the 1951 Convention only: Madagascar, Monaco, Namibia and Saint Vincent and the Grenadines

States Parties to the 1967 Protocol only: Cape Verde, Swaziland, USA and Venezuela

States Parties which maintain the geographical limitation: Congo, Madagascar, Monaco, Hungary, Malta, Turkey.

Albania	Cape Verde	Finland
Algeria	Central African Republic	France
Angola	Chad	Gabon
Antigua & Barbuda	Chile	Gambia
Argentina	China	Germany
Armenia	Colombia	Ghana
Australia	Congo	Greece
Austria	Costa Rica	Guatemala
Azerbaijan	Côte d'Ivoire	Guinea
Bahamas	Croatia	Guinea-Bissau
Belgium	Cyprus	Haiti
Belize	Czech Republic *	Holy See
Benin	Denmark	Honduras
Bolivia	Djibouti	Hungary
Bosnia and Herzegovina	Dominica	Iceland
Botswana	Dominican Republic	Iran, Islamic Republic of
Brazil	Ecuador	Ireland
Bulgaria	Egypt	Israel
Burkina Faso	El Salvador	Italy
Burundi	Equatorial Guinea	Jamaica
Cambodia	Estonia	Japan
Cameroon	Ethiopia	Kenya
Canada	Fiji	Korea, Republic of

Kyrgyzstan
Lesotho
Liberia
Liechtenstein
Lithuania
Luxembourg
Macedonia, Former
  Yugoslav Republic of
Madagascar
Malawi
Mali
Malta
Mauritania
Monaco
Morocco
Mozambique
Namibia
Netherlands
New Zealand
Nicaragua
Niger
Nigeria
Norway

Panama
Papua New Guinea
Paraguay
Peru
Philippines
Poland
Portugal
Romania
Russian Federation
Rwanda
Saint Vincent and the
  Grenadines
Samoa
Sao Tome and Principe
Senegal
Seychelles
Sierra Leone
Slovak Republic *
Slovenia **
Solomon Islands
Somalia
South Africa
Spain

Sudan
Suriname
Swaziland
Sweden
Switzerland
Tajikistan
Togo
Tunisia
Turkey
Tuvalu
Uganda
United Kingdom
United Republic of
  Tanzania
United States of America
Uruguay
Venezuela
Yemen
Yugoslavia
Zaire
Zambia
Zimbabwe

* The succession by the Governments of Czech and Slovak Republics took effect on 1 January 1993, the date on which the Republics assumed responsibility for their international relations.

** The succession by the Government of the Republic of Slovenia took effect on 25 June 1991, the date on which Slovenia assumed responsibility for its international relations.

2. States Parties to the 1969 OAU Convention

Date of entry into force: 20 June 1974
Number of States Parties: 43*

Algeria
Angola
Benin
Botswana
Burundi
Burkina Faso
Cameroon
Cape Verde
Central African Republic
Chad

Congo
Egypt
Equatorial Guinea
Ethiopia
Gabon
Gambia
Ghana
Guinea
Guinea Bissau
Kenya

Lesotho
Liberia
Libya
Malawi
Mali
Mauritania
Mozambique
Niger
Nigeria
Rwanda

Senegal	Togo	Zambia
Seychelles	Tunisia	Zimbabwe
Sierra Leone	Uganda	
South Africa	United Republic of	
Sudan	Tanzania	
Swaziland	Zaire	

* Morocco, formerly a party, withdrew from the OAU in 1984, following admission of the Sahrawi Arab Democratic Republic.

3. Government Delegations participating in the 1984 Cartagena Declaration

Adopted 22 November 1984
Number of Governments participating: 10

Belize	Colombia	Costa Rica
El Salvador	Guatemala	Honduras
Mexico	Nicaragua	Panama
Venezuela		

4. States Members of the Executive Committee of the High Commissioner's Programme

Number of Member States: 53

Algeria	India	Russian Federation
Argentina	Iran, Islamic Republic of	Somalia
Australia	Ireland	South Africa
Austria	Israel	Spain
Bangladesh	Italy	Sudan
Belgium	Japan	Sweden
Brazil	Lebanon	Switzerland
Canada	Lesotho	Thailand
China	Madagascar	Tunisia
Colombia	Morocco	Turkey
Denmark	Namibia	Uganda
Ethiopia	Netherlands	United Kingdom
Finland	Nicaragua	United Republic of
France	Nigeria	Tanzania
Germany	Norway	United States of America
Greece	Pakistan	Venezuela
Holy See	Philippines	Yugoslavia
Hungary	Poland	Zaire

SELECT BIBLIOGRAPHY

Books and Monographs

Achermann, A., & Hausammann, C. *Handbuch des Asylrechts*, 2 Aufl. Haupt, Bern, 1991
——, Bieber, R., Epiney, A., & Wehner, R. *Schengen und die Folgen*, Verlag Stämpfli & Cie AG, Bern, 1995
Aitchison, C.U., *A Collection of Treaties, Engagements and Sanads Relating to India and Neighbouring Countries*, 4th edn., Calcutta, 1909
Aleinikoff, T.A. & Martin, D.A., *Immigration: Process and Policy*, 2nd edn., West Publishing Co., St. Paul, Minn., 1991
Alston, P., *The United Nations and Human Rights: A Critical Appraisal*, Clarendon Press, Oxford, 1992
American Law Institute, *Restatement of the Law, Third, Foreign Relations Law of the United States*, 2 vols., St. Paul, Minn., 1987
Amnesty International, *Annual Reports*, Amnesty International Publications, London
Baehr, P. R. & Tessenyi, G., eds., *The New Refugee Hosting Countries: Call for Experience-Space for Innovation*, Netherlands Institute of Human Rights, Utrecht, 1991
Bar-Yaacov, N., *The Handling of International Disputes by Means of Inquiry*, Royal Institute of International Affairs, Oxford University Press, London, 1974
Bassiouni, M.C., *Crimes against Humanity in International Criminal Law*, Martinus Nijhoff, Dordrecht, 1992
Bau, I., *This Ground is Holy*, Paulist Press, Mahwah, N.J., 1985
Beach, H. & Ragvald, L., *A New Wave on the Northern Shore: The Indo-chinese Refugees in Sweden*, Statens Invandrarverk; Arbetsmarknadsstyrelsen, Norrköping, 1982
Bethell, N., *The Last Secret*, André Deutsch, London, 1974
Bhabha, J. & Coll, G., eds., *Asylum Law and Practice in Europe and North America*, Federal Publications Inc., Washington, D.C., 1992
Bossuyt, M., *L'interdiction de la discrimination dans le droit international des droits de l'homme*, Bruylant, Bruxelles, 1976
Brownlie, I., *Principles of Public International Law*, 4th edn., Clarendon Press, Oxford, 1990
——, *System of the Law of Nations: State Responsibility, Part I*, Clarendon Press, Oxford, 1983
——, *International Law and the Use of Force by States*, Clarendon Press, Oxford, 1963
Brownlie, I., ed., *Basic Documents in International Law*, 4th edn., Clarendon Press, Oxford, 1995
Carlier, J.-Y., *Droit des réfugiés*, E. Story-Scientia, Brussels, 1989
Chan, K.B. & Indra, D.M., eds., *Uprooting, Loss and Adaptation: The Resettlement of Indo-Chinese Refugees in Canada*, Canadian Public Health Association, Ottawa, 1987
Citizenship and Immigration Canada, *Into the 21st Century: A Strategy for Immigration and Citizenship*, Ottawa, 1994
Clark, L., *Early Warning of Refugee Flows*, Refugee Policy Group, Washington, D.C., 1989
Cohn, I. & Goodwin-Gill, G.S., *Child Soldiers*, Clarendon Press, Oxford, 1994

Cuny, F.C., Stein, B.N., & Reed, P., eds., *Repatriation during Conflict in Africa and Asia*, Center for the Study of Societies in Crisis, Dallas, 1992

Drüke, L., *Preventive Action for Refugee Producing Situations*, Peter Lang, Frankfurt-am-Main, 1990

European Council on Refugees and Exiles, *Asylum in Europe*, 2 vols., London, 1994

Fawcett, J., *The Application of the European Convention on Human Rights*, 2nd. edn., Clarendon Press, Oxford, 1987

Foreign Language Press, *Those who Leave*, Hanoi, 1979

——, *The Hoa in Vietnam*, Dossiers I and II, Hanoi, 1978

——, *With Firm Steps: Southern Vietnam since Liberation 1975–1977*, Hanoi, 1978

Garcia-Mora, M.R., *International Law and Asylum as a Human Right*, Public Affairs Press, Washington D.C., 1956

Goodwin-Gill, G.S., *International Law and the Movement of Persons between States*, Clarendon Press, Oxford, 1978

Gordenker, L., *Refugees in International Politics*, Croom Helm, London, 1987

Gowlland-Debbas, V., ed., *The Problem of Refugees in the Light of Contemporary International Law Issues*, Martinus Nijhoff, The Hague, 1995

Grahl-Madsen, A., *The Status of Refugees in International Law*. vols. 1 and 2, Sijthoff, Leyden, 1966, 1972

——, *Territorial Asylum*, Swedish Institute of International Affairs, Uppsala, 1980

Grant, B., *The Boat People*. Penguin, Melbourne, Middx., 1979

Hambro, E., *The Problem of Chinese Refugees in Hong Kong*, Sijthoff, Leyden, 1955

Hathaway, J., *The Law of Refugee Status*, Butterworths, Toronto, 1991

Henckaerts, J.-M., *Mass Expulsion in Modern International Law and Practice*, Martinus Nijhoff, The Hague, 1995

Holborn, L.W., *Refugees: A Problem of our Time. The Work of the UNHCR: 1951–1972*. 2 vols., Metuchen, Scarecrow Press, 1975

——, *The International Refugee Organization: A Specialized Agency of the United Nations. Its History and Work 1946–1952*, Oxford University Press, London, 1956

Independent Commission on International Humanitarian Issues, *Refugees: The Dynamics of Displacement*, Zed Books, London, 1986

International Commission of Jurists, *The Events in East Pakistan, 1971*, Geneva, 1972

International Refugee Organization, *Manual for Eligibility Officers*, Imprimeries Populaires, Geneva, n.d.

Jaeger, G., *Study on Irregular Movements of Asylum Seekers and Refugees*, Working Group on Irregular Movements of Asylum Seekers and Refugees, Geneva, 1985

Kälin, W., *Grundriss des Asylverfahrens*, Helbing & Lichtenhahn, Basel, 1990

——, *Das Prinzip des Non-Refoulement*, Peter Lang, Bern, 1982

Kimminich, O., *Der internationale Rechtsstatus des Flüchtlings*, Carl Heymans Verlag, Cologne, 1962

Köfner, G. & Nicolaus, P., *Grundlagen des Asylrechts in der Bundesrepublik Deutschland*, Kaiser, Grünewald, Mainz, Munich, 1986

Kouchner, B., *Le malheur des autres*, Editions de la Seine, Editions Jacob, 1992

Koziebrodski, L.B., *Le droit d'asile*, Sijthoff, Leyden, 1962

La Protección Internacional de los Refugiados en América Central, México y Panamá: Problemas Jurídicos y Humanitarios, National University of Colombia, 1984

Larkin, M.A., Cuny, F.C., & Stein, B.N., *Repatriation under Conflict in Central America*, CIPRA and Intertect, Washington, D.C., 1991

Lauterpacht, H. *The Development of International Law by the International Court*, Stevens, London, 1958

——, *International Law and Human Rights*, Stevens, London, 1950

Loescher, G., *Beyond Charity: International Co-operation and the Global Refugee Crisis*, Oxford University Press, New York, 1993

—— & Monahan, L., eds., *Refugees and International Relations*, Oxford University Press, Oxford, 1989

—— & Scanlan, J.A., *Calculated Kindness*, The Free Press, Macmillan, New York, 1986

Macalister-Smith, P., *International Humanitarian Assistance: Disaster Relief Actions in International Law and Organization*, Martinus Nijhoff, Dordrecht, 1985

Malarek, V., *Haven's Gate: Canada's Immigration Fiasco*, Macmillan, Toronto, 1987

Marrus, M., *The Unwanted: European Refugees in the Twentieth Century*, Oxford University Press, New York, 1985

Martin, D.A., ed., *The New Asylum-Seekers*, Martinus Nijhoff, Dordrecht, 1988

Marx, R., *Kommentar zum Asylverfahrensgesetz*, 3. Aufl. Luchterhand, Berlin, 1995

——, *Asylrecht*, 5. Aufl. Nomos, Baden-Baden, 1991

McGoldrick, D., *The Human Rights Committee: Its Role in the Development of the International Covenant on Civil and Political Rights*, Clarendon Press, Oxford, 1991

McNair, Lord (Arnold Duncan McNair), *The Law of Treaties*, Clarendon Press, Oxford, 1961

Meijers, H. et al, *Schengen: Internationalisation of Central Chapters of the Law on Aliens, Refugees, Security and the Police*, W.E.J. Tjeenk Willink, Kluwer, Dordrecht, 1991

Meron, T., *Human Rights and Humanitarian Norms as Customary Law*, Clarendon Press, Oxford, 1989

Minority Rights Group, London, Various titles; *see* below, Country Information Sources

Muntarbhorn, V., *The Status of Refugees in Asia*, Clarendon Press, Oxford, 1992

Nash, A., ed., *Human Rights and the Protection of Refugees under International Law*, Institute for Research on Public Policy, Canadian Human Rights Foundation, Halifax, NS, 1988

O'Connell, D.P., *The International Law of the Sea*, 2 vols. (Shearer, I. ed.), Clarendon Press, Oxford, 1982, 1984

——, *State Succession in Municipal Law and International Law*, vol. 1, Cambridge University Press, Cambridge, 1967

Palley, C., *Constitutional Law and Minorities*, Minority Rights Group, Report No. 36, London, 1978

Plaut, W.G., *Refugee Determination in Canada*, Minister of Supply and Services, Ottawa, 1985

Ratushny, E., *A New Refugee Status Determination Process for Canada*, Minister of Supply and Services, Ottawa, 1984

Reiterer, M., *The Protection of Refugees by their State of Asylum*, Wilhelm Braumüller, Vienna, 1984

Ressler, E.M., *Evacuation of Children from Conflict Areas: Considerations and Guidelines*, UNHCR/UNICEF, Geneva, 1992

——, Boothby, N., & Steinbock, D., *Unaccompanied Children: Care and Protection in Wars, Natural Disasters and Refugee Movements*, Oxford University Press, New York, 1988

Reynolds, E.E., *Nansen,* rev. edn., Penguin, London, 1949

Robinson, N., *Convention relating to the Status of Refugee: A Commentary,* Institute of Jewish Affairs, New York, 1953

Ruthström-Ruiz, C., *Beyond Europe: The Globalization of Refugee Aid,* Lund University Press, Lund, 1993

Rutledge, P.J., *The Vietnamese Experience in America,* Indiana University Press, Bloomington, 1992

Rystad, G., ed., *The Uprooted: Forced Migration as an International Problem in the Post-War Era,* Lund University Press, Lund, 1990

Salomon, K., *Refugees in the Cold War: Toward a New International Refugee Regime in the Early Postwar Era,* Lund University Press, Lund, 1991

Schwarzenberger, G. & Brown, L., *A Manual of International Law,* 6th edn., Professional Books, Milton, 1976

Sharpe, R.J., *The Law of Habeas Corpus,* Clarendon Press, Oxford, 1976

Shearer, I.A., *Extradition in International Law,* Manchester University Press, 1971

Simpson, J.H., *The Refugee Problem,* Royal Institute of International Affairs, Oxford University Press, London, 1939

Sinha, S.P., *Asylum and International Law,* Nijhoff, The Hague, 1971

Sjöberg, T., *The Powers and the Persecuted: The Refugee Problem and the Intergovernmental Committee on Refugees (IGCR), 1938–1947,* Lund University Press, Lund, 1991

Skran, C., *Refugees in Inter-War Europe: The Emergence of a Regime,* Oxford University Press, Oxford, 1995

Spijkerboer, T., *Women and Refugee Status: Beyond the public/private distinction,* Emancipation Council, The Hague, 1994

Stein, B.N., Cuny, F.C., & Reed, P., eds., *Refugee Repatriation during Conflict,* Center for the Study of Societies in Crisis, Dallas, 1995

Stenberg, G., *Non-Expulsion and Non-Refoulement,* Iustus Förlag, Uppsala, 1989

Takkenberg, A. and Tahbaz, C.C., *The Collected Travaux Préparatoires of the 1951 Convention relating to the Status of Refugees,* 3 volumes, Dutch Refugee Council/European Legal Network on Asylum, Amsterdam, 1988

Tiberghien, F., *La protection des réfugiés en France,* 2e éd., Economica, Presses Universitaires d'Aix-Marseille, 1988

Tolstoy, N., *Victims of Yalta,* Hodder & Stoughton, 1977; rev. edn., Corgi, London, 1979

US Committee for Refugees, *World Refugee Survey,* Washington, D.C., annually

US Department of State, *Country Reports on Human Rights Practices,* Washington, D.C., annually

UNHCR/Centre for Documentation on Refugees, CD-ROM, *RefWorld/RefMonde,* Geneva, 1996

UNHCR, *Refugee Children: Guidelines on Protection and Care,* Geneva, 1994

——, *The State of the World's Refugees: The Challenge of Protection,* Penguin, London, 1993

——, *Guidelines for the Disembarkation of Refugees,* Geneva, 1983

——, UNHCR, *Collection of International Instruments concerning Refugees,* 2nd edn., Geneva, 1979

——, *Handbook on Procedures and Criteria for Determining Refugee Status,* Geneva, 1979

——, *A Mandate to Protect and Assist Refugees,* Geneva, 1971

Vernant, J., *The Refugee in the Post-War World,* Yale Press, New Haven, 1953

Veuthey, M., *Guérilla et droit humanitaire,* Comité International de la Crois Rouge, Geneva, 1983

Vierdag, E.W., *The Concept of Discrimination in International Law*, Nijhoff, The Hague, 1973
Wain, B., *The Refused: The Agony of the Indo-china Refugee*, Simon and Schuster, New York, 1982
Weis, P., *Nationality and Statelessness in International Law*, 2nd edn., Sijthoff, Leyden, 1979
Woodbridge, G., *UNRRA: The History of the United Nations Relief and Rehabilitation Administration*, 3 vols., Columbia University Press, New York, 1950
de Zayas, A., *Nemesis at Potsdam: The Anglo-Americans and the Expulsion of the Germans*, Routledge and Kegan Paul, London, 1977
Zolberg, A.R., Suhrke, A., & Aguayo, S., *Escape from Violence: Conflict and the Refugee Crisis in the Developing World*, Oxford University Press, New York, 1989

Articles, Chapters, Reports and Occasional Papers

Ablard, T. & Novak, A., 'L'évolution du droit d'asile en Allemagne jusqu'à la réforme de 1993', 7 *IJRL* 260 (1995)
Achermann, A., 'Schengen und Asyl: Das Schengener Übereinkommen als Ausgangspunkt der Harmonisierung europäischer Asylpolitik', in Achermann, A., Bieber, R., Epiney, A., Wehner, R., *Schengen und die Folgen*, (1995), 79
——, 'Neuansetzung einer Ausreisefrist für "Tolerierte" — Bemerkungen zum Entscheid der Europäischen Menschenrechtskommission i. S. X. c. Schweiz vom 1.10.1990, Beschwerde Nr. 14912/89', *Asyl*, 1991/2, 19–20
—— & Gattiker, M., 'Safe Third Countries: European Developments', 7 *IJRL* 19 (1995)
Adelman, H., 'Humanitarian Intervention: The Case of the Kurds', 4 *IJRL* 4 (1992)
Aga Khan, Sadruddin, 'Legal Problems relating to Refugees and Displaced Persons', Hague *Recueil* (1976–I) 287
Akhavan, P., 'Punishing War Crimes in the Former Yugoslavia: A Critical Juncture for the New World Order', 15 *HRQ* 262 (1993)
Aleinikoff, T.A., 'Aliens, due process and "community ties": A response to Martin', 44 *Uni. Pittsburgh L.R.* 237 (1983)
Allen, R. & Hiller, H.H., 'Social Organization of Migration: An Analysis of the Uprooting and Flight of Vietnamese Refugees', 23 *Int. Mig.* 439 (1985)
Alston, P., 'The Committee on Economic, Social and Cultural Rights', in Alston, P., *The United Nations and Human Rights*, (1992), 473
Alvarez, L. & Loucky, J., 'Inquiry and Advocacy: Attorney-Expert Collaboration in the Political Asylum Process', 11 *NAPA Bulletin* 43 (1992) (American Anthropological Association)
Amnesty International, 'Turkey—Selective Protection: Discriminatory treatment of non-European refugees and asylum-seekers', Mar. 1994, AI Index EUR 44/16/94
——, 'Japan: Inadequate Protection for Refugees and Asylum Seekers', (1993); also published in 5 *IJRL* 205 (1993)
——, '5000 years in prison: Conscientious objectors in Greece', Mar. 1993
——, 'Europe: Harmonization of asylum policy. Accelerated procedures for "manifestly unfounded" asylum claims and the "safe country" concept.' AI EC Project, Brussels, Nov. 1992
——, 'Memorandum to the Governments of Hong Kong and the United Kingdom regarding the protection of Vietnamese Asylum-seekers in Hong Kong', Jan. 1990, AI Index ASA 19/01/90

Amnesty International, 'Sri Lanka: Continuing Human Rights Violations', May 1989, AI Index: ASA 37/04/89

Amnesty International British Section, *Playing Human Pinball: Home Office Practice in "Safe Third Country" Asylum Cases*, London, 1995

——, 'United Kingdom: Deficient Policy and Practice for the Protection of Asylum Seekers,' London, Nov. 1990

Anker, D.E., 'First Asylum Issues under United States Law', in Bhabha, J. & Coll, G., eds., *Asylum Law and Practice in Europe and North America*, (1992), 150

——, 'Determining Asylum Claims in the United States: Report of the Findings and Recommendations of an Empirical Study of Adjudication before the Immigration Court', 2 *IJRL* 252 (1990)

——, 'Discretionary Asylum: A Protection Remedy for Refugees under the Refugee Act of 1980', 28 *Virg. JIL* 1 (1987)

——, Blum, C.P. & Johnson, K.R., '*INS v. Zacarias:* Is There Anyone Out There?' 4 *IJRL* 266 (1992)

Arboleda, E., 'The Cartagena Declaration of 1984 and its Similarities to the 1969 OAU Convention—A Comparative Perspective,' 7 *IJRL Special Issue—Summer 1995* (1995)

——, 'Refugee Definition in Africa and Latin America: The Lessons of Pragmatism,' 3 *IJRL* 185 (1991)

—— & Hoy, I., 'The Convention Refugee Definition in the West: Disharmony of Interpretation and Application', 5 *IJRL* 66 (1993)

Avery, C., 'Refugee Status Decision-making: The Systems of Ten Countries', 19 *Stan. JIL*, 235 (1983)

Bach, R.L., 'Third Country Resettlement', in Loescher, G. & Monahan, L., eds., *Refugees and International Relations*, (1989), 313

Bagambiire, D., 'Terrorism and Convention Refugee Status in Canadian Immigration Law: The Social Group Category according to *Ward v. Canada*', 5 *IJRL* 183 (1993)

Baha'i International Community, *The Baha'is in Iran: A Report on the Persecution of a Religious Minority*, New York, 1982

Bakwesegha, C.J., 'The Role of the Organization of African Unity in Conflict Prevention, Management and Resolution', 7 *IJRL Special Issue—Summer 1995* 207 (1995)

Banks, D.L., 'The Analysis of Human Rights Data over Time', 8 *HRQ* 654 (1986)

Barcroft, P., 'Immigration and Asylum Law in the Republic of Ireland: Recent Developments and proposed Statutory Reform', 7 *IJRL* 84 (1995)

Bari, S., 'Refugee Status Determination under the Comprehensive Plan of Action (CPA)', 4 *IJRL* 487 (1992)

Barsh, R.L., 'Measuring Human Rights: Problems of Methodology and Purpose', 15 *HRQ* 87 (1993)

Batchelor, C.A., 'Stateless Persons: Some Gaps in International Protection', 7 *IJRL* 232 (1995)

Bettati, M., 'The right of humanitarian intervention or the right of free access to victims?' ICJ *Review*, No. 49, 1 (Dec. 1992)

Beyer, G.A., 'Establishing the United States Asylum Officers Corps: A First Report', 4 *IJRL* 455 (1992)

——, 'Affirmative Asylum Adjudication in the United States', 6 *Geo. Imm. L.J.* 253 (1992)

——, 'Monitoring Root Causes of Refugee Flows and Early Warning: The Need for Substance', 2 *IJRL Special Issue—September 1990* 71

——, 'Human Rights Monitoring and the Failure of Early Warning: A Practitioner's View', 2 *IJRL* 56 (1990)

——, 'Improving International Response to Humanitarian Situations,' Refugee Policy Group, Washington, D.C., Dec. 1989

Blay, S.K.N. & Tsamenyi, B.M., 'Reservations and Declarations under the 1951 Convention and the 1967 Protocol relating to the Status of Refugees', 2 *IJRL* 527 (1990)

—— & Zimmermann, A., 'Recent Changes in German Refugee Law: A Critical Assessment', 88 *AJIL* 361 (1994)

Blum, C.P., 'License to Kill: Asylum Law and the Principle of Legitimate Governmental Authority to "Investigate its Enemies" ', 28 *Willamette L.R.* 719 (1992)

——, 'Refugee Status based on Membership in a Particular Social Group: A North American Perspective', in Bhabha, J. & Coll, G., eds., *Asylum Law and Practice in Europe and North America*, (1992), 98

——, 'The Ninth Circuit and the Protection of Asylum Seekers since the Passage of the Refugee Act of 1980', 23 *San Diego L.R.* 327 (1986)

Bodart, S., 'Les réfugiés apolitiques: guerre civile et persécution de groupe au regard de la Convention de Genève', 7 *IJRL* 39 (1995)

Bois, P., 'La non-entrée en matière selon l'art. 16 I litt. a LAS et le recours contre le retrait de l'effet suspensif', *Asyl*, 1990/4, 11

Borgen, J. et al, 'Institutional Arrangements for Internally Displaced Persons: The Ground Level Experience,' Norwegian Refugee Council, 1 *Report* (1995)

Bovard, A., 'La procédure d'asile suisse', *Doc. réf.*, no. 213, supp., 30 mars/12 avr. 1993

Bronée, S.A., 'The History of the Comprehensive Plan of Action', 5 *IJRL* 534 (1993)

Buzan, B., 'Negotiating by Consensus: Developments in Techniques at the United Nations Conference on the Law of the Sea', 75 *AJIL* 324 (1981)

Byrnes, A., 'The Committee against Torture', in Alston, P., ed., *The United Nations and Human Rights*, (1992), 509

Campiche, M.-P., 'Entrée illégale et séjour irrégulier des réfugiés et requérants d'asile: La pratique des cantons', *Asyl*, 1994/3, 51

Carlier, J.-Y., 'La demande d'asile introduite par un mineur non accompagné', *RDDE*, 19–20 mai 1994, 94

Castel, J.R., 'Rape, Sexual Assault and the Meaning of Persecution', 4 *IJRL* 39 (1992)

Centre for Refugee Studies, York University, Toronto, 'Towards Practical Early Warning Capabilities concerning Refugees and Displaced Persons', 4 *IJRL* 84 (1992)

Cervenak, C.M., 'Promoting Inequality: Gender-Based Discrimination in UNRWA's Approach to Palestine Refugee Status', 16 *HRQ* 300 (1994)

Chandrahasan, N., 'Use of Force to ensure Humanitarian Relief — A South Asian Precedent examined', 42 *ICLQ* 664 (1993)

Charlesworth, H., 'The Declaration on the Elimination of All Forms of Violence against Women', *ASIL Insight*, No. 3, (1994)

Chimni, B.S., 'The Meaning of Words and the Role of UNHCR in Voluntary Repatriation', 5 *IJRL* 442 (1993)

——, 'Perspectives on Voluntary Repatriation: A Critical Note', 3 *IJRL* 541 (1991)

Citizenship and Immigration, International Refugee and Migration Policy Branch, 'Resettlement from Abroad Class', Discussion Paper, Apr. 1995

Clark, T., 'Human Rights and Expulsion: Giving Content to the Concept of Asylum', 4 *IJRL* 189 (1992)

Cohen, C.P., 'The Rights of the Child: Implications for Change in the Care and Protection of Refugee Children', 3 *IJRL* 675 (1991)

Cohen, R., 'Human Rights Protection for Internally Displaced Persons', Refugee Policy Group, (1991)

Cohn, I., 'The Convention on the Rights of the Child: What it Means for Children in War', 3 *IJRL* 291 (1991)

Commission de l'immigration et du statut de réfugié, 'Ahmadis du Pakistan: mise à jour décembre 1991 à octobre 1993', (1994)

Corey, J.M., 'INS v Doherty: The Politics of Extradition, Deportation and Asylum', 16 *Maryland J.Int'l. L & Trade* 83 (1992)

Corliss, S., 'Asylum State Responsibility for the Hostile Acts of Foreign Exiles', 2 *IJRL* 181 (1990)

Crawford, J., 'Australian Immigration Law and Refugees: The 1989 Amendments', 2 *IJRL* 626 (1990)

—— & Hyndman, P., 'Three Heresies in the Application of the Refugee Convention', 1 *IJRL* 152 (1989)

Cuellar, R., García-Sayán, D., Montaño, J., Diegues, M. & Valladares Lanza, L., 'Refugee and Related Developments in Latin America: The Challenges Ahead', 3 *IJRL* 482 (1991)

D'Alotto, A. & Garretón, R., 'Developments in Latin America: Some Further Thoughts', 3 *IJRL* 499 (1991)

D'Amato, A., 'On Consensus', 8 *Can. YIL* 104 (1970)

Degni-Ségui, R., 'Rapports sur la situation des droits de l'homme au Rwanda du 28 juin 1994 et du 12 août 1994', 13 *RSQ*, Nos. 2 & 3, 116 (1994)

Deng, F.M., 'The International Protection of the Internally Displaced', 7 *Special Issue—Summer 1995* 74 (1995)

Dieng, A., 'Addressing the Root Causes of Forced Population Displacements in Africa: A Theoretical Model', 7 *IJRL Special Issue—Summer 1995* 119 (1995)

Dignam, Q., 'The Burden of Proof: Torture and Testimony in the Determination of Refugee Status in Australia', 4 *IJRL* 343 (1992)

Dimitrichev, T.F., 'Conceptual Approaches to Early Warning: Mechanisms and Methods—A View from the United Nations', 3 *IJRL* 264 (1991)

Donnelly, J. & Howard, R.E., 'Assessing Nations Human Rights Performance: A Theoretical Framework', 10 *HRQ* 214 (1988)

Eggleston, Sir Richard, 'What is Wrong with the Adversary System?' 49 *Australian Law Journal* 428 (1975)

——, 'Is Your Cross-Examination Really Necessary?' *Proceedings of the Medico-Legal Society of Victoria*, vol. IX, 84 (1961)

Einarsen, T., 'The European Convention on Human Rights and the Notion of an Implied Right to *de facto* Asylum,' 2 *IJRL* 361 (1990)

Epps, V., 'The Validity of the Political Offence Exception in Extradition Treaties in Anglo-American Jurisprudence,' 20 *Harv. ILJ* 61 (1979)

European Council on Refugees and Exiles, 'Safe Third Countries: Myths and Realities', (1995)

——, 'A European policy in the light of established principles,' Apr. 1994

——, 'Fair and Efficient Procedures for Determining Refugee Status: A Proposal', 2 *IJRL Special Issue—September 1990* 112 (1990)

Fan, R., 'Hong Kong and the Vietnamese Boat People: A Hong Kong Perspective', 2 *IJRL Special Issue—September 1990* 144 (1990)

Federal Ministry of the Interior, 'Recent Developments in the German Law on Asylum and Aliens', 6 *IJRL* 265 (1994)

Fehervary, A., 'Citizenship, Statelessness and Human Rights: Recent Developments in the Baltic States', 5 *IJRL* 392 (1993)

Feliciano, F.P., 'The Principle of *Non-Refoulement*: A Note on International Legal Protection of Refugees and Displaced Persons,' 57 *Philippine L.J.* 598 (1982)

Feller, E., 'Carrier Sanctions and International Law', 1 *IJRL* 48 (1989)

Fisher Williams, J., 'Denationalization', 8 *BYIL* 45 (1927)

Fitzpatrick, J. & Pauw, R., 'Foreign Policy, Asylum and Discretion', 28 *Willamette L.R.* 751 (1992)

Fong, Chooi, 'Some Legal Aspects of the Search for Admission into other States of Persons leaving the Indo-Chinese Peninsular in Small Boats', 52 *BYIL* 53

Fonteyne, J.-P., 'Overview of Refugee Determination Procedures in Australia', 6 *IJRL* 253 (1994)

——, 'Burden-Sharing: An Analysis of the Nature and Function of International Solidarity in Cases of Mass Influx of Refugees', 8 *Aust. YB Int'l Law* 162 (1983)

Frelick, B., '"Preventive Protection" and the Right to Seek Asylum: A Preliminary Look at Bosnia and Croatia', 4 *IJRL* 439 (1992)

Frowein, J. Abr. & Kühner, R., 'Drohende Folterung als Asylgrund und Grenze für Auslieferung und Ausweisung', 35/36 *ZaöRV* 538

Fullerton, M., 'A Comparative Look at Refugee Status based on Persecution due to Membership in a Particular Group', 26 *Cornell Int'l L.J.* 505 (1993)

——, 'Persecution due to membership in a particular social group: Jurisprudence in the Federal Republic of Germany', 4 *Georgetown Imm.L.J.* 381 (1990)

Garcia Marquez, G., 'The Vietnam Wars', *Rolling Stone*, May 1980

Gasarasi, C.P., 'The Mass Naturalization and further Integration of Rwandese Refugees in Tanzania: Process, Problems and Prospects', 3 *JRS* 88 (1990)

Gattiker, M. & Illes, R., 'Kosovo: Trends in der deutschen und schweizerischen Asylrechtsprechung', *Asyl* (1993/2), 32

Gersony, R., 'Why Somalis flee,' 2 *IJRL* 4 (1990)

——, 'Summary of Mozambican Refugee Accounts of Principally Conflict-Related Experience in Mozambique', US Department of State, US Government Printing Office, Washington, D.C., Apr. 1988

Gibney, M., 'A "Well-founded Fear" of Persecution', 10 *HRQ* 109 (1988)

Gold, M.E., 'Non-extradition for political offences: the Communist perspective,' 11 *Harv. ILJ* 191 (1970)

Goldstein, R.J., 'The Limitations of Using Quantitative Data in Studying Human Rights Abuses', 8 *HRQ* 607 (1986)

Goodwin-Gill, G.S., 'The Right to Leave, the Right to Return and the Question of a Right to Remain', in Gowlland-Debbas, V., *The Problem of Refugees in the Light of Contemporary International Law Issues*, (1995), 95

——, 'Asylum: The Law and Politics of Change', 7 *IJRL* 1 (1995)

——, 'UNHCR and International Protection: Old Problems—New Directions', 5 *IJRL* 1 (1993)

——, 'Chi é un rifugiato', *Politica internazionale*, No. 5, sett-ott, 1991, 41

Goodwin-Gill, G.S., 'Different Types of Forced Migration Movements as an International and National Problem', in Rystad, G., ed., *The Uprooted: Forced Migration as an International Problem in the Post-War Era*, (1990), 15

——, 'Voluntary Repatriation: Legal and Policy Issues', in Loescher, G. & Monahan, L., *Refugees and International Relations*, (1989), 255

——, 'The Language of Protection,' 1 *IJRL* 6 (1989)

——, 'International Law and Human Rights: Trends concerning International Migrants and Refugees', 23 *Int.Mig.Rev.* 526 (1989)

——, 'Refugees: The Functions and Limits of the Existing Protection System,' in Nash, A., *Human Rights and the Protection of Refugees under International Law*, (1988), 149

——, '*Non-refoulement* and the New Asylum Seekers,' 26 *Virg. JIL* 897 (1986)

——, 'The detention of non-nationals, with particular reference to refugees and asylum-seekers', 9 *In Defense of the Alien* 138 (1986)

——, 'International Law and the detention of refugees and asylum-seekers', 20 *Int. Mig. Rev.* 193 (1986)

Gordenker, L., 'Early Warning of Disastrous Population Movements', 20 *Int. Mig. Rev.* 170 (1986)

Gorlick, B., 'Refugee Protection and the Committee against Torture', 7 *IJRL* 504 (1995)

Gorman, R., 'Poets, Playwrights, and the Politics of Exile and Asylum in Ancient Greece and Rome', 6 *IJRL* 402 (1994)

——, 'Revenge and Reconciliation: Shakespearean Models of Exile and Banishment', 2 *IJRL* 211 (1990)

Gortázar C.F., 'The Implementation Rules of the new Spanish Asylum Law', 7 *IJRL* 506 (1995)

Gowlland-Debbas, V., 'Security Council Enforcement Action and Issues of State Responsibility', 43 *ICLQ* 55 (1994)

Grahl-Madsen, A., 'Protection of Refugees by their Country of Origin', 11 *Yale JIL* 362 (1986)

Grant, S., 'Protection Mechanisms and the Yugoslav Crisis', *Interights Bulletin*, 8:1 (1994)

Greene, I. & Schaffer, P., 'Leave to Appeal and Leave to commence Judicial Review in Canada's Refugee Determination System: Is the Process Fair?' 4 *IJRL* 71 (1992)

Groenendijk, C.A., 'The Competence of the EC Court of Justice with respect to inter-governmental Treaties on Immigration and Asylum', 4 *IJRL* 531 (1992)

Gros Espiell, H., Picado, S. & Valladares Lanza, L., 'Principles and Criteria for the Protection of and Assistance to Central American Refugees, Returnees and Displaced Persons in Central America', 2 *IJRL* 83 (1990)

Guedalla, V., 'Representing unaccompanied refugee children in the asylum process', *Childright*, Dec. 1994, No. 112

Guest, I., 'The United Nations, the UNHCR, and Refugee Protection—A Non-Specialist Analysis', 3 *IJRL* 585 (1991)

Hailbronner, K., 'The Concept of "Safe Country" and Expeditious Asylum Procedures: A Western European Perspective', 5 *IJRL* 31 (1994)

——, 'Rechtsfragen der Aufnahme von "Gewaltflüchtlingen" in Westeuropa—am Beispiel Jugoslawien', (1993) *Schweizerische Zeitschrift für internationales und europäisches Recht*, 517

——, 'Perspectives of a Harmonization of the Law of Asylum after the Maastricht Summit,' 29 *CMLR* 917 (1992)

——, 'The Right to Asylum and the Future of Asylum Procedures in the European Community', 2 *IJRL* 341 (1990)

——, '*Non-refoulement* and "Humanitarian" Refugees: Customary International Law or Wishful Legal Thinking?', 26 *Virg JIL* 857 (1986)

Hamerslag, R.J., 'The Schiphol Refugee Centre Case', 1 *IJRL* 395 (1989)

Hampson, F.J., 'The Concept of an "Arguable Claim" under Article 13 of the European Convention on Human Rights', 39 *ICLQ* 891 (1990)

Hathaway, J., 'A Reconsideration of the Underlying Premise of Refugee Law', 31 *Harv. Int.L.J.* 129 (1990)

——, 'The Evolution of Refugee Status in International Law: 1920–1950', 33 *ICLQ* 348 (1984)

Hausammann, C., 'Die Beurteilung frauenspezifischer Verfolgung in Asylverfahren', Erster Teil, *Asyl*, 1991/4 7; Zweiter Teil, 1992/1, 3

Helton, A.C., 'Refugee Determination under the Comprehensive Plan of Action; Overview and Assessment', 5 *IJRL* 544 (1993)

——, 'Persecution on Account of Membership in a Social Group as a Basis for Refugee Status', 15 *Col. Hum. Rts.L.R.* 39 (1983)

Hernandez, C.E., 'Asylum and Refugee Status in Spain', 4 *IJRL* 57 (1992)

Higgins, R., 'The United Nations and Former Yugoslavia', 69 *International Affairs* 3 (1993)

——, 'Derogations under Human Rights Treaties', 48 *BYIL* 281 (1976–77)

Hofmann, R., 'Voluntary Repatriation and UNHCR', 44 *ZaöRV* 327 (1984)

Houle, F., 'The Credibility and Authoritativeness of Documentary Information in Determining Refugee Status: The Canadian Experience', 6 *IJRL* 6 (1994)

Hyndman, P., 'Asylum and *Non-Refoulement*—Are these Obligations owed to Refugees under International Law?', 57 *Philippine L.J.* 43 (1982)

Immigration and Naturalization Service, Department of Justice, *Worldwide Guidelines for Overseas Refugee Processing*, (Aug. 1983)

Immigration and Refugee Board of Canada, 'IRB: Guidelines on Gender-Related Persecution', 5 *IJRL* 278 (1993)

Immigration and Refugee Board Documentation Centre (IRBDC), 'CIS, Baltic States and Georgia: Nationality Legislation (April 1992)', 4 *IJRL* 230 (1992)

——, 'Haiti: The Impact of the September 1991 Coup (June 1992)', 4 *IJRL* 217 (1992)

——, 'Bulgaria: The Impact of Reform (May 1991)', 3 *IJRL* 288 (1991)

——, 'Bulgaria: Political Parties and Groups (April 1991)', 3 *IJRL* 273 (1991)

——, 'Lebanon: Country Profile', 1 *IJRL* 331 (1989)

International Commission of Jurists/Centre for the Independence of Judges and Lawyers, 'The Civilian Judicial System in the West Bank and Gaza: Present and Future', June 1994

Iogna-Prat, M., 'The Notion of "Membership of a Particular Social Group" from the Point of View of European Jurisprudence', in Bhabha, J. & Coll, G., eds., *Asylum Law and Practice in Europe and North America*, (1992), 87

——, 'L'Affaire Bereciartua-Echarri', 1 *IJRL* 403 (1989)

Iza, A.O., 'The Asylum and Refugee Procedure in the Argentine Legal System', 6 *IJRL* 643 (1994)

Jackman, B., 'Well-founded fear of persecution and other standards of decision-making: A North American perspective', in Bhabha, J. & Coll, G., *Asylum Law and Practice in Europe and North America*, (1992), 44

Jackson, I.C., 'The 1951 Convention relating to Status of Refugees: A Universal Basis for Protection', 3 *IJRL* 403 (1991)

Jahn, E. 'The Work of the Asian-African Legal Consultative Committee on the Legal Staus of Refugees', 27 *Zeitschrift für ausländishes offentliches Recht und Völkerrecht* 122 (1967)

Jennings, R.Y., 'Some International Law Aspects of the Refugee Question', 20 *BYIL* 98 (1939)

Johnson, D.H.N. 'Refugees, Departees and Illegal Migrants', 9 *Sydney LR* 11 (1980)

Johnsson, A.B., 'The Duties of Refugees', 3 *IJRL* 579 (1991)

——, 'The International Protection of Women Refugees', 1 *IJRL* 221 (1989)

Joly, D., 'The Porous Dam: European Harmonization on Asylum in the Nineties', 6 *IJRL* 159 (1994)

Julien-Laferrière, F., 'Droit d'asile et politique d'asile en France', *Asyl* 1993/4, 75

——, 'Commentaire des résolutions et conclusions adoptées par le Conseil européen d'Edimbourg sur le pays où il n'existe pas de risques sérieux de persécution, les pays tiers d'accueil et les demandes manifestement infondées', *Doc. réf.* no. 205–6, supp., 17 déc. 1992

——, 'Le contentieux en matière de réfugiés en France: deux arrêts récents', *Doc. réf.*, no. 139, 27 fevr./8 mars 1991, Suppl., 7

Kälin, W., 'The Legal Condition of Refugees in Switzerland,' 24 *Swiss Reports presented at the XIVth International Congress of Comparative Law*, 57 (1994)

——, 'Safe Return for Refugees of Violence: A Blueprint for Action,' in Gowlland, V. and Sampson, K., *Problems and Prospects of Refugee Law*, (1992), 125

——, 'Refugees and Civil Wars: Only a Matter of Interpretation?' 3 *IJRL* 435 (1991)

——, 'Troubled Communication: Cross-Cultural Misunderstandings in the Asylum Hearing', 20 *Int. Mig. Rev.* 230 (1986)

Kelly, N., 'Guidelines for Women's Asylum Claims', 6 *IJRL* 517 (1994)

——, 'Report on the International Consultation on Refugee Women, held in Geneva, 15–19 November 1988', 1 *IJRL* 233 (1989)

Kennedy, D., 'International Refugee Protection', 8 *HRQ* 1 (1986)

Kirişçi, K., 'Asylum seekers and Human Rights in Turkey', 10 *Neth.Q.H.R.* 447 (1992)

Kiss, A., 'La convention européenne et la clause de la nation la plus favorisée', *Ann. Fr.* 478 (1957)

Kjaerum, M., 'Temporary Protection in Europe in the 1990s', 6 *IJRL* 444 (1994)

——, 'The Concept of Country of First Asylum', 4 *IJRL* 514 (1992)

Kooijmans, P. H., 'Ambiguities in Refugee Law: Some Remarks on the Concept of the Country of First Asylum', in Nowak, M., Steurer, D., & Tretter, H., eds., *Fortschritt im Bewusstsein der Grund-und Menschenrechte. Progress in the Spirit of Human Rights. Festschrift für Felix Ermacora*, (1988), 401

Kussbach, E., 'The 1991 Austrian Asylum Law', 6 *IJRL* 227 (1994)

Landgren, K., 'Safety Zones and International Protection: A Dark Grey Area', 7 *IJRL* 436 (1995)

Le Xuan Khoa, 'Forced Repatriation of Asylum Seekers: The Case of Hong Kong', 2 *IJRL Special Issue—September 1990*, 137 (1990)

LeBlanc, L. J., 'The Intent to Destroy Groups in the Genocide Convention: The Proposed U.S. Understanding', 78 *AJIL* 369 (1984)

Lee, L.T., 'The declaration of principles of international law on compensation to refugees: its significance and implications', 6 *JRS* 65 (1993)

——, 'The right to compensation: Refugees and countries of asylum', 80 *AJIL* 532 (1986)

Legomsky, S.H., 'Political Asylum and the Theory of Judicial Review', 73 *Minnesota L.R.* 1205 (1989)

Lillich, R., 'Notes and Comments: The *Soering* Case', 85 *AJIL* 128 (1991)

——, 'Civil Rights', in Meron, T., ed., *Human Rights in International Law*, (1984), 15

Luca, D., 'Questioning Temporary Protection, together with a Selected Bibliography on Temporary Refuge/Temporary Protection', 6 *IJRL* 535 (1994)

——, 'La notion de "solution" au problème des réfugiés', *Revue de droit international*, janv.-mars 1987, 1

Macklin, A., '*Canada (Attorney-General) v. Ward:* A Review Essay', 6 *IJRL* 362 (1994)

Mahmoud, S., 'The Schengen Information System: An Inequitable Data Protection Regime', 7 *IJRL* 179 (1995)

Maluwa, T., 'The Domestic Implementation of International Refugee Law: A Brief Note on Malawi's Refugee Act of 1989', 3 *IJRL* 503 (1991)

Martin, D.A., 'Reforming Asylum Adjudication: On Navigating the Coast of Bohemia', 138 *Uni. Penn. L.R.* 1247 (1990)

——, 'Effects of International Law on Migration Policy and Practice', 23 *Int. Mig. Rev.* 547 (1989)

——, 'Due Process and the treatment of aliens', 44 *Uni. Pittsburgh L.R.* 165, (1983)

——, 'Large Scale Migrations of Asylum Seekers,' 76 *AJIL* 598 (1982)

Marx, R., '*Non-refoulement*, Access to Procedures and Responsibility to Determine Claims', 7 *IJRL* 383 (1995)

——, 'Temporary Protection—Refugees from Former Yugoslavia: International Protection or Solution Orientated Approach?', ECRE, June 1994

——, 'The Criteria for the Determination of Refugee Status in the Federal Republic of Germany', 4 *IJRL* 151 (1992)

Mawani, N., 'Introduction to the Immigration and Refugee Board of Canada Guidelines on Gender-Related Persecution', 5 *IJRL* 240 (1993)

McAllister, D.M., 'Refugees and Public Access to Immigration Hearings in Canada: A Clash of Constitutional Values', 2 *IJRL* 562 (1990)

McCallin, M., 'Living in Detention: A review of the psychological well-being of Vietnamese children in the Hong Kong detention centres', International Catholic Child Bureau, Geneva, (1992)

——, 'The Convention on the Rights of the Child: An Instrument to Address the Psychosocial Needs of Refugee Children', 2 *IJRL Special Issue—September 1990* 82 (1990)

McDowall, R., 'Co-ordination of Refugee Policy in Europe', in Loescher, G. and Monahan, L., *Refugees and International Relations*, (1989), 179

McKean, W.A., 'The Meaning of Discrimination in International and Municipal Law', 44 *BYIL* 177 (1970)

McLeod, M., 'Legal Protection of Refugee Children separated from their Parents: Selected Issues', 27 *Int. Mig.* 295 (1989)

McNair, Lord (Arnold Duncan McNair), 'Extradition and Exterritorial Asylum', 28 *BYIL* 172 (1951)

McNamara, D., 'The Origins and Effects of "Humane Deterrence" Policies in South-east Asia', in Loescher, G. & Monahan, L., eds., *Refugees and International Relations*, (1989), 123

Médecins sans Frontières/Artsen zonder Grenzen, 'Awareness Survey: Rohingya Refugee Camps, Cox's Bazar District, Bangladesh, 15 March 1995', The Netherlands, 1995

Melander, G., 'The Principle of "Country of First Asylum" from a European Perspective', in Bhabha, J. & Coll, G., eds., *Asylum Law and Practice in Europe and North America*, (1992), 122

Mendiluce, J.-M., 'War and Disaster in the Former Yugoslavia: The Limits of Humanitarian Action', in US Committee for Refugees, *World Refugee Survey—1994*, 10

Menjivar, C., 'Salvadorian Migration to the United States in the 1980s: What can we learn *about* it and *from* it?', 32 *Int. Mig.* 371 (1994)

Meron, T., 'Rape as a Crime under International Humanitarian Law', 87 *AJIL* 424 (1993)

——, 'On a Hierarchy of International Human Rights', 80 *AJIL* 1 (1987)

Merrills, J.G., 'Interim Measures of Protection in the Recent Jurisprudence of the International Court of Justice', 44 *ICLQ* 90 (1995)

Mirdal, G.M., 'The Interpreter in Cross-Cultural Therapy', 26 *Int. Mig.* 327 (1988)

Mooney, E.D., 'Presence, *ergo* protection? UNPROFOR, UNHCR and the ICRC in Croatia and Bosnia and Herzegovina', 7 *IJRL* 407 (1995)

Morgenstern, F., 'The Right of Asylum', 26 *BYIL* 327 (1949)

Morris, N., 'Refugees: Facing Crisis in the 1990s—A Personal View from within UNHCR', 2 *IJRL Special Issue—September 1990*, 38 (1990)

Mtango, E.-E., 'Military and Armed Attacks on Refugee Camps', in Loescher, G. & Monahan, L., eds., *Refugees and International Relations*, (1989), 87

Musalo, K., 'Irreconcilable Differences? Divorcing Refugee Protections from Human Rights Norms', 15 *Mich. J. Int. Law* 1179 (1994)

——, 'Swords into Ploughshares: Why the United States should provide refuge to young men who refuse to bear arms for reasons of conscience', 26 *San Diego L.Rev.* 849 (1989)

Mushkat, R., 'Implementation of the CPA in Hong Kong: Compatibility with International Standards?', 5 *IJRL* 559 (1993)

——, 'Refuge in Hong Kong', 1 *IJRL* 449 (1989)

——, 'Hong Kong as a country of temporary refuge: an interim analysis', 12 *Hong Kong LJ* 157 (1982)

Nagy, B., 'Asylum Seekers and Refugees: Hungarian Dilemmas', 34 *Acta Juridica Hungarica*, (1992), No. 1-2, 27

——, 'Before or After the Wave? The Adequacy of the New Hungarian Refugee Law', 3 *IJRL* 529 (1991)

Nascimbene, B., 'The Case of Albanians in Italy: Is the Right of Asylum under Attack?', 3 *IJRL* 714 (1991)

Nobel, P., 'What Happened with Sweden's Refugee Policies?', 2 *IJRL* 265 (1990)

Norway, 'Temporary Protection: Summary and Recommendations from the Report of the Inter-Ministerial Working Group, Norway, April 1993', 5 *IJRL* 477 (1993)

Norwegian Refugee Council & Refugee Policy Group, 'Roundtable Discussion on United Nations Human Rights Protection for Internally Displaced Persons', Nyon, Switzerland, Feb. 1993

Note, 'The indefinite detention of excluded aliens: statutory and constitutional justifications and limitations', 82 *Mich. L. Rev.* 61 (1983)

OAU/UNHCR, 'The Addis Ababa Symposium 1994', 7 *IJRL Special Issue—Summer 1995*, (1995)

O'Donnell, D., 'Resettlement or Repatriation: Screened-out Vietnamese Child Asylum Seekers and the Convention on the Rights of the Child', 6 *IJRL* 382 (1994)

Oliver, P., 'The French Constitution and the Treaty of Maastricht', 43 *ICLQ* 1 (1994)

Oloka-Onyango, J., 'The Place and Role of the OAU Bureau for Refugees in the African Refugee Crisis', 6 *IJRL* 34 (1994)

——, 'Human Rights, the OAU Convention and the Refugee Crisis in Africa', 3 *IJRL* 453 (1991)

Opsahl, T., 'The Human Rights Committee', in Alston, P., *The United Nations and Human Rights*, (1992), 369

Osborne, M., 'The Indo-chinese Refugees: Causes and Effects', *International Affairs*, (1980), 37

Perluss, D. and Hartman, J., 'Temporary Refuge: Emergence of a Customary International Norm', 26 *Virg. JIL* 551 (1986)

Perruchoud, R., 'Persons falling under the Mandate of the International Organization for Migration, to Whom the Organization may Provide Migration Services', 4 *IJRL* 205 (1992)

——, 'From the Intergovernmental Committee for European Migration to the International Organization for Migration', 1 *IJRL* 501 (1989)

Petrasek, D., 'New Standards for the Protection of Internally Displaced Persons: A Proposal for a Comprehensive Approach', 14 *RSQ*, Nos. 1 & 2, 285 (1995)

Physicians for Human Rights, *Winds of Death: Iraq's use of Poisonous Gas against its Kurdish Population*, (1989)

Piper, T., 'Myanmar: Exodus and Return of Muslims from Rakhine State', 13 *RSQ*, No. 1, 11 (1994)

Plender, R., 'The Legal Basis of International Jurisdiction to act with regard to the Internally Displaced', 6 *IJRL* 345 (1994)

Pompe, C.A., 'The Convention of 28 July 1951 and the international protection of refugees', HCR/INF/42 (May 1958) 10, n. 3; originally published in Dutch in *Rechtsgeleerd Magazyn Themis*, (1956), 425

Prunier, G., 'La crise rwandaise: Structures et déroulement', 13 *RSQ*, Nos. 2 & 3, 13 (1994)

Pugash, J.Z., 'The Dilemma of the Sea Refugee: Rescue without Refuge', 18 *Harv. ILJ* 577 (1977)

Radley, K.R., 'The Palestinian Refugees: The Right to Return in International Law', 72 *AJIL* 586 (1978)

Ramcharan, B.G., 'Early Warning at the United Nations: The First Experiment', 1 *IJRL* 379 (1989)

Raoul Wallenberg Institute, *Responsibility for Examining an Asylum Request*, Report of a Seminar in Lund, 24–26 April 1985, Report No. 1 (1986)

Reale, E., 'Le droit d'asile', Hague *Recueil* (1938–I), 473

——, 'Le problème des passeports', Hague *Recueil* (1934–IV), 89

Refugee Policy Group, 'Internally Displaced Persons in Africa: Assistance Challenges and Opportunities', (1992)

——, 'Humanitarian Action in the Post Cold War Era', Background Paper and Conference Summary, Bellagio, Italy, May 1992

——, 'Human Rights Protection for Internally Displaced Persons', Report of an International Conference, 24–25 June 1991

Refugee Policy Group, 'Improving International Response to Humanitarian Situations', (1989)

——, 'U.S. Refugee Admissions: Processing in Europe', (Mar. 1985)

Reiter, R.B., Zunzunequi, M.V. & Quiroga, J., 'Guidelines for Field Reporting of Basic Human Rights Violations', 8 *HRQ* 628 (1986)

Rikhof, J., 'War Crimes, Crimes against Humanity and Immigration Law', 19 *Imm. L.R.* (2d) 18

Riveles, S., 'Diplomatic Asylum as a Human Right: The Case of the Durban Six', 11 *HRQ* 139 (1989)

Rizvi, Z., 'Causes of the Refugee Problem and the International Response', in Nash, A.E., ed., *Human Rights and the Protection of Refugees under International Law*, (1988), 107

Ruff, A., 'The United Kingdom Immigration (Carriers' Liability) Act 1987: Implications for Refugees and Airlines', 1 *IJRL* 481 (1989)

Ruiz, H.A., 'Early Warning Is Not Enough: The Failure to Prevent Starvation in Ethiopia, 1990', 2 *IJRL Special Issue—September 1990* 83 (1990)

Rusu, S., 'Refugees, Information and Solutions: The Need for Informed Decision-Making', 13 *RSQ*, No. 1, 4 (1994)

——, 'The Role of the Collector in Early Warning', 2 *IJRL Special Issue—September 1990* 65 (1990)

——, 'The Development of Canada's Immigration and Refugee Board Documentation Centre', 1 *IJRL* 319 (1989)

Rwelamira, M., '1989—An Anniversary Year: The 1969 OAU Convention on the Specific Aspects of Refugee Problems in Africa', 1 *IJRL* 557 (1989)

Samuels, H., 'The Detention of Vietnamese Asylum Seekers in Hong Kong: *Re Pham Van Hgo and 110 Others*', 41 *ICLQ* 422 (1992)

Sandoz, Y., '"Droit" or "devoir" d'ingérence and the right to assistance: the issues involved', ICJ *Review*, No. 49, 12 (Dec. 1992)

Schnyder, F., 'Les aspects juridiques actuels du problème des réfugiés', Hague *Recueil* (1965–I) 339

Singer, S., 'The protection of children during armed conflict situations', *International Review of the Red Cross*, May–June 1986, 133

Steenbergen, H.D.M., 'The Relevance of the European Convention on Human Rights for Asylum Seekers', in Baehr, P. R. & Tessenyi, G., eds., *The New Refugee Hosting Countries: Call for Experience-Space for Innovation*, (1991), 45

Stevens, D., 'Re-introduction of the United Kingdom Asylum Bill', 5 *IJRL* 91 (1993)

Stohl, M., Carleton, D., Lopez, G., & Samuels, S., 'States' Violation of Human Rights: Issues and Problems of Measurement', 8 *HRQ* 592 (1986)

Stravropoulou, M., 'Refugee Law in Greece', 6 *IJRL* 53 (1994)

Sztucki, J., 'The Conclusions on the International Protection of Refugees adopted by the Executive Committee of the UNHCR Programme', 1 *IJRL* 285 (1989)

Takkenberg, L., 'Detention and other restrictions of the freedom of movement of refugees and asylum seekers: The European perspective', in Bhabha, J. & Coll, G., *Asylum Law and Practice in Europe and North America*, (1992), 178

——, 'The Protection of Palestine Refugees in the Territories Occupied by Israel', 3 *IJRL* 414 (1991)

Tang Lay Lee, 'Stateless Persons and the Comprehensive Plan of Action-Part 1: Chinese Nationality and the Republic of China (Taiwan)', 7 *IJRL* 201 (1995)

Thayer, C., 'Vietnam—Beleaguered Outpost of Socialism', 79 *Current History*, No. 461, (1980)

——, 'Dilemmas of Development in Vietnam', 75 *Current History*, No. 442, (1978)

Thomas, D.Q. & Beasley, M.E., 'Domestic Violence as a Human Rights Issue', 15 *HRQ* 36 (1993)

Thorburn, J., 'Transcending Boundaries: Temporary Protection and Burden-Sharing in Europe', 7 *IJRL* 459 (1995)

Tiberghien, F., 'La crise yougoslave devant la Commission des recours', *Doc. réf.*, no. 223, 17/30 août 1993, Suppl., CJ, 1

——, 'La Commission des recours et l'article 1er, F de la Convention de Genève', *Doc. réf.* no. 169, 19 dec. 1991/1er janv. 1992, Suppl., JC, 1

——, 'L'expulsion des réfugiés: Problèmes legislatifs et jurisprudentiels', *Doc. réf.*, no. 73, 5/14 mars 1989, Suppl., CJ, 1

——, 'Le lieu d'exercice des persecutions', *Doc. réf.* no. 67, 6/15 mars 1989, 1

——, 'L'étendue du contrôle du Conseil d'Etat sur les decisions de la Commission des Recours', *Doc. réf.*, no. 55, Suppl., CJ, 1

——, 'Le champ d'application de l'article 1er, A, 2 de la Convention de Genève', *Doc. réf.* no. 49, 7/16 sept. 1988, Suppl., CJ, 1

——, 'L'article 1er, F de la Convention de Geneve: Tendances récentes de la jurisprudence', *Doc. réf.* no. 43, 9/18 juillet 1988, Suppl., CJ, 1

Trenholme, N.M., 'The Right of Sanctuary in England', 1 *Univ. Missouri Studies*, No. 5 (1903)

Troeller, G.G., 'UNHCR Resettlement as an Instrument of International Protection', 3 *IJRL* 564 (1991)

Uibopuu, H.-J., 'Ss. 7(2) Asylgesetz und der "anderweitige Schutz" des Asylbewerbers', 34 *Österr. Z. Recht und Völkerrecht* 30 (1984)

UNHCR, 'The Concept of "Protection Elsewhere" ', 7 *IJRL* 123 (1995)

United Kingdom Delegation, Geneva, 'Sending Asylum Seekers to Safe Third Countries', 7 *IJRL* 119 (1995)

US Committee for Refugees, 'Genocide in Rwanda: Documentation of two Massacres during April 1994', (1994)

——, 'The Usual People: Refugees and Internally Displaced Persons from Sierra Leone', (1995)

——, 'Transition in Burundi: The Context for a Homecoming', (1993)

——, 'Left out in the Cold: The perilous homecoming of Afghan refugees', (1992)

——, 'Croatia's Crucible: Providing Asylum for Refugees from Bosnia and Herzegovina', (1992)

——, 'Refugees at our Borders: The U.S. Response to Asylum Seekers', (1989)

——, 'Uncertain Harbors: The Plight of Vietnamese Boat People', (1987)

——, 'Despite a Generous Spirit: Denying Asylum in the United States', (1986)

——, 'The Asylum Challenge to Western Nations', (1984)

Van den Wyngaert, C., 'Applying the European Convention on Human Rights to Extradition: Opening Pandora's Box?', 39 *ICLQ* 757 (1990)

von Sternberg, M.R., 'Political Asylum and the Law of Internal Armed Conflict: Refugee Status, Human Rights and Humanitarian Law Concerns', 5 *IJRL* 153 (1993)

——, 'Emerging Bases of "Persecution" in American Refugee Law: Political Opinion and the Dilemma of Neutrality', 13 *Suffolk Transnat'l L.J.* 1 (1989)

Ward, I., 'The Story of M: A Cautionary Tale from the United Kingdom', 6 *IJRL* 194 (1994)

Weil, P., 'Towards Relative Normativity in International Law?', 77 *AJIL* 413 (1985)

Weinman, S.C., '*INS v. Stevic*: A Critical Assessment', 7 *HRQ* 391 (1985)

Weis, P., 'Legal Aspects of the Convention of 28 July 1951 relating to the Status of Refugees', 30 *BYIL* 478 (1953)

——, 'The International Protection of Refugees', 48 *AJIL* 193 (1954)

——, 'The International Status of Refugees and Stateless Persons', *Journal du Droit International* 4 (1956)

——, 'Refugee Seamen', 7 *ICLQ* 340 (1958)

——, 'The Concept of the Refugee in International Law', *Journal du droit international*, (1960) 1

——, 'The Convention relating to the Status of Stateless Persons', 10 *ICLQ* 255 (1961)

——, 'The United Nations Convention on the Reduction of Statelessness, 1961', 11 *ICLQ* 1073 (1962)

——, 'Territorial Asylum', 6 *Indian Journal of International Law* 173 (1966)

——, 'The 1967 Protocol relating to the Status of Refugees and some Questions of the Law of Treaties', 42 *BYIL* 39 (1967)

——, 'The United Nations Declaration on Territorial Asylum', 7 *Can. YIL* 92 (1969)

——, 'The Legal Aspects of the Problems of *de facto* Refugees', in International University Exchange Fund, *Problems of Refugees and Exiles in Europe*, (1974)

——, 'The Draft United Nations Convention on Territorial Asylum', 50 *BYIL* 151 (1980)

Wierzbicki, B., 'Political Asylum in International Law', *Revue héllenique de droit international*, 1985–1986, 11, (1988)

Wiseberg, L.S., 'Protecting Human Rights Activists and NGOs: What More can be Done?', 13 *HRQ* 525 (1991)

Wolf, D., 'A Subtle Form of Inhumanity: Screening of the Boat People in Hong Kong', 2 *IJRL Special Issue—September 1990* 161 (1990)

Yahya Hassan Bajwa, 'Zur Situation der Ahmadi-Muslime in Pakistan', *Asyl*, 1994/3, 65

Yamagami, S., 'Determination of Refugee Status in Japan', 7 *IJRL* 60 (1995)

de Zayas, A., 'International Law and Mass Population Transfers', 16 *Harv. ILJ* 207 (1975)

Zolberg, A., 'The Refugee Crisis in the Developing World: A Close Look at Africa', in Rystad, G., *The Uprooted: Forced Migration as an International Problem in the Post-War Era*, (1990), 87

Selected United Nations documents

Aga Khan, Sadruddin. Study on Human Rights and Massive Exoduses: UN doc. E/CN.4/1503 (1981)

Capotorti, F., Study on the Rights of Persons belonging to Ethnic, Religious and Linguistic Minorities: UN doc. E/CN/4/Sub.2/384/Rev. 1 (1978)

Daes, E.-I., Study of the Individual's Duties to the Community and the Limitations of Human Rights and Freedoms under Article 29 of the Universal Declaration of Human Rights: UN doc. E/CN.4/Sub.2/432/Rev.1 and Add. 1–7 (1980)

Deng, F., Comprehensive Study on the Human Rights Issues relating to Internally Displaced Persons: UN doc. E/CN.4/1993/35 (1993)

——, Internally Displaced Persons, Report of the Representative of the Secretary-General: UN doc. E/CN.4/1994/44 (1994)

——, Profiles in Displacement: Sri Lanka: UN doc. E/CN.4/1994/44/Add.1 (25 Jan. 1994); Colombia: UN doc. E/CN.4/1995/50/Add.1 (3 Oct. 1994); Burundi: UN doc. E/CN.4/1995/50/Add.2 (28 Nov. 1994); also published in 14 *RSQ*, Nos. 1 & 2, (1995)

Elles, Baroness, International Provisions protecting the Human Rights of Non-Citizens: UN doc. E/CN.4/Sub.2/392/Rev.1 (1980)

Ingles, J., Study of Discrimination in Respect of the Right of Everyone to leave any Country, including his own, and return to his Country: UN doc. E/CN.4/Sub.2/229/Rev.1 (1964)

Martinez Cobo, J.R., Study of the Problem of Discrimination against Indigenous Populations: UN doc. E/CN.4/Sub.2/L.707 (1979)

Mazowiecki, T., Special Rapporteur on former Yugoslavia of the UN Commission on Human Rights: UN docs. E/CN.4/1992/S-1/9 (28 Aug. 1992); E/CN.4/1992-/S-1/10 (27 Oct. 1992)

Ruhashyankiko, N., Study of the Question of the Prevention and Punishment of the Crime of Genocide: UN doc. E/CN.4/Sub.2/416 (1978)

Report of the Secretary-General. Strengthening of the Coordination of Humanitarian and Disaster Relief Activities, etc.: UN doc. A/50/203; E/1995/79 (14 June 1995); also Add.1 (27 June 1995)

Elimination of All Forms of Religious Intolerance. *Note* by the Secretary-General: UN doc. A/8330 (1971)

Internally Displaced Persons. *Analytical Report* of the Secretary-General: UN doc. E/CN.4/1992/23, 14 Feb. 1992

Report of the Group of Governmental Experts on International Co-operation to Avert New Flows of Refugees: UN doc. A/41/324 (May 1986)

Report of the Secretary-General on the Meeting on Refugees and Displaced Persons in South East Asia, Geneva, 20–21 July 1979, and subsequent developments: UN doc. A/34/637 (1979)

Report of the Secretary-General on Methods of Fact-Finding: UN docs. A/5694 (1964); A/6228 (1966)

Report of the Secretary-General. The Role of Youth in the Promotion and Protection of Human Rights, including the Question of Conscientious Objection to Military Service: UN doc. E/CN.4/1989/30 (20 Dec. 1988)

Human Rights Committee, General Comments, No. 15: UN doc. CCPR/C/21/ Rev.1 (19 May 1989)

Human Rights Committee, General Comment No. 22 (48) on art. 18(1): UN doc. CCPR/C//21/Rev.1/Add.4, (27 Sept. 1993)

International Law Commission, Draft Articles on the Draft Code of Crimes against the Peace and Security of Mankind: UN doc. A/46/405, (11 Sept. 1991)

International Law Commission, Draft Statute of the International Criminal Court (1994): Text in *Report of the International Law Commission,* (1994), UN GAOR, 49th Sess., Suppl. No. 10 (A/49/10)

Multilateral Treaties deposited with the Secretary-General: Status as at 31 December 1994: UN doc. ST/LEG/SER.E/13 (1995)

A Select Bibliography on Territorial Asylum: UN doc. ST/GENEVA/LIB/SER.B/ Ref.9 (1977)

A Study of Statelessness: UN doc. E/1112 and Add. 1 (1949)

UN Commission on Human Rights, Working Groups and Special Rapporteurs—additional documents

Report of the United Nations Commission on Human Rights: UN doc. E/CN.4/1989/L.10/Add.15 (9 Mar. 1989)

Report on extrajudicial, summary or arbitrary executions: UN doc. E/CN.4/1994/7 (7 Dec. 1993)

Report on developments in the human rights situation in El Salvador: UN doc. E/CN.4/1994/11 (3 Feb. 1994)

Report of the Special Rapporteur on Torture: UN doc. E/CN.4/1994/26 (22 Dec. 1993) E/CN.4/1994/31 (6 Jan. 1994);

Report on the Situation of Human Rights in the Sudan: UN doc. E/CN.4/1994/48 (1 Feb. 1994)

Report of the Working Group on Enforced or Involuntary Disappearances: UN doc. E/CN.4/1993/25 (7 Jan. 1993)

Report on the visit to Sri Lanka by three members of the Working Group on Enforced or Involuntary Disappearances: UN doc. E/CN.4/1993/25/Add.1 (30 Dec. 1992)

Report on extrajudicial, summary or arbitrary executions: UN doc. E/CN.4/1993/ 46 (23 Dec. 1992)

Rights of Persons belonging to National and Ethnic, Religious and Linguistic Minorities: UN doc. E/CN.4/1994/72 (13 Dec. 1993)

Final Report on the Situation of Human Rights in Iran: UN docs. E/CN.4/1993/41 (28 Jan. 1993), E/CN.4/1994/50 (2 Feb. 1994)

Reports of the Special Rapporteur of the Commission on Human Rights on religions and intolerance: UN doc. E/CN.4/1993/62 (6 Jan. 1993); Add.1 (29 Jan. 1993)

Sub-Commission on the Prevention of Discrimination and the Protection of Minorities. Conscientious Objection to Military Service: UN doc. E/CN.4/Sub.2/1983/30/Rev.1 (1983)

Selected Council of Europe documents

Parliamentary Assembly. Report on deserters and draft resisters from the republics of the former Yugoslavia. Rapporteur: Mr. Franck. CE Doc. 7102, 10 Jun. 1994

Parliamentary Assembly. Report on the right of asylum. Rapporteur: Mr. Franck. CE Doc. 7052, 23 Mar. 1994

Parliamentary Assembly. Report on migratory flows in Czechoslovakia, Hungary and Poland. Rapporteurs, Miss Guirado, Miss Szelényi. CE Doc. 6633, 16 Jun. 1992

Parliamentary Assembly. Report on Europe of 1992 and refugee policies. Rapporteur: Sir John Hunt. CE Doc. 6413, 12 Apr. 1991

Conscientious Objection to Military Service. Explanatory Report: CE Doc. 88.C55 (1988)

European Agreement on Transfer of Responsibility. Explanatory Report. Strasbourg. 1980

European Consultative Assembly. Report on the Political Rights and Position of Aliens. CE Doc. 3834. 1976

Supplementary Report of the Committee of Experts on Extradition to the Committee of Ministers. CE Doc. CM(57) 52. 1957

Country Information Sources

Good information on the legal and human rights situation in countries producing refugees and asylum seekers is an essential foundation for good decisions, whether on individual applications for refugee status and asylum, or on broader, policy concerns. Experience shows that a coherent understanding of the background to actual or imminent flight depends on accurate and authoritative reports on political, economic, and social conditions. Fortunately, many experienced organizations now produce such information on a regular basis, and it is increasingly available in print (many UN and WriteNet country reports, for example, are published in the *Refugee Survey Quarterly*, available from Oxford University Press for UNHCR/CDR: http://www.oup.co.uk/journals), and in electronic form. Several of the more common sources referred to throughout the text now maintain Internet Gopher or WorldWideWeb sites:

Amnesty International
International Secretariat
1 Easton Street
London WC1X 8DJ
United Kingdom

Lawyers Committee for Human Rights
330 Seventh Avenue, 10th Fl.
New York
NY 10001
United States of America

Human Rights Watch
485 Fifth Avenue
New York
NY 10017–6104
United States of America

Minority Rights Group International
279 Brixton Road
London SW9 7DE
United Kingdom

Physicians for Human Rights
100 Boylston Street, Suite 702
Boston
MA 02116
United States of America

P.O. Box 20147
Ottawa
Ontario K1N 9P4
Canada

United States Committee for Refugees
1025 Vermont Ave. N.W.
Suite 920
Washington D.C. 20005
United States of America
Human Rights Internet

International and government sources also produce information on asylum-related issues according to generally accepted standards of credibility and authoritativeness, although distribution may be limited, particularly by costs. These include:

UN Commission on Human Rights
Centre for Human Rights
Palais des Nations
1211 Geneva 19
Switzerland

UNHCR/Centre for Documentation on Refugees
CP 2500
1211 Geneva 2 Dépôt
Switzerland

Immigration and Refugee Board of Canada
Documentation, Information and Research Branch
222 Nepean Street
Ottawa
ONT. K1A 0K1
Canada

Immigration and Naturalization Service/Resource Information Center (INS/RIC)
425 I Street N.W.
Ullico Building 3rd Fl.
Washington D.C. 20536
United States of America

US Department of State
Washington D.C. 20520–7526
United States of America

Refugee Legal Centre
Sussex House
39–45 Bermondsey Street
London SE1 3XF
United Kingdom

Office fédéral des réfugiés/Federal Office for Refugees
Taubenstrasse 16
3003 Bern
Switzerland

Online and Electronic Access

Various organizations, such as Amnesty International, distribute information electronically, through the Internet/WorldWideWeb; for useful links, see, for example, *The Humanitarian HomePage* at the University of Aberwystwyth: http://www.aber.ac.uk/~bbr94. During 1995, UNHCR/CDR opened access to several databases (country information, refugee literature and refugee case law) through its Internet Gopher site (RefWorld). At the same time, work was completed on the CD-ROM, *RefWorld/Refmonde*, and a web site replaced the Gopher in 1996: http://www.unhcr.ch/refworld

The UNHCR/CDR CD-ROM contains a wealth of information, including United Nations General Assembly and Security Council resolutions, UNHCR Executive Committee documents and conclusions, various databases, including REFLIT—refugee literature; REFCAS—refugee case law; REFINT—international instruments; country reports from UNHCR, reports from UN Commission on Human Rights rapporteurs and working groups, WriteNet Consultants, Amnesty International (also the annual reports from 1994 and 1995), Human Rights Watch, INS/RIC (USA), US Department of State *Annual Reports on Human Rights Practices*, IRB/DIRB (Canada), Refugee Legal Centre (United Kingdom), Federal Office for Refugees (Switzerland).

Many primary sources also now maintain their own web sites; see for example:
    Amnesty International: www.amnesty.org
    Human Rights Watch: www.hrw.org
    UN Commission on Human Rights: www.unhchr.ch
and for disaster-related information generally, see:
    ReliefWeb: www.reliefweb.int

Related legal information

Besides the law abstracts published by UNHCR/CDR, a selection of which appears regularly in the *International Journal of Refugee Law* published by Oxford University Press: http://www.oup.co.uk/reflaw, refugee jurisprudence is also available online through a variety of commercially available legal database services. Among these, QL Systems Limited, through its well-known QuickLaw service, has pioneered a number of refugee-specific databases, including selected decisions from Canada's Convention Refugee Determination Division (database code CRDD; version française DSSR). QuickLaw databases contain other relevant case law and are fully linked to related judgments in the Canadian Federal and Supreme Courts.

QL Systems Ltd.
St Andrew's Tower
275 Sparks Street
Ottawa
Ontario K1R 7X9
Canada
http://www.qlsys.ca

INDEX